Time Out

Berlin

timeout.com/berlin

Time Out Guides

Published by Time Out Guides Ltd, a wholly owned subsidiary of Time Out Group Ltd.
Time Out and the Time Out logo are trademarks of Time Out Group Ltd.

Previous editions 1993, 1995, 1998, 2000, 2002

10 9 8 7 6 5 4 3 2 1

This edition first published in Great Britain in 2004 by Ebury
Ebury is a division of The Random House Group Ltd,
20 Vauxhall Bridge Road, London SW1V 2SA

Random House Australia Pty Limited, 20 Alfred Street, Milsons Point, Sydney, New South Wales 2061, Australia
Random House New Zealand Limited, 18 Poland Road, Glenfield, Auckland 10, New Zealand
Random House South Africa (Pty) Limited, Endulini, 5A Jubilee Road, Parktown 2193, South Africa

Random House UK Limited Reg. No. 954009

Distributed in USA by Publishers Group West
1700 Fourth Street, Berkeley, California 94710

Distributed in Canada by Penguin Canada Ltd
10 Alcorn Avenue, Toronto, Ontario, Canada M4V 3B2

For further distribution details, see www.timeout.com

ISBN 1-904978-14-2

A CIP catalogue record for this book is available from the British Library

Colour reprographics by Icon, Crowne House, 56-58 Southwark Street, London SE1 1UN

Printed and bound by Cayfosa-Quebecor, Ctra. De Caldes, KM 3 08 130 Sta, Perpètua de Mogoda, Barcelona, Spain

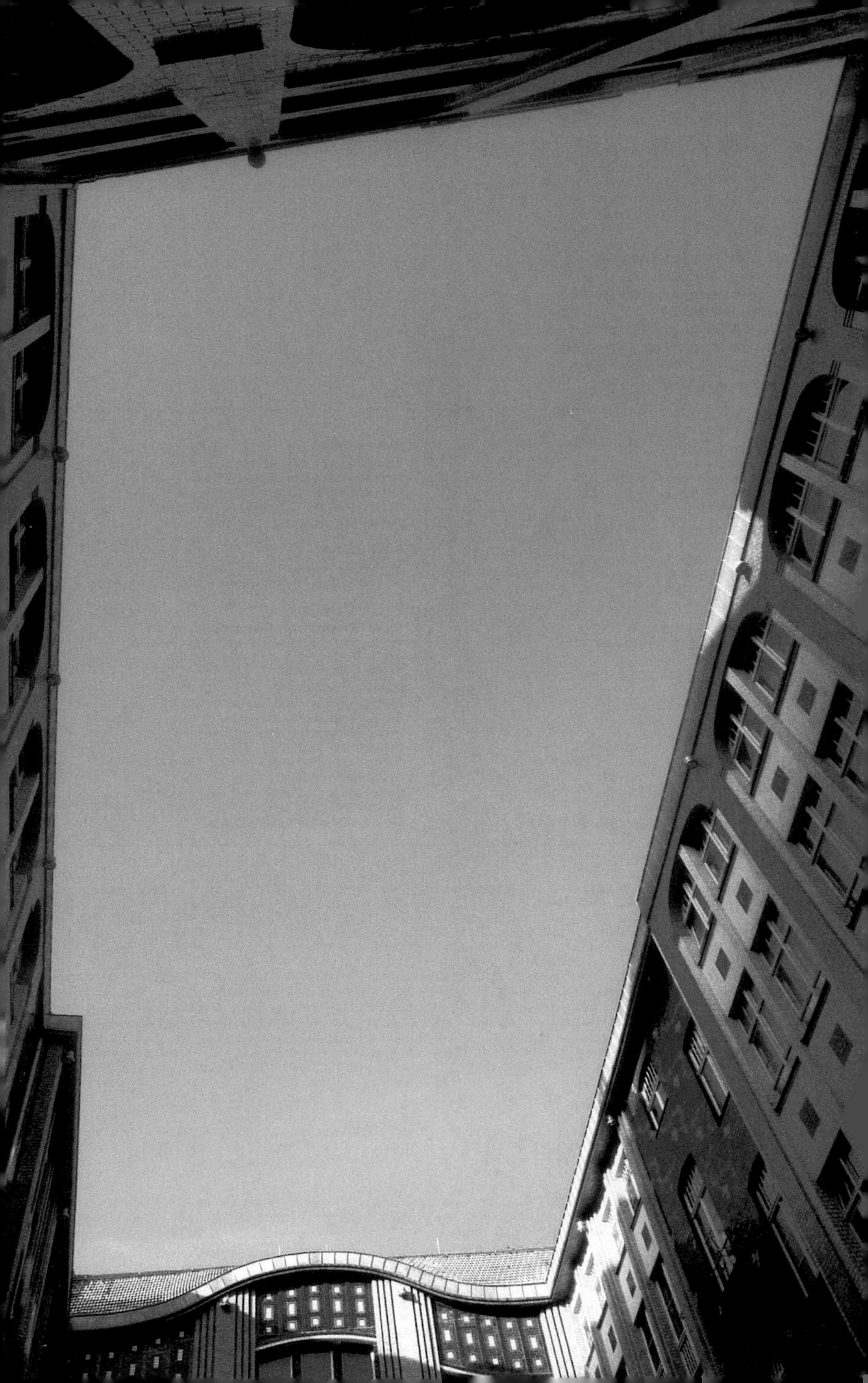

Time Out Guides Limited
Universal House
251 Tottenham Court Road
London W1T 7AB
Tel + 44 (0)20 7813 3000
Fax + 44 (0)20 7813 6001
Email guides@timeout.com
www.timeout.com

Editorial
Editor Dave Rimmer
Deputy Editor Hugh Graham
Listings Checker Manon Kahle
Proofreader Charlie Godfrey-Faussett
Indexer Cathy Heath

Editorial/Managing Director Peter Fiennes
Series Editor Ruth Jarvis
Deputy Series Editor Lesley McCave
Guides Co-ordinator Anna Norman
Accountant Sarah Bostock

Design
Art Director Mandy Martin
Acting Art Director Scott Moore
Acting Art Editor Tracey Ridgewell
Acting Senior Designer Astrid Kogler
Designer Sam Lands
Junior Designer Oliver Knight
Digital Imaging Dan Conway
Ad Make-up Charlotte Blythe

Picture Desk
Picture Editor Jael Marschner
Deputy Picture Editor Kit Burnet
Picture Researcher Ivy Lahon
Picture Desk Assistant/Librarian Laura Lord

Advertising
Sales Director Mark Phillips
International Sales Manager Ross Canadé
International Sales Executive James Tuson
Advertising Sales (Berlin) In Your Pocket
Advertising Assistant Lucy Butler

Marketing
Marketing Manager Mandy Martinez
US Publicity & Marketing Associate Rosella Albanese

Production
Guides Production Director Mark Lamond
Production Controller Samantha Furniss

Time Out Group
Chairman Tony Elliott
Managing Director Mike Hardwick
Group Financial Director Richard Waterlow
Group Commercial Director Lesley Gill
Group Marketing Director Christine Cort
Group General Manager Nichola Coulthard
Group Art Director John Oakey
Online Managing Director David Pepper
Group Production Director Steve Proctor
Group IT Director Simon Chappell

Contributors
Introduction Dave Rimmer. **History** Frederick Studemann (*Knight fever* Kevin Cote; *Uncommon currency* Dave Rimmer; *The Good German* Paul Hockenos). **Berlin Today** Kevin Cote. **Architecture** Michael Lees, Francesca Roger (*A tale of two squares* Michael Lees). **Where to Stay** Sophie Lovell. **Sightseeing** Kevin Cote, Manon Kahle, Dave Rimmer, Ed Ward (*Essential Berlin* Jonathan Cox; *A walk on the Wall side* Julie Gregson; *On the waterfront, Miles of files* Kevin Cote; *Home for 'Heroes', Pillars of publicity, The Russian zone* Dave Rimmer). **Restaurants** Kevin Cote, Natalie Gravenor, Chris Hoff, Patrick Lonergan, Sophie Lovell, Dave Rimmer, Ed Ward (*Pig and stodge* Ed Ward). **Cafés, Bars & Pubs** Natalie Gravenor, Chris Hoff, Dave Rimmer, David Strauss (*A different corner* Dave Rimmer). **Shops & Services** Susan Hannaford, Julie Wedow (*Design for living rooms* Julie Wedow; *Lenin's on sale again* Susan Hannaford, Dave Rimmer). **Festivals & Events** Natalie Gravenor. **Children** Kevin Cote, Rudi Teichmann (*The great indoors* Kevin Cote). **Film** Andrew Horn. **Galleries** Neal Wach. **Gay & Lesbian** Jens Friedrich. **Music: Rock, World & Jazz** Natalie Gravenor. **Nightlife** Natalie Gravenor. *Cabaret* Priscilla Be. **Performing Arts** *Music: Classical & Opera* David Canisius, Rick Perera (*Roll over Beethoven* Dave Rimmer). *Theatre* Priscilla Be, Marianne Torrance. *Dance* Petra Roggel. **Sport & Fitness** Don Mac Coitir. **Trips Out of Town** Julie Gregson, Ed Ward (*Hollywood Babelsberg* Julie Gregson). **Directory** Jonathan Cox, Natalie Gravenor, Manon Kahle, Biba Kopf, Dave Rimmer (*Watching the wildlife, Beautiful party evening!* Dave Rimmer).

Maps JS Graphics (john@jsgraphics.co.uk).

Photography Hadley Kincade, except: page 3 Christoph Petras; page 6 Getty News and Sport; page 9 Bridgeman Art Library; pages 12, 17, 20, 25 Hulton Getty; pages 32, 68, 69, 183 www.berlin-tourist-information.de/Koch; page 184 Photoart/Rainer J. Stevens and Frank Loehmer; page 218 Foto Sahin; page 242 Thomas Aurin.The following images were provided by the featured establishments/artists: pages 29, 233.

The editor would like to thank Chris Bohn, Kevin Cote, Peterjon Cresswell, Kevin Ebbutt, Omar Elshami, John Fitzsimons, Aziz Hashmi, Volker Hauptvogel, Paul Hockenos, Sarah Horton, Doris Jaud, Patrick Lonergan, Sophie Lovell, Russ Newburgh, Sandra Portman, Mark Reeder, Colin Shepherd, Neil Tennant, Neal Wach, Annette Wilson, Trevor Wilson.

Contents

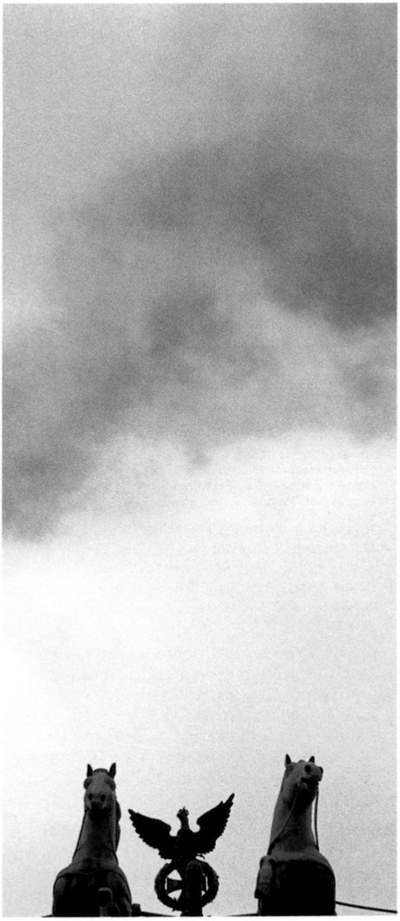

Introduction

Stroll up Unter den Linden, past all those Schinkel buildings you're obliged to admire, and on to Museumsinsel, island where Berlin was born. On the north side, the neo-classical colonnade of the Altes Museum fronts a cluster of revered cultural institutions. To the south, alone and unloved, dismantled while its neighbours get renovated, hunches the poor old Palast der Republik.

This was the site of the Stadtschloss, home of the Kaisers. Damaged in World War II, it was demolished by the Communists and replaced in 1976 with the glass and concrete Palast. This housed the East German parliament, bars and restaurants, a bowling alley and, in its vast foyer, such a profligacy of bulbous light fittings that it was nicknamed *Erichs Lampenladen* – Erich (Honecker)'s Light Shop. It was a fun kind of palace.

But since the early 1990s there has been a campaign to knock it down and recreate the old Prussian pile. During arguments over which piece of history to recreate or erase, the Palast was cleansed of asbestos, which left it looking more like something you'd find in Chernobyl than at the head of Berlin's grand ceremonial avenue.

For now, stalemate. The government has voted to replace it with something that looks like the Stadtschloss, but there's no money so it'll have to wait, probably for years. In the interim, an organisation aims to open up the dramatically gutted interior (*pictured*) for cultural events. Which is all very early 21st-century Berlin, right down to the cranky name of the organisation – Zwischenpalastnutzung, 'Between Palace Utilisation'.

A while ago one would have read all this as a parable of Berlin's shifty historical nature, or of its capacity to regenerate from ruin. But the Berlin surveyed by this guide seems beyond all that now. We're as far from the Wall coming down as the Wall going up was from the end of World War II. Few Berliners under 20 remember much of division and, while east-west tensions linger, they're slowly being sidelined by population turnover. Most new building is finished, the government has set up shop and the new social map is now pretty much redrawn. It might be bankrupt or need a few more tweaks, but this right here is the New Berlin.

In the middle all this, the Between Palace stands as a massive anomaly – a reminder not just of Berlin's uncertainty about how far to turn back the clock, and of its uncertain finances, but also that however much some might wish to make out that the 20th century never happened, communism played a huge part in forming the Berlin we know today. It's reflected in everything from the current retro-futurist design craze through Balkan Beats and Russian Disco club nights to Berlin's developing role as the cultural and economic capital of eastern Europe.

Certainly, as the old Warsaw Pact nations join the European Union, there's no other city that can in the same way bridge east and west, communist past and capitalist future, with all the attendant tensions and possibilities. Berlin is becoming its own kind of melting pot, a creative confusion on the cusp of the new Europe that is reflected in every aspect of this guide. Enjoy.

ABOUT THE TIME OUT CITY GUIDES

This is the sixth edition of *Time Out Berlin,* one of an expanding series of *Time Out* guides produced by the people behind the successful listings magazines in London and New York. Our guides are written and updated by resident experts to provide you with all the up-to-date information you need to explore the city or read up on its background, whether you're a local or a first-time visitor.

THE LIE OF THE LAND

Berlin is a big, sprawling city. For ease of use, we've split many chapters in this guide into districts. The first page of each sightseeing chapter contains a small locator map, so you can see how each area relates to those around it, and there are detailed street maps at the back of this guide. Wherever possible, a map reference is provided for each venue, indicating the page and grid reference at which it can be found on the street maps. The most convenient public transport options are also listed.

ESSENTIAL INFORMATION

For all the practical information you might need for visiting Berlin, including emergency phone numbers, visa and customs information, useful websites and details of local transport, turn to the **Directory** chapter at the back of the guide. It starts on page 269.

THE LOWDOWN ON THE LISTINGS

We have tried to make this book as useful and as easy to use as possible. Addresses, phone numbers, websites, transport, opening times and admission prices are all included in our listings. However, owners and managers can change their arrangements at any time. Before you go out of your way, we'd advise phoning ahead to check opening times and other particulars. While every effort has been made to ensure the accuracy of the information in this guide, the publishers cannot accept responsibility for any errors it may contain.

PRICES AND PAYMENT

The prices we've supplied were correct at press time, but should be treated as guidelines, not gospel. If prices vary wildly from those we've quoted, ask whether there's a good reason and please write to let us know. We aim to give the best advice, so we always want to know if you've been badly treated or overcharged.

We have noted where shops, restaurants and hotels accept the following credit cards: American Express (**AmEx**), Diners Club (**DC**), MasterCard (**MC**) and Visa (**V**). Credit cards are not as widely accepted in Berlin (particularly in bars and cafés) as in many other European and US cities. Some shops, restaurants and attractions take travellers' cheques.

Advertisers

We would like to stress that no establishment has been included in this guide because it has advertised in any of our publications and no payment of any kind has influenced any review. The opinions given in this book are those of Time Out writers and entirely independent.

TELEPHONE NUMBERS

The code for Berlin is 030, dialled before the relevant number when calling the city from within Germany. From abroad, you need to dial the international access code followed by 49 for Germany, 30 for Berlin and then the number. For more information on telephones, *see p284*.

LANGUAGE

Many Berliners, particularly younger ones, speak some English, and many speak it very well, but you can't assume that you will be understood. A few basic German phrases can go a long way, and in restaurants it's useful to have a dictionary – outside tourist areas, many places only have menus in German.

MAPS

The map section at the back of this book starts with an overview of the greater Berlin area, and follows with eight pages of detailed street maps of the central districts. The back page contains a close-up map of Mitte, the area within which many visitors spend the majority of their time. On page 88, there is a map of the Friedrichshain district. There is also a map of the U- and S-Bahn network. The maps start on page 298.

LET US KNOW WHAT YOU THINK

We hope you enjoy *Time Out Berlin,* and we'd like to know what you think of it. We welcome tips for places that you consider we should include in future editions and take note of your criticism of our choices. You can email us at guides@timeout.com.

There is an online version of this book, along with guides to 45 other international cities, at **www.timeout.com**.

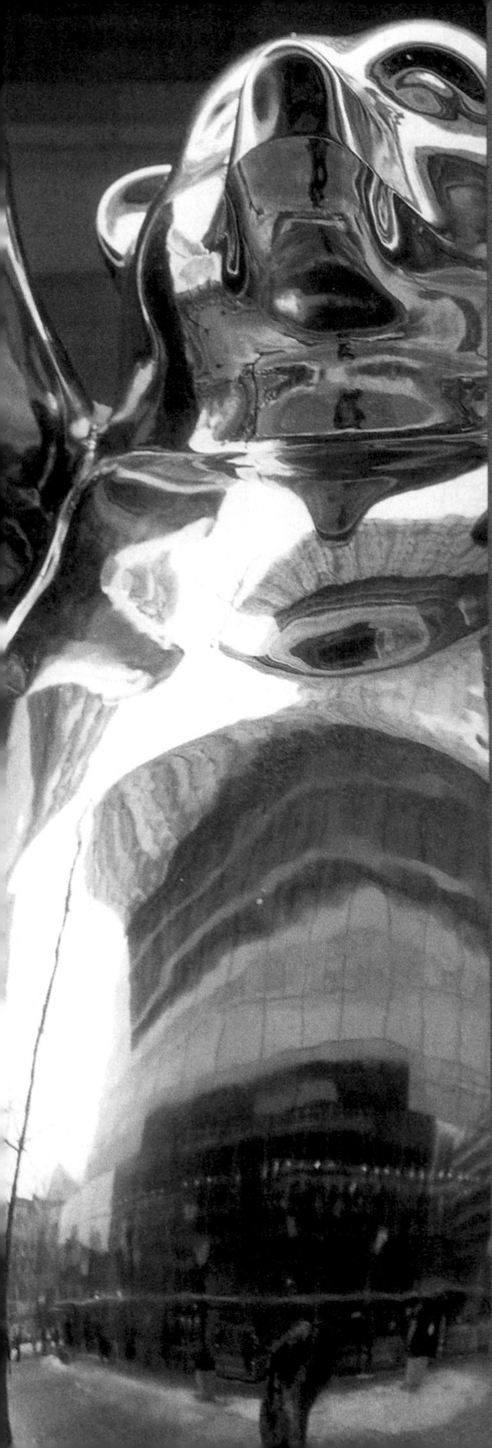

In Context

Features

History

From medieval swamp to modern capital, calling at wars, revolutions and assorted evil empires on the way.

Berlin's origins are neither remarkable nor auspicious. A settlement emerged sometime in the 12th century on unpromising, swamplands that pioneering German knights had wrested from the Slavs. The name Berlin is believed to be derived from the Slav word birl, meaning swamp.

Facing off across the Spree river, Berlin and its twin settlement Cölln (on what is now the Museumsinsel) were founded as trading posts halfway between the older fortress towns of Spandau and Köpenick. Today the borough of Mitte embraces Cölln and old Berlin, and Spandau and Köpenick are outlying suburbs. The town's existence was first recorded in 1237, when Cölln was mentioned in a church document. In the same century, construction began on the Marienkirche and Nikolaikirche churches, both of which still stand.

The Ascanian family, who held the title of Margraves of Brandenburg, ruled over the twin towns and the surrounding region. Eager to encourage trade, they granted special rights to merchants with the result that Berlin and Cölln emerged as prosperous trading centres linking east and west Europe. In 1307 the two towns were officially united.

Early years of prosperity came to an end in 1319 with the death of the last Ascanian ruler. This opened the way for robber barons from outlying regions, eager to take control of Berlin. But, despite political upheaval and the threat of invasion, Berlin's merchants continued business. In 1359 the city joined the Hanseatic League of free-trading northern European cities.

FROM TRADING POST TO CAPITAL

But the threat of invasion remained. In the late 14th century two powerful families, the Dukes of Pomerania and the brutal von Quitzow brothers, began to vie for control of the city.

Salvation came with Friedrich of Hohenzollern, a nobleman from southern Germany sent by the Holy Roman Emperor in 1411 to bring peace to the region. Initially, Friedrich was well received. The bells of the Marienkirche were melted down and made into weapons for the fight against the aggressors. (In an echo of history, the Marienkirche bells were again transformed into tools of war in 1917, in the reign of Kaiser Wilhelm II, the last of the Hohenzollerns to rule.)

Having defeated the von Quitzow brothers, Friedrich officially became Margrave. In 1416 he took the further title of Elector of Brandenburg, denoting his right to vote in the election of the Holy Roman Emperor – titular head of the German-speaking states.

Gradually, Berlin was transformed from an outlying trading post to a small-sized capital (in 1450 the population was 6,000). In 1442 foundations were laid for Berlin Castle and a royal court was established.

With peace and stability came the loss of independent traditions as Friedrich consolidated power. Disputes rose between the patrician classes (representing trade) and the guilds (representing crafts). Rising social friction culminated in the 'Berlin Indignation' of 1447-8 when the population rose up in rebellion. Friedrich's son, Friedrich II, and his courtiers were locked out of the city and the foundations of the castle were flooded, but within months the uprising collapsed and the Hohenzollerns returned triumphant. Merchants faced new restrictions and the city lost economic impetus.

REFORM AND DEBAUCHERY

The Reformation arrived in Berlin and Brandenburg under the reign of Joachim I Nestor (1535-71), the first Elector to embrace Protestantism. Joachim strove to improve the cultural standing of Berlin by inviting artists, architects and theologians to work in the city.

In 1538 Caspar Theyss and Konrad Krebbs, two master-builders from Saxony, began work on a Renaissance-style palace. The building took 100 years to complete, and evolved into the bombastic Stadtschloss, which stood on what is now Museuminsel in the Spree until the East German government demolished it in 1950.

Joachim's studious nature was not reflected in the behaviour of his subjects; self-indulgence characterised life in the late 16th-century city. Attempts to clamp down on drinking, gambling and loose morals had little effect. Visiting the city, Abbot Trittenheim remarked that 'the people are good, but rough and unpolished; they prefer stuffing themselves to good science'.

After stuffing itself with another 6,000 people, Berlin left the 16th century with a population of 12,000.

THE THIRTY YEARS WAR

The outbreak of the Thirty Years War in 1618 dragged Berlin on to the wider political stage. Although initially unaffected by the conflict between Catholic forces loyal to the Holy Roman Empire and the Swedish-backed Protestant armies, Berlin was eventually caught up in the war, which left the German-speaking states ravaged and divided for two centuries. In 1626 imperial troops occupied Berlin and plundered the city. Berliners were soon forced to pay special taxes to the occupying forces. Trade collapsed and its hinterland was laid waste. To top it all, there were four serious epidemics between 1626 and 1631 that killed thousands. By the end of the war in 1648, Berlin had lost a third of its housing and the population had fallen to less than 6,000.

THE NEW IMMIGRANTS

Painstaking reconstruction was carried out under Friedrich Wilhelm, 'the Great Elector.' He succeeded his father in 1640, but sat out the war in exile. Influenced by Dutch ideas on town planning and architecture (he was married to a Princess of Orange), Wilhelm embarked on a policy that linked urban regeneration, economic expansion and solid defence.

'The growing cosmopolitan mix laid the foundations for a flowering of intellectual and artistic life.'

New fortifications were built around the city, and a garrison of 2,000 soldiers established as Friedrich expanded his 'Residenzstadt'. In the centre of town, the Lustgarten was laid out opposite the palace. Running west from the palace, the first Lindenallee ('Avenue of Lime Trees' or Unter den Linden) was created.

To revive the economy, housing and property taxes were abolished in favour of a sales tax. With the money that was raised, three new towns – Friedrichswerder, Dorotheenstadt and Friedrichstadt – were built. (Together with Berlin and Cölln, these now make up the district of Mitte.) In the 1660s a canal was constructed linking the Spree and Oder rivers, establishing Berlin as an east–west trading centre.

But Friedrich Wilhelm's most inspired policy was to encourage refugees to settle in the city. First to arrive were over 50 Jewish families from Vienna. In 1672 Huguenot settlers arrived from France. Both groups brought new skills and industries to Berlin.

The growing cosmopolitan mix laid the foundations for a flowering of intellectual and artistic life. By the time the Great Elector's son Friedrich III took the throne in 1688, one in five Berliners spoke French. Today, French words still pepper Berlin dialect, such as boulette ('hamburger') and étage ('floor').

In 1695 work commenced on Schloss Charlottenburg to the west of Berlin. A year later the Academy of Arts was founded, and, in 1700, intellectual life was further stimulated by the founding of the Academy of Sciences under Gottfried Leibniz. The building of the German and French cathedrals at Gendarmenmarkt in 1701 gave Berlin one of its loveliest squares. Five years later the Zeughaus ('Armoury'), now housing the Deutsches Historisches Museum, was completed on Unter den Linden.

In 1701 Elector Friedrich III had himself crowned Prussian King Friedrich I (not to be confused with the earlier Elector).

THE PRUSSIANS ARE COMING

The common association of Prussia with militarism can broadly be traced back to the 18th century and the efforts of two men in particular: King Friedrich Wilhelm I and his son Friedrich II (also known as Frederick the Great). Although father and son hated each other, and had different sensibilities (Friedrich Wilhelm was boorish and mean, Friedrich II sensitive and philosophical), together they launched Prussia as a major military power, and, in turn, gave Berlin the character of a garrison city.

King Friedrich Wilhelm I (1713-40) made parsimony and militarism state policy – and almost succeeded in driving Berlin's economy into the ground. The only thing that grew was the army, which by 1740 numbered 80,000 troops. Many of these were deployed in Berlin and billeted in the houses of ordinary citizens.

With a king much more interested in keeping the books than reading them, intellectual life suffered. Friedrich Wilhelm had no use for art, so he closed down the Academy of Arts; instead he collected soldiers, and swapped a collection

Knight fever

Berlin's Tempelhof district is so closely identified with Tempelhof Airport and its role in the 1948 airlift (*see p21*) that few are aware of the area's medieval heritage as an outpost of the Knights Templar, the warrior monks who gave this part of town its name.

The history of Tempelhof stretches back earlier than the founding of Berlin, when a German order of the 'Poor Knights of the Temple of Solomon' set up a franchise here. Remnants of the Templars' tenure are among the oldest structures in Berlin: these include a 13th-century chapel in Alt-Marienfelde, and another one near Rathaus Tempelhof.

The Templars were founded during the Crusades to protect pilgrims travelling to the Holy Land. They also blended two of mankind's most powerful urges – to worship and to fight – into an institution with spiritual legitimacy, political clout and extraordinary wealth. Their trademark white tunics with red crosses were as recognisable then as the logo of any global corporation today.

The knights were feared as ferocious fighters, but they also set up possibly the world's first formal banking scheme: pilgrims could deposit gold and silver at their nearest Templar outpost, collect a voucher, and cash it in at a Templar office near their destination. The Templars were probably invited to settle Tempelhof by the Markgraf Otto II precisely because of their money management skills.

But they were a weird lot, even by medieval standards. They had secret initiation rituals, took vows of poverty and celibacy, were big on collecting holy relics, and wore sheepskin underwear they were forbidden to change.

In 1307, France's Philip IV arrested all the Templars at their Paris headquarters, charging them with heresy, based on stories of homosexuality and idol worship. The reality was that Pope Clement felt threatened by the Templar's power, and Philip wanted their cash for his war against England. After Templars confessed under torture, their Grand Master was burned at the stake and their land holdings, including those at Tempelhof, were turned over to other religious orders.

Templar legends are central to many esoteric systems, and why they went down without a fight is an enduring source of speculation for occultists. Some believe a chosen few went underground to preserve a secret knowledge, and re-emerged in the 17th century as the Freemasons.

One surviving piece of Templar stonemasonry is the ancient Templar Cross carved above the door of the 1220 Alte-Dorfkirche on Alt-Marienfelde (S2 Buckower Chaussee/bus 172), Berlin's oldest church. Other structures of Templar origin are the 1230 Dorfkirche at Alt-Mariendorf, outside the station (U6 Alt-Mariendorf), and the former chapel of the Templars' local headquarters, standing in a small park on Parkstrasse (U6 Alt-Tempelhof).

27 October 1806: **Napoleon** marches through the Brandenburg Gate. *See p10.*

of oriental vases for one of the King of Saxony's regiments. The Tsar received a small gold ship in exchange for 150 Russian giants.

But the obsession with all things military did have some positive effects. The King needed competent soldiers, so he made school compulsory; the army needed doctors, so he set up medical institutes. Berlin's economy also picked up on the back of demand from the military. Skilled immigrants (mostly from Saxony) met the increased demand. The result was a population boom (from 60,000 in 1713 to 90,000 in 1740) and a growth in trade.

FREDERICK THE GREAT

While his father collected soldiers, Frederick the Great (Friedrich II) deployed them – in a series of wars with Austria and Russia (from 1740-42, 1744-5 and 1756-63; the latter known as the Seven Years War) in a bid to win territory in Silesia in the east. Initially, the wars proved disastrous. The Austrians occupied Berlin city in 1757, the Russians in 1760. However, thanks to a mixture of good fortune and military genius, Frederick finally emerged victorious from the Seven Years War.

When not fighting, the King devoted his time to forging a modern state apparatus (he liked to call himself 'first servant of the state'; Berliners simply called him 'Old Fritz') and transforming Berlin and Potsdam. This was achieved partly through conviction – the King was friends with Voltaire and saw himself very much as an aesthetically minded figure of the Enlightenment – but it was also a political necessity. He needed to convince both enemies and subjects that even in times of national crisis he was able to afford grand projects.

So Unter den Linden was transformed into a grand boulevard. At the palace end, the Forum Fridericianium, designed and constructed by the architect von Knobelsdorff, comprised the Staatsoper, St Hedwigskathedrale, Prince Heinrich Palace (now housing Humboldt-Universität) and the Staatsbibliotek. Although it was never fully completed, the Forum remains one of Berlin's main attractions today.

To the west of Berlin, the Tiergarten was landscaped and a new palace, Schloss Bellevue (now the Berlin residence of the German president), was built. Frederick also decided to replace a set of barracks at Gendarmenmarkt with a theatre, now called the Konzerthaus.

To encourage manufacturing and industry (particularly textiles), advantageous excise laws were introduced. Businesses such as the KPM (Königliche Porzellan-Manufaktur) porcelain works were nationalised and turned into prestigious and lucrative enterprises.

Legal and administrative reforms also characterised Frederick's reign. Religious freedom was enshrined in law, torture was abolished and Berlin became a centre of the Enlightenment. Cultural and intellectual life blossomed around figures such as philosopher Moses Mendelssohn and poet Gottfried Lessing.

By the time Friedrich died in 1786, Berlin had a population of 150,000 and was the capital of one of Europe's grand powers.

ENLIGHTENMENT'S END

The death of Frederick the Great also marked the end of the Enlightenment in Prussia. His successor, Friedrich Wilhelm II, was more interested in spending money on classical architecture than wasting his time with political philosophy. Censorship was stepped up and the King's extravagance plunged the state into an economic crisis. By 1788 14,000 Berliners were dependent on state and church aid. The state apparatus crumbled under the weight of greedy administrators. When he died in 1797 Friedrich Wilhelm II left his son with huge debts.

However, the old King's love of classicism left Berlin with its most famous monument: the Brandenburger Tor (Brandenburg Gate). It was built by Karl Gottfried Langhans in 1789, the year of the French Revolution, and modelled on the Propylaea in Athens. Two years later, Johann Schadow added the Quadriga, a sculpture of a bare-chested Victoria riding a chariot drawn by four horses. Originally one of 14 gates marking Berlin's boundaries, the Brandenburger Tor is now the geographical and symbolic centre of the city.

If the King did not care for intellect, then the emerging bourgeoisie did. Towards the turn of the century, Berlin became a centre of German Romanticism. Literary salons flourished, and remained a feature of Berlin's cultural life into the middle of the 19th century.

Despite censorship, Berlin still had a platform for liberal expression. The city's newspapers welcomed the French Revolution so enthusiastically that in the southern German states Jacobins were referred to as 'Berliners'.

THE NAPOLEONIC WARS

In 1806 Berlin came face to face with the effects of revolution in France: following the defeat of the Prussian forces in the battles of Jena and Auerstadt on 14 October, Napoleon's army headed for Berlin. The King and Queen fled to Königsberg and the garrison was removed from the city. On 27 October Napoleon and his army marched through the Brandenburger Tor. Once again Berlin was an occupied city.

Napoleon set about changing the political and administrative structure. He called together 2,000 prominent citizens and told them to elect a new administration ('the Comité Administratif'), which oversaw the city's administration until the French troops left in 1808.

Napoleon decreed that property belonging to the state, the Hohenzollerns and many aristocratic families be expropriated. Priceless works of art were removed from palaces in Berlin and Potsdam and sent to France; even the Quadriga was taken from the Brandenburg Gate and shipped to Paris. At the same time, the city was hit by crippling war reparations.

When the French left, a group of energetic, reform-minded aristocrats, grouped around Baron vom Stein, introduced a series of reforms in a bid to modernise the moribund Prussian state. One key aspect was the clear separation of state and civic responsibility, which gave Berlin independence to manage its own affairs. A new council was elected (though only property owners and the wealthy were entitled to vote). In 1810 the philosopher Wilhelm von Humboldt founded the university. All remaining restrictions on the city's Jewish population were removed. Generals Scharnhorst and Gneisenau completely overhauled the army.

Although the French occupied Berlin again in 1812 on their way home from the disastrous Russian campaign, this time they were met with stiff resistance. A year later the Prussian King finally joined the anti-Napoleon coalition and thousands of Berliners signed up to fight.

'For the majority, the post-Napoleonic era was a period of frustrated hopes and bitter poverty.'

When Napoleon tried to capture the city once more, he was defeated at nearby Grossbeeren. This, together with a subsequent defeat for the French in the Battle of Leipzig, marked the end of Napoleonic rule in Germany.

In August 1814 General Blücher brought the Quadriga back to Berlin, and restored it to its place on the Brandenburger Tor. One symbolic addition was made to the statue: an Iron Cross and Prussian eagle were added to the staff in Victoria's hand.

THE RISE OF THE POLICE STATE

The burst of reform initiated in 1810 was short-lived. Following the Congress of Vienna (1814-15), which established a new order for post-Napoleonic Europe, King Friedrich Wilhelm III reneged on promises of constitutional reform. Instead of a greater unity among the German states, a loose alliance came into being; dominated by Austria, the German Confederation was distinctly anti-liberal.

In Prussia itself state power increased. Alongside the normal police, a secret service and vice squad were set up. The police president even had the power to issue directives to the city council. Book and newspaper censorship increased. The authorities sacked von Humboldt from the university he had created.

With their hopes for lasting change frustrated, the bourgeoisie withdrew into their salons. It is one of the ironies of this time that, although political opposition was quashed, a vibrant cultural movement flourished. Academics like Hegel and Ranke lectured at the university and enhanced Berlin's reputation as an intellectual centre.

The period became known as Biedermeier, after a fictional character embodying bourgeois taste, created by Swabian comic writer Ludwig Eichrodt. Another legacy of this period is the range of neo-classical buildings designed by Schinkel, such as his Altes Museum and the Neue Wache on Unter den Linden.

For the majority, however, the post-Napoleonic era was a period of frustrated hopes and bitter poverty. Industrialisation swelled the ranks of the working class. Between 1810 and 1840, the city's population doubled to 400,000. But most of the newcomers lived in conditions that would later lead to riot and revolution.

THE INDUSTRIAL REVOLUTION

Prussia was ideally equipped for the industrial age. By the 19th century it had grown dramatically and boasted one of the greatest abundances of raw materials in Europe.

It was the founding of the Borsig Werke on Chausseestrasse in 1837 that established Berlin as the workshop of continental Europe. August Borsig was Berlin's first big industrialist. His factories turned out locomotives for the new Berlin-to-Potsdam railway network, which opened in 1838. Borsig also left his mark through the establishment of a suburb (Borsigwalde) that still carries his name.

The other great pioneering industrialist, Werner Siemens, set up his electrical engineering firm in a house by Anhalter Bahnhof. The first European to produce telegraph equipment, Siemens personified the German industrial ideal, with his mix of technical genius and business savvy.

The Siemens company also left a permanent imprint on Berlin through the building of a new suburb (Siemensstadt) to house its workers.

1848 AND ALL THAT

Friedrich Wilhelm IV's accession to the throne in 1840 raised hopes of an end to repression; and, initially, he did appear to want real change. He declared an amnesty for political prisoners, relaxed censorship, sacked the hated justice minister and granted asylum to refugees.

Political debate thrived in coffee houses and wine bars. The university was another focal point for discussion. In the late 1830s Karl Marx spent a term there, just missing fellow alumnus Otto von Bismarck. In the early 1840s Friedrich Engels came to Berlin to do his military service.

The thaw didn't last long. It soon became clear that Friedrich Wilhelm IV shared his father's opposition to constitutional reform. Living and working conditions for the majority of Berliners worsened. Rapid industrialisation brought the horrors of sweatshops, 17-hour days and child labour.

These poor conditions were compounded in 1844 by harvest failure. Food riots broke out on Gendarmenmarkt, when a crowd stormed the market stalls.

Things came to a head in 1848, the year of revolutions. Berliners seized the moment. Political meetings were held in beer gardens and in the Tiergarten, and demands made for internal reform and a unification of German-speaking states. At the end of one demonstration in the Tiergarten, there was a running battle between police and demonstrators on Unter den Linden.

'Bismarck strove to bring the states together under the authoritarian dominance of Prussia.'

On 18 March the King finally conceded to allowing a new parliament, and made vague promises about other reforms. Later that day, the crowd of 10,000 that gathered to celebrate the victory were set upon by soldiers. Shots were fired and the revolution began. Barricades went up throughout central Berlin and demonstrators fought with police for 14 hours. Finally the King backed down (again). In exchange for the dismantling of barricades, the king ordered his troops out of Berlin. Days later, he took part in the funeral service for the 'March Dead' – the 183 revolutionaries who had been killed – and also promised more freedoms.

Berlin was now ostensibly in the hands of the revolutionaries. A Civil Guard patrolled the city, the King rode through the streets wearing the revolutionary colours (black, red and gold), seeming to embrace liberalism and nationalism. Prussia, he said, should 'merge into Germany'.

But the revolution proved short-lived. When pressed on unification, the King merely suggested that the other German states send representatives to the Prussian National Assembly, an offer that was rebuffed.

Leading liberals instead convened a German National Assembly in Frankfurt in May 1848, while a new Prussian Assembly met in what is now the Konzerthaus on Gendarmenmarkt to debate a new constitution. At the end of 1848 reforming fervour took over Berlin.

THE BACKLASH

The onset of winter, however, brought a change of mood to the city. Using continuing street violence as the pretext, the King ordered the National Assembly to be moved to Brandenburg. In early November, he brought troops back into the city and declared a state of siege. Press freedom was once again restricted. The Civil Guard and National Assembly were dissolved. On 5 December the King delivered his final blow to the liberals by unveiling a new constitution fashioned to his own tastes.

Throughout the winter of 1848-9 thousands of liberals were arrested or expelled. A new city constitution, drawn up in 1850, reduced the number of eligible voters to five per cent of the population. The police president became more powerful than the mayor.

By 1857 Friedrich Wilhelm had become senile. His brother Wilhelm acted as regent until becoming king on Friedrich's death in 1861.

Once again, the people's hopes were raised: the new monarch began his reign by appointing liberals to the cabinet. The building of the Rotes Rathaus ('Red Town Hall') gave the city council a headquarters to match the size of the royal palace. Completed in 1869, the Rathaus was named for the colour of its bricks, and not (yet) the political persuasion of its members.

But by 1861 the King was locked in a dispute with parliament over proposed army reforms. He wanted to strengthen his control of the armed forces. Parliament refused, so the King went over its members' heads and appointed a new prime minister: Otto von Bismarck.

THE IRON CHANCELLOR

An arrogant genius who began his career as a diplomat, Bismarck was well able to deal with unruly parliamentarians. Using a constitutional loophole to rule against the majority, he quickly pushed through the army reforms. Extra-parliamentary opposition was dealt with in the usual manner: oppression and censorship. Dissension thus suppressed, Bismarck turned his mind to German unification.

Unlike the bourgeois revolutionaries of 1848, who desired a Germany united by popular will and endowed with political reforms, Bismarck strove to bring the states together under the authoritarian dominance of Prussia. His methods involved astute foreign policy and outright aggression.

Wars against Denmark (1864) and Austria (1866) brought post-Napoleonic order to an abrupt end. Prussia was no longer the smallest of the Great Powers, but an aspiring initiator of geopolitical change. Austria's defeat confirmed the primacy of Prussia among German-speaking states. Victory on the battlefield boosted Bismarck's popularity across Prussia – but not in Berlin itself. He

GUILLAUME II SUR SON
NOUVEAU CHEVAL DE BATAILLE.
ZEPPELIN 1908
Orens 08
...NOTRE AVENIR EST EN L'AIR!
(GARE A TOI LA LUNE...)

The Wilhelmine period: showy militarism and ridiculous moustaches.

was defeated in his Berlin constituency in the 1867 election to the new North German League. This was a Prussian-dominated body linking the northern states and a stepping stone towards Germany's overall unification.

Bismarck's third war – against France in 1870 – revealed his scope for intrigue and opportunism. He exploited a dispute over the succession to the Spanish throne to provoke France into declaring war on Prussia. Citing the North German League and treaties signed with the southern German states, Bismarck brought together a united German army under Prussian leadership.

Following the defeat of the French army on 2 September, Bismarck turned a unified military into the basis for a unified nation. The Prussian king would be German emperor: beneath him would be four kings, 18 grand-dukes and assorted princes from the German states, which would retain some regional powers. (This arrangement formed the basis for the modern federal system of regional *Länder*.)

On 18 January 1871 King Wilhelm was proclaimed German Kaiser ('Emperor') in the Hall of Mirrors in Versailles.

In just nine years, Bismarck had united Germany, forging an empire that dominated central Europe. The political, economic and social centre of this new creation was Berlin.

IMPERIAL BERLIN

The coming of empire threw Berlin into one of its greatest periods of expansion and change. The economic boom (helped by five billion gold francs extracted from France as war reparations) led to a wave of speculation. Farmers in Wilmersdorf and Schöneberg became millionaires overnight as they sold off their fields to developers.

During the decades following German unification, Berlin emerged as Europe's most modern metropolis. This period was later dubbed the *Gründerzeit* ('Foundation Years').

The *Gründerzeit* were marked by a move away from traditional Prussian values of thrift and modesty, towards the gaudy and bombastic. In Berlin, the change of mood manifested itself in numerous monuments and buildings. Of these the Reichstag, the Siegessäule ('Victory Column'), the Berliner Dom and the Kaiser-Wilhelm-Gedächtniskirche are the most prominent.

Superficially, the Reichstag (designed by Paul Wallot, and completed in 1894) represented a weighty commitment to parliamentary democracy, but, in reality, Germany was still in the grip of conservative, backward-looking forces. The authoritarian power of the Kaiser remained intact, as was demonstrated by the decision of Wilhelm II to sack Bismarck in 1890 following a number of disagreements over policy.

THE 'RED MENACE'

When Bismarck began his premiership in 1861 his offices on Wilhemstrasse overlooked potato fields. By the time he lost his job in 1890 they were in the centre of Europe's most congested city. Economic boom and growing political and social importance attracted hundreds of thousands of new inhabitants. At the time of unification in 1871 820,000 people lived in Berlin; by 1890 this number had nearly doubled.

The growing numbers of the working class were shoved into hastily built *Mietskasernen* tenements (literally, 'rental barracks') that mushroomed across the city – particularly in Kreuzberg, Wedding and Prenzlauer Berg. Poorly ventilated and overcrowded, the *Mietskasernen* (many of which still stand), became a breeding ground for social unrest.

The Social Democratic Party (SPD), founded in 1869, quickly became the voice for the city's have-nots. In the 1877 general election it won 40 per cent of the Berlin vote. Here was born the left-wing reputation of *Rotes Berlin* ('Red Berlin') that has persisted to the present day.

In 1878 two assassination attempts on the Kaiser gave Bismarck an excuse to classify socialists as enemies of the state. He introduced restrictive laws to curb the 'red menace', banning the SPD and other progressive parties.

The ban existed until 1890 – the year of Bismarck's sacking – but did not stem support for the SPD. In the 1990 general election, the SPD dominated the vote in Berlin. And in 1912 it won more than 70 per cent of the Berlin vote, becoming the largest party in the Reichstag.

KAISER BILL

Famed for his ridiculous moustache, Kaiser Wilhelm II came to the throne in 1888, and soon became the personification of the new Germany: bombastic, awkward and unpredictable. Like his grandmother Queen Victoria, he gave his name to an era. Wilhelm's epoch is associated with showy militarism and foreign policy bungles leading to a world war that cost the Kaiser his throne and Germany its stability.

The Wilhelmine years were also notable for explosive growth in Berlin (the population rose to four million by 1914) and a blossoming of the city's cultural and intellectual life. The Bode Museum was built in 1904, and in 1912 work began next door on the Pergamon Museum. In 1912 a new Opera House was unveiled in Charlottenburg (later to be destroyed in the war; the Deutsche Oper now stands on the site). Expressionism took off in 1910 and the

Kurfürstendamm became filled with art galleries. Although Paris was still Europe's art capital, the German city was fast catching up.

By the time of Wilhelm's abdication in 1918, Berlin had become a centre of scientific and intellectual development. Six Berlin scientists (including Albert Einstein and Max Planck) were awarded Nobel Prizes.

In the years immediately preceding World War I Berlin appeared to be loosening its stiff collar of pomposity. Tangoing became all the rage in new clubs around Friedrichstrasse – though the Kaiser promptly banned officers in uniform from joining in the fun. Yet, despite the progressive changes, growing militarism and international tension overshadowed the period.

Germany was not alone in its preparedness for war. By 1914 Europe was well and truly armed and almost waiting to tear itself apart. In June 1914 the assassination of Archduke Franz Ferdinand provided the excuse. On 1 August war was declared on Russia, and the Kaiser appeared on a balcony of the royal palace to tell a jubilant crowd that from that moment onwards, he would not recognise any parties, only Germans. At the Reichstag the deputies, who had virtually unanimously voted in support of the war, agreed.

WORLD WAR I AND REVOLUTION

No one was prepared for the disaster of World War I. After Bismarck, the Germans had come to expect quick, sweeping victories. The armies on the Western Front settled into their trenches for a war of attrition that would cost over a million German lives. Meanwhile, the civilian population began to adapt to austerity and shortages. After the 1917 harvest failed there

Uncommon currency

Of all the disasters that hit Berlin in the 20th century, nothing was as mad as the hyperinflation of 1923. It wasn't a sudden catastrophe. The German government had been dallying with inflation for years, funding its war effort by printing bonds. In 1914 a dollar was buying 4.2 marks; by late 1922, it was buying 7,000. And then the French occupied the Ruhr and things got really out of hand. By 20 November 1923, the rate had reached a boggling 4,200,000,000,000 marks to the dollar.

Images of the crisis are vaguely comic: children using bundles of notes as building blocks, a wheelbarrow of currency for a loaf of bread. At its height, over 300 paper mills and 2,000 printing presses worked around the clock to supply the Reichsbank with notes – in denominations of one million, then one billion, then a hundred billion. Some companies paid their employees twice a day, so they could shop at lunch to beat the afternoon inflation.

A little hard currency could buy anything or anyone. Foreign visitors splashed out in an orgy of conspicuous consumption. Entrepreneurs created whole business empires from ever cheaper marks. And the homes of peasants in nearby villages filled up with Meissen porcelain and fine furniture as Berliners traded valuables for eggs or bread.

But although it was absurd, it wasn't funny. People starved as all their possessions vanished. The suicide rate shot up, as did infant mortality. Teenagers prostituted themselves after school, often with parental approval. Nothing made sense anymore. And as the simple fabric of everyday life was seen to unravel, so did people's faith in government. Among the worst hit were those who had most trusted the idea of Germany: the middle-class patriots who had sunk their money into war bonds, only to be paid back in useless paper.

The crisis was eventually brought under control, but the result had been a mass transfer of wealth to a handful of adventurers, big business and government. And as a pauperised people wondered who to blame, the hard right had found a cause. Nothing prepared the ground for Hitler better than the literal and moral impoverishment of the inflationary period.

Currency issues would continue to rumble through Berlin's 20th century. The formal division of Germany and Berlin followed the introduction of zonal currencies in 1948. The destabilisation of the east mark was one factor behind the later decision to build the Wall. For the rest of the Cold War, foreign visitors whooping it up on hard currency once again became a feature of city life, at least in its eastern half. And the true end of the GDR came not when the Wall was breached, but on the July 1990 day when the east mark was absorbed by its western counterpart – at a one-to-one rate so unrealistic that it promptly caused the collapse of East German industry. And these days, of course, everyone's moaning about the euro.

were outbreaks of famine. Soon dog and cat meat started to appear on the menu in the capital's restaurants.

The SPD's initial enthusiasm for war evaporated, and in 1916 the party refused to pass the Berlin budget. A year later, members of the party's radical wing broke away to form the Spartacus League. Anti-war feeling was voiced in mass strikes in April 1917 and January 1918. These were brutally suppressed, but, when the Imperial Marines in Kiel mutinied on 2 November 1918, the authorities were no longer able to stop the anti-war movement.

The mutiny spread to Berlin where members of the Guards Regiment came out against the war. On 9 November the Kaiser was forced into abdication and, later, exile. This date is weirdly layered with significance in German history; it's the anniversary of the establishment of the Weimar Republic (1918), Kristallnacht (1938) and the fall of the Wall (1989).

It was on this day that Philip Scheidemann, a leading SPD member of parliament and key proponent of republicanism, broke off his lunch in the second-floor restaurant of the Reichstag. He walked over to a window overlooking Königsplatz (now Platz der Republik) where a crowd had massed and declared to them: 'The old and the rotten have broken down. Long live the new! Long live the German Republic!'

At the other end of Unter den Linden, Karl Liebknecht, who, together with Rosa Luxemburg, headed the Spartacus League, declared Germany a socialist republic from a balcony of the occupied royal palace. (The balcony was the same one the Kaiser used when he spoke to Berliners on the eve of the war, and has been preserved as part of the *Staatratsgebäude* ('State Council building') of the East German government.)

Liebknecht and the Spartacists wanted a Communist Germany; Scheidemann and the SPD favoured a parliamentary democracy. Between them stood those still loyal to the vanished monarchy. All were prepared to fight. Street battles ensued throughout the city.

It was in this climate of turmoil and violence that the Weimar Republic was born.

THE WEIMAR REPUBLIC

The revolution in Berlin may have brought peace to the Western Front, where hostilities were ended on 11 November, but in Germany it unleashed a wave of political terror and instability. Berlin's new masters, the SPD under the leadership of Friedrich Ebert, ordered renegade battalions of soldiers returning from the front (known as the Freikorps) to quash the Spartacists, who launched a concerted bid for power in January 1919.

Within days, the uprising had been bloodily suppressed, and Liebknecht and Luxemburg went into hiding. On 15 January Freikorps officers traced them to a house in Wilmersdorf. They were arrested and taken to a hotel near Zooligischer Garten for interrogation. The officers then murdered them, dumping Luxemburg's body over the Liechtenstein Bridge into the Landwehr Canal. Today a plaque marks the spot.

Four days later, the national elections returned the SPD as the largest party: the Social Democrats' victory over the extreme left was complete. Berlin was deemed too dangerous for parliamentary business, so the government swiftly decamped to the quaint provincial town of Weimar, from which the first German republic took its name.

Germany's new constitution ended up being full of good liberal intentions, but riddled with technical flaws, and this left the country wide open to weak coalition government and quasi-dictatorial presidential rule.

'During the 1920s the city overtook Paris as Europe's arts and entertainment capital.'

Another crippling blow to the new republic was the Versailles Treaty, which set the terms of peace. Reparation payments (set to run until 1988) blew a hole in an already fragile economy. Support for the right-wing nationalist lobby was fuelled by the loss of territories in both east and west. And restrictions placed on the German military led some right-wingers to claim that Germany's soldiers had been 'stabbed in the back' by Jews and left-wingers.

In March 1920 a right-wing coup was staged in Berlin under the leadership of Wolfgang Kapp, a civil servant from east Prussia. The recently returned government once again fled the city. For four days Berlin was besieged by roaming Freikorps. Some of them had taken to adorning their helmets with a new symbol: the *Hakenkreuz* or swastika.

Ultimately, a general strike and the refusal of the army to join Kapp brought an end to the putsch. But the political and economic chaos in the city remained. Political assassinations were commonplace. Food shortages lead to bouts of famine. Inflation started to escalate (*see p14* **Uncommon currency**).

There were two main reasons for the precipitate devaluation of the Reichsmark. To pay for the war, the desperate imperial government had resorted simply to printing more money, a policy continued by new republican rulers. The burden of reparations also lead to an outflow of foreign currency.

In 1923, the French government sent troops into the Ruhr industrial region to take by force reparation goods that the German government said it could no longer afford to pay. The Communists planned an uprising in Berlin for October, but lost their nerve.

In November, a young ex-corporal called Adolf Hitler, who led the tiny National Socialist Party (NSDAP or Nazi Party), launched an attempted coup from a beer-hall in Munich.

His programme called for armed resistance against the French, an end to the 'dictatorship of Versailles' and punishment for all those – especially the Jews – who had 'betrayed' Germany at the end of the war.

Hitler's first attempt at power came to nothing. Instead of marching on Berlin, he went to prison. Inflation was finally brought down with the introduction of a new currency (one new mark was worth one trillion old ones).

But the overall decline of moral and social values that had taken place in the five years since 1918 was not so easy to restore.

THE GOLDEN TWENTIES

Joseph Goebbels came to Berlin in 1926 to take charge of the local Nazi Party organisation. On arriving, he observed: 'This city is a melting pot of everything that is evil – prostitution, drinking houses, cinemas, Marxism, Jews, strippers, negroes dancing and all the offshoots of modern art.'

Omitting the word 'evil', Goebbels' description of 1920s Berlin was not far wrong. During that decade the city overtook Paris as continental Europe's arts and entertainment capital, and added its own decadent twist. 'We used to have a first-class army,' mused Klaus Mann, the author of *Mephisto*; 'now we have first-class perversions.'

By 1927 Berlin boasted more than 70 cabarets and nightclubs. At the Theater des Westens, near Zoo, cabaret artist Josephine Baker danced to a packed house. She also danced naked at parties thrown by playwright Karl Volmoeller in his flat on Pariser Platz. 'Berlin was mad! A triumph!' she later recalled.

While Brecht's *Dreigroschenoper* played at the Theater am Schiffbauerdamm, Berlin's Dadaists gathered at the Romanisches Café on Tauentzienstrasse (later destroyed by bombing – the Europa-Center now stands on the site). There was a proliferation of avant-garde magazines focusing on new art and literature.

But the flipside of all the frenetic enjoyment was an underbelly of raw poverty and glaring social tension, reflected in the works of painters like George Grosz and Otto Dix. In the music halls, Brecht and Weill used a popular medium to ram home points about social injustices.

In architecture and design, the revolutionary ideas emanating from the Bauhaus school in Dessau (it briefly moved to Berlin in 1932, but was closed down by the Nazis a year later) were taking concrete form in building projects such as the Shell House building on the Landwehr Canal, the Siemenstadt new town, and the model housing project Hufeisensiedlung ('Horse Shoe Estate') in Britz. Art created in the Bauhaus workshop from 1919-1933 is kept in the Bauhaus Archiv-Museum für Gestaltung.

STREET-FIGHTING YEARS

The stock market crash on Wall Street and the onset of global depression in 1929 ushered in the brutal end of the Weimar Republic.

The fractious coalition governments that had just managed to hold on to power in the prosperous late 1920s were no match for rocketing unemployment and a surge in support for extremist parties.

By the end of 1929 nearly one in four Berliners were out of work. The city's streets became a battleground for clashes between Nazis, Communists and social democrats. Increasingly, the police relied on water cannons, armoured vehicles and guns to quell street fighting across the city. One May Day demonstration left 30 dead and several hundred wounded. At Bülowplatz (now Rosa-Luxemburg-Platz) where the Communist Party, the KPD, had its headquarters, there were regular battles between Communists, the police and Nazi stormtroopers (the SA). In August 1931, two police officers were murdered on Bülowplatz. One of the men accused of the murders (and later found guilty, albeit by a Nazi court) was Erich Mielke, a young Communist, later to become the head of East Germany's secret police, the Stasi.

In 1932 the violence in Berlin reached crisis level. In one six-week period, 300 street battles left 70 people dead. In the general election in July the Nazis took 40 per cent of the vote and became the largest party in the Reichstag. Hermann Göring, one of Hitler's earliest followers, and a wounded veteran of the beer-hall putsch, was appointed Reichstag president.

But the prize of government still eluded the Nazis. At the elections held in November, the Nazis lost two million votes across Germany and 37,000 in Berlin, where the Communists emerged as the strongest party. (In 'Red' Wedding, 60 per cent voted for the KPD.)

The election had been held against the backdrop of a strike by some 20,000 transport employees, who were protesting against planned wage cuts. The strike had been called by the Communists and the Nazis, who vied with each other to capture the mass vote and bring the Weimar Republic to an end. Under orders from Moscow, the KPD shunned all co-operation with the SPD, ending any possibility of a broad left-wing front.

As Berlin headed into another winter of depression, almost every third person was out of work. A city survey recorded that almost half of Berlin's inhabitants were living four to a room, and that a large proportion of the city's housing stock was unfit for human habitation. Berlin topped the European table of suicides.

The new government of General Kurt von Schleicher ruled by presidential decree. Schleicher had promised President von Hindenburg he could tame the Nazis into a coalition. When he failed, his rival Franz von Papen successfully overcame Hindenburg's innate dislike for Hitler and manoeuvred the Nazi leader into power. On 30 January 1933 Adolf Hitler was named Chancellor and moved from his headquarters in the Hotel Kaiserhof in Glinkastrasse (it was central and his favourite band played there) to the Chancellery two streets away in Wilhelmstrasse.

That evening, the SA staged a torchlight parade through the Brandenburger Tor and along to the Chancellery. Looking out from the window of his house next to the Gate, the artist Max Liebermann remarked to his dinner guests: 'I cannot eat as much as I'd like to puke.'

THE NAZIS TAKE CONTROL

The government Hitler now led was a coalition of Nazis and German nationalists, led by the media magnate Alfred Hugenberg. Together their votes fell just short of a parliamentary majority, so another election was called for March. In the meantime Hitler continued to rule by decree.

The last free election of the Republic was also the most violent. Open persecution of Communists began. The Nazis banned meetings of the KPD, shut down Communist newspapers and broke up SPD election rallies.

On 27 February a fire broke out in the Reichstag. It was almost certainly started by the Nazis, who used it as an excuse to step up the persecution of opponents. Over 12,000 Communists were arrested. Spelling it out in a speech at the Sportspalast two days before the election, Goebbels said: 'It's not my job to practise justice, instead I have to destroy and exterminate – nothing else.'

The Nazis still didn't achieve an absolute majority (in Berlin they polled 34 per cent), but that didn't matter. With the support of his coalition allies, Hitler passed an Enabling Law giving him dictatorial powers. By summer Germany had been declared a one-party state.

Already ad hoc concentration camps – known as brown houses after the colour of the SA uniforms – had sprung up around the city. The SS established itself in Prinz Albrecht

The Nazis burn books in May 1933. *See p18.*

Jewish memorial in **Grosse Hamburger Strasse**. *See p19.*

Palais where it was later joined by the secret police, the Gestapo. Just to the north of Berlin near Oranienburg, a concentration camp, Sachsenhausen, was set up.

Along the Kurfürstendamm squads of SA stormtroopers would go 'Jew baiting', and on 1 April 1933 the first boycott of Jewish shops began. A month later Goebbels, who became Minister for Propaganda, organised a book-burning, which took place in the courtyard of the university on Unter den Linden. Books by Jews or writers deemed degenerate or traitors were thrown on to a huge bonfire.

Berlin's unemployment problem was tackled through a series of public works programmes, growing militarisation, which drew new recruits to the army, and the 'encouragement' of women to leave the workplace.

Following the policy of *Gleichschaltung* (co-ordination), the Nazis began to control public life. With a few exceptions, party membership became obligatory for doctors, lawyers, professors and journalists.

During the Night of the Long Knives in July 1934, Hitler settled old scores with opponents within the SA and Nazi Party. At Lichterfelde barracks, officers of the SS shot and killed over 150 SA members. Hitler's predecessor as Chancellor, General von Schleicher, was shot with his wife at their home in Wannsee.

After the death of President Hindenburg in August 1934 Hitler had himself named Führer ('Leader') and made the armed forces swear an oath of allegiance to him. Within less than two years, the Nazis had subjugated Germany.

THE VITAL AND THE DEGENERATE

A brief respite came with the Olympic Games in August 1936. In a bid to persuade foreign spectators that all was well in the Reich, Goebbels ordered the removal of anti-Semitic slogans from shops. 'Undesirables' were moved out of the city, and the pavement display cases for the racist Nazi newspaper *Der Stürmer* ('The Stormtrooper') were dismantled.

The Games, mainly held at the newly built Olympiastadion in Charlottenburg, were not such a success for the Nazis. Instead of blond Aryan giants sweeping the field, Hitler had to watch the African-American Jesse Owens clock up medals and records.

The Games did work, however, as a public relations exercise. Foreign observers left glowing with reports about a strident and healthy nation. But had any of the foreign visitors stayed, they would have seen the reality of Hitler's policy of co-ordinating all facets of life in Berlin within the Nazi doctrine.

As part of a nationwide campaign to remove what the Nazis considered to be *Entartete*

Kunst ('Degenerate Art') from German cultural life, works of modern art were collected and brought together in a touring exhibition designed to show the depth of depravity in contemporary ('Jewish-dominated') culture.

But Nazi hopes that these 'degenerate' works would repulse the German people fell flat. When the exhibition arrived at Berlin's Zeughaus in early 1938 thousands queued for admission. The people loved the paintings.

After the exhibition, the paintings were sent to auction in Switzerland. Those that remained unsold were burnt in the fire station in Köpenicker Strasse. More than 5,000 paintings were destroyed.

TOTALITARIAN TOWN PLANNING

After taking power, Hitler ordered that the lime trees on Unter den Linden be chopped down to give the boulevard a cleaner, more sanitised form – the first step in Nazi urban planning.

Hitler's plans for the redesign of Berlin reflected the hatred the Nazis felt for the city. Hitler entrusted young architect Albert Speer with the job of recreating Berlin as a metropolis to 'out-trump Paris and Vienna'. The heart of old Berlin was to be demolished, and its small streets replaced by two highways stretching 37 kilometres (23 miles) from north to south and 50 kilometres (30 miles) from east to west. Each axis would be 90 metres (295 feet) wide. Crowning the northern axis would be a huge *Volkshalle* ('People's Hall') nearly 300 metres (1,000 feet) high with space for 150,000 people. Speer and Hitler also had grand plans for a triumphal arch three times the size of the Arc de Triomphe, and a Führer's Palace 150 times bigger than the one occupied by Bismarck. The new city was to be called Germania.

The onset of war meant that Speer only built a fraction of what was intended. Hitler's new Chancellery, completed in early 1939, was constructed in under a year. (It was demolished after the war.) On the proposed east–west axis, a small section around the Siegessäule was widened for Hitler's 50th birthday in April 1939.

KRISTALLNACHT

Of the half-a-million Jews living in Germany in 1933 over a third lived in Berlin. The Jewish community had played an important role in Berlin's development, especially in the financial, artistic and intellectual circles of the city.

The Nazis wiped out these centuries-old traditions in 12 years of persecution and murder. Arrests soon followed the initial boycotts and acts of intimidation. From 1933 to 1934 many of Berlin's Jews fled to exile abroad. Those who stayed were to be subjected to legislation (the Nuremberg Laws of 1935) that banned Jews from public office, forbade them to marry Aryan Germans and stripped them of citizenship. Jewish cemeteries were desecrated and the names of Jews chipped off war memorials.

Berlin business institutions that had been owned by Jews – such as the Ullstein newspaper group and the Tietz and Wertheim department stores – were 'Aryanised'. The Nazis either expropriated them from the owners or forced them to sell at ridiculously low prices.

On 9 November 1938 'Kristallnacht' (named after the broken glass), a wave of 'spontaneous' acts of vandalism and violence against Jews and their property, began in response to the assassination of a German diplomat in Paris by a young Jewish émigré. Jewish businesses and houses across Berlin were stoned, looted and set ablaze. A total of 24 synagogues were set on fire. The Nazis rounded up 12,000 Jews and took them to Sachsenhausen concentration camp.

WORLD WAR II

Since 1935 Berliners had been taking part in practice air-raid drills, but it was not until the Sudeten crisis of 1938 that the possibility of war became real. At that juncture Hitler was able to get his way and persuade France and Britain to let him take over the German-speaking areas of northern Czechoslovakia.

'They joked and drank brandy as they sat around discussing mass murder.'

But a year later, his plans to repeat the exercise in Poland were met with resistance in London and Paris. Following Germany's invasion of Poland on 1 September 1939 Britain and France declared war on the Reich.

Despite the propaganda and early victories, most Berliners were horrified by the war. The first air raids came with the RAF bombing of Pankow and Lichtenberg in early 1940.

In 1941, following the German invasion of the Soviet Union, the 75,000 Jews remaining in Berlin were required to wear a yellow Star of David and the first systematic deportations to concentration camps began. By the end of the war only 5,000 Jews remained in Berlin.

Notorious assembly points for the deportations were Putlitzstrasse in Wedding, Grosse Hamburger Strasse and Rosenstrasse in Mitte. On 20 January 1942 a meeting of the leaders of the various Nazi security organisations in the suburb of Wannsee agreed on a 'final solution' to the Jewish question. They joked and drank brandy as they sat around discussing mass murder.

The *Trummerfrauen* start cleaning the rubble of post-war Berlin. *See p21.*

The turning point in the war came with the surrender at Stalingrad on 31 January 1943. In a bid to grab some advantage from this crushing defeat, Goebbels held a rally in the Sportpalast where he announced that Germany had now moved into a state of 'total war'. By summer women and children were being evacuated from Berlin and schools were shut down. By the end of 1943 over 700,000 people had fled Berlin.

The Battle of Berlin, which the RAF launched in November 1943, reduced much of the city centre to rubble. Between then and February 1944 more than 10,000 tonnes of bombs were dropped on the city. Nearly 5,000 people were killed and around 250,000 were made homeless.

THE JULY PLOT

On 20 July 1944 a group of officers, civil servants and former trades unionists launched a last-ditch attempt to assassinate Hitler. But Hitler survived the explosion of a bomb placed at his eastern command post in East Prussia by Colonel Count von Stauffenberg.

That evening Stauffenberg was killed by firing squad in the courtyard of army headquarters in Bendlerstrasse, now Stauffenbergstrasse. The other members of the plot were rounded up and put on trial at the People's Court near Kleistpark and subsequently executed at Plötzensee Prison.

In early January 1945 the Red Army launched a major offensive that carried it on to German soil. On 12 February the heaviest bombing raid yet on Berlin killed over 23,000 people in little more than an hour.

As the Red Army moved into Berlin's suburbs Hitler celebrated his last birthday on 20 April in his bunker behind Wilhelmstrasse. Three days later Neukölln and Tempelhof fell. By 28 April Alexanderplatz and Hallesches Tor were in the hands of the Red Army.

The next day Hitler called his last war conference. He then married his companion Eva Braun and committed suicide with her the day after. As their bodies were being burnt by loyal SS officers, a few streets away a red flag was raised over the Reichstag. The city officially surrendered on 2 May. Germany's unconditional surrender was signed on 8 May at the Red Army command centre in Karlshorst.

DEVASTATION AND DIVISION

When the playwright Bertolt Brecht returned to Berlin in 1948 he encountered 'a pile of rubble next to Potsdam'. Nearly a quarter of all buildings in the city had been destroyed. The human cost of the war was equally startling – around 80,000 Berliners had been killed, not including the thousands of Jews who would not return from the concentration camps.

There was no gas or electricity and only the suburbs had running water. Public transport had broken down. In the first weeks following capitulation, Red Army soldiers went on a rampage of random killings and rapes. Thousands of men were transported to labour camps in the Soviet Union. Food supplies were used up and later the harvest in the war-scarred land around the city failed. Come winter, the few remaining trees in the Tiergarten and other parks were chopped down for firewood.

Clearing the rubble was to take years of dull, painstaking work. The *Trummerfrauen* ('rubble women') cleared the streets and created mountains of junk – such as the Teufelsberg, one of seven such hills that still exist today.

The Soviets stripped factories across Berlin as part of a programme to dismantle German industry and take it back home. As reparation, whole factories were moved to Russia.

Under the terms of the Yalta Agreement, which divided Germany into four zones of Allied control, Berlin was also split into four sectors, with the Soviets in the east and the Americans, British and French in the west. A Kommandatura, made up of each army's commander and based in the building of the People's Court in Elssholzstrasse, dealt with the administration of the city.

Initially, the administration worked well in getting basics, like the transport network, back to running order. But tensions between the Soviets and the Western Allies began to rise as civilian government of city affairs returned. In the eastern sector a merger of the Communist and Social Democratic parties (which had both been refounded in summer 1945) was pushed through to form the Socialist Unity Party (SED). In the western sector, however, the SPD continued as a separate party.

Events came to a head after elections for a new city government in 1946. The SED failed to get more than 20 per cent of the vote, while the SPD won nearly 50 per cent of all votes cast. The Soviets vetoed the appointment to office of the SPD's mayoral candidate, Ernst Reuter, who was a committed anti-Communist.

THE BERLIN AIRLIFT

The situation worsened in spring 1948. In response to the decision by the Western Allies to merge their respective zones in western Germany into one administrative entity and introduce a new currency, the Soviets walked out of the Kommandatura. In late June all transport links to West Berlin were cut off and the blockade of the city by Soviet forces began. Three 'air-corridors' linking West Berlin with western Germany became lifelines as Allied aircraft transported food, coal and industrial components to the beleaguered city.

Within Berlin the future division of the city began to take permanent shape as city councillors from the west were drummed out of the town hall. They moved to Rathaus Schöneberg in the west. Fresh elections in the western sector returned Reuter as mayor. The Freie Universität was set up in response to Communist dominance of the Humboldt University in the east.

Having failed to starve West Berlin into submission, the Soviets called off the blockade after 11 months. The blockade also convinced the Western Allies that they should maintain a presence in Berlin and that their sectors of the city should be linked with the Federal Republic, founded in May 1949. The response from the East was the founding of the German Democratic Republic on 7 October. With the birth of the 'first Workers' and Peasants' State on German soil', the formal division of Germany into two states was complete.

THE COLD WAR

During the Cold War, Berlin was the focal point for stand-offs between the United States and the Soviet Union. Far from having any control over its own affairs, the city was wholly at the mercy of geopolitical developments. Throughout the 1950s the 'Berlin Question' remained prominent on the international agenda.

Technically, the city was still under Four-Power control, but since the Soviet departure from the Kommandatura, and the setting up of the German Democratic Republic with its capital in East Berlin (a breach of the wartime agreement on the future of the city), this counted for little in practice.

'The US poured millions of dollars into West Berlin to maintain it as a counterpoint to Communism.'

In principle, the Western Allies adhered to these agreements by retaining ultimate authority in West Berlin, while allowing the city to be integrated into the West German system. (There were notable exceptions, such as the exemption of West Berliners from conscription, and the barring of city MPs from voting in the West German parliament.)

Throughout the 1950s the two halves of Berlin began to develop separately as the political systems in East and West evolved.

In the East, Communist leader Walter Ulbricht set about creating Moscow's most hardline ally in eastern Europe. Work began on a Moscow-style boulevard – called Stalinallee – running east from Alexanderplatz. Industry was nationalised and subjected to rigid central planning. Opposition was kept in check by the new Ministry for State Security: the Stasi.

West Berlin landed the role of 'Last Outpost of the Free World' and, as such, was developed into a showcase for capitalism. As well as the Marshall Plan, which paid for much of the reconstruction of West Germany, the US poured millions of dollars into West Berlin to maintain it as a counterpoint to Communism. The West German government, which at the time refused to recognise East Germany as a legitimate state, demonstrated its commitment to seeing Berlin reinstated as German capital by holding occasional parliamentary sessions in the city. The prominence accorded West Berlin was later reflected in the high profile of its politicians (Willy Brandt, for example) who were received abroad by prime ministers and presidents – unusual for mere mayors.

Yet despite the emerging divisions the two halves of the city continued to co-exist in some abnormal fashion. City planners on both sides of the sectoral boundaries initially drew up plans with the whole city in mind.

'Soviet tanks rolled into the centre of East Berlin, where they were met by stones thrown by demonstrators.'

The transport system crossed between East and West, with the underground network being controlled by the West and the S-Bahn by the East. Movement between the sectors (despite 'border' checks) was relatively normal, as Westerners went East to watch a Brecht play or buy cheap books. Easterners travelled West to work, shop or see the latest Hollywood films.

The secret services of both sides kept a high presence in the city, and there were frequent acts of sabotage. Berlin became espionage capital of the world.

RECONSTRUCTION AND REFUGEES

As the effects of US money and the West German 'economic miracle' took hold, West Berlin began to recover. A municipal housing programme meant that by 1963 200,000 new flats had been built. Unemployment dropped from 30 per cent in 1950 to virtually zero by 1961. The labour force also included about 50,000 East Berliners who commuted over the inter-sector borders.

In the East reconstruction was slower. Until the mid 1950s East Germany paid reparations to the Soviet Union. And to begin with there seemed to be more acts of wilful destruction than positive construction. The old palace, only slightly damaged by bombing, was blown up in 1950 to make way for a parade ground, which later evolved into a car park.

In 1952 the East Germans sealed off the border with West Germany. The only way out of the 'zone' was through West Berlin and the number of refugees from the East rose dramatically from 50,000 in 1950 to 300,000 in 1953. Over the decade, one million refugees from the East came through West Berlin.

THE 1953 UPRISING

In June 1953, partly in response to the rapid loss of skilled manpower, the East German government announced a ten per cent increase in working 'norms' – the number of hours and volume of output that workers were required to fulfil each day. In protest, building workers on Stalinallee (now Karl-Marx-Allee) downed tools on 16 June and marched to the government offices on Leipziger Strasse. The government refused to relent, and strikes soon broke out across the city. Communist Party offices were stormed and red flags torn from public buildings. By midday the government had lost control of the city and it was left to the Red Army to restore order. Soviet tanks rolled into the centre of East Berlin, where they were met by stones thrown by demonstrators.

By nightfall the uprising was crushed. According to official figures 23 people died, though other estimates put the figure at over 200. There followed a wave of arrests across East Berlin, with more than four thousand people detained. The majority went on to receive stiff prison sentences.

The 17 June uprising only furthered the wave of emigration. And by the end of the 1950s it seemed likely that East Germany would cease to function as an industrial state through the loss of skilled labour. Estimates put the loss to the East German economy through emigration at some DM100 billion. Ulbricht increased his demands on Moscow to take action.

In 1958 the Soviet leader Nikita Khrushchev tried to bully the Allies into relinquishing West Berlin with an ultimatum calling for an end to the military occupation of the city and a 'normalisation of the situation in the capital of the GDR', by which he meant Berlin as a whole. The ultimatum was rejected and the Allies made clear their commitment to West Berlin. Unwilling to provoke a world war, but needing to prop up his ally, Khrushchev backed down and sanctioned Ulbricht's alternative plan for a solution to the Berlin question.

THE WALL

During the early summer of 1961 rumours spread in town that Ulbricht intended to seal off West Berlin with a barrier or reinforced border. Emigration had reached a high point as 1,500 East Germans fled to the West each day.

However, when in the early hours of 13 August units of the People's Police (assisted by

'Working Class Combat Groups') began to drag bales of barbed wire across Potsdamer Platz, Berlin and the world were caught by surprise.

In a finely planned and executed operation (overseen by Erich Honecker, then Politburo member in charge of security affairs), West Berlin was sealed off within 24 hours. As well as a fence of barbed wire, trenches were dug, the windows in houses straddling the new border were bricked up, and tram and railway lines were interrupted: all this under the watchful eyes of armed guards. Anyone trying to flee West risked being shot; in the 29 years the Wall stood, nearly 80 people died trying to escape. Justifying their actions, the East Germans said they had erected an 'Anti-Fascist Protection Rampart' to prevent a world war.

Days later the construction of a wall began. When it was completed, the concrete part of the 160-kilometre (100-mile) fortification ran to 112 kilometres (70 miles); 37 kilometres (23 miles) of the Wall ran through the city centre. Previously innocuous streets like Bernauer Strasse (where houses on one side were in the East, those on the other in the West) suddenly became the location for one of the world's most sophisticated and deadly border fortifications.

The initial stunned disbelief of Berliners turned into despair as it became clear that (as with the 17 June uprising) the Western Allies could do little more than make a show of strength. President Kennedy dispatched American reinforcements to Berlin, and, for a few tense weeks, American and Soviet tanks squared off at Checkpoint Charlie.

'As fortifications along the Wall were improved... escape became nearly impossible.'

Moral support from the Americans came with the visit of Vice-President Lyndon Johnson a week after the Wall was built. And two years later Kennedy himself arrived and spoke to a crowd of half-a-million people in front of Rathaus Schöneberg. His speech linked the fate of West Berlin with that of the free world and ended with the now famous statement 'Ich bin ein Berliner!' (Literally, alas, 'I am a doughnut').

In its early years the Wall was the scene of daring escape attempts (featured in the Museum Haus Am Checkpoint Charlie). People abseiled off buildings, swam across the Spree, waded through sewers or tried to climb over.

But as the fortifications along the Wall were improved with mines, searchlights and guard dogs, and as the guards were given orders to shoot, escape became nearly impossible. By the time the Wall fell in November 1989 it had been 'updated' four times to incorporate every conceivable deterrent.

In 1971 the Four Powers met and signed the Quadrapartite Agreement, which formally recognised the city's divided status. Border posts (such as the infamous Checkpoint Charlie) were introduced and designated to particular categories of visitors – one for foreigners, another for West Germans, and so on.

A TALE OF TWO CITIES

During the 1960s, with the Wall as infamous and ugly backdrop, the cityscape of modern Berlin (both East and West) began to take shape. On Tauentzienstrasse in the West the Europa-Center was built, and the bomb-damaged Kaiser-Wilhelm-Gedächtniskirche was given a partner – a new church made up of a glass-clad tower and squat bunker.

Hans Scharoun laid out the Kulturforum in Tiergarten as West Berlin's answer to the Museuminsel complex in the East. The first building to go up was Scharoun's Philharmonie, completed in 1963. Mies van der Rohe's Neue Nationalgalerie (which he had originally designed as a Bacardi factory in Havana) was finished in 1968.

In the suburbs work began on concrete mini-towns, Gropiusstadt and Märkisches Viertel. Conceived as solutions to housing shortages, they would develop into alienating ghettos.

Alexanderplatz in the East was rebuilt along totalitarian lines and the Fernsehturm ('Television Tower') was finished. The historic core of Berlin was mostly cleared to make way for parks (such as the Marx-Engels Forum) or new office and housing developments. On the eastern outskirts of the city in Marzahn and Hohenschönhausen work began on mass-scale housing projects.

In 1965 the first sit-down was staged on the Kurfürstendamm by students protesting low grants and expensive accommodation. This was followed by several student political demonstrations against the state in general and the Vietnam war in particular. The first communes were set up in Kreuzberg, sowing the seeds of a counter-culture that was to make the district famous.

The student protest movement came into violent confrontation with the police in 1967 and 1968. One student, Benno Ohnesorg, was shot dead by police at a demonstration against the Shah of Iran, who visited the city in June 1967. A year later the students' leader, Rudi Dutschke, was shot by a right-winger. Demonstrations were held outside the offices of the newspaper group Springer, whose papers were blamed for inciting the shooting. It was out of this movement that the Red Army Faction (also known as the Baader-Meinhof gang) was to emerge. It was to make headlines often in the 1970s, not least through a series of kidnappings of high-profile city officials.

NORMALISING ABNORMALITY

The signing of the Quadrapartite Agreement confirmed West Berlin's abnormal status and ushered in an era of decline, as the frisson of Cold War excitement and 1960s rebellion petered out. More than ever West Berlin depended on huge subsidies from West Germany to keep it going.

Development schemes and tax breaks were introduced to encourage businesses to move to the city (Berliners also paid less income tax), but still the economy and population declined.

At the same time there was growth in the number of *Gastarbeiter* ('guest workers') who arrived from southern Europe and particularly Turkey, to take on menial jobs. Today there are over 120,000 Turks in the city, largely concentrated in Kreuzberg.

By the late 1970s Berlin was mired in the depths of decline. In the West, the city government was discredited by a number of scandals, mostly connected with property deals. In East Berlin Erich Honecker's regime (he succeeded Ulbricht in 1971), which had begun in a mood of reform, became repressive. Some of East Germany's best writers and artists, who had previously supported socialism, left the country. From its headquarters in Normannenstrasse (a building that now houses the Stasi Museum), the Stasi directed its policy of mass observation, and permeated every part of East German society. Between East and West

The good German

If any one figure stands for the Berlin Republic, it's Germany's 55-year-old foreign minister, Joschka Fischer. Leader of the Green Party, which came to power in 1998 as junior coalition partner of the Social Democrats, Fischer is the government's No.2 after Chancellor Gerhard Schröder. He's also both the country's most popular politician and the darling of the international community. Remarkably, this former street-fighting man, notoriously pictured attacking a riot cop back in the early 1970s, has now come to represent 'the Good German'.

Fischer's history – from revolutionary Marxist, to Green MP, to debonair international statesman – roughly parallels the course of a generation. The Greens emerged in the late 1970s Federal Republic, an amalgam of feminist and environmental groups, anti-nuclear protesters, peaceniks and Marxist splinter groups. Fischer came from one of the latter, a Frankfurt faction called Revolutionär Kampf (Revolutionary Struggle). In the late 1960s, they tried to challenge the state from the streets. When the revolution didn't happen, Fischer's generation changed tack and took positions as teachers, lawyers and social workers, hoping to change Germany's political culture from within. They never guessed that their 'long march through the institutions' would lead to the foreign ministry of a united Berlin.

The Green Party was born in 1980. By 1983, it had won representation in the Bundestag. One MP who quickly singled himself out as a talented orator and media-friendly *enfant terrible* was 35-year old ex-rebel Joschka Fischer. His little 'anti-party' made electoral gains throughout the 1980s, participating in regional coalitions and slowly becoming a fixture of the political landscape.

After 1998, the 'red-green' coalition's first term saw a host of green initiatives: a liberal citizenship law, a phasing-out of nuclear power, arms exports restrictions, the legalization of gay partnerships and an ecological tax. Measures such as these are changing Germany and defining the Berlin Republic. And while Fischer has taken his share of domestic flak, particularly over the 1999 decision to send German troops to Kosovo, his presence on the world stage, by turns plain-speaking and visionary, has provided Germany with its image as a modern, liberal state.

Fischer's vision is of a democratic Europe from the Baltic to the Balkans, the Atlantic to the Urals. Only a unified Europe with a single foreign policy, he argues, can tackle the global issues of the day or pose an alternative to US dominance in world affairs.

For the time being, Fischer and the Berlin Republic have their hands full selling long-overdue welfare state reforms to their sceptical constituencies. But whether or not Joschka eventually lands the job of European foreign minister, it's clear that a career of colourful transformations is far from over.

13 August 1961: another brick in the Wall.

there were squalid exchanges of political prisoners for hard currency.

The late 1970s and early 1980s saw the rise of the squatter movement (centred in Kreuzberg), which brought violent political protest back on to the streets.

In 1987 Berlin celebrated its 750th birthday twice, as East and West vied to outdo each other with exhibitions and festivities. In the East, the Nikolaiviertel was restored in time for the celebrations, and Honecker began a programme to do the same for the few remaining historical sites that had survived both wartime bombing and post-war planning. The statue of Frederick the Great riding his horse was returned to Unter den Linden.

THE FALL OF THE WALL

But restored monuments were not enough to stem the growing discontent of East Berliners. The arrival of perestroika in the USSR had been ignored by Honecker, who stuck hard to his Stalinist instincts. Protest was strong and only initially beaten back by the police.

By the spring of 1989 the East German state was no longer able to withstand the pressure of a population fed up with Communism. Throughout the summer thousands fled the city and the country via Hungary, which had opened its borders to the West. Those who stayed began demonstrating for reforms.

By the time Honecker was hosting the celebrations in the *Volkskammer* ('People's Chamber') to mark the 40th anniversary of the GDR on 7 October 1989 crowds were demonstrating outside, chanting 'Gorby! Gorby!' to register their opposition. Honecker was ousted days later. His successor, Egon Krenz, could do little to stem the tide of opposition. In a bid to defend through attack, he decided to grant the concession East Germans wanted most – freedom to travel. On 9 November 1989 the Berlin Wall was opened, just over 29 years after it had been built. As thousands of East Berliners raced through to the sound of popping corks, the end of East Germany and the unification of Berlin and Germany had begun.

REUNIFYING BERLIN

With the Wall down Berlin was once again the centre stage of history. Just as the division of the city defined the split of Europe so the freedom to move again between east and west marked the dawn of the post-Cold War era.

Unsurprisingly, such an auspicious moment went to Berlin's head, and for more than a year the city was in a state of euphoria. Between November 1989 and October 1990 the city witnessed the collapse of Communism and the first free elections (March 1990) in the east for more than 50 years; economic unification with the swapping of the tinny Ostmark for the Deutschmark (July 1990); and the political merger of east into west with formal political unification on 3 October 1990. (It was also the year West Germany picked up its third World Cup trophy. The team may have come from the west, but in a year characterised by outbursts of popular celebration, easterners cheered too.)

But Unification also brought problems, especially for Berlin, where the two halves had to be made into one whole. While western infrastructure in the form of roads, telephones and other amenities was in decent working order, in the east it was falling apart. Challenges also came from the collapse of a command economy where jobs were provided regardless of cost or productivity. The Deutschmark put hard currency into the wallets of easterners, but it also exposed the true state of their economy. Within months thousands of companies cut jobs or closed down altogether.

The restructuring of eastern industry was placed with the Treuhandanstalt, a huge state agency that, for a while, was the world's largest industrial holding company. In Goering's old air ministry on the corner of Leipziger Strasse and Wilhelmstrasse (now the Finance Ministry), the Treuhand gave high-paid employment to thousands of western yuppies and put hundreds of thousands of easterners on the dole.

'The giddy excitement of post-Unification soon gave way to disappointment.'

Easterners soon turned on the Treuhand, vilified as the agent of a brutal western takeover. The situation escalated when Detlev Karsten Rohwedder, a western industrialist who headed the agency, was assassinated in spring 1991 – most probably by members of the Red Army Faction, the left-wing terror group.

The killing of another state employee, Hanno Klein, an influential city planner not always loved by the city's construction sector, drew attention to another dramatic change brought about by unification: the property boom. With the Wall down and – after a 1991 parliamentary decision – the federal government committed to moving from Bonn to Berlin, a wave of construction and investment swept the city.

DRIFTING TO NORMALITY

The giddy excitement of the post-Unification years soon gave way to disappointment. The sheer amount of construction work, the scrapping of federal subsidies and tax breaks to West Berlin, rising unemployment and a delay in the arrival of the government all contributed to dampening spirits. In 1994 the last Russian, US, British and French troops left the city. With them went Berlin's unique Cold War status, and the also the internationalism that came with occupation. After decades of being different, Berlin was becoming like any other big European capital.

The 1990s were characterised by the regeneration of the east. In the course of the decade the city's centre of gravity shifted towards Mitte. The government and commercial districts were revitalised. On their fringes, especially around Oranienburger Strasse, the Hackesche Höfe and into Prenzlauer Berg, trendy bars, restaurants, galleries and boutiques sprouted in streets that under Communism had been grey and crumbling.

Fast-track gentrification in the east was matched by the decline of West Berlin. The proprietors of upmarket shops and bars began to desert Charlottenburg and Schöneberg. Kreuzberg, once the inelegantly wasted symbol of a defiant West Berlin, in places degenerated to slum-like conditions, while a new bohemia developed across the Spree in Friedrichshain.

Westerners did, however, benefit from the reopening of the Berlin hinterland. Tens of thousands left the city for greener suburbs in the surrounding state of Brandenburg.

THE BERLIN REPUBLIC

Having spent the best part of a decade doing what it had done so often in the past – regenerating itself out of the wreckage left by history – Berlin left the 20th century with a flourish. Many of the big and symbolic construction projects – Potsdamer Platz, the Adlon, the Reichstag – were finished off. Other major landmarks such as Daniel Libeskind's Judisches Museum and IM Pei's extension to the Zeughaus on Unter den Linden soon followed.

The turn of the century also saw Berlin return to the centre of German politics. Parliament, the government, the lobbyists and journalists finally arrived from Bonn. From Chancellor Gerhard Schröder down, everyone marked the transition as the beginning of the 'Berlin Republic' – for which read a peaceful, democratic and self-confident Germany distinct from the chaos of the Weimar years and the self-conscious timidity of the Bonn era.

The Kosovo crisis of 1999, the attacks of September 11, 2001, and wars in Afghanistan and Iraq saw the Berlin government called upon to play a more active role on the world stage. And with this came marked differences from the past. President George W Bush's visit to Berlin in May 2002 was a world away from previous visits by US leaders. Where Kennedy brought a boost in a time of crisis, Reagan a bit of supportive straight talking ('Mr Gorbachev, tear down this wall!') and Bush senior a nod to Germany's emerging importance, George W came to tell Europe to fall into line over Iraq. He was soon disappointed. Schröder made opposition to action in Iraq a centrepiece of his September 2002 re-election campaign – which helped the 'red-green' coalition of Social Democrats and Greens squeak back into power.

Meanwhile, Berlin's financial problems got worse, setting the stage for a depressing period of perpetual agonising about cuts. Matching this was the ineptitude of the city's political establishment, which appeared caught in a time warp – addicted to central government subsidies, desperate to hang on to old privileges and unwilling to face up to tough choices. These woes were brought together in the fate of the Bankgesellschaft Berlin – a bank largely owned by the city. In summer 2001 it was felled by a raft of dud and corrupt real estate loans. As well sparking further deterioration in public finances, the scandal brought down the Senate, a 'grand coalition' of Christian Democrats and SPD that had governed since 1990.

The resulting elections went some way towards a new start. With lingering divisions made clear in the strong showing of the Party of Democratic Socialism, which took almost half the vote in the east, Klaus Wowereit, head of the SPD, broke one of the great post-unification taboos and invited the successors to East Germany's Communist Party into a Social Democrat-led coalition. The attending hullabaloo all but drowned out Wowereit's other bit of taboo-breaking: the unapologetic homosexuality which made him the first openly gay politician to be elected to high office.

But unfinished historical business continued to set the agenda. The urge to transcend old divisions played a part in municipal reforms in 2001. These saw the number of boroughs slashed as *Bezirke* were merged, across the former east–west divide. The construction of the Denkmal für die ermordeten Juden Europas, the Holocaust memorial, finally got under way after years of anguished debate – and was immediately engulfed by scandal. In late 2003 it emerged that the graffiti-proofing contract had gone to a firm that had used slave labour during the Third Reich.

Perhaps the most curious 'historical' project, however, was the plan to rebuild the Hohenzollern Stadtschloss, a palace which had stood at the top end of Unter den Linden until demolished by the Communists in 1950. What started in the early 1990s as a campaign by a Hamburg businessman, ended up a decade later in the Bundestag where deputies backed a motion calling for the reconstruction of the palace. In reality the new palace, earmarked as yet another cultural forum, was set to be just that: brand new. Fragments of the Stadtschloss will be used to provide a façade. Add that to guarded wording from parliament – offering its backing in principle while pleading for delay due to lack of funds – and the whole episode just about summed up early 21st century Berlin.

Käthe Kollwitz's sculpture remembers the victims of war at **Neue Wach**. *See p76.*

Key events

1237 Town of Cölln first mentioned in a church document.
1307 Towns of Berlin and Cölln officially united under the rule of the Ascanian family.
1319 Last of the Ascanians dies.
1359 Berlin joins the Hanseatic League.
1411 Friedrich of Hohenzollern is sent by the Holy Roman Emperor to bring peace to the region.
1447-8 The 'Berlin Indignation'. Citizens rebel and lock Friedrich II out of the city.
1535 Accession of Joachim I Nestor,the first protestant Elector. Start of Reformation.
1538 Work begins on the Stadtschloss.
1618-48 Berlin and Brandenburg are ravaged by the Thirty Years War; population halves.
1640-88 Reign of Friedrich Wilhelm, the Great Elector.
1662-8 Construction of the Oder–Spree canal.
1672 Jewish and Huguenot refugees arrive.
1695 Work starts on Schloss Charlottenburg.
1701 Elector Friedrich III, son of the Great Elector, has himself crowned Friedrich I, King of Prussia. Work begins on the German and French cathedrals at the Gendarmenmarkt.
1713-40 Reign of King Friedrich Wilhelm I; Berlin becomes a garrison city.
1740-86 Reign of Frederick the Great (Friedrich II), a time of military expansion.
1756-63 Seven Years War ends triumphantly for Prussia.
1788-91 Construction of Brandenburg Tor.
1806 Napoleon marches into Berlin. Two years of French occupation. The Quadriga taken to Paris.
1809 Wilhelm von Humboldt founds the university.
1813 Napoleon defeated at Grossbeeren and Leipzig.
1814 General Blücher brings the Quadriga back to Berlin; restored to Brandenburg Tor.
1837 Foundation of the Borsig Werke marks the beginning of Berlin's expansion towards becoming Europe's largest industrial city.
1838 First railway line in Germany, from Berlin to Potsdam.
1840 Friedrich Wilhelm IV accedes to the throne. With a population of around 400,000, Berlin is the fourth largest city in Europe.
1848 The 'March Revolution' breaks out. Berlin briefly ruled by revolutionaries.
1861 Accession of King Wilhelm I.
1862 Appointment of Otto von Bismarck as Prime Minister of Prussia.
1871 After victory in the Franco-Prussian war, King Wilhelm I is proclaimed German Emperor (Kaiser). Berlin becomes the Imperial capital.
1879 Electric lighting comes to Berlin, which also boasts the world's first electric railway. Telephone services arrive in 1882. Berlin becomes Europe's most modern metropolis.
1888 Kaiser Wilhelm II comes to the throne.
1890 Wilhelm II sacks Bismarck.
1894 Completion of the Reichstag.
1902 First underground line is opened.
1914-18 World War I.
1918 9 Nov: the Kaiser abdicates, Philip Scheidemann proclaims Germany a republic and Karl Liebknecht declares Germany a socialist republic. Chaos ensues.
1919 Spartacist uprising suppressed.
1923 Hyperinflation – at one point $1 is worth 4.2 billion marks.
1926 Josef Goebbels comes to Berlin to take charge of the local Nazi Party organisation.
1927 Berlin boasts more than 70 cabarets.
1933 Hitler takes power.
1936 11th Olympic Games held in Berlin.
1938 Kristallnacht, 9 Nov Jewish homes, businesses and synagogues in Berlin are looted and set ablaze.
1939 Outbreak of World War II, during which Berlin suffers appalling devastation.
1944 A group around Colonel Count von Stauffenberg attempts to assassinate Hitler.
1945 Germany signs unconditional surrender.
1948-9 The Berlin Blockade. The Soviets cut off all transport links to west Berlin. For 11 months city is supplied by the Allied Airlift.
1949 Foundation of Federal Republic in May and German Democratic Republic in October.
1953 17June East Berlin uprising crushed.
1961 The Wall goes up on 13 August.
1968 Student leader Rudi Dutschke is shot.
1971 Erich Honecker succeeds Walter Ulbricht as GDR head of state. Quadrapartite Agreement formalises Berlin's divided status.
1980-81 'Hot Winter': squatter protests.
1987 Berlin's 750th birthday.
1989 9 Nov: the Wall comes down.
1990 3 Oct: formal German Reunification.
1994 Last of the Allied military leave Berlin.
1999 German government moves from Bonn and 'Berlin Republic' born.
2001 Gay Klaus Wowereit elected mayor. Boroughs merge across east-west divide.
2002 'Red-Green' coalition elected for second term.

World class? IM Pei's block for the **Deutsches Historisches Museum**.

Berlin Today

Once upon a time, the Wall was Berlin's defining reality. These days it's the budget deficit.

When British folks go to London they see the British Museum and the Crown jewels and do a bit of shopping in Harrods. Americans travelling to Washington DC visit the memorials to Lincoln, Jefferson and Washington. When the French go to Paris, they stop by the Bastille, and eat in great restaurants. One of the functions of a capital city is to make you feel good about being British, American or French. But what if you're German? Why would you visit Berlin?

Begin thinking about that question, and you're carrying the baggage you need to discover the Berlin of today. First off, let's establish that the Berlin often mentioned in the same breath as London and Paris is not always the same Berlin of today. Some of the same buildings are around, sure, but Berlin has changed allegiances several times since the days, when, like London or Paris, it was both the cradle of nationhood and the country's premier urban centre. It started out as capital of Prussia, then it was capital of the German Reich, then of the Weimar Republic, and then of the Third Reich. After World War II, half of the divided city was the capital of the German Democratic Republic, then after 1991, a united Berlin was voted over Bonn as the capital of an expanded Federal Republic. It's hardly surprising that Germans don't necessarily see it as the natural centre of things.

The protean nature of the city and its role in history is of course a part of its enduring attraction to outsiders. But among Germans it has triggered a full-blown case of national soul-searching known broadly as the *Hauptstadtdebatte* – the capital debate.

Though the debate has many facets, it all boils down to money. Berlin is in the middle of a major financial crisis, not that unusual for many cities. But here the debate is not just about how to solve the problem. It's also about who is responsible for solving it.

Meanwhile, the shimmering capital of Europe's biggest economy is flat out of cash. Educational standards are plummeting as a

Berlin's fiscal disaster isn't reflected in the futuristic new complex at Potsdamer Platz.

hiring freeze has left kids with ageing, jaded teachers. Civil servants are demotivated and unable to cope with new cost-saving procedures. The police force has to shed 3,000 officers by attrition. Grass isn't cut. Roads aren't repaired. Fountains run dry.

Around 250,000 manufacturing jobs have been lost since 1990. Unemployment runs at 19 per cent. Empty shop fronts are common even on the Ku'damm, once West Berlin's glitzy shopping centrepiece. Newspaper circulations have plummeted, as have advertising revenues. Discount chains and own-brand supermarkets sway over the retail landscape; a consumer electronics discounter hit a nerve with the slogan: *Geiz ist Geil!* Miserliness is cool!

'Far from "flourishing landscapes", it turned into a bottomless pit.'

It wasn't always this way, and that's part of the problem. During the Cold War days, both East and West Berlin offered fairly cushy lifestyles. Large employers were attracted to West Berlin by generous subsidies; East Berlin was kept afloat as a showcase of socialist urban achievement. In West Berlin, politicians and civil servants were basically charged with distributing huge monthly transfers from Bonn. The situation bred fraud and corruption, a legacy which continues. East Berlin was different, but residents had enough privileges to be resented by other East Germans living in drab villages or over-industrialised cities.

When the Wall was breached in 1989, the rug was yanked from under the feet of Berliners, East and West. Initially, there was euphoria. People talked of the government moving lock, stock and moneybags into Berlin by 1995. East Berliners converted their east marks to deutschmarks at the phenomenal official one-to-one rate, and the city was awash in cash. Chancellor Helmut Kohl told Germans unification would result in a huge economic upswing – 'flourishing landscapes' were what he famously envisaged – and Berlin would be in the middle of it all. International investors would flock to the city, building a commercial gateway to the east. Berlin would have a new international airport, dwarfing the three existing ones. Population would grow to five million by the turn of the century.

None of this happened. When the government finally did take up residence, it was in 1999, not 1995, and not all of the federal ministries and offices moved from Bonn. East Germany turned out to have a lot fewer assets than anticipated and the one-to-one currency conversion helped bring about the near total collapse of eastern industry. Far from flourishing landscapes, it turned into a bottomless pit. An end to subsidies drove out various big western employers and potential new investors got spooked by the government's delay in moving and the lack of an international airport. Today only 15 companies employ more than 500 people in Berlin. Plans to expand the airport in Schönefeld have stalled repeatedly over financing and planning issues. And the population has barely budged.

The problem for Berliners was that as the euphoria of unification wore off, as the billions from Bonn dried up and one employer after another closed shop, their elected representatives continued with business as usual. They borrowed money to replace lost

There might be a shortage of money, but Berlin hasn't stopped moving yet.

funds from Bonn and local leaders failed to make the politically sensitive cutbacks needed for the city to meet its payroll. Remember, these were bureaucrats specialised at spending money, not saving it. And they got the city involved in a number of bank and real estate projects that have since gone bust.

The bottom line is that the city is now saddled with about €44 billion of debt, and the current budget deficit is running about €4.3 billion. By comparison, New York has a deficit approaching €2.8 billion, but over twice as many residents as Berlin.

While Berliners struggle to come to terms with the new reality, many Germans have little sympathy. Considering the city's ongoing corruption scandals and poor track record at cutting the fat out of bureaucracy, leaders of some German states say they no longer want to transfer part of their revenue to impoverished Berlin, as required in Germany's federal system.

Berliners counter that at least some of the burdens facing the city are not of its own doing, that many arise from Berlin's new status as a capital city. Those on this side of the *Hauptstadtdebatte* say Berlin needs to maintain a vibrant cultural scene, with world-class museums and concert halls. The city has to have a big police force to keep order when, say, hundreds of thousands of trade unionists from all over the nation rally at the Brandenburg Gate. Why should Berliners pay?

But Germany's national economy has been sputtering for years. With reforms in everything from pension payments, working conditions and healthcare costs being introduced, Berlin's chances of relief from the federal government are bleak.

In the meantime, the city has brought a case before Germany's highest court demanding a partial release from its debt over a ten-year period. If granted, this might pave the way for a merger with the surrounding state of Brandenburg, which could result in a better distribution of the city's costs. There's also some hope that federal ministries still in Bonn may eventually relocate, so Berlin would lose some of its current image as an incomplete capital – an undisputed brake on investment.

'Within the next few years a third of the population will have rotated.'

Though Berlin seems to have reached the end of the line with its finances, the fiscal disaster does not always show up at street level. The futuristic complex at Potsdamer Platz throngs with moviegoers and shoppers. Development on adjacent Leipziger Platz is nearly complete, adding dimension to the new downtown. The government quarter by the Reichstag is finished. And, just across the river, the new Lehrter Bahnhof station – centrepiece of another massive development – looms on the edge of the future. Get off the train here and take in the views to the south: the Reichstag with its glass dome, the Kanzleramt, Potsdamer Platz. This view didn't exist three years ago.

Soon Lehrter Bahnhof will be the city's central rail station, funneling in travellers from all of Europe. And this will be what they see first.

Berlin remains a city of neighbourhoods, but the neighbourhoods have evolved. Districts in the east have seen the most change. Prenzlauer Berg and Mitte are preferred by 'new Berliners'. Young families are attracted to the leafy streets and parks of Prenzlauer Berg. Working singles are drawn by the boutiques and bars of northern Mitte. Berlin's total population level has not changed, but the demographics have. Within the next few years around third of the population will have rotated. Hundreds of thousands have packed up and moved out; hundreds of thousands are moving in.

This upheaval is part of what keeps Berlin dynamic. The newcomers bring enthusiasm and add to the buzz. They're drawn by the arts and nightlife, as well as by cheap rents (one benefit of an ailing economy). Creative people burnt out on the pace and expense of life in London or New York increasingly find respite in Berlin.

Germans coming to Berlin mostly find a city transformed from their last visit, one that lives up to the spectacular photo spreads they've seen in the national press. But they haven't really got used to the idea of Berlin as their capital, the fixed point around which the nation revolves. So far they are tolerating the prospect that this may one day be the case. But someone has to figure out a way to pay for it first.

Ostalgia ain't what it used to be

The crumbling of the Berlin Wall in 1989 was part of a much wider process in which Warsaw Pact nations rose up peaceably against their Soviet-imposed oppressors. But while Poland, Hungary, the Czech Republic and all the other nations of 'New Europe' have eagerly embraced free-market principles and peered towards the future, the former East Germans are alone in exhibiting a strange, post-Cold War Peter Pan complex known as *Ostalgie* or Ostalgia – a yearning for the little things that made life in the former East so warm and fuzzy.

Though few East Germans would genuinely want to go back to secret police, travel restrictions and queues for bananas, there are plenty who long for the days of a regular wage, free medical and childcare services – and especially for the friendly image of a little man in a hat who lit up green at traffic intersections from Dresden to Rostock.

Ostalgia kicked off in the mid 1990s as East German pedestrian crossing signals began to be replaced with the kind used throughout West Germany. Two enterprising souvenir sellers in East Berlin, whose Mondo Arts shop (*see p180*) specialised in GDR memorabilia, launched a spoof campaign to 'Save the Little Traffic Light Man'. People took the jest seriously, however, and authorities were swamped with letters and petitions pleading to strike the *Ampelmännchen* from the endangered species list. In Berlin and the state of Saxony-Anhalt, the traffic authorities even relented.

Since then, Ostalgia has occasionally approached hysteria. There are Ostalgia parties where guests dress up in communist-era uniforms. They drink Rottkäpchen Sekt, East Germany's favourite sparkling wine, and dance to 1970s GDR rockers such as the Phudys. Radio and television broadcasts Ostalgia specials, reviving personalities from the GDR's stage and screen.

Most East German brands were long ago bought up by multinationals, but many are still available, and selling well in reformulated versions. F6 cigarettes, for example, Florena cosmetic cream or Spee detergent powder. In Dresden there's even a department store called (N)Ostalgie-Warenhaus – on seven floors! For more Ostalgic retail, *see p177* **Lenin's on sale again**.

Leander Haussmann's film *Sonnenallee* made Ostalgia a media phenomenon in 2000. It's a feel-good tale of growing up in the 1970s in an East Berlin neighbourhood near the Wall, and it broke taboos by sympathetically portraying a way of life which had vanished overnight. More recently, *Goodbye Lenin!* by Wolfgang Becker has swept up awards across the globe. Also set in Berlin, it's the story of a young man whose devoutly communist mother wakes from a coma, and the lengths he goes to prevent her learning that her beloved GDR is no more.

These films have helped Ostalgia become a national affliction, waking memories all east Germans share. But most Ostaligic manifestations have a kind of freak-show quality about them. East German writer Christa Wolf says the phenomenon is much like the other side of the same coin: the demonisation of the GDR in the early 1990s. Both are based on misconceptions of what it was actually like.

Architecture

How has the birthplace of modern architecture risen to the new urban challenge?

Berlin may be one of Europe's younger capitals, but the city can boast a long and distinguished tradition of architectural experimentation. During the 1910s and 1920s, Berlin was home to some of the century's greatest architects and designers, such as Peter Behrens, Bruno Taut, Ludwig Mies van der Rohe and Walter Gropius. But the path to modernism was launched, on the heels of the Napoleonic occupation, by Karl Friedrich Schinkel, who many still consider to be Berlin's greatest builder. In addition, fine specimens of nearly every style since the baroque age can be found here, from neo-Renaissance to neo-Rationalism.

Though the Berlin we see today was largely shaped by the rise of the modern era, just about every political and economic transformation of the city, before and since, has also been accompanied by a new set of architectural and planning principles. Another factor is that until the fall of the Wall, Berlin had been a military post of one kind or another for centuries.

But it wasn't until the late 19th century that Berlin as a whole was finally able to hold its own with grander European capitals, thanks to a construction boom known as the *Gründerzeit*, triggered by the rapid progress in industry and technology that followed German unification in 1871. The city acquired a massive scale, with wide streets and large blocks. These followed a rudimentary geometry and were filled in with five-storey *Mietskaserne* ('rental barracks') built around linked internal courtyards. The monotony – and the smoke and noise of nearby factories – was partially relieved by a few public parks, while later apartment houses gradually became more humane and eventually got rather splendid. During the 1920s, this method of development was rejected in favour of Bauhaus-influenced slabs and towers, which were used to fill out the peripheral zones at the edge of the forests. The post-war years saw even more radical departures from the earlier tradition in all sectors of the city.

The post-Wall building boom has now deposited a new layer, a mixture of contemporary design and historic emulation. Some of it uses new environmental strategies and much of it attempts to restore a sense of continuity to an urban fabric ruptured by division and heavy-handed reconstruction. Many of Berlin's older architectural landmarks are more important as historical markers than as masterpieces. Much was lost to the war, including Messel's Wertheim department store at Leipziger Platz and Mendelsohn's Columbushaus at Potsdamer Platz. The new buildings in these areas have been reworked with these losses in mind.

The spirit of historic revival has even taken in the city's most famous landmark, **the Wall** (*see p72*), which was dismantled with breathtaking speed after 1989. It is now being commemorated in public art, from the Gedenkstätte Berliner Mauer at Bernauer Strasse to Frank Thiel's portraits of the last Allied soldiers, suspended above Checkpoint Charlie. The former line of the Wall is also marked in many places by a cobblestone strip, such as that visible to the west of the Brandenburg Gate. But with so much new architecture from all over the globe, the memory of the Wall is fading away.

THE FIRST FEW HUNDRED YEARS

Berlin's long journey to world city status began in two tiny settlements on the Spree named Berlin and Cölln, originally Wendish/Slavic towns that were colonised by Germans around 1237. Among their oldest surviving buildings are the parish churches **Marienkirche** and **Nikolaikirche** (for both, *see p86*). The latter was rebuilt in the district known as the Nikolaiviertel, along with other landmarks, such as the 1571 pub Zum Nussbaum and the baroque **Ephraim-Palais** (*see p85*). The Nikolaiviertel, between Alexanderplatz and the Spree, is the only part of central Berlin to give any idea of how the medieval city might have felt – except it's a clumsy fake, rebuilt by the East Germans in 1987, just a few decades after they had levelled the district.

Thanks to the GDR's subtractive planning ideology, little survives of the massive **Stadtschloss** ('City Palace', 1538-1950; *see p77*), other than recently excavated foundations in front of the Palast der Republik, dating to the reign of Elector Joachim II. The Schlossbrücke crossing to Unter den Linden, adorned with sensual figures by Christian Daniel Rauch, and the **Neptunbrunnen** ('Neptune Fountain', now relocated south of Marienkirche), modelled on Bernini's Roman fountains, were designed to embellish the palace.

In 1647 the Great Elector Friedrich Wilhelm II (1640-88) hired Dutch engineers to transform the route to the Tiergarten, the royal hunting forest, into the tree-lined boulevard of **Unter den Linden**. It led west toward **Schloss Charlottenburg** (*see p108*), built in 1695 as a summer retreat for Queen Sophie-Charlotte. Over the next century, the Elector's 'Residenzstadt' expanded to include Berlin-Cölln and the extension of Friedrichswerder to the south-west. Traces of the old stone **Stadtmauer** ('city wall') that enclosed them can still be seen on Waisenstrasse in Mitte. Two further districts, Dorotheenstadt (begun 1673, named after the Great Elector's Dutch queen) and Friedrichstadt (begun 1688), expanded the street grid north and south of Unter den Linden.

Andreas Schlüter built new palace wings for Elector Friedrich Wilhelm III (1688-1713, crowned King Friedrich I of Prussia in 1701) and supervised the building of the **Zeughaus** (Armoury; Nering and de Bodt, 1695-1706; now home to the **Deutsches Historisches Museum**; *see p76*). Bellicose ornamentation embodies the Prussian love of militarism, with Schlüter's 22 masks of dying warriors in the courtyard.

City life changed when Wilhelm I, the Soldier King (1713-40), imposed conscription and subjugated the town magistrate to the court and military elite. The economy now catered to an army comprising 20 per cent of the population (a fairly constant percentage until 1918). To spur growth in gridded Friedrichstadt – and to quarter his soldiers cheaply – the King forced people to build new houses, mostly in a stripped-down classical style. He permitted one open square, Gendarmenmarkt, where twin churches were built in 1701, one of which now houses the **Hugenotten Museum** (*see p81*).

After the population reached 60,000 in 1710, a new customs wall enclosed four new districts – the Spandauer Vorstadt, Königstadt, Stralauer Vorstadt and Köpenicker Vorstadt; all now parts of Mitte. The 14-kilometre (nine-mile) border remained the city limits until 1860.

Geometric squares later marked three of the 14 city gates in Friedrichstadt. At the square-shaped **Pariser Platz**, axial gateway to the Tiergarten, Langhans built the **Brandenburger Tor** (Brandenburg Gate) in 1789, a triumphal arch later topped by Schadow's **Quadriga** (*see p72*). The stately buildings around the square were levelled after World War II, but have now largely been reconstructed or replaced, including the **Adlon Hotel** (Patzschke, Klotz, 1997; *see p47*), on an expanded version of its original site, and the buildings flanking the gate, **Haus Sommer** and **Haus Liebermann** (Kleihues, 1998).

Konzerthaus: Schinkel's finest.

SCHINKEL AND CO

Even with the army, Berlin's population did not reach 100,000 until well into the reign of Frederick the Great (1740-86). Military success inspired the French-speaking 'philosopher king' to embellish Berlin and Potsdam; many of the monuments along Unter den Linden stem from his vision of a **'Forum Fredericianum'**. Though never completed, the unique ensemble of neo-classical, baroque and rococo monuments includes the vine-covered **Humboldt-Universität** (Knobelsdorff/Boumann, 1748-530; *see p283*); the **Staatsoper** (Knobelsdorff, Langhans, 1741-3; *see p238*); the **Prinzessinnenpalais** (1733, now the Operncafé; *see p145*) and the **Kronprinzen-palais** (Unter den Linden 3; 1663, expanded 1732). Set back from the Linden on Bebelplatz are the **Alte Bibliothek**, reminiscent of the curvy Vienna Hofburg (Unger, 1775-81, part of Humboldt-Universität) and the pantheon-like, copper-domed **St Hedwigs-Kathedrale** (Legeay and Knobelsdorff, 1747-73; *see p76*).

Not long after the Napoleonic occupation, the prolific Karl Friedrich Schinkel became Berlin's most revered architect under Prince Friedrich Wilhelm IV. Drawing on early classical and Italian precedents, his early stage-sets experimented with perspective, while his inspired urban visions served the cultural aspirations of an ascendant German state. His work includes the colonnaded **Altes Museum** (1828; *see p78*), regarded by most architects as his finest work, and the **Neue Wache** (New Guardhouse, 1818; *see p76*), next to the Zeughaus, whose Roman solidity lent itself well to Tessenow's 1931 conversion into a memorial to the dead of World War I.

Other Schinkel masterpieces include the **Schauspielhaus**, a theatre to replace one lost to fire at Gendarmenmarkt (1817-21, now the **Konzerthaus**; *see p237*); the neo-Gothic brick **Friedrichwerdersche Kirche** (1830, now the **Schinkel-Museum**; *see p76*); and the cubic **Schinkel-Pavillon** (1825; *see p110*) at Schloss Charlottenburg. Among his many collaborations with garden architect Peter Joseph Lenné is the picturesque ensemble of classical follies at **Schloss Glienecke**, near the Glieneckebrücke, which connects Berlin with Potsdam.

After Schinkel's death in 1841, his many disciples propagated his architectural lessons in brick and stone. Friedrich August Stüler most notably satisfied the King's desire to complement the Altes Museum with the **Neues Museum** (1841-59, Bodestrasse 1-3, Mitte). Originally home of the Egyptian collection, it mixed new wrought-iron technology with classical architecture, terracotta ceiling coffers and elaborate murals. By 1910, Museumsinsel comprised the neo-classical **Alte Nationalgalerie** (also Stüler, 1864; *see p77*) with an open stairway framing an equestrian statue of the King; the triangular **Bode Museum** (von Ihne, 1904; Am Kupfergraben/Monbijoubrücke; *see p77*); and the sombre grey **Pergamonmuseum** (Messel and Hoffmann, 1906-9; *see p78*). These are a stark contrast to the neo-Renaissance poly-chromy of the **Martin-Gropius-Bau** across town (Gropius and Schmieden, 1881, *see p95*).

WILD ECLECTICISM

As the population boomed after 1865, doubling to 1.5 million by 1890, the city began swallowing up neighbouring towns and villages. Factory complexes and worker housing gradually moved to the outskirts. Many of the new market halls and railway stations used a vernacular brick style with iron trusses, such as **Arminiushalle** in Moabit (Blankenstein, 1892; Bremer Strasse 9) and Franz Schwechten's Romanesque **Anhalter Bahnhof** (1876-80, now a ruin; Askanischer Platz, *see p94*). Brick was also used for civic buildings, like the neo-Gothic **Rotes Rathaus** (1861-9; *see p85*), while the orientalism of the gold-roofed **Neue Synagoge** on Oranienburger Strasse (Knoblauch, Stüler, 1859-66; *see p84*) made use of colourful masonry and mosaics.

Restrained historicism gave way to wild eclecticism as the 19th century marched on, in public buildings as well as apartment houses with plain interiors, dark courtyards and overcrowded flats behind decorative façades. Eclecticism was also rampant among lavish Gründerzeit villas in the fashionable suburbs to the south-west, especially Dahlem and Grunewald. In these areas the modest yellow-brick vernacular of Brandenburg was rejected in favour of stone and elaborate stucco.

The **Kurfürstendamm**, a tree-lined shopping boulevard built in the 1880s, soon helped the 'new west' rival the finery of Leipziger Strasse. Further out, in Nikolassee and Wannsee, private homes hit new heights of scale and splendour. Many were inspired by the English country house, such as **Haus Freudenberg** in Zehlendorf (Muthesius, 1908; Potsdamer Chaussee 48).

THE NEW METROPOLIS

In anticipation of a new age of rationality and mechanisation, an attempt at greater stylistic clarity was made after 1900, in spite of the bombast of works such as the new **Berliner Dom** (Raschdorff, 1905; *see p78*) and the **Reichstag** (Wallot, 1894; *see p100*). The Wilhelmine era's paradoxical mix of reformism and conservatism yielded an architecture of *Sachlichkeit* ('objectivity') in commercial and public buildings. In some cases, such as Kaufmann's **Hebbel-Theater** (1908; now part of HAU, *see p240*), or the **Hackesche Höfe** (Berndt and Endell, 1906-7; Rosenthaler Strasse 40-41, Mitte), *Sachlichkeit* meant a calmer form of art nouveau (or *Jugendstil*); elsewhere it was more sombre, with heavy, compact forms, vertical ribbing, and low-hanging mansard roofs. One of the most severe examples is the stripped-down classicism of Alfred Messel's Pergamon-museum; even Bruno Schmitz's **food automat** at Friedrichstrasse 167 (1905), with its three central bays, is pretty dry.

The style goes well with Prussian bureaucracy in the civic architecture of Ludwig Hoffmann, city architect from 1896 to 1924. Though he sometimes used other styles for his many schools, courthouses and city halls, his towering **Altes Stadthaus** in Mitte (1919; Jüdenstrasse) and the **Rudolf-Virchow-Krankenhaus** in Wedding (1906; Augustenburger Platz 1), then innovative for its pavilion system, epitomise Wilhelmine architecture.

In housing after 1900, Sachlichkeit led to early modernism to serve the masses of the metropolis, now totalling three million. Messel became architect to some of the first successful housing co-ops, designing with a country-house flair (Sickingenstrasse 7-8, Moabit, 1895; and Stargarder Strasse 30, Prenzlauer Berg, 1900). Paul Mebes launched his long career in housing,

Restrained historicism gives way to wild eclecticism on *Gründerzeit* façades.

beginning with a double row of apartments with enclosed balconies (Fritschweg, Steglitz, 1907-8). He and others moved on to larger ensembles, forerunners of the Weimar-era housing estates. Schmitthenner explored a vernacular style with gabled brick terraces arranged like a medieval village in **Staaken**, built near Spandau for World War I munitions workers (1917). Taut and Tessenow substituted coloured stucco for ornament in the terraced housing of **Gartenstadt Falkenberg** in Altglienicke (1915), part of an unbuilt larger town plan.

Prior to the incorporation of Berlin in 1920, many suburbs had full city charters and sported their own town halls, such as the massive **Rathaus Charlottenburg** (1905; Otto-Suhr-Allee 100) and **Rathaus Neukölln** (1909; Karl-Marx-Strasse 83-5). Neukölln's Reinhold Kiehl also built the **Karl-Marx-Strasse Passage** (1910, now home of the **Neuköllner Oper**; *see p239*), and the **Stadtbad Neukölln** (1914), with niches and mosaics evoking a Roman atmosphere. Special care was also given to suburban rail stations of the period, such as the **S-Bahnhof Mexikoplatz** in Zehlendorf, set on a garden square with shops and restaurants (Hart and Lesser, 1905), and the **U-Bahnhof Dahlem-Dorf**, whose half-timbered style goes a step further to capture a countrified look.

WEIMAR'S NEW FORMS

The work of many pioneers brought modern architecture to life in Berlin. One of the most important was Peter Behrens, who reinterpreted the factory with a new monumental language in the façade of the **Turbinenhalle** at Huttenstrasse in Moabit (1909) and several other buildings for the AEG. After 1918, the turbulent birth of the Weimar Republic offered a chance for a final aesthetic break with the Wilhelmine style.

A radical new architecture gave formal expression to long-awaited social and political reforms. The *Neues Bauen* ('new buildings') began to exploit the new technologies of glass, steel and concrete, inspired by the early work of Tessenow and Behrens, Dutch modernism, cubism, Russian constructivism, civil engineering and even a bit of Japanese design.

Berlin architects could explore the new functionalism to their hearts' content, using clean lines and a machine aesthetic bare of ornament. This was thanks to post-war housing demand, and a new social democrat administration that put planner Martin Wagner at the helm after 1925. The city became the builder of a new form of social housing, and, in spite of rampant inflation, several hundred thousand units were completed. The *Siedlung* ('housing estate') was developed within the framework of a 'building exhibition' of experimental prototypes – often collaborations among architects, such as Luckhardt, Gropius, Häring, Salvisberg and the brothers Taut. Standardised sizes kept costs down and amenities like tenant gardens, schools, public transport and shopping areas were offered when at all possible.

Among the best known 1920s estates are Bruno Taut's **Hufeisen-Siedlung** (Bruno-Taut-Ring, Britz, 1927), arranged in horseshoe shape around a communal garden, and **Onkel-Toms-Hütte** (Haring, Taut, 1928-9; Argentinische Allee, Zehlendorf), with Salvisberg's linear U-Bahn station at its heart. Most *Siedlungen* were housing only, such as the **Ringsiedlung** (Goebelstrasse, Charlottenburg) or **Siemensstadt** (Scharoun and others, 1929-32). Traditional-looking 'counter-proposals' with pitched roofs were made by more conservative designers at **Am Fischtal** (Tessenow, Mebes, Emmerich, Schmitthenner et al, 1929; Zehlendorf).

Larger infrastructure projects and public works were also built by avant-garde architects under Wagner's direction. Among the more interesting are the rounded U-Bahn station at **Krumme Lanke** (Grenander, 1929), the totally rational **Stadtbad Mitte** (1930; Gartenstrasse 5-6), the **Messegelände** (Poelzig, Wagner, 1928; Messedamm 22, Charlottenburg), the ceramic-tiled **Haus des Rundfunks** (Poelzig, 1930; Masurenallee 10, Charlottenburg), and twin office buildings on the southern corner of Alexanderplatz (Behrens, 1932).

Beginning with his expressionist **Einsteinturm** in Babelsberg, Erich Mendelsohn distilled his own brand of modernism, characterised by the rounded forms of the **Universum Cinema** (1928; now the **Schaubühne**; *see p240*) and the elegant corner solution of the **IG Metall** building (1930; Alte Jacobstrasse 148, Kreuzberg). Before emigrating – as did many architects, Jewish and non-Jewish – Mendelsohn built a few private homes, including his own at Am Rupenhorn 6 in Charlottenburg (1929).

GRAND DESIGN & DEMOLITION

In the effort to remake liberal Berlin in their image, the Nazis undertook a form of spatial re-education. This included banning modernist trademarks such as flat roofs and slender columns in favour of traditional architecture, and shutting down the Bauhaus school shortly after it was banished from Dessau. Modern architects fled Berlin as Hitler dreamt of refashioning it into the mega-capital

'Germania', designed by Albert Speer.The crowning glory was to be a grand axis with a railway station at its foot and a massive copper dome at its head, some 16 times the size of St Peter's in Rome. Work was halted by the war, but not before demolition was begun in Tiergarten and Schöneberg.

Hitler and Speer's fantasy was that Germania would someday leave picturesque ruins as per ancient Rome. But ruins came sooner than expected. Up to 90 per cent of the inner city was destroyed by Allied bombing. Mountains of rubble cleared by women survivors rose at the city's edge, such as the **Teufelsberg** in the west and **Friedrichshain** in the east. During bombing and reconstruction, many apartment buildings lost their decoration, leaving the blunted lines characteristic of Berlin today.

Fascism left an invisible legacy of a bunker and tunnel landscape. The more visible fascist architecture can be recognised by its stripped-down, abstracted classicism, typically in travertine: in the west, **Flughafen Tempelhof** (Sagebiel, 1941; *see p93 and p270*) and the **Olympiastadion** (March, 1936; *see p244*); in the east, the marble-halled **Reichsluftfahrtministerium** (now the Bundesministerium der Finanzen; Sagebiel, 1936; Wilhelmstrasse 97, Mitte) and the downright scary **Reichsbank** (now the Auswärtiges Amt; Wolff, 1938; Werderscher Markt, Mitte).

Reichsbank: downright scary.

BERLIN, BERLIN

The **Berlin Wall**, put up in a single night in 1961, introduced a new and cruel reality that rapidly acquired a sense of permanence. The city's centre of gravity shifted as the Wall cut off the historic centre from the west, suspending the Brandenburger Tor and Potsdamer Platz in no-man's land, while the outer edge followed the 1920 city limits.

Post-war architecture is a mixed bag, ranging from the crisp linear brass of 1950s storefronts to concrete 1970s mega-complexes. Early joint planning efforts led by Hans Scharoun were scrapped, and radical interventions cleared out vast spaces. Among the architectural casualties in the East were Schinkel's Bauakademie and much of Fischerinsel, clearing a sequence of wide spaces from Marx-Engels-Platz to Alexanderplatz. In West Berlin, Anhalter Bahnhof was left to stand in ruins but Schloss Charlottenburg narrowly escaped demolition.

Though architects from East and West shared the same modernist education, their work became the tool of opposing ideologies, and housing was the first battlefield. The GDR adapted Russian socialist realism to Prussian culture in projects built with great effort and amazing speed as a national undertaking. First and foremost was Stalinallee (1951-4; now **Karl-Marx-Allee**, Friedrichshain). The Frankfurter Tor segment of its monumental axis was designed by Herman Henselmann, a Bauhaus modernist who briefly agreed to switch styles. In response, West Berlin called on leading International Style architects such as Gropius, Niemeyer, Aalto and Jacobsen to build the **Hansaviertel**. A loose arrangement of inventive blocks and pavilions at the edge of the Tiergarten, it was part of the 1957 Interbau Exhibition for the 'city of tomorrow', which included Le Corbusier's Unité d'Habitation in Charlottenburg (Corbusierhaus, just south S-Bahnhof Olympiastadion). Oddly, today both the Hansaviertel and Karl-Marx-Allee contain highly sought-after housing.

East and West stylistic differences diminished in the 1960s and 1970s, as new *Siedlungen* were built to even greater dimensions. The **Gropiusstadt** in Britz and **Märkisches Viertel** in Reinickendorf (1963-74) were mirrored in the East by equally massive (if shoddier) prefab housing estates in Marzahn and Hellersdorf.

To replace cultural institutions then cut off from the West, Dahlem became the site of various museums and of the new **Freie Universität**, with its daring rusted-steel exterior (Candilis Woods Schiedhelm, 1967-79; *see p282*). Scharoun conceived a 'Kulturforum' on the site cleared for Germania, designing two masterful pieces: the **Philharmonie** (1963; *see p237*) and the **Staatsbibliothek** (1976; *see p278*). Other additions were Mies van der Rohe's slick **Neue Nationalgalerie** (1968; *see p102*) and the **Gemäldegalerie** (Hilmer & Satler, 1992-8; *see p102*).

The US presented Berlin with Hugh Stubbin's **Kongresshalle** in the Tiergarten (1967, now the **Haus der Kulturen der Welt**; *see p99*), an entertainingly futuristic work, which rather embarrassingly required seven years' repair after its roof collapsed in 1980. East German architects brewed their own version of futuristic modernism in the enlarged, vacuous Alexanderplatz with its **Fernsehturm** (TV Tower, 1969; *see p86*), the nearby **Haus des Lehrers** (Henselmann, 1961-4; Grunerstrasse/Karl-Marx-Allee, Mitte) with its restored frieze, and the impressive cinemas, **Kino International** (Kaiser, 1964; Karl-Marx-Allee 33, Mitte) and **Kosmos** (Kaiser, 1962; Karl-Marx-Allee 131, Friedrichshain).

POSTMODERN RENEWAL

Modernist urban renewal gradually gave way to historic preservation after 1970. In the West, largely in response to the squatting movement, the city launched a public-private enterprise within the **Internationale Bauausstellung** (IBA), to conduct a 'careful renewal' of the Mietskaserne and 'critical reconstruction' with infill projects to close the gaps left in areas along the Wall.

Within the huge catalogue of IBA architects are many brands of postmodernism, both local and foreign, from Ungers, Sawade and Behnisch, to Krier, Moore and Hertzberger; many had never built anywhere. It is a truly eclectic collection: the irreverent organicism of the prolific **Ballers** (Fraenkelufer, Kreuzberg, 1982-4) contrasts sharply with the neo-rationalist work of **Eisenman** (Kochstrasse 62-63, Kreuzberg, 1988) and **Rossi** (Wilhelmstrasse 36-8, Kreuzberg, 1988); a series of projects was also placed along Friedrichstrasse. IBA thus became a proving-ground for contemporary architectural theories.

In the East, urban renewal slowed to a halt when funds for the construction of new housing ran dry; and towards the end of the 1970s, inner-city areas became again politically and economically attractive. Most East-bloc preservation focused on run-down 19th-century buildings on a few streets and squares in Prenzlauer Berg. Some infill buildings were also added on Friedrichstrasse in manipulated grids and pastel colours, so that the postmodern theme set up by IBA architects on the street south of Checkpoint Charlie was continued over the Wall. But progress was slow, and when the Wall fell in 1989 many sites still stood half-finished.

MISSING LINKS

Rejoining east and west became the new challenge, requiring work of every kind, from massive infrastructure to commercial and residential projects. There were two key decisions. The first was to eradicate the Wall zone with projects that would link urban structures on either side. The second was to pursue a 'critical reconstruction' of the old city block structure, using a contemporary interpretation of Prussian scale and order.

There are three main projects intended to link east and west: the area around Potsdamer Platz and Leipziger Platz; the government quarter and the 'Band des Bundes'; and the new central station at Lehrter Bahnhof. Standalone projects such as these were outside the discussion on critical reconstruction, and their architecture reflects this in a greater freedom of approach.

Potsdamer Platz (*see p101*) was the first of the three, designed as a new urban area based on the old geometries of Potsdamer and **Leipziger Platz**. This former swathe of no-man's land was redeveloped not only to forge a link between Leipziger Strasse to the east and the Kultur-forum to the west, but also to supply Berlin with a new central focus in an area that was formerly neither one side or the other.

The twin squares of Potsdamer Platz and Leipziger Platz have been reinstated and five small quarters radiate to the south and west. Leipziger Platz is rising again as an enclosed octagonal set-piece, with modern terrace buildings such as Christoph Langhof's **No.9** (2003) or Axel Schultes and Charlotte Frank's **No.10** (2000). Potsdamer Platz is by contrast once more an open intersection, entrances to the various quarters beyond staked out with major buildings by Hans Kollhoff, Hilmer Sattler and Albrecht, Helmut Jahn, Renzo Piano and Schweger and Partner (1999-2003).

The closed metal and glass block of Helmut Jahn's **Sony Center** (2000) is a singular piece, organised around a lofty central forum with a tented glass and textile roof as its spectacular focus. Offices and apartments look down on to an oval public space with cinemas, bars, restaurants and the glass-encased remnants of the old **Esplanade Hotel**. But a lack of diversity makes it an entertainment centre that doesn't entertain for long.

The **Daimler Chrysler** area on the other side of Potsdamer Strasse, largest of the new quarters, is a network of tree-lined streets with squares and pavement cafés. It's also the work of various architects, though Renzo Piano got all the key pieces, notably the **Arkaden shopping mall**, the **Debis headquarters**, and the **Musicaltheater and Spielbank** on Marlene-Dietrich-Platz (all 1999), all in a language of terracotta and glass. The quarter's south-west flank facing on to Tilla-Durieux-Park is a rich architectural mix, with **Richard Rogers**' two buildings of cylinders, blocks and wedges (Linkstrasse, 1998), and **Arata Isozaki's** concoction of ochre and brown stripes topped with a wavy glass penthouse (Linkstrasse, 1998).

Though these can be interesting quarters in themselves, they are somewhat introspective for a development intended as a linking project. There aren't even any cross-relationships which would cause you to wander from one quarter to another, let alone between east and west Berlin. *See below* **A tale of two squares**.

The **'Band des Bundes'**, the linear arrangement of new government buildings north of the Reichstag, is another project

A tale of two squares

In Wim Wenders' *Wings of Desire*, an old man wanders through high grass looking for Potsdamer Platz. Just over the Wall, the octagonal outline of Leipziger Platz lies visible on the death strip. After the war, the Wall and the passage of time, only romantic memories remained of Berlin's two busiest squares.

Then the Wall fell and prompted a major urban project to reinstate the old pulse of the city, to forge a link between east and west, a fusion of Friedrichstadt and Tiergarten. The international architectural glitterati were asked for ideas and Hilmer and Sattler's master plan for the area was chosen. The overall idea was to replace the closed octagonal form of **Leipziger Platz**, and to radiate urban blocks from the adjoining **Potsdamer Platz** to meet the Kulturforum in the west. This new urban quarter was to pick up the old memories and become a spectacular hub for working, living, entertainment and transport. It's more or less complete now. Has it succeeded?

Leipziger Platz, panelled with fine buildings, once worked as a sort of reception room for Friedrichstadt. Beyond it was the commercial chaos of Potsdamer Platz. The new buildings on Leipziger Platz work like their predecessors, enclosing the square in a regular wallpaper of harmonious styles.

Potsdamer Platz is contrastingly wide open and the towers on its edges are a hysterical mix of styles and colours, from Hans Kollhoff's Chicago School towers, to Renzo Piano's layered glass elegance, to Helmut Jahn's seductive, glazed curves. But they all should have been much higher to really put the place on the map. Someone lost their nerve here.

Helmut Jahn's **Sony Center** is the only quarter that is all of one piece – an introspective triangular block framed with strong forms of layered glass, steel and mesh with an oval forum at its core. The complex is an urban entertainment centre with apartments and offices including Sony's own European headquarters. The Mount Fuji form of the canopy, the central fountain, the glazed chasm to the subterranean cinemas and the careful showcase for the remains of the **Esplanade hotel** are all very fine, but from a functional standpoint it falls short. There isn't enough entertainment in it, the forum is obstructed, there's no clear link to the **Kulturforum** and, worst of all, the early promise of Sony-quality, Times Square-type technology was left unrealised.

On the other side of the notably dead stretch of Potsdamer Strasse that divides rather than connects the two, the **Daimler-Chrysler area** hits most of the right notes. It's big enough to allow a network of tree-lined streets with bars and restaurants, and the use of a variety of architects within a masterplan has provided visual diversity. Renzo Piano as master planner and architect to some of the buildings was able to put a bit of backbone into the area. But ultimately it all feels as contrived and sterile as a new town or theme park and little is likely to change this. It also offers no outgoing links to the other quarters or to the Kulturforum.

So the Wall is gone and buildings have risen again, but Wenders' old man could still be wandering around looking for Potsdamer Platz. There might be a letting plan, but they'll have to work hard to retrieve the romance.

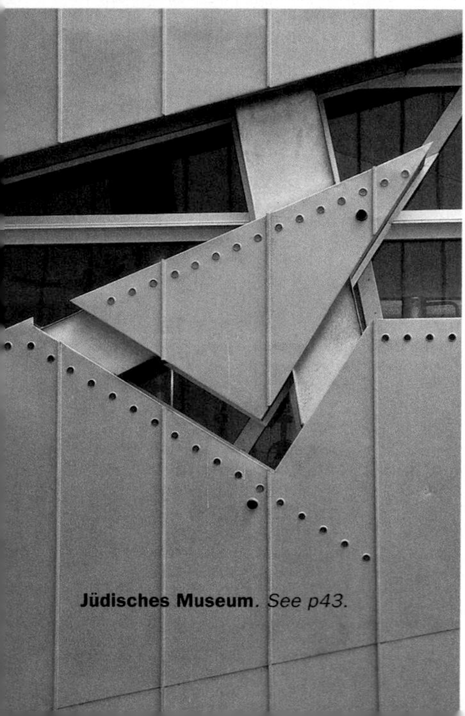

Jüdisches Museum. *See p43.*

linking east and west. The result of a competition won by Axel Schultes and Charlotte Frank, it straddles the Spree and the former border, resembling a giant paper clip that binds the two halves of the city. The centrepiece is the **Bundeskanzleramt** (Federal Chancellery; Schlutes and Frank, 2000; Willi-Brandt-Strasse, Tiergarten) flanked by buildings with offices for parliamentary deputies. The arrangement reads like a unity thanks to a common and simple language of concrete and glass.

North of this is the partially completed new central station, **Hauptbahnhof-Lehrter Bahnhof** (Von Gerkan, Marg), which will form a huge new intersection for local, regional and international trains. The platform hall is some 430 metres (1411 foot) long and covered by a barrel vault of delicately gridded glass. The building stands as a functional and symbolic link between east and west Germany and, indeed, as a hub of the continental rail network, eastern and western Europe.

To the South is the **Reichstag**, gutted, remodelled, and topped with a new glass dome by Norman Foster (1999) to bring a degree of public access and transparency to a building with a dark past. The dome or its public roof terrace offer clear views of the city centre.

CRITICAL RECONSTRUCTION?

The historic areas around the Pariser Platz and Friedrichstrasse to the north and mainly to the south of Unter den Linden through to Leipziger Strasse were peppered with empty sites following reunification. These became a primary focus for the Senate in hammering out its policy of critical reconstruction.

Pariser Platz (*see p71*) has been almost completely rebuilt to its old proportions. Some of the buildings are a pale blend of modern and historic but there are exceptions such as the **DG Bank** by Frank Gehry (Pariser Platz 3, Mitte; 2000) with its witty use of a rational façade in front of the spectacular free forms in its internal court, or Christian Portzamparc's **French Embassy** (Pariser Platz 5, Mitte; 2002), which plays with classical composition but uses contemporary materials. Round the corner in the Wilhelmstrasse, Michael Wilford's **British Embassy** (*see p275*; 2000) also came to terms with the city's strict planning limitations by raising a conformist punched stone façade, which he then broke open to expose a rich and colourful set of secondary buildings in the central court.

The first major commercial project in the Friedrichstrasse stuck with the required city scale but took the game rules lightly. The various buildings of the **Friedrichstadt-**

Passagen (Friedrichstrasse 66-75, Mitte; 1996), despite their subterranean mall link, offer separate approaches. Pei Cobb Freed and Partner's **Quartier 206** (*see p162*) is a confection of architectural devices reminiscent of 1920s Berlin, while Jean Nouvel's **Galeries Lafayette** (*see p161*) is a smooth and rounded glass form. Only the third building, **Quartier 205** by Oswald Mathias Ungers, uses a current German style with its sandstone solidity and rigorous square grid. Good examples of the emerging Berliner Architektur, based on the solidity of the past but with modern detail and expressive use of materials, are to be found in Thomas van den Valentyn and Matthias Dittmann's monumental **Quartier 108** (Friedrichstrasse/Leipziger Strasse, Mitte, 1998) and in the **Kontorhaus Mitte** (Friedrichstrasse 180-90, Mitte, 1997) by Josef Paul Kleihues, Vittorio Magnago Lampugnani, Walther Stepp and Klaus Theo Brenner.

On both sides of the city, much historic substance was lost in World War II and the sweeping changes that followed. Today, the rebuilding of the former imperial areas around Unter den Linden, the Museuminsel and Schlossplatz revolve around a choice between critical reconstruction or straightforward replicas of the past. The debate rumbles on about whether to rebuild the Stadtschloss. The abandoned hulk of the Palast der Republik is still on its site, but with no Kaiser available and a bankrupt city a rebuilt Stadtschloss will have to take a commericial use internally, with only its outer shell referring to the original.

The Kommandenthaus, next to the Staatsoper on Unter den Linden, rebuilt by Thomas van den Valentyn as the **Stiftung Bertelsmann** (2004) is another example of this tendency towards historical replication, as is the mooted reconstruction of Friedrich Schinkel's **Bauakademie** next door.

Thankfully some decisions have been taken in favour of contemporary architecture, particularly the new entrance building to the **Auswärtiges Amt** (Foreign Office; Werdescher Markt 1, 1999) by Thomas Müller and Ivan Reimann, and IM Pei's triangular block for the **Deutsches Historisches Museum** (*see p76*; 2003) with its curved foyer and cylindrical stair tower.

Berlin's return to capital city status has brought with it a number of interesting new embassies, consulates and representations which lie in and around a revived diplomatic quarter on Tiergartenstrasse and in the area north of Leipziger Platz. Notable among the Tiergartenstrasse embassies are the solid red stone **Indian Embassy** by Leon Wohlhage Wernik (2001), and the extension of the existing **Japanese Embassy** by Ryohel Amemiya (2000). There are other intriguing examples around the corner in Klingelhöferstrasse: the monumental, louvre-fronted **Mexican Embassy** by Teodore Gonzalez de Leon and J. Francisco Serrano (2000); and the encircling copper wall of the five **Nordic Embassies**, containing work by various Scandinavian architects after a plan by Alfred Berger and Tiina Parkkinen (1999).

Other embassies which seem to symbolise their countries include Rem Koolhaas' **Dutch Embassy** (Rolandufer/Klosterstrasse, 2004) with its transparency and juxtaposition of elements; and Diener and Diener's clean-lined cubic extension to the **Swiss Embassy** (2000), at Otto-von-Bismarck Allee 4.

BEST OF THE REST

The transformations of the last decade also produced work which had nothing to do with the linking of the two cities or the debate on critical reconstruction. And outside of those arguments are some of the city's best new buildings. Daniel Libeskind's **Jüdisches Museum** (*see p95*; 1999) in Kreuzberg is a symbolic sculpture in the form of a lightning bolt. Peter Eisenmann's controversial **Denkmal für die ermordeten Juden Europas** (2004), south of Pariser Platz, is a departure from a traditional memorial, with its open and sunken grid of 2,700 steles.

Nicholas Grimshaw's **Ludwig-Erhard-Haus** for the stock exchange (Fasanenstrasse 83-84; 1998) breaks with convention by taking the form of a glass and steel armadillo, though a city-required fire wall obscures the structure. On the corner at Kantstrasse 55, Josef Paul Kleihues' **Kant-Dreieck** (1995) extends the sculptural response with its huge metal weather vane. Dominique Perrault's **Velodrome** (*see p244*; 1997) sinks into the landscape in the form of a disc and a flat rectangular box of glass, concrete and gleaming steel mesh.

For all of these big, highly visible projects, the true fabric of the city is in the architecture of the everyday. The Berlin Senate's Director of Building, Hans Stimmann, in charge of Berlin's reconstruction from the early 1990s, has actually done well in the unglamorous aspects of re-establishing a well mannered and well scaled city. But now it's time to think about exceptional new projects that reflect the power, confidence and imagination of Berlin. Sauerbruch and Hutton's striking 21-storey headquarters for the **GSW** (Kochstrasse 22a, Kreuzberg; 1999) with its translucent sailed top and colourful and constantly changing façade, shows how singular buildings can take the city's urban quality to the next level.

Where to Stay

Features

Where to Stay

More choice than ever, and cheaper than comparable capitals. It's true what they say – Berlin is good in bed.

The number of hotel beds in Berlin has more than doubled since 1992; there are now about 67,000 in the city. And a steadily increasing flow of visitors (there were around 11 million overnight stays in 2002, according to Berlin Tourismus Marketing) continues to attract heavy investment in the market. Just about every major hotel chain from Ritz-Carlton to Hyatt, Raffles and Marriott has recently built a new hotel in the city.

This boom, however, has been decidedly top heavy, primarily in the four- and five-star department. This means that it's getting tough for smaller, independent establishments, who don't have a multinational chain behind them to swallow the losses during the inevitable slump.

The good news for visitors, though, is that the average price of a Berlin hotel room is, at €98 (2001 figures), lower than in most other European cities. You will pay a lot more in Prague (€109), Amsterdam (€143), London (€173) or Paris (€183) (source: The Andersen Hotel Industry Benchmark Survey, 2002).

But don't be lulled into a false sense of security. A new hotel doesn't necessarily mean a good hotel and good hotels have a tendency to be full. So book ahead, especially at times when there are major cultural events such as the Berlin Marathon (*see p185*) in September, the FilmFest in February (*see p186*) or the Love Parade in July (*see p183*).

Most hotels have websites, which are worth checking for information about deals. Some, for example, offer cheaper rates at weekends. The concept of bed and breakfast is also catching on and many small *Pensionen*, especially in the Charlottenburg area (*see p48* **West end pearls**) offer good value.

Hotels are mainly concentrated around the Gendarmenmarkt and Potsdamer Platz in the eastern city centre and around the Zoo and Savignyplatz in the west end. The selection of cheaper options in the east side of the city has dramatically improved in the last few years with pensions such as the Honigmond (*see p53*) alongside a variety of new backpacker hostels. While it's good to stay in a central location, Berlin's public transport is also excellent: unless you really are out in the suburbs, you're rarely more than half an hour from anywhere you might want to be.

PRICES

Our price categories work as follows: a **Deluxe** hotel is one in which the cheapest double room costs **€175 or more** per night; in an **Expensive** hotel it costs **€115 to €174**; **Moderate** is **€65 to €114**; and a double in a **Cheap** hotel or hostel costs **under €65**. All prices given are room prices, unless specified. Note that hotel rates tend to drop at weekends.

Remember to add breakfast to your room price if it is not included. Most hotels offer breakfast as a buffet which can be as simple as coffee and rolls (called *Schrippen*) with cheese and salami, or the full works complete with smoked meats, muesli with fruit and yoghurt, and even a glass of sparkling wine.

For accommodation catering to a predominantly gay clientele, *see p209*.

Berlin Tourismus Marketing

Europa-Center, Budapester Strasse, Charlottenburg, 10787 (reservations/information 250 025/fax 2500 2424/www.berlin-tourist-information.de). S3, S5, S7, S9, S75, U2, U9 Zoologischer Garten. **Open** 10am-7pm Mon-Sat; 10am-6pm Sun. **Map** p305 D4.

This privatised tourist information service can sort out hotel reservations as well as tickets for shows and travel arrangements to Berlin. It provides a free listings booklet of over 400 hotels – but note that the hotels therein have paid to be included. It also has lists for campsites, apartments and holiday homes (the latter costs €1.20). Their website is quite comprehensive and you can download most information as PDF files, although they're often in German. It contains no phone numbers or direct links to the hotels, though – you have to book through BTM. But this can work to your advantage as they make deals with hotels and often offer discounts. Allow plenty of time if you decide to visit one of the Berlin BTM branches: staff are notoriously inattentive. Booking online or by telephone is therefore recommended and saves you a €3 fee.

Other locations: *Brandenburger Tor; Pariser Platz, Mitte; Fernsehturm (TV Tower), Alexanderplatz, Mitte; Tegel airport.*

Mitte

Mitte is still a work in progress as far as accommodation is concerned and new hotels are springing up all the time. The first wave of post-Wall, five-star establishments now have to compete with assorted newcomers

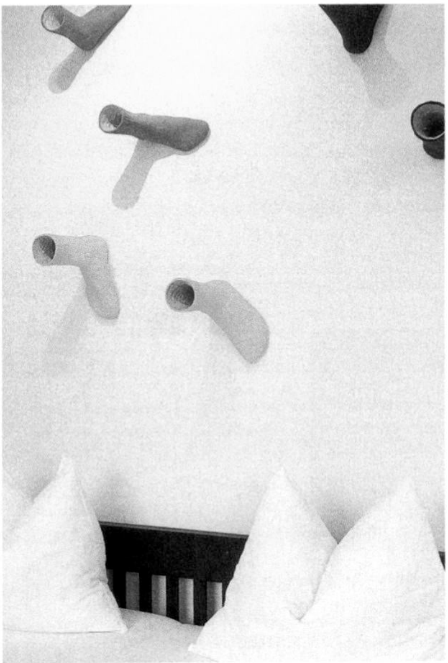
Künstlerheim Luise: a work of art. *See p53.*

around Potsdamer Platz and the freshly renovated standards in the Zoo area. For smaller, independent places it's a case of adapt or die. You won't find much of the historic pension charm of, say, Charlottenburg here but it's the most exciting part of Berlin to stay.

Deluxe

Adlon Hotel Kempinski Berlin

Unter den Linden 77, 10117 (22610/fax 2261 2222/www.hotel-adlon.de). S1, S2, S25 Unter den Linden. **Rates** €280-€440 single; €330-€490 double; €440-€8,500 suite. **Credit** AmEx, DC, MC, V. **Map** p316/p302 F3.

The original Hotel Adlon, renowned for its luxurious interiors and discreet atmosphere, opened in 1907 but burned down after World War II. The new Adlon, rebuilt by the Kempinski group on the original site, opened in 1997. Right next to the Brandenburg Gate and handy for the diplomatic quarter, it's Berlin's top hotel these days and first choice for heads of state, movie stars and anyone keen to make an impression. The rooms are decorated in a sort of international executive style; the presidential suites look like a cross between the White House and *Dallas*. There are 337 rooms, including 81 suites, six rooms for allergy sufferers, two for travellers with disabilities and two bulletproof presidential suites. Drawbacks are that the staff can be a little frosty if you don't look the part and the lobby and restaurant sometimes tend to get a bit crowded with gawkers.

Hotel services *Air-conditioning. Bar. Business services. Conference facilities. Gym. Parking. Restaurants (3). Swimming pool.* **Room services** *Hi-fi. Telephones. TV.*

Four Seasons Hotel

Charlottenstrasse 49, 10117 (20338/fax 2033 6166/www.fourseasons.com). U6, S1, S2, S3, S5, S7, S25, S75, S9 Friedrichstrasse. **Rates** €325 single; €300-€360 double; €395-€2,750 suite; breakfast €27. **Credit** AmEx, DC, MC, V. **Map** p316/p302 F3.

This is what five-star luxury is all about: marble bathrooms, huge soft towels and dressing gowns, king-size beds with pure wool blankets and elegant, impeccably trained staff who know what you need before you do. The decor is English/French country house style: wood panelling, open fireplaces, porcelain vases and oil paintings of flowers and Scottish landscapes. The effect is one of having been invited up to a country estate for the weekend and it's hard to believe that this place only opened in 1996. Pop stars love it here, both for its old-world atmosphere and for its marvellously discreet staff.

Hotel services *Bar. Concierge. Conference facilities. Disabled: adapted rooms. Gym. Laundry. No-smoking rooms. Parking (€21/day). Safe.* **Room services** *Air-conditioning. Hairdryer. Minibar. Telephone. TV: cable.*

Royal Dorint am Gendarmenmarkt

Charlottenstrasse 50, 10117 (203 750/fax 203 75100/www.dorint.de/berlin-gendarmenmarkt). U2, U6 Stadtmitte. **Rates** €197-€280 single; €218-€295 double; €255-€510 suites; €21 breakfast. **Credit** AmEx, DC, MC, V. **Map** p316/302 F3.

It's not easy to get a room here and for good reason: it really is very lovely. A great deal of attention has been paid to detail, from the calming colour scheme to the excellent lighting. The atmosphere is intimate and each room is beautifully styled, with perhaps the best-looking bathrooms in Berlin. Conference rooms are superb and the 'wellness' area is a delight, complete with plunge pools and picturesque views across the Gendarmenmarkt.

Hotel services *Bar. Conference facilities. Gym. Laundry. Lift. Parking (€15). Restaurants (2). Sauna. Solarium.* **Room services** *Bathrobe. Hairdryer. Minibar. Room service. TV.*

Expensive

Hotel Albrechtshof

Albrechtstrasse 8, 10117 (308 860/fax 3088 6100/ www.albrechtshof-hotels.de). U6, S1, S2, S3, S5, S7, S9, S25, S75 Friedrichstrasse. **Rates** (breakfast included) €118-€169 single; €148-€199 double; €230 suite. **Credit** AmEx, DC, MC, V. **Map** p316/p302 F3.

Although it doesn't make a song and dance about it, this place is a member of the Verband Christlicher Hotels (Christian Hotels Association). Naturally,

West end pearls

Hotel Garni Askanischer Hof

Compared to other European cities, Berlin is a bit short on palazzo hotels or grand, nostalgic guest houses. And with a few exceptions, the decor in most new Berlin hotels is about as exciting as an IKEA showroom. But not all of the city's bedrooms are lacking in romance. If you don't mind doing without room service and halogen lighting, then a few nights in a Charlottenburg *Pension* could be just the ticket. This district is full of atmospheric private guest houses, often cheaper than regular hotels. But not all '*Zimmer Frei*' signs in west end sidestreets are gateways to little gems. There are dodgy dives too. So look at your room before booking it – or try one of the following.

Hotel-Pension Funk (*see p63*), the former abode of a Danish silent movie star, was converted into a guest house by the Funk sisters in the 1950s. Manager Michael Pfund scours auction rooms and antique shops to maintain the retro ambience. It's a favourite with Film Festival visitors – hardly surprising as the whole place resembles a movie set.

Hotel-Pension Dittberner (*see p62*), on the other hand, feels like a beautifully decorated

Hotel-Pension Dittberner

private house. Elly Lange has been running it since 1958, and her colour schemes and furnishings – both antique and contemporary – have been blended with the precision of a master interior decorator. The walls are also adorned with art – her husband, Ludwig Lange, owns a gallery on the ground floor.

The **Hotel Garni Askanischer Hof** (*see p61*) has long been a favourite with actors and musicians – notable guests have included Robert Wilson, Georg Tabori, David Bowie, Luc Bondi and Marianne Sägebrecht. And the eclectic decor, a sort of greatest-hits medley of 20th-century styles, has interiors editors going weak at the knees: a chesterfield under a 1970s lamp, say, beside a Caspar David Friedrich print.

The bohemian charm of the **Pension Kettler** (*see p64*) is another highlight. Owner Frau Josipovici is a flamboyant character who would seem more at home in Swinging London than Charlottenburg. Her glamorous life story is a whirl of art exhibitions and literary guests. In short, she is the epitome of a fascinating guest-house proprietress – you wouldn't get staff like her at the Holiday Inn.

then, it's got its own chapel. There's also a pleasant *Hof* garden, where breakfast is served in summer, and a restaurant specialising in Berlin cuisine. The hotel is situated in the government quarter, close to Friedrichstrasse station and several theatres. The decor isn't much to write home about, but it's agreeably smart and clean, and staff are friendly. The owners also have two other hotels nearby: the Augustinenhof and the Allegra. Both can be booked at the above number; check website for more details.
Hotel services *Conference facilities. Disabled: adapted rooms. Parking (€11/day). Restaurants.* **Room services** *Minibar. TV.*

Alexander Plaza Berlin

Rosenstrasse 1, 10178 (240 010/fax 2400 1777/ www.hotel-alexanderplaza.com). S3, S5, S7, S75, S9 Hackescher Markt. **Rates** €140 single; €150 double; €155-€215 suite; €15 breakfast buffet. **Credit** AmEx, DC, MC, V. **Map** p316/p303 G3.
Well located between Alexanderplatz, Museuminsel and Hackescher Markt, this handsome, renovated building houses a comfortable modern establishment. Despite its proximity to one of the liveliest parts of Mitte, the hotel stands in an oasis of quiet not far from the river. Staff are polite and the decor is not bad. There are 92 rooms, 32 of which are non-smoking. Each room has modem facilities and there is also a fitness centre.
Hotel services *Beauty salon. Gym. No-smoking rooms. Parking. Restaurant. Sauna.* **Room services** *Hairdryer. Minibar. TV: pay movies.*

Hotel Garni Gendarm

Charlottenstrasse 61, 10117 (206 0660/fax 206 06666/www.hotel-gendarm-berlin.de). U2, U6. Stadtmitte. **Rates** (breakfast included) €124 single; €149 double; €164-€250 suite. **Credit** AmEx, DC, MC, V. **Map** p316/p306 F4.
If you fancy a five-star location but don't want to blow a fortune, then this place is just the ticket. It hasn't got a lot of extras, but the rooms are smart and it's close to the Gendarmenmarkt and an assortment of top restaurants. The Staatsoper is just down the road, too, so it's well placed for cultural visits. For less than half the price of the nearby Dorint, Four Seasons or Hilton, you can't really go wrong – unless you bring the car. In this neighbourhood parking could end up costing as much as your room.
Hotel services *Bar. Gym. Lift.* **Room services** *Hairdryer. Minibar. TV.*

Hotel Hackescher Markt

Grosse Präsidentenstrasse 8, 10178 (280 030/fax 280 03111/www.hackescher-markt.com). S3, S5, S7, S9, S75 Hackescher Markt. **Rates** €120-€150 single; €155-€185 double; €185-€205 suite. **Credit** AmEx, DC, MC, V. **Map** p316/p303 G3.
An elegant hotel in a nicely renovated town house that solves the noise problem at its Hackescher Markt location by having most rooms face inwards on to a tranquil green courtyard. Some rooms have balconies, most have their own bath with underfloor heating, and the suites are spacious and comfortable. The staff speak good English and are kind, smiling and helpful. Not cheap though.
Hotel services *Bar. No-smoking floor. Parking. (€15).* **Room services** *Minibar. Hairdryer. Internet. Safe. TV.*

Hotel-Pension Kastanienhof

Kastanienallee 65, 10119 (443 050/fax 4430 5111/ www.hotel_kastanienburg_berlin.de). U8 Rosenthaler Platz or U2 Senefelder Platz/Bus 143/tram 13, 52, 53. **Rates** (breakfast included) €93 single; €128 double; €138 apartment. **Credit** AmEx, MC, V. **Map** p303 G2.
If you can handle the pastel peach and pink decor, rooms here are generously proportioned and well equipped. Staff are friendly and there are three breakfast rooms and a bar. The hotel is also well situated for exploring Prenzlauer Berg and Mitte, as it lies on the border between the two districts.
Hotel services *Bar. Conference facilities. Lift. Parking (€7).* **Room services** *Hairdryer. Minibar. Radio. Safe. Telephone. TV: satellite.*

Maritim proArte Hotel Berlin

Friedrichstrasse 151, 10117 (203 35/fax 2033 4209/www.maritim.de) U6, S1, S2, S3, S5, S7, S9, S25, S75 Friedrichstrasse. **Rates** €149-€265 single; €168-€278 double; €300-€1900 suites; €18 breakfast. **Credit** AmEx, DC, V, MC. **Map** p316/p302 F3.
On the former site of the Hotel Metropol, this gleaming edifice was one of Berlin's first 1990s 'designer hotels'. Though it has since been somewhat eclipsed by more recent arrivals, it's still a decent place with a central location. Adorned with huge paintings and designer furniture, the foyer, three restaurants and bar are pretty swish. The 403 rooms, apartments and suites all have fax and PC connections, air-conditioning and marble bathrooms. Staff are polite and helpful. The Brandenburg Gate and Reichstag are within walking distance, as are Unter den Linden, the swanky shops of Friedrichstrasse and the bars and galleries of the Scheunenviertel.
Hotel services *Air-conditioning. Bar. Conference facilities. Disabled: adapted rooms. Gym. Lifts. Massage. Parking (€13/day). Restaurants (3). Sauna. Swimming pool.* **Room services** *Minibar. Room service. TV: pay movies.*

Radisson SAS Berlin

Karl-Liebknecht-Strasse 5, 10178 (238 280/fax 238 2810/www.berlin.radissonsas.com). U6, S1, S2, S25, S3, S5, S7, S75, S9 Friedrichstrasse. **Rates** €160-€235 single; €160-€235 double; €230-€650 suite; €19 breakfast buffet. **Credit** AmEx, DC, MC, V. **Map** p316/p303 G3.
With two other huge five-star hotels opening their doors in central Berlin, the Radisson SAS realised it needed a little extra something to make a big splash. So now they have the world's largest free-standing aquarium in the middle of their atrium (*see p85*). Each bedroom has a guaranteed 'sea view' on to the breathtaking 25m- (82ft-) high tank, which houses 2,500 varieties of fish in over a million litres of salt water. For guests longing to dip their own toes, the

hotel also has a large spa complete with swimming pool and sauna, and you can wet your whistle in the Aqua Lounge bar and restaurant. German-born designer Yasmine Mahmoudieh (she also did the new Airbus A380 interiors) has worked wonders with the 427 rooms, which are fresh, uncluttered and free of the blandness so typical of big chain hotels.
Hotel services *Bar. Beauty salon. Disabled: adapted rooms. Gym. Parking. Restaurant. Swimming pool.* **Room services** *Minibar. Room service. TV: movies.*

Westin Grand

Friedrichstrasse 158-164, 10117 (20 270/fax 2027 3362/www.westin.com/berlin). U6, S1, S2, S3, S5, S7, S9, S25, S26, S75 Friedrichstrasse. **Rates** €131-€350 single; €165-€375 double; €397-€1930 suite; €18 breakfast buffet. **Credit** AmEx, DC, V. **Map** p316/302 F3.
Just around the corner from Unter den Linden, the Westin Grand is pure five-star international posh (the Stones stay here when they are in town). Despite prefabricated East German construction, the hotel lives up to its name rather well: the decor is gratifyingly elegant with lots of glass and polished brass. The staircase and foyer are especially bombastic. Its 35 suites, meanwhile, are individually furnished with period decor themed after their names (try the Schinkel or Lessing suites). The regular rooms are decorated in a tasteful, traditional style. There's also a lovely garden and patio, plus a couple of bars and restaurants. On the negative side, the claustrophobic corridors seem to go on for ever.
Hotel services *Bar. Beauty salon. Conference facilities. Laundry. No-smoking floor. Pool. Restaurant.* **Room services** *Air-conditioning. Minibar. Room service. TV: cable/pay movies.*

Moderate

Hotel am Scheunenviertel

Oranienburger Strasse 38, 10117 (282 2125/ 2830 8310/fax 282 1115/www.hotelamscheunen viertel.de). U6 Oranienburger Tor or S1, S2, S25 Oranienburger Strasse. **Rates** (breakfast included) €70 single; €80 double. **Credit** AmEx, DC, MC, V. **Map** p316/p302 F3.
In the historical heart of town and the old Jewish Quarter, this 18-room hotel is a good base for exploring Berlin. The Museuminsel, Friedrichstrasse and Hackesche Höfe are all close by, and by night the area is alive with bars and restaurants. Rooms are clean and comfortable, if a bit dark and dingy; each has a WC and good shower. Downsides are the uninspiring buffet breakfast and noise from the nightclub next door. But helpful staff make up for it.
Room services *Telephone. TV.*

Art'otel Berlin Mitte

Wallstrasse 70-73, 10179 (240 620/fax 2406 2222/ www.artotel.de). U2 Märkisches Museum. **Rates** (breakfast included) €70-€180 single; €100-€210 double; €240-€260 suite. **Credit** AmEx, DC, MC, V. **Map** p316/p307 G4.
On the banks of the Spree, this is a delightful fusion of old and new, housing both immaculately restored rococo reception rooms and ultra-modern bedrooms designed by Nalbach & Nalbach. The hotel is a showcase for the work of artist Georg Baselitz: all the rooms and corridors contain originals of his work as well as others by AR Penck and Andy Warhol. Besides the art, every detail of the decor has been meticulously attended to, from Philippe Starck bathrooms to the Marcel Breuer chairs in the conference rooms. Service is friendly and the views from the top suites across Mitte are stunning.
Hotel services *Babysitting. Bar. Business services. Laundry. Parking. Restaurant.* **Room services** *Hairdryer. Radio. Telephone. TV: pay movies.*

Boardinghouse Mitte

Mulackstrasse 1-2, 10119 (2838 8488/ fax 2838 8489/www.home-from-home.com). U8 Weinmeisterstrasse or S3, S5, S7, S9, S75 Hackescher Markt. **Rates** €70-€250 single apartment; €77-€250 double apartment; €87-€286 maisonette; €6 breakfast. **Credit cards** AmEx, MC, V. **Map** p303 G3.
More of a place to stay in for a week or more, offering small but modern and fully kitted out, German designer-style serviced apartments. It's not cheap, but prices get lower the longer you stay and it's well located in the pretty Scheunenviertel and heart of the fashion district. There are lots of good cafés and restaurants on the doorstep and it's just a short walk from Hackescher Markt. If they are fully booked here, they now have an extra 39 new apartments near the Lehrter Bahnhof on Invalidenstrasse (no.32-33; see the website) but this is a different district so check first into which building they are booking you.
Hotel Services *Babysitter. Laundry. Parking (€9/day).* **Room services** *Cooking facilities. Hi-fi. Iron. TV: video.*

Dietrich-Bonhoeffer-Haus

Ziegelstrasse 30, 10117 (284 670/fax 2846 7145/ www.hotel-dbh.de). U6 Friedrichstrasse or S1, S2, S25, S26 Oranienburger Strasse. **Rates** (breakfast included) €85 single; €110 double; €140 triple. **Credit** AmEx, MC, V. **Map** p316/p302 F3.
Built in 1987 as a meeting place for Christians from the east and west, this hotel is named after a theologian executed by the Nazis for alleged participation in the Hitler assassination attempt of 1944. The building is centrally located in a quiet side street near the Museuminsel, and there's a friendly atmosphere – everyone says hello and smiles a lot, which is unusual in this town. Rooms are enormous, the breakfast is good and the day's weather forecast is helpfully posted in the lift. A good place to stay.
Hotel services *Conference facilities. Restaurant.* **Room services** *Radio. Telephone.*

Honigmond Garden Hotel

Invalidenstrasse 122, 10115 (2844 5577/fax 2844 5588/www.honigmond-berlin.de). U6 Oranienburger Tor. **Rates** (breakfast included) €89-€109 single; €109-€159 double. **Credit** V. **Map** p302 F2/3.

Pension Acksel Haus is an oasis in Prenzlauer Berg. *See p55.*

Why doesn't Berlin have more new hotels like this? The sister to Honigmond Pension just up the road (*see below*), this place is charming and doesn't cost an arm and a leg. Choose between big rooms facing the street (loud if you open your windows), or smaller ones facing the Tuscan-style garden. There are also spacious apartments. Rooms are furnished with attention to detail: pine floors, iron bedsteads, oil paintings and antiques. There's also a sitting room for putting your feet up at the end of the day. As the brochure points out, 'all the sights worth seeing in East Berlin can be reached by foot from here'.
Hotel services *Parking (€7).* **Room services** *Hairdryer. Iron. Telephone. TV.*

Honigmond Pension

Borsigstrasse 28, 10115 (284 4550/fax 284 4551/ www.honigmond.com). U6 Oranienburger Tor. **Rates** €49-€89 single; €69-€119 double; €7.50 breakfast. **Credit** V. **Map** p302 F2.
The 20 recently renovated rooms in this 1899 building are spacious and attractive, though only nine have their own shower and WC. But don't let that put you off: this is probably the best budget hotel east of the Zoo. Breakfast is served in the Honigmond restaurant (*see p121*), running since 1920. The lunchtime buffet (€6.50) varies in quality but the evening menu is worth sampling. Overall, the hotel is friendly and good for families. It's also within walking distance from the Scheunenviertel.
Hotel services *Bar. Restaurant.* **Room services** *Hair dryer. Iron. TV.*

Künstlerheim Luise

Luisenstrasse 19, 10117 (284 480/fax 280 6942/2844 8448/www.kuenstlerheim-luise.de). U6 Oranienburger Tor. **Rates** €48-€95 single; €79-€139 double; €130-€149 suite; €7 breakfast. **Credit** MC, V. **Map** p316/p302 E3.
A pension with a difference and a well-deserved reputation as one of the city's most imaginative small hotels. Each room is the creation of a different artist. They vary from very basic on the top floor – a bed, telephone and art with shared bathroom facilities and communal kitchen – to grand rooms and suites on the first floor. Try the Oliver Jordan suite, Dieter Mammel's room with the huge bed, or the Rainer Gross Shaker room. Some rooms get a bit of noise from the S-Bahn, but don't be put off: this is a great location – within a stone's throw of the Reichstag.
Hotel services *Bar. Restaurant.* **Room services** *Telephone.*

Hotel Märkischer Hof

Linienstrasse 133, 10115 (282 7155/fax 282 4331/ www.maerkischer-hof-berlin.de). U6 Oranienburger Tor. **Rates** (breakfast included) €60-€70 single; €75-€90 double; €120 triple. **Credit** MC, V. **Map** p316/p302 F3.
This quiet, family-run hotel opposite the Tacheles arts centre is within walking distance of several cultural attractions, including the Berliner Ensemble, the Metropoltheater and the Staatsoper. It's an unremarkable place with a pension atmosphere and comfortable rooms in an apricot hue.
Hotel services *Parking.* **Room services** *Telephone. TV.*

mitArt Pension

Friedrichstrasse 127, 10117 (2839 0430/fax 2839 0432/www.mitart.de). U6 Oranienburger Tor. **Rates** (breakfast included) €55-€88 single; €88-€105 double. **Credit** AmEx, MC, V. **Map** p316/p302 F3.
Opposite Tacheles, this elegant pension is also a gallery; the friendly owner started out by letting his rooms to artists. The grand breakfast room is typical of a 19th-century Berlin town house and a healthy 'naturkost' breakfast is served here. The

best room is the *Mädchenkammer*: a set of wooden steps up to a platform and simple white unadorned walls where the servant used to sleep. This is a good base for gallery-hopping: Auguststrasse is around the corner and the owner knows the art scene. It's tricky to find though: look at the labels on the door-bell and go up the main staircase to the first floor.
Room services *Telephone.*

Park Inn Hotel

Alexanderplatz 8, 10178 (2389 4333/fax 2389 4305/www.parkinn.de) U2, U5, U8, S3, S5, S7, S75, S9 Alexanderplatz. **Rates** €89-€175 single; €89-€190 double; €150-€250 suite; €15 breakfast. **Credit cards** AmEx, MC, V. **Map** p316/p303 G3.
It's hard to find something nice to say about any of the 1006 rooms here, which are generally cramped and expensive, though the new owners (this used to be the Forum Hotel) have tried to smarten things up. That said, the views are spectacular. If you can get an *Eckzimmer* (corner room) above the 16th floor, overlooking the Fernsehturm and Karl-Marx-Allee, the sunsets can be sensational. On the other hand, you could just go up and have a meal in the Panorama restaurant or play in the top-floor casino and save yourself the horror and expense of actually having to stay overnight. Otherwise only recommended for convention groups, for whom they have specially priced packages.
Hotel Services *Bar. Conference facilities. Disabled: adapted rooms. Gym. Laundry. No-smoking floors. Parking (€15). Restaurants (2).* **Room services** *Hairdryer. Minibar. TV: pay movies, satellite.*

Taunus Hotel

Monbijouplatz 1, 10178 (283 5254/fax 283 5255/ www.hotel-taunus.de). S3, S5, S7, S9, S75 Hackescher Markt. **Rates** (breakfast included) €88 single; €99 double. **Credit** AmEx, DC, MC, V. **Map** p316/p302 F3.
Tucked away behind Hackescher Markt S-Bahn station, this small hotel has a great location, near the Museuminsel and ideally placed for exploring Mitte nightlife. It's a little near to the main tram terminus to be recommended for light sleepers in summer, but you can't beat it for city hustle and bustle. Ask for a room with a view of the Dom cathedral.
Hotel services *Bar. Parking (€15).* **Room services** *Telephone. TV.*

Cheap

Circus Hostel

Weinbergsweg 1a, 10119 (2839 1433/fax 2839 1484/www.circus-berlin.de). U2 Rosa Luxemburg Platz. **Rates** (per bed per night) €14 6-7-bed room; €17 4-5-bed room; €20 3-bed room; €24 2-bed room; €30 1-bed room; €65-€120 2-4-bed apartment with balcony; €2 bedlinen (compulsory). €1.50-€4.50 breakfast. **No credit cards**. **Map** p316/p303 G3.
The Circus now has two locations (the other is in nearby Rosa-Luxemburg-Strasse; see website). Both are a short walk from Mitte's best bars and clubs. They're friendly hostels with clean and bright rooms – a rarity for backpacker places. The owners are young travellers themselves and work hard to offer value for money. Staff can arrange discount club and concert tickets and travel cards. Best of all, they do special tours to underground bunkers and normally inaccessible archives; the Stasi tour should not be missed. For longer stays, the apartments on the top floor are well priced and have fine views. Single-sex rooms are also available. But be sure to book ahead: this place is deservedly popular.
Hostel services *Bar. Disabled: adapted rooms. Laundry. Pay phone. Safe. TV.*
Other locations: Rosa-Luxemburg-Strasse 39, Babelsberg, 2839 1433.

Hotel Garni Transit Loft: party on. *See p55.*

The Clubhouse Hostel

Kalkscheunenstrasse 2, 10117 (2809 7979/fax 2809 7977/www.clubhouse-berlin.de). U6, S1, S2, S3, S5, S7, S9, S25, S26, S75 Friedrichstrassee. **Rates** (per bed per night) €14-€17 dormitory; €20 for 3-bed room; €46 double, €32 single; €2 bedlinen (compulsory); €3 breakfast buffet (plus drinks). **No credit cards**. **Map** p316/p302 F3.
Centrally located, the Clubhouse Hostel is housed in a historic building and culture centre, the Kalkscheune ('chalk barn') just behind the infamous Tacheles arts centre. The rooms smell a bit like dirty socks, but that's budget travelling for you. No matter, the staff are friendly and speak English. Other highlights include an attractive communal room.
Hostel services *Internet. Guided tours. Payphone. Safe. Storage.*

Mitte's Backpacker Hostel

Chausseestrasse 102, 10115 (2839 0965/fax 2839 0935/www.backpacker.de). U6 Zinnowitzer Strasse. **Rates** (per bed per night) €15-17dormitory; €19 4-

bed room; €20 3-bed room; €22-€27 double; €29 single; bedlinen €2.50; €3.75 breakfast.
Credit AmEx, MC, V. **Map** p302 F2.
Open since 1994, this is the oldest backpacker hostel in Mitte. It's got a homely, student digs kind of atmosphere. The rooms are all decorated by artistically minded former guests and have been named accordingly. The 'Berlin room' is amusing, with light fittings in the shape of Berlin's two television towers and the green poem room is good for insomniacs (the walls are covered in lengthy poems). There's a kitchen and a video room with English films. The staff are multilingual, friendly and helpful.
Hostel services *Cooking facilities.*

Prenzlauer Berg

This charming borough has a surprising dearth of decent accommodation. But the atmospheric architecture and lively bar and café culture make this one of Berlin's most desirable places to live. So if you intend to stay for a while, try renting a private apartment or room from an accommodation agency – it can be cheaper than a hotel and really give you a feel for the place.

Moderate

Pension Acksel Haus

Belforter Strasse 21, 10405 (4433 7633/fax 441 6116/www.ackselhaus.de). U2 Senefelder Platz.
Rates €66-€95 single; €77-€105 double.
No credit cards (cash only). **Map** p303 G2.
An oasis in Prenzlauer Berg, this pension now has ten apartments. Each has a bedroom, sitting room, bathroom and kitchenette, complete with lovely old wooden floorboards, white walls, antique furniture and a Mediterranean feel. The blue and white 'maritime apartment', with its mahogany furniture and seafaring paintings, is a particular gem. Most of the rooms have two beds, and one larger apartment is suitable for four to five people. Delightful back garden in summer. Recommended, but book ahead.
Hotel services *Garden.* **Room services** *Cooking facilities. Telephone. TV.*

Hotel Greifswald

Greifswalder Strasse 211, 10405 (442 7888/fax 442 7898/www.hotel-greifswald.de). Tram 2,3,4 Hufelandstrasse. **Rates** (breakfast included) €65-€78 single; €78-€88 double. **Credit** AmEx, DC, MC, V. **Map** p303 H2.
A clean, no-nonsense hotel near Kollwitzplatz and a short tram hop from Alexanderplatz. Rooms are cheerful with bright curtains and good-sized beds; staff are helpful. There is an interesting collection of signed photographs from unknown bands and musicians in the foyer. The hotel is close to the Knaack and Magnet clubs (for both *see p227*). In summer, breakfast is served in the courtyard.
Hotel services *Parking.* **Room services** *Telephone. TV.*

Myer's Hotel

Metzer Strasse 26, 10405 (440 140/fax 4401 4104/www.myershotel.de). U2 Senefelderplatz.
Rates (breakfast included) €80-€130 single; €100-€165 double. **Credit** AmEx, MC, V. **Map** p303 G2.
This fully renovated, traditional Berlin town house could have done with a good interior designer. It's not that it's unattractive: it's just somewhat bland and a bit overpriced. However, the lovely Kollwitzplatz is around the corner and it's within walking distance of Mitte.
Hotel services *Bar. Garden.* **Room services** *Hairdryer. Minibar. Telephone. TV.*

Cheap

Hotel Garni Transit Loft

Greifswalder Strasse 219, 10405 (entrance: Immanuelkirchstrasse 14) (4849 3773/fax 4405 1074/www.transit-loft.de). Tram 2,3,4 Hufelandstrasse. **Rates** (breakfast included) €90 3-bed room; €120 4-bed room; €150 5-bed room; €69 double; €59 single; €15 dormitory.
Credit AmEx, MC, V. **Map** p303 H2.
In an old, renovated factory, this newish loft hotel caters for backpackers and groups of young travellers. The rooms all have en suite bathrooms, which means no wandering up and down the corridor in your towel, bumping into strangers. In the same building are a sauna, gym and billiard salon, which all have special rates for guests. There's also good wheelchair access. Another huge plus: the bar is open all night. Party on.
Hotel services *Bar. Disabled: adapted rooms. TV.*

Lette'm Sleep Hostel

Lettestrasse 7, 10437 (4473 3623/fax 4473 3625/ www.backpackers.de). U2 Eberswalder Strasse.
Rates (per person bed per night) €14-€19 7-bed room to 3-bed room; €48 double; €66 apartment; €3 bedlinen (optional); breakfast self catering, special rates for longer stays. **Credit** MC, V. **Map** p303 G1.
Run by Australians, this small hostel is slap in the middle of Prenzlauer Berg. Breakfast is not provided but you can make your own in the kitchen. The whole place feels a bit run-down, but there are disabled facilities. A beer garden is supposed to be ready by summer 2004.
Hostel services *Cooking facilities. Disabled: adapted rooms. Internet. Payphone.*

Friedrichshain

Friedrichshain is the city's new bohemia, as students and creative types colonise the area in between the Stalinist architecture of Karl-Marx-Alle and the old industrial area around the Warschauer Brücke. With its decent transport connections, nostalgic 'Eastie' feel, fantastic café breakfasts, reasonably priced bars and cafés, clubs and live music venues, it's a great area to stay, especially if you're on a budget.

Hotel Riehmer's Hofgarten: a real gem.

Moderate

East Side City Hotel

Mühlenstrasse 6, 10243 (293 833/fax 2938 3555/ www.eastsidecityhotel.de). U1, U15, S3, S5, S7, Warschauer Strasse. **Rates** (breakfast included) €60 single; €85 double. **Credit** AmEx, MC, V. **Map** p307 H4.

Directly opposite the famous East Side gallery, this modest, simply decorated hotel is great if you want to get some idea of what Berlin felt like 15 years ago. Get a room at the back if you want peace and quiet, but then you'll miss a sunset view across the old red-brick factory buildings, the Warschauer Bridge and one of the last remaining stretches of the Berlin Wall.

Hotel services *Bar. Lift. Parking (free). Restaurant.* **Room services** *Telephone. TV.*

Cheap

A & O Backpackers

Boxhagener Strasse 73, 10245 (297 7810/fax 2977 8-20/www.aohostel.com). U5 Samariter Strasse or S3, S5, S6, S7, S8, S9, S75 Ostkreuz. **Rates** (per bed per night) €13-€18 for 8-10-bed room; €22 for 6-bed room; €22 for 4-bed room (breakfast included); €30 double (breakfast included); €58 single (breakfast included); €3 bedlinen (optional); €4 breakfast buffet. **Credit** MC, V. **Map** p88.

This hostel has a bit of a school camp atmosphere. Rooms are clean and the pine furniture is attractive. There is also a budget 'easy dorm': no locker, no shower, no booking, just a bed (€10). In summer, guests hang out in the courtyard. See website for details about sister hostels at Zoo and in Mitte.

Hostel services *Cooking facilities. DVD player. Internet. Laundry. Safe. TV.*

Odyssee Globetrotter Hostel

Grünberger Strasse 23, 10243 (2900 008/fax 2900 3311/www.hostel-berlin.de). U5 Frankfurter Tor. **Rates** (per person per bed per night) €13 for 8-bed room; €13-€15 for 6-bed room; €17 for 4-bed room; €19 for 3-bed room; €45-€52 double; €35 single; €3 breakfast buffet. **No credit cards.**

Just off the former Stalin Allee, this friendly place is located in the studenty area of town, which has good alternative clubs and bars. No wonder the twentysomething backpacker brigade love it. The entrance is in a pretty courtyard; the interior is cosy and decorated with imagination, even if the rooms have a slight whiff of trainer about them. Very helpful international staff. For longer stays, there's a dorm with its own kitchen.

Hostel services *Luggage room. Safe.*

Kreuzberg

Before the Wall came down Kreuzberg was *the* alternative place to be in Berlin, if not the whole of Europe. Now most people tend to overlook its charms in their rush for the 'new Mitte'. They are making a mistake, though. That's because Kreuzberg has some of Berlin's most picturesque streets, lively markets, nicest cafés and interesting alternative venues.

Expensive

Hotel Riehmer's Hofgarten

Yorckstrasse 83, 10965 (780 98800/fax 780 98808/www.hotel-riehmers-hofgarten.de). U6, U7 Mehringdamm. **Rates** (breakfast included) €98-€108 single; €123-€138 double. **Credit** AmEx, MC, V. **Map** p306 E5.

In an historic building with one of Berlin's prettiest courtyards, this place is a real gem. The styling is exquisite, the staff are charming and the rooms airy and well furnished. The bathrooms were recently refurbished too. Surprisingly, the prices are pretty reasonable. The only drawback is the location, which is just a little off the beaten track. Nevertheless, Viktoria Park and the shops and cafés of Bergmannstrasse are nearby, and Mitte is only ten minutes away by U-Bahn.

Hotel services *Bar. Parking (€8). Restaurant.* **Room services** *Minibar. TV: cable.*

Cheap

BaxPax Berlin

Skalitzer Strasse 104, 10997 (6951 8322/fax 6951 8372/www.baxpax.de). U1 Görlitzer Bahnhof. **Rates** (per person per room) €29 single; €22 triple; €17-€19 4-bed room; €12-16 dormitory; €2.50 bedlinen. **Credit** AmEx, MC, V. **Map** p307 H5.

Opened in 2001, Baxpax belongs to the same people as the Backpacker Hostel in Mitte (*see p54*). It follows the usual Berlin backpacker formula: there are friendly, English-speaking staff, a young,

party atmosphere and self-service kitchen. There's also a good pool nearby, which is a boon in summer after a hard morning of sightseeing. Female-only dorms need to be booked in advance.
Hotel services *Bar. Cooking facilities. Laundry. TV: VCR.* **Room services** *Safe.*

Die Fabrik

Schlesische Strasse 18, 10997 (611 7116/fax 618 2974/www.diefabrik.com). U1 Schlesisches Tor. **Rates** (per room) €32-€38 single; €42-€52 double; €60-€69 triple; €76-€84 quadruple; €15-€18 dormitory; bedlinen free. **No credit cards**. **Map** p307 H5.
Fabrik is German for 'factory' and this hostel, like most others in Berlin, is in a 19th-century former factory building. But unlike the other backpacker hostels, this one has none of the little extras that make you feel like family; no kitchen, TV room, billiards or whatever. It's just a bed and a locker; breakfast in the café next door costs extra.
Hotel services *Internet. Lift. Locker.*

Pension Kreuzberg

Grossbeerenstrasse 64, 10963 (251 1362/fax 251 0638/www.pension-kreuzberg.de). U7, U6 Mehringdamm. **Rates** (breakfast included) €40 single; €52 double; €22.50 per person 3-5-bed room. **No credit cards**. **Map** p306 F5.
A small, friendly 12-room pension in a typical old Berlin building. It's not for the lazy or infirm, as you have to climb four steep flights of stairs to reception. And only two rooms have their own bathrooms (there's a communal one on each floor), although they all have wash basins. Nevertheless, there's a cheap and cheerful vibe and a breakfast room with buffet. Worth considering if you are a family travelling on a budget.

Hotel Transit

Hagelberger Strasse 53-54, 10965 (789 0470/ fax 7890 4777/www.hotel-transit.de). U6, U7 Mehringdamm. **Rates** (breakfast included) €52 single; €60 double. **Credit** AmEx, MC, V. **Map** p306 F5.
Another converted factory, another budget hotel, this one very bright and airy and in one of the most beautiful parts of Kreuzberg, handy for Viktoria Park and a variety of cafés and restaurants. The 49 rooms are basic but clean and the €15 dormitory is good value (book in advance; women-only dorms are also available). All rooms have showers and the staff speak English.
Hotel services *Bar. Internet. Lift. Safe.*

Tiergarten

Just to confuse everyone, Tiergarten, like Wedding, is now officially part of Mitte but nobody seems to pay much attention apart from civil servants. Some of the following establishments are dotted around the edge of the huge park which gives this district its name. Tiergarten also contains a whole bunch of embassies, cultural institutions and of course, Potsdamer Platz, where various glitzy five-star palaces are now clustered.

Deluxe

The Berlin Marriott Hotel

Inge-Beisheim-Platz 1, 10785 (220 000/ fax 22000 1000/www.marriott.de/BERMC). U2, S1, S25, S2, S9 Potsdamer Platz. **Rates** €180 single; €225 double; €305 suites; breakfast buffet included. **Credit** AmEx, MC, V, DC. **Map** p306 E4.
More modest than its sister hotel, the Ritz-Carlton next door, the Marriott also has five stars but is more reasonably priced and decorated in what they call a 'modern designer' style. The cool white interior of the enormous atrium is impressive. By contrast, the room decor is disappointingly bland and, as for the bathrooms, they're downright boring. Still, the restaurant isn't too bad. Close proximity to the Tiergarten means you can go for a spectacular run past the Brandenburg Gate and Reichstag.
Hotel services *Air-conditioning. Bar. Business services. Conference facilities. Gym. Pool.* **Room services** *Hairdryer. Iron. Room service. Minibar. TV: cable/satellite.*

Grand Hotel Esplanade

Lützowufer 15, 10785 (254 780/fax 254 788 222/www.esplanade.de). U2, U4, U15 Nollendorfplatz. **Rates** €230-€280 single; €255-€305 double; €420-€2300 suite; €20 breakfast. **Credit** AmEx, DC, MC, V. **Map** p305 D4.
One of Berlin's better luxury hotels, next to the Landwehr canal and close to the Tiergarten. The entrance lives up to the name, with a huge, gushing wall of water and hundreds of lights glittering overhead. The lobby is spacious and beautifully decorated; art exhibitions adorn some of the walls. The rooms are tasteful and gratifyingly free of frilly decor; 30 have been set aside for non-smokers. An added benefit of staying here is being within stumbling-back-to-bed distance of Harry's New York Bar – it's on the ground floor, underlining the distinctly American feel of the place.
Hotel services *Bar. Beauty salon. Disabled: adapted rooms. Laundry. No-smoking rooms. Parking. Pool. Restaurant.*

Grand Hyatt

Marlene-Dietrich-Platz 2, 10785 (2553 1234/fax 2553 1235/www.berlin.grand.hyatt.com). U2, S1, S25, S2, S25, S9 Potsdamer Platz. **Rates** (breakfast included) €180 single; €225 double; €490-€3500 suites. **Credit** AmEx, DC, MC, V. **Map** p306 E4.
Despite the pleasure-seeking, Potsdamer-Platz-visiting tourist throng outside, the Hyatt is quite a classy hotel. The lobby is all matte black, slick surfaces and wood panelling with the odd minimalist art touch – a refreshing change from the usual five-star marble or country mansion look. The rooms are spacious and elegant without a floral print in sight; the internet TV is also a nice touch. The rooftop spa

The Berlin Marriott Hotel. *See p58.*

Hotel Alt Berlin: where everything old is new.

and gym has a splendid pool with views across the city. The lobby restaurant, the Tizian Lounge, is truly excellent with a menu of international classics and a good wine list.
Hotel services *Air-conditioning. Bar. Disabled: adapted rooms. Gym. Parking (€16). Pool. Restaurant.* **Room services** *Hairdryer. Minibar. TV.*

Hotel Intercontinental

Budapester Strasse 2, 10787 (26020/fax 2602 2600/www.interconti.com). U2, U9, S3, S5, S6, S7, S9 Zoologischer Garten/Bus 200 vor Haus. **Rates** €195-€260 single; €199-€294 double; €374-€2100 suite; €20 breakfast. **Credit** AmEx, DC, MC, V. **Map** p305 D4.

Extremely plush and spacious, the 'Interconti' exudes luxury. The rooms are large, tastefully decorated and graced with elegant bathrooms. The airy lobby, with its soft leather chairs, is ideal for reading the paper; the restaurant, Hugo's (*see p136*), is currently rated Berlin's best, and the gym and spa have just received a major overhaul. Visiting heads of state take note: they claim the President Suite is the safest in the city.
Hotel services *Bar. Beauty salon. Conference facilities. Gym. Laundry. Parking (€18.50). Pool.* **Room services** *Minibar. Room service. TV.*

The Ritz-Carlton

Potsdamer Platz 3 (10785 33 7777/fax 33 777 5555/www.ritzcarlton.com). U2, S1, S2, S25, S26 Potsdamer Platz. **Rates** (breakfast included) €250-280 single; €280-€310 double; €305-€5,000 suite; €22 breakfast. **Credit** AmEx, DC, MC, V. **Map** p306 E4.

It's flashy, it's trashy, it's Vegas meets Versailles. The brand new Ritz-Carlton is so choc-a-bloc with black marble, gold taps and taffeta curtains that the rooms seem stuffy, small and cramped. It's supposedly done up in an art deco style, but the overall impression is more upmarket shopping mall. Still, the oyster and lobster restaurant is decadently delicious. And the service is fantastic: the technology butler will sort out bugs in your computer connection and the bath butler will run your bath. Bring a fat wallet, and get ready to be pampered.
Hotel services *Bar. Disabled: adapted rooms. Gym. Parking (€18). Pool. Restaurants (3).* **Room services** *DVD player. Hi-fi. Minibar. Room service. TV: pay movies, satellite.*

Moderate

Hotel Alt Berlin

Potsdamer Strasse 67, 10785 (260 670/fax 2606 7445/www.altberlin-hotel.de). U1, U15 Kurfürstenstrasse. **Rates** (breakfast included) €85-€110 single; €99-€145 double; free under-12s. **Credit** AmEx, DC, MC, V. **Map** p306 E5.

This 'turn-of-the-century-Berlin' hotel actually opened just a couple of years ago – the furnishings in the spacious rooms might look retro but they're actually modern. The restaurant downstairs, meanwhile, resembles a cluttered museum and serves up hearty Berlin traditional food. The hotel is within walking distance of Potsdamer Platz.
Hotel services *Bar. Parking. Restaurant.* **Room services** *Minibar. Telephone. TV.*

Charlottenburg

You may not find the hippest nightlife or café culture around here, but there's plenty of fine dining and elegant shopping in Berlin's west end, plus an assortment of museums and attractions. This smart end of town, within easy reach of anything you might want to do, offers either five-star luxury or traditional charm in one of the many great little pensions, often housed in grand turn-of-the-century town houses. *See p48* **West end pearls**.

Deluxe

Bristol Hotel Kempinski Berlin

Kurfürstendamm 27, 10719 (884 340/fax 883 6075/www.kempinskiberlin.de). U15, U9 Kurfürstendamm. **Rates** €197.50-€272.50 single; €230-€305 double; €360-€1,250 triple; €23 breakfast buffet. **Credit** AmEx, DC, MC, V. **Map** p305 C4.

Perhaps Berlin's most famous hotel, if not its best, the Kempinski exudes a faded charm. But even though the rooms are plush, you never really feel as if you're living in the lap of luxury – as you should at these prices. The Bristol Bar on the ground floor, with its fat leather sofas and dark wood furnishings, has a long cocktail list and snooty waiters. The two restaurants, the Kempinski Eck and the Kempinski Grill, are nothing special. The swimming pool's lovely though: in the mornings, you can take breakfast lounging beside it, which is a rare treat on a bleak Berlin winter day.

Hotel services *Bar. Beauty salon. Conference facilities. Gym. Laundry. Pool. Restaurants.* **Room services** *Minibar. Room service. TV: pay movies.*

Savoy Hotel Berlin

Fasanenstrasse 9-10, 10623 (311 030/fax 311 03 333/www.hotel-savoy.com). U2, U9, S3, S5, S7, S9, S75 Zoologischer Garten. **Rates** (breakfast included) €142-€192 single; €192-€242 double; €232-€302 triple. **Credit** AmEx, MC, V. **Map** p305 C5.

This smart, stylish hotel is set back from the hustle and bustle of Zoologischer Garten. Erected in 1929, it was the hotel of choice for author Thomas Mann and still continues to impress. The rooms are divided into two styles: romantic or business-like. The beautiful restaurant serves South American cuisine; best of all is the fabulous Savoy Bar, with its own library and excellent collection of Cuban cigars. The Savoy lives up to its name both in decor and service and is well situated for business visitors on a tight schedule who may need to meet and wine and dine clients on site.

Hotel services *Babysitting. Restaurant.* **Room services** *Minibar. Hairdryer. Room service. TV: cable.*

Swissotel Berlin

Am Kurfürstendamm Augsburger Strasse 44, 10789 (220 100/fax 220 102 222/www.swissotel-berlin.de). U2, U9, S5, S7, S9, S75 Zoologischer Garten or U15 Kurfürstendamm. **Rates** €180 single; €320 double; €330-€450; €21 breakfast. **Credit** AmEx, DC, MC, V. **Map** p305 C4.

You know Berlin's being taken seriously when the Raffles chain wants a look-in. The hotel's styling is elegant and the second-floor foyer – away from the bustle and hassle of the Ku'damm – is an architectural stroke of genius. Rooms overlook the inner courtyard or the Ku'damm. Choose the latter type of room on a high floor if you want a great sunset view. The Restaurant 44 (*see p139*) is one of Berlin's top gourmet spots. There's no pool, but the option of having a massage in your room should compensate.

Hotel services *Bar. Beauty salon. Business services. Gym. Laundry. Restaurant.* **Room services** *Hairdryer. Iron. Minibar. Room s ervice. TV: pay movies/satellite.*

Expensive

Hotel Bleibtreu

Bleibtreustrasse 31, 10707 (884 740/fax 8847 4444/www.bleibtreu.com). U15 Uhlandstrasse or S3, S5, S7, S9, S75 Savignyplatz. **Rates** (breakfast included) €137-€237; €162-€262 double. **Credit** AmEx, D, MC, V. **Map** p305 C4.

The Bleibtreu is a cosy and smart establishment popular with media and fashion visitors. The rooms are a little on the small side but they're all individually and lovingly decorated with environmentally friendly materials. A pleasant relief from the posh-bland look of so many hotels in this category. Good service, nice food and lots of pampering and attention? What more could you want?

Hotel services *Parking (pay). Restaurant.* **Room services** *Minibar. TV.*

Concept Hotel

Grolmanstrasse 41-43, 10623 (884 260/fax 8842 6500/www.concept-hotel.com).U15 Uhlandstrasse or S3, S5, S7, S9, S75 Savignyplatz. **Rates** (breakfast included) €115-€145 single; €145-€180 double; €180-€260 suite. **Credit** AmEx, DC, MC, V. **Map** p305 C4.

Generally pretty smart. Ask for a room in the new wing if you want internet access and air-conditioning in your room. There are conference facilities and a restaurant and bar. The hotel is quiet and on a lovely street in the smart shopping area with a good restaurant selection nearby. Boring bar.

Hotel services *Bar. Parking (€10.50).* **Room services** *Disabled: adapted rooms. Minibar. TV.*

Hotel Garni Askanischer Hof

Kurfürstendamm 53, 10707 (881 8033/34/fax 881 7206). U7 Adenauerplatz or S3, S5, S7, S9, S75 Savignyplatz. **Rates** (breakfast included) €95-€110 single; €117-€145 double; €200 suite. **Credit** AmEx, D, MC, V. **Map** p305 C4.

One of the city's best kept secrets, the friendly Askanischer Hof has hosted visiting actors and literary types since well before the war. The breakfast room doesn't seem to have changed a jot since 1910 and each room spans a century of European interiors: 1970s chrome standard lamps teamed with overstuffed leather chesterfields, heavy Prussian desks and 1940s wallpaper. Full of atmosphere and in dodgy taste, this is vintage Berlin. Recommended.

Hotel services *Bar. Lift. Parking (free).* **Room services** *Telephone. TV.*

Hecker's Hotel

Grolmanstrasse 35, 10623 (88900/fax 889 0260/ www.heckers-hotel.com). U15 Uhlandstrasse or S3, S5, S7, S9, S75 Savignyplatz. **Rates** €150-€170 single; €120-€190 double; €310-€350 suite; under-12s free; €15 breakfast. **Credit** AmEx, DC, MC, V. **Map** p305 C4.

A smart, high-quality hotel with a stylish lobby and an air of privacy. Rooms are spacious and comfortable, especially the suites; the latter come with air-conditioning and Bang & Olufsen DVD TVs. Bathrooms are clean and well lit with marble tiling. Other highlights include the roof terrace and the Cassambalis House restaurant, which serves decent Mediterranean cuisine.

Hotel services *Bar. Conference facilities. No-smoking floors. Parking (€12). Restaurant.* **Room services** *Minibar. TV.*

Sorat Art'otel Berlin

Joachimstaler Strasse 29, 10719 (884 470/ fax 8844 7700/www.SORAT-Hotels.com). U9, U15 Kürfurstendamm. **Rates** (breakfast included) €124-€194 single; €146-€216 double. **Credit** AmEx, DC, MC, V. **Map** p305 D4.

Just off the Ku'damm in the heart of the west end, this hotel's theme is the work of artist Wolf Vostell, whose collages and prints adorn the walls. It has lost a little of its shine of late and the Sottsass-like styling is somewhat dated but, on the plus side, the rooms are modern and large with far-out bathrooms. Ask to see a couple of them first, because they range from good to great without any apparent relation to the price. Note: the *Eckzimmer* (corner rooms) are the best. The breakfast room is very pleasant: in summer, it opens on to an attractive garden and the buffet really is splendid.

Hotel services *Bar (24hrs). Conference facilities. Disabled: adapted rooms. No-smoking floors. Parking (€11). Restaurant.* **Room services** *Minibar. TV: cable.*

Moderate

Hotel Art Nouveau

Leibnitzstrasse 59, 10629 (327 7440/34/fax 3277 4440/www.hotelartnouveau.de). U7 Adenauerplatz or S3, S5, S7, S9, S75 Savignyplatz. **Rates** (breakfast included) €95-€140 single; €110-€165 double; €175-€230 suite. **Credit** AmEx, D, MC, V. **Map** p305 C4.

A real gem, this has to be just about the loveliest small hotel in Berlin. The rooms are decorated with flair in a mix of Conran-modern and antique furniture. The en suite bathrooms are well integrated into the rooms without disrupting the elegant town-house architecture. Even the TVs are stylish. The breakfast room has a cooking area and a refrigerator full of goodies if you should you feel peckish in the wee hours. To top things off, staff are utterly charming. Highly recommended.

Hotel services *Lift. Conference facilities. Parking (€4).* **Room services** *Telephone. TV.*

Berlin Plaza Hotel

Knesebeckstrasse 62, 10719 (884 130/fax 8841 3754/www.plazahotel.de). U15 Uhlandstrasse. **Rates** (breakfast included) €70-€120 single; €79-€150 double. **Credit** AmEx, DC, MC, V. **Map** p305 C4.

International bland, you-could-be-anywhere styling makes this hotel visually unmemorable. Its 131 rooms are decorated in pink, maroon and white and are rather small and plain. Still, all doubles and some singles come equipped with both shower and bath. And the breakfast buffet is good, particularly the mix-your-own muesli and fresh bread which is baked on the premises regularly. German specialities, meanwhile, are served in the restaurant and bar. Another bonus: children under 16 stay in their parent's room for free.

Hotel services *Bar. Conference facilities. Laundry. Lift. Parking (€5-€10). Restaurant.* **Room services** *Hairdryer. Minibar. Safe. Telephone. TV: pay movies.*

Hotel Bogota

Schlüterstrasse 45, 10707 (881 5001/fax 883 5887/www.hotelbogota.de). S3, S5, S7, S9, S75 Savignyplatz. **Rates** (breakfast included) €44-€72 single; €69-€98 double; €87-€120 3-bed room, €134 4-bed room. **Credit** AmEx, DC, MC, V. **Map** p305 C4.

The stylish and attractive foyer of this characterful two-star belies rooms more functional than fancy. That said, this place is terrific value with a great atmosphere, interesting history and wonderfully friendly staff. There is a variety of rooms available hence the price range, about half of the doubles have their own showers and toilets and all have at least a washbasin. Cosy sitting rooms on each floor are also a nice touch.

Hotel services *Lift. TV.* **Room services** *Telephone. TV (some rooms).*

Hotel-Pension Dittberner

Wielandstrasse 26, 10707 (884 6950/fax 885 4046/ www.hotel_ditterberner.de). U7 Adenauerplatz or S3, S5, S6, S7, S9, S75 Savignyplatz. **Rates** (breakfast included) €66.50 single; €92.50-€107.50 double; suite €118; extra bed €23. **Map** p305 C4. **No credit cards**.

Stylish, eclectic and grand, this pension is full of fine original art works from the gallery downstairs. It has enormous crystal chandeliers and comfortable rooms furnished with love and care. Owner Frau Lange is friendly and helpful and goes out of her way to make guests feel right at home, which is a rare treat in Berlin. What's more, some of the rooms and suites are truly palatial. Without question, one of the best pensions in the city.

Hotel services *Internet. Lift.* **Room services** *Telephone. TV.*

Hotel Gates

Knesebeckstrasse 8-9, 10623 (311 060/fax 312 2060/www.hotel-gates.de). U2 Ernst-Reuter-Platz. **Rates** €85-€190 single; €110-€120 double; €35 extra bed. **Credit** AmEx, DC, MC, V. **Map** p305 C4.

We were ready to be critical here because of the name alone, but surprisingly this hotel turns out to be a pretty good four-star. It's particularly good for business travellers who use Windows: there's a PC in every room with unlimited free internet access. The superior and deluxe rooms are especially comfortable: they offer huge bathrooms and plenty of work space. The hotel is a great place to stay if you are in town for one of the trade fairs at the Messegelände and there's also a fine selection of restaurants down the road around Savignyplatz. Discounts are available at weekends. Note: there are no disabled facilities.
Hotel services *Laundry. Lift. Parking (€15). TV.* **Room services** *Computer. Hairdryer. Internet. Minibar. TV.*

Pension-Gästezimmer Gudrun

Bleibtreustrasse 17, 10623 (881 6462/fax 883 7476/pensiongudrun@aol.com). S3, S5, S7, S9, S75 Savignyplatz. **Rates** €47.50 single; €67.50-€72.50 double. **No credit cards. Map** p305 C4.
This tiny pension has huge rooms and friendly, helpful owners who speak English, French, Arabic and German. The rooms are decorated with lovely turn-of-the-century Berlin furniture and for families or small group travelling together they are really good value. Nice place.
Hotel services *Lift. Refrigerator.* **Room services** *TV.*

Hotel-Pension Imperator

Meinekestrasse 5, 10719 (881 4181/fax 885 1919). U9, U15 Kurfürstendamm. **Rates** (breakfast included) €45-€65 single; €75-€98 double. **No credit cards. Map** p305 C4.
The building is a huge, traditional Berlin town house and the Imperator occupies the second floor. Its 11 bedrooms are large and furnished quite well with a mixture of antique and modern furniture with a predominantly black and white colour scheme. The pension is also notable for the various musicians and artists who have stayed here, Cecil Taylor and John Cage among them. Despite the arty ambience, the place is spotless and the rooms are capacious. Highly recommended.
Hotel services *Conference facilities. Laundry. Lift. Parking (€4). TV.* **Room services** *Room service.*

Hotel-Pension Modena

Wielandrstrasse 26, 10707 (885 7010/fax 881 529). U7 Adenauerplatz or S3, S5, S7, S9, S75 Savignyplatz. **Rates** €41-€65 single; €95 double. **Credit** AmEx, DC, MC, V. **Map** p305 C4.
It may not be as glamorous as the Dittberner, its upstairs neighbour, but this pension is nevertheless a very friendly place and it's also slightly cheaper than its rival. The bedrooms are a bit plain and uninspired, but freshly decorated, and the bathrooms are all new. All in all, this is a good budget option for small groups travelling together who want to be in the heart of the west.
Hotel services *Lift. TV room.* **Room services** *Telephone.*

Cheap

Hotel Pension Castell

Wielandstrasse 24, 10707 (882 7181/fax 881 5548/www.hotel-castell.de). U7 Adenauerplatz, U15 Uhlandstrasse **Rates** €65 single; €60-€80 double; €90-€120 3-5-bed room. **Credit** AmEx, V. **Map** p305 C4.
Tucked away just off the Ku'damm, this 30-room pension has friendly, if somewhat haphazard, staff and clean, tidy, good-sized rooms. There's no danger of it gracing the pages of an interiors magazine, though, and you need to be quite keen on the colour tangerine to stay here. All rooms have a shower and TV but some haven't their own WC.
Hotel services *Lift.* **Room services** *Telephone. TV.*

Hotel Charlot am Kurfürstendamm

Giesebrechtstrasse 17, 10629 (323 4051/fax 3279 6666/www.hotel-charlot.de). U7 Adenauerplatz or S3, S5, S6, S7, S9 Charlottenburg. **Rates** €52-€75 single; €62-€118 double. **Credit** MC, V. **Map** p304/p305 B/C4.
This is a moderately priced hotel that your mum might like to stay in. It's in a nice residential area full of chic shops and good cafés. The historical Jugendstil building has been well restored, it has friendly management and the 42 bedrooms are spotless although the decor is quite pink and frilly. Not all rooms have showers and toilets, but the communal facilities aren't too bad. Despite its name, the hotel is actually about a five-minute walk from the Kurfürstendamm.
Hotel services *Bar. Parking (€6.50). TV.* **Room services** *Telephone. TV.*

Hotel-Pension Columbus

Meinekestrasse 5, 10719 (tel 881 5061/fax 88132 00). U1, U9 Kurfürstendamm or S5, S7, S9, S75 Zoologischer Garten. **Rates** (breakfast included) €35-€55 single; €65-€85 double. **Credit** AmEx, MC, V. **Map** p305 C4.
A higgledy-piggledy, third-floor, family hotel, right next to the Ku'damm. The rooms were once charmingly eclectic but the place got infected with the IKEA virus. However, the prices are unbeatable for this area and the owners are extremely kind and friendly. The beds are good too.
Hotel services *Lift.* **Room services** *Telephone. TV.*

Hotel-Pension Funk

Fasanenstrasse 69, 10719 (882 7193/fax 883 3329/www.hotel-pensionfunk.de). U15 Uhlandstrasse. **Rates** (breakfast included) €34-€82 single; €52-€112 double. **Credit** AmEx, MC, V. **Map** p305 C4/5.
Despite its upmarket address, opposite Cartier and next door to Gucci, this pension offers extremely good value. It's actually the former apartment of the Danish silent movie star Asta Nielsen, and the charming proprietor does his best to maintain the ambience of a graceful pre-war flat. The 14 large and comfortable rooms are furnished to cosy effect with

Hotel Brandenburger Hof.

elegant pieces from the 1920s and 1930s: satinwood beds and matching wardrobes. The only niggle is that some of the showers are somewhat antiquated, but then that's also part of the charm. A romantic place. Recommended.
Hotel services *Lift.* **Room services.** *Room service. Telephone.*

Pension Kettler

Bleibtreustrasse 19, 10623 (883 4949/5676/fax 882 4228/www.kurfurstendamm.de). U15 Uhlandstrasse or S3, S5, S7, S9, S75 Savignyplatz. **Rates** (breakfast included) €50-72.50 single; €60-€90 double. **No credit cards. Map** p305 C4.
The Pension Kettler has been around since 1936 but current owner, Isolde Josipovici, has imbued this little hotel with her own distinctive style. The four rooms are a cosy blend of art deco and *Gründerzeit* with a touch of hippy. The corridor walls are festooned with mixed-media art, including a chunk of Berlin Wall. The owner's life story – which she is happy to share – is an epic. Recommended for writers in search of inspiration.
Room services *Telephone.*

Pension Viola Nova

Kantstrasse 146, 10623 (315 7260/fax 312 3314/ www.violanova.de). S3, S5, S7, S9, S75 Savignyplatz. **Rates** €40-€70 single; €60-€85 double. **No credit cards. Map** p305 C4.
One of many similar pensions in the Savignyplatz district. Like the others, this is in an old, converted Berlin house, but the Viola Nova is particularly notable for its friendly owners and value for money. It has a wide variety of clean, spacious rooms ranging from good backpacker standards to a couple of doubles decorated with antique furniture. Ask about prices for large rooms with several beds; these are good for small groups travelling together. Breakfast is included in the room price when staying more than one night.
Room services *Telephone. TV.*

Wilmersdorf

It may not be the most interesting of areas, but it's not very far from the rest of town and Wilmersdorf can proudly claim to host Berlin's most decadent luxury hotel (Schlosshotel Vierjahreszeiten Berlin), its most discreet hotel (Hotel Brandenburger Hof, Relais & Chateaux), the coolest new designer hotel (Ku'damm 101), and the city's wackiest hotel (Propeller Island). So it can't be all that bad.

Deluxe

Hotel Brandenburger Hof

Eislebener Strasse 14, 10789 (214 050/fax 214 05100/www.brandenburger-hof.com). U1 Augsburger Strasse. **Rates** (breakfast included) €165-€245 single; €240-€280 double; €450 suite; extra bed €55. **Credit** AmEx, DC, MC, V. **Map** p305 D4.
A discreet jewel tucked away in a quiet side street behind KaDeWe. From the moment you set foot inside the foyer you know that you are going to like this place. Staff are friendly and not at all aloof, a rarity in luxury hotels. There's a pretty winter garden with a bistro and if you duck under the trailing vine and go into the small intimate dining room you will find yourself in the Michelin-starred Quadriga restaurant. Upstairs, the 82 rooms and suites are decorated with panache and the bed-making is an art form in itself. For a binge, check for details of their weekend special offers which include visits to the opera, six-course gourmet meals and sightseeing tours of Berlin in a chauffeur-driven limo.
Hotel services *Bar. Beauty salon. Conference facilities. Parking (pay). Restaurant (2).* **Room Services** *Hairdryer. Minibar. TV: VCR.*

Schlosshotel Vierjahreszeiten Berlin

Brahmsstrasse 10, 14193 (895 840/fax 8958 4800/www.schlosshotelberlin.com). S7 Grunewald. **Rates** €275-€305 single; €295-€375 double; €460-€3000 suite; €23 breakfast. **Credit** AmEx, DC, MC, V. **Map** p304 A6.
If you are not the potentate of a small country, an industry mogul or a titled aristocrat, you won't feel at home in this place. This is the sort of luxury that whole countries revolted against. Designed down to the smallest detail by Karl Lagerfeld, the Schlosshotel is in a restored 1914 villa on the edge of the Grunewald – about 15 minutes' drive from the Ku'damm. It has a swimming pool, a couple of restaurants, a golf course and dining on the beautiful lawn in the summer. There are 12 suites and 54 rooms, a limousine and butler service, elegant mar-

ble bathrooms and flocks of well-trained staff running around after you. A beautiful place in a beautiful setting but so exclusive that it might as well be on another planet.
Hotel services. *Air-conditioning. Bar. Conference facilities. Disabled: adapted rooms. Gym. Parking. Pool. Restaurants (2). Tennis.* **Room Services** *Bathrobes. Hairdryer. Minibar. TV:VCR.*

Expensive

Ku'damm 101

Kurfürstendamm 101, 10711 (52 00 550/fax 5200 55555/www.kudamm101.com). U7 Adenauerplatz or S41, S42, S45 Halensee. **Rates** €101-€195 single; €118-€215 double; €13 breakfast. **Credit** AmEx, DC, MC, V. **Map** p304 B5.
Part of the small chain that owns the Bleibtreu (*see p61*) and the Savoy (*see p61*), this new designer hotel is a huge hit with style-conscious travellers. The funky lobby, the work of Berlin designers Vogt and Weizenegger, is more like a cool club than hotel. The rooms, meanwhile, were designed by Swiss interior designer Franziska Kessler, whose mantra is clarity and calm. It works well. The 171 rooms are simply decorated with linoleum floors and bespoke contemporary furniture; the colour scheme is chosen strictly from Le Corbusier's palette. Added bonuses include high-speed wireless internet access and a breakfast terrace garden. The Lounge 101, meanwhile, is good for a variety of occasions: a quick breakfast, daytime snacks, and cocktails and groovy sounds by night.
Hotel services *Air-conditioning. Bar. Disabled: adapted rooms. Parking (€13).* **Room services** *TV.*

Moderate

Hotel-Pension München

Güntzelstrasse 62, Wilmersdorf, 10717 (857 91222/fax 853 2744/www.hotel-pension-muenchen-in-berlin.de). U9 Güntzelstrasse. **Rates** (breakfast included) €40-€75 single; €70-€80 double. **Credit** AmEx, MC, V. **Map** p305 C5.
This pension is a really charming place. The artist owner has decorated the rooms beautifully and there are original prints all over the clean white walls. All double rooms come with shower and WC and it's well located: a five-minute walk will connect you to the U-Bahn. A welcome change from the average pension. Recommended.
Hotel services *Lift. Parking (€5).* **Room services** *Telephone. TV: cable.*

Propeller Island City Lodge

Albrecht Achilles Strasse 58, 10709 (891 9016/fax 892 8721/www.propeller-island.com). U7 Adenauerplatz. **Rates** €70-€200; €8 breakfast. **Credit cards** MC, V. **Map** p304 B5.
Propeller Island is a guest house straight out of *Alice in Wonderland*. More than just a hotel: it's a work of art. Designed by artist owner Lars Stroschen, the 30 rooms are a collection of jaw-dropping theatre sets. The Upside Down Room, for example, has all of its furniture on the ceiling. The Flying Room has tilted walls and floor and a double bed seemingly suspended in thin air. Other highlights include the disorienting Mirror Room for narcissists and a Prison Cell for those who feel the need to be punished. Rooms lack the usual hotel accoutrements, such as room service or telephones. The reservation process is also surreal. View the rooms on the website, and then choose your three favourites. Bookings are taken only by fax and your expected time of arrival must be included. There is no reception and the office is only officially open from 8am until noon. Check-in is generally until 11.30am and payment is normally by cash on arrival. All this might sound a bit strange but nothing about this place is remotely normal. Highly recommended.
Room services *Hi-fi, TV (some rooms).*

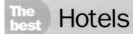

The best Hotels

For affordable charm
The **Honigmond Garden Hotel** has both garden rooms and spacious apartments that won't cost an arm and a leg. *See p52.*

For sheer upmarket class
The **Grand Hyatt** is the best of Berlin's new five-stars. *See p58.*

For budget-conscious backpackers
Circus Hostel is clean, bright, friendly and helpful. *See p54.*

For internet addicts
Why bother with sightseeing when the **Hotel Gates** offers a PC in every room with unlimited free internet access? *See p62.*

For landlocked sea views
Rooms at the **Radisson SAS Berlin** now overlook the world's largest free-standing aquarium. *See p51.*

For a romantically retro ambience
The **Hotel-Pension Funk** is in the former apartment of a silent movie star. *See p63.*

For potentates and plutocrats
The **Schlosshotel Vierjahreszeiten Berlin** is so exclusive it might as well be on another planet. *See p64.*

For hotel life through the looking-glass
Propeller Island City Lodge is the craziest hotel in town. *See left.*

Camping

If you want to explore the camp sites of Berlin or surrounding Brandenburg, ask for a camping map from the BTM information offices in Berlin (*see p285*) or download a PDF from their website. They are all located far out of the city, so check timetables for last buses if you want to enjoy Berlin nightlife. Prices don't vary much between sites: for tents, you'll pay about €3.75; for caravans €6.45, plus €4.95 per person (€2.35 children aged 6-14). More info can be obtained from the German Camping Club below.

Landesverband des DCC (Deutscher Camping Club)

Geisbergstrasse 11, Schöneberg, 10777 (218 6071/ 72/www.dccberlin.de). **Open** 10.30am-6pm Mon; 8am-4pm Wed; 8am-1pm Fri. **Map** p305 D5.

Youth Hostels

Official youth hostels in Berlin (there are three: **Jugendgästehaus-Berlin**; **Jugendgästehaus am Wannsee** and **Jugendherberge Ernst Reuter**) are crammed most of the year so book ahead. If you book more than two weeks in advance use the central reservations office on 262 3024. You have to be a member of the YHA to stay in these and they all have single-sex dormitories. To obtain a YHA membership card, go to the **Mitgliederservice des DJH Berlin-Brandenburg** (also known as the Jugend-Zentrale) listed below. Remember to take your passport and a passport-sized photo. Individual youth hostels also have a day membership deal where you pay an extra €3 per day if you can't be bothered with the whole membership palaver. Check the website address below for further youth hostel info.

Mitgliederservice des DJH Berlin-Brandenburg

Tempelhofer Ufer 32, 10963 (264 9520/fax 262 0437/www.djh.de or *www.jugendherberge.de). U2, U7 Möckernbrucke, U1, U15, U2 Gleisdreieck.* **Open** 9am-4pm Mon, Wed, Fri; 9am-6pm Tue, Thur.

Longer stays

For a longer stay, try calling a *Mitwohnagentur* – a flat-seeking agency – to see what they have on offer, but remember to ask what the total price will be, including agency fees. The agencies listed below can find you a room in a shared house or a furnished flat for anything from a week to a couple of years. In summer, when Berlin is crowded, they are useful for finding short-term accommodation. Most agencies accept advance bookings and you may want to consider different offers, so start looking a month ahead especially at busy holiday times. Don't forget that this is all private accommodation so you will be living in someone's home, often with their books, furniture and belongings. This can be a great way to get to know people, but take your time talking to the owners and looking at the places before you choose. For student accommodation, look on the noticeboards in the foyer of the Hochschule der Kunst at Hardenbergstrasse 33 in Charlottenburg, or pin up your own notice there. Prices vary wildly, but if you look for something '*auf Zeit*' (for a limited period) you can often get something quite reasonable.

If you're staying for a couple of weeks and manage to find something through a *Mitwohnagentur*, you will probably pay €20-€40 a night. For longer stays, agencies charge different rates. It is always a good idea to ask for the total figure for comparison. Another alternative is looking for ads in *Zweite Hand*, *tip*, *Zitty* and the *Berliner Morgenpost*. Prices vary wildly, but if you look for something 'auf Zeit' (for a limited period) you can often find something quite reasonable. Expect to pay €400-€700 per month for a two-bedroom flat in the more central districts of Kreuzberg, Prenzlauer Berg and Schöneberg. Mitte can be more pricey, but sometimes you can get lucky.

Erste Mitwohnzentrale

Sybelstrasse 53, Charlottenburg, 10629 (324 3031/fax 324 9977/www.mitwohn.com). U7 Adenauerplatz. **Open** 9am-8pm Mon-Fri; 10am-4pm Sat. **No credit cards. Map** p304 B4.

fine + mine Internationale Mitwohnagentur

Neue Schönhauser Strasse 20, 10178 (235 5120/fax 2355 1212/www.fineandmine.com). U8 Weinmeisterstrasse or S3, S5, S7, S75 Hackescher Markt. **Open** 10am-6pm Mon-Fri. **Credit** V. **Map** p316/p303 G3.

Freiraum

Wiener Strasse 14, Kreuzberg, 10999 (618 2008/ fax 618 2006/www.frei-raum.com). U1, U15 Görlitzer Bahnhof. **Open** Mon-Fri 9am-7pm, Sat 10am-2pm. **Credit** MC, V. **Map** p307 G5.

HomeCompany

Joachimstalerstrasse 17, Charlottenburg, 10719 (19 445/fax 882 6649/www.homecompany.de). U15, U9, Kurfürstendamm. **Open** 9am-5pm Mon-Fri; 11am-2pm Sat. **Credit** AmEx, V. **Map** p305 C4.

Zeitraum Wohnkonzepte

(Agentur Streicher & Burg Immobilien) Immanuelkirchstrasse 8, 10405 (4416 622/ fax 4416 623/www.zeit-raum.de). Tram 1 Knaackstrasse. **Open** 10am-1pm, 3-6pm Mon-Fri; by appointment Sat. **Credit** V. **Map** p303 G2.

Sightseeing

Features

Maps

Introduction

Berlin's bounteous attractions are diverse, scattered and offbeat.

Brandenburger Tor.

Not the most ancient of cities and never a particularly beautiful one, Berlin is not a conventional sightseeing destination in the same way as Paris or Rome. But that isn't to say that there's nothing to see. Berlin's turbulent history has left scars and reminders all over this huge town, while a future as capital of unified Germany is now signalled by a brand new selection of architectural landmarks.

Most Berlin sights that could properly be described as unmissable – either because you really ought to see them or simply because you couldn't avoid them if you tried – are in and around the central Mitte district. But this is only a small segment of this enormous, sprawling city – carved up by rivers and canals, and fringed with lakes and forest.

After Mitte, **Prenzlauer Berg** and **Friedrichshain** are the two districts of former East Berlin that have changed most. The former retains pockets of radical energy but is now mostly gentrified. There are few conventional sights here, but it's a relaxed place for a meal or drink. Friedrichshain is Berlin's new bohemia, managing both a firm connection with the old East and a forward-looking, youthful scene.

Kreuzberg has correspondingly lost its monopoly on the arty and anarchic, but remains fascinatingly diverse and currently seems to be staging a recovery. Neighbouring **Schöneberg** is quiet and residential, but contains some great bars and cafés in its northern reaches, and is a major hub of the city's gay scene.

Tiergarten is dominated by the park of the same name. Along its southern fringe are some fine museums, the zoo, the reborn diplomatic quarter and the new Potsdamer Platz.

Charlottenburg has a lot to offer visitors. The shop-rich area around Bahnhof Zoo and the Ku'damm was the centre of old West Berlin, and, to the west, Schloss Charlottenburg and its surrounding museums are a major draw.

Beyond these central districts, attractions include the Dahlem museums complex, the vast Grunewald woods and the Havel river in the south-west, the proud town of Spandau in the north-west or the villagey charms of Köpenick and Müggelsee in the south-east.

Essential Berlin

... in one day

The key sights

• Pick a café for breakfast in the Scheunenviertel area of Mitte (*see p82*).
• Get your bearings from the top of the **Fernsehturm** on Alexanderplatz (*see p86*).
• Walk across to Museuminsel and check the architectural treasures at the **Pergamonmuseum** (*see p78*).
• Stroll along Unter den Linden (*see p71*), detouring to the **Gendarmenmarkt** (*see p79*) along the way, ending at the **Brandenburger Tor** (*see p71*).
• Ascend the dome of the **Reichstag** (*see p98*).
• Walk south to **Potsdamer Platz** (*see p101*), taking in the **Denkmal für die ermordeten Juden Europas** (*p75*).
• Head west, either through **Tiergarten** (*see p98*), ending up at the **Zoo and Aquarium** (*see p103*), or via the **Kulturforum** complex (lovers of Old Masters should take in the **Gemäldegalerie** – *see p102*; modern art fans head for the **Neue Nationalgalerie** (*see p101*).
• Late afternoon shopping on and around the **Ku'damm** (*see p104*)
• U-Bahn to Kreuzberg to see the extraordinary **Jüdisches Museum** (*see p95*).
• Evening: sample the restaurants and bars of rejuvenated Mitte (*see p120* and *p142*).

... in two days

Museums, palaces, greenery and a beach

• Head for **Schloss Charlottenburg** (*see p108*). Apart from the palace and grounds, there are first-rate museums in the area, including the **Ägyptisches Museum** (*see p107*), the **Bröhan-Museum** (*see p108*) and the **Sammlung Berggruen** (*see p108*).
• Then, on a fine day, escape to the leafy surrounds of the **Grunewald** (*see p115*) and/or the watery pleasures of the **Wannsee** (*see p116*).
• Evening: experience the laid-back cafés and nightlife of Prenzlauer Berg.

... in three days

Great escapes

• If you've had enough of museums, take a boat trip from Mitte through the old East down to the **Müggelsee** (*see p70, p118* and *p272*).
• If you want more culture, the museum complex at Dahlem includes the brilliant **Ethnologisches Museum** (*see p113*) and the **Brücke Museum** (*see p116*) and **Allierten Museum** (*see p116*) are nearby.
• Head on to the parks and palaces of **Potsdam** (*see p256*).
• Evening: try the youthful nightlife of Friedrichshain (*see p223*) or decent dining in Kreuzberg or Schöneberg (*see p120*).

... in four days

Wartime and Cold War Berlin

• Get a historical overview at the **Deutsches Historisches Museum** (*see p76*) or the **Story of Berlin** (*see p107*).
• Those interested in Nazi architecture should head for the **Olympiastadion** (*see p39*) or **Flughafen Tempelhof** (*see p39*). For an insight into the Nazi terror machine, check out the **Topographie des Terrors** (*see p96*), the **Gedenkstätte Plötzensee** (*see p110*) or **Sachsenhausen** (*see p262*), a former concentration camp north of Berlin.
• If the Cold War is more alluring, make for the **Gedenkstätte Berliner Mauer** (*see p111* or *p73*) to see one of the few remaining stretches of Wall, or go to the **Haus am Checkpoint Charlie** (*see p95*). The **Stasi Museum** (*see p117*) and the **Museum Berlin-Karlshorst** (*see p118*) also offer fascinating insights into the way both sides operated.
• Evening: return to your favourite bar – you'll certainly have one by now.

The **Reichstag** dome.

A 2001 administrative rejig amalgamated many of Berlin's historic districts into larger political units. But no Berliner would say that they live in 'Friedrichshain-Kreuzberg', so in this guide we use the old district names in the same way as the locals.

For ideas on how to spend your time in the city, *see p69* **Essential Berlin**.

MUSEUMS & GALLERIES

If you're planning to do a lot of sightseeing and museum visiting, then you may want to invest in a discount card. Many museums and galleries are administered by the **Staatliche Museen zu Berlin (SMPK)**, including the Pergamonmuseum, the Gemäldegalerie, the Ethnologisches Museum and the Ägyptisches Museum. SMPK offers both a **one-day card** (€10, €5 concessions) and a **three-day card** (€12, €6 concessions), available from any of its museums. (SMPK museums are free on the first Sunday of the month; most are closed on Mondays but open late on Thursdays.

Another deal is the **WelcomeCard** (€21; valid for one adult and up to three children under 14), which combines three days free public transport with reduced or free entry to sightseeing walks, tours and boat trips, museums, theatres and attractions in Berlin and Potsdam. Cards are available from BTM (*see p285*), S-Bahn offices and many hotels.

Tours

On foot

If you're pushed for time but want a good overview of the city, go for an **Insider Tour** (692 3149/www.insidertour.com) or try **The Original Berlin Walks** (301 9194/www.berlinwalks.com), whose three-and-a-half-hour Discover Berlin tour expertly whips through some 700 years of history.

If you've more time and want more detail, the seven-hour walking tour by **Brewer's Best of Berlin** (www.brewersberlin.com) explores the city's history in depth (there is also a tour of Potsdam). **Berlin Sightseeing Tours** (7974 5600/www.berlin-sightseeing-tours.de) have come up with an interactive five-kilometre (three-mile) walking tour that takes in all major sights, plus many lesser-known ones.

By bike

Largely flat, Berlin is perfect for getting around by bike. **Berlin Expedition** (4849 5325/www.berlinexpedition.de) organises three- to four-hour tours for groups of five or more, including one along the former line of the Wall. **Fahrradstation** (see p273) offers themed city tours including 'Cold War Berlin', 'Architecture in Berlin' and a Sunday trip to the countryside. **Insider Tour** (*see above*) offers four-hour bike excursions covering similar ground as their walking tours. **Pedal Power** (5515 3270) organises tours for two people at a time.

For places to hire bikes, *see p273*. Remember that you may need to leave some ID as deposit.

By bus

A cheap and flexible option is bus 100, a standard public transport route running from Zoo to Prenzlauer Berg, passing major sights along the way. **Berolina** (8856 8030/www.berolina-berlin.com), on the other hand, offers the works – wraparound windows, commentary in a choice of languages and a handy 'hop on hop off' arrangement. **Top Tour Berlin** (2652 6570/stadttouristik@bvg.de) is just as flexible but uses open-top buses, and **Zille Bus** (2652 6570/www.bvg.de/service/citytours05.html) operates tours on vintage open-top buses.

By boat/ship

Reederei Bruno Winkler (3499 5935) tours ply the Spree, the Wannsee and venture as far west as Brandenburg. If you haven't got time for a leisurely cruise then **Historical City Tour** (536 3600) covers a fair few sights in just an hour, including the Reichstag, Palast der Republik and the Berliner Dom. **Berliner Wassertaxi-Stadtrundfahrten** (BWTS) (6588 0203/www.berlinerwassertaxi.de) does tours on Amsterdam-style 'Grachten' boats.

From Berlin's neighbour, Potsdam (*see p256*), there are more opportunities for sightseeing by boat; for instance, **Havel Dampfschiffahrt** (0331 275 9233) organises 90-minute cruises on the Havel river.

See also p272.

Specialist

City Guide Tour (614 397) offers tailor-made tours, where you can choose both theme and mode of transport, including helicopter, plane or balloon. **Berlin Starting Point** (3062 721303/www.berlin-starting-point.de) also devises customised tours.

Among other specialists, **Susanne Oschmann** (782 1202) focuses on the musical history of Berlin, **Spielball** (8507 5390) does supervised tours for children, **Sta Tours** (3010 5151/www.sta-tours.de) shows you the houses of famous people, and **Berliner Unterwelten** (4991 0517/www.berliner-unterwelten.de) organises tours of subterranean sites.

Mitte

Culturally, scenically, administratively, historically – whichever way you want to look at it, Mitte is the centre of Berlin.

Back when the Wall was up, the idea of this part of town calling itself Mitte – 'middle' – seemed ludicrous. True, it was the place where the city was born on the sand islands in the Spree, and before World War II it had been the hub of the city. But it was by no means central to East Berlin, and, despite a few international-quality hotels and big public buildings, it simply didn't seem that important. But in the last 15 years, Mitte has regained its title as centre of the city, culturally, scenically and administratively. With the historic old buildings scrubbed until they shine, an influx of capital promoting new construction, and a new energy from moneyed settlers (particularly in the previously ratty north part), Mitte is very much back in the middle again.

Brandenburger Tor.

Unter den Linden

Map p302 & p316

From before the Hohenzollern dynasty through the Weimar Republic, and from the Third Reich to the GDR, the entire history of Berlin can be found on or close to this celebrated street.

Originally laid out to connect the town centre with the Tiergarten (*see p98*), **Unter den Linden**, running east from the Brandenburger Tor to Museumsinsel (*see p76*), got its name from the *Linden* (lime trees) that shaded its central walkway. Hitler, concerned that the trees obscured the view of his parades, had them felled, but they were later replanted.

During the 18th and 19th centuries, the Hohenzollerns erected no-nonsense baroque and neo-classical buildings along their capital's showcase street. (Most of these were rubble after World War II, but many were restored.) The side streets were laid out in a grid by the Great Elector Friedrich Wilhelm for his Friedrichstadt (*see p7*).

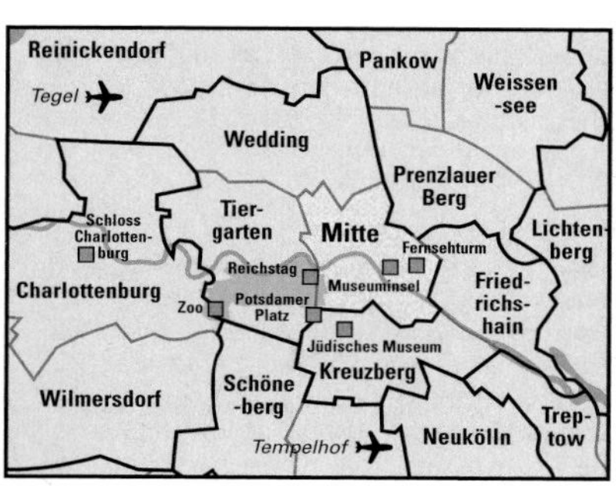

Brandenburger Tor & Pariser Platz

The focal point of Unter den Linden's western end is the **Brandenburger Tor** (Brandenburg Gate). Constructed in 1791, and designed by Carl Gotthard Langhans after the Propylaea gateway into ancient Athens, the Gate was built as a triumphal arch celebrating Prussia's capital city. It was initially called the Friedenstor ('Gate of Peace') and is the only remaining city gate left from Berlin's original 18. (Today, a handful of U-Bahn stations are named after other city gates, such as Frankfurter Tor or Schlesisches Tor).

A walk on the Wall side

Little remains of the Berlin Wall today. Most of it was demolished between June and November 1990. What had become the symbol of the inhumanity of the East German regime was prosaically crushed and re-used for road-fill.

This walk sets out to trace the course of a small stretch of the Wall on the northern border of Mitte. Along the way you can see some of the remnants – including the **Gedenkstätte Berliner Mauer** in the Bernauer Strasse (*see p111*) – and gain an impression of how brutally the border carved its way through the city.

The starting point is Hauptbahnhof-Lehrter Bahnhof in former West Berlin. Leave the S-Bahn station by the Invalidenstrasse exit, turning right on to the street. From the viewing platform here you can admire the huge international railway station under construction, a key piece of the reunified city's new infrastructure. Continue eastwards, passing on your left a Wilhelmine building, now a regional court, and the railway station turned contemporary art gallery **Hamburger Bahnhof, Museum für Gegenwart** (*see p82*).

A little further on is the **Sandkrugbrücke**, located on the former border crossing into East Berlin. A stone by the bridge commemorates Günter Litfin, the first person to be shot dead attempting to escape to West Berlin. The *Invalidenhaus* on the eastern side long predates the Cold War. Built in 1747 to house disabled soldiers, it was used in East German times as a military and government hospital, as well as the state's ministry of health and Supreme Court. Today it houses the **Bundesministerium für Wirtschat und Arbeit** (Federal Ministry of Economics and Labour). Keeping this complex on your right, turn down the canalside promenade, continuing along until you get to the Invalidenfriedhof.

The Wall once ran straight through this graveyard – and a section still remains. Headstones of the graves in the 'death strip' were removed so as not to impair the sightlines of border guards. The graveyard, more evidence of the area's military links, is a fascinating microcosm of Berlin history. Metres from the splendid **18th-century tombs of Prussian generals**, there is a plaque commemorating members of the anti-Hitler resistance. Victims of air raids and the Battle of Berlin are buried in an adjacent mass grave. And it was here in 1962 that West Berlin police shot dead an East Berlin border guard to save a 15-year-old boy who was in the process of escaping.

Just outside the graveyard, you will find a former **watchtower** improbably nestling in front of a new apartment building at the corner of Kieler Strasse. Opening times are unpredictable, but sometimes you can look inside the observation post. Between here and the corner of Chausseestrasse there are few traces left of the Wall, which ran roughly parallel to the canal before veering right close to the present helipad. At the end of Boyenstrasse, pavement markings indicating the Wall's former course briefly appear before vanishing under the new corner building.

Looking down Chausseestrasse note the line of powerful street lights indicating the site of another checkpoint. The **Liesenstrasse Friedhof** is the graveyard where 19th-century writer Theodor Fontane is buried. It was also part of East Berlin's border strip. A short section of the Wall appears before the railway bridge at the junction with Gartenstrasse.

The last leg of the walk takes us up Bernauer Strasse. Desperate scenes took place here in August 1961 as people leaped – three of them to their deaths – from the windows of houses that then stood on the street's eastern side. The buildings were in East Berlin, but the pavement before their doors was in the West. The iconic photograph of a border guard leaping over barbed wire into the West was snapped days earlier at the street's northern end. In the 1960s and 1970s a number of tunnels were dug from cellars in this area and dozens successfully escaped.

The **Quadriga** statue, a four-horse chariot driven by Victory and designed by Johann Gottfried Schadow, sits on top of the gate. It has had an eventful life. When Napoleon conquered Berlin in 1806 he carted the Quadriga off to Paris and held it hostage until his defeat in 1814. The Tor was later badly damaged during World War II, and during subsequent renovations, the GDR removed the Prussian Iron Cross and turned it around so that the chariot faced west. The current Quadriga is actually a 1958 copy of the 18th-century original, and was stranded in no-man's land for 30 years. After the Wall came down, during

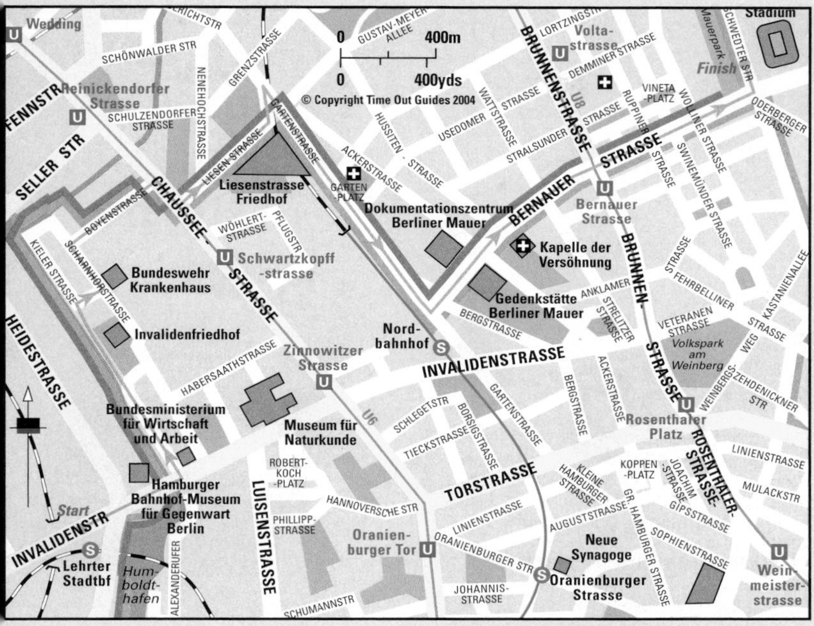

At the Gedenkstätte Berliner Mauer you can gain an impression of what the border installation looked like – from below or above. The **Dokumentationszentrum** opposite, an information centre about the Wall, has a viewing platform. A little further on is the oval **Kapelle der Versöhnung** (Chapel of Reconciliation) built on the site of an older church that was left stranded in the death strip and finally blown up in 1985 by the East German authorities.

The swathe of former borderland beyond lies largely derelict despite its prime location. Redevelopment has been slow because of legal challenges to its appropriation by the Federal Government. The old tarmacadam patrol road remains in places as do some of the border illuminations. Note, for instance, the lights on No.20 Swinemünder Strasse. The plasterwork on the building at the corner of Wolliner Strasse also clearly reveals where the eastern side of the Wall abutted existing apartment blocks.

Between Wolliner and Schwedter Strasse, you can still see the turning circle once used by West Berlin buses. On the eastern side, the tram still comes to an abrupt halt in Eberswalder Strasse. Even so, it's hard to believe that this whole area was once part of the world's most heavily fortified border. In the **Mauerpark**, a popular meeting place for younger folk in summer, you can have one last stroll along the Wall before heading to the Eberswalder Strasse underground station.

which process the Tor was the scene of much celebration, there had to be further repairs. The Iron Cross was replaced and the Quadriga was turned back around to face into Mitte again.

West of the Gate stretches the vast expanse of the **Tiergarten** (*see p98*), Berlin's central park. Just to the north is the reborn **Reichstag** (*see p98*), while ten minutes' walk south is the even more dramatically reconceived **Potsdamer Platz** complex (*see p101*).

Immediately east of the Brandenburger Tor is **Pariser Platz**, which was given its name in 1814 when Prussia and its allies conquered Paris. This square, once more enclosed by

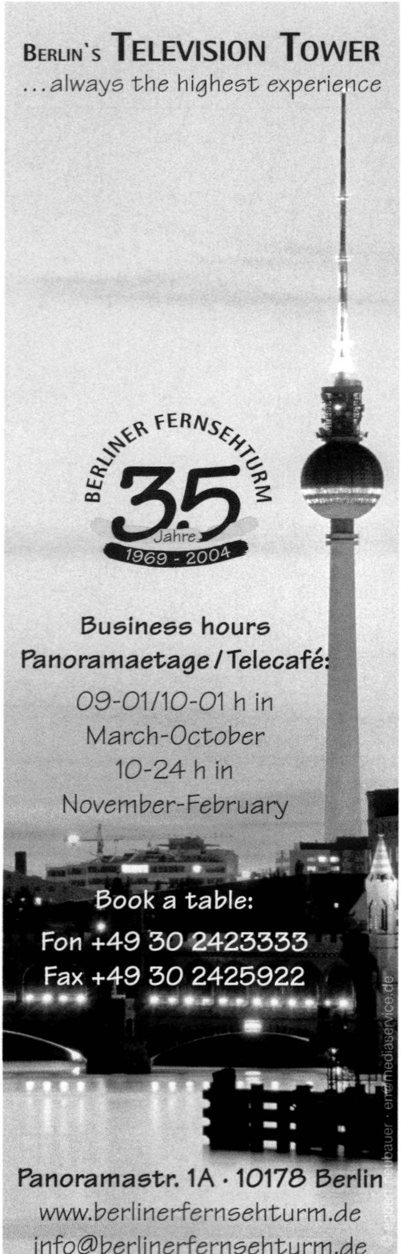
BERLIN'S TELEVISION TOWER
...always the highest experience
BERLINER FERNSEHTURM
35 Jahre
1969 - 2004
Business hours
Panoramaetage / Telecafé:
09-01/10-01 h in
March-October
10-24 h in
November-February
Book a table:
Fon +49 30 2423333
Fax +49 30 2425922
Panoramastr. 1A · 10178 Berlin
www.berlinerfernsehturm.de
info@berlinerfernsehturm.de

The most
up to date
source of
information
in Berlin
Berlin
inyourpocket
Essential city guides
From punks to yuppies
Prenzlauer Berg
Fever pitch
Updated every two
months, In Your Pocket is
the perfect local
companion to Time Out
Berlin, and can be picked
up at tourist offices, all
good bookshops and
hotels.
inyourpocket
www.inyourpocket.com

embassies and bank buildings, was once seen as Berlin's *Empfangssaal* – its reception room. Foreign dignitaries would ceremoniously pass through it on their way to visit tyrants and dictators in the palaces downtown.

In 1993, plans were drawn up to revive Pariser Platz, with new buildings on the same scale as the old ones, featuring conservative exteriors and contemporary interiors. Some old faces are back on the historical sites they occupied before World War II: the reconstructed **Adlon Hotel** (*see p47*) is now at its old address, as is Michael Wilford's new **British Embassy** (around the corner at Wilhelmstrasse 70-1; open for visits by appointment 9am-4.30pm; 2045 7254; *see p275*).

While outwardly conforming to the restrictions, inside, many buildings harbour flights of fancy prohibited at street level. Frank Gehry's **DG Bank** at No.3 has a huge, biomorphic interior dome hidden behind its regular façade. The **Dresdner Bank** opposite is virtually hollow, thanks to another interior atrium. Next door, Christian de Portzamparc's **French Embassy** features a space-saving 'vertical garden' on the courtyard wall, and 'french windows' extending over two storeys.

The south-west corner of the square is supposed to accommodate the new US Embassy. But since a return to its old address was announced back in 1993, building of the embassy has been delayed first by budgetary miscalculation, and then by new US State Department regulations stipulating a minimum 30-metre (98-foot) security zone between US embassies and adjoining streets. With existing plans approved and budgeted, the only way to achieve that would be to move all the roads around, and that's what the US expected Berlin to do. But after years of having to acquiesce to whatever the US occupying forces wanted, today's city authorities have not been so accommodating. In 1999, then mayor Eberhardt Diepgen caused a minor diplomatic scandal by suggesting that the US build a McDonald's here instead. Since then there has been much talk of compromise, but the site looks likely to remain vacant for the time being.

South of the US Embassy site is another area that has been mired in controversy. Before the end of 2004, the **Denkmal für die ermordeten Juden Europas** – 'Memorial to the Murdered Jews of Europe' – will be unveiled here. Peter Eisenmann's design was the result of a second competition, the winner of the first one having been rejected by then Chancellor Kohl. There have also been arguments over content (many feel the memorial should honour all victims of the Holocaust, not only Jewish ones), location (the chosen site has no particular link to the Holocaust), and function (should such a monument draw a line under history, or aim to stimulate debate and discussion?) The memorial as built is a field of 2,700 stone pillars. The most recent scandal was that the graffiti-proofing contract had gone to a company which had used slave labour during the Third Reich.

Between the Denkmal and Leipziger Platz is an area filled with representations from Germany's various *Länder*.

East along Unter den Linden

Heading east along Unter den Linden, passing the 1950s monolithic, Stalinist wedding cake-style **Russian Embassy** on your right, and, on the next block, the box office of the **Komische Oper** (*see p236*), you reach the crossroads with Friedrichstrasse, once a café-strewn focus of Weimar Berlin.

On the other side of the junction, on the right, housed in the ground floor of a 1920 building now occupied by Deutsche Bank, is the **Deutsche Guggenheim Berlin** (*see p76*), somewhat more modest in size and scope than its big sisters in New York and Bilbao. Facing the art gallery across Unter den Linden stands the grandiose **Staatsbibliotek** (it's open to all, and there's a small café within), usually filled with students from the next-door **Humboldt-Universität** (*see p283*). The university's grand old façade has been restored, as have the two statues of the Humboldts (founder Wilhelm and his brother Alexander), between which booksellers set up tables in good weather.

Across the street is **Bebelplatz**, the site of the huge Nazi book-burning, commemorated by Micha Ullmann's wonderful monument set into the Platz itself. At press time the site was inaccessible because of work on an underground carpark, scheduled for completion towards the end of 2004.

Dominating the square's eastern side is the **Staatsoper** (*see p238*), built in neo-classical style by Georg Wenzeslaus von Knobelsdorff in 1741-3. The present building actually dates from 1955, but remains faithful to the original. Established as Frederick the Great's Royal Court Opera, it is now one of Berlin's three major opera houses. The west side of the square is taken up by the late 18th-century **Alte Bibliotek**, commonly known as the 'Kommode', after its resemblance to a curvy piece of baroque furniture.

Alongside it, in the centre of Unter den Linden, stands a restored equestrian statue of Frederick the Great, originally removed by the GDR, and then replaced one night when the Party line changed on Prussian history.

Just south of the Staatsoper (and also designed by Knobelsdorff, in 1747) is **Sankt-Hedwigs-Kathedrale** (*see below*), a curious circular Roman Catholic church, inspired by the Pantheon in Rome. A minute's walk east of here brings you to another church, **Friedrichs-Werdersche-Kirche**, which now contains the **Schinkel-Museum** (see below), a homage to the building's architect.

North of here, back on Unter den Linden by the River Spree, is the baroque **Zeughaus**, a former armoury with a deceptively peaceful pink façade. After renovation is completed in 2005, the Zeughaus will once again house the **Deutsches Historisches Museum** (see below). The new wing by IM Pei (of Louvre glass pyramid fame) hosts changing exhibitions, and has a fine café on the top floor.

Just west of the Zeughaus stands the **Neue Wache** (New Guardhouse), constructed by Schinkel in 1816-18, which originally served as a guardhouse for the royal residences in the area. Today, it is a hauntingly plain memorial to the 'victims of war and tyranny', with an enlarged reproduction of a Käthe Kollwitz sculpture, *Mother with Dead Son*, at its centre. Beneath this are the remains of an unknown soldier and an unknown concentration camp victim, surrounded by earth from World War II battlefields and concentration camps.

Deutsche Guggenheim Berlin

Unter den Linden 13-15 (202 0930/www.deutsche-guggenheim-berlin.de). U6 Französische Strasse. **Open** 11am-8pm Mon-Wed, Fri-Sun; 11am-10pm Thur. **Admission** €3; €2 concessions; free Mon; free under-12s. **No credit cards**. **Map** p316/p302 F3.

In partnership with the Deutsche Bank (and housed in one of its buildings) this is the least impressive European branch of the Guggenheim. Big bucks, big ads, big boring. Huge, safe, famous name, glossy corporate art that you can take your granny to and buy a catalogue afterwards. The exhibition space is disappointingly small. Recent exhibitions have featured Miwa Yangi, Bruce Nauman and Tom Sochs.

Deutsches Historisches Museum

Zeughaus, Unter den Linden 2 (203 040/www.dhm.de). U6 Französische Strasse. **Open** 10am-6pm Mon, Tue, Fri-Sun; 10am-10pm Thur. **Admission** €2; under-18s free. **Map** p316/p302 F3.

Housed within the ex-armoury known as the Zeughaus, the revamped Museum of German History is, at press time, scheduled to reopen in early 2005. The core of the permanent exhibition (extending over three floors) will be the chronological 'period rooms', focusing on crucial times in German history. There will also be 'topic rooms', dealing with such subjects as 'The Relationship between the Sexes' or 'Changes in Work and Profession'. Temporary exhibitions are held in the new wing by IM Pei, which has already opened.

Friedrichswerdersche-Kirche/Schinkel-Museum

Werderscher Markt (208 1323/www.smpk.de). U2 Hausvogteiplatz. **Open** 10am-6pm Tue-Sun. **Admission** €3; €1.50 concessions; free 1st Sun of mth. **No credit cards**. **Map** p316/p302 F3.

This brick church, designed by Karl Friedrich Schinkel, was completed in 1831. Its war wounds were repaired in the 1980s and it reopened in 1987 as a homage to its architect. Inside are statues by Schinkel, Schadow and others, bathed in soft light from stained-glass windows. Pictures of Schinkel's works that didn't survive the war (like the Prinz-Albert-Schloss) are also displayed.

Sankt-Hedwigs-Kathedrale

Hinter der katholischen Kirche 3 (203 4810/www.hedwigs-kathedrale.de). U2 Hausvogteiplatz or U6 Französische Strasse. **Open** 10am-5pm Mon-Sat; 1-5pm Sun. **Admission** free; guided tour €1.50. **Map** p316/p302 F3.

Constructed in 1747 for Berlin's Catholic minority, this circular Knobelsdorff creation was bombed out during the war and only reconsecrated in 1963. Its modernised interior contains a split-level double altar. The crypt contains the remains of Bernhard Lichtenberg, who preached here against the Nazis, was arrested, and died while being transported to Dachau in 1943.

Museumsinsel

Map p302 & p316

The eastern end of Unter den Linden abuts the island in the Spree where Berlin was born (*see p6*). The northern part, with its collection of museums and galleries, is known as **Museumsinsel** (Museum Island), while the southern half (much enlarged by landfill), once a neighbourhood for the city's fishermen (and known as Fischerinsel), is now dominated by a clutch of grim tower blocks.

The five Museumsinsel museums (the Pergamonmuseum, Altes Museum, Alte Nationalgalerie, Neues Museum and Bode Museum) have been undergoing a massive restoration programme for many years; the first three are open, while work remains to be done on the latter two. Such is the importance of the site that it was added to UNESCO's World Cultural Heritage list in 1999.

One of the must-see attractions while you are in Berlin is the **Pergamonmuseum** (*see p78*). It's a showcase for three huge and important examples of ancient architecture: the Hellenistic Pergamon Altar (a Greek temple complex in what is now western Turkey), the Babylonian Gate of Ishtar and the Roman Market Gate of Miletus. The museum also contains the **Museum fur Islamische Kunst** (Museum of Islamic Art).

The **Berliner Dom** has been restored to its former glory. *See p78.*

Schinkel's superb **Altes Museum** (Old Museum; *see p78*), from 1830, has a small permanent collection and hosts some excellent temporary exhibitions. The most recently opened museum is the **Alte Nationalgalerie** (Old National Gallery; see below), which, since December 2001, has once again become home to a wide-ranging collection of 19th-century painting and sculpture.

The **Bode Museum** had a strange mixture of displays, including the half a million coins of the **Münzkabinett** numismatic collection (some of which is currently on display in the Pergamonmuseum) and the **Museum für Spätantike und Byzantinische Kunst** (Museum of Late Antique and Byzantine Art); it is due to reopen May 2006.

The **Neues Museum** is finally having its severe war-time bomb damage repaired – it is due to reopen in October 2009 as a home for the **Ägyptisches Museum** (*see p107*) and the **Museum für Vor- und Frühgeschichte** (*see p108*), both currently in Charlottenburg.

Dominating the Museumsinsel skyline is the the huge, bombastic **Berliner Dom** (*see p78*). It's worth climbing up to the cathedral's dome for fine views over the city. In front of here, and lined on one side by the Altes Museum, is the **Lustgarten**, an elegant green square.

Across the main road bisecting the island stands Schlossplatz and the shell of the **Palast der Republik**. This once-asbestos-contaminated relic of the GDR has been closed to the public since 1990. Built in the mid 1970s as the main parliamentary chamber of the GDR, it also contained discos, bars and a bowling alley. The Palast replaced the remains of the war-ravaged Stadtschloss, residence of the Kaisers, which was heavily damaged in World War II and demolished by the GDR in 1952. Arguments have rumbled on for years about whether or not to rebuild the Stadtschloss. At the end of 2003 it was decided to demolish the Palast and leave a green space here until funding for a rebuilt Stadtschloss (or at least, for a Stadtschloss-style façade over a more modern structure) could be found. For the time being, a company called Zwischen Palast Nutzung (www.zwischenpalastnutzung.de) is looking to organise temporary uses for the existing, gutted Palast.

Alte Nationalgalerie

Bodestrasse 1-3 (2090 5801/www.smpk.de). S3, S5, S7, S9, S75 Hackescher Markt. **Open** 10am-6pm Tue, Wed, Fri-Sun; 10am-10pm Thur. **Admission** €8; €4 concessions. **No credit cards**. **Map** p316/p302 F3.

The Old National Gallery reopened in December 2001 after three years of careful restoration. With its ceiling and wall paintings, fabric wallpapers and marble staircase, it provides a sparkling home to one of the largest collections of 19th-century art and sculpture in Germany. Among the 440 paintings and 80 sculptures, which span the period from Goethe to the beginning of the Modern, German artists such as Adolph Menzel, Caspar David Friedrich and Carl

Spitzweg are well represented. There are also some first-rank early Impressionist works from Manet, Monet and Rodin. Although it's worth a visit, don't expect to see the definitive German national collection. This is a big country and you would also have to take in the vast museums of Stuttgart, Weimar, Munich and Hamburg to get a true overall view.

Altes Museum

Lustgarten (2090 5245/www.smpk.de). S3, S5, S7, S9, S75 Hackescher Markt. **Open** 10am-6pm Tue-Sun. **Admission** €8; €4 concessions; free 1st Sun of month. **No credit cards**. **Map** p316/p302 F3.

Opened as the Royal Museum in 1830, the Old Museum originally housed all the art treasures on Museumsinsel. It was designed by Schinkel and is considered one of his finest buildings, with a particularly magnificent entrance rotunda. Like most of the Museumsinsel museums, it is being renovated, slowly, but continues to show a good range of temporary exhibitions; a recent one was dedicated to the Berlin years of architect Ludwig Mies van der Rohe. In May 2005, the Ägyptische Museum moves here from Charlottenburg, and will stay until 2009.

Berliner Dom

Lustgarten (2026 9133/guided tours 2026 9119/www.berliner-dom.de). S3, S5, S7, S9, S75 Hackescher Markt. **Open** *Apr-Sept* 9am-8pm Mon-Sat; noon-8pm Sun. *Oct-Mar* 9am-7pm Mon-Sat; noon-7pm Sun. **Admission** €5; €3 concessions; free under-14s. **No credit cards**. **Map** p316/p302 F3.

The dramatic Berlin Cathedral is now finally healed of its war wounds. Built around the turn of the 20th-century in Italian Renaissance style, it was destroyed during World War II and remained a ruin until 1973, when extensive restoration work began. It has always looked fine from the outside, but now that the internal work is complete, it is fully restored to its former glory. Crammed with Victorian detail, and containing dozens of statues of eminent German Protestants, it is now holding weekly services after several decades of existing in the face of GDR displeasure. Its lush 19th-century interior is hardly the perfect acoustic space for the frequent concerts that are held here, but it's worth a visit to see the crypt containing around 90 sarcophagi of the Hohenzollern dynasty, or to clamber up for splendid views from the cupola.

Pergamonmuseum

Am Kupfergraben (2090 5566/www.smpk.de). U6, S1, S2, S3, S5, S7, S9, S25, S26, S75 Friedrichstrasse. **Open** 10am-6pm Tue, Wed, Fri-Sun; 10am-10pm Thur. **Admission** €8; €4 concessions; free 1st Sun of month. **No credit cards**. **Map** p316/p302 F3.

One of the world's major archaeological museums, the Pergamon shouldn't be missed. Its treasures are made up of the **Antikensammlung** (Collection of Classical Antiquities) and the **Vorderasiastisches Museum** (Museum of Near Eastern Antiquities) and contain three major draws. The first is the Hellenistic Pergamon Altar. This dates from 170-159 BC, when Pergamon was one of the major cities of Asia Minor; huge as it is, the museum's partial re-creation represents only one third of its original size. The altar's outstanding feature is the stunning original frieze that once wound 113 metres (371 feet)

Friedrichstrasse. *See p79.*

around the base of the structure. A remarkable proportion of it survives, and depicts the epic battle between gods and titans with a vividness and vitality that make the frieze one of the greatest artistic legacies of classical antiquity.

In an adjoining room, and even more architecturally impressive, is the towering two-storey Roman Market Gate of Miletus (29 metres/95 feet wide and almost 17 metres/56 feet high), erected in AD 120. This leads through (and back in time) to the third of the big three attractions – the extraordinary blue-and-ochre tiled Gate of Ishtar and the Babylonian Processional Street, dating from the reign of King Nebuchadnezzar (605-562 BC). There are plenty of other gems in the museum, including some stunning Assyrian reliefs, but it's an admirably digestible and focused place.

The museum is also now home to the **Museum für Islamische Kunst** (Museum of Islamic Art) which takes up 14 rooms in the southern wing. The collection is wide-ranging, including applied arts, crafts, books and architectural details (the latter are particularly notable) produced by Islamic peoples from the eighth to the 19th century. Entrance is included in the overall admission price.

An excellent audio guide (included in the price of entrance) gives plenty of interesting, non-patronising background info on the exhibits throughout the museum.

Heckmann Höfe: star courtyard. *See p83.*

South of Unter den Linden

Map p302 & p316

What the Kurfürstendamm tried to be in post-war West Berlin, **Friedrichstrasse** had been and may be again: the city's glitziest shopping street. Like Unter den Linden, the north–south street (starting at Mehringplatz in Kreuzberg and ending at Oranienburger Tor in Mitte) was laid out as part of the baroque late 17th-century expansion of the city.

The liveliest, sleekest stretch of the street is that between **Checkpoint Charlie** (*see p95*) and Friedrichstrasse station. A huge amount of money has been poured into redevelopment here, with office buildings and upmarket shopping malls galore, though opinions differ as to the effectiveness of the architecture. Look out for the all-glass façade of the modernist-style **Galeries Lafayette** (No.75; *see p161*), the acute angles of the expressionist **Quartier 206** (Nos.71-4; *see p162*) and the monolithic geometric mass of **Quartier 205** (Nos.66-70). Otherwise there are auto showrooms for Rolls Royce, Bentley, Volkswagen, Audi and Mercedes-Benz, boutiques for Mont Blanc, Cartier, DKNY and countless other high-class concerns.

Just to the east of this stretch lies the square of **Gendarmenmarkt**, one of the high points of Frederick the Great's vision for the city. Here, two churches, the **Französischer Dom** ('French Cathedral'; home of the Hugenottenmuseum; *see p81*) and the **Deutscher Dom** (home of the 'Questions on German History' exhibition; see below) frame the **Konzerthaus** (*see p237*), home to the Deutsches Symphonie-Orchester Berlin.

Just west of Friedrichstrasse on Leipzigerstrasse is the **Museum für Kommunikation** (*see p81*). There are many other interesting sights close by over the Mitte border with Kreuzberg. For these, *see p91*.

Deutscher Dom

Gendarmenmarkt, entrance in Markgrafenstrasse (227 30431/www.webmuseen.de). U2, U6 Stadtmitte. **Open** 10am-10pm Tue; 10am-6pm Wed-Sun; guided tours 11am & 1pm daily. **Admission** free. **Map** p316/p302 F3.

Both this church and the Französischer Dom were built in 1780-85 by Carl von Gontard for Frederick the Great, in imitation of Santa Maria in Montesanto and Santa Maria dei Miracoli in Rome. The Deutscher Dom was intended for Berlin's Lutheran community. Its neo-classical tower is topped by a 7m (23ft) gilded statue representing Virtue. Inside is the 'Questions on German History' exhibition.

Französischer Dom/Hugenottenmuseum

Gendarmenmarkt (229 1760/www.franzoesische-kirche.de). U2, U6 Stadtmitte. **Open** *Museum* noon-5pm Tue-Sat; 11am-5pm Sun. *Tower* (summer) 10am-7pm; (winter) 10am-6pm daily. **Admission** *Museum & tower* €2; €0.50 concessions. **No credit cards. Map** p315/p302 F3.

Built in the early 18th century for Berlin's 6,000-plus-strong French Protestant community (known as Huguenots, expelled from France by Louis XIV in 1685), the church was later given a baroque tower, which offers fine views over Mitte. The tower is purely decorative and unconsecrated – and, therefore, not part of the church, which is known as the **Französischen Friedrichstadt Kirche** (noon-5pm Mon-Sat, after service-5pm Sun).

An exhibition on the history of the French Protestants in France and Berlin-Brandenburg is displayed within the building (note: the modest church itself has a separate entrance at the western end). The museum chronicles the religious persecution suffered by Calvinists (note the bust of Calvin on the outside of the church) and their subsequent immigration to Berlin after 1685, at the behest of the Hohenzollerns. The development of the Huguenot community is also detailed with paintings, documents and artefacts. One part of the museum is devoted to the church's history, particularly the effects of World War II – it was bombed during a Sunday service in 1944 and remained a ruin until the mid-1980s. Other exports from France can be found in the wine restaurant upstairs.

Museum für Kommunikation

Leipziger Strasse 16 (202 940/www.museumsstiftung.de/berlin). U2 Mohrenstrasse or U2, U6 Stadtmitte. **Open** 9am-5pm Tue-Fri; 11am-7pm Sat, Sun. **Admission** free. **Map** p316/p306 F4.

Tracing its origins back to the world's first postal museum (founded in 1872), this once-dispersed collection only reopened in 2000 and covers a lot more than stamps. It traces the development of telecommunications up to the current internet era, though philatelists might want to head straight to the basement to check out the 'Blue Mauritius', one of the world's rarest stamps. The lovely, airy interior of the museum is worth a look in itself. Three robots welcome visitors in the main atrium.

North of Unter den Linden

Map p302 & p316

The continuation of Friedrichstrasse north of Unter den Linden is less appealing and lively than its southern stretch. Friedrichstrasse station has been turned into a Deutsche Bahn shopping mall, the formerly grim building having been totally gutted in the process. The station interior was once notable mostly for its ability to confuse, since its role as the only East-West border crossing point open for all categories of citizen (East and West Germans, West Berliners, citizens of Allied countries, and other foreigners) involved a warren of passageways and interior spaces.

Looming over the nearby plaza is the former **Internationales Handelzentrum** ('International Trade Centre', now just known as the IHZ). This was built by the Japanese as a base from which their companies could trade with the GDR.

Following the line of the train tracks east along Georgenstrasse, you come upon the **Berliner Antik & Flohmarkt** (*see p176*) – a succession of antiques stores, bookshops and cafés in the Bogen ('arches'), underneath the railway.

The building just to the north of the train station is known as the **Tränenpalast** ('Palace of Tears'), since it was where departing visitors left their Eastern friends and relations who could not follow them through the border. Today, this former checkpoint is a concert and cabaret venue, and a piece of the Wall can be seen in its beer garden.

Across Friedrichstrasse stands the **Admiralspalast**, originally a luxurious bathhouse and a survivor of the bombing. In the 1920s, the Metropol Theater, a former venue for translated Broadway hits and home to the Distel Cabaret, was opened here.

Crossing the river on the wrought-iron **Weidendammer Brücke**, a left turn on Schiffbauerdamm brings you to the **Berliner Ensemble** (*see p240*), with its bronze statue of Bertolt Brecht, who directed the company from 1948 to 1956, surrounded by quotations from his works. A couple of minutes' walk north-west of here, on Schumannstrasse, stands the **Deutsches Theater** (*see p240*), another of the city's important companies.

Back on Friedrichstrasse stands the **Friedrichstadtpalast** (*see p231*), a large cabaret venue that was an entertainment hotspot during the days of the GDR, since it took hard currency; it still pulls the crowds today, albeit mostly grannies from out of town. Further north is the **Brecht-Weigel-Gedenkstätte** (*see p82*), home to Bertolt Brecht (until his death in 1956) and his wife Helene Weigel. Both are buried in the **Dorotheenstädtische Friedhof** (Apr-Sept 8am-7pm, Oct-Mar 8am-4pm daily) next door, along with the architect Schinkel, the author Heinrich Mann and the philosopher Georg Hegel.

Two worthwhile museums are five and ten minutes' walk from here : the **Museum für Naturkunde** (Natural History Museum; *see p82*) and the **Hamburger Bahnhof, Museum für Gegenwart** (Hamburg Station

Museum of Contemporary Art; *see below*), which puts on a series of excellent, varied temporary exhibitions within the atmospheric confines of a converted railway station.

Brecht-Weigel-Gedenkstätte

Chausseestrasse 125 (2830 57044/www.adk.de). U6 Oranienburger Tor. **Open** *Guided tours* every half-hour 10-11.30am Tue, Wed, Fri; 10am-noon, 5-6.30pm Thur; 9.30am-1.30pm Sat; every hour 11am-6pm Sun. **Admission** €3; €1.50 concessions. **No credit cards. Map** p302 F2.

Brecht's home from 1948 until his death in 1953 has been preserved exactly as he left it. Tours of the house last about half an hour and give interesting insights into the life and reading habits of the playwright. The window at which he worked overlooked the grave of Hegel in the neighbouring cemetery. Brecht's wife, actress Helene Weigel, continued living here until she died in 1971. The Brecht archives are kept upstairs. Phone in advance for a tour in English. The Kellerrestaurant near the exit serves 'select wines and fine beers and Viennese cooking in the style of Helene Weigel', in case you want to extend your Brecht-Weigel experience. *See p121.*

Hamburger Bahnhof, Museum für Gegenwart

Invalidenstrasse 50-51 (397 8340/www.smpk.de). S3, S5, S7, S9, S75 Lehrter Stadtbahnhof. **Open** 10am-6pm Tue-Fri; 11am-6pm Sat, Sun. **Admission** €6; €3 concessions. **No credit cards. Map** p302 E3.

The Hamburg Station Museum of Contemporary Art opened with much fanfare in 1997. Housed within a huge and expensive refurbishment of a former railway station, the exterior features a stunning fluorescent light installation by Dan Flavin. The permanent exhibition comes principally from the bequested Erich Marx Collection, which, despite its distinctly 1980s monolithic, monotone feel, is lightened by a good, varied range of temporary exhibitions and retrospectives. There are wings for works by Andy Warhol and Joseph Beuys, along with pieces by Bruce Nauman, Anselm Kiefer and many others. Upstairs you'll find the sculptures of Rosemarie Trockel and charming pre-pop Warhol drawings from the 1950s. The museum has one of the best art bookshops in Berlin and an Aktionraum, hosting various events, such as performances and symposia, plus a video archive of all Joseph Beuys' taped performances. And a café, too.

Museum für Naturkunde

Invalidenstrasse 43 (2093 8591/www.museum.hu-berlin.de). U6 Zinnowitzer Strasse. **Open** 9.30am-5pm Tue-Fri; 10am-6pm Sat, Sun. **Admission** €3.50; €2 concessions; €7 family; free under-6s. **No credit cards. Map** p302 E3.

The Natural History Museum is one of the world's largest and best organised – it's also one of the oldest, and looks it: the core of the collection dates from 1716, and the dull, dusty layout has changed little from GDR days. A tall skeleton of a brachiosaurus greets you in the dinosaur-filled first room, which also contains perhaps the most perfectly preserved skeleton of an archaeopteryx yet unearthed. Another room has a vast display of fossils, from trilobites to lobsters, while other highlights include the skeleton of a giant armadillo. The immense stuffed animal collection, assembled in the 1920s, is equally impressive, and the huge mineral collection is a geologist's playground: row upon row of rocks, set up just as they were when the building first opened in 1889. Don't miss the meteor chunks in the back. Part of Humboldt University, the museum contains more than 60 million exhibits.

The Scheunenviertel

If the area south of Friedrichstrasse station is the new upmarket face of Mitte, the **Scheunenviertel** (stretching around the north side of the curve of the Spree, running east from Friedrichstrasse to Hackescher Markt) is the face of its moneyed bohemia. This is Berlin's main nightlife district and art quarter, littered with bars and galleries. Once so far out of town that the highly flammable hay barns (*Scheunen*) were built here, this was also historically the centre of Berlin's immigrant community, including many Jews from eastern Europe. During the 1990s it again began to attract Jewish immigrants, including both young Americans and Orthodox Jews from the former Soviet Union.

In the 1990s, the Scheunenviertel became a magnet for squatters with access to the list of buildings supposedly wrecked by lazy urban developers, who had checked them off as gone in order to meet quotas – but had actually left them standing. With many other buildings in disrepair, rents were cheap, and the new residents soon learned how to take advantage of city subsidies for opening galleries and other cultural spaces. Result: the Scheunenviertel became Berlin's hot cultural centre.

The first of these art-squats was **Tacheles** on Oranienburger Strasse, the spine of the Scheunenviertel. Built in 1907, the building originally housed the Friedrichstrasse Passagen, an early attempt at a shopping mall, which in the 1930s was used by various Nazi organisations. It stood vacant for years – at one point the GDR tried to demolish it, but, so the story goes, ran out of dynamite halfway through the job – and was falling apart when it was squatted by artists immediately following the fall of the Wall. It then became a rather arrogant arbiter of hip in the neighbourhood, offering studio space to artists, performance spaces for music, a cinema, and several bars and discos. In 1997, the city presented the squatters with an opportunity to buy it cheaply and was spurned. In 1998, Tacheles was bought by a German company which has recently reconstructed a big portion of the building, now housing new galleries and an 'office of cultural marketing'. In some form or another, Tacheles will be around for a long while yet.

Across Tucholskystrasse at Oranienburger Strasse 32 is an entrance to the **Heckmann Höfe** (the other is on Auguststrasse), a series of restored courtyards formerly belonging to an engineering firm. The courtyards have been delightfully restored to accommodate shops and restaurants. The free-standing building with the firm's coat of arms in the pavement in front of it was once the stables, as indicated by the sculpture of a horse's head, positioned as if peering out of the building.

A little further down the block stands the **Neue Synagoge** (*see p84*), with its gleaming golden Moorish-style dome. Turning into Grosse Hamburger Strasse, you find yourself surrounded by Jewish history. On the right, on the site of a former old people's home, there is a memorial to the thousands of Berlin Jews who were forced to congregate here before being shipped off to concentration camps. Following Jewish tradition, many visitors put a stone on the memorial in remembrance of those who died. Behind the memorial is a park that was once Berlin's oldest Jewish cemetery; the only gravestone left is that of the father of the German Jewish renaissance, Moses Mendelssohn, founder of the city's first Jewish school, next door at No. 27. That the school has heavy security fencing and a permanent police presence, even today, only adds to the poignancy of this place.

Equally moving, across the street at Nos. 15-16 is **The Missing House**, an artwork by Christian Boltanski, in which the walls of a bombed-out house have the names and occupations of former residents inscribed on the site of each one's apartment. A little further on, the **Sophienkirche**, from which nearby Sophienstrasse gets its name, is one of Berlin's few remaining baroque churches. It is set back from the street behind wrought-iron fences, and, together with the surrounding ensemble, is one of the prettiest architectural sites in the city. The interior is a little disappointing though.

At the end of Oranienburger Strasse, at the corner of Rosenthaler Strasse, is the famous **Hackesche Höfe**. Built in 1906-7 by some young Jewish idealists, these form a complex of nine interlinking *Jugendstil* courtyards with elegant ceramic façades. The Höfe symbolise Berlin's new Mitte: having miraculously survived two wars, the forgotten, crumbling buildings were restored in the mid-1990s using the old plans. Today, they house an upmarket collection of shops, galleries, theatres, cabarets, cafés, restaurants and cinemas and are just about Berlin's top tourist attraction. Try to avoid visiting at the weekend.

A few doors up Rosenthaler Strasse is a tumbledown alley alongside the Central cinema, in which a workshop for the blind was located during World War II. Its owner managed to stock it fully with 'blind' Jews, and helped them escape or avoid the camps. Now it houses alternative galleries and bars. Across the street from the Hackesche Höfe, and under the S-Bahn arches, there is a welter of bars, restaurants and shops as well as the **British Council** building in the Neue Hackesche Höfe, which has a great library and internet lounge.

There are still more fashionable bars and shops along Rosenthaler Strasse and around the corner on Neue Schönhauser Strasse as well as some good sandwich and coffee bars. This area has settled into being Berlin's hip centre with many cool little shops. Most of the original houses have now been renovated and the former gaps left by wartime bombing raids have had some extensive dental treatment in the form of slick new buildings. Even the **Plattenbauten**, the East German prefabs, have been spruced up. Watch out for the pavements though, they still have craters the size of Prada handbags dotted around, waiting to trip the unwary.

Leading off Rosenthaler Strasse, **Sophienstrasse** has to be Mitte's most picturesque little side road. Built in the 18th century, it was restored in 1987 for the city's 750th anniversary, with craftworkers' ateliers that have replicas of old merchants' metal signs hanging outside them. This pseudo-historicism has now become part of a more interesting mix of handcraft shops: the excellent woodwind instrument makers, a traditional wooden toy and figurine shop, a whisky and cigar shop, bakers and a number of art galleries. The brick façade of the **Handwerker Verein** at No.18 is particularly impressive. If you wander into the courtyard (as you can with most courtyards that aren't private), you'll find the **Sophiensaele** (*see p241*), an interesting performing arts space in an old ballroom. The Sophiensaele was also the location of the first German Communist Party HQ.

At Nos.20-21 are the **Sophie-Gips Höfe**, which came into being when wealthy art patrons Erika and Rolf Hoffmann were denied permission to build a gallery in Dresden for their huge collection of contemporary art. Instead, they bought this complex between Sophienstrasse and Gipsstrasse, restored it, and installed the art here, along with their spectacular private residence. Tours of the

Sammlung Hoffmann (*see below*) are available on Saturdays, by appointment. There are also text, earth and light artworks integrated into the building complex (which can be seen until 10pm), as well as galleries, cafés and offices.

Running between the west end of Oranienburger Strasse and Rosenthaler Strasse, Auguststrasse is the core of Berlin's eastern gallery district; it was here that the whole Mitte scene originated less than a decade ago, with such important venues as **Eigen + Art** (*see p200*) and **Kunst-Werke** (*see p200*) among many others. This became known as Mitte's 'Art Mile', and the street still makes a good afternoon's stroll, although many of the cutting-edge galleries have moved on to fresh pastures. If you are lucky, you might catch a *Rundgang* or 'walkaround', generally held on the first Saturday evening of every other month (check in the galleries for details). These gallery crawls are pleasant on summer evenings as galleries open their doors late and sometimes serve wine.

Neue Synagoge

Centrum Judaicum, Oranienburger Strasse 28-30 (8802 8451/www.cjudaicum.de). S1, S2, S25, S26 Oranienburger Strasse. **Open** *Sept-Apr* 10am-6pm Mon-Thur, Sun; 10am-2pm Fri. *May-Aug* 10am-8pm Mon, Sun; 10am-6pm Tue-Thur; 10am-5pm Fri. **Admission** €3; €2 concessions. **No credit cards**. **Map** p316/p302 F3.

Built in 1857-66 as the Berlin Jewish community's showpiece (and inaugurated in the presence of Bismarck), it was the New Synagogue that was attacked during Kristallnacht in 1938, but not too badly damaged – Allied bombs did far more harm in 1945. The façade remained intact and the Moorish dome has been rebuilt. Inside is a permanent exhibition about Jewish life in Berlin and a glassed-in area protecting the ruins of the sanctuary. The dome is also open to visitors in summer.

Sammlung Hoffman

Sophienstrasse 21, Mitte (2849 9121/www.sophie-gips.de). U8 Weinmeisterstrasse. **Open** (by appointment only) 11am-4pm Sat. **Admission** €6. **No credit cards**. **Map** p316/p302 F3.

This is Erika and Rolf Hoffmann's private collection of international contemporary art, including a charming floor installation work by Swiss video artist Pippilotti Rist and work by Douglas Gordon, Felix Gonzalez-Torres and AR Penck. The Hoffmans offer guided tours through their apartment every Saturday by appointment – felt slippers supplied.

Alexanderplatz & around

Map p303 & p316

Visitors who have read Alfred Döblin's *Berlin Alexanderplatz* or seen the television series by Fassbinder may arrive here and wonder what has happened. What happened was that in the early 1970s Erich Honecker decided that this historic area should reflect the glories of socialism, and tore it all down. He replaced it with a masterpiece of commie kitsch: wide boulevards; monotonous white buildings filled with cafés and shops; and, of course, the impressive golf-ball-on-a-knitting-needle, the **Fernsehturm** (Television Tower; *see p86*).

At ground level, capitalism's neon icons sit incongruously on Honecker's erections. The goofy clock topped with the 1950s-style atom design signals the time in (mostly) former socialist lands; water cascades from the **Brunnen der Völkerfreundschaft** ('Fountain of the Friendship of Peoples'); at the **Markthalle** you can sink a beer or bite into a brand-name burger. There are plans to replace most of Alexanderplatz with a dozen or so skyscrapers, among which the Fernsehturm will remain standing, but it's not at all certain when, or if, such plans will come to fruition.

One of the few survivors from pre-war Alexanderplatz sits in the shadow of the Fernsehturm: the **Marienkirche** (*see p86*), Berlin's oldest parish church, dating from the 13th century. Later 15th-century (the tower) and 18th-century (the upper section) additions enhance the building's harmonious simplicity.

Just south of here stands the extravagant **Neptunbrunnen**, an 1891 statue of the trident-wielding sea god, surrounded by four female figures representing the most important German rivers – the Elbe, the Rhine, the Oder and the Vistula. This was moved here from the Stadtschloss when the Communists demolished it in 1950. Overlooking Neptune from the south-east is the huge red-brick bulk of the **Berliner Rathaus** (Berlin Town Hall; *see p85*), while to the south-west is the open space of **Marx-Engels Forum**, one of the few remaining monuments to the old boys – the huge statue of Karl and Fred begs you to take a seat on Karl's lap. On Spandauer Strasse behind the Radisson Hotel, opposite what used to be the university bookshop but is now **Zentralbüro** (*see p198*), an alternative art venue, is the entrance to the **Aquadom and Sea Life** (*see p85*), one of Mitte's more eccentric new attractions.

For a vague impression of what this part of the city might have looked like before Allied bombers and the GDR did their work, take a stroll around the Nikolaiviertel, just south of Alexanderplatz. This is Berlin's oldest quarter, centred around **Nikolaikirche** (dating from 1220; *see p86*). The GDR's reconstruction involved bringing the few undamaged buildings from this period together into what is essentially a fake assemblage of history. There are a couple of historic residences, including the **Knoblauch-Haus** (*see p86*), and the **Ephraim-Palais** (*see below*), which once belonged to the court jeweller. You'll also find **Gottfried Lessing's** house, restaurants, cafés (including a reconstruction of Zum Nussbaum, a contender for the oldest bar in Berlin) and overpriced shops. On the southern edge of the district is the **Hanf Museum** (Hemp Museum; *see p86*).

Long before the infamous Wall, Berlin had another one: the medieval **Stadtmauer** (City Wall) of the original 13th-century settlement. There's almost as much left of this wall (a couple of minutes' walk east of the Nikolaiviertel, on Littenstrasse/Waisenstrasse) as there is of the more recent one. Built along the wall is the old (and extremely popular) restaurant **Zur Letzten Instanz**, which takes its name from the neighbouring law court from which there was no further appeal. There has been a restaurant on this site since 1525, Napoleon among its customers. The building is one of four old houses that have been reconstructed.

Just over the Spree from here is the church-like red-brick **Märkisches Museum** (*see p86*), which houses a rambling, but not uninteresting, collection tracing the history of the city, and the small neighbouring Köllnischer Park. You'll see multi-hued bear statues all over the city, but the park's bearpit is home to Schnute, Maxi and Tilo, Berlin's trio of flesh-and-blood brown bears – and official symbols of the city.

Around the corner on Wallstrasse is the **Museum Kindheit und Jugend** (*see p86*), with its not especially thrilling displays of old toys and school life over the last two centuries.

Aquadom & Sea Life

Spandauer Strasse 3 (992 800/www.sealife.de). S3, S5, S7, S9, S75 Hackescher Markt. **Open** 10am-6pm daily. **Admission** €13.50; under-14s €10; €12.60 concessions. **No credit cards. Map** p316/p303 G3.

Billed as two attractions in one, but both of them involving lots of water and plenty of fish. Sea Life leads one through 13 themed aquaria offering fish in different habitats, starting with the kinds you'd find in the nearby Spree, then in the nearby Wannsee, then in Hamburg Harbour, and finally beyond in the North Sea and Atlantic Ocean. The Aquadom is the world's largest free-standing aquarium – a spacey stucture that looks like it might just have landed from the Planet Aqua. What you do is take a lift up through the middle of this giant cylindrical fishtank – a million litres of saltwater that is home to 2,500 colourful creatures – and enfolded by the atrium of the Radisson Hotel (*see p51*).

Berliner Rathaus

Rathausstrasse 15 (902 60/guided tours 9026 2523). U2, U5, U8, S3, S5, S7, S9, S75, Alexanderplatz. **Open** 9am-6pm Mon-Fri; tours by appointment. **Admission** free. **Map** p316/p303 G3.

Neue Synagoge: a true survivor. *See p84.*

This magnificent building was built of terracotta brick during the 1860s. The history of Berlin up to that point is illustrated in a series of 36 reliefs on the façade. During Communist times, it served as East Berlin's town hall – which made its old nickname, Rotes Rathaus ('Red Town Hall'), after the colour of the façade, doubly fitting. West Berlin's city government workers moved here from their town hall, Rathaus Schöneberg, in 1991. For security reasons, admission is restricted to small parts of the building; bring some ID.

Ephraim-Palais

Poststrasse 16 (2400 2121/www.stadtmuseum.de). U2, U5, U8, S3, S5, S7, S9, S75 Alexanderplatz. **Open** 10am-6pm Tue-Sun. **Admission** €3; €1.50 concessions; free Wed. *Combined ticket* (with Knoblauch-Haus & Nikolaikirche) €5; €3 concessions. **No credit cards. Map** p316/p303 G3.

Built in the 15th century, remodelled in late baroque style in the 18th century, demolished by the Communists, and then rebuilt by them close to its original location for the 750th anniversary of Berlin in 1987, the Ephraim-Palais is today home to temporary exhibitions. Recent ones have been about KMP porcelain 1800-1900 or children's clothing of the Wilhelmian era 1871-1918. Soft, chandelier lighting and parquet floors add a refined touch to exhibited works without overwhelming them.

Fernsehturm

Panoramastrasse 1A (242 3333/www.berlinerfernsehturm.de). U2, U5, U8, S3, S5, S7, S9, S75 Alexanderplatz. **Open** *Mar-Oct* 9am-1am daily. *Nov-Feb* 10am-midnight daily. **Admission** €6.80; €3.50 concessions; free under-3s; last entry 30mins before closing. **Credit** AmEx, DC, MC, V. **Map** p316/p303 G3.

Built in the late 1960s at a time when relations between East and West Berlin were at their lowest ebb, the 365m (1,198ft) Television Tower – its ball-on-spike shape visible all over the city – was intended as an assertion of Communist dynamism and modernity. A shame then that such television towers were a West German invention. A shame, too, that they had to get Swedish engineers to build the thing. Communist authorities were also displeased to note a particular phenomenon: when the sun shines on the tower, reflections on the ball form the shape of a cross. Berliners dubbed this stigmata 'the Pope's revenge'. Nevertheless, the authorities were proud enough of their tower to make it one of the central symbols of the East German capital; its silhouette even formed the 'i' in 'Berlin' on the GDR's tourist information logo. Take an ear-popping trip in the lift to the observation platform at the top: a great way to orient yourself early on a visit to Berlin. The view is unbeatable by night or day – particularly looking westwards, where you can take in the whole of the Tiergarten and surrounding area. If heights make you hungry, take a twirl in the revolving restaurant, which offers an even better view plus a menu of snacks and meals.

Hanf Museum

Mühlendamm 5 (242 4827/www.hanflobby.de/hanfmuseum). U2, U5, U8, S3, S5, S7, S9, S75 Alexanderplatz. **Open** 10am-8pm Tue-Fri; noon-8pm Sat, Sun. **Admission** €3; free under-10s. **No credit cards**. **Map** p316/p303 G3.

The world's largest hemp museum aims to teach the visitor about the uses of hemp throughout history, as well as touching on the controversy surrounding the herb today. There are a few booklets to leaf through in English. The café (doubling as a video- and reading-room) has cakes made with and without hemp. Everything, though, is THC-free.

Knoblauch-Haus

Poststrasse 23 (2345 9991/www.stadtmuseum.de). U2, U5, U8, S3, S5, S7, S9, S75 Alexanderplatz. **Open** 10am-6pm Tue-Sun. **Admission** *Combined ticket* (with Ephraim-Palais & Nikolaikirche) €5; €3 concessions; free Wed. **No credit cards**. **Map** p316/p303 G3.

This neo-classical mid 18th-century town house was home to the influential Knoblauch family and contains an exhibition about some of their more prominent members. However, the real draw is the striking *haute bourgeoise* interior of the house. The building also houses a reconstructed 19th-century wine restaurant and, from August 2004, will also host a museum of hairdressing.

Marienkirche

Karl-Liebknecht-Strasse 8 (242 4467/www.marienkirche-berlin.de). U2, U5, U8, S3, S5, S7, S9, S75 Alexanderplatz. **Open** *Apr-Oct* 10am-6pm daily. *Nov-Mar* 10am-4pm daily. **Admission** free. **Map** p316/p303 G3.

Begun in 1270, this is one of Berlin's few remaining medieval buildings. Just inside the door is a wonderful Dance of Death fresco dating from 1485 (though it's in need of restoration) and the 18th-century Walther organ here is considered that famous builder's masterpiece. Marienkirche hit the headlines in 1989 when the civil rights movement chose it for one of their first sit-ins, since churches were among the few places where people could congregate without state permission. Tours available.

Märkisches Museum

Am Köllnischen Park 5 (3086 6215/www.stadtmuseum.de). U2 Märkisches Museum. **Open** 10am-6pm Tue-Sun. **Admission** €4; €2 concessions; free Wed. **Map** p316/p307 G4.

This extensive, curious and somewhat old-fashioned museum traces the history of Berlin through a wide range of historical artefacts. Different sections examine themes such as Berlin as newspaper city, women in Berlin's history, intellectual Berlin and the military. There are models of the city at different times, and some good paintings, including works by members of the Brücke group, such as Kirchner and Pechstein. Some section descriptions are in English.

Museum Kindheit und Jugend

Wallstrasse 32 (275 0383/www.berlin-kindheitundjugend.de). U2 Märkisches Museum or U8 Heinrich-Heine-Strasse, S3, S5, S7, S9, S75 Jannowitzbrücke. **Open** 9am-5pm Tue-Fri; 10am-6pm Sat, Sun. **Admission** €2; €1 concessions; free Wed. Family ticket €2.50. **No credit cards**. **Map** p316/p307 G4.

The place to come if you want to show kids how lucky they are to be going to school today and not 50 years ago. Apart from old toys, it displays artefacts from classrooms during the Weimar Republic, the Nazi era and under Communism.

Nikolaikirche

Nikolaikirchplatz (2472 4529/www.stadtmuseum.de). U2, U5, U8, S3, S5, S7, S9, S75 Alexanderplatz. **Open** 10am-6pm Tue-Sun. **Admission** €1.50; free Wed. *Combined ticket* (with Knoblauch-Haus & Ephraim-Palais) €5; €3 concessions. **No credit cards**. **Map** p316/p303 G3.

Inside Berlin's oldest congregational church, from which the Nikolaiviertel takes its name, is an interesting historical collection chronicling Berlin's development from its founding (c1230) until 1648. Old tiles, tapestries, stone and wood carvings – even old weapons and punishment devices – are on display. The collection includes photographs of the extensive wartime damage, plus examples of how the stones melted together in the heat of bombardment. Reconstruction was completed in 1987 for Berlin's 750th anniversary.

Prenzlauer Berg & Friedrichshain

Between gentrified elegance and post-industrial nightlife, Berlin still marches eastwards on café-studded streets.

Abutting Mitte to the north-east and south-east respectively, the districts of Prenzlauer Berg and Friedrichshain present very different faces of east Berlin. The former is now largely gentrified, with tree-lined and café-studded streets, evoking something of pre-war Berlin. The latter, stretching out from the Stalinist spine of Karl-Marx-Allee into waterfront and post-industrial quarters, feels more a product of the Communist era. Both districts have lively bar and club scenes; neither offer much in the way of conventional sightseeing.

Prenzlauer Berg

Map p303

Once thought of as a grey, depressing working-class district, in the last decade and a half Prenz'lberg (as the locals call it) has had its façades renovated, its streets cleaned, and its buildings newly inhabited by everyone from Russian artists to west German office workers. Galleries and cafés have sprouted, and 100-year-old buildings have finally had central heating, bathrooms and telephones installed. Hardcore alternative types might now have moved out to rawer Friedrichshain, feeling the district has lost its edge, but, for many Berliners, there's no cooler part of town.

Laid out at the turn of the 20th century, Prenzlauer Berg seems to have had more visionary social planners than other

The gloomy **Jüdischer Friedhof**. *See p89.*

neighbourhoods of the period. It has wider streets and pavements, giving the area a distinctive, open look. Although some buildings still await restoration, the scrubbed and painted streets give the impression of a 19th-century boulevard.

The district's focal point is pretty **Kollwitzplatz**, named after Käthe Kollwitz, the socially minded artist who lived much of her life around here The square is lined with bars, cafés and restaurants, and hosts an organic-type market on Thursday and Saturday. It was here in the Café Westphal (now a Greek restaurant) that the first meetings of East Berlin dissidents were held in the early 1980s.

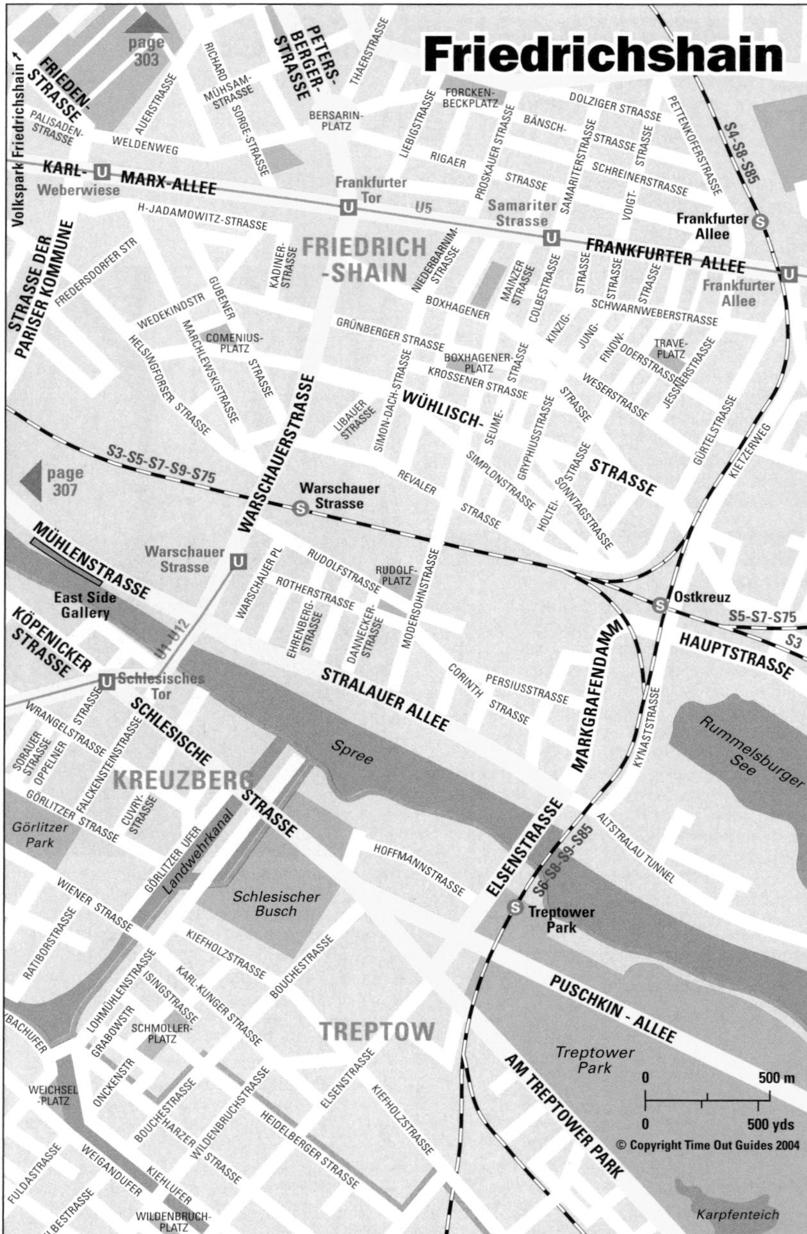
Friedrichshain
page 303
page 307
Volkspark Friedrichshain
FRIEDEN-STRASSE
PALISADEN-STRASSE
AUERSTRASSE
WELDENWEG
RICHARD MÜHSAM-STRASSE
SORGE-STRASSE
PETERS-BERGER-STRASSE
THAERSTRASSE
BERSARIN-PLATZ
LIEBIGSTRASSE
FORCKEN-BECKPLATZ
RIGAER
STRASSE
PROSKAUER STRASSE
BÄNSCH-
STRASSE
DOLZIGER STRASSE
SAMARITERSTRASSE
VOIGT-
STRASSE
SCHREINERSTRASSE
PETTENKOFERSTRASSE
S4-S8-S85
KARL-MARX-ALLEE
Weberwiese
Frankfurter Tor
U5
Samariter Strasse
Frankfurter Allee
FRANKFURTER ALLEE
H-JADAMOWITZ-STRASSE
STRASSE DER PARISER KOMMUNE
FREDERSDORFER STR
KADINER-STRASSE
FRIEDRICH-SHAIN
NIEDERBARNIM-STRASSE
MAINZER STRASSE
COLBESTRASSE
STRASSE
STRASSE
STRASSE
Frankfurter Allee
BOXHAGENER
SCHWARNWEBERSTRASSE
WEDEKINDSTR
GUBENER
COMENIUS-PLATZ
GRÜNBERGER STRASSE
KINZIG-
JUNG-
FINOW-
ODERSTRASSE
TRAVE-PLATZ
JESSNERSTRASSE
HELSINGFORSER STRASSE
MARCHLEWSKISTRASSE
STRASSE
BOXHAGENER-PLATZ
STRASSE
KROSSENER STRASSE
WESERSTRASSE
SIMON-DACH-STRASSE
WÜHLISCH-
STRASSE
LIBAUER STRASSE
SEUME-
GRYPHIUSSTRASSE
STRASSE
GÜRTELSTRASSE
KIETZERWEG
WARSCHAUERSTRASSE
S3-S5-S7-S9-S75
SIMPLONSTRASSE
REVALER
STRASSE
HOLTEI-
SONNTAGSTRASSE
Warschauer Strasse
MÜHLENSTRASSE
Warschauer Strasse
East Side Gallery
WARSCHAUER PL
RUDOLFSTRASSE
RUDOLF-PLATZ
ROTHERSTRASSE
EHRENBERG-STRASSE
DANNECKER-STRASSE
MODERSOHNSTRASSE
Ostkreuz
S5-S7-S75
S3
HAUPTSTRASSE
MARKGRAFENDAMM
KÖPENICKER STRASSE
U1-U12
Schlesisches Tor
STRALAUER ALLEE
CORINTH
STRASSE
PERSIUSSTRASSE
KYNASTSTRASSE
Rummelsburger See
SCHLESISCHE STRASSE
WRANGELSTRASSE
STRASSE
SORAUER STRASSE
OPPELNER
FALCKENSTEINSTRASSE
KREUZBERG
Spree
GÖRLITZER STRASSE
CUVRY-STRASSE
Görlitzer Park
ELSENSTRASSE
S6-S8-S9-S85
ALTSTRALAU TUNNEL
GÖRLITZER UFER
Landwehrkanal
HOFFMANNSTRASSE
WIENER STRASSE
Schlesischer Busch
Treptower Park
RATIBORSTRASSE
KIEFHOLZSTRASSE
BOUCHESTRASSE
PUSCHKIN - ALLEE
LOHMÜHLENSTRASSE
ISINGSTRASSE
KARL-KUNGER STRASSE
TREPTOW
BACHUFER
GRABOWSTR
SCHMOLLER-PLATZ
Treptower Park
0
500 m
0
500 yds
AM TREPTOWER PARK
WEICHSEL-PLATZ
ONCKENSTR
BOUCHESTRASSE
WILDENBRUCHSTRASSE
ELSENSTRASSE
KIEFHOLZSTRASSE
HARZER STRASSE
HEIDELBERGER STRASSE
© Copyright Time Out Guides 2004
FULDASTRASSE
WEIGANDUFER
KIEHLUFER
ELBESTRASSE
WILDENBRUCH-PLATZ
Karpfenteich

Karl-Marx-Allee – communism's answer to the Champs Elysées.

Knaackstrasse, heading south-east from Kollwitzplatz, brings you to one of the district's main landmarks, the **Wasserturm**. This circular water tower, constructed by English architect Henry Gill in 1852-75, provided running water for the first time in Germany. During the war the Nazis used its basement as a prison and torture chamber. A plaque commemorates their victims; the tower has now been converted into apartments. If you want to know more about the district's history, look in at the **Prenzlauer Berg Museum** (*see below*).

The north-west extension of Knaackstrasse from Kollwitzplatz leads to the vast complex of the **Kulturbrauerei**, an old brewery that now houses galleries, artists' studios, a food market and a cinema. South-west of here, the area around Kastanienallee has plenty of good bars, restaurants and shops. And to the north-east, the so-called 'LSD' area around Lychener Strasse, Stargarder Strasse and Dunckerstrasse is another of Prenzlauer Berg's hot spots.

South-west of Kollwitzplatz is the **Jüdischer Friedhof** (Jewish Cemetery), Berlin's oldest, and fairly gloomy due to its closely packed stones and canopy of trees. Close by on Rykestrasse is the **Synagoge Rykestrasse**, a neo-Romanesque turn-of-the-20th-century structure, badly damaged during Kristallnacht (*see p19*) in 1938, and, after repairs in 1953, the only working synagogue in old East Berlin.

Heading north on Prenzlauer Allee, you come to **Ernst-Thälman-Park**, named after the leader of the pre-1933 German Communist Party. In its north-west corner stands the **Zeiss-Grossplanetarium** (*see below*), a fantastic GDR interior space that once hymned Soviet cosmonauts and still runs programmes on what's up there in space.

The **Vitra Design Museum** (www.design-museum.de) on Kopenhagener Strasse recently closed but should reopen at new premises in the Pfefferburg (Schönhauser Allée 176) in 2005.

Prenzlauer Berg Museum

Prenzlauer Allee 227 (4240 1097/www.kulturamt-pankow.de). U2 Senefelderplatz. **Open** 11am-5pm Tue, Wed; 1-7pm Thur; 2-6pm Sun. **Admission** free. **Map** p303 G2.

An interesting museum on the history and culture of the district, with temporary exhibitions.

Zeiss-Grossplanetarium

Prenzlauer Allee 80 (4218 4512/www.astw.de). S4, S8, S85 Prenzlauer Allee. **Open** 8am-noon, 1-3pm Mon-Fri. **Admission** varies. **No credit cards**. **Map** p303 H1.

This vast planetarium was built in the 1980s. Though changing exhibitions are only in German, the shows in the auditorium are entertaining for all.

Friedrichshain

Map p89 & p303

As Prenzlauer Berg and Mitte became gentrified, Berlin's bohemia edged south-east into Friedrichshain. It's convenient for the centre and the incoming trains at Ostbahnhof, and the next step for an eastward-growing city.

That said, much of Friedrichshain is pretty bleak, dominated as it is by big Communist-era housing blocks – more than half of its buildings were destroyed during World War II. Originally known as Stralau, this was historically a largely industrial district, with Berlin's central wheat and rye mill, its first hospital, and Osthaven, its eastern port. Much of its southern portion bordering the Spree contains the remains of industrial buildings.

On the waterfront

If it weren't for the water, there wouldn't be Berlin. The city grew out of swampy outposts on either side of the Spree some 800 years ago, and ever since then, this unspectacular workhorse of a river has served the city silently, diligently and, packed with slithering eels, without a trace of self-consciousness.

It is an industrial river. The Spree transported raw materials to Berlin's 19th-century factories and carried their finished goods to market. Connecting with the Havel river to the west, the Spree is part of a 200-kilometre (124 miles) urban waterway network, unique in central Europe.

Following the fall of the Berlin Wall, and the subsequent de-industrialisation of East Berlin, the scrappy Spree is being reinvented. Planners and architects put the river at the centre of a couple of Berlin's six official 'development areas', hoping to attract big-time investors and home buyers alike.

The most ambitious project is on the stretch of Spree that divides Kreuzberg and Friedrichshain, at sites which used to form a border between East and West Berlin. It includes the Osthafen (East Harbour) with its derelict warehouses and wharfs, and a greener residential area around Rummelsburg Bay, where the city envisions town houses, floating homes and offices. Think London's Docklands, and divide by three.

In many ways, the area has already been discovered. The approach here from the river to downtown, impossible for anyone but barge captains when the Wall was up, affords the only view of the city's skyline anywhere. The twin-peaked Oberbaumbrücke, spanning the river between the Schlesisches Tor and Warschauer Strasse U-Bahn stations, has been redesigned by Santiago Calatrava. The next bridge up, Schillingbrücke, is the new home of Maria am Ufer, a top electronic music dance club (*see p220*). To the south, at the tip of Treptower Park, is the Arena (*see p218*), a cavernous concert venue, formerly a garage for East Berlin's buses. After-gig parties often take place on the MS *Hoppetosse*, a docked riverboat with dance floors and two bars. Close by, on either side of a narrow inlet called the Flutgraben, are Verein der Visionare and Freischwimmer, popular waterside cafés in summer.

On the Friedrichshain side, one of the first retrofitted warehouses in the Osthafen is the new home of Universal Music in Germany. The company was lured out of Hamburg not so much by waterfront views or proximity to Berlin's vibrant underground, but by the large subsidies that come with the harbour's status as an EU investment area. Ditto for MTV-Europe's German operation, which moved here from Munich in spring 2004.

That's liable to be it though, for now. Berlin's lack of an international airport and infrastructural deficiencies are holding back the investment necessary to transform the Spree from a 19th-century logistical asset into a 21st-century lifestyle attraction.

There is an agglomeration of bars, clubs, restaurants and natural food stores on Simon-Dach-Strasse and nearby streets. North of Frankfurter Allee is another concentration of hangouts in the Rigaer Strasse area.

The best way to get a feeling for both Friedrichshain and the old GDR is to walk east from Alexanderplatz down Karl-Marx-Allee. The Kino International (No.33) gives hints, but it's only at Lichtenberger Strasse that the street truly shows its socialist past, with endless rows of Soviet-style apartment blocks, stretching as far as Proskauer Strasse. The **Internationales Berliner Bierfestival** (*see p184*) is held on the street every August, a good time to see the neighbourhood come out in force.

To the south, on Mühlenstrasse (the name means 'Mill Street'; the old mill is at No.8) along the north bank of the Spree is the **East Side Gallery**, a stretch of former Wall given over to international artists. The industrial buildings here have been renovated and rechristened Oberbaum City, and are now home to loft spaces, offices and studios. Confirming the area's hipness, the International Design Zentrum (IDZ) has moved here. Property development is now big business; if the new international airport is built south of the city, Friedrichshain's riverside is likely to blossom further. *See above* **On the waterfront**.

There are no tourist attractions, but green relief can be found in the district's north-west corner in the **Volkspark Friedrichshain**. This huge park is scattered with socialist realist art, and has a couple of hills, an open-air stage, a fountain of fairy-tale characters and the popular Café Schönbrunn (*see p152*). The graves of fighters who fell in March 1848 in the battle for German unity are here. It's also a popular gay cruising zone.

Kreuzberg & Schöneberg

Ethnically mixed neighbourhoods, a variety of nightlife, interesting museums, decent dining and the hub of gay Berlin.

Bordering Mitte to the south is the district of Kreuzberg. Though now administratively joined to Friedrichshain across the Spree, it maintains the independence of spirit that drew so many hippies, punks and other seekers of alternative lifestyle in the 1970s and 1980s. Many of these have moved on, many of the rest have grown up, and Kreuzberg is now better known for its sizeable Turkish community and relaxed and varied nightlife. To its west lies the wealthier, largely residential district of Schöneberg. Much of Berlin's irrepressible gay life is focused in its northern reaches.

Kreuzberg

Map p306 & p307

Back in November 1994, one of the last Kreuzberg demonstrations attempted to prevent the opening of the Oberbaumbrücke to motor traffic. During the Cold War, this bridge over the Spree was a border post and spy-exchange venue. Only pedestrians could cross. Its renovation by Santiago Calatrava and its opening to traffic was effectively the fall of one of the last pieces of the Wall. But it was also the fall of the Kreuzberg of old.

East Kreuzberg

In the 1970s and 1980s, the eastern half of Kreuzberg north of the Landwehrkanal was off at the edge of inner West Berlin. Enclosed on two sides by the Wall, on a third by the canal, and mostly ignored by the rest of the city, its

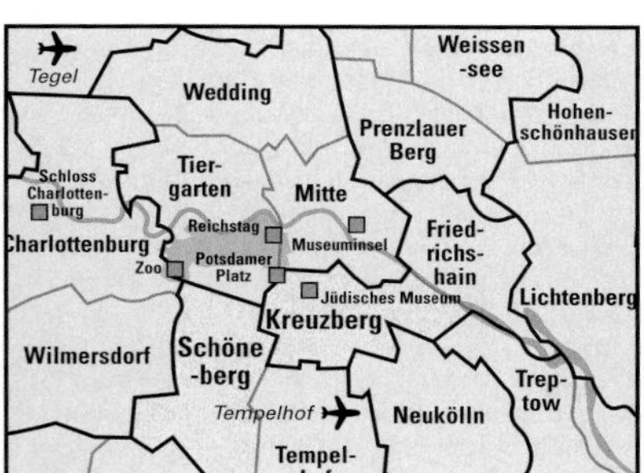

decaying tenements came to house Berlin's biggest, and most militant, squat community. The area was full of punky left-wing youth on a draft-dodging mission and Turks who came here because the rents were cheap and people mostly left them alone.

No area of west Berlin has changed quite so much since the Wall came down. This once-isolated pocket found itself recast as desirable real estate. Much of the alternative art scene shifted north to the Scheunenviertel in Mitte, and even the May Day Riots – long an annual Kreuzberg tradition (*see p182*) – began taking place in Prenzlauer Berg.

Oddly enough, gentrification never really took off in this end of Kreuzberg, but it did so in Prenzl'berg, and now the riots have moved back. Though Kreuzberg is no longer a magnet for young bohemia, enough of the anarchistic old guard stayed behind to ensure that the area still has a distinct atmosphere. It's an earthy kind of place, full of cafés, bars and clubs, dotted with independent cinemas, and is an important nexus for the city's gay community.

And it's still the capital of Turkish Berlin, the world's fifth-largest Turkish city. The scruffy area around Kottbusser Tor bustles with kebab shops and Anatolian travel agents. The open-air **Türkischer Markt** (*see p176*) stretches along the Maybachufer every Tuesday and Friday. **Görlitzer Park**, once an important train station, turns into a huge Turkish barbecue on fine weekends.

Oranienstrasse is the area's main drag, dotted with bars and clubs, and the blocks to the north and west of here are home to even more places to booze and boogie. South across Skalitzer Strasse, Oranienstrasse changes into Wiener Strasse, running alongside the old Görlitzer Bahnhof, where more bars and cafés welcome what's left of the Kreuzberg crowd. A couple of blocks further south lies Paul-Linke-Ufer, lined with canal-bank cafés that provide a favourite spot for weekend brunch.

The U1 line runs overhead through the neighbourhood along the middle of Skalitzer Strasse. The onion-domed Schlesisches Tor station was once the end of the line. These days the train continues one more stop across the Spree to Warschauer Strasse. You can also walk across the Oberbaumbrücke into Friedrichshain and the post-industrial nightlife district around Mühlenstrasse. But nowadays traffic is also coming the other way. Courtesy of riverside development on the Spree (*see p90* **On the waterfront**), and simply of an overspill from Friedrichshain, the area around Schlesisches Tor station and along Schlesische Strasse towards Treptow is Berlin's newest hot spot. Cafés and bars are opening up, property prices are soaring, and Kreuzberg looks to be regaining some of its old atmosphere.

Schlesische Strasse leads over the canal and into the borough of Treptow. There are several cafés and venues along Puschkinallee and **Treptower Park**, with its **Sowjetisches Ehrenmal** (Soviet War Memorial), lies beyond.

South-west Kreuzberg

The southern and western part of Kreuzberg contains some of the most picturesque corners of west Berlin, including the 'cross hill' (the

Home for 'Heroes'

Someday they'll put up a plaque outside Hauptstrasse 155 in Schöneberg, where David Bowie kept an apartment in 1976-78. Iggy Pop also lived at the same unglamorous address – first as Bowie's lodger, later in his own small Hinterhof flat.

Like many who washed up on the geopolitical island that was West Berlin, the pair were seeking refuge. But where others came to dodge the draft, escape poverty or oppression, Bowie and Iggy were running from from the drug-fuelled celebrity culture of glitter-era Los Angeles. Bowie had spent a year strung out on cocaine and dabbling in diabolism. Iggy sank so low that he checked himself into LA's Neuropsychiatric Institute, from where Bowie hauled him off on the spring 1976 Station to Station tour. Producer Tony Visconti later reckoned that the two had made 'some kind of pact to get healthy'.

Bowie and Iggy passed through Berlin in April. There were reports of Nazi literature found in Bowie's luggage at the Soviet border. In Stockholm he allegedly told a journalist that 'Britain could benefit from a Fascist leader'. On 2 May there was the famous 'Hitler salute' as Bowie arrived at London's Victoria station. Though the fascination with fascism would soon run its course, no one was terribly surprised when that autumn Bowie was discovered living in Schöneberg.

The peace and isolation of West Berlin suited a Bowie determined to keep a 'low' profile. Reports found him revelling in the ordinary: reading in the local library, looking at Expressionist paintings, dining at Exil in Kreuzberg. But this was also an extraordinarily productive period. With *Low* and *'Heroes'*, Bowie not only made the two most original and influential albums of his career, but also redirected the Berlin myth from colourful decadence to romantic desolation. The stillness and melancholy of pieces such as 'Neuköln' or 'Weeping Wall' really did finger one aspect of Cold War Berlin. 'Heroes' fingered another: the defiance of everyday humanity against politics written in concrete and barbed wire.

Bowie also produced and co-wrote Iggy's *The Idiot* and *Lust For Life*, two classic, career-reviving albums. Here too Berlin can be heard in the ghostly revellers of 'Nightclubbing' or the 'city's ripped back sides' of 'The Passenger', evoking Iggy's roaming on the S-Bahn system. The thunderous drum pattern of 'Lust For Life' originated in the morse-code theme tune of an AFN news show, heard in the kitchen at Hauptstrasse and transcribed on a ukelele.

Little is left of the West Berlin that Iggy and Bowie inhabited. The bars and restaurants are mostly gone, save for what is now **Neues Ufer** (*see p207*), then Café Nemesis, where Bowie often breakfasted, and the **Pinguin Club** (*see p155*), which Bowie knew in its earlier incarnation as Harlekin. The **Brücke Museum** (*see p116*) was where Bowie fell in love with the paintings of Erich Heckel and derived inspiration for the covers of both *The Idiot* and *'Heroes'*. And what used to be Hansa Studio 2, where *'Heroes'* and *Lust For Life* were recorded, now hosts classical concerts as the **Meistersaal** (*see p239*).

Iggy would stick around a bit longer, and Schöneberg would later host the scene that included Nick Cave and Einstürzende Neubauten, but Bowie was gone by mid 1978. His appearance in David Hemmings' *Just A Gigolo* (some of it shot in Riehmer's Hofgarten; *see p93*) is best forgotten; while his concert performance in *Christiane F.* was actually shot in New York. In 1981 he returned once more to Hansa to record his wonderful interpretations of the songs from Bertolt Brecht's *Baal*, for the BBC production in which he took the title role.

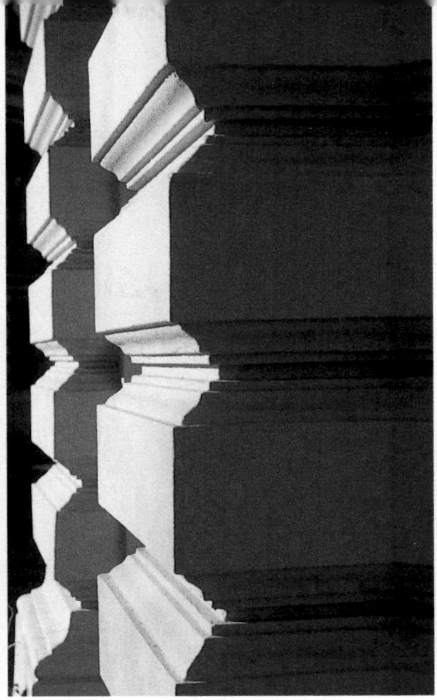

Riehmers Hofgarten is one of Berlin's most picturesque courtyard complexes.

literal meaning of 'Kreuzberg') in Viktoriapark after which the borough is named.

Viktoriapark is the natural way to enter the area. In summer it has a cheery, fake waterfall cascading down the Kreuzberg, and paths wind their way to the summit, where Schinkel's 1821 monument commemorates victories in the Napoleonic Wars – many of the streets nearby are named after battles and generals of that era. From this commanding view over a mainly flat city, the landmarks of both east and west spread out before you: Friedrichstrasse dead ahead, the Europa-Center off to the left, the Potsdamer Platz high-rises in between, the Fernsehturm over to the right. The view is clearer in winter, when the trees are bare.

Back on ground level, the streets north of the park lead to one of Berlin's most picturesque courtyard complexes. Riehmers Hofgarten is cobbled, closed to traffic and often used as a film location for its 19th-century feel. It's also home to one of Berlin's nicest small hotels, the **Hotel Riehmers Hofgarten** (*see p57*).

Around the corner on Mehringdamm is the **Schwules Museum** (Gay Museum; *see p96*). Bergmannstrasse, which runs to the east from here, is the main hub of local activity. Bucking the tendency for everything to move eastwards, this street of cafés and junk shops, grocery stores and record shops is livelier than ever by day, although the area is relatively lacklustre at night. It leads down to Marheinekeplatz, site of one of Berlin's busiest market halls. Zossener Strasse (north from here) also bustles.

Bergmannstrasse continues east to Südstern, past a large cemetery, and eventually comes to the **Volkspark Hasenheide**, the other of the neighbourhood's large parks, with another good view from atop the Rixdorfer Höhe.

The streets just south of Bergmannstrasse are like another movie set. Many buildings survived wartime bombing and the area around Chamissoplatz has been immaculately restored. The cobbled streets are lined with houses still sporting their Prussian façades and illuminated by gaslight at night. This is one of the most beautiful parts of this largely unbeautiful city.

South of here, just across the border into the borough of the same name, stands the enormous **Tempelhof Airport**. Once the central airport for the city, it was begun in the 1920s and later greatly expanded by the Nazis. The largest building in Berlin – and one of the largest in the world – its curving bulk looms with an authoritarian ominousness.

Tempelhof Airport was where German national carrier Lufthansa started, but its place in the city's affections was cemented during the Airlift of 1948-9, when it served as the base for the 'raisin-bombers', which flew in and out at a rate of one a minute, bringing supplies to the blockaded city and tossing sweets and raisins to waiting kids. The monument forking towards the sky on Platz der Luftbrücke commemorates

Schwules Museum. *See p96.*

those who flew these missions, as does a photo-realist painting in the terminal. In the early 1970s, Tempelhof became the US Air Force base in Berlin. Today, it's once more a civil airport catering to small airlines running small planes on short-hop European routes.

This facility uses only a tiny fraction of the Tempelhof's enormous structure, some parts of which have been converted into entertainment venues, such as the **La Vie en Rose** cabaret (*see p232*). On the other side of Columbiadamm are the **Columbiahalle** and **ColumbiaFritz** concert venues (for both, *see p219*). The latter was built by the US Air Force as a cinema for use by their personnel, and is a classic example of 1950s cinema architecture.

North-west Kreuzberg

The north-west portion of Kreuzberg, bordering Mitte, is where you will find most of the area's museums and tourist sights. The most prominent is the extraordinary **Jüdisches Museum** (*see p95*) on Lindenstrasse, an example of architecture at its most cerebral and a powerful sensory experience. West of here, close to the Landswehrkanal, is the quirky and enjoyable **Deutsches Technikmuseum Berlin** (German Museum of Technology; *see p95*).

Over the canal to the north is the site of **Anhalter Bahnhof**, once the city's biggest and busiest railway station. Only a tiny piece of façade remains, preserved in its bombed state near the S-Bahn station that bears its name. The **Grusel Kabinett** (*see p95*), a chamber of horrors, occupies an old air-raid shelter on the Schöneberger Strasse side of the area where platforms and tracks once stood. The **Tempodrom** venue (*see p220*) and its **Liquidrom** (*see p253*) sauna complex are opposite on Möckernstrasse.

On Stresemannstrasse, the Bauhaus-designed **Europahaus** was heavily bombed during World War II, but the lower storeys remain. Nearby, on the north side of the street, Berlin's parliament, the **Abgeordnetenhaus von Berlin** (Berlin House of Representatives), meets in what was formerly the Prussian parliament. Dating from the 1890s, the building was renovated in the early 1990s. Opposite stands the **Martin-Gropius-Bau** (*see p95*), a venue for major art shows. The building was modelled on London's South Kensington museums – the figures of craftspeople on the external reliefs betray its origins as an applied arts museum.

Next to it is a deserted patch of ground that once held the Prinz Albrecht Palais, which the Gestapo took over as its headquarters. In the basement's 39 cells, political prisoners were held, interrogated and tortured. The land was flattened after the war. In 1985, during an acrimonious debate over the design of a memorial to be placed here, a group of citizens and staged a symbolic 'excavation'. To their surprise, they hit the Gestapo's basement, and plans were then made to reclaim the site. Today, the **Topographie des Terrors** (*see p96*) exhibition is undergoing renovation and a document centre is due to open in 2007. Along the site's northern boundary is one of the few remaining stretches of the **Berlin Wall**, pitted and threadbare after thousands of 1990 souvenir-hunters pecked away at it with hammers and chisels.

From here, it's a short walk down Kochstrasse – once Berlin's Fleet Street – to Friedrichstrasse, where Checkpoint Charlie once stood and where the **Haus am Checkpoint Charlie** (*see below*) documents the history of the Wall. Most of the space where the border post once stood has been claimed by new buildings. The actual site of the borderline itself is memorialised by Frank Thiel's photographic portraits of an American and a Soviet soldier. The small white building that served as gateway between East and West is now in the **Alliierten Museum** (*see p116*) – the one in the middle of the street is a replica.

Deutsches Technikmuseum Berlin

Trebbiner Strasse 9 (902 540/www.dtmb.de). U1, U7, U15 Möckernbrücke. **Open** 9am-5.30pm Tue-Fri; 10am-6pm Sat, Sun. **Admission** €4.50; €2.50 concessions. **Map** p306 E5.

Opened in 1983 in the former goods depot of the once-thriving Anhalter Bahnhof, the German Museum of Technology is a quirky collection of industrial objects. The rail exhibits have pride of place, with the station sheds providing an ideal setting for locomotives and rolling stock from 1835 to the present. Also on view are exhibitions about the industrial revolution; street, rail, water and air traffic; computer technology and printing technology. Behind the main complex is an open-air section with two functioning windmills and a smithy. Oddities, such as vacuum cleaners from the 1920s, make this a fun place for implement enthusiasts. The Spectrum annex, in an old railway administrative building at Möckernstrasse 26, houses 200 interactive devices and experiments. In late 2003, the Maritime wing was opened with vessels and displays on both inland waterways and international shipping. A similar section that will focus on aircraft and space travel is scheduled to open in early 2005.

Grusel Kabinett

Schöneberger Strasse 23A (2655 5546). S1, S2 Anhalter Bahnhof. **Open** 10am-7pm Mon-Tue, Thur, Sun; 10am-8pm Fri; noon-8pm Sat. **Admission** €7; €5 concessions. **No credit cards**. **Map** p306 F4.

This 'Chamber of Horrors' is housed in the city's only visitable World War II air-raid shelter. Built in 1943, the five-level bunker was part of an underground network connecting various similar concrete structures throughout Berlin, and today houses both the Grusel Kabinett and an exhibit on the bunker itself. The latter includes a few personal effects found here after the war and a video documentary in German only. The actual structure is the most interesting thing. The 'horrors' begin at ground level with an exhibit on medieval medicine (mechanical figures amputate a leg to the sound of canned screaming). Elsewhere there's a patented coffin designed to advertise your predicament should you happen to be buried alive. Upstairs is scarier: a musty labyrinth with a simulated cemetery, strange cloaked figures, lots of spooky sounds and a few surprises. Kids love it, but not those under ten.

Martin-Gropius-Bau

Niederkirchnerstrasse 7 (254 860/www.martin gropiusbau.de). S1, S2, S25, S26 Anhalter Bahnhof. **Open** varies. **Admission** varies. **Credit** AmEx, MC, V. **Map** p306 F4.

Cosying up to where the Wall once ran (there is still a short, pitted stretch running along the south side of nearby Niederkirchnerstrasse), the Martin-Gropius-Bau is named after its architect, uncle of the more famous Walter. Built in 1881, it has been renovated and serves as a venue for large-scale art exhibitions and touring shows, for which it is ideal. Recent exhibitions have included a Canadian photography retrospective and a selection of winners of the Gabriel Munter Prize. It's also a venue for the Berlin Biennale. No permanent exhibition.

Haus am Checkpoint Charlie

Friedrichstrasse 43-5 (253 7250). U6 Kochstrasse. **Open** 9am-10pm daily. **Admission** €7.50; €4.50 concessions. **No credit cards**. **Map** p306 F4.

A little tacky, but essential for anyone interested in the Wall and the Cold War. This private museum opened not long after the GDR erected the Berlin Wall in 1961 with the purpose of documenting the events that were taking place. The exhibition charts the history of the Wall, and gives details of the ingenious and hair-raising ways people escaped from the GDR – as well as exhibiting some of the contraptions that were used, such as suitcases and a weird car with a propeller.

Jüdisches Museum

Lindenstrasse 9-14 (2599 3300/guided tours 2599 3333/www.jmberlin.de). U1, U6, U15 Hallesches Tor. **Open** 10am-10pm Mon; 10am-8pm Tue-Sun. Closed Jewish holidays & Christmas Eve. **Admission** €5; €2.50 concessions; family ticket €10. **No credit cards**. **Map** p306 F4.

The idea of a Jewish museum in Berlin was first mooted in 1971, 300th birthday of the city's Jewish community. In 1975 an association was formed to acquire materials for eventual display. In 1989, the Jewish Department of the Berlin Museum held a competition for designs for an extension to house these materials. Daniel Libeskind emerged as the winner, the foundation stone was laid in 1992, the building was completed in 1998, and on 9 September 2001, the permanent exhibition finally opened.

The ground plan of Libeskind's remarkable building is in part based on an exploded Star of David, in part on lines drawn between the site and former addresses of figures in Berlin's Jewish history, such as Mies van der Rohe, Arnold Schönberg and Walter

Benjamin. The entrance is via a tunnel from the Kollegienhaus next door. The underground geometry is startlingly independent of the above-ground building. One passage leads to the exhibition halls, two others intersect en route to the Holocaust Tower and the ETA Hoffmann Garden, a grid of 49 columns, tilted to disorientate. Throughout, diagonals and parallels carve out surprising spaces, while windows slash through the structure and its zinc cladding like the knife-wounds of history. And then there are the 'voids' cutting through the layout, negative spaces that can be viewed or crossed but not entered, standing for the emptiness left by the destruction of German Jewish culture.

The permanent exhibition struggles at times with such powerful surroundings. And the problem with telling the story of German Jewish history is that we all know only too well what it was leading up to. What makes the exhibit engaging is its focus on the personal. It tells the stories of prominent Jews, what they contributed to their community and to the cultural and economic life of Berlin and Germany. After centuries of prejudice and pogroms, the outlook for German Jews seemed to be brightening and full civil equality had been achieved under the Weimar Republic. Then came the Holocaust. This part of the exhibit is the most harrowing. The emotional impact of countless stories of the eminent and ordinary, and the fate that almost all shared, is hard to convey adequately in print.

The museum is a must-see, but expect long queues and big crowds. Last entrance is one hour before closing. From September 2004 to January 2005 there's an exhibition on 'Fashioning the Family'; from May 2005, another on 'Jewish Identity in Contemporary Architecture'.

Schwules Museum

Mehringdamm 61 (6959 9050/www. schwulesmuseum.de). U6, U7 Mehringdamm. **Open** 2-6pm Mon, Wed-Sun. Tours 5pm Sat. **Admission** €5; €3 concessions. **No credit cards**. **Map** p306 F5.

The Gay Museum, opened in 1985, is still the only one in the world dedicated to the research and public exhibition of homosexual life in all of its forms. The museum, its library and archives are staffed by volunteers and function thanks to private donations and bequests (such as the archive of GDR sex scientist Rudolf Klimmer). On the ground floor is the actual museum, housing temporary exhibitions. The library and archives are on the third floor. Here are around 8,000 books (around 500 in English), 3,000 international periodicals, collections of photos, posters, plus TV, film and audio footage, all available for lending. Information is available in English.

Topographie des Terrors

Niederkirchnerstrasse 8 (2548 6703/www. topographie.de). S1, S2, S25, S26 Anhalter Bahnhof. **Open** *Oct-Apr* 10am-dusk daily. *May-Sept* 10am-8pm daily. **Admission** free. **Map** p306 F4.

Essentially a piece of waste ground where once stood the Prinz Albrecht Palais, headquarters of the Gestapo. It was from here that the Holocaust was directed, and where the Germanisation of the east was dreamt up. You can walk around – small markers explain what was where – before examining the exhibit documenting the history of Nazi state terror. This is in some former basement cells of the Gestapo complex. The catalogue (available in English) is excellent. A surviving segment of the Berlin Wall runs along the northern boundary of the site. When the new building complex and documentation centre are completed in 2007, the entire site will be open to the public and there will be four different exhibition areas. Call to arrange tours in English.

Schöneberg

Map p305 & p306

Both geographically and atmospherically, Schöneberg lies between Kreuzberg and Charlottenburg. It's a diverse and vibrant part of town, mostly built in the late 19th century. Though largely devoid of conventional sights, Schöneberg is rich in reminders of Berlin's recent history.

Schöneberg means 'beautiful hill' – oddly, because the borough is flat. It does have an 'island', though: the triangular **Schöneberger Insel**, carved out by the two broad railway cuttings that carry S-Bahn line 1 and lines 2, 25 and 26, with an elevated stretch of line S4, 45 and 46 providing the southern boundary. In the 1930s the areas was known as Rote Insel ('Red Island'), because, approached mostly over bridges and thus easy to defend, it was one of the last bits of Berlin to resist Nazification. There's a fine view of central east Berlin from Monumentenbrücke, on the east side of the island going towards Kreuzberg's Viktoriapark. On the north-west edge of the island is **St Matthäus-Kirchhof**, a large graveyard and last resting place of the Brothers Grimm.

West along Langenscheidtstrasse – named after the dictionary publishers whose offices stand close by– leads you towards the Kleistpark. Here Schöneberg's main street is called Hauptstrasse to the south and Potsdamer Strasse to the north. Hauptstrasse leads south-west in the direction of Potsdam. David Bowie and Iggy Pop once resided at No.155 (*see p92* **Home for 'Heroes'**). Further south, **Dominicuskirche** is one of Berlin's few baroque churches.

North-west along Dominicusstrasse is **Rathaus Schöneberg**, outside of which John F Kennedy made his famous 'Ich bin ein Berliner' speech. The square now bears Kennedy's name. This was the West Berlin's town hall during the Cold War, and the place where mayor Walter Momper welcomed East Berliners in 1989.

Winterfeldtplatz market – bustle and 'bio' produce every Wednesday and Saturday.

From here, Belziger Strasse leads back towards **Kleistpark**. The entrance on Potsdamer Strasse is an 18th-century double colonnade, moved here from near Alexanderplatz in 1910. The mansion in the park was originally a law court, and during the Cold War became headquarters for the Allied Control Council. After the 1972 treaty which formalised the separate status of East and West Germany, the building stood virtually unused. But there were occasional Allied Council meetings, before which the Americans, British and French would observe a ritual pause, as if expecting the Soviet representative, who had last attended in 1948, to show up. In 1990 a Soviet finally did wander in and the Allies held a last meeting to formalise their withdrawal from the city in 1994. This may be the place where the Cold War officially ended.

On the north-west corner of Potsdamer Strasse's intersection with Pallasstrasse stood the **Sportpalast**, site of many Nazi rallies and the scene of Goebbels' famous 'Total War' speech of 18 February 1943. West along Pallasstrasse is a block of flats straddling the road and resting on top of the huge hulk of a concrete Nazi air-raid shelter, which planners were unable to destroy. This featured in Wim Wenders' 1987 film *Wings of Desire*.

At the west end of Pallasstrasse stands **St-Matthias-Kirche**. South from here, Goltzstrasse is lined with cafés, bars and interesting shops. To the north of the church is **Winterfeldtplatz**, site of bustling Wednesday and Saturday morning markets, engendering a particularly lively café life. Winterfeldtstrasse has many antiquarian bookshops and at night the area is alive with bars and restaurants.

Nollendorfplatz, to the north is the hub of Schöneberg's nightlife. Outside Nollendorfplatz U-Bahn, the memorial to the homosexuals killed in concentration camps is a reminder of the area's history. Christopher Isherwood chronicled Berlin from his rooming house at Nollendorfstrasse 17; Motzstrasse is a major centre of Berlin's gay life. Gay Schöneberg continues around the corner and across Martin-Luther-Strasse into Fuggerstrasse.

Schöneberg's most famous daughter is screen icon Marlene Dietrich, now buried just over the district's southern boundary, in the tiny **Friedhof Friedenau** on Fehlerstrasse (*see map p305 C6*).

Tiergarten

Berlin's central park is fringed with government buildings, embassies and heavyweight cultural attractions.

The huge green swathe of the Tiergarten park dominates and gives its name to this district. The Wall once ran along its eastern side, but now Tiergarten once again forms the link between Mitte and Charlottenburg, the park stretching from the Reichstag in the north-east to the Zoo in the south-west. Along the park's northern boundary the Spree meanders (above this is the largely residential area of Moabit), while south of the park is a host of cultural, architectural and commercial attractions, including the reborn Potsdamer Platz and the museums and galleries of the Kulturforum.

The park & the Reichstag

Map p301 p302, p305, p306 & p316

A hunting ground for the Prussian electors since the 16th century, Tiergarten, the park that stretches west from the Brandenburg Gate, was opened to the public in the 18th century. During the war it was badly damaged, and, in the desperate winter of 1945-6, almost all the surviving trees were cut down for firewood. It wasn't until 1949 that Tiergarten started to recover – towns from all over Germany donated trees (as did Queen Elizabeth II) and are commemorated by an inscribed stone on the Grosser Weg, a large path that snakes through the park. Today, joggers, nature lovers, gay cruisers and picnickers pour into the park in fine weather, yet its 167 hectares (412 acres), much of which feels quite wild, rarely seem crowded. There is no nicer place from which to appreciate it all than the gardens of the Café am Neuen See on Lichtensteinallee (*see p156*).

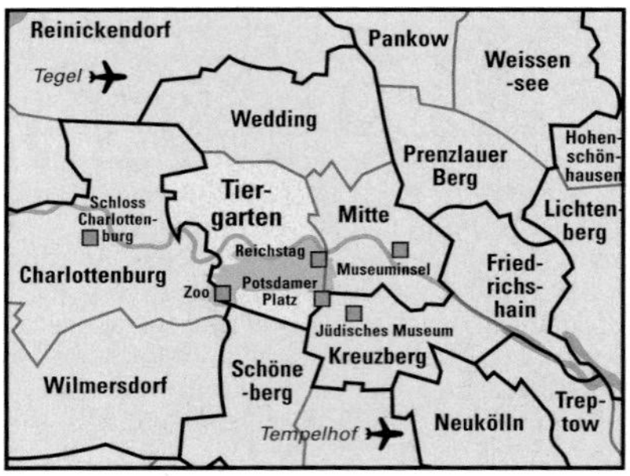

All roads entering Tiergarten lead to the park's largest monument, the **Siegessäule** (Victory Column; *see p100*), which celebrates late 19th-century Prussian military victories. The park's main thoroughfare, Strasse des 17.Juni (named after the date of the East Berlin workers' strike of 1953) is one of the few pieces of Hitler's plan for 'Germania' that actually got built – a grand east–west axis, lined with Nazi lampposts, and linking Unter den Linden to Neu-Westend. The Siegessäule was moved here from its original position in front of the Reichstag.

Towards the eastern end of Strasse des 17.Juni stands the **Sowjetisches Ehrenmal** (Soviet War Memorial). Once the only piece of Soviet property in West Berlin, it was built in 1945-6 out of granite and marble from the ruins of Hitler's Neue Reichskanzlei and posed something of a political problem. Standing in the British Zone, it was surrounded by a British military enclosure, which was in turn guarded by the Berlin police, and all to protect the monument and the two Soviet soldiers who stood 24-hour guard there. The tanks flanking the monument are said to have been the first two Soviet tanks into Berlin, but this is probably just legend.

At the north-eastern corner of the park, just north of the Brandenburger Tor (*see p71*), stands the **Reichstag** (*see p100*). Described by Kaiser Wilhelm II as the 'Imperial Monkey House', scene of unseemly Weimar squabblings, left as a burnt-out ruin during the Third Reich, regarded by the Red Army as its main prize, and stranded for forlorn decades beside the Wall that divided the Deutsches Volk whose representatives it was intended to house, the Reichstag hasn't exactly had a happy history.

In 1995, the artist Christo wrapped it in aluminium-coated fabric, drawing a somewhat ironic line under all that, and then in 1999, Sir Norman Foster's brilliant refitting of the building was unveiled to the public. His crowning achievement is the new glass cupola – a trip up to the top should be a must-do on any visitor's agenda.

When the decision was made in 1991 to make Berlin the German capital, the area north of the Reichstag was picked as the central location for new government buildings. Designed by Axel Schultes and Charlotte Frank, the immense

An angel over Berlin – the **Siegessäule**. *See p100.*

Spreebogen complex, also known as the **Band des Bundes**, is built over a twist in the River Spree (Bogen means 'bend'). It crosses the river twice and the old east-west border once, symbolising the reunion of Berlin. The most notable building in the new complex is Schultes and Frank's Bundeskanzleramt (Federal Chancellery).

South of that building's western end is the **Haus der Kulturen der Welt** (*see below*; formerly the Kongresshalle), an impressive piece of modern architecture whose reflecting pool contains a Henry Moore sculpture. Formerly known as the Kongresshalle, the HdKdW was designed by Hugh Stubbins. A gift from the Americans, and known to the locals as the 'pregnant oyster', it opened in 1957, and its roof collapsed in 1980 – an event that gave the name to one of Berlin's best-known bands, Einstürzende Neubauten ('collapsing new buildings'). Today, it hosts exhibits from cultures around the world.

Also on the park's northern boundaries, further west, stands **Schloss Bellevue**, a minor palace from 1785, now home to the German President when he's in town (his presence is indicated by a flag flying on the roof). His employees work next door in a new elliptical office building, hidden from the street.

Across the river, a serpentine 718-apartment residence for Federal employees, nicknamed **'Die Schlange'** (the Snake), winds its way across land formerly used as a goods yard.

West of Schloss Bellevue is the **Englischer Garten**, which got laid out after King Ludwig I of Bavaria decided that the lack of revolutions in England was due to the abundance of open green spaces in the cities. The idea caught on, and these gardens became such an integral part of German life that Lenin once commented that revolution in Germany was impossible because it would require people to step on the grass.

Just north of here the **Akademie der Künste** (*see p238*) offers an impressively varied programme of arts events and classical concerts. The district between the Akademie and the loop of the Spree is known as the **Hansaviertel**, a post-war housing project whose buildings were designed by a Who's Who of architects. This complex is a source of great interest to specialists, but others may see little more than a group of sterile-looking modernist slabs.

Haus der Kulturen der Welt

John-Foster-Dulles-Allee 10 (397 870). S3, S5, S7, S9, S75 Bellevue/bus 100. **Open** 10am-9pm Tue-Sun. **Admission** varies. **No credit cards**.
Map p302 E3.

Funded by the Federal government and the Berlin Senate, the 'House of World Cultures' was set up in 1989 to promote artists from developing countries, mounting spectacular large-scale exhibitions such as contemporary Indian art, Bedouin culture or the Chinese avant-garde. One recent show featured contemporary Iranian artists. Black Atlantic (Sep-Nov 2004) is about diaspora art. The HdKdW's programme also involves film festivals, readings, lectures, discussions, concerts and dance performances. Hugh Stubbins' oyster-like building was erected in 1957 as America's contribution to Berlin's first international building exhibition. A unique Berlin cultural institution. Decent café too.

Pillars of publicity

On the cover of children's classic *Emil and the Detectives*, two boys hide behind one. In *The Third Man*, Orson Welles makes his entrance from inside another. In Berlin, these tall advertising columns, festooned with posters, are almost as ubiquitous as lampposts – and often almost as invisible.

The German for one of these things is *Litfasssäule* – *Säule* meaning 'column' and Litfass being the name of he who invented this primitive advertising vehicle. And on 5 December 2004, the *Litfasssäule* celebrates its 150th anniversary. It was on this day in 1854 that Ernst Litfass, a book printer, distressed at slapdash posters on walls but also with an eye for a profit, negotiated the right to erect 100 prototypical *Litfasssäulen* all over Berlin. Litfass set up a further 50 in 1865, and retained a lucrative monopoly on sales of poster space until 1880.

But they weren't only used for advertising. There was space for public notices, and during the Franco-Prussian War they were first used for war telegrams. They also found double usage as housing for electrical or phone switches. Soon they spread beyond Berlin and today can be found all over continental Europe. There are reckoned to be 100,000 in Germany alone.

Back in their home town, once you start noticing them, a whole history of Berlin is written in the language of the *Litfasssäule* – from crenellated 19th-century towers in traditional dark green, to silvery postmodern numbers topped with a nut-and-bolt motif. These cunning cylinders are trying all sorts of tricks to keep up with the information age. Many recent ones revolve and are backlit.

On the Gendarmenmarkt, near the Französische Dom (*see p81*), the Wall company (one of several that run Berlin's *Litfasssäule* racket) is demonstrating a new prototype. From a central light source in the roof via an integrated reflector system the entire exterior structure is evenly and economically illuminated. The *Litfasssäule*, Wall claims, is the perfect advertising medium for small businesses and cultural enterprises. Other *Litfasssäule* companies seem more interested in tobacco money. Either way, it's clear that these pillars of publicity are far from dead yet.

The most garish new *Litfasssäulen* can be found around Potsdamer Platz. The old streets of Prenzlauer Berg are good for models of an earlier vintage. Children may enjoy the board game, *Emil and the Litfasssäule Labyrinth*.

Reichstag

Platz der Republik (2270). S1, S2, S25, S26 Unter den Linden/bus 100. **Open** *Dome* 8am-midnight daily; last entry 10pm. **Admission** free. **Map** p316/p302 E3.

The hugely imposing Reichstag was controversial from the very beginning. Architect Paul Wallot struggled to find a style that would symbolise German national identity at a time – 1884-94, shortly after Unification – when no such style (or identity) existed. It was burned on 17 February 1933 – an event the Nazis may or may not have done themselves, but which they blamed on the Dutchman Marius van der Lubbe, and certainly used as an excuse to clamp down on Communists and suspend basic freedoms. Today, after its celebrated renovation by Sir Norman Foster, the Reichstag is again home to the Bundestag (the German parliament), and open to the public. Foster conceived his architectural approach as a 'dialogue between old and new'. Graffiti scrawled by Russian soldiers in 1945, for example, has been left in view and there has been no attempt to clean up or even deny the building's turbulent history. No dome appeared on his original competition-winning plans, but the German government insisted upon one. Foster, in turn, insisted that, unlike the structure's original dome (damaged in the war and demolished in the 1950s), the new one should be a public space, open to visitors.

A trip to the top of the dome is a must, but beware of queues: come first thing or in the evening if possible. A lift whisks you to the roof, where there's also a decent restaurant, and from there ramps lead to the top of the dome, affording fine views of the capital. At its centre is a funnel of mirrors, angled so as to shed light on the workings of democracy below. They also have an almost funhouse effect: on the spiral walkways, the visitor can see his head in this mirror, his legs in that one. Foster has created a space that is open, playful and defiantly democratic.

Siegessäule

Strasse des 17. Juni (391 2961). S3, S5, S7, S9 Bellevue. **Open** *Summer* 9am-6pm Mon-Sat. *Winter* 9.30am-5pm Mon-Sat. **Admission** €2.20; €1.50 concessions. **No credit cards**. **Map** p301 D3.

Tiergarten's biggest monument was built in 1871-3 to commemorate the Prussian campaigns against Denmark (1864), Austria (1866) and France (1870-71). Originally planted in front of the Reichstag, it was moved here by Hitler to form a centrepiece for the east-west axis connecting western Berlin with the palaces and ministries of Mitte. On top of the column is an 8m (26ft) gilded Goddess of Victory by Friedrich Drake; captured French cannons and cannonballs, sawn in half and gilded, provide the decoration of the column proper. It's 285 steps to the viewing platform at the top.

South of the park

Map p305 & p306

At the south-east corner of the Tiergarten is what was for many years following reunification Europe's largest building site: the now reborn **Potsdamer Platz**, intended as the city's new commercial centrepiece. Since this once-bustling intersection was bombed flat and then found itself just on the east side of the Wall, it was a no-man's land for many years. Fierce debate ensued over whether the redevelopment should be in keeping with the typical scale of a 'European' city or American-style high-rise or truly avant-garde. In the end the former was the favoured option, with medium-height development except at Potsdamer Platz itself, where high-rises up to 90 metres (295 feet) were allowed.

Opinions are mixed as to the success of the finished article. In the Cold War, this area was neither one thing nor the other – half on one side of the Wall, half on the other, and barren no-man's land on both sides. Neither east nor west, it sounds like a good candidate for a unifying centre. But actually it's an isolated island of redevelopment, connecting to no area around it, still neither one thing nor the other.

And despite the presence of so many architectural heavyweights, there's little here to excite. Helmut Jahn's soaring **Sony Center**, homogenous in steel and glass, contains the Forum, conceived as an urban entertainment complex. In this, at least, it has succeeded, containing the CineStar and CinemaxX multiplexes (*for both see p195*), the more offbeat Arsenal cinema (*see p194*) and the excellent **Filmmuseum Berlin** (*see p196*). It is also now the main venue for the Berlin International Film Festival (*see p192*). But there is little to recommend around here in terms of eating, drinking or shopping.

One of only two Potsdamer Platz buildings to survive World War II and the subsequent clearout was here on the Sony site: the Kaisersaal Café from the old Grand Hotel Esplanade, a listed building. When plans for the area solidified, the café was found to be in a bad position, so the whole structure was moved 75 metres (246 feet) to its present position on the north side of the building, where it has been integrated into the apartment complex on Bellevuestrasse.

The other major corporate presence at Potsdamer Platz is Daimler-Chrysler, which is responsible for most of the development south of the Sony Center. This includes buildings by Richard Rogers, Renzo Piano and Hans Kollhof. The company's major cultural contribution is the **Sammlung DaimlerChrysler** (*see p103*), which exhibits 20th-century works from the auto manufacturer's big-name art collection.

In anticipation of the increased human traffic through Potsdamer Platz, the Potsdamer Platz Arkaden – a three-storey American-style shopping mall – were grafted on to the U-Bahn and S-Bahn stations. Just outside the Arkaden, on Alte Potsdamer Strasse, the other survivor of the bombing, Weinhaus Huth, is back selling wine at its old location.

Immediately west of the Potsdamer Platz development is one of the city's major concentrations of museums, galleries and cultural institutions. Collectively known as the **Kulturforum**, this quarter was based on the designs of Hans Scharoun (1946-57). Scharoun himself was responsible for the building of the **Staatsbibliotek** (State Library) and the unmistakeable gold **Philharmonie** (*see p237*), home to the Berlin Philharmonic Orchestra, and famous for offering near-perfect acoustics and sightlines from all of its 2,200 seats. Adjacent is the **Musikinstrumentenmuseum** (Musical Instrument Museum; *see p102*).

One block to the west is a low-rise museum complex. Its biggest draw is the wonderful collection of 13th- to 18th-century art in the **Gemäldegalerie** (Picture Gallery; *see p102*). The **Kunstgewerbemuseum** (Museum of Applied Art; *see p102*) is also worth a peek. Here too is the **Kunstbibliotek** (Art Library) and a decent café and shop.

Next door stands the **Matthäuskirche** (Matthias Church) and, on its south side, the bold glass cube of the **Neue Nationalgalerie** (New National Gallery; *see p102*). The latter hosts major temporary shows, such as the current exhibition of 200 masterworks from the Permanent Collection of New York's Museum of Modern Art (until September 2004).

Between the north flank of the Kulturforum and the south flank of Tiergarten runs Tiergartenstrasse, main drag of Berlin's revived diplomatic quarter. Part of Albert Speer's plan for 'Germania', the original embassy buildings were designed by German architects. Damaged by bombing, they were largely abandoned, and Tiergartenstrasse became an eerie walk past decaying grandeur. But with the land often still the property of the respective governments, embassies were reconstructed at their old addresses during the diplomatic relocation from Bonn. Today, this area is embassy row again.

The **Gedenkstätte Deutscher Widerstand** (Memorial to the German Resistance; *see below*) is south on Stauffenbergstrasse – a street named after the leader of the July 1944 plot to kill Hitler. At the corner of this street and Reichpietschufer is **Shell House**, a curvaceous masterpiece by Emil Fahrenkamp (1932). It survived the war and is now offices for the BEWAG electricity company.

Five minutes' walk west along the Landswehrkanal is the gleaming white building of the **Bauhaus Archiv – Museum für Gestaltung** (*see below*); a further ten minutes' walk west leads to the less highbrow attractions of the Zoologischer Garten (*see p103*) and the hub of west Berlin around Bahnhof Zoo and the Ku'damm (*see p104*).

Bauhaus Archiv – Museum für Gestaltung

Klingelhöferstrasse 13-14 (254 0020). Bus 100, 129, 187, 341. **Open** 10am-5pm Mon, Wed-Sun. **Admission** €4; €2 concessions. **No credit cards**. **Map** p305 D4.

Walter Gropius, founder of the Bauhaus school, designed the elegant white building which now houses this absorbing design museum. It presents furniture, ceramics, prints, sculptures, photographs and sketches created in the Bauhaus workshop between 1919 and 1933 (when the school was closed down by the Nazis). There are first-rate temporary exhibitions too. A computerised introduction in German and English provides a useful context, and translations of text panels are available.

Gedenkstätte Deutscher Widerstand

Stauffenbergstrasse 13-14 (2699 5000/www.gdw-berlin.de). U2, S1, S2, S25, S26 Potsdamer Platz. **Open** 9am-6pm Mon-Wed, Fri; 9am-8pm Thur; 10am-6pm Sat, Sun. **Admission** free. **Map** p306 E4.

The Memorial of the German Resistance chronicles the German resistance to National Socialism. The building is part of a complex known as the Bendlerblock, which was owned by the German military from its construction in 1911 until 1945. At the back is a memorial to the conspirators killed during their attempt to assassinate Hitler at this site on 20 July 1944. Also occasional temporary exhibitions.

Gemäldegalerie

Stauffenbergstrasse 40 (266 2101/www.smpk.de). U2, S1, S2, S25, S26 Potsdamer Platz. **Open** 10am-6pm Tue, Wed, Fri-Sun; 10am-10pm Thur. **Admission** €6; €3 concessions. **No credit cards**. **Map** p306 E4.

The Picture Gallery's first-rate early European painting collection features a healthy selection of the biggest names in Western art. Although many fine Italian, Spanish and English works are on display, highlights are the Dutch and Flemish pieces. Fans of Rembrandt can indulge themselves with around 20 paintings – the best of which are the portrait of preacher and merchant Cornelis Claesz Anslo and his wife, and an electric Samson confronting his father-in-law. Two of Franz Hals' finest works are here – the wild, fluid, almost impressionistic *Malle Babbe* ('Mad Babette') and the detailed portrait of the one-year-old Catharina Hooft and her nurse. Other highlights include a couple of unflinching portraits by Robert Campin (early 15th century), a version of Botticelli's *Venus Rising*, and Corregio's brilliant *Leda with the Swan*. Look out also for a pair of Lucas Cranach Venus and Cupid paintings and his *Fountain of Youth*. Pick up the excellent (free) English-language audio guide.

Kunstgewerbemuseum

Kulturforum, Matthäikirchplatz (266 2902/www.smpk.de). U2, S1, S2, S25, S26 Potsdamer Platz. **Open** 10am-6pm Tue-Fri; 11am-6pm Sat, Sun. **Admission** €6; €3 concessions. **No credit cards**. **Map** p306 E4.

The Museum of Applied Art contains a frustrating collection of European arts and crafts, stretching from the Middle Ages through Renaissance, baroque and rococo to Jugendstil and art deco. There are some lovely pieces on display, particularly furniture and porcelain, but labelling is only in German and the layout of the building is confusing.

Musikinstrumentenmuseum

Tiergartenstrasse 1 (2548 1139/www.smpk.de). U2, S1, S2, S25, S26 Potsdamer Platz. **Open** 9am-5pm Tue-Fri; 10am-5pm Sat, Sun. **Admission** €3; €1.50 concessions; free under-12s; free 1st Sun of mth. **No credit cards**. **Map** p306 E4.

Over 2,200 string, keyboard, wind and percussion instruments dating back to the 1500s are crammed into this small museum next to the Philharmonie. Among them are rococo musical clocks, for which 18th-century princes commissioned jingles from Mozart, Haydn and Beethoven. Museum guides play obsolete instruments such as the Kammerflugel. On Saturdays at noon the wonderful Wurlitzer organ – salvaged from an American silent movie house – is cranked up for a performance.

Neue Nationalgalerie

Potsdamer Strasse 50 (266 2651/www.smpk.de). U2, S1, S2, S25, S26 Potsdamer Platz. **Open** 10am-6pm Tue, Wed, Fri; 10am-10pm Thur; 11am-6pm Sat, Sun. **Admission** €6; €3 concessions; special exhibitions varies. **No credit cards**. **Map** p306 E4.

The building was designed in the 1960s by Mies van der Rohe, and houses German and international paintings from the 20th century. It's strong on German expressionists and surrealists such as Max Beckmann, Otto Mueller, Ernst Ludwig Kirchner, Paul Klee and Max Ernst. The Neue Sachlichkeit is also well represented by George Grosz and Otto Dix. Many major non-German 20th-century artists are featured, including Picasso, de Chirico, Léger, Munch and Dalí. There are also lesser-known artists such as Ludwig Meidner, whose apocalyptic post-World War I landscapes exert the garish power of an action-packed comic centrefold. Be warned that

Bauhaus Archiv. *See p102.*

the permanent collection is sometimes put into storage during big shows, such as the massive MOMA New York exhibit that runs to September 2004.

Sammlung DaimlerChrysler

Alte Potsdamer Strasse 5, Tiergarten (2594 1420/www.sammlung.daimlerchrysler.com). U2, S1, S2, S25, S26 Potsdamer Platz. **Open** 11am-6pm daily. *Guided tours* 3pm Sat. **Admission** free; guided tours €2.50. **Map** p306 E4.

As you'd expect from one of the world's largest car manufacturers, this collection is serious stuff. It has stuck to the 20th century, and covers abstract, constructivist, conceptual or minimal art; its collection numbers around 1,300 works from artists such as Josef Albers, Max Bill, Walter de Maria, Jeff Koons and Andy Warhol. The gallery rotates different portions of the collection periodically, typically between 30-80 works at a time. They also host temporary exhibitions, most recently of photographs and video under the name 'Museum Africa'.

Zoologischer Garten & Aquarium

Hardenbergplatz 8 (254 010/www.zoo-berlin.de). U2, U9, S3, S5, S7, S9, S75 Zoologischer Garten. **Open** *Zoo* Jan-March 9am-5.30pm daily; Apr-Sep 9am-6.30pm; Oct 9am-6pm; Nov, Dec 9am-5pm. *Aquarium* 9am-6pm daily. **Admission** *Zoo* €9; €4.50-€7 concessions. *Aquarium* €9; €4.50-€7 concessions. *Combined admission* €14; €7-€11 concessions. **No credit cards**. **Map** p305 D4.

Germany's oldest zoo was opened in 1841 to designs by Martin Lichtenstein and Peter Joseph Lenné. With almost 14,000 creatures, it's one of the world's largest and most important zoos, with more endangered species in its collection than any in Europe save Antwerp's. It's beautifully landscaped, and there are plenty of places for a coffee, beer or snack. Some enclosures are too small (the polar bear seems far from happy), but other animals seem content. A new bear enclosure is in the works for late 2005. Also under construction is a new cage for birds of prey.

The aquarium can be entered either from within the zoo or from its own entrance on Olof-Palme-Platz by the Elephant Gate. More than 500 species are arranged over three floors, and it's a good option for a rainy day. On the ground floor are the fish (and some impessive sharks); on the first you'll find reptiles (the crocodile hall is the highlight); while insects and amphibians occupy the second. The dark corridors and liquid ambience, with colourful tanks lit from within and curious aquarian creatures floating by, are as absorbing as many an art exhibit.

Charlottenburg

The city's west end includes the Ku'damm's crucible of commerce, the bustle of Bahnhof Zoo and the cluster of culture at Schloss Charlottenburg.

This huge swathe of the city, once the centre of West Berlin, stretches from the Tiergarten to Spandau, from Tegel Airport in the north down to Wilmersdorf to the south. It has two main focal points – the commercial cauldron around Bahnhof Zoo, extending west along the Kurfürstendamm, and the cluster of cultural treasures in and around Schloss Charlottenburg.

Bahnhof Zoo & the Ku'damm

Map p305

Hymned by U2 and centrepiece of the film *Christiane F*, **Bahnhof Zoo** (Zoo Station – Bahnhof Zoologischer Garten, to give it its full name) was long a spooky anomaly – slap in the middle of West Berlin but policed by the East, which controlled the intercity rail system – and a seedy hangout for junkies and old soaks. Today, it has spruced-up facades and a postmodernised interior full of chain stores and fast-food outlets. The original building was designed in 1882 by Ernst Dircksen; the modern glass sheds were added in 1934.

The surrounding area, with its sleaze and shopping, huge cinemas and bustling crowds is the gateway to the Kurfürstendamm, the main shopping street of western Berlin. The discos and bars along Joachimstaler Strasse are best avoided – the opening of the **Beate-Uhse Erotik-Museum** (*see p106*) actually added a touch of class to the area.

The most notable nearby landmark is the fractured spire of the **Kaiser-Wilhelm-Gedächtniskirche** (Kaiser Wilhelm Memorial Church; *see p107*) in Breitscheidplatz. Close by is the 22-storey **Europa-Center**, whose Mercedes star can be seen from much of the rest of the city. It was built in 1965 and looks it. Intended as the anchor for the development of a new western downtown, it was the first of Berlin's genuinely tall buildings; now it's the grande dame of the city's shopping malls. Its exterior looks best when neon-lit at night. The strange sculpture in front was erected in 1983. It is officially called *Weltenbrunnen* (Fountain of the Worlds), but, like almost everything else in Berlin, it has a nickname: *Der Wasserklops* (Water Meatball).

Just north of here is the entrance to the enjoyable **Zoologischer Garten** (Zoo) and **Aquarium** (for both, *see p103*).

Running along the south of the Europa-Center, Tauentzienstrasse is the westernmost piece of the *Generalzug*, a sequence of streets laid out by Peter Joseph Lenné to link the west end with Kreuzberg and points east. Constructed around 1860 they are all named after Prussian generals from the Napoleonic wars: Tauentzien, Kleist, Bülow, Yorck and Gneisenau. The tubular steel sculpture in the central reservation along Tauentzienstrasse was commissioned for the city's 750th anniversary and represents the then divided city in that the two halves twine around each other but never meet.

The street continues east past **KaDeWe** (*see p161*), the largest department store in continental Europe. Its full title is Das Kaufhaus des Westens (Department Store of the West), and it was founded in 1907 by Adolf Jandorf, acquired by Herman Tietz in 1926 and later 'Aryanised' and expropriated by the Nazis. KaDeWe is the only one of Berlin's famous turn-of-the-century department stores to survive the war intact, and has been extensively modernised over the last decade. Its most famous feature is the sixth-floor food hall.

Tauentzienstrasse ends at Wittenburgplatz. The 1911 neo-classical U-Bahn station here (by Alfred Grenander) is a listed building and has been wonderfully restored with wooden kiosks and old ads on the walls. A block further is the huge steel sculpture at An der Urania with its grim monument to children killed in traffic by Berlin's drivers. This marks the end, or the beginning, of the western 'downtown'.

As hymned by U2, the spruced-up former centre of sleaze: **Bahnhof Zoologischer Garten**.

Leading south-west from the Kaiser-Wilhelm-Gedächtniskirche, the Kurfürstendamm (or Ku'damm, as it's universally known), west Berlin's tree-lined shopping boulevard is named after the Prussian Kurfürst ('Elector') – and for centuries it was nothing but a track leading from the Elector's residence to the royal hunting palace in the Grunewald. In 1881 Bismarck insisted it be widened to 5.3 metres (17 feet). To the south of the street, many villas were put up, and, though few survive today, one sizeable exception contains the **Käthe-Kollwitz-Museum** (*see p107*), the Villa Griesbach auction house and the Literaturhaus Berlin with its **Wintergarten am Literaturhaus café** (*see p156*) on Fasanenstrasse. The villas were soon replaced by upmarket tenement buildings with huge apartments – sometimes upwards of ten large rooms. About half of the original buildings were destroyed in the war and replaced by functional offices, but many bombastic old structures remain.

The ground-level Ku'damm soon developed into an elegant shopping boulevard. It remains so today with cinemas (mostly showing dubbed Hollywood fare), restaurants (from the classy to assorted burger joints) and upmarket fashion shops – the Ku'damm is dedicated to separating you from your cash. If you tire of spending, check out the **Story of Berlin** (*see p107*), which offers an entertaining trip through the history of the city.

Side streets to the south are quieter but even more upmarket, and Bleibtreustrasse to the north has more shops and a number of outrageous examples of 19th-century *Gründerzeit* architecture.

At the north-west corner of the intersection of Ku'damm and Joachimstaler Strasse is the **Neues Kranzler-Eck**, a Helmut Jahn-designed ensemble built around the famous old Café Kranzler, with a 16-storey tower and pedestrian courtyards including a habitat for various exotic birds.

Other notable new architecture in the area includes Josef Paul Kleihues' **Kant-Dreieck** (Fasanenstrasse/Kantstrasse), with its large metal 'sail', and Nicholas Grimshaw's **Ludwig-Erhard-Haus** for the Stock Exchange at Fasanenstrasse 83-4. Back towards the Kurfürstendamm end of Fasanenstrasse is the **Jüdisches Gemeindehaus** (Jewish Community House), and, opposite, the **Zille-Hof flea market** (*see p176*).

The Russian zone

The softly seductive sound of Russian is often heard in Berlin, and nowhere more so than in Charlottenburg. Back in the 1920s there were estimated to have been around 300,000 Russian emigrés in Berlin – monarchists fleeing the October Revolution, but also Mensheviks and anarchists, as well as artists and intellectuals attracted to what was then the crucible of modernism. Artists such as Marc Chagall, El Lissitzky and Vassily Kandinsky, writers such as Ilya Ehrenburg, Maxim Gorky and Vladimir Nabokov, all sojourned in the city, adding to Weimar Berlin's experimental edge.

The majority of them settled in Charlottenburg, earning this district the nickname 'Charlottengrad'. This was the most significant Russian exile community in Europe, surpassing even that of Paris. Schools, restaurants, shops, churches, libraries, galleries and newspapers catered to the Russians and enriched the city's cosmopolitan mix. The Blauer Vogel cabaret gained renown beyond expat circles and the Bauhaus simply wouldn't have been the same without Kandinsky and El Lissitzky.

Yet the expats seem to have taken less than they gave. Few Russian writers, for example, refer to their host city in works from this time – Nabokov's *The Gift* being one notable exception, and that was written in the 1930s, after the heyday of Charlottengrad. Many shared El Lissitzky's sentiment that Berlin was merely a 'transit station', and by the mid 1920s the creative exiles had either returned home to the Soviet Union or moved on to Paris or the US. The rise of the Nazis and World War II essentially severed Berlin's old Russian connection.

East Berlin was populated by diplomats, KGB agents and other Soviet functionaries throughout the life of the GDR. The **Museum Berlin-Karlshorst** (*see p118*), in the building where the German surrender was signed in 1945, dates from the Cold War period and documents German-Russian relations in the 20th century. In the 1990s, there came a new wave of immigration, mostly of Russian Jews and Russian Germans. This is the backdrop for Wladimir Kamisky's best-selling collection of tales, *Russian Disco* (*see p287*). While nowhere near the high-water mark of the 1920s there are now officially around 25,000 Russians and other nationals of European former Soviet states in Berlin – constituting Berlin's fourth-largest non-German community after Turks, ex-Yugoslavs and Poles. The true number is likely to be much higher.

And once again, more Russians live in Charlottenburg than in any other district in Berlin. The 'Russendisko' might be at **Kaffee Burger** in Mitte (*see p225*) and Prenzlauer Berg may be home to the **Gagarin** café (*see p149*) and the **Pasternak** restaurant (*see p130*), but Charlottenburg has the established **Samowar** (Luisenplatz 3, 341 4154, www.restaurant-samowar.de), the **Knigi Russkiye** book shop (Kantstrasse 82, 323 4815), and the extraordinary selection of Russian CDs for sale at **Musik-Welt** (Wilmersdorfer Strasse 158, 3470 5295). It also has all the Mafia bars and glossy discos favoured by the Russian *nouveau riches*. though these venues are not exactly welcoming to outsiders, and the luxury retailers of Fasanenstrasse seem to run these days on Russian cash.

Kantstrasse runs more or less parallel to the Ku'damm at the Zoo end, and contains the grandiloquent **Theater des Westens** and more shops. Since the opening of the **stilwerk** design centre (*see p164* **Design for living rooms**), the stretch around Fasanenstrasse has become a centre for designer homeware stores. The environs of leafy Savignyplatz, meanwhile, are dotted with numerous chic restaurants, cafés and shops, particularly on Grolmanstrasse and in the Savignypassage. Nearby Knesebeckstrasse is the place to come for book shops. The northern stretch, which includes several antiquarian dealers, is a particularly good place.

Beate-Uhse Erotik-Museum

Joachimstaler Strasse 4 (886 0666/www. erotikmuseum.de). U2, U9, S3, S5, S7, S9, S75 Zoologischer Garten. **Open** 9am-midnight daily. **Admission** €5; €4 concessions. **Credit** AmEx, MC, V. **Map** p305 C4.

The three floors of this collection (housed above a flagship Beate-Uhse retail outlet offering the usual videos and sex toys) contain oriental prints, some daft showroom-dummy tableaux, and glass cases containing such delights as early Japanese dildos, Andean penis flutes, Javanese erotic dagger hilts, 17th-century chastity belts, a giant coconut that looks like an arse and a vase used in the film *Caligula*. There's a small exhibit on pioneering sex researcher Magnus Hirschfeld, sadly comprising nothing more than a few boards of dry documentary material. The only other things with any connection to Berlin are an inadequate item on Heinrich Zille and a corner documenting the career of Frau Uhse herself, who went from Luftwaffe pilot and post-war potato-picker to annual sex-aid sales of €50 million. All oddly respectable, given the subject.

Kaiser-Wilhelm-Gedächtniskirche

Breitscheidplatz (218 5023/www.gedaechtniskirche.com). U2, U9, S3, S5, S7, S9, S75 Zoologischer Garten. **Open** 9am-7pm daily. *Guided tours* 1.15pm, 2pm, 3pm Mon-Sat. **Admission** free. **Map** p305 D4.

The Kaiser Wilhelm Memorial Church is one of Berlin's best-known sights, and one of its most dramatic at night. The neo-Romanesque church was built in 1891-5 by Franz Schwechten in honour of – you guessed it – Kaiser Wilhelm I. Much of the building was destroyed during an Allied air raid in 1943. These days the church serves as a stark reminder of the damage done by the war, although some might argue that the bombing has improved what was originally a profoundly ugly structure. Inside the rump of the church is a glittering art nouveau-style ceiling mosaic depicting members of the House of Hohenzollern going on pilgrimage towards the cross. Here, you'll also find a cross made from the nails from the destroyed cathedral at Coventry, and photos of the church before and after the war. The ruin of the tower is flanked by ugly modern concrete extensions, yet inside the chapel the wraparound blue stained glass in the windows is quite stunning.

Käthe-Kollwitz-Museum

Fasanenstrasse 24, Wilmersdorf (882 5210/www.kollwitz.de/museum.htm). U9, U15 Kurfürstendamm. **Open** 11am-6pm Mon, Wed-Sun. **Admission** €5; €2.50 concessions. **No credit cards. Map** p305 C4.

Käthe Kollwitz's powerful, deeply empathetic work embraces the full spectrum of life, from the joy of motherhood to the pain of death (with rather more emphasis on the latter than the former). The collection includes her famous lithograph *Brot!*, as well as charcoal sketches, woodcuts (a medium particularly suited to her style) and sculptures, all displayed to good effect in this grand villa off the Ku'damm. Some labelling is in English.

Story of Berlin

Kurfürstendamm 207-8 (8872 0100/www.story-of-berlin.de). U15 Uhlandstrasse. **Open** 10am-8pm daily; last entry 6pm. **Admission** €9.30; €7.50 concessions. **No credit cards. Map** p305 C4.

If you're interested in the city's history, the Story of Berlin should not be missed. The huge floor space is filled with well designed rooms and multimedia exhibits created by authors, designers and film and stage specialists, telling Berlin's story from its founding in 1237 to the present day. A headset provides an audio commentary, but this only comes in German. No matter, as the 20 themed displays are labelled in both German and English. Underneath all this is a massive nuclear shelter. Built by the Allies in the 1970s, this low-ceilinged, oppressive bunker is still a fully functional shelter and can hold up to 3,500 people. Guided tours (€3.50; children free) every hour on the hour.

Schloss Charlottenburg & around

Map p300

The palace that gives Charlottenburg its name lies about three kilometres (two miles) north-west of Bahnhof Zoo. In contrast to the commercialism and crush of the latter, this part of the city is quiet, wealthy and serene. **Schloss Charlottenburg** (*see p108*) was built in the 17th century as a summer palace for Queen Sophie-Charlotte, wife of Friedrich III (later King Friedrich I), and was intended as Berlin's answer to Versailles. It's not a very convincing answer, but there's plenty of interest in the buildings and grounds of the palace – the apartments of the New Wing and the gardens are the main attractions.

Next to the palace's west wing is the **Museum für Vor- und Frühgeschichte** (Primeval and Early History Museum; *see below*); in front of the Schloss entrance is a trio of first-rate museums – the **Sammlung Berggruen: Picasso und seine Zeit** (Berggruen Collection: Picasso and his Time; *see p108*), the art nouveau and art deco **Bröhan-Museum** (*see below*) and the superb **Ägyptisches Museum** (Egyptian Museum; *see below*).

There are few eating, drinking or shopping opportunities in the immediate vicinity of the palace, but if you head down Schlossstrasse and over Bismarckstrasse, the streets south of here, particularly those named after philosophers (Leibniz, Goethe) have a lot of interesting small shops selling antiques, books and the fashions that well-to-do residents sport around Charlottenburg's cafés and restaurants.

Ägyptisches Museum

Schlossstrasse 70 (3435 7311/www.smpk.de). U2 Sophie-Charlotte-Platz or U7 Richard-Wagner-Platz. **Open** 10am-6pm Tue-Sun. **Admission** €6; €3 concessions; free Sun. **No credit cards. Map** p300 B3.

Just across the street from Schloss Charlottenburg is this deservedly popular museum, slated to close here in March 2005 and reappear on the top floor of the Altes Museum *(see p78)* in May 2005. The collection's most celebrated exhibit is the bust of Nefertiti, dating from around 1350 BC, and the portrayal of the human face is one of the most compelling aspects of the museum (a nearby, damaged bust looks remarkably like a Francis Bacon creation). Particularly notable in this respect is a series of characterful model faces, and also the vivid 'Berlin Green Head', which may date from around 500 BC – it looks disconcertingly like a bad-tempered nightclub bouncer. By the time we reach Graeco-Roman Egypt, there are examples of arresting realistic portraits being painted on mummies. Another unique treasure is a piece of papyrus with the only known example of Cleopatra's handwriting. Labelling is only in German – it's worth buying the enlightening Egyptian Art in Berlin booklet from the shop before wandering around.

Bröhan-Museum

Schlossstrasse 1A (3269 0600/www.broehan-museum.de). U2 Sophie-Charlotte-Platz or U7 Richard-Wagner-Platz. **Open** 10am-6pm Tue-Sun. **Admission** €4; €3 concessions. Free 1st Wed of mth. Guided tours call for details. **No credit cards**. **Map** p300 B3.

Opposite the Ägyptisches Museum, this quiet, private museum contains three well laid out levels of international art nouveau and art deco pieces that businessman Karl Bröhan began collecting in the 1960s and donated to the city of Berlin on his 60th birthday. The wide array of paintings, furniture, porcelain, glass, silver and sculptures dates from 1890 to 1939. Hans Baluschek's paintings of social life in the 1920s and 1930s, and Willy Jaeckel's series of portraits of women are the pick of the fine art bunch; the furniture is superb too. The third floor hosts special exhibitions, such as a recent one on flowers as a decorative motif. Labelling is only in German. Good website, though.

Museum für Vor- und Frühgeschichte

Langhansbau, Schloss Charlottenburg (3267 4811/www.smpk.de). U2 Sophie-Charlotte-Platz or U7 Richard-Wagner-Platz. **Open** 9am-5pm Tue-Fri; 10am-5pm Sat, Sun. **Admission** €6; €3 concessions. **No credit cards**. **Map** p300 B3.

The Primeval and Early History Museum – spread over six galleries – traces the evolution of Homo sapiens from 1,000,000 BC to the Bronze Age. The highlights are the replicas (and some originals) of Heinrich Schliemann's famous treasure of ancient Troy, including works of ceramics and gold, as well as weaponry. Keep an eye out also for the sixth-century BC grave of a girl buried with a gold coin in her mouth. Information is available in English.

Sammlung Berggruen: Picasso und seine Zeit

Westlicher Stülerbau, Schlossstrasse 1 (3269 5815/www.smpk.de). U2 Sophie-Charlotte-Platz or U7 Richard-Wagner-Platz. **Open** 10am-5pm Tue-Sun. **Admission** €3; €1.50 concessions. **No credit cards**. **Map** p300 B3.

Heinz Berggruen was an early dealer in Picassos in Paris, and the subtitle of this museum 'Picasso and his Time' sums up this satisfying and important collection. Displayed over an easily digestible three circular floors, it's inevitable that Pablo's works dominate (taking up much of the ground floor, and almost all of the first); his astonishingly prolific and diverse output is well represented. Highlight is perhaps the 1942 *Reclining Nude*. There are also works by Braque, Giacometti, Cézanne and Matisse, and most of the second floor is given over to wonderful paintings by Paul Klee. Audio guide available.

Schloss Charlottenburg

Luisenplatz & Spandauer Damm (320 911/www.spsg.de). U2 Sophie-Charlotte-Platz or U7 Richard-Wagner-Platz. **Open** *Old Palace* 9am-5pm Tue-Fri; 10am-5pm Sat, Sun. Last tour 4pm. *New Wing* 10am-6pm Tue-Fri; 11am-6pm Sat, Sun. *New Pavilion* 10am-5pm Tue-Sun. Last entrance 4.30pm. *Mausoleum* Apr-Oct 10am-noon, 1-5pm Tue-Sun. Last entrance 4.30pm. *Belvedere* (Apr-Oct) 10am-5pm Tue-Sun. (Nov-Mar) noon-4pm Tue-Fri; noon-5pm Sat, Sun. Last entrance 4.30pm. **Admission** *Combination tickets* €5-€9; €4-€6 concessions. Individual sights call for details. **No credit cards**. **Map** p300 B3.

Queen Sophie-Charlotte was the impetus behind this sprawling palace and gardens (and gave her name to both the building and the district) – her husband Friedrich III (later King Friedrich I) built it in 1695-9 as a summer home for his queen. Later kings also summered here, tinkering with, and adding to the buildings. It was severely damaged during World War II, but has now been restored, and stands as the largest surviving Hohenzollern palace.

There are a number of parts of the palace to which the public are admitted, though the bafflingly complicated individual opening times and admission prices have many a visitor scratching their heads. The easiest option is to go for the combination ticket that allows entrance to all parts of the palace, with the exception of the state and private apartments of King Friedrich I and Queen Sophie-Charlotte in the **Altes Schloss** (Old Palace), which are only accessible on a guided tour (€8; €5 concessions; in German only). This tour, through more than 20 rooms, some of staggering baroque opulence, has its highlights (particularly the Porcelain Cabinet), but can be skipped – there's plenty of interest elsewhere. The upper apartments in the old palace can be visited without a guided tour, but, frankly, they are pretty dull and are really only of interest to silver and porcelain junkies.

The one must-see is the **Neue Flügel** (New Wing). Also known as the Knobeldorff Wing (after its architect), the upper floor of the wing contains the State Apartments of Frederick the Great and the Winter Chambers of his successor King Friedrich Wilhelm II. Pick up the free audio guide as you enter – it really brings the apartments alive. The contrast between the two sections is particularly interesting – Frederick's rooms are all excessive rococo exuberance (the wildly over-the-top Golden Gallery literally drips gilt), while Friedrich Wilhelm's far more modestly proportioned rooms reflect the more

Kaiser-Wilhelm-Gedächtniskirche.
See p107.

restrained classicism of his time. Frederick the Great was a big collector of 18th-century French painting, and some choice canvases hang from the walls, including Watteau's masterpiece *The Embarkation for Cythera*. Also worth a look are the apartments of Friedrich Wilhelm III in the New Wing.

By the east end of the New Wing stands the **Neue Pavillon** (New Pavilion). Also known as the Schinkel Pavilion, it was built by the Schinkel in 1824 for Friedrich Wilhelm III – the King liked it so much that he chose to live here in preference to the grandeur of the main palace.

The huge gardens are one of the palace's main draws. Laid out in 1697 in formal French style, they were reshaped in a more relaxed English style in the 19th century. Within them you'll find the Belvedere, a three-storey structure built in 1788 as a teahouse, now containing a collection of Berlin porcelain. Also in the gardens is the sombre **Mausoleum**, containing the tombs of Friedrich Wilhelm III, his wife Queen Luise, Kaiser Wilhelm I and his wife. Look out for temporary exhibitions in the Orangery. Café and restaurant at the front of the palace. Note: the entire palace is closed on Mondays.

Elsewhere in Charlottenburg

Map p301 & p304

About three kilometres (two miles) north-east of Schloss Charlottenburg is a reminder of the terror inflicted by the Nazi regime on dissidents, criminals and anybody else they deemed undesirable. The **Gedenkstätte Plötzensee** (Plötzensee Memorial; *see below*) preserves the execution shed of the former Plötzensee prison, wherein more than 2,500 people were killed between 1933 and 1945.

A couple of kilometres south-west of Schloss Charlottenburg, at the western end of Neue Kantstrasse, stands the futuristic **International Conference Centre** (ICC). Built in the 1970s, it is used for pop concerts, political rallies and the like. Next door, the even larger **Messe- und Ausstellungsgelände** (Trade Fair and Exhibition Area) plays host to trade fairs ranging from electronics to food to aerospace (*see p219* **Pop komms to Berlin**). Within the complex, the **Funkturm** (Radio Tower; *see below*) offers panoramic views. Nearby, Hans Poelzig's **Haus des Rundfunks** (Masurenallee 9-14) is an expressive example of monumental brick modernism.

Another couple of kilometres north-west is the **Olympiastadion** (*see below*). One of the few pieces of fascist-era architecture still intact in Berlin, it's a surprisingly pleasing structure, despite its unpalatable origins. Immediately south of Olympiastadion S-Bahn station is a huge apartment block designed by Le Corbusier. The **Corbusierhaus**, with its multicoloured paint job, was constructed for the International Building exhibition of 1957, and hailed as a model for contemporary urban living. From here, a ten-minute walk along Sensburger Allee brings you to the sculptures of the **Georg-Kolbe-Museum** (*see below*).

Funkturm

Messedamm (3038 1905). U2 Theodor-Heuss-Platz or Kaiserdamm. **Open** 10am-9pm Mon; 10am-11pm Tue-Sun; closed July. **Admission** €3.60; €1.80 concessions. **No credit cards. Map** p304 A4.

The 138m (453ft) high Radio Tower was built in 1926 and looks not unlike a smaller version of the Eiffel Tower. The Observation Deck stands at 126m (413ft); vertigo sufferers should seek solace in the restaurant, only 55m (180ft) from the ground.

Gedenkstätte Plötzensee

Hüttigpfad (344 3226). Bus 123. **Open** *Mar-Oct* 9am-5pm daily. *Nov-Feb* 9am-4pm daily. **Admission** free. **Map** p301 C2.

This memorial stands on the site where the Nazis executed over 2,500 (largely political) prisoners. In a single night in 1943, 186 people were hanged in groups of eight. In 1952 it was declared a memorial to the victims of fascism, and a memorial wall was constructed. There is little to see today, apart from the execution area, behind the wall, with its meat hooks from which victims were hanged (many were also guillotined), and a small room with an exhibition. Excellent (if depressing) booklets in English available. The stone urn near the entrance is filled with earth from concentration camps. Today, the rest of the prison is a juvenile corrective centre.

Georg-Kolbe-Museum

Sensburger Allee 25 (304 2144/www.georg-kolbe-museum.de). S5, S75 Heerstrasse/bus X34, X49, 149. **Open** 10am-5pm Tue-Sun. **Admission** €4; €2.50 concessions. Special exhibitions €5; €3 concessions. **No credit cards**.

Georg Kolbe's former studio has been transformed into a showcase for his work. The Berlin sculptor, regarded as Germany's best in the 1920s, mainly focused on naturalistic human figures. The museum features examples of his earlier, graceful pieces, as well as his later sombre and larger-than-life works created in accordance with the ideals of the Nazi regime. One of his most famous pieces, *Figure for Fountain*, is outside in the sculpture garden.

Olympiastadion

Olympischer Platz 3 (3006 3430/museum 301 1100). U2 Olympia-Stadion or S5 Olympiastadion. **Open** *Exhibition* 10am-6pm Wed, Sun. **Admission** *Exhibition* €2.50; €1.50 concessions. *Tours* call for details. **No credit cards**.

Originally designed by Werner March and opened in 1936 for the Olympics, the 76,000-seat stadium has been undergoing major renovations for the 2006 World Cup, due to be completed at end 2004. Home of Hertha BSC (*see p245*), it also hosts the German Cup Final, plus other sporting events and concerts.

Other Districts

Berlin sprawls into lakes and forest, Communist blocks and bourgeois villas, museums and monuments of all stripes.

Because the underlying soil is sandy, until recently large buildings could not be built in Berlin, which means that the city sprawls for miles. However, public transport can quickly whisk you to lesser-known neighbourhoods, many of which have easy access to lakes and woods. Here are some suggestions for further exploration.

North of the centre

To the north, the city eventually gives itself up to block after block of industrial buildings and worker housing; it's hard to summon much enthusiasm for districts like Wedding and Reinickendorf, though some might find the area's industrial legacy interesting.

Wedding

Map p302

Following recent reorganisation of the *Bezirke* (city administrative districts), the working-class industrial district of Wedding is now officially part of Mitte, but few visitors venture into its largely grim fastnesses. Apart from a couple of low-key attractions – the **Anti-Kriegsmuseum** (Anti-war Museum; see below) and the nearby **Zucker Museum** (Sugar Museum; see below) – there is also one of the few remaining stretches of the Wall at the **Gedenkstätte Berliner Mauer** (Berlin Wall Memorial; *see below* and *p72* **A walk on the Wall side**).

Anti-Kriegsmuseum

Brüsseler Strasse 21 (4549 0110/tours 402 8691/ www.anti-kriegs-museum.de). U9 Amrumer Strasse. **Open** 4-8pm daily. **Admission** free. **Map** p301 D1.

The original anti-war Museum was founded in 1925 by Ernst Friedrich, author of the book *War Against War*. It was destroyed in 1933 by the Nazis, and Friedrich fled to Brussels. There he had another museum from 1936 to 1940, at which point German troops once again showed up and trashed the place. In 1982 a group of teachers including Tommy Spree, grandson of Friedrich, re-established the museum in West Berlin. It now hosts films, discussions, lectures and exhibitions as well as a permanent display including grim World War I photos and artefacts from the original museum, children's war toys, information on German colonialism in Africa and pieces of anti-Semitic material from the Nazi era. Copies of *War Against War* are available in English, but exhibitions are only in German. Call ahead to arrange a tour in English with British director Tommy Spree. Though admission is free, donations are welcomed.

Gedenkstätte Berliner Mauer

Bernauer Strasse 111 (464 1030/www.berliner-mauer-dokumentationszentrum.de). U8 Bernauer Strasse or S1, S2 Nordbahnhof. **Open** *Documentation centre* 10am-5pm Wed-Sun. **Admission** free. **Map** p302 F2.

Immediately upon Unification, the city bought this stretch of the Wall to maintain as a memorial, and it was finally dedicated in 1998. Impeccably restored (graffiti disappears virtually overnight), it is also as sterile a monument as Berlin boasts, with a brass plaque decrying the Communist 'reign of terror', which is regularly defaced. A documentation centre, featuring displays on the Wall and a database of escapees, is to be found across the street at Bernauer Strasse 111, and from its roof you can view the Wall, and the Kapelle der Versöhnung (Chapel of

The best Views

Teufelsberg

The Grunewald and western lakes from the city's biggest rubble-mountain. *See p115.*

Siegessäule

An angel's eye over the Tiergarten. *See p100.*

Reichstag

The city's new buildings from Foster's splendid dome. *See p100.*

Kreuzberg

The city centre spreads below the peak of Viktoriapark's 'Cross Hill'. *See p93.*

Humboldthain

City skyline from the north, atop the World War II flak tower in Humboldthain park. *See map p302 F1.*

Fernsehturm

Berlin's most dramatic view, but also its most detached. *See p85.*

Reconciliation) – built on the site of a church destroyed by the East Germans. *See p72* **A walk on the Wall side**.

Zucker Museum

Amrumer Strasse 32 (3142 7574/www.dtmb.de/Zucker-Museum). U6 Seestrasse or U9 Amrumer Strasse. **Open** 9am-4.30pm Mon-Thur; 11am-6pm Sun. **Admission** €2.30; €1 concessions; family ticket €3.50. **No credit cards. Map** p301 D1.

Any museum devoted to the chemistry, history and politics of sugar would have problems thrilling the punters. But this place does have an unusual collection of sugar paraphernalia. Most interesting is a slide show on the slave trade, on which the sugar industry was so dependent. The museum celebrated its 100th birthday in January 2004.

Sightseeing

West of the centre

To the west of the city is the once independent settlement of Spandau. The district of the same name stretches from the Tegeler See in the north to the Havel in the south.

Spandau

Berlin's western neighbour and eternal rival, **Spandau** is a little baroque town that seems to contradict everything about the city of which it is now, reluctantly, a part. Spandauers still talk about 'going into Berlin' when they head off to the rest of the city. Berliners, for their part, basically consider Spandau to be part of west Germany, though travelling there is easy on the U7, alighting at either Zitadelle or Altstadt Spandau, depending on which sights you want to visit. None is thrilling, but they make for a low-key escape from the city.

The **Zitadelle** (Citadel; *see below*) contains in one of its museums Spandau's original town charter, which dates from 1232, a fact Spandauers have relied on ever since to assert their historical primacy over Berlin. Spandau's old town centre is mostly pedestrianised, with 18th-century town houses interspersed with burger joints and department stores. One of the prettiest is the former Gasthof zum Stern in Carl-Schurz-Strasse; older still are houses in Kinkelstrasse and Ritterstrasse; but perhaps the best-preserved district is north of Am Juliusturm in the area bounded by Hoher Steinweg, Kolk and Behnitz. Steinweg contains a fragment of the old town wall from the first half of the 14th century; Kolk has the **Alte Marienkirche** (1848); and in Behnitz, at No.5, stands the elegant baroque **Heinemannsche Haus**. At Reformationsplatz, the brick nave of the **Nikolaikirche** dates from 1410-50; the west tower was added in 1468, and there were later additions by Schinkel.

One of the most pleasant times to visit is at Christmas, when the market square houses a life-size Nativity scene with real sheep and the Christmas market is in full swing. The café and bakery on Reformationsplatz are excellent.

For many visitors Spandau is chiefly known for its association with Rudolf Hess. Hitler's deputy was held in the Allied jail after the Nuremberg trials, where he remained (alone after 1966) until his suicide at age 93 on 17 August 1987. Once he'd gone, the 19th-century brick building at Wilhelmstrasse 21-4 was demolished to make way for a supermarket for the (also now departed) British forces.

Some distance south of Spandau, and a long and convoluted journey by public transport, is the Luftwaffenmuseum (*see below*).

Luftwaffenmuseum

Gross-Glienicker Weg, Gatow (811 0769/www.luftwaffenmuseum.de). U7, S5, S75 Rathaus Spandau, then bus 134 to Alt-Gatow, then bus 334 to Luftwaffenmuseum (last stop) or bus X34 from Bahnhof Zoo to Alt-Gatow, then bus 334 to Luftwaffenmuseum (last stop). **Open** 9am-5pm Tue-Sun. **Admission** free.

On the western fringes of the city at one of the airbases integral to the Airlift, this sizeable collection (more than 150 aircraft) is housed in an old hangar. It includes information on the history of the Luftwaffe plus fighter and surveillance planes from the early 20th century through to 1970s NATO equipment. There's a World War I tri-plane, a restored Handley Page Hastings (as used in the Airlift) and an Antonov An-2 from the GDR Air Force. Outside are more recent aircraft. The museum also has uniforms and personal equipment galore; English guided tours by prior arrangement.

Zitadelle

Am Juliusturm, Spandau (354 944 200/tours 334 6270/www.zitadelle-spandau.net). U7 Zitadelle. **Open** 9am-5pm Tue-Fri; 10am-5pm Sat, Sun. **Admission** €4; €2.50 concessions. **No credit cards.**

The oldest structure in the citadel (and the oldest secular building in Berlin) is the Juliusturm, probably dating back to an Ascanian fortress from about 1160. The present tower was home until 1919 to the 120-million Goldmark reparations, stored in 1,200 boxes, which the French paid to Germany in 1874 after the Franco-Prussian War. (In German financial circles, state reserves are still referred to as Juliusturm.) The bulk of the Zitadelle was designed in 1560-94, in the style of an Italian fort, to dominate the confluence of the Spree and Havel rivers. Since then it has been used as everything from garrison to prison to laboratory. Today, much of the huge site is under restoration and not accessible to the public, except for its museums. One tells the story of the citadel with models and maps; the other is a museum of local history and of limited interest – neither have any English labelling.

Gedenkstätte Berliner Mauer. *See p111.*

South-west of the centre

The huge, largely residential district of Zehlendorf is chiefly of interest to visitors for the cluster of museums in Dahlem, and the bucolic and aquatic attractions of the Grunewald, Wannsee and Glienicke.

Zehlendorf & the Dahlem museums

South-west Berlin was the American Sector, and districts like **Steglitz** and **Zehlendorf** contain some of the city's wealthier residences. A major draw is the clutch of museums at **Dahlem**, including the **Ethnologisches Museum** (Museum of Ethnology; see below), one of the world's finest such collections. In the same building are the **Museum für Indische Kunst** (Museum of Indian Art) and the **Museum für Ostasiatisches Kunst** (Museum of East Asian Art; for both, see below). Nearby is also the **Museum Europäischer Kulturen** (Museum of European Cultures; *see p114*).

Dahlem is also home to the **Freie Universität**, some of whose departments occupy former villas seized by the Nazis from their Jewish owners. North-west of the U-Bahn station, opposite the Friedhof Dahlem-Dorf (cemetery), is the **Domäne Dahlem** working farm (*see below*) – a great place to take kids.

Ten minutes' walk east from Dahlem along Königin-Luise-Strasse brings you to the **Botanischer Garten and Botanisches Museum** (Botanical Garden and Museum; see below), while taking the same street for a kilometre or so west of Dahlem to the edge of the Grunewald (*see p115*) brings you closer to a couple of other interesting spots: the **Alliierten Museum** (Allied Museum; *see p116*) and the **Brücke-Museum** (*see p116*).

Botanischer Garten & Museum

Königin-Luise-Strasse 6-8 (8385 0100/www.bgbm.fu-berlin.de/BGBM). S1 Botanischer Garten. **Open** *Botanischer Garten* 9am-dusk daily. *Botanisches Museum* (Oct-Feb) 10am-6pm daily. **Admission** Combined €5; €2.50 concessions. *Museum only* €2; €1 concessions. **No credit cards**.

The Botanical Garden was landscaped at the beginning of the 20th century. Today, it is home to 18,000 plant species, 16 greenhouses and a museum. The latter is intended to explain the plant kingdom, but there's no information in English, and the place looks like it hasn't been decorated since the Wall went up, but it's free with a ticket for the gardens, and they make a pleasant stroll. Note that the Garden is a 15-minute walk from the S-Bahn station.

Domäne Dahlem

Königin-Luise-Strasse 49 (666 3000/www.domaene-dahlem.de). U1 Dahlem-Dorf. **Open** 10am-6pm Mon, Wed-Sun. **Admission** free. **No credit cards**.

On this organic working farm, children can see how life was lived in the 17th century. Craftspeople – blacksmiths, carpenters, bakers and potters – preserve and teach their skills. Best to visit during one of several festivals held during the year, when children can ride ponies, tractors and hay-wagons.

Ethnologisches Museum

Lansstrasse 8 (830 1438/www.smpk.de). U1 Dahlem-Dorf. **Open** 10am-6pm Tue-Fri; 11am-6pm Sat, Sun. **Admission** €4; €2 concessions. **No credit cards**.

The Ethnological Museum is a stunner – extensive, authoritative, beautifully laid out and lit. It encompasses cultures from Oceania to Central America to Africa to the Far East, and also has an educational department, including a junior museum and museum for the blind. Only the true ethno-fan should

Miles of files

Nobody's exactly sure how many unofficial informers were on the payroll of East Germany's Ministerium für Staatssicherheit, better known as the Stasi. There were something like 90,000 full-time agents, and about 175,000 *Inoffizielle Mitarbeiter* – unofficial informers – otherwise known as IMs. For certain, the secret police apparatus was the most pervasive in the history of state-sponsored repression; in its 1940s heyday, the Gestapo only had about 30,000 members.

Though its grip on everyday life in the GDR was exhaustive, the Stasi must go down in history as a flawed institution. In spite of its secret prisons, hidden cameras and microphones, and burgeoning network of IMs, the Stasi ultimately failed to prevent the peaceful revolution of 1989. Still, only a few weeks after the Wall was breached, crowds fell on the Stasi headquarters at Normannenstrasse, venting anger and frustration at their former tormentors.

In the preceding days, Stasi agents were working overtime, using up to 100 shredding machines to destroy documents. They barely put a dent in the 6 million or so files, which are now administered by a special authority charged with reviewing them and making them available to prosecutors and everyday people who are simply curious to know what the Stasi knew about them.

Not surprisingly, the files contained embarrassing revelations for many politicians, journalists, athletes and other folks trying to get on with life in united Germany. Most of the charges involve people being listed as unofficial informers, a status hard to dispute or verify. West German investigative reporter Günther Wallraff and Germany's current transport minister Manfred Stolpe are among those who have been implicated in discussions about the Stasi files. Stolpe has explained that it was necessary to be a double agent in order to retain his contacts with the dissident movement. Wallraff has flatly denied any Stasi connection at all.

Many could have been falsely implicated by over-ambitious Stasi career types, whose rank and pay were pegged to their success at recruiting spies. Even former chancellor Helmut Kohl and East German figure-skater Katarina Witt have been in the courts fighting to have their files kept under lock and key.

There are thousands of Germans who readily own up to their double lives with the Stasi. They have to, in fact, to get their pensions – one major function of the agency minding the Stasi files is to determine who qualifies for retirement payments.

One of those qualifying was Erich Meilke, the Stasi supremo. Meilke collected about €400 monthly until he died in an old-age home in May 2000 at the age of 92. Meilke was sentenced to prison in 1993 for murdering two policemen in Berlin in 1931, but was set free a few years later due to senility and declining health. His former office is now the centrepiece of the **Forschungs- und Gedenkstätte Normannenstrasse** (*see p117*), otherwise known as the Stasi Museum.

attempt to see it all, but no one should miss the Südsee (South Sea) room. Here you'll find New Guinean masks and effigies, and a remarkable collection of original canoes and boats – some huge and elaborate. The African rooms are also impressive – look out for the superb carvings from Benin and the Congo, and beaded artefacts from Cameroon. An enlightening small exhibit explores the influence of African art on the German expressionists. The museum only has space to exhibit two per cent of its 500,000 items, and is hoping to move to the Stadtschloss in Mitte, should that ever get rebuilt.

This building also houses the **Museum für Indische Kunst** (Museum of Indian Art) and the **Museum für Ostasiatische Kunst** (Museum of East Asian Art). The former represents more than 3,000 years of Indian culture and is strong in terracottas, stone sculptures and bronzes and Central Asian wall paintings and sculptures from Buddhist cave temples along the Silk Route. The latter features archaeological objects and works of fine art from Japan, China and Korea from the early Stone Age to the present. An audio guide in English is available for the Indian and East Asian museums.

Museum Europäischer Kulturen

Im Winkel 6-8 (8390 1287/www.smpk.de). U1 Dahlem-Dorf. **Open** 10am-6pm Tue-Fri; 11am-6pm Sat, Sun. **Admission** €4; €2 concessions. **No credit cards**.

Very near the Dahlem Museum complex, the Museum of European Cultures aims to 'trace cultural phenomena common to all of Europe and specify their particular ethnic, regional, and national characteristics'. In mid-2005 it moves into the same building as the Ethnologisches Museum; until then it's only hosting small, temporary exhibitions.

Grunewald

The western edge of Zehlendorf is formed by the Havel river and the extensive **Grunewald**, largest of Berlin's many forests. On a fine Sunday afternoon, its lanes and paths are as packed as the Ku'damm, but with walkers, runners, cyclists, horse riders and dog walkers. This is because it's so easily accessible by S-Bahn. There are several restaurants next to Grunewald rail and S-Bahn station, and on the other side of the motorway at Schmetterlingsplatz, open April to October.

One popular destination is the **Teufelsee**, a tiny lake packed with bathers in summer, reached by heading west from the station along Schildhornweg for 15 minutes. Close by is the mound of the **Teufelsberg**, a product of wartime devastation – a railway was laid from Wittenbergplatz to carry the rubble that forms it. There are great views from the summit. The disused American electronic listening post that stood on the top is being dismantled, and there is talk of a hotel and conference centre.

South of the station, at Grunewaldsee, the 16th-century **Jagdschloss Grunewald** (Grunewald Hunting Lodge) is an example of the kind of building that once maintained the country life of the landed gentry, the Prussian Junkers. Here, you can find bathing by the lake in the summer, including a nudist section. The Grunewaldsee is also a favourite promenade for dogs and their owners, who refresh themselves in the deer-horn-bedecked Forsthaus Paulsborn.

A further kilometre south-east through the forest, you'll find **Chalet Suisse**, an over-the-top Swiss-themed restaurant popular with families because of its playground and petting zoo. Continuing for a further ten-minute walk takes you to the **Alliierten Museum** (Allied Museum; *see p116*) on Clayallee. A kilometre north of here is the **Brücke-Museum** (*see p116*), housing many surviving works by the influential Brücke group, including Kirchner, Heckel and Schmidt-Rottluff.

Further south, **Krumme Lanke** and **Schlachtensee** are pleasant urban lakes along the south-eastern edge of the Grunewald, perfect for picnicking, swimming or rowing – and each with its own station: U1 for Krumme Lanke, S1 for Schlachtensee.

On the west side of the Grunewald, halfway up Havelchaussee, is the **Grunewaldturm**, a tower built in 1897 in memory of Wilhelm I. It has an observation platform 105 metres (344 feet) above the lake, with views as far as Spandau and Potsdam. There is a restaurant at the base, and another over the road, both with garden terraces. A short walk south along Havelufer leads to the ferry to Lindwerder Insel (island), which also has a restaurant.

Sightseeing

Alliierten Museum

Clayallee 135, corner of Huttenweg (818 1990/ www.alliiertenmuseum.de). U1 Oskar-Helene-Heim/bus 115. **Open** 10am-6pm Mon, Tue, Thur-Sun. **Admission** free.

The Allies arrived as conquerors, kept West Berlin alive during the 1948 Airlift and finally went home again in 1994. In what used to be a US Forces cinema, this museum is mostly about the period of the Blockade and Airlift, documented with photos, tanks, jeeps, planes, weapons and uniforms. Outside is the building that was once the stop-and-search centrepiece of Checkpoint Charlie. Guided tours in English can be booked in advance. It's ten minutes' walk north up Clayallee from the U-Bahn station.

Brücke-Museum

Bussardsteig 9 (831 2029/www.bruecke-museum.de). U1 Oskar-Helene-Heim, then bus 115 to Pücklerstrasse. **Open** 11am-5pm Mon, Wed-Sun. **Admission** €5; €3 concessions. **No credit cards**.

This interesting museum is dedicated to the work of Die Brücke ('The Bridge'), an expressionist movement of painters founded in Dresden in 1905 before moving to Berlin. On display are oils, watercolours, drawings and sculptures by the main members: Schmidt-Rottluff; Heckel; Kirchner; Mueller and Pechstein. The Brücke is definitely worth seeing: a connoisseur's museum, small but satisfying .

Wannsee & Pfaueninsel

At the south-west edge of the Grunewald, you'll find boats and beaches in summer, castles and forests all through the year. **Strandbad Wannsee** is the largest inland beach in Europe. Between May and September, there are boats and pedaloes and hooded, two-person wicker sunchairs for hire, a playground and a separate section for nudists. Service buildings house showers, toilets, cafés, shops and kiosks.

The waters of the Havel (the Wannsee is an inlet of the river) are extensive and in summer warm enough for comfortable swimming; there is a strong current, so do not stray beyond the floating markers. The rest of the water is in constant use use by ferries, sailboats, speedboats and waterskiers.

A small bridge north of the beach leads to Schwanenwerder, once the exclusive private island retreat of Goebbels and now home to the international think-tank, the Aspen Institute.

The town of Wannsee to the south is clustered around the bay of the Grosser Wannsee and is dominated by the long stretch of promenade, Am Grossen Wannsee, scattered with hotels and fish restaurants. On the west side of the bay is the **Gedenkstätte Haus der Wannsee-Konferenz** (*see p117*). At this elegant *Gründerzeit* mansion, now a museum, a January 1942 meeting of prominent Nazis laid out plans for the extermination of the Jews.

A short distance from S-Bahn Wannsee along Bismarckstrasse is a little garden where German dramatist Heinrich von Kleist shot himself in 1811; the beautiful view of Kleiner Wannsee was the last thing he wanted to see.

On the other side of the railway tracks is **Düppler Forst**, a forest including a nature reserve at Grosses Fenn at the south-western end. Travelling three S-Bahn stops to Mexikoplatz, then taking the 629 or 211 bus, brings you to the reconstructed 14th-century village at **Museumsdorf Düppel** (*see p117*).

From Wannsee, bus 218 scoots through the forest to a ferry pier on the Havel, and then it's a brief ferry ride to **Pfaueninsel** (Peacock Island). This 98-hectare (242-acre) island was inhabited in prehistoric times, but isn't mentioned in archives until 1683. Two years later the Grand Elector presented it to Johann Kunckel von Löwenstein, a chemist who experimented with alchemy but instead of gold produced 'ruby glass', examples of which are on view in the castle. But it was only at the start of the Romantic era that the island's windswept charms began to attract more serious interest. In 1793 Friedrich Wilhelm II purchased it and built a Schloss for his mistress, but died in 1797 before they had a chance to move in. Its first residents were the happily married couple Friedrich Wilhelm III and Queen Luise, who spent much of their time together on the island, even setting up a working farm there.

A royal menagerie was later developed. Most of the animals were moved to the new

Tiergarten Zoo in 1842, and only peacocks, pheasants, parrots, goats and sheep remain. Surviving structures include the **Jakobsbrunnen** (Jacob's Fountain), a copy of a Roman temple; the **Kavalierhaus** (Cavalier's House), built in 1803 from an original design by Schinkel; and the Swiss cottage, also based on a Schinkel plan. All are linked by winding, informal paths laid out in the English manner by Peter Joseph Lenné. A walk around the island, with its monumental trees and rough meadows, and views over the Havel, provides one of the most complete sensations of escape to be had within the borders of Berlin.

Back on the mainland, a short walk south along is the **Blockhaus Nikolskoe**, a huge wooden chalet built in 1819 by Friedrich Wilhelm II for his daughter Charlotte, and named after her husband, the future Tsar Nicholas of Russia. There is a magnificent view from the terrace, where you can enjoy mid-priced Berlin cuisine or coffee and cakes.

Gedenkstätte Haus der Wannsee-Konferenz

Am Grossen Wannsee 56-8 (805 0010/ www.ghwk.de). S1, S7 Wannsee, then bus 114. **Open** 10am-6pm daily. **Admission** free.

On 20 January 1942, a collection of prominent Nazis, chaired by Heydrich, gathered here to draw up plans for the Final Solution, making jokes and sipping brandy as they sorted out the practicalities of genocide. Today, this infamous villa has been converted into the Wannsee Conference Memorial House, a place of remembrance, with a photo exhibit on the conference and its consequences. Call in advance if you want to join an English-language tour (8050 1026), otherwise all information is in German.

Museumsdorf Düppel

Clauertstrasse 11 (802 6671/www.dueppel.de). S1 Mexikoplatz then bus 211, 629. **Open** *early Apr-late Oct* 3-7pm Thur; 10am-5pm Sun. **Admission** €2; €1 concessions. **No credit cards**.

At this 14th-century village, reconstructed around archaeological excavations, workers demonstrate handicrafts, medieval technology and farming techniques. Ox-cart rides for kids. Small snack bar.

Glienicke

West of Wannsee, and only a couple of kilometres from Potsdam, Glienicke was once the south-westernmost tip of West Berlin. The suspension bridge over the Havel here was named '**Brücke der Einheit**' (Bridge of Unity) because it joined Potsdam with Berlin. After the building of the Wall, it was painted different shades of olive green on the East and West sides and used only by Allied soldiers and for top-level prisoner and spy exchanges – Anatoly Scharansky was one of the last in 1986.

The main reason to come here is **Park Glienicke**. The centrepiece is **Schloss Glienicke** (not open to the public), originally a hunting lodge designed by Schinkel for Prinz Carl von Preussen, who banned all women visitors, adorned the garden walls with ancient relics collected on his Mediterranean holidays, and decided to simulate a walk from the Alps to Rome in the densely wooded park, laid out by Pückler in 1824-50. The summer houses, fountains and follies are all based on original Italian models, and the woods and fields surrounding them make an ideal place for a Sunday picnic, since this park is little visited.

At nearby Moorlake, there's a restaurant in a 1842 hunting lodge, which is good for game dishes or afternoon coffee and cakes.

East & south-east of the centre

The eastern side of the city is often considered a wasteland of decaying Communist blocks – and much of it truly is depressing – but there's still a lot of the flavour of old Berlin in the east. There are a couple of decent museums and parks in **Lichtenberg** and **Treptow**, but for the most rewarding escapism in the east, head for characterful **Köpenick**.

Lichtenberg & Treptow

Many neighbourhoods of the old east have little to offer the visitor. East of Prenzlauer Berg and Friedrichshain, **Lichtenberg** isn't very appealing, though it does contain the **Tierpark Berlin-Friedrichsfelde** (Berlin-Friedrichsfelde Zoo; *see p118*) and the **Stasi Museum**, otherwise known as the **Forschungs- und Gedenkstätte Normannenstrasse** (see below and p114 **Miles of files**). Further south is the **Museum Berlin-Karlshorst** (*see p118*), documenting 20th-century Russian-German relations.

South of Lichtenberg and bordering Neukölln, **Treptow** is chiefly of note for **Treptower Park**, containing the massive **Sowjetisches Ehrenmal** (Soviet War Memorial). From here, several boats leave in the summer for trips along the Spree. The park continues to the south, where it becomes the **Plänterwald** and houses a big amusement park.

Forschungs- und Gedenkstätte Normannenstrasse (Stasi Museum)

Ruschestrasse 103 (553 6854/www.stasimuseum.de). Frankfurter Allee or U5 Magdalenenstrasse. **Open** 11am-6pm Mon-Fri; 2-6pm Sat, Sun. **Admission** €3.50; €2.50 concessions. **No credit cards**.

In what used to be part of the headquarters of the Ministerium für Staatssicherheit (the Stasi), you can look round the old offices of secret police chief Erich Mielke – his old uniform still hangs in his wardrobe – and view displays of bugging devices and spy cameras concealed in books, plant pots and Trabant car doors. There's also a lot of Communist kitsch, including banners and busts of Marx and Lenin. Documentation is in German. Tours in English can be booked in advance. *See p114* **Miles of files**.

Museum Berlin-Karlshorst

Zwieseler Strasse 4, corner Rheinsteinstrasse (5015 0810/www.museum-karlshorst.de). S3 Karlshorst. **Open** 10am-6pm Tue-Sun. **Admission** free.

After the Soviets took Berlin, they commandeered this former German officers' club as HQ for the military administration and it was here, on the night of 8-9 May 1945, that German commanders signed the final and unconditional surrender, ending the war in Europe. The museum looks at the German-Soviet relationship over 70 years. Divided into 16 rooms including the conference room where the Nazis surrendered, it takes us through two world wars and one cold one, plus assorted pacts, victories and capitulations. Exhibits includes photos, memorabilia, maps, videos and propaganda posters. Buy a guide in English; exhibits are labelled in German and Russian. English tours can be booked in advance.

Tierpark Berlin-Friedrichsfelde

Am Tierpark 125 (515 3170/www.tierpark-berlin.de). U5 Tierpark. **Open** *Jan, Feb, mid Oct-Dec* 9am-5pm daily. *Mar, mid Sept-mid Oct* 9am-6pm daily. *Apr-mid Sept* 9am-7pm daily. **Admission** €9; €4 concessions. **No credit cards**.

Köpenick.

One of Europe's largest zoos, with plenty of roaming space for some animals, though others are kept in distressingly small cages. Animals include bears, elephants, big cats and penguins. In the zoo's north-west corner is the baroque Schloss Friedrichsfelde.

Köpenick

The name **Köpenick** is derived from the Slavonic *copanic*, meaning 'place on a river'. The old town, around 15 kilometres (nine miles) south-east of Mitte, stands at the confluence of the Spree and Dahme, and, having escaped bombing, decay and development by the GDR, still maintains much of its 18th-century character. This is one of the most sought-after areas of east Berlin, with handsome shops, cafés and restaurants clustered around the old centre. With its old buildings and extensive riverfront, it's a fine place for a Sunday afternoon wander.

The imposing **Rathaus** (Town Hall) is a good example of Wilhelmine civic architecture. It was here in 1906, two years after the building's completion, that Wilhelm Voigt, an unemployed cobbler who'd spent half his life in jail, dressed up as an army captain and ordered a detachment of soldiers to accompany him into the Treasury, where they emptied the town coffers. He instantly entered popular folklore, Carl Zuckmeyer immortalised him in a play as *Der Hauptmann von Köpenick* ('Captain of Köpenick'), and the Kaiser pardoned him because he had shown how obedient Prussian soldiers were. His theft is re-enacted every June during the Köpenicker summer festival.

Close by on Schlossinsel, **Schloss Köpenick**, with its medieval drawbridge, Renaissance gateway and baroque chapel, contains the **Kunstgewerbemuseum** (Museum of Applied Art; 266 2902; an outpost of its namesake in Tiergarten, *see p102*). Open-air concerts are held in the Schloss in summer.

Friedrichshagen & the Müggelsee

A couple of kilometres east of Köpenick, the village of **Friedrichshagen** has retained its independent character. The main street, Bölschestrasse, is lined with steep-roofed Brandenburg houses, and ends at the shores of a large lake, the **Grösser Müggelsee**.

Friedrichshagen is particularly enjoyable when the Berliner Burgerbräu brewery, family-owned since 1869, throws open its gates for its annual summer celebration. Booths line Bölschestrasse, the brewery lays on music, and people sit on the shores with cold beer and look out over the lake. Boat tours are available, and the restaurant Braustubl, next to the brewery, serves especially good Berlin cuisine.

Eat, Drink, Shop

Features

Restaurants

Pork may still dominate local menus, but there's more to pig out on than pig.

French food and high fashion are part of the pattern at **Borchardt**. *See p121.*

Berlin could never be described as a haven of gastronomy, but it's possible to dine well here. And if you're after a hearty hunk of roast pork, you should relish the prospect. There's no doubt the city's eating-out scene has improved since Reunification, but the starting point was low. There are many reasons for this. First, Germany's colonial experience didn't last very long, so there has been no long-term link with a foreign cuisine, as with India and Britain or Indonesia and the Dutch. Second, the basic building blocks of a great cuisine just aren't found in Prussian food (*see p129* **Pig and stodge**). Third, many locals are highly conservative in their tastes, and flatly reject foreign influences and strong flavours. Fourth, there's no great ethnic presence here besides the Turks, and they mostly prefer to eat at home and sell snacks to the general public.

Compared to a decade ago, though, it's a paradise. For one thing, the opening of the east meant a lot of cheap real estate that young restaurateurs found irresistible, so some of the most adventurous dining in Berlin is now found in Mitte and Prenzlauer Berg. For another, it's always the young and affluent who dictate dining trends, and Berlin's young and affluent have visited places like London, California and Tuscany, where they go for work and play, and have returned with demands for lighter, healthier and better seasoned eating. The Italian influence in particular is felt everywhere; it's hard to find a restaurant that doesn't offer *caprese* (tomato, mozzarella and basil salad), a pasta dish, or something with rucola (rocket) in it.

No longer is going out to dinner with a vegetarian in tow a chore for Berliners: it's now hard to walk into a decent restaurant here without finding several vegetarian options on the menu. There's still plenty missing, though. Chinese food is rare; good Chinese food even rarer. Sushi places have erupted in the past couple of years, but other Japanese food is hard to find. Indian restaurants too have proliferated, but the fare is so Germanised that Indians would have trouble recognising it. Neither would a Mexican recognise nearly all Berlin's 'Mexican' cuisine. And Americans are perfectly within their rights to decry what's sold as American food, right down to the frozen hockey-pucks universally used in the hamburgers. Still, they're better off than the British, whose cuisine doesn't get a look in.

Lunch in Berlin tends to be lunch, unlike in other parts of Germany, where the day's main meal is served at noon. Bakeries usually offer a variety of sandwiches, all on fresh *Brötchen*. If you're after more, try an *Imbiss*, or snack bar. The term embraces just about anywhere you get food but not table service, from stand-up street corner stalls to self-service snack bars offering all manner of exotic cuisines. Quality varies wildly, but some excellent, cheap food can be found. The Turkish *Imbisse* will offer the ubiquitous *Kebap*, Turkish 'pizza', half chickens and salads, while German *Imbisse* will tempt you with various kinds of sausage.

In the evenings, of course, there's much more choice. Take heed, though: Berliners like to eat out, particularly at weekends, and a place empty on a Tuesday may well be packed when you decide to go on a Friday. Reservations are a good idea, especially at more upmarket places.

In restaurants, a service charge of 17 per cent is added to the bill, but unless service has been awful (not impossible in Berlin, alas), diners usually round up the bill or, in classier joints, add ten per cent. Tips are handed to the server (or you tell staff how much to take) and never left on the table, which is considered by some to be insulting. When you hand over the cash, never say 'danke' unless you want staff to keep the change.

Mitte

German

Borchardt

Französische Strasse 47 (2038 7110). U6 Französische Strasse. **Open** 11.30am-late daily. **Main courses** €16-€22. **Credit** V. **Map** p316/p302 F3.

In the late 19th century, the original Borchardt opened next door at No.48. It became the place to be for politicians and society folk, but was destroyed in World War II. But now Roland Mary and Marina Richter have reconstructed a highly fashionable, Maxim's-inspired bistro which serves respectable French food. So why not snorkel down a dozen oysters and tuck into a fillet of pike-perch or beef after a cultural evening at the Komische Oper, the Staatsoper or the Konzerthaus?

Gambrinus

Linienstrasse 133 (282 6043). U6 Oranienburger Tor/bus N6. **Open** noon-4am Mon-Sat; 3pm-4am Sun. **Main courses** €6-€16. **No credit cards**. **Map** p303 G3.

Traditional Berlin local restaurant serving variations on the meat, potato and cabbage theme, and usefully open until four in the morning.

Honigmond

Borsigstrasse 28 (2844 5512/www.honigmond-berlin.de). U6 Zinnowitzer Strasse. **Open** 7.30am-1am daily. **Main courses** €6-€13.50. **No credit cards**. **Map** p302 F2.

This quiet, neighbourhood place serves up traditional German food alongside an innovative bi-weekly menu ranging from kangaroo to Swiss fondue. Noteworthy are the *Königsberger Klöpse* (east Prussian meatballs in a creamy caper sauce), and a very good Caesar salad. If the decor falls short of the 1920s nostalgia it tries to evoke, the excellent wine list and remarkable home-made bread (and butter!) make up for it. Small hotel upstairs too (*see p53*).

Kellerrestaurant im Brecht-Haus

Chausseestrasse 125 (282 3843/www.brechtkeller.de). U6 Oranienburger Tor. **Open** 6pm-1am daily. **Main courses** €9-€15. **No credit cards**. **Map** p316/p302 F3.

Bertholt Brecht got that sleek, well-fed look from the cooking his partner Helene Weigel learned in Vienna and Bohemia. This atmospheric place, crammed with model stage sets and Brecht memorabilia, serves a number of her specialities (indicated on the menu), including *Fleischlabberln* (spicy meat patties) and a mighty Wiener Schnitzel. In summer, the garden more than doubles the place's capacity.

Lutter & Wegner

Charlottenstrasse 56 (202 9540/www.lutter-wegner-gendarmenmarkt.de). U2, U6 Stadtmitte. **Open** 11am-3am daily. **Main courses** €15-€22. **Credit** AmEx, MC, V. **Map** p316/p306 F4.

This place has it all: history (one of Berlin's earliest wine merchants, its champagne became known locally as 'Sekt', now the common German term for any sparkling white wine); atmosphere in its airy, elegant rooms with plenty of fresh flowers; great German/Austrian/French cuisine; and excellent service. The wine list is justifiably legendary, and if the prices look high, just head for the bistro, where the same list holds sway along with perfect salads, cheese and ham plates, and excellent desserts.

Margaux

Unter den Linden 78 (2265 2611/www.hoffmann margaux-berlin.de). S1, S2, S25, S26 Unter den Linden. **Open** 7-10.30pm Mon-Wed; noon-2pm, 7-10.30pm Thur-Sat. **Main courses** €30-€40. **Credit** AmEx, DC, MC, V. **Map** p316/p302 F3.

The ultimate 'new Berlin' dining temple, this top-flight restaurant features Michael Hoffman's slightly avant-garde take on classic French cooking. Try the stewed shoulder of venison seasoned with coriander, anise and saffron. The spacious interior is lit by glowing columns of honey-hued onyx, which reflect in the black marble floors. Named for its extraordinary wine list, which includes some 30 vintages of Château Margaux. Service is first-rate.

Maxwell

Bergstrasse 22 (280 7121/www.restaurant-maxwell.de). U6 Oranienburger Tor. **Open** 6pm-midnight daily. **Main courses** €15-€20. **Credit** AmEx, DC, MC, V. **Map** p302 F2.

Set in a handsome old brewery, Maxwell's plates of food imitate the art on the walls. Witness the polka-dotted platter, Duck à la Hirst, created by chef Uwe Popall. The duck's black pepper sauce supposedly brings out the subliminal dark side of Hirst's works. Service is slow, the portions are small, but nobody seems to mind.

stäV

Schiffbauerdamm 8 (282 3965/www.stäv.de). U6, S1, S2, S3, S5, S7, S9, S25, S26, S75 Friedrichstrasse. **Open** 10am-1am daily. **Main courses** €7-€12.50. **Credit** MC, V. **Map** p316/p302 F3.

A 'ständige Vertretung' (the term West Germany used for their non-Embassy in the East) of the Rhineland in Berlin, stäV caters to homesick Bonners in what has become a quarter full of them. Both Berliners and Rhinelanders can sink their teeth into Himmel und Äade ('heaven and earth': Blutwurst with mashed potatoes and apples), raisiny Rhinish Sauerbraten, and drink Cologne's sneakily powerful beer, Kölsch, while puzzling over the political in-jokes on the wall. There's also a good list of Rhine wines.

Vau

Jägerstrasse 54-5 (202 9730/www.vau-berlin.de). U6 Französische Strasse. **Open** noon-2.30pm, 7pm-10pm Mon-Sat. **Menus** €78-€110. **Credit** AmEx, DC, MC, V. **Map** p316/p306 F4.

The love of innovation and inspiration from all corners of the globe make chef Kolja Kleeberg's menu one of the best in town. His lobster with mango and black olives with a tapenade, and braised pork belly with grilled scallops, are complemented by an extensive wine list (starting at €26). A glass of Banyuls to go with your wine tart with red wine ice-cream is no shabby finish. Downstairs, the fake-library bar is terrific for special occasions. Booking essential.

Weinbar Rutz

Chausseestrasse 8 (2462 8760/www.rutz-weinbar.de). U6 Zinnowitzer Strasse. **Open** 5pm-midnight Mon-Sat. **Main courses** €19.50-€24. **Credit** AmEx, DC, MC, V. **Map** p302 E2.

The impressive ground-floor bar has a whole wall showcasing fine wines from around the globe – not obscure New World vintages, but the best of the best. No tasting notes on the exhaustive list, though. In the second-floor restaurant, TV chef Ralf Zacherl serves a limited nouvelle menu, all of it beautifully presented. Snacks downstairs. Booking essential.

Americas

¡Viva México!

Chausseestrasse 36 (280 7865). U6 Zinnowitzer Strasse. **Open** noon-11pm Mon-Fri; 5pm-midnight Sat, Sun. **Main courses** €3-€11. **No credit cards. Map** p302 E2.

A valuable find: a Mexican woman and her family preparing authentic interior Mexican food in Berlin. Highlights include the own-made refried beans and at least four salsas (three of which are good and spicy) to put on tacos, burritos and tortas, and the decent range of dinner items. This place would be good in Mexico, let alone Germany.

French

Entrecote Fred's

Schutzenstrasse 5 (2016 5496/www.entrecote.de). U2, U6 Stadtmitte. **Open** noon-midnight Mon-Fri, 6pm-midnight Sat. **Main courses** €12-€24. **Credit** AmEx, DC, MC, V. **Map** p306 F4.

Steak and frites in a brasserie ambience close to Checkpoint Charlie. The food here is simple but very well prepared and Fred's Special Sauce, a mixed herb remoulade, is excellent. The long wine list encompasses all French regions, and there are half bottles. Professional service, classic desserts and plenty of room.

Greek

Skales

Rosenthaler Strasse 12 (283 3006). U8 Weinmeisterstrasse. **Open** 5pm-late daily. **Main courses** €6.50-€13.50. **Credit** AmEx, DC, MC, V. **Map** p316/p302 F3.

To look at this huge, high-ceilinged room, you'd never guess it was once a storage space for uniforms and other paraphernalia of the Freie Deutsche Jugend, the GDR's youth organisation. It has since gone through a severe ideological change: snooty service matches the often snooty customers, but the Greek food is well prepared.

Imbiss/fast food

Der Imbiss W

Kastanienallee 49 (4849 2657). U8 Rosenthaler Platz. **Open** *Winter* 1pm-midnight daily. *Summer* noon-midnight daily. **Main courses** €4-€6.50. **No credit cards. Map** p303 G2.

Owned by 103 (*see p142*), the bar next door, this vogueish place is named for Gordon W, the minor celebrity chef from Canada, who devised its wacky fusion menu of 'naan pizzas', 'rice shells' and international 'dressings'. The food tries hard to be clever but it's not actually that well executed and, with a few wok dishes in preparation, the open kitchen can be a bit much in the small space. For a bit of air, grab an outside table in summer.

Maxwell, where food imitates art and dishes are named after Damien Hirst. *See p122.*

Misuyen Asia-Bistro

Torstrasse 22 (247 7269). U2 Rosa-Luxemburg-Platz. **Open** noon-11pm Mon-Sat. **Main courses** €2.50-€6. **No credit cards**. **Map** p303 G2

Sometimes, if you look behind the surface of one of Berlin's many Asian *Imbisse*, you'll find the unexpected. In Misuyen's case, it's Laotian food, albeit mixed with the usual greatest hits: Thai, Indonesian, Chinese. Lighter and with more fresh vegetables than the usual Asian fare, the Laotian dishes can also be made without MSG if you say the magic words: 'Ohne Glutamat, bitte'.

RNBS

Oranienburger Strasse 27 (0179 540 2505/ www.rnbs.de). S1, S2, S25, S26 Oranienburger Strasse. **Open** noon-midnight daily. **Main courses** €2.50-€3.90. **No credit cards**. **Map** p316/p302 F3.

Contemporary interior in eau de nil and orange for a selection of pan-Asian ricepaper rolls, noodles, meat- and fishballs, and soups – all made without artificial ingredients or flavourings.

International

Liberta

Weinbergsweg 27 (4405 7337). U8 Rosenthaler Platz/bus N2, N8. **Open** 10am-1am Mon-Sat; 10am-1am Sun. **Main courses** €5.50-€11. **No credit cards**. **Map** p302 F2.

Kurdish owner Erdal offers a solid menu veering from Mediterranean to Tex-Mex. Many of the dishes are vegetarian and prepared with home-made yogurt. Generous portions are usually preceded by toasted Turkish bread with tomato yogurt dressing. The place also serves as a bar; cocktails are professionally concocted. Tables outside in summer and on Sundays a brunch buffet with bangers, eggs and oriental delicacies (11am-6pm; €7 a head).

Urban Comfort Food

Zionskirchstrasse 5 (4862 3131). U8 Rosenthaler Platz. **Open** noon-1am Mon-Fri; 6pm-late Sat; 10am-6pm Sun. **No credit cards**. **Map** p303 G2.

This small, cosy eatery next to Roberta (*see p145*) and Hotelbar (*see p224*) resolves the oxymoronic implications of its name with great aplomb. The decor is a *Five Easy Pieces*-era diner imagined by a hip designer, and the menu puts an urban spin on filling, nourishing 'comfort' food. Think ravioli variations, hearty spiced soups based on potato or pumpkin, or home-baked bread that's crispy on the outside and slightly gooey in the middle. For breakfast and lunch there are classic Italian-American deli sandwiches with fresh ingredients. In the evenings, a selection of soups, salads and meat, fish and veggie dishes. Menu changes every Wednesday.

Italian

Cantamaggio

Alte Schönhauser Strasse 4 (283 1895). U8 Rosa-Luxemburg-Platz. **Open** 6pm-midnight Mon-Sat. **Main courses** €10-€18. **Credit** AmEx, DC, MC, V. **Map** p316/p303 G3.

A quick perusal of Cantamaggio's menu will give you an idea of its wild mix of fancy new dishes and old standbys. Among the former, how about rose petal pan-fried duck breast with strawberry vinaigrette on lamb's lettuce, or duck liver with yellow chanterelles? Or perhaps you'd rather stick to the classic cannelloni with beef or fettuccine with lamb ragout. Desserts are of the classic variety. This is a well-loved restaurant, and elegant if a mite spartan; the loud floral arrangements don't help much to absorb the loud chatter of habitués.

Cibo Matto

Rosenthaler Strasse 44 (283 85170/www.cibomatto.de). S3, S5, S7, S9, S75 Hackescher Markt. **Open** 9am-late daily. **Main courses** €10-€21. **Credit** MC, V. **Map** p316/p302 F3.

Decent food in a blandly chichi setting just across from the Hackesche Höfe. The menu is intelligent Italian with lightly seasoned fish and fowl, and by far the best bet is the daily lunch special including a starter for about €6.50. We were told Cibo Matto means something like 'Crazy Kitchen' in Italian. That suggests a level of creativity largely unattained, but still, you'll get a well-crafted platter that smells and tastes good without being pretentious. Cocktail lounge off to the side of the bar; great summer terrace in the back.

Malatesta

Charlottenstrasse 59 (2094 5071/www.restaurant-malatesta.de). U2, U6 Stadtmitte. **Open** noon-midnight Mon-Sat. **Main courses** €7-€21. **Credit** AmEx, MC, V. **Map** p306 F4.

Nice location at the end of the Gendarmenmarkt and with food and prices that you would expect from a first-class Italian. The restaurant is spread out over two floors. Downstairs there is a small bar for an aperitif or coffee. Meanwhile, starters such as grilled artichoke hearts or antipasto misto, the usual suspects in terms of home-made pastas, daily fish specialities and meat dishes such as oxtail filled with truffles, are among the reasons to linger upstairs. Service is attentive but not intrusive. The third in a trilogy of Piero De Vetis' restaurants (after Osteria No.1, *see p133*, and Sale e Tabbachi, *see p133*) and definitely the best.

Rosmini Pastamanufaktur

Rosmini Pastamanufaktur Invalidenstrasse 151 (2809 6844/www.rosmini.de). U8 Rosenthaler Platz. **Open** noon-midnight Mon-Fri; 10am-4pm, 5.30pm-midnight Sat, Sun. *Cocktail bar* 6pm-2am Tue-Thur; 6pm-3am Fri, Sat. **Main courses** €8-€17. **No credit cards**. **Map** p302 F2.

Appealing, affordable southern Italian food emerges from Rosmini's kitchens, and, yes, pasta is made on the premises. Although the starters and secondi here are wonderful, it's obvious that pasta is a passion, and the chefs seem to come up with endless variations; try the asparagus ravioli in the spring.

Salumeria Culinario

Tucholskystrasse 34 (2809 6767). S1, S2, S25, S26 Oranienburger Strasse. **Open** 10am-midnight Mon-Fri; 11am-late Sat, Sun. **Main courses** €8-€19. **No credit cards**. **Map** p316/p302 F3.

The daily changing lunch menu here is a great way to recharge depleted batteries after a morning of shopping or gallery-hopping. Pick up a bottle of wine, some cheese, olives and salami, or ponder the many panettones stocked in the Italian import section, or simply grab a plate to go. The size of this small café belies the 18 staff members needed to keep up with demand for the home-made gnocchi and busy catering service for small parties in the neighbourhood. There is space for 60 at the busy beer tables on the pavement.

Schwarzenraben

Neue Schönhauser Strasse 13 (2839 1698/www.schwarzenraben.de). U8 Weinmeisterstrasse. **Open** *Café* 10am-2am Mon-Thur, Sun; 10am-4am Fri, Sat. *Restaurant* 11.30am-late Mon-Sat; 2pm-late Sun. **Main courses** €13-€23. **Credit** AmEx, MC, V. **Map** p316/p303 G3.

Some contend that so many of Berlin's young film and theatre stars eat here because they're non-paying bait to draw other punters to owner Rudolf H Girolo's chicest of Berlin's Italo-Mediterranean joints. It may be hugely popular, yet it's hugely overrated. Still, the downstairs club sometimes features some interesting events.

Japanese

Kuchi

Gippstrasse 3 (2838 6622/www.kuchi.de). U8 Weinmeisterstrasse. **Open** noon-midnight Mon-Thur; 12:30pm-12:30am Fri-Sun. **Main courses** €7-€16. **Credit** AmEx, MC, V. **Map** p316/p302 F3.

It's the quality of the ingredients here that makes the food special. And there's not only fish in the sushi rolls: one maki, for example, is filled with chicken, mandarin oranges and poppy seeds. Delicate tempura, yakitori chicken hearts or shiitake mushrooms are all excellently served by a young, cool and multinational team. Packed at lunch. The private tatami room downstairs can be booked for parties or large groups. The Kantstrasse branch has a takeaway next door which also delivers.

Other locations: Kantstrasse 30 (3150 7815/delivery service 3150 7816).

Jewish

Café Oren

Oranienburger Strasse 28 (282 8228). S1, S2, S25, S26 Oranienburger Strasse. **Open** noon-1am Mon-Fri; 10am-1am daily Sat, Sun. **Main courses** €6-€14. **Credit** AmEx, V. **Map** p316/p302 F3.

A Jewish (not kosher) restaurant next to the Neue Synagoge offering standard fish and vegetarian dishes with Middle Eastern specialities. The garlic cream soup is thick and tasty; the salad fresh and crispy; and the soya cutlet breaded with sesame, in a light curry sauce served with fried banana and rice, is absolutely heavenly. There is an excellent vegetarian borscht and the Orient Express platter (a

Heavenly Jewish food is served up next to the Neue Synagogue at **Café Oren**. *See p124.*

large choice of meze) is great value. Tables appear in the courtyard every summer. Breakfast is served at weekends. Booking is advised.

North African

Fanous

Brunnenstrasse 3 (4435 2503). U8 Rosenthaler Platz/bus N2, N8. **Open** 11am-1am Mon-Thur, Sun; 11am-3.30am Fri, Sat. **Main courses** €4.50-€6.50. **No credit cards**. **Map** p302 F1/2.

Moroccan snack bar convenient for the Rosenthaler Platz nightlife hood. The deep-fried halloumi cheese with salad in pita bread, topped off with a choice of mango or sesame sauce, is the vegetarian's best bet. Carnivores should try the delicious mergez (lamb sausages). Also couscous, served warm and as tabbouleh salad. Free tea with your meal.

Oriental

Good Time

Chausseestrasse 1 (280 46015/www.goodtime-berlin.de). U6 Oranienburger Tor. **Open** noon-midnight daily. **Main courses** €8.50-€17. **Credit** AmEx, MC, V. **Map** p302 F3.

We've hardly tried the Thai offerings at this Thai/Indonesian restaurant because Indonesian food is so rare in Berlin, and Good Time does it well. The *rijstafel* is excellent, the soup and the *rendang* (a beef dish) being particularly notable. German tastes are catered to with a wide range of noodle dishes. Service is wonderfully friendly. If you get a window seat, there are great people-watching opportunities at this busy corner site.

Mirchi

Oranienburger Strasse 50 (2844 4480/www.mirchi.de). U6 Oranienburger Tor. **Open** noon-1am Mon-Thur, Sun; noon-2am Fri, Sat. **Main courses** €7-€14. **Credit** AmEx, MC, V. **Map** p316/p302 F3.

An ambitious 'Singapore fusion' concept sees Indian, Chinese, Thai and Malay ideas rubbing shoulders on a longish, creative menu. The hearty Thai-Indian soups, based in coconut and curry spices, show the kitchen at its simple, tasty best. Nice entrance, lots of space, useful location.

Pan Asia

Rosenthaler Strasse 38 (2790 8811/www.panasia.de). U8 Weinmeisterstrasse or S3, S5, S7, S9, S75 Hackescher Markt. **Open** noon-1am daily. **Main courses** €6-€14. **Credit** AmEx, DC, MC, V. **Map** p316/p302 F3.

You may hear mixed reports about service and waiting times at this large and fashionably minimalist place to see, be seen and eat modern Asian food. Japanese beers and Chinese teas complement excellent wun tun, kim chi salad and a variety of soups and wok dishes. Hidden in a pleasant courtyard off busy Rosenthaler, with tables outside in summer. Self-conscious crowd, unbelievable bathrooms.

Swiss

Nola's am Weinberg

Veteranenstrasse 9 (4404 0766/www.nola.de). U8 Rosenthaler Platz. **Open** 10am-2am daily. **Main courses** €7.50-€14. **No credit cards**. **Map** p302 F2.

In a former park pavilion, with a quiet terrace overlooking the leafy Volkspark Weinberg and a spacious bar and dining-room within, the original intention here was to rotate the 'one world' menu from cuisine to cuisine. At press time, however, they'd decided to stick with Swiss. This makes sense to us, having sampled excellently hearty dishes such as venison goulash with mushrooms and spinach noodles, or rosti with spinach and cheese with fried eggs. The goats' cheese mousse with rucola starter is big enough for two and it's worth noting that, with a little thought, it's possible to eat quite cheaply here. Kitchen can sometimes drag its feet. Nice bar.

Vietnamese

Manngo

Mulackstrasse 29 (2804 0558). U8 Weinmeisterstrasse. **Open** noon-midnight Mon-Fri; 4pm-midnight Sat. **Main courses** €5. **No credit cards**. **Map** p303 G3.

Well positioned to catch the overspill from Monsieur Vuong around the corner, but also more relaxed than its neighbour and worth a visit for a selection of restrained but commendable noodle dishes. Stand-up and sit-down sections have separate entrances, but both are served by the same kitchen.

Monsieur Vuong

Alte Schönhauser Strasse 46 (3087 2643/www.monsieurvuong.de). U2 Rosa-Luxemburg-Platz. **Open** noon-midnight Mon-Sat; 2pm-midnight Sun. **Main courses** €5-€9. **No credit cards**. **Map** p316/p303 G3.

Something of an institution now, serving astonishingly toothsome and bitingly fresh Vietnamese soups and noodles. A couple of daily specials supplement a handful of regular dishes. Once you've tried the glass noodle salad, you'll understand why less is more. Chic, cheap, cheery and full of charm. But often packed to the rafters.

Prenzlauer Berg

German

Gugelhof

Knaackstrasse 37 (442 9229/www.gugelhof.com). U2 Senefelderplatz. **Open** 4pm-1am Mon-Fri; 10am-1am Sat, Sun. **Main courses** €12-€18. **Credit** AmEx, MC, V. **Map** p303 G2.

An Alsatian restaurant that pretty much pioneered the Kollwitzplatz scene in the 1990s, the Gugelhof is now a mature place. The food is refined but filling, the service is formal and smooth but friendly, and the furnishings feel comfortably worn in. The choucroute contains the best charcuterie in town, and the *backöfe* (meat and potatoes with root vegetables) uses superb riesling subtly to underpin its simplicity. There's also a selection of Alsatian *tartes flambées*. Commonly known as the restaurant where Gerhard Schröder took Bill Clinton for dinner. Reservations recommended.

Offenbach-Stuben

Stubbenkammerstrasse 8 (445 8502/www.offenbachstuben.de). S4, S8, S10 Prenzlauer Allee. **Open** 6pm-late daily. **Main courses** €10-€15. **Credit** AmEx, DC, MC, V. **Map** p303 G2.

An eccentric survivor from the old East Berlin, this was a private (non-state-owned) restaurant catering largely to the theatre crowd – and it has made the transition gracefully. There's nothing fancy in the kitchen, just classic German cuisine prepared with top-notch ingredients and the sure skill that comes from long practice. A fine Saxon wine list helps the food down. The walls are covered with memorabilia relating to the French composer from which the place takes its name.

Villa Groterjan

Milastrasse 2 (5471 3330/www.villa-groterjan.de). U2, S8, S10 Schönhauser Allee. **Open** noon-1am daily. **Main courses** €8-€14. **Credit** AmEx, MC, V. **Map** p303 G1.

The food here isn't worth a rave: it's standard east Berlin fare. But the place itself is a gem: all Old German architecture and vaulted ceilings. It was once a brewery, then a cinema in the 1920s, then a canteen for the DEFA film studio. Whether you're in the huge dining hall, the beer garden, or at the astonishing bar, it's a very special place.

Chinese

Ostwind

Husemannstrasse 13 (441 5951). U2 Senefelderplatz. **Open** 6pm-1am Mon-Sat; 10am-1am Sun. **Main courses** €6.50-€13. **No credit cards**. **Map** p303 G2.

Good Chinese food is rare in Berlin, so Ostwind's stabs at authenticity are welcome. Some of it might be bland, but such light dishes as dan-dan noodles sauced with spicy meat and bean sauce, or steamed dumplings with pork and vegetables, make a good lunch. Main courses are, by Chinese tradition, keyed to the seasons and change four times a year. It's not all great, but choose carefully and you will be rewarded with superb country cooking.

French

Bistro Chez Maurice

Bötzowstrasse 39 (425 0506). S4, S8, S10 Greifswalder Strasse. **Open** 5pm-midnight Mon, Sun; 11am-midnight Tue-Sat. **Main courses** €10-€17. **No credit cards**. **Map** p303 H2.

Maurice is gone, and so is the deli next door and the confusing 'menu and supplement' system that made for such chaos once upon a time. But at least the idea of serving solid, working class French fare – a rare thing in Berlin – is intact.

Imbiss/fast food

Cubandres

Danzigerstrasse 61 (0179 671 3086). U2 Eberswalder Strasse/tram 20. **Open** 12.30pm-midnight Mon-Thur; 12.30pm-1am Fri; 1pm-1am Sat; 1pm-midnight Sun. **Main courses** €4-€6. **No credit cards. Map** p303 G/H2.

Cuban snack bar with standing tables. Not very cosy seating, but a good place to fill up on variations of rice, beans, plaintain and choice of pork or chicken (rarely duplicating what's listed on the menu) before heading off into Prenzlauer Berg nightlife.

Konnopke's Imbiss

Under U-Bahn tracks, corner Danziger Strasse/Schönhauser Allee (no phone). U2 Eberswalder Strasse. **Open** 5am-7pm Mon-Sat. **Main courses** €1.25-€3.50. **No credit cards**. **Map** p303 G1.

When the BSE scare hit Berlin, Chancellor Schröder headed straight here, ordered one of the famous Currywursts, and said: 'I eat what I want!' A brilliant political move: not only did he say something savvy, but he went to an east Berlin *Wurstbudde* that has been under the same family management since 1930, and ordered the same thing as most of its customers. A quintessentially Berlin experience.

Indian

Desi

Wichertstrasse 57 (4471 8376/www.desiberlin.com). S8, S41, S42 Prenzlauer Allee. **Open** noon-midnight Mon-Sat; 11am-10pm Sun. **Main courses** €6-€14. **Credit** AmEx, DC, MC, V. **Map** p303 G1.

A bit out of the way but Desi has plenty going for it: the cooks here have all worked in London, sauces are prepared dish by dish, and despite a tandoori menu that's only adventurous in places, it's still a cut above most Berlin curry houses. Sunday brunch buffet from noon-9pm, €9 per head.

Italian

Trattoria Paparazzi

Husemannstrasse 35 (440 7333). U2 Eberswalder Strasse. **Open** 6pm-1am daily. **Main courses** €8-€15. **No credit cards**. **Map** p303 G2.

Hiding behind a daft name and ordinary façade is one of Berlin's best Italians. Cornerstone dishes are *malfatti* (pasta rolls seasoned with sage) and *strangolapretti* ('priest stranglers' of pasta, cheese and spinach with slivers of ham), but pay attention to daily specials. The southern Italian waiters can seem a bit spaced-out. House wines are excellent, though there are few other choices. Booking essential.

Pig and stodge

If you've eaten at a 'German restaurant' outside the German-speaking world, it's almost certain you've had Bavarian cuisine. This style of cooking encompasses several kinds of roasted pork, pork pot-roasted as *Sauerbraten*, creative ways with *Sauerkraut*, dumplings, potatoes, and desserts piled high with whipped cream.

Within Germany, one of the favourite regional cuisines is Swabian, from the southwest. Italian influences abound here, especially pasta, with which the Swabians have done great things. In Germany's wine-growing regions – Saxony, the Mosel and Rhine valleys – you'll also discover some fine cooking.

But Berlin is in the north-east, and, as the French will tell you, the cuisine is the soil. Berlin's soil is very sandy, which makes it poor for growing crops. Besides the ubiquitous pork, little but cabbage and potatoes is successful.

History also plays a part. Frederick the Great, who put Berlin on the map, was a Francophile. This Gallic influence is still felt in Berlin argot, but not on its tables (except in the higher price range). For instance, the hamburger-like patty known in most places as a *Frikadelle* is here called a *Boulette*, as it is in French. Sadly, Berlin's Francophilia helped deter the city from producing an haute cuisine of its own.

To the extent that there is a Berlin cuisine, it is working people's food, so it's cheap. Berlin's signature dish is *Eisbein*, yet this delicacy – pig's trotter with leathery skin and an overwhelming abundance of fat – is often enough to send people scurrying elsewhere for nourishment all by itself. However, once you get inside the gelatinous mass of the *Eisbein*, there are morsels of flesh that, having been cooked with all that fat around them, are delicious and moist. Some people spoon the fat into their mouths, but we wouldn't recommend it. *Eisbein* is sometimes pickled, and is served with puréed peas, *Erbsenpuree*.

If you'd rather have more meat than fat, try a *Kasseler*. Invented in Berlin by a butcher called Kassel, this delicately smoked pork chop or steak can be quite delicious, although it's not often found on menus. Another popular main course is liver, onions and apples, a Berlin tradition that's even harder to find if you're eating out.

A good lunch can be made from the *Currywurst*, where the meat is treated with curry powder, as is the heated ketchup that's poured over the top. It sounds horrible, but has its charms. The ur-Currywurst can be found at Prenzlauer Berg's Konnopke's Imbiss (*see p128*).

In many ways, Berlin cuisine epitomises everything that's wrong with German cooking in general: pig and stodge. No wonder Berliners flock to Italian restaurants. Nevertheless, once you've lived through a winter here and experienced coming out of the snow to a good hearty Berliner feast, you realise there's a time and place for everything. Even the heaviest food is sometimes a comfort.

Japanese

Oki

Oderberger Strasse 23 (4985 3130). U2 Eberswalder Strasse. **Open** 3pm-11pm Tue-Sun. **Main courses** €8.50-€16.50. **No credit cards**. **Map** p303 G2.

Small, bright local that successfully fuses north German food with Japanese delights in dishes such as potato soup with shiitake mushrooms or *Tafelspitz* with stir-fried vegetables and rice. Traditional sashimi, sushi, tempura and noodle udon are also on the small menu.

Sumo Sushi

Kastanienallee 24 (4435 6130/www.sumosushi.de). U2 Eberswalder Strasse/bus N2. **Open** noon-midnight Mon-Fri; 3pm-midnight Sat, Sun. **Main courses** €9-€12. **No credit cards**. **Map** p303 G2.

Stands out for its sashimi, made with really fresh-tasting tuna or salmon, and California maki, rice rolls with crabmeat and avocado rolled in red caviar. Plus they have an offer fish-lovers won't be able to refuse: all-you-can-eat sushi for €15 on weekday evenings. Take-away and online delivery services are available too.

Other locations: Chausseestrasse 19, Mitte U6 Zinnowitzer Strasse (2404 8910).

Mongolian

Chinggis-Khan

Bornholmer Strasse 10 (4471 5604/www.chinggis.de). S1, S2, S8, S25 Bornholmer Strasse/tram 50. **Open** 4.30-midnight Mon-Fri; noon-midnight Sat, Sun. **Main courses** €5-€10. **No credit cards**. **Map** p302 F1.

Off the beaten path, but worth seeking out: the ample helpings of rice, fried beef and vegetarian dishes can fuel hordes. A particular delicacy are the pelmeni-like ravioli filled with meat.

Russian

Pasternak

Knaackstrasse 22-4 (441 3399). U2 Senefelderplatz. **Open** noon-1am daily. **Main courses** €12-€15. **Credit** MC. **Map** p303 G2.

Book if you want to dine in this small bar and Russian restaurant on Prenzlauer Berg's most chic corner. It's often crammed, which can be irritating at some tables as people brush past you looking for places. Try for a table in the small side room. But the atmosphere is friendly and the food fine and filling. Kick off with borscht or the ample fish plate, then broach the hearty beef stroganoff.

Sri Lankan

Suriya Kanthi

Knaackstrasse 4 (442 5301). U2 Senefelderplatz Knaackstrasse/tram 1. **Open** noon-1am daily. **Main courses** €5-€9. **No credit cards. Map** p303 G2.

Authentic Sri Lankan and south Indian food is to be had at both of these locations. Dishes include fiery curries, many involving exotic vegetables such as jackfruit; others feature organic Neuland meat. Try the hoppers – similar to crêpes – instead of rice, and cool down afterwards with an avocado milkshake.

Other locations: Chandra Kumari, Gneisenaustrasse 4 (694 3056).

Thai

Bangkok

Prenzlauer Allee 46 (443 9405). U2 Eberswalder Strasse/Marienburger Strasse/tram 1. **Open** noon-11pm daily. **Main courses** €4-€8. **No credit cards. Map** p303 G2.

This popular little Thai, with beach-hut decor and authentic dishes, is a firm local favourite. Informal, friendly and fun. Booking recommended.

Mao Thai

Wörther Strasse 30 (441 9261). U2 Senefelderplatz. **Open** noon-midnight daily. **Main courses** €10-€20. **Credit** AmEx, DC, MC, V. **Map** p303 G2.

Charming service and excellent food comes with a 'to whom it may concern' testimonial from the Thai ambassador, framed on the stairs down to the lower level. Classics such as Tom Kai Gai, vegetarian spring rolls, green papaya salad with peanuts and sweet vinegar dressing, and glass noodle salad with minced pork are all spectacular, and the red tofu and vegetable curry is the best in town. Comfortable, well established and friendly.

Other locations: Toans Hütte, Dirkstenstrasse 40, Mitte (283 6940).

Turkish

Miro

Raumerstrasse 29 (4473 3013). S8, S41, S42 Prenzlauer Allee. **Open** 10am-late daily. **Main courses** €8-€17. **Credit** V. **Map** p303 G2.

Named, they say, not after the painter but in honour of a 'Mespotamian natural philosopher', this cool, roomy place serves Anatolian specialities and well priced drinks. The menu is long and intriguing, with many vegetarian possibilities, legions of warm and cold starters and a good salad selection – all of which arrive in generous proportions. Friendly service. Breakfast until 3pm.

Friedrichshain

German

Fritz Fischer

Stralauer Allee 1 (520 072 202/www.fritz-fischer.de). U1, U15, S3, S5, S6, S7, S9, S75 Warschauer Strasse. **Open** 6.30pm-late Mon-Sat. **Main courses** €13-€17. **Credit** MC, V. **Map** p316/p303 G3.

On the ground floor of a 19th-century egg warehouse shared with the new European headquarters of Universal Music, light and well-prepared new German dishes are served up with impressive views of an eclectic riverside landscape. At lunchtime, the restaurant doubles as Universal's company canteen, but in the evening the lighting changes, tables are set and the atmosphere becomes more intimate for the seasonal, fish-dominated menu composed by Rainer Mennig.

Czech

Prager Hopfenstube

Karl-Marx-Allee 127 (426 7367). U5 Weberwiese. **Open** 11am-midnight daily. **Main courses** €7-€22. **Credit** V. **Map** p303 G3/H3.

Czech food on the former socialist Champs Elysées. You'll find all the faves from your last Prague holiday on the menu here: *svickova* (roast beef), *veprova pecene* (roast pork), *knedliky* (dumplings) and the lone but tasty prospect for vegetarians: *smazeny syr* or breaded and deep-fried hermelin cheese served with remoulade sauce and fries. Wash down your heavy meal with mugs of Staropramen beer; afterwards, a Becherovka herbal digestif should help stave off the worst indigestion. Fast and friendly service from the slyly funny waitress is a pleasingly inauthentic touch.

Imbiss/fast food

Nil

Grünberger Strasse 52 (2904 7713). U1, U15, S3, S5, S6, S7, S9, S75 Warschauer Strasse or U5 Frankfurter Tor. **Open** 11am-1am daily. **Main courses** €2.50-€4. **No credit cards. Map** p88.

Markthalle: a Kreuzberg legend. *See p132.*

Sudanese *Imbiss* offering well-priced lamb and chicken dishes and an excellent vegetarian selection, including great falafel, halloumi and aubergine salad. Hot peanut sauces are the speciality of this small, friendly place. Stand-up only, though.

Italian

Kingston Pizzerei

Simon-Dach-Strasse 12 (2977 6494). U1, U15, S3, S5, S6, S7, S9, S75 Warschauer Strasse or U5 Samariterstrasse. **Open** noon-10pm daily. **Main courses** €1.50-€3. **No credit cards. Map** p88.

They've only got five dishes on the menu and two of 'em are pizza. You're definitely getting your euro's worth for the €1.50 mini and €3 biggie pizza, whose ultra-thin and light, crispy crust is a welcome change for this district. A big plus is that you can pile on as many of their 18 toppings as you like for no extra charge. Tables are limited, but in summer there's plenty of outdoor seating.

Mediterranean

Pi Bar

Gabriel-Max-Strasse 17 (2936 7581). U1, U15, S3, S5, S6, S7, S9, S75 Warschauer Strasse or U5 Samariterstrasse. **Open** 4pm-late daily; 10am-midnight Sun. **Main courses** €6-€18.50. **No credit cards. Map** p88.

An amazing variety of seafood and vegetarian dinners are served at this restaurant and bar, and this is the only place in the area where you can find crab or scampi. Pi Bar is relatively new and draws a thirtysomething crowd, many less interested in the food than in the 6-8.30pm Happy Hour featuring 70 different cocktails and long drinks.

Umspannwerk Ost

Palisadenstrasse 48 (4280 9497/www.umspannwerk-ost.de). U5 Weberwiese. **Open** 11:30am-late daily. **Main courses** €8.50-€16. **Credit** AmEx, MC, V. **No credit cards. Map** p303 H3.

Formerly a transformer station, this amazing 1900 tiled hall was high enough to have an open gallery for additional seating constructed within it. Instead of conserving the building's industrial charm, the owners turned it into something elegant. The impressive show-kitchen is not separated from the dining area, so you can peek over to check whether the cook is working on your pasta. The menu is short, but well thought out; it changes weekly, with a fuzzy focus on Mediterranean cuisine. Portion sizes seem dwarfed by the surroundings, however.

Middle Eastern

Shisha

Krossener Strasse 19 (2977 1995). U1, U15, S3, S5, S6, S7, S9, S75 Warschauer Strasse or U5 Samariterstrasse. **Open** 10am-late daily. **Main courses** €5-€13. **No credit cards. Map** p88.

Arabic restaurant/bar serving exotic vegetarian and meat dishes from Lebanon, Syria and Iraq. Hookahs are the real attraction for the twentysomething crowd: take advantage of the ten flavoured tobaccos and huge elevated couch to smoke yourself silly from 4-8pm daily at €3.50 per hookah.

North African

Meyman

Krossener Strasse 11a (0162 469 4708). U1, U15, S3, S5, S6, S7, S9, S75 Warschauer Strasse or U5 Samariterstrasse. **Open** noon-midnight Mon-Thur, Sun; noon-2am Fri, Sat. **Main courses** €2.50-€6.50. **No credit cards. Map** p88.

Moroccan and Arabic specialities plus fresh fruit shakes and pizza are served in this warm and comfortable *Imbiss* where there are usually plenty of tables. It's a bit pricier than comparable places, but fresh ingredients and a wide variety of dishes keep them coming – and few others are open this late.

Vegetarian

Volkswirtschaft

Krossener Strasse 17 (2900 4604). U1, U15, S3, S5, S6, S7, S9, S75 Warschauer Strasse or U5 Samariterstrasse. **Open** 1pm-late Thur-Sat; 10am-late Sun; 6pm-late Mon-Wed. **Main courses** €5-€10. **No credit cards. Map** p88.

A little of everything here: occasional live music, film nights, readings, vegetarian and vegan Sunday brunches and Pinkus, a seldom-found organic beer. As a restaurant, it prides itself on healthy, hearty dishes and an extensive menu that changes daily. Every day of the week has a culinary theme: Friday's fish and Tuesday's creative home cooking are especially good.

Kreuzberg

German/Austrian

Austria

Bergmannstrasse 30, on Marheineke Platz (694 4440). U7 Gneisenaustrasse. **Open** *Sept-May* 6pm-1am daily. *June-Aug* 7pm-1am daily. **Main courses** €13.50-€17.50. **Credit** MC, V. **Map** p306 F5.

With an awesome collection of antlers, this place does its best to look like an Austrian hunting lodge. The meat is organic, and there's a list of organic wines as well. From the Kapsreiter or Zipfer beer on tap to the famous, over-the-top schnitzel – and not forgetting the *Obstler* (fruit brandy) as the finishing touch to a hearty meal – this place is well worth a visit. Outdoor seating under a red-striped awning on a tree-lined square makes it a pleasant summer venue too. Book at weekends and in summer.

Grossbeerenkeller

Grossbeerenstrasse 90 (251 3064). U1, U7, U15 Möckernbrücke. **Open** 4pm-2am Mon-Fri; 6pm-2am Sat. **Main courses** €7-€16. **No credit cards**. **Map** p306 F5.

In business since 1862, Grossbeerenkeller serves good home cooking of a solid Berlinisch bent, and the Hoppel-Poppel breakfast is legendary.

Henne

Leuschnerdamm 25 (614 7730/www.henne-berlin.de). U1, U8 Kottbusser Tor. **Open** 7pm-1am Tue-Sun. **Main courses** €2-€6. **No credit cards**. **Map** p307 G4.

Only one thing on the menu: half a roast chicken. What sets it apart from other *Imbisse* with chickens rotating in their windows is that Henne's birds are organically raised, milk-roasted and, in short, the Platonic ideal of roast chicken. The only other decisions are whether to have cabbage or potato salad (we'd say cabbage) and which beer to wash it down with (try the Monchshof). Check the letter from JFK over the bar, regretting missing dinner here.

Markthalle

Pücklerstrasse 34 (617 5502). U1, U15 Görlitzer Bahnhof. **Open** 9am-3am Mon-Thur; 8am-4am Fri, Sat; 10am-3pm Sun. **Main courses** €8-€14. **Credit** AmEx, MC, V. **Map** p307 H4.

This unpretentious schnitzel restaurant and bar, with chunky tables and wood-panelled walls, has become a Kreuzberg institution – all the more so since its recent starring role in the novel and movie *Herr Lehmann*. Breakfast is served until 5pm, salads from noon, and, in the evening, a selection of filling and reasonably priced meals. It's also fun just to sit at the long bar and sample their impressive selection of grappas. After dinner, see what's on at the Privat Club downstairs (*see p229*).

French

Le Cochon Bourgeois

Fichtestrasse 24 (693 0101). U7 Südstern. **Open** 6pm-1am Tue-Sat. **Main courses** €15-€21. **No credit cards**. **Map** p307 G5.

A calm and welcoming oasis of excellent French cuisine tucked in a quiet and unassuming corner of Kreuzberg. People come from all over Berlin to sample dishes such as perch with a lentil salad, followed by quail with wild mushroom risotto, or guinea-fowl with winter vegetables and a saffron ginger sauce. Fantastic wines from the Alsace, plus a good selection of digestifs, round off an evening of quiet piano music and attentive service.

Imbiss/fast food

Kulinarische Delikatessen

Oppelner Strasse 4 (618 6758). U1, U15 Schlesisches Tor. **Open** 11am-11pm daily. **Main courses** €2-€3. **No credit cards**. **Map** p307 H5.

Why do Berliners eat such bad Turkish food? Maybe because they know in their hearts that some day they'll come upon a place like this, where the same old leaden selections are transmuted into gold. The doners aren't bad, but it's the vegetarian offerings that really shine. Try an aubergine-falafel combo kebab, a courgette kebab or even one of the salads.

Italian

Der Goldener Hahn

Pücklerstrasse 20 (618 8098/www.goldenerhahn.de). U1, U15 Görlitzer Bahnhof. **Open** 7pm-late daily. **Main courses** €9-€15. **Credit** V. **Map** p307 H4.

A small bar with brick walls, old wooden pharmacists' fittings and lots of stuffed chickens front a small restaurant with a reasonably priced selection of light Italian meals. Good spot for a discreet rendezvous. Couple of tables outside in summer.

Gorgonzola Club

Dresdener Strasse 121 (615 6473/www.gorgonzolaclub.de). U1, U8, U15 Kottbusser Tor. **Open** 6pm-midnight Mon-Thur, Sun; 6pm-2am Fri, Sat. **Main courses** €7-€13.50. **No credit cards**. **Map** p307 G4.

Popular place with a simple Italian menu. The authentic pizzas are well priced; spaghetti, linguini, gnocchi and ravioli are served with a choice of basic sauces, including, of course, gorgonzola. The walnut-gorgonzola dressing on the salads is excellent. The rush between movies at the English-language cinema Babylon (*see p194*) down the street gives this trattoria the air of a theatre district restaurant.

Watch the Thai ladies whip up sensational red and green curries at **Pagoda**. *See p135.*

Osteria No 1

Kreuzbergstrasse 71 (786 9162). U6, U7 Mehringdamm. **Open** noon-1am daily. **Main courses** €7.50-€19. **Credit** AmEx, DC, MC, V. **Map** p306 F5.

Most of Berlin's best Italian chefs paid their dues as waiting staff at this 1977-founded establishment, learning their lessons from a family of restaurateurs from Lecce. Osteria is run by Fabio Angilè, nephew of the owner of Sale e Tabacchi (*see p133*). The daily changing menu surprises even regulars who love taking advantage of the three-course lunch menu. In summer, one of Berlin's loveliest garden courtyards welcomes you. Staff are super-friendly. Booking recommended.

Sale e Tabacchi

Kochstrasse 18 (252 1155/2529 5003). U6 Kochstrasse. **Open** 9am-2am Mon-Fri; 10am-2am Sat, Sun. **Main courses** €7-€20. **Credit** MC, V. **Map** p306 F4.

Architects, journalists and politicians fill the long hall and back room with VIP chatter. The café up front keeps the quiet lingerers happy too. The restaurant is well known for fish dishes (tuna and swordfish carpaccio or loup de mer) and for the pretty courgette flowers filled with ricotta and mint, not to mention its large, impressive selection of Italian wines. The interior design is meant to reflect a time when salt (sale) and tobacco (tabacchi) were sold exclusively by the state. In summer, enjoy a leisurely lunch or dinner in the garden under lemon, orange and pomegranate trees.

Japanese

Sumo

Bergmannstrasse 89 (6900 4963/www.s-u-m-o.com). U7 Gneisenaustrasse. **Open** noon-midnight. **Main courses** €7-€16. **No credit cards**. **Map** p306 F5.

Quick, fresh food and intensive flavours in a well-lit modern interior spread over two floors. The sushi is masterfully prepared but you can also enjoy standards such as tempura udon soup, warm bean salad, chicken yakitori or grilled tuna on rice. The feeling is modern Japanese toned down for German tastes. DJs regularly rock the house; wide variety of teas.

Jewish

Liebermanns

Judisches Museum, Lindenstrasse 9-14 (2593 9760/www.liebermanns.de). U1, U6, U15 Hallesches Tor. **Open** 10am-8pm Mon; noon-10pm Tue-Sun. **Main courses** €5-€11. **Credit** AmEx, DC, MC, V. **Map** p306 F4.

The best dishes at the self-service, non-kosher (but kosher style) canteen of the Judisches Museum (*see p95*) are the mixed entrée plates that the staff lovingly put together at the buffet. From 4pm it's teatime with authentic Jewish pastries. In summer, tables are set outside in the courtyard. On Monday evenings there is an oriental buffet with live music (€22.50). For this we recommend booking.

Mediterranean

Svevo

Lausitzer Strasse 25 (6107 3216). U1, U15 Görlitzer Bahnhof. **Open** 6pm-late Mon-Sat. **Main courses** €12-€20. **Credit** AmEx, DC, MC, V. **Map** p307 H5.

Once this was a well kept secret. Now you have to book days in advance. No wonder. Chef Claudio Andretta balances the best of European cuisine on his menu. Imagine mountain trout wrapped in bacon and chopped egg on a bed of cress, beef fillet poached in sour cream served on black salsify and potato gnocchi, and, if you behave, a pyramid of rich chocolate with cassis sauce for dessert. The interior is simple but cramped. Good service.

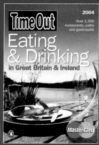

Middle Eastern

Baraka

Lausitzer Platz 6 (612 6330). U1, U15 Görlitzer Bahnhof. **Open** noon-midnight Mon-Thur, Sun; noon-1am Fri, Sat. **Main courses** €6-€10. **No credit cards. Map** p307 H4/5.

North African and Egyptian specialties such as couscous and foul (red beans and chickpeas in sesame sauce) enhance a menu also including oriental standards such as falafel, schwarma and kofte. You can take away your meal or eat in the cavernous restaurant, with its cosy seating on embroidered cushions. Vegetarian dishes are available too.

Thai

Pagoda

Bergmannstrasse 88 (691 2640). U7 Gneisenaustrasse. **Open** noon-midnight daily. **Main courses** €5.50-€9.50. **No credit cards. Map** p306 F5.

You can watch the gaggle of Thai ladies whipping up your meal behind the counter and ensure that everything is fresh and authentic. Red and green curries here are sensational and the pad Thai is heavenly. If the place looks crowded, don't worry: there's extra seating in the basement where you can watch the residents of a huge fish tank glide around.

Turkish

Hasir

Adalbertstrasse 10 (614 2373/www.hasir.de). U1, U8 Kottbusser Tor. **Open** 24hrs daily (often closes 2-3 hours early morning). **Main courses** €6-€11. **No credit cards. Map** p307 G4.

All hail the mother church of the doner kebab! You thought the Turks had been chewing on this tasty sandwich-like item for ages? Sorry: it was invented in Germany in 1971 by Mehmet Aygun, who eventually opened this highly successful chain of Turkish restaurants. While you'll get one of the best doners in Berlin here, you owe it to yourself to check out the rest of the menu, which involves various other skewered meats in sauce, and some agreeably addictive bread rolls. The dessert menu is also a winner – especially the rice pudding.

Other locations: Nürnberger Strasse 46, Wilmersdorf (217 7774); Breite Strasse 43, Spandau (353 04792); Maasenstrasse 10, Schöneberg (215 6060); Oranienburger Strasse 4, Mitte (2804 1616).

Merhaba

Wissmannstrasse 32 (692 1713/www.merhaba-restaurant.com). U7, U8 Hermannplatz. **Open** noon-midnight daily. **Main courses** €7-€14. **Credit** AmEx, DC, MC, V. **Map** p307 G6.

Turkish hotspot heavy on authentic wines and good traditional food. Ignore the main courses and share a selection of spicy appetisers instead. Effusive service but uninspiring decor of mirrors and chrome.

Vegetarian

Abendmahl

Muskauer Strasse 9 (612 5170/www.abendmahl-berlin.de). U1, U15 Görlitzer Bahnhof. **Open** 6pm-1am daily. **Main courses** €8-€16. **No credit cards. Map** p307 H4.

No matter whether you translate the name as 'evening meal', 'last supper' or 'communion', this is Berlin's temple of vegetarian gastronomy (although there is fish on the menu too). Dishes change according to the seasons and the weird and wonderful names they're given form part of the restaurant's off-beat charm: I Shot Andy Warhol for dessert anyone? The Flammendes Inferno (a Thai fish curry) isn't exactly flaming, but the soups are wonderful, there are great things done with *seitan*, and creativity is at a very high level throughout. The dessert selection looks so mouth-watering it's even available as a postcard series. Booking is recommended.

Lon Men

Grossbeerenstrasse 57a (7700 8037/www.lon-men-vegetarisch.de.vu). U6, U7 Mehringdamm. **Open** 6pm-midnight daily. **Buffet** €8 Mon-Thur; €10 Fri-Sun. **Credit** AmEx, MC, V. **Map** p306 F5.

Simply excellent all-you-can-eat Asian vegetarian buffet. No frills, no waiting, and plenty of tables to eat at, including some outside in summer.

Schöneberg

German

Storch

Wartburgstrasse 54 (784 2059/www.storch-berlin.de). U7 Eisenacher Strasse. **Open** 6pm-1am Mon-Sat. **Main courses** €8-€15. **Credit** AmEx MC,V. **Map** p305 D5.

It's hard to recommend Storch too highly. The Alsatian food – soup and salad starters, a sausage and sauerkraut platter, plus varying meat and fish dishes from the place where German and French cuisines rub shoulders – is finely prepared and generously proportioned. The house speciality is *tarte flambée*: a crispy pastry base cooked in a special oven and topped with either a combination of cheese, onion and bacon or (as a dessert) with apple, cinnamon and flaming Calvados. The cosmopolitan front-of-house staff are among the best and nicest crews in Berlin. Long wooden tables are shared by different parties and the atmosphere nearly always buzzes. Booking essential.

African

Bejte-Ethiopia

Zietenstrasse 8 (262 5933). U1, U2, U15 Nollendorfplatz or U2 Bülowstrasse/bus N19. **Open** 4pm-1am Mon-Fri; 2pm-2am Sat, Sun. **Main courses** €6-€10. **Credit** MC, V. **Map** p306 E4.

Ethiopian home cooking in a homey atmosphere. The food is essentially a variety of spiced meats and vegetables in varying states of stewedness, which are scooped on a piece of enjera bread and shovelled to the mouth. The wait staff is unobtrusive but happy to show the uninitiated the ropes. Not one for the cleanliness fanatic, though, as the restaurant has a somewhat gamey, but not unappetising feel.

Indian

India Haus

Feurigstrasse 38/corner Dominicusstrasse (781 2546/www.restaurant-indiahaus.de). U4, S4 Innsbrucker Platz. **Open** 2pm-midnight Mon-Fri; noon-midnight Sat, Sun. **Main courses** €5.50-€13. **Credit** AmEx, DC, V. **Map** p305 D6.

Proximity to the English-language Odeon cinema (*see p196*) redeems an out-of-the-way location, but food is good here and a long menu offers many vegetarian choices. The almond soup is excellent and the Malay kofta delicious. Cheaper *Imbiss* attached.

Italian

Café Aroma

Hochkirchstrasse 8 (782 5821/www.café-aroma.de). U7, S1, S2, S25, S26 Yorckstrasse. **Open** 6pm-midnight Mon-Fri; noon-midnight Sat; 11am-midnight Sun. **Main courses** €11-€15. **No credit cards. Map** p306 E5.

A temple of Tuscanophilia, Café Aroma has informal language classes on Sunday mornings, a wide selection of Italian magazines to read, and, oh yes, some of the best northern Italian food in Berlin. Appetisers and pastas are so good you may never stray over to the *secondi* (where all of the meat is organic). The wine list – including a wide variety by the glass – matches the standard set by the food. Booking is advised.

Petite Europe

Langenscheidtstrasse 1 (781 2964). U7 Kleistpark. **Open** 5pm-1am daily. **Main courses** €7-€13. **Credit** MC, V. **Map** p306 E5.

You may have to queue for a table in this popular, friendly place, but the turnover's fast. Weekly specials are first-rate, as are the pasta dishes. Salads could be better and none of this is haute cuisine, but it's all well made and inexpensive.

Middle Eastern

Habibi

Goltzstrasse 24, on Winterfeldtplatz (215 3332). U1, U2, U4 Nollendorfplatz. **Open** 11am-3am Mon-Thur, Sun; 11am-5am Fri, Sat. **Main courses** €4-€11. **No credit cards. Map** p305 D5.

Freshly made Middle Eastern specialities including falafel, kibbeh, tabouleh and various combination plates. Wash it down with freshly squeezed orange or carrot juice, and finish up with a complimentary tea and one of the wonderful pastries. The premises are light, bright and well run. Everything is excellently presented. This branch can get very full.

Other locations: Akazienstrasse 9, Schöneberg (787 4428); Körtestrasse 35, Kreuzberg (692 2401); Oranienstrasse 30, Kreuzberg (6165 8346).

Vegetarian

Hakuin

Martin-Luther-Strasse 1a (218 2027/www.restaurant-hakuin.de). U1, U2, U15 Wittenbergplatz. **Open** 5-11.30pm Tue-Sat; noon-11.30pm Sun. **Menu** €14.80-€16.20. **Credit** V. **Map** p305 D5.

Excellent but expensive Buddhist vegetarian food. In the beautiful main room people eat quietly amid a jungle of plants and a fish pool with a fountain. Fruit curries are often served on bamboo plates.

Tiergarten

German

Café Einstein

Kurfürstenstrasse 58 (261 5096). U2 Kurfürstenstrasse. **Open** 9am-1am daily. **Main courses** €9-€20. **Credit** AmEx, DC, V. **Map** p305 D4.

Red leather banquettes, parquet flooring and the crack of wooden chairs all contribute to the old Viennese Café Einstein experience. Fine Austrian cooking is produced alongside several nouveau cuisine specialities. Alternatively, you could simply order Apfelstrudel and coffee and soak up the atmosphere of this elegant 1878 villa. The other location has considerably less charm than the original.

Other locations: Unter den Linden 42, Mitte (204 3632).

Hugo's

Intercontinental Hotel, Budapester Strasse 2 (2602 1263/www.hugos-restaurant.de). U2, U9, S3, S5, S7, S9, S75 Zoologischer Garten. **Open** 6-10.30pm Mon-Sat. **Main courses** €33-€37. **Credit** AmEx, DC, MC, V. **Map** p305 D4.

Undoubtedly Berlin's best restaurant right now, and with the awards to prove it. Chef Thomas Kammeier juxtaposes classic haute cuisine with an avant-garde new German style. Dishes such as cheek of ox with beluga lentils and filled calamares, goose liver with mango, and Canadian lobster salad bring out the best of a mature kitchen and well-balanced menu. The beautiful room occupies the entire top floor of the Intercontinental (*see p60*), and has absorbing views in all directions. Service is formal but good.

Tiergarten Quelle

Stadtbahnbogen 482, Bachstrasse, near Haydnstrasse (392 7615). S3, S5, S7, S9 Tiergarten. **Open** noon-midnight Mon-Fri; noon-1am Sat, Sun. **Main courses** €7-€13. **No credit cards. Map** p301 D3.

Zen and the art of Buddhist cooking at **Hakuin.** *See p136.*

Students jam this funky bar for huge servings of food Grandma used to make: pork medallions with tomatoes and melted cheese with *Käsespätzle*; mixed grilled with sauerkraut; *Maultaschen* on spinach. To drink there are stone steins of foaming Schultheiss beer. The *Kaiserschmarren* is a meal in itself.

Australian

Corroboree

Sony Center, Bellevuestrasse 5 (2610 1705/www.corroboree.com). U2, S1, S2, S25, S26 Potsdamer Platz. **Open** 10.30am-1am daily. **Main courses** €7-€16. **Credit** MC, V. **Map** p306 F4.

The only decent place to go in the overpriced Sony Center. Not that Corroboree is cheap, mind you, but the selection of good Australian wines and tasty Australian dishes made with high quality fish and game such as kangaroo is worth shelling out for. And the atmosphere is stylish but relaxed, offering cosy sofas for intimate seating.

Imbiss/fast food

Cornwall Pasty Co

Beisheim Center, Auguste-Hauschner-Strasse 1 (2693 0811/www.cornwallpasty.de). U2, S1, S2, S25 Potsdamer Platz. **Open** 8am-7pm Mon-Sat; noon-6pm Sun. **Main courses** €2-€4. **No credit cards. Map** p306 F4.

Nothing particularly authentic about the pasties, and they're about twice what they'd cost in the UK, but they're tasty and freshly baked and make a change from more obvious franchise fodder in the Potsdamer Platz area.

Spätzle

S-Bahnbogen 390, Lüneberger Strasse (394 2057). S3, S5, S7, S9 Bellevue. **Open** 7am-11pm Mon-Fri; 6pm-11pm Sat; 2pm-11pm Sun. *Buffet* €8.50. **No credit cards. Map** p301 D3.

A lovely little place serving the pastas of Swabia, including *Spätzle* (a dish with Bratwurst, lentils or meatballs), *Käsespätzle* (with cheese), *Maultaschen* (resembles giant ravioli) and *Schupfnudelen* (a cross between pasta and chips). Wash your food down with a dark Berg beer.

Thai

Edd's

Lützowstrasse 81 (215 5294). U1, U15 Kurfürstenstrasse. **Open** 11.30am-3pm, 6pm-midnight Mon-Fri; 5pm-midnight Sat; 2pm-midnight Sun. **Main courses** €14-€21. **No credit cards. Map** p306 E4.

Known and loved by many, so bookings are essential for this comfortable, elegant Thai. A husband and wife team know how to please their guests with well balanced but somewhat spicy creations. Original is banana flower and prawn salad or try the duck no.18, double cooked and excellent.

Charlottenburg & Wilmersdorf

German/Austrian/Swiss

Alt-Luxemburg

Windscheldstrasse 31 (323 8730/www.altluxembourg.de). U2 Sophie-Charlotte-Platz. **Open** 5pm-late Mon-Sat. **Main courses** €24-€27. **Credit** AmEx, DC, V. **Map** p304 B4.

Karl Wannemacher combines classic French flavours with Asian influences in a wonderfully romantic dining room. Sample such wonders as horseradish terrine with smoked eel, or monkfish with a succulent saffron sauce informed with tomato. But this pretty little restaurant's wine list could do with more moderately priced bottles.

Understanding the menu

USEFUL PHRASES
I'd like to reserve a table for... people.
Ich möchte einen Tisch für...
Personen reservieren.
Are these places free?
Sind diese Plätze frei?
The menu, please. **Die Speisekarte, bitte.**
I am a vegetarian. **Ich bin Vegetarier.**
I am a diabetic. **Ich bin Diabetiker.**
We'd/I'd like to order.
Wir möchten/Ich möchte bestellen.
We'd/I'd like to pay. **Bezahlen, bitte.**

BASICS
Frühstück breakfast
Mittagessen lunch
Abendessen dinner
Imbiss snack
Vorspeise appetiser
Hauptgericht main course
Nachspeise dessert
Brot/Brötchen bread/rolls
Butter butter
Ei/Eier egg/eggs
Spiegeleier fried eggs
Rühreier scrambled eggs
Käse cheese
Nudeln/Teigwaren noodles/pasta
Sosse sauce
Salz salt
Pfeffer pepper
gekocht boiled
gebraten fried/roasted
paniert breaded/battered

SOUPS (SUPPEN)
Bohnensuppe bean soup
Brühe broth
Erbsensuppe pea soup
Hühnersuppe chicken soup
klare Brühe mit Leberknödeln clear broth with liver dumplings
Kraftbrühe clear meat broth
Linsensuppe lentil soup

MEAT, POULTRY AND GAME (FLEISCH, GEFLÜGEL UND WILD)
Ente duck
Gans goose
Hackfleisch ground meat/mince
Hirsch venison
Huhn/Hühnerfleisch chicken
Hähnchen chicken (when served in one piece)
Kaninchen rabbit
Kohlrouladen cabbage-rolls stuffed with pork
Kotelett chop
Lamm lamb
Leber liver
Nieren kidneys
Rindfleisch beef
Sauerbraten marinated roast beef
Schinken ham
Schnitzel thinly pounded piece of meat, usually breaded and sautéed
Schweinebraten roast pork
Schweinefleisch pork
Speck bacon
Truthahn turkey
Wachteln quail
Wurst sausage

FISH (FISCH)
Aal eel
Forelle trout
Garnelen prawns
Hummer lobster

First Floor

Hotel Palace, Budapester Strasse 45 (2502 1020/ www.palace.de). U2, U9, S3, S5, S7, S9, S75 Zoologischer Garten. **Open** noon-3pm, 6pm-10:30pm Mon-Fri, Sun; 6pm-10.30pm Sat. **Main courses** €32.50-€36.50. **Menus** €66.50-€104. **Credit** AmEx, DC, MC, V. **Map** p305 D4.

Now under the sway of hot young chef Mathias Bucholz, this is the place to come for refined French/European cuisine. Try, for example, Bresse pigeon served with chanterelles and a ragout of potatoes, or venison richly stuffed with foie gras – to say nothing of his loup de mer and Breton lobster served with saffron and tomato confit. The frozen Grand Marnier soufflé is as honourable as the unobtrusive service. Three menus are offered daily. Don't let the fact this is a hotel dining room put you off; it's one of Berlin's top tables.

Florian

Grolmanstrasse 52 (313 9184). S3, S5, S7, S9, S75 Savignyplatz. **Open** 6pm-3am daily. **Main courses** €10-€18. **Credit** MC, V. **Map** p305 C4.

Florian has anchored this quietly posh street for a couple of decades now. The two sisters who started the place knew what they were doing: offering fine south German food to the neighbourhood. The fact that the neighbourhood was filled with media types didn't hurt, of course. The cooking is hearty, the service impeccable. Yes, staff will put you in Siberia if they don't like your looks, but they'll also welcome you back if you're good.

Kabeljau cod
Karpfen carp
Krabbe crab or shrimp
Lachs salmon
Makrele mackerel
Matjes/Hering raw herring
Miesmuscheln mussels
Schellfisch haddock
Scholle plaice
Seezunge sole
Thunfisch tuna
Tintenfisch squid
Venusmuscheln clams
Zander pike-perch

HERBS AND SPICES (KRAUTER UND GEWÜRZE

Basilikum basil
Kümmel caraway
Mohn poppyseed
Nelken cloves
Origanum oregano
Petersilie parsley
Thymian thyme
Zimt cinnamon

VEGETABLES (GEMÜSE)

Blumenkohl cauliflower
Bohnen beans
Bratkartoffeln fried potatoes
Brechbohnen green beans
Champignons/Pilze mushrooms
Erbsen green peas
Erdnüsse peanuts
grüne Zwiebel spring onion
Gurke cucumber
Kartoffel potato
Knoblauch garlic
Knödel dumpling
Kohl cabbage
Kürbis pumpkin
Linsen lentils
Möhren carrots
Paprika peppers
Pommes chips
Rosenkohl Brussels sprouts
Rösti grated roast potatoes
rote Bete beetroot
Rotkohl red cabbage
Salat lettuce
Salzkartoffeln boiled potatoes
Sauerkraut shredded white cabbage
Spargel asparagus
Tomaten tomatoes
Zwiebeln onions

FRUIT (OBST)

Ananas pineapple
Apfel apple
Apfelsine orange
Birne pear
Erdbeeren strawberries
Heidelbeeren blueberries
Himbeeren raspberries
Kirsch cherry
Limette lime
Zitrone lemon

DRINKS (GETRÄNKE)

Bier beer
dunkles Bier/helles Bier dark beer/lager
Glühwein mulled wine
Kaffee coffee
Mineralwasser mineral water
Orangensaft orange juice
Saft juice
Tee tea
Wein wine

Marjellchen

Mommsenstrasse 9 (883 2676). S3, S5, S7, S9, S75 Savignyplatz. **Open** 5pm-midnight Mon-Sat. **Main courses** €10-€20. **Credit** AmEx, DC, MC, V. **Map** p305 C4.

There aren't many places like this around any more, serving specialities from East Prussia, Pomerania and Silesia in an atmosphere of old-fashioned *Gemütlichkeit*. Beautiful bar, great service. Larger-than-life owner recites poetry and sometimes sings.

Restaurant 44

Swiss Ôtel, Augsburger Strasse 44 (2201 02288). U9, U15 Kurfürstendamm. **Open** noon-11pm daily. **Main courses** €15-€34. **Credit** AmEx, DC, MC, V. **Map** p305 D4.

Chef Tim Raue offers two separate menus: one traditional French, the other radical Neue Deutsche Kuche. The latter includes the likes of sandalwood goat's cheese with lobster tail, or schnitzel with apple and beetroot salad and a remoulade of white truffle. Cool and comfortable room, elegantly framed desserts, and a fine selection of wines by the glass.

Julep's

Giesebrechtstrasse 3 (881 8823/www.juleps.de). U7 Adenauerplatz. **Open** 5pm-1am Mon-Wed, Sun; 5pm-2am Thur-Sat. **Main courses** €9-€15 **Credit** MC, V. **Map** p304 B4.

Most European restaurants' take on 'American' food misses the point by not acknowledging that dishes across the Atlantic today involve a fusion of flavours and aromas, traditional ingredients combined with exotic additives. Julep's gets it right, partly because the manager is Canadian and the new cook is from Philadelphia and both are probably homesick. Start with duck prosciutto or quesadillas with rhubarb and apple chutney, and move on to teriyaki chicken with lemon grass and basmati rice or Cajun-style red snapper. The Caesar salad is a classic, and recommended desserts include chocolate brownies made with Jack Daniels. Happy Hour is from 5pm to 8pm, and all night Sunday.

Chinese

Tai Ji

Uhlandstrasse 194 (313 2881). U2, U9, S3, S5, S7, S9, S75 Zoologischer Garten. **Open** noon-midnight daily. **Main courses** €8-€14. **Credit** MC, V. **Map** p305 C4.

Fashionable folk cluster at Good Friends around the corner, but the food is actually far better and much more authentic here. The room, a peaceful, semi-circular pavilion overlooking a garden courtyard, is showing its age, but starters such as daugoo and button mushrooms and onion, or wun tun in a red chilli sauce, are simply sensational. Main courses have bizarre names like Meeting on a Magic Bridge or Eight Drunken Immortals Cross the Sea, but don't let that put you off. Note: half the Beijing-Sichuan dishes are vegetarian.

French

Paris Bar

Kantstrasse 152 (313 8052). S3, S5, S7, S9, S75 Savignyplatz. **Open** noon-2am daily. **Main courses** €9-€25. **Credit** AmEx. **Map** p305 C4.

Owner Michel Wurthle's friendship with Martin Kippenberger and other artists is obvious from the art hanging over every available inch of wall and ceiling. Paris Bar, with its old-salon appeal, is one of Berlin's tried and true spots. It attracts a crowd of rowdy regulars, but newcomers can feel left out when seated in the rear. The food, to be honest, isn't nearly as good as the staff pretend. The adjoining Bar du Paris Bar opened in May 2001 and has yet to gain that settled-in feel. To experience the often rude service and pricey food, you'll need to book.

Indian

Surya

Grolmanstrasse 22 (312 9123). S3, S5, S7, S9, S75 Savignyplatz. **Open** noon-11pm daily. **Main courses** €5.50-€12.50. **No credit cards**. **Map** p305 C4.

You've probably had these dishes before, but not cooked so well – at least, not in Berlin. That's probably why Surya is in its second decade on flashy Grolmanstrasse, while many ritzier places come and go. It's related to both the *Imbiss* across the street and the grocery shop down the block. With a little bit of encouragement, the chef will amp up the spice levels for you. Service is top-drawer.

Italian

Enoteca Il Calice

Walter-Benjamin-Platz 4 (324 2308/www.enoiteca-il-calice.de). U7 Adenauerplatz. **Open** noon-2am daily. **Main courses** €18-€25. **Credit** AmEx, MC, V. **Map** p304 B5.

One for the oenophile – a relaxed place that serves mostly Italian food conceived to complement its 40-page list of wines. Many bottles are listed with full and rather fruity descriptions; there's also a selection of rather complicated offers, including seasonal menus which are accompanied by recommended bottles, and the friendly staff will organise a Weinkarusell with four wines for your own private tasting. Carpaccio is a speciality.

XII Apostoli

Savigny Passage, Bleibtreustrasse 49 (312 1433). S3, S5, S7, S9 Savignyplatz. **Open** 24 hrs daily. **Main courses** €10-€20. **No credit cards**. **Map** p305 C4.

It's overcrowded, it's cramped, it's pricey, the service varies from rushed to rude, the music is trad jazz doodling irritatingly at the edge of perception – but the pizzas are excellent and it's open 24 hours.

Other locations: S-Bahnbogen 177-180, Georgenstrasse, Mitte, 10117 (201 0222); Frankfurter Allee 108, Friedrichshain (2966 9123).

Japanese

Sachiko Sushi

Grolmanstrasse 47 (313 2282). S3, S5, S7, S9, S75 Savignyplatz. **Open** 11am-midnight daily. **Main courses** €12-€24. **No credit cards**. **Map** p305 C4.

Berlin's first *kaiten* sushi ('revolving sushi') joint. The scrummy morsels come round on little boats that circumnavigate a chrome and black stone bar. Sachiko is invariably packed with upmarket Charlottenburg thirtysomethings, undoubtedly due to its location in the Savignypassagen.

Turkish

Hitit

Corner Danckelmannstrasse/Knobelsdorffstrasse (322 4557). U2 Sophie-Charlotte-Platz. **Open** 8am-midnight daily. **Main courses** €7-€13. *Breakfast* €4.99. **Credit** MC, V. **Map** p304 B4.

Completely different from most of the other Turkish restaurants in the city, Hitit serves excellent Anatolian/Turkish food in an elegant setting, complete with Hittite wall-reliefs. You can choose from more than 150 dishes, with plenty of options for vegetarians. Service is friendly and the atmosphere is calm and soothing, embellished by the small waterfall running at the front of the restaurant.

Paris Bar. *See p140.*

Cafés, Bars & Pubs

Beer, breakfast, bounteous brunch buffets, baked goodies, bowls of *Milchkaffee*, booze and even bowling alleys – right around the clock.

In Berlin it's often a blurry line that separates the café from the bar. You can get breakfast, lunch, *Kaffee und Kuchen*, dinner and then horribly drunk into the small hours, all in the same place. But then it's also a blurry line that separates the bar from the club – if late drinking is your objective, then many more options will be found in the Nightlife chapter (*see p223*) – and sometimes the bar and/or café from the restaurant. Many places where you might go out for dinner will also have a decent bar and there's no law that says you have to eat to have a drink there. And just about anywhere that's open in the morning is going to serve some kind of breakfast – unless it's one of those places where the night before tends to stretch well beyond rush hour of the morning after.

Breakfast is a big ritual in Berlin. At weekends, people will have big breakfast parties and invite their friends around. Many cafés offer a big variety of ways to start the day, from croissants and jam or a simple selection of rolls, cheeses and cold cuts through to themed extravaganzas it could take all morning to devour. At weekends, all-you-can-eat brunch buffets are the thing, usually served from around 10am until sometime in late afternoon. *See p145* **Places for breakfast**.

At the other end of the day, Berliners do like a drink. The capital's changing social composition means that cocktails are on the increase, and there have always been plenty of wine bars, but this is Germany and beer remains the main tipple, even though local brews are a sorry substitute for those of Bavaria and Bohemia. People tend to pay their own way and drink at their own pace – partly because in many places bills are only totted up as you leave – but ceremonial rounds of vodka, Jägermeister or tequila are a feature of the Berlin night.

If you're used to British licensing laws, it might be wise to pace yourself at first. Here no one is going to shout 'time' in your ear, even though the general tendency is for bars to close earlier these days. If you feel like carrying on when the staff finally do get around to putting the chairs up on the tables and pointedly offering to call you a taxi, there's bound to be somewhere else open nearby. Just ask the bar staff – it's probably where they're going.

Mitte

In the centre of Berlin, there's no shortage of confidence, ostentation or fun. Squatters in **Oranienburger Strasse** were the first to open cafés after the Wall fell, but these days it's the tourist industry that dictates the pace of the Scheunenviertel's main drag. Things are both quieter and funkier up on **Auguststrasse**, and the corner with **Tucholskystrasse** bustles of an evening, but **Gipstrasse** is probably the most happening nexus in this neighbourhood.

Hackescher Markt promises everything and draws a lot of tourists. The restored courtyards across from the S-Bahn station are indeed impressive, but their renovation has chased out the offbeat and left behind rather too many over-designed identikit bars. Some decent cafés by day, though.

Torstrasse and the **Mitte-Nord** area beyond it are happier hunting grounds, especially the quarter around Veteranenstrasse, Rosenthaler Platz and the beginning of Kastanienallee, which is home to an assortment of eccentric establishments.

103

Kastanienallee 49 (4849 2651). U8 Rosenthaler Platz/bus N2, N8, N84. **Open** 9am-2am Mon-Fri; 10am-2am Sat, Sun. **No credit cards**. **Map** p303 G2.

Born from the wreckage of the legendary 103 club, this bar is L-shaped, well-lit and airy (for Berlin). It competes with Schwarz-Sauer to be the primary Kastanienallee hangout for the Mitte crowd: numbered T-shirts, tracksuits and Border Patrol shades abound. The food is generally excellent, an odd mix of Asian and Italian. But more importantly, it's the perfect summer location to sit outside with a beer and watch well-coiffed local freaks strut their stuff.

Café Aedes East

Hof II, Hackesche Höfe, Rosenthaler Strasse 40-41 (285 8275). S3, S5, S7, S9, S75 Hackescher Markt/bus N2, N5, N8, N48, N54, N65, N92. **Open** *Summer* 10am-10pm Mon-Thur, Sun; 10am-1am Fri, Sat. *Winter* 11am-10pm Mon-Fri, Sun; 11am-1am Fri, Sat. **Credit** AmEx, MC, V. **Map** p316/p302 F3.

This small and stylish Hackesche Höfe café fills with insiders who know that the food here is better – and better-priced – than the stuff in the larger places in the first Hof. Aedes attracts a mixture of people from the nearby theatres, bars and offices.

Altes Europa

Gipsstrasse 11 (2404 8650/www.alteseuropa.com). U8 Weinmeisterstrasse/bus N2, N5, N8. **Open** noon-1am daily. **No credit cards. Map** p316/p302 F3.
A relatively blank, relatively new and relatively spacious space in which there usually seems to be some kind of party going on. The gentle minimalism of the decor is kind of restful – basic furnishings and nothing but a few old maps on the walls – and the sense of humour informing the name also keeps the staff's eyes twinkling. The decent bar serves light meals (€4.50-€7.50), Ukrainian vodka and draught Krusovice in both dark and light varieties to a hip, good-looking youngish crowd. Sounds are mostly rat-packish classics of cool.

Barcomi's

Sophienstrasse 21, Sophie-Gips-Höfe, 2 Hof (2859 8363/www.barcomi.de). U8 Weinmeisterstrasse. **Open** *Winter* 9am-8pm Mon-Thur; 10am-8pm Fri-Sun. *Summer* 9am-10pm Mon-Thur; 10am-8pm Fri-Sun. **No credit cards. Map** p316/p302 F3.
Prominent in the renovated courtyard downstairs from the Sammlung Hoffmann (*see p84*), and serving American-style coffee and snacks and light meals, this is a popular stop for lunch or an afternoon break. Decent but overrated and often packed.
Other locations: Bergmannstrasse 21, Kreuzberg (694 8138).

Bergstübl

Veteranenstrasse 25 (4849 2268/www.bergstuebl.de). U8 Rosenthaler Platz/bus N2, N8, N84. **Open** 4pm-5am Mon-Thur, Sun; 4pm-late Fri, Sat. **No credit cards. Map** p302 F2.
Perhaps the most popular spot on popular Veteranenstrasse and certainly the oddest. A former fascist hangout, with old wood panelling still intact, it's now owned by an African and is strangely popular with a cruisy gay crowd. But the clientele is resolutely mixed, with hipsters sharing small tables with hardcore alkies and neighbourhood eccentrics while an eclectic selection of DJs spin over a lousy sound system. Try a bottle of Tannen Zapfel, one of Germany's best beers, but difficult to find in Berlin.

Bantu Bar

Brunnenstrasse 172 (4404 3657). U8 Rosenthaler Platz/bus N2, N8, N84. **Open** 6pm-4am daily. **No credit cards. Map** p302 F1/2.
Friendly bar decorated in an interesting mishmash of African steppe straw and vintage rare groove record covers. A great place to sip a cheap, well-mixed Mojito before or after checking out the neighbouring KingKongKlub (*see p225*) or the rest of the still pleasantly under-hyped nightlife north of Torstrasse. Good drinks list, free peanuts, and spliffs tolerated, complementing the reggae that sometimes pulses in the background.

Gorki Park. *See p144.*

Burns Night at **Jarman**.

Erdbeer
Max-Beer-Strasse 56 (no phone). U8 Rosa-Luxemburg-Platz/bus N2, N54. **Open** *Summer* 2pm-late daily. *Winter* 5pm-late daily. **No credit cards. Map** p303 G2/3.
The name means strawberry in German, and this dark, spacious (and a bit dingy) bar off Rosa-Luxemburg-Platz has earned a reputation for its powerful and delicious fresh fruit drinks. There are other eccentric mixtures on offer, as well as the usual beers, both bottled and from the *Fass*. Nightly DJs are of wildly differing styles and quality.

FC Magnet
Veteranenstrasse 26 (no phone/www.fcmagnet.de). U8 Rosenthaler Platz/bus N2, N8, N84. **Open** 8pm-late daily **No credit cards. Map** p302 F2.
A few years ago, Berliners began transforming old-style East Berlin social clubs into fancy new bars. The slacker entrepreneurs behind FC Magnet have taken it a step further, creating a fashionable football bar complete with its own team. Though the drinks aren't exceptional, beautiful people pack the spot on weekends to play *Kicker* (table football) under a giant photograph of 'Der Kaiser', Franz Beckenbauer. But despite all the numbered T-shirts, one suspects that most patrons get their only exercise by lifting drink to mouth.

Galao
Weinbergsweg 8 (4404 6882). U8 Rosenthaler Platz/bus N2, N8, N84. **Open** *Summer* 8am-8pm Mon-Fri; 10am-8pm Sat, Sun. *Winter* 8am-7pm Mon-Fri; 10am-7pm Sat, Sun. **No credit cards. Map** p302 F2/3.
Every few years Berliners grab at a food trend, and panini fever recently swept the city. The inexpensive Galao serves the best in the area, with delicious *Milchkaffee* to accompany. It's small but makes a virtue of it by tossing a few cushions on to the steps, transforming what could be a cramped, tableless restaurant into an outdoor meeting place in summer.

Gorki Park
Weinbergsweg 25 (448 7286). U8 Rosenthaler Platz/bus N2, N8, N84. **Open** 9.30am-2am daily. **No credit cards. Map** p302 F2.
Tiny Russian-run café with surprisingly tasty and authentic snacks – blini, pierogi and the like. Guests range from students and loafers to the occasional guitar-toting Ukrainian and scenesters having a quiet coffee before heading down to pose at more centrally located bars. Interesting weekend brunch buffet includes a selection of warm dishes.

Greenwich
Gipsstrasse 5 (0177 280 8806/www.cookies.ch.de). U8 Weinmeisterstrasse/bus N2, N5, N8. **Open** 8pm-6am daily. **No credit cards. Map** p316/p302 F3.
It wasn't too long ago that east Berlin nightlife was mostly squats and bunkers serving cheap beer and industrial vodka. But when club pioneer Cookie opened this place, still referred to as 'Cookie's Bar', the city began its half-hearted romance with glam-flecked exclusivity. Of course, this being Berlin, an Adidas jacket and an ironed shirt will probably get you in. The interior looks like a set from *Barbarella*. Increasingly a yuppie hangout, but the cocktails are top-notch and the clientele is easy on the eyes.

Hackbarth's
Auguststrasse 49A (282 7706). U8 Weinmeisterstrasse/bus N2, N5, N8. **Open** 9am-3am daily. *Breakfast* 9am-2pm. **No credit cards. Map** p316/p302 F3.
Popular spot for a leisurely breakfast among ex-squatters, art-world scenesters and other long-time Scheunenviertel residents. By night, it's less a café than a local scene bar, where the large intruding V-shaped brass counter gives the place the feel of a landlocked ship. The golden light can flatter the pale, and facilitates the pick-up tendency of Berlin's late-night fun seekers.

Jarman
Bergstrasse 25 (2804 7378/www.jarman.de). U8 Rosenthaler Platz/bus N2, N8, N84. **Open** 5pm-1am Tue-Thur, Sun; 5pm-late Fri, Sat. **No credit cards. Map** p316/p302 F3.
Engaging, cultish bar removed from the passive, be-seen places south of Torstrasse, Jarman is subdued, intimate and as idiosyncratic as its artsy, Vienna-educated proprietor Daniel Jarman (cousin of the late film director Derek). His porcelain teapot and quirky figurine collection fill shelves above others full of tasty Austrian beers and bottles of smoky whisky from his native Scotland. Occasional DJs, readings and special events, such as the Persian Buffet or the Robert Burns Night, with haggis on the menu.

Kapelle

Zionskirchplatz 22-4 (4434 1300/www.cafekapelle.de). U8 Rosenthaler Platz/bus N2, N8, N84. **Open** 9am-3am daily. **No credit cards. Map** p302 F2.

A comfortable, high-ceilinged café-bar across from the Zionskirch, Kapelle takes its name from Die Rote Kapelle, 'The Red Orchestra'. This was a clandestine anti-fascist organisation and in the 1930s and 1940s the Kapelle's basement was a secret meeting place for the resistance. The regularly changing menu features organic meat and vegetarian dishes, and the proceeds are donated to local charities and social organisations.

KMA 36

Karl-Marx-Allee 36 (no phone). U5 Schillingstrasse/bus N5. **Open** 6.30pm-2am Mon-Thur, Sun; 6.30pm-6am Fri, Sat. **No credit cards. Map** p303 G3.

If it must, this bar with no name will answer to the above terse abbreviation of its official street address. In part of the same GDR-constructed edifice as the excellent WMF (*see p227*), KMA 36 makes effective use of the building's retro design without pandering to the banalities of *Ostalgie*. The decor unites communist-era wooden panelling and a wondrous glass façade that lets in the city lights and allows you to observe the flotsam and jetsam on Karl-Marx-Allee. Most nights DJs spin electronica and lounge. Occasional lo-fi live performances.

Operncafé im Opernpalais

Unter den Linden 5 (2026 8433/www.opernpalais.de). U6 Französische Strasse/bus N6. **Open** 8am-midnight daily. **Credit** AmEx, MC, V. **Map** p316/p302 F3.

A traditional coffee-and-cake stop in literally palatial surrounds. Choose from a huge selection of beautifully displayed cakes, then relax over a *Milchkaffee* in the elaborate interior, or sit outside in summer and watch Unter den Linden go by.

Pony Bar

Alte Schönhauser Strasse 44 (no phone). U8 Weinmeisterstrasse/bus N2, N5, N8. **Open** noon-late Mon-Sat; 6pm-late Sun. **No credit cards. Map** p303 G3.

This austere and edgy watering hole is an ideal place to end an evening with affordable cocktails. *Au courant* electrolounge sounds provide a stylish soundtrack but don't drown conversation. Garden seating in summer.

Roberta

Zionskirchstrasse 7 (4405 5580/www.bar-roberta.de). U8 Bernauer Strasse/bus N8, N42. **Open** 6pm-4am daily. **No credit cards. Map** p302 F2.

All the elements seem to be here – high ceilings, apricot walls, civilised drink prices and DJs playing house, easy listening, funk, soul and other music dear to the pleasantly mixed, straight and gay crowd's heart. And yet there's something hip-bar-by-numbers about the place.

Schokoladen

Ackerstrasse 169-70 (282 6527/www.schokoladenmitte.de). U8 Rosenthaler Platz/bus N2, N8, N84. **Open** 8pm-late Mon-Thur, Sun; 9pm-late Fri, Sat. **No credit cards. Map** p302 F2.

This eastern scene stalwart, located in the former ZAR chocolate factory, is still going strong and never fails to amaze with its adventurous mix of theatre, poetry and off-the-beaten-track music, both live and from turntables. Attracts a knowing, student and intellectual-artsy crowd with humane drink prices and a playful, yet down-to-earth atmosphere.

The best Places for breakfast

Café 100Wasser

The all-you-can-eat brunch buffet is a spectular start to any day of the week. *See p150.*

Café Atlantic

Eleven different ways to have your eggs scrambled on the sunny side of the street. *See p152.*

Barcomi's

American-style coffee any way you can imagine it, with bagels and other baked goodies to match. *See p143.*

Café Einstein

There are few more peaceful places to scarf up some eggs benedict than the Einstein's beautiful garden. *See p155.*

Gagarin

The newest of several choices for breakfast by the Wasserturm, all of them with pavement tables. *See p149.*

Café Bar Morena

Famous for fine breakfasts on a characterful Kreuzberg corner. *See p153.*

Schwarzes Café

Berlin nightlife can seriously mess up your body clock, but whatever time it screams for breakfast, this place is there to serve it. *See p156.*

Strandbad Mitte

Hearty Scheunenviertel breakfasts in a simulated seaside style environment. *See p147.*

KMA 36. *See p145.*

Strandbad Mitte

Kleine Hamburger Strasse 16 (283 6877). S1, S2, S25, S26 Oranienburger Strasse/bus N84. **Open** 9am-2am Mon-Sat; 10am-2am Sun. **No credit cards. Map** p302 F3.

'Strandbad' means bathing beach, and this café adds a touch of seaside resort to this dead-end street off Auguststrasse. In summer, beach chairs strewn on the pavement in front of the entrance are great to sink in to – if you can get one. If not, try to grab a seat on the divan inside to sip your *Milchkaffee* or enjoy one of the hearty breakfasts served until 4pm.

White Trash Fast Food

Torstrasse 201 (0179 473 2639/www.whitetrash fastfood.com). U8 Rosenthaler Platz/bus N2, N8, N84. **Open** 9pm-late Tue-Sun. **No credit cards. Map** p302 F2/3.

The remnants of a garish Chinese restaurant provide the stage set for what has over the last couple of years become as much a centre of expat American nightlife as of the Berlin underground. The music is loud, usually nu electro or heavy metal, the clientele is tattooed, and everyone looks like they're falling out of their clothes. Meanwhile, the beer is mediocre and overpriced and the service absolutely awful. You'll find the American-style food surprisingly good, however, when it eventually arrives.

Prenzlauer Berg

A centre of pre-war Jewish life and the one truly bohemian district in communist East Berlin, Prenzlauer Berg takes its cultural status very seriously. Most of its splendid *Grunderzeit* buildings have now been renovated and there are dozens of small shops at ground level selling health food, scented candles, designer crockery and baby clothes.

Kollwitzplatz is a leafy square fringed with cafés and bars. There is more of the same around the Wasserturm, at the junction of **Rykestrasse** and **Knaackstrasse**. The cafés near **Helmholtzplatz** (in the so-called **'LSD'** neighbourhood, standing for the initial letters of Lychener Strasse, Schliemannstrasse and Dunckerstrasse) stray a bit further downmarket, stay open later and are somewhat more spontaneous than those around Kollwitzplatz. The Prater beer garden in nearby **Kastanienallee** is a pleasant place on a warm summer evening, and a good starting point for crawls down Kastanienallee and into Mitte.

8mm

177b Schonhauser Allee (4050 0624/www.8mmbar.com). U2 Senefelderplatz/bus N2. **Open** 9pm-late daily. **No credit cards. Map** p303 G2.

This purple-walled dive exists to remind travellers that Berlin isn't Stuttgart. The attractive, young and poor go for that fifth nightcap into incoherence around 6am, and local scenesters rub shoulders with anglophone expats. There seems to be more hard alcohol consumed here than in your average Berlin hangout, which might explain why the DJs tend to play the same Peaches track over and over. And, yes, sometimes films are shown, should you still be able to raise your head to watch.

Café Anita Wronski

Knaackstrasse 26-8 (442 8483). U2 Senefelderplatz/bus N2. **Open** 9am-2am Mon-Sat; 10am-2am Sun. **No credit cards. Map** p303 G2.

Friendly café on two levels with scrubbed floors, beige walls, hard-working staff and as many tables crammed into the space as the laws of physics allow. Excellent brunches, and plenty of other cafés on this stretch if there's no room here. Quiet in the afternoon and a good spot to sit and read.

Headbanging made hip at **Paule's Metal Eck**. *See p151.*

August Fengler

Lychener Strasse 11 (4435 6640/www.augustfengler.de). U2 Eberswalder Strasse/bus N42. **Open** 7pm-late daily. **No credit cards. Map** p303 G1.

Big, fun local pub with a colourful public, unradical, crowd-pleasing DJs most nights and an ancient, slightly dank two-lane *Kegelbahn* (German-style bowling alley) in the basement. If you want to bowl, book in advance via the website (€13 per lane per hour). Lots of space upstairs, and an excellent bar to perch at when the place isn't too crowded, but it all turns into one big cheerful drink-endangering jostle on a weekend night.

Dr Pong

Eberswalder Strasse 21 (no telephone). U2 Eberswalder Strasse/bus N42. **Open** 9pm-late Tue-Sat; 2pm-late Sun. **No credit cards. Map** p303 G2.

Bring your table tennis bat and prepare for ping-pong madness. The action doesn't start until around midnight, but when it does you can expect around 30 players – some good, some bad – circling around the table in a game of Chinese table tennis. Beer, soda, tea and juice are available, and sometimes cakes or pastries, but otherwise no food. No tables either. Just a bunch of chairs and two couches in a smoked-out, garage-like room. Lots of fun. Be warned that opening hours are unreliable.

Eckstein

Pappelallee 73 (441 9960). U2 Eberswalder Strasse/bus N42. **Open** 9am-1am Mon-Thur, Sun; 9am-2am Fri, Sat. **No credit cards. Map** p303 G1.

This beautiful café, with its broad corner front and deco-ish look, draws a mixed crowd but maintains a following among less well-scrubbed locals, adding a pleasingly bohemian feel to a place otherwise clean enough to take your parents.

EKA

Dunckerstrasse 9 (4372 0612/www.eka-leka.de). U2 Eberswalder Strasse/bus N42. **Open** noon-late daily. **No credit cards. Map** p303 G1.

This new-ish and comfortable addition to the café scene around Helmholztplatz looks something like a 1940s American soda shop reimagined as a burnished livery stable. Berlin always finds a way to sneak beer into an afternoon of coffee and cake, and EKA is of course no exception, serving both Bock and Portuguese brews. Although in no way set up for it, it also manages sometimes to sneak in a DJ or two. In short, this inexpensive spot is the apotheosis of Berlin casual.

Gagarin

Knaackstrasse 22 (442 8807/www.bar-gagarin.de). U2 Senefelderplatz/bus N2. **Open** 10am-2am daily. **Credit** AmEx, V. **Map** p303 G2.

Brought to you by the folks who run Gorki Park (*see p144*) and Pasternak (*see p130*), adding a bar to the troika of Russian hospitality. Vogue-ish retro futurist space-age decor (with colourful planets and the likeness of Yuri himself adorning the walls) and cool minimal techno and clicks 'n' cuts provide the backdrop for Baltika beer and a selection of tasty Russian pub grub like pelmeni or blini.

Hausbar

Rykestrasse 54 (no phone). U2 Senefelderplatz/ bus N2. **Open** 7pm-5am daily. **No credit cards. Map** p303 G2.

All bright red and gold, with a glorious cherub-filled sky on the ceiling, this small pocket of fabulousness seats about 15 people at a push. Hausbar is much more fun than all the wanky cafés with Russian literary names you'll find around the corner, and it's particularly inviting at three or four in the morning.

Klub der Republik

Pappelallee 81 (no phone). U2 Eberswalder Strasse/ bus N42. **Open** 8pm-4am daily. **No credit cards. Map** p303 G1.

Above a Yamaha music school and accessed via a wobbly staircase in the courtyard, this spacious bar manages to mix the best of the *Wohnzimmer* (living room) retro design craze with the sort of lively revelry associated with the east back in the mid-1990s. The bartenders are knowledgeable and the beer selection is gratifyingly big – try the Augustiner, one of Munich's best brews, which they neglect to display. The DJs are top-notch, usually eschewing current electronica trends for everything from 1960s soul to jazz fusion.

Luxus

Belforter Strasse 18 (4434 1514). U2 Senefelderplatz/bus N2. **Open** 8pm-late daily. **No credit cards. Map** p303 G2.

This tiny, tiled bar, one of Berlin's hidden treasures, has an almost Mediterranean feel. Patrons gather at the bar, or sit against the wall in close proximity, which often results in drunken argument, banter or something better. Although the quality of the drinks isn't really the point, a glass of cheap table wine will often lead to three or four more.

Café Maurer

Templiner Strasse 7 (4404 6077). U2 Senefelderplatz/bus N2. **Open** noon-12:30am Tue-Fri; 3pm-12:30am Sat; 10.30am-12:20am Sun. **No credit cards. Map** p303 G2.

Big, high-ceilinged space and a clever location in a leafy street behind the Pfefferberg, but there's nothing Moroccan about this place except for the name and the light fittings. The cakes are German, the evening menu is Italian (main courses €8-€15), and the customers are mostly families from the neighbourhood. Good quality stuff, plenty of room.

Nemo

Oderberger Strasse 46 (448 1959). U2 Eberswalder Strasse/bus N42. **Open** 6pm-3am Mon-Sat; 11am-3am Sun. **No credit cards. Map** p303 G2.

Decent dive with decorative art by a local comic illustrator, Mexican and Bavarian beers, table football, and Sunday brunch for €5 a head. If it's crowded, you'll find other cheap eats and drinks on a street that hosts a dozen other places.

Café November

Husemannstrasse 15 (442 8425/www.cafe-november.de). U2 Eberswalder Strasse/bus N42. **Open** 9am-2am daily. **No credit cards. Map** p303 G2.

Friendly place that's especially nice during the day when light floods in through picture windows offering views of beautifully restored Husemannstrasse.

Prater

Kastanienallee 7-9 (448 5688/www.pratergarten.de). U2 Eberswalder Strasse/bus N42. **Open** 6pm-11pm Mon-Sat; 10am-11pm Sun. **No credit cards. Map** p303 G2.

Almost any evening this huge and immaculately restored swing-era bar, across the courtyard from the theatre of the same name (*see p241*), attracts a smart, high-volume crowd. The beer-swilling lustiness, big wooden tables, and primeval platefuls of meat and veg (main courses €7-€14) can almost make you feel like you've been teleported to Munich. In summer the shady beer garden makes for an all-day buzz. Brunch is served from 10am-4pm on Saturdays and Sundays.

Schwarz-Sauer

Kastanienallee 13 (448 5633). U2 Eberswalder Strasse/bus N42. **Open** 8am-6am daily. **No credit cards. Map** p303 G2.

Quite possibly the most popular bar on the well-travelled Kastanienallee and currently the main meeting place for those who inhabit the twilight zone between Prenzlauer Berg and Mitte. Strangely, its ambience is sort of plain, its wait staff Berlin surly, and its food and drink of only adequate quality. But in summer the outside tables overflow day and night with what would appear to be three-quarters of the neighbourhood. As for winter, a tolerance for cigarette smoke is helpful.

Cafe Torpedokäfer

Dunckerstrasse 69 (4365 9820). U2 Eberswalder Strasse/bus N42. **Open** 1pm-late Mon-Fri; 6pm-late Sat; 11am-late Sun. **No credit cards. Map** p303 G1.

This place has been around a while and many regulars have roots in the legendary Dunckerstrasse squat, making it something of a decompression chamber after too much exposure to nearby gentrification. Buffet breakfast on Sundays.

Wohnzimmer

Lettestrasse 6 (445 5458). U2 Eberswalder Strasse/bus N42. **Open** 10am-4am daily. **No credit cards. Map** p303 G1.

Days can be sluggish at this shabbily elegant café. Visitors who make it past the poignantly drunken, would-be anarchists sunning in Helmholtzplatz will find, behind the door to this 'living room', a suspiciously bar-like structure made from an inspired ensemble of kitchen cabinets. Threadbare divans and artsy bar girls make this the perfect place to discuss Dostoevsky with career students over a tepid borscht. Evening light from candelabra reflects on gold-sprayed walls as students and maudlin poets chase brandies with Hefeweizen and bodily fluids. The capacity was recently doubled by the opening of a second room.

Friedrichshain

Friedrichshain currently carries the flag for youthful Berlin bohemia. The area around **Simon-Dach-Strasse** is full of fun bars, cheap cafés and ethnic takeaways. But it's also begun to acquire a kind of settled feel and its orbit has begun expanding east towards **Ostkreuz** S-Bahn station and **Sonntagstrasse**, an area hitherto dotted only with down-at-heel *Eck-Kneipen* (*see p151* **A different corner**).

Rigaer Strasse and **Mainzer Strasse** were once hubs of the militant squatting scene, and an element of disgruntled radicalism persists around here. Locals may sneer if you wear your best designer togs or attempt to pay with a credit card.

Down by the Spree it's a different scene as the waterfront is developed and the area inches upmarket (*see p90* **On the waterfront**). Here Friedrichshain begins to connect with a reviving Kreuzberg over the river.

Meanwhile, the former socialist showcase boulevard that is **Karl-Marx-Allee** is also beginning to develop into a nightlife area, but more as an eastern extension of the Mitte scene than a western annex of the Friedrichshain one.

Café 100Wasser

Simon-Dach-Strasse 39 (2900 1356). U5 Frankfurter Tor or U1, U15, S3, S5, S6, S7, S9, S75 Warschauer Strasse/bus N5, N29. **Open** 10am-late daily. **No credit cards. Map** p88.

The all-you-can-eat brunch buffet (€8.50, 10am-4pm daily) has a cult following among students and other late risers. Take your time and don't panic as the buffet gets plundered. Just when the food seems to be finished, out comes loads of new stuff.

Conmux

Simon-Dach-Strasse 35 (291 3863). U5 Frankfurter Tor or U1, U15, S3, S5, S6, S7, S9, S75 Warschauer Strasse/bus N5, N29. **Open** 9am-late daily. **No credit cards. Map** p88.

For those who love outdoor tables: here, even in winter there are seats outside on Simon-Dach-Strasse, and the waiters will light one of the big gas heaters to warm you up. Inside there are sewing-machine tables and pieces of scrap-metal art. The menu offers a variety of well-priced light meals. Service is at best monosyllabic, at worst downright indifferent.

Ehrenburg

Karl-Marx-Allee 103 (4210 5810). U5 Weberwiese/bus N5. **Open** 10am-late daily. **No credit cards. Map** p303 H3.

Named after Russian-Jewish novelist Ilja Ehrenburg, a committed socialist, this newish café and espresso bar, with its sober, geometric decoration, is one of the few stylish places around Weberwiese U-Bahn station. Although the library looks like it's part of the decorative style, you're free to pick up a book and study the works of Ehrenburg, Lenin, Stalin, Engels or Marx as you enjoy a latte macchiato and other capitalist achievements.

Fargo

Grünberger Strasse 77 (2900 5720/www.bergwerk.de). U5 Frankfurter Tor or U1, U15, S3, S5, S6, S7, S9, S75 Warschauer Strasse/bus N5, N29. **Open** 5pm-late Mon-Fri; 10am-late Sat, Sun. **No credit cards.**

Any place with a happy hour and a 'hungry hour' can't be bad. From 6-8pm every day you can buy cheap drinks and also get a hearty meal for just €2.90. Fargo also features an ample Sunday brunch buffet from 10am to 4pm. The pool table and amiable wait staff should keep you entertained and its modest late-night kitchen (open until midnight) will leave you satisfied. Happy hour also all day Monday; Tuesday is Caipirinha day – €3.60 a pop.

Fischladen

Rigaer Strasse 83 (no telephone). U5 Samariterstrasse/bus N5. **Open** 5pm-late Tue-Sun. **No credit cards. Map** p88.

In an abandoned house and run by squatters, this is one of the few places of its kind surviving in Friedrichshain. It offers numerous bottled beers, a limited bar, and on Saturday and Sunday from 7pm there's a *Volksküche* ('people's kitchen') offering a vegetarian meal for €1.50; otherwise expect junk food. Occasionally there's live (acoustic) music and sometimes a DJ. The anarchistic crowd is young and obvious – pirate flags and posters for demos hang on the walls (one for an anti-Nazi protest reads 'Grandpa, shut the fuck up') – so strap on your combat boots. Very smoky.

Intimes

Boxhagener Strasse 107 (2966 6457). U5 Samariterstrasse/bus N5. **Open** 10am-late daily. **No credit cards. Map** p88.

Next to the cinema of the same name, decorated with painted tiles and offering a good variety of Turkish and vegetarian food as well as breakfast at reasonable prices. Pleasures can be as simple as fried potatoes with garlic sausage; best deal is the Wednesday special. Decent selection of beers, friendly service.

Paule's Metal Eck

Krossener Strasse 15 (291 1624). U5 Frankfurter Tor or U1, U15, S3, S5, S6, S7, S9, S75 Warschauer Strasse/bus N5, N29. **Open** 7pm-late Mon-Fri; 3pm-late Sat, Sun. **No credit cards. Map** p88.

Neither a typical heavy metal bar, nor remotely typical for this area, the Egyptian-themed Eck attracts a young, hip crowd with relentless metal videos, a decent selection of beers, and both pool and table football. Inoperative disco balls, mummy overhead lamps and formidable dragon busts deck an interior half designed like a mausoleum, and half in gloomy medieval style. A small menu changes weekly and there's live Bundesliga football on weekend afternoons. Happy hour 7-9pm daily.

A different corner

On unfashionable corners, down certain streets, you'll run across a genre of drinking establishment known as the *Eck-Kneipe* – corner pub. As it goes, these places need not actually be on corners, though many are. They are often named, with an entirely typical lack of imagination, after the name of the street or some nearby feature – Brücke-Eck, Wasserturm-Eck. Other common suffixes, usually on a brewery-sponsored sign, are Klause (den) or Krug (inn). But sometimes they sport names that are simply bizarre (Zum Blauen Affen – 'to the blue ape') or else downright creepy (Zum Alten Kamaraden – 'at the old comrades').

From the outside, it can be hard to tell what's happening within. Grubby net curtains will cover the windows. Sometimes, on the window ledge, like totems to ward you off, there will be a row of wooden trolls brandishing miniature swords and spears – the drinking equivalent of that other great German invention, the garden gnome. Looking for a little local colour, you may be tempted to wander inside. Be prepared.

It will probably be dark and smoky. Even in mid-afternoon it might be hard to make out what's going on in the far corners. Don't worry, this may be a blessing in disguise. Strange German pop music oom-pahs from a jukebox somewhere. Indigenous gambling machines with incomprehensible arrangements of spinning discs, click and whirr to themselves as someone absently feeds in coins. Grimy knick-knacks and nasty ornaments will clutter every surface. There will be antlers on the wall and a few pictures of Hertha BSC.

The locals are mostly male, and mostly drunk out of their faces. They all know each other and bellow in thick, barely intelligible Berlin accents, following arcane native rituals it would take an anthropologist to unravel while downing industrial quantities of Schnapps and beer. '*Verdammte Scheisse*!' they call one to the other. '*Verdammte Scheisse*!!'

Then you walk in. You are a stranger and you have dared to invade their inner sanctum. Everyone will stare. Sometimes you can expect outright hostility. Even worse, they might try and talk to you. Expect daft conversational openings about the Royal Family (a German obsession), World War II, English food or the fact that in Britain, as everyone in Germany learns at school, it is raining cats and dogs.

Perhaps not surprisingly, these places are beginning to disappear. Their regulars are ageing. Younger folk have more complex demands of a good night out. Soon the Eck-Kneipe will have gone the way of the dodo or the slide rule.

In the meantime, if you must sample one, we'd recommend the **Metzer Eck** (Metzer Strasse 33, Prenzlauer Berg, 442 7656, www.metzer-eck.de). It reckons itself to be the oldest bar in the borough and the people there are super-nice. Which isn't exactly typical, but there you go.

Sanatorium

Frankfurter Allee 23 (4202 1193). U5 Frankfurter Tor. **Open** 4pm-late Tue-Sat; 2pm-late Sun. **No credit cards. Map** p88.

Yuppies and twentysomething welfare recipients rub shoulders and sip from one of the many cocktails or five different beers. Sit on Japanese-style floor mats at art deco tables or sprawl out on one of the many red or white elevated futon beds. No chairs allowed. Occasionally you can get a full body massage (€10 per 20 minutes or €55 for the full hour) while DJs spin electronica or drum 'n' bass. Every last Sunday of the month listen to a German band that actually sings in German.

Café Schönbrunn

Am Schwanenteich, Volkspark Friedrichshain (4679 3893). Bus 200. **Open** 10am-1am Mon-Fri; 10am-2am Sat, Sun. **No credit cards. Map** p303 H3.

Not for those afraid to walk in the park at night, but for everyone else it's a favoured hangout. A couple of years ago, this place by the lake sold coffee and *Würstchen* to an elderly crowd. With a change of management, the music and food improved dramatically. The unspectacular concrete front was left as it was, and the (new) lounge furniture is pure 1970s. On a sunny afternoon, older park-goers take their first afternoon beer on the terrace next to the in-crowd having breakfast. For your first visit come in daytime – just to make sure you find it.

Supamolly

Jessner Strasse 41 (2900 7294). U5, S4, S8, S10 Frankfurter Allee/bus N5. **Open** 8pm-late Tue-Sun. **No credit cards. Map** p88.

Having opened in the early 1990s as a semi-legal bolthole fronting a lively squat, Supamolly (or Supamolli) is a miracle of survival. The frequent live punk and ska shows in the club behind the bar dictates only some of the clientele; a healthy mix of young and ageing punks, unemployed activists and music lovers of all types gather in this dim, mural-smeared, candlelit watering hole until the early morning. DJs at weekends (€3 admission).

Tagung

Wühlischstrasse 29 (2977 3788). U5 Samariterstrasse/bus N5. **Open** 7pm-late daily. **No credit cards. Map** p88.

Small bar decked in GDR memorabilia and still serving things like Club Cola, the old Eastern brand. The patrons are 20- and 30-somethings and the place seems to provide good laughs and drunken nights for all. The small club downstairs is likewise 'ostalgically' decorated and offers mainstream dance music and occasional one-off events.

Kreuzberg

Enough ageing scenesters and alternative types hung on in west Berlin's former art and anarchy quarter to ensure that some kind of atmosphere remained in these parts. But lately there have been signs of a revival in the area around **Schlesisches Tor**, where Kreuzberg faces off against Friedrichshain across the Spree.

The district around **Oranienstrasse** and **Wiener Strasse** offers a variety of opportunities for drinking, partying or breakfasting, and is also one of the city's gay hubs. Tucked away behind the concrete mess that is Kottbusser Tor, Dresdener Strasse has more than its fair share of decent places to drink and dally.

Though lively by day, the Bergmannstrasse neighbourhood is sadly somnolent after dark, with **Haifischbar** (*see p153*) providing the only really decent late-night option. But the two gay places on Mehringdamm – **Café Melitta Sundström** (*see p207*) and **Bargelb** (*see p210*) – are inclusive and fun.

Café Adler

Friedrichstrasse 206 (251 8965). U6 Kochstrasse/bus N29, N84. **Open** 10am-midnight Mon-Sat; 10am-7pm Sun. **Credit** AmEx, V. **Map** p306 F4.

Next to what used to be Checkpoint Charlie, you could once watch history in the making from this elegant corner café. Today, it's a bustling, businesslike corner and Adler is a well-lit oasis of calm, coffee and decent light meals.

Anker-Klause

Kottbusser Brücke/corner Maybachufer, Neukölln (693 5649). U8 Schönleinstrasse/bus N8. **Open** 4pm-late Mon; 10am-late Tue-Sun. **No credit cards. Map** p307 G5.

Although looking over Kreuzberg's Landwehrkanal, the only thing nautical about this 'anchor den' is the midriff-tattooed, punk-meets-portside swank of the bar staff. A slamming jukebox (rock, sleaze, beat), a weathery terrace and good sandwich melts offer ample excuse to dock here from afternoon until whenever they decide to close. Convivial during the week, packed at weekends.

Atlantic

Bergmannstrasse 100 (691 9292). U6, U7 Mehringdamm/bus N19. **Open** 9am-2am daily. **No credit cards. Map** p306 F5.

On the south side of the street, the pavement café thrives in the summer, and a beer as late as 8pm will still have you sitting in a ray of light, if you're lucky enough to get a table. Breakfast, including 11 different ways to have your eggs scrambled, is served until 5pm. There are also daily lunch specials, and dinner is a cheap but decent affair. The staff change every two days, as does the music.

Cake

Schlesische Strasse 32 (6162 4610/www.cake-bar.de). U1, U15 Schlesisches Tor/bus N29. **Open** 4pm-late daily. **No credit cards. Map** p307 H4.

A diverse crowd in age and nationality – the hostel across the street lends a youthful international air–

Mutter. See p154

mill about in this lounge equipped with old easy chairs, sofas, art-bedecked walls and a dark red, musty interior. Music gently hums overhead, providing a great atmosphere for relaxing and conversing. They've even got a vintage jukebox equipped with a variety of oldies. DJs most weekends for free. Happy hour 7pm-9pm daily.

Careca Bar & Café

Falkenstein 42 (no telephone). U1, U15 Schlesisches Tor/bus N29. **Open** *Summer* 1pm-4am daily. *Winter* 6pm-4am daily. **No credit cards. Map** p88.

New cocktail bar and café with ultra-modern decor offers a comprehensive selection of cocktails, long drinks and wine as well as tea and excellent coffee. Don't come for the three varieties of bottled beer, though, or the paltry snack selection. Women often dominate the scene, possibly because this is one of the few bars in the area that isn't dingy. Sit at petite, low, well-lit tables in the front room or lounge out on plush couches in the side room.

Haifischbar

Arndtstrasse 25 (691 1352/www.haifischbar-berlin.de). U6, U7 Mehringdamm/bus N19.
Open 8pm-3am Mon-Thur, Sun; 8pm-5am Fri, Sat.
No credit cards. Map p306 F5.

Well-run and friendly bar where the staff are expert cocktail-shakers, the music's hip and tasteful in a trancey groove kind of way, and the back room, equipped with a sushi bar, is a good place to chill out at the end of an evening. Certainly the most happening place in the Bergmannstrasse *Kiez*, and with some kind of crowd any night of the week.

Madonna

Wiener Strasse 22 (611 6943). U1, U15 Görlitzer Bahnhof/bus N29, N44. **Open** 3pm-late daily.
No credit cards. Map p307 H5.

With over a hundred whiskies and frescoes detailing a lascivious pageant of falling angels and clerical inebriation, this bar and café offers a friendly vantage on the debauched, counterculture erudition of Kreuzberg thirtysomethings who don't care if or where the government resides. Particularly interesting as neutral ground for subcultures that, until Berlin's modernisation frenzy gave them common cause, had differing opinions on the proper way to burn a car, squat a building or play a guitar.

Milagro

Bergmannstrasse 12 (692 2303/www.milagro.de). U7 Gneisenaustrasse/bus N4, N19. **Open** 9am-1am Mon-Thur, Sun; 9am-2am Fri, Sat. **No credit cards. Map** p306 F5.

Light and friendly café, famous for its excellent breakfasts, served until 4pm. There are also cheap but classy dishes (soups, pasta) served until midnight. Disorienting stairs lead to hospital-like toilets. On a winter's afternoon, the front room can be too dim to read your daily paper.

Montecruz

Skalitzer Strasse 80 (6953 4190/www.montecruz.de). U1, U15 Schlesisches Tor/bus N29, N65. **Open** 9am-midnight Mon-Fri; 10am-midnight Sat, Sun.
No credit cards. Map p307 H5.

Come for the breakfast or Sunday brunch, stay for the second-hand clothes. This homey new café/bar bakes a quality muffin and bagel and freshly squeezes all its juices, making it a favourite with the area's tree-hugging types. But there's also plenty of beer, wine, and drinks. If all else fails, peruse Montecruz's impressive selection of second-hand clothes. T-shirts, sweaters, coats and dresses can all be picked up at a good price. Take advantage of the small patio when the weather's nice.

Café Bar Morena

Wiener Strasse 60 (611 4716/www.morena-berlin.de). U1, U15 Görlitzer Bahnhof/bus N29, N44. **Open** 9am-late daily. **No credit cards. Map** p307 H5.

Famous breakfasts are served to people who wake up at all hours, and these are the main reason to come here. In the evening it bustles and service can be slow. The music isn't overpowering and the half-tiled walls and parquet flooring lend an art deco feel. Outside tables in summer.

Mysliwska

Schlesische Strasse 35 (611 4860). U1, U15 Schlesisches Tor/bus N29, N65. **Open** 6pm-late daily. **No credit cards. Map** p88.

This small, dark bar draws a mixed local crowd and doesn't get going until late. The spartan interior boasts old, small, poker-like tables and stiff wooden chairs. Except for a pistachio dispenser and frequently unpopulated, disco-balled side room, frills are kept to a minimum. Live music once or twice a month and DJs most weekends (no entrance fee).

The Old Emerald Isle

Erkelenzdamm 49 (615 6917/www.old-emerald-isle.de). U1, U8, U15 Kottbusser Tor/bus N8, N29. **Open** noon-2am Mon-Thur, Sun; noon-4am Fri, Sat. **Map** p307 G5. **No credit cards.**

Decent all-purpose Irish pub with draught Guinness and Kilkenny, a big selection of hearty meals, plenty of televisions for watching British and Irish football and rugby matches, a pleasant beer garden on the quiet street outside and a cheerfully rowdy atmosphere throughout. Live music, pub quizzes and bingo nights aim to keep regulars coming back.

Wiener Blut

Wiener Strasse 14 (618 9023). U1, U15 Görlitzer Bahnhof/bus N29, N44. **Open** 6pm-late Mon-Fri, Sun; 3:30pm-late Sat. **No credit cards. Map** p307 H5.

A narrow, darkish bar equipped with lazy booths and a well-abused table football table, Wiener Blut sometimes features DJs who pack the place with wild beats and wild friends. Otherwise it's just another red bar. Tables out front in the summer are a good alternative to the overcrowded terrace of Morena (*see p153*) up the street.

Würgeengel

Dresdener Strasse 122 (615 5560). U1, U8, U15 Kottbusser Tor/bus N8. **Open** 7pm-late daily. **No credit cards. Map** p307 G4.

Red walls and velvet upholstery convey an atmosphere aching for sin, while well-mixed cocktails and a fine wine list served by smartly dressed waiting staff make this a place for the more discerning drinker. The glass-latticed ceiling and a 1920s chandelier elegantly belie the fairly priced drinks and tapas on offer. Daily specials from the adjoining Gorgonzola Club (*see p132*) can also be ordered. Ideal in summer when a canopy of greenery curtains outdoor picnic tables.

Schöneberg

A smart, pleasantly gentrified borough where residents greet each other jovially in the street and spend long afternoons reading the international papers over a *Milchkaffee*.

Civilised, tolerant and cosmopolitan, Schöneberg retains just a hint of its more radical past and celebrates the summer with an assortment of street festivals.

Motzstrasse and **Fuggerstrasse** are the centre of gay life in Berlin (*see p210*), with numerous bars and shops catering to all tastes and fetishes. The more conventional **Winterfeldtplatz** is excellent for summer carousing and the bars on and around nearby **Goltzstrasse** fill up in the evenings with a cosmopolitan and convivial crowd. There is more going on behind discreet doors on these quiet, tree-lined streets than is immediately apparent to the untutored eye.

Bilderbuch

Akazienstrasse 28 (7870 6057/www.bilderbuch.de). U7 Eisenacher Strasse/bus N4, N48. **Open** 9am-1am Mon-Thur; 9am-2am Fri, Sat; 10am-1am Sun. **No credit cards. Map** p305 D5.

Cavernous book-lined labyrinth whose inner dimensions surprise after the storefront entrance. Vast spaces between the tables allow a certain privacy, though some parts of the café are so far from the kitchen it's a surprise the food isn't cold by the time it reaches your table. Usefully located on one of Schöneberg's more interesting shopping streets.

Green Door

Winterfeldtstrasse 50 (215 2515/www.greendoorbar.de). U1, U2, U4, U15 Nollendorfplatz/bus N2, N5, N19, N26. **Open** 6pm-3am Mon-Fri, Sun; 6pm-4am Sat. **No credit cards. Map** p305 D5.

It really does have a green door, and behind it there's a whole lotta cocktail shaking going on – the drinks menu is enormous and impressive. There's also a nice long and curvy bar, perhaps a few too many yuppies, and a good location off Winterfeldtplatz.

Mister Hu

Goltzstrasse 39 (217 2111). U7 Eisenacher Strasse/bus N4, N48. **Open** 5pm-4am Mon-Thur, Sun; 5pm-5am Fri, Sat. **No credit cards. Map** p305 D5.

Dark and cosy bar decorated in greens and blues and named after one of its owners, cigar-smoking Chinese-Indonesian writer Husen Ciawi. Long cocktail list, so at its best during happy hour (5-8pm Mon-Sat, all day Sun).

Mutter

Hohenstaufenstrasse 4 (216 4990). U1, U2, U4 Nollendorfplatz/bus N2, N5, N19, N26. **Open** 10am-4am daily. **Credit** AmEx, MC, V. **Map** p305 D5.

'Mother' tries to do everything at once: two bars; an enormous selection of wines, beers and cocktails; breakfasts until 4pm; a sushi bar from 6pm, plus other snacks throughout the day. It's a big place, but it can be difficult to find a seat on weekend nights, when trancey house plays in the front bar (there are more sedate sounds in the café area at the back). It's roomy, the decor is heavy on gold paint and the spectacular corridor to the toilets is worth a visit in itself.

Pinguin Club

Wartburgstrasse 54 (781 3005/www.pinguin-club.de). U7 Eisenacher Strasse/bus N4, N48. **Open** 9pm-4am daily. **No credit cards. Map** p305 D5.

Though a little past its heyday, this is still one of Berlin's finest and friendliest institutions. It's decorated with original 1950s Americana and rock 'n' roll memorabilia, and the owners all have punk roots. Good sounds are a feature. Take your pick from 156 spirits, and don't be surprised if everyone begins to dance to disco or sing along to Nick Cave tunes.

Potemkin

Viktoria-Luise-Platz 5 (2196 8181). U4 Viktoria-Luise-Platz/bus N46. **Open** 8am-1am Mon-Sat; 8am-midnight Sun. **No credit cards. Map** p305 D5.

Film stills and the likeness of *Battleship Potemkin* director Eisenstein adorn the wall, and the red and black decor has a constructivist feel. Breakfasts also sport titles of Eisenstein films, from the basic 'Ivan the Terrible' to 'Viva Mexico' with marinated chicken breast served with pineapple and cheese on toast. There's also a daily lunch special and snacks such as mozzarella rolls stuffed with serrano ham.

Savarin

Kulmer Strasse 17 (216 3864). U7, S1, S2 Yorckstrasse/bus N19. **Open** 10am-midnight Mon-Thur; 10am-9pm Fri-Sun. **No credit cards. Map** p306 E5.

Cosy café with a sophisticated edge and famously excellent cakes and pies. On Sundays it's not just that you can't find a seat – you can't even get in the door for all the people queuing to take away cheesecake slices and apple tarts.

Tim's Canadian Deli

Maassenstrasse 14 (2175 6960). U1, U2, U4 Nollendorfplatz/bus N2, N5, N19, N26. **Open** 8am-1am Mon-Fri; 8am-late Sat; 9am-1am Sun. **Credit** AmEx, MC, V. **Map** p305 D5.

Against the odds, this place seems to have conquered the Winterfeldtplatz area, though there's not a café round here that's not full on a market day. Lots of bagels and muffins, egg breakfasts until 4pm, various light meal options.

Zoulou Bar

Hauptstrasse 4 (no phone). U7 Kleistpark/bus N4, N48. **Open** 8pm-6am daily. **No credit cards. Map** p306 E5.

Small bar with a funky vibe and occasional DJs. It can get packed between 10pm and 2am; after that the crowd thins and late is the best time for a visit.

Tiergarten

The area around **Potsdamer Strasse** is kind of a northern Schöneberg, its scene overlapping with that of the neighbouring borough. Around **Lützowplatz** it's rather more upmarket. There are one or two bars inside the Tiergarten itself – **Café am Neuen See** is a splendid spot in summer – but alas we can find nothing to recommend among all the shiny new franchises of **Potsdamer Platz**.

Bar am Lützowplatz

Lützowplatz 7 (262 6807/www.baramlützowplatz.com). U1, U2, U4, U15 Nollendorfplatz/bus N2, N5, N19, N26. **Open** 2pm-late daily. **Credit** AmEx, MC, V. **Map** p305 D4.

Long bar with a long drinks list and classy customers in Chanel suits sipping expensive, well-made cocktails as they compare bank balances.

Café Einstein

Kurfürstenstrasse 58 (261 5096/www.cafeeinstein.com). U1, U2, U4 Nollendorfplatz/bus N2, N5, N19, N26. **Open** 9am-1am daily. **Credit** AmEx, DC, MC, V. **Map** p305 D4.

Victoria Bar. *See p156.*

Viennese-style coffeehouse with waiters in bow ties, international papers to read and an *Apfelstrudel* of legend. In summer you can enjoy a leisurely garden breakfast (served all day). *See also p145.*
Other locations: Unter den Linden 42, Mitte (204 3632).

Café am Neuen See
Lichtensteinallee 2 (254 4930). U2, U9, S3, S5, S7, S9, S75 Zoologischer Garten. Bus X9, 100, 187, 341. **Open** *Mar-Oct* 10am-11pm. *Nov-Feb* 10am-8pm daily. **Credit** AmEx, V. **Map** p305 D4.
Stretch out at one of the outside tables by a leafy Tiergarten lake and it feels like you've slipped right outside of the city. Coffee, cakes, drinks, light meals and rowing boats for hire nearby.

Kumpelnest 3000
Lützowstrasse 23 (261 6918). U1, U15 Kurfürstenstrasse/bus N2, N5, N48. **Open** 5pm-late daily. **No credit cards**. **Map** p306 E4.
This perennially popular and studiedly tacky establishment is at its best at the end of a long Saturday night, when it's crowded and chaotic and everyone is attempting to dance to disco classics.

Schleusenkrug
Müller-Breslau-Strasse/Unterschleuse (313 9909/ www.schleusenkrug.de). S3, S5, S7, S9, S75 Tiergarten/bus N9. **Open** 10am-1am daily. **No credit cards**. **Map** p305 C4.
Bar and beer garden directly on the canal in the Tiergarten, with easy listening, mod and indie pop nights. During the day the place retains much of its original flavour, hingeing on nautical themes and large glasses of Pils.

Victoria Bar
Potsdamer Strasse 102 (2575 9977/www. victoriabar.de). U1, U15 Kurfürstenstrasse/bus N2, N5, N48. **Open** 6pm-3am Mon-Thur, Sun; 6pm-4am Fri, Sat. **No credit cards**. **Map** p306 E4/5.
Funky, grown-up cocktail bar for a relaxed, mixed crowd. The low-key concept – long bar, subdued lighting, restrained colours, muffled funk, and staff who know what they're mixing – is successful enough that this place feels like it's been here for ever, though it actually only opened in 2003.

Charlottenburg/Wilmersdorf

There are pockets of life around **Savignyplatz** and **Karl-August-Platz**, but Charlottenburg is a place where nothing much happens these days. The last decent club checked out some time in the late 1980s and the borough's ageing bars are no match for neighbouring Schöneberg, let alone Mitte. Those places that do business cater mostly to tourists, businesspeople and a big Russian population. Plenty of café life by day, though – as there also is around **Ludwigkirchplatz**, south of the Ku'damm, in Wilmersdorf.

Galerie Bremer
Fasanenstrasse 37 (881 4908). U1, U9 Spichernstrasse/bus N9. **Open** 8pm-late Tue-Sun. **No credit cards**. **Map** p305 C5.
In the back room of a tiny gallery, this bar has the air of a well-kept secret. The room is painted in deep, rich colours with a beautiful ship-like bar designed by Hans Scharoun. When the assistant barman takes your coat and welcomes you, it's meant to make you feel at home, and it's also the done thing to make a little conversation with the majestically bearded owner – he'll remember next time you drop in. Then you can sit back, feel privileged, and watch the odd member of parliament entering incognito.

Diener
Grolmanstrasse 47 (881 5329). S3, S5, S7, S9, S75 Savignyplatz/bus N27, N49. **Open** 5pm-late daily. **No credit cards**. **Map** p305 C4.
An old-style Berlin bar, named after a famous boxer. The walls are adorned with faded hunting murals and photos of famous Germans you won't recognise. You could almost be in 1920s Berlin. Almost.

Café Hardenberg
Hardenbergstrasse 10 (312 2644/www.cafe-hardenberg.de). U2 Ernst-Reuter-Platz/bus N45. **Open** 9am-1am Mon-Thur, Sun; 9am-1am Fri, Sat. **Main courses** €3.50-€7. **Credit** V. **Map** p305 C4.
Across from the Technical University and usually packed with students drinking coffee. Simple, decent pasta, salads and sandwiches at reasonable prices.

Leysieffer
Kurfürstendamm 218, Wilmersdorf (885 7480). U15 Uhlandstrasse. **Open** 10am-7pm Mon-Sat; 11am-6pm Sun. **Credit** AmEx, DC, MC, V. **Map** p305 C4.
Exquisite tortes and fruitcakes are served upstairs in the high-ceilinged café. Tempting mounds of truffles and bonbons are sold downstairs in the shop.

Café im Literaturhaus
Fasanenstrasse 23 (882 5414/www.literatur-berlin.de). U15 Uhlandstrasse/bus N10, N19, N21, N27. **Open** 9.30am-1am daily. **No credit cards**. **Map** p305 C4.
The café of the Literaturhaus, which has lectures, readings and a bookshop. The greenhouse-like winter garden or salon rooms are great for ducking into a book over breakfast or a snack.

Schwarzes Café
Kantstrasse 148 (313 8038). S3, S5, S7, S9, S75 Savignyplatz/bus N27, N49. **Open** midnight-3am Mon; 10am-late Tue; 24hrs Wed-Sun. **No credit cards**. **Map** p305 C4.
Open all hours for breakfasts and meals, it was once all black and anarchistically inclined (hence the name) but these days the decor has been brightened and the political crowd moved elsewhere ages ago. Service can get overstretched when it's crowded, such as early on a weekend morning, when clubbers stop for breakfast on their way home.

Shops & Services

Upmarket or underground? It depends on the neighbourhood. Berlin is a patchwork of shopping experiences.

Berlin has never had one single downtown, and these days things are more mixed up than ever. Parts of the city march upmarket. Other bits cling to their origins in the offbeat, alternative and underground. Berliners tend to prefer shopping in their own *Kiez*, or neighbourhood, and most districts have a lively high street that meets the needs of any given day.

There are two top-of-the-line international high streets, one east and one west. The relevant bit of Friedrichstrasse in Mitte stretches from the station of the same name south to Checkpoint Charlie, with Dussmann Das KulturKaufhaus (*see p161*), Galeries Lafayette (*see p161*), and Quartier 206 (*see p162*) as anchors. And then there's the Kurfürstendamm in the west end, which actually begins on Tauentzienstrasse with KaDeWe (*see p161*) and stretches westward with one big brand name after another. There are more individualistic shops in the streets between Ku'damm and Kantstrasse, itself a centre for interior design and household goods.

Potsdamer Platz is stuck in the middle with a boring arcade and a big bunch of chain stores, a shopping experience so international that you could be anywhere. The other extreme is the concentration of eccentric enterprises and cutting-edge boutiques around Alte and Neue Schönhauser Strasse and the Hackesche Höfe in Mitte, which couldn't be anywhere else.

A further assortment of idiosyncratic retail can be found on and around Kastanienallee in Prenzlauer Berg. In Friedrichshain, the Boxhagener/Simon-Dach-Strasse axis offers lots of small boutiques and second-hand stuff. Kreuzberg's Oranienstrasse area is good for a variety of specialist shops; and the same borough's Bergmannstrasse *Kiez* has a great concentration of book and music shops. Winterfeldtplatz in Schöneberg is known for its lively market (*see p176*), and good antique shops on Goltzstrasse to the south.

Antiquarian booksellers, second-hand clothing warehouses, basements of pre-war furniture, and small *Trödeler* spilling bric-a-brac on to the pavement can be found in every area. Berlin's vibrant cultural life feeds demand for books and music, art and fashion. And a cosmopolitan population ensures a steady supply of international food and drink.

No, it can't really compete with Paris or London. But Berlin shopping has its own character and diversity. The treasures are out there, and an unusual assortment they are too.

OPENING HOURS

Shops can sell goods until 8pm on weekdays and up to 4pm on Saturdays (6pm for supermarkets). Retailers in central areas tend to keep these hours, but shops in residential areas begin shutting at 6pm on weekdays and as early as 3pm on Saturday. But generally, the tendency is for more and more shops to stay open longer and longer. Most big stores open between 8.30am and 9am; newsagents and bakeries as early as 6am; smaller or independent shops tend to open around 10am or later. Many bakeries are open for a few hours on Sundays. Many all-purpose neighbourhood shops find legal loopholes to stay open late.

Antiques

Collectors and browsers with an interest in the 18th and 19th centuries will find many of the better dealers on **Keithstrasse** and **Goltzstrasse** in Schöneberg. The streets around **Fasanenplatz** in Wilmersdorf are good, as is **Suarezstrasse** in Charlottenburg. In the east, **Kollwitzstrasse** and **Husemannstrasse** in Prenzlauer Berg are home to small, unpretentious *Antiquariaten*. *See also p180* **Souvenirs** and *p176* **Flea markets**.

Deco Arts

Motzstrasse 6, Schöneberg (215 8672). U1, U2, U4, U15 Nollendorfplatz. **Open** 3-6.30pm Wed-Fri; 11am-3pm Sat. **No credit cards. Map** p305 D5.

Shell-shaped 1930s sofas and other art deco furniture at fair prices, as well as the odd piece by Marcel Breuer and Carl Jacobs, and treasures from the 1950s and 1960s. If an American bar is too big to take home, pick up a stylish tea set, vase or ashtray.

Emma Emmelie

Schumannstrasse 15A, Mitte (2838 4884). U6 Oranienburger Tor. **Open** 1-7.30pm Mon-Fri. **Credit** AmEx, DC, MC, V. **Map** p316/p302 E3.

In an area that's undergone a major facelift because of its proximity to the seat of government, this subterranean treasure has the atmosphere of a lost era. Antique linens and clothes from the first half of the 20th century, and dolls, jewellery, glasses and china.

Comic relief at **Modern Graphics**. *See p159.*

Fingers

Nollendorfstrasse 35, Schöneberg (215 3441). U1, U2, U4, U15 Nollendorfplatz. **Open** 2.30-6.30pm Tue-Fri; 11am-2.30pm Sat. **No credit cards. Map** p305 D5.

Splendid finds from the 1940s, 1950s and 1960s, including lipstick-shaped cigarette lighters, vintage toasters, weird lighting and eccentric glassware.

Lehmanns Colonialwaren

Grolmanstrasse 46, Charlottenburg (883 3942). S3, S5, S7, S9, S75 Savignyplatz. **Open** 2-7pm Tue-Fri; 11am-2pm Sat. **No credit cards. Map** p305 C4.

Turn-of-the-20th-century luggage, clothing and furniture clutter this small shop like a Victorian parlour. The eccentric stock follows a colonial theme, so don't be surprised to find snakeskin suitcases or a guide to hunting big game.

Radio Art

Zossener Strasse 2, Kreuzberg (693 9435). U7 Gneisenaustrasse. **Open** noon-6pm Thur, Fri; 10am-1pm Sat. **Credit** AmEx, MC, V. **Map** p306 F5.

A fine collection of antique radios, from big 1930s wooden-cased specimens, designed as sitting-room centrepieces, to tiny 1970s transistors in shocking pink plastic by names such as Blaupunkt, RCA and Telefunken. Half a century of receivers in perfect working order.

Wolfgang Haas

Suarezstrasse 3, Charlottenburg (321 4570/ www.haasberlin.de). U2 Sophie-Charlotte-Platz/ bus 204. **Open** 3-7pm Tue-Fri; 11am-4pm Sat. **No credit cards. Map** p304 B4.

Period timber furniture, glassware, ceramics and other small antiques dating from 1800 to 1960. There are classic tables, chairs and cabinets, as well as some appealing art nouveau pieces. The selection of German crystal is particularly good.

Beauty salons

Hautfit Bio Kosmetik

Goltzstrasse 18, Schöneberg (216 5259). U1, U2, U4, U15 Nollendorfplatz. **Open** 10am-6.30pm Mon-Fri; 10am-2pm Sat. **Credit** MC, V. **Map** p305 D5.

This salon uses only plant-based products including the brand considered the purest of the pure, from German anthroposophical company Dr Hauschka. Products used vary according to skin type: treatments include the algae-based Sea Treatment, the flower essence facial or – the whole hog – a two-hour Dr Hauschka treatment including facial, foot bath and hand massage. Products are for sale in the shop, a *fin-de-siècle* butcher's tiled in Jugendstil ceramics.

Marie France

Fasanenstrasse 42, Charlottenburg (881 6555). U15 Uhlandstrasse. **Open** 9am-6pm Mon- Fri; 9am-3pm Sat. **Credit** MC, V. **Map** p305 C5.

The cosmeticians speak reasonable English and use luxurious French products at this clean, pleasant salon, which has been glamming up Berliners for more than 30 years. Hot-wax depilation is a speciality, and staff also offer a wide range of relaxing and beautifying treatments.

Vivera

Leibnitzer Strasse 60, Charlottenburg (8867 8512). U7 Wilmersdorfer Strasse. **Open** 10am-8pm Mon-Fri; 10am-4pm Sat. **Credit** AmEx, DC, V. **Map** p305 C4.

Berlin businesspeople frequently extend their lunch breaks to treat themselves to a Comforting Eye Treatment or a Himalayan Rejuvenation Treatment at Vivera. At the back of this cosmetics shop, the hair and beauty salon offers first-rate hair styling, cutting and colouring, aromatherapy massage, manicures, facials and a range of body treatments, using products based on natural flower essences.

Books

Though the chains are spreading, Berlin still has a lively independent book-shop scene. For gay book shops, *see p215*.

Berlin Story

Unter den Linden 10, Mitte (2045 3840/ www.berlinstory.de). U6 Französische Strasse. **Open** 10am-7pm daily. **Credit** AmEx, MC, V. **Map** p316/p302 F3.

You won't find a better source of Berlin-related books (in both German and English). Subjects range from the history of the Hohenzollerns or the GDR to Prussian architecture and Norman Foster's Reichstag. Also historical maps, posters, videos, CDs, and souvenirs such as mounted wall chunks.

Bücherbogen

Savignyplatz Bogen 593, Charlottenburg (3186 9511/www.buecherbopgen.com). S3, S5, S7, S9, S75 Savignyplatz. **Open** 10am-8pm Mon-Fri; 10am-6pm Sat. **Credit** MC, V. **Map** p305 C4.

This great art book shop is a prime browsing spot. This branch stocks books on painting, sculpture, photography and a little architecture; the branch at S-Bahnbogen 585 does film; the Kochstrasse branch has architecture, and in Knesebeckstrasse there are discounted books and remainders.

Other locations: S-Bahnbogen 585, Charlottenburg (312 1932); Kochstrasse 19, Kreuzberg (251 1345); Knesebeckstrasse 27, Charlottenburg (8868 3695).

Hammett

Friesenstrasse 27, Kreuzberg (691 5834/www. hammett-krimis.de). U7 Gneisenaustrasse. **Open** 10am-8pm Mon-Fri; 9am-4pm Sat. **Credit** V. **Map** p306 F5/6.

Small, friendly store specialising in crime and mystery novels, both new and second-hand, with plenty of English titles.

Kohlhaas & Company

Fasanenstrasse 23, Wilmersdorf (882 5044). U15 Uhlandstrasse. **Open** 10am-8pm Mon-Fri; 10am-6pm Sat. **Credit** MC, V. **Map** p305 C4.

Elegantly housed beneath the Literaturhaus, this small book shop aims towards the high-brow. German literature predominates. Service is helpful.

Modern Graphics

Oranienstrasse 22, Kreuzberg (615 8810/www. modern-graphics.de). U1, U15 Kottbuser Tor. **Open** 10am-8pm Mon-Thur; 10am-6pm Fri; 10am-4pm Sat. **Credit** AmEx, MC, V. **Map** p316/p302 F3.

Large selection of imported and alternative comics. Also T-shirts, graphic novels, Anime and calendars.

Other locations: Bundesallee 83, Friedenau (8599 9054).

ProQM

Alte Schönhauser Strasse 48, Mitte (2472 8520/ www.pro-qm.de). U8 Weinmeisterstrasse. **Open** noon-8pm Mon-Fri; noon-6pm Sat. **Credit** MC, V. **Map** p316/p303 G3.

The artist owners offer a cosmopolitan and well-informed selection of books and magazines on architecture, art, design, pop culture, town planning and cultural theory – including many titles in English. Cool decor with fabulous old 'sentry-box' cash desk.

Storytime Books

Schmargendorfer Strasse 36-37, Friedenau (8596 7004/www.storytime-books.com). U9 Friedrich-Wilhelm-Platz. **Open** 10am-6pm Mon-Fri; 9.30am-1.30pm Sat. **Credit** AmEx, MC, V.

American owner Diane Pentaleri-Otto specialises in children's books and works hard to make the shop child- and parent-friendly. Events for kids include a weekly story time in English (4pm Wed) and singalongs in English and German (4pm Tue, 4pm, 5.45pm Fri). Coffee and muffins for the grown-ups.

Antiquarian & second-hand books

Knesebeckstrasse in Charlottenburg, **Winterfeldtstrasse** in Schöneberg and **Kollwitzstrasse** and **Husemannstrasse** in Prenzlauer Berg all offer rich literary pickings.

Antiquariat Senzel

Knesebeckstrasse 13-14, Charlottenburg (312 5887). U2 Ernst-Reuter-Platz. **Open** noon-6.30pm Mon-Fri; 11am-2pm Sat. **No credit cards**. **Map** p305 C4.

Most of the books are in German, though odd English and French volumes can be found. Also some beautifully leather-bound tomes and old maps.

Düwal

Schlüterstrasse 17, Charlottenburg (313 3030/ www.duewal.de). S3, S5, S7, S9, S75 Savignyplatz. **Open** noon-6.30pm Mon-Fri; 11am-2pm Sat. **Credit** DC, MC, V. **Map** p305 C4.

Large store with everything from recent bestsellers to rare first editions. Good selection of foreign titles.

English-language books

Another Country

Riemannstrasse 7, Kreuzberg (6940 1150/www. anothercountry.de). U7 Gneisenaustrasse. **Open** 11am-8pm Mon-Fri; 11am-6pm Sat. **No credit cards. Map** p306 F5.

Spacious premises housing an ambitious book shop and private library stocked with more than 10,000 English-language titles – around half of them science fiction – from the collection of British owner Alan Raphaeline. A small membership fee allows you to use the reading room downstairs and help yourself to tea and coffee, or borrow books for varying fees. Return them to recoup a deposit, or else hang on to the book.

Books in Berlin

Goethestrasse 69, Charlottenburg (313 1233/www. booksinberlin.de). S3, S5, S7, S9, S75 Savignyplatz. **Open** noon-8pm Mon-Fri; 10am-4pm Sat. **Credit** V. **Map** p305 C4.

Run by a Bostonian, with a small but solid selection of new and used history and politics, classical and modern fiction, reference and travel books.

Fair Exchange

Dieffenbachstrasse 58, Kreuzberg (694 4675). U8 Schönleinstrasse. **Open** 11am-7pm Mon-Fri; 10am-6pm Sat. **No credit cards. Map** p307 G5.
Large selection of second-hand English-language books, with an emphasis on literature.

Hugendubel

Tauentzienstrasse 13, Charlottenburg (214 060/ www.hugendubel.de). U1, U2, U15 Wittenbergplatz. **Open** 9.30am-8pm Mon-Fri; 9am-4pm Sat. **No credit cards. Map** p305 D4.
Berlin's largest book shop houses more than 140,000 books, including a big English-language section.
Other locations: Friedrichstrasse 83, Mitte (2063 5100).

Le Matou

Husemannstrasse 29, Prenzlauerberg, Mitte (2809 9601). U6 Eberswalderstrasse. **Open** 10am-6.30pm Mon-Fri; 10am-2pm Sat. **No credit cards. Map** p303 G2.
International books for children and young people in English, French, Italian, Spanish, Arabic and Russian, with some 3,000 titles in stock.

Marga Schoeller Bücherstube

Knesebeckstrasse 33, Charlottenburg (881 1112/ 1122). S3, S5, S7, S9, S75 Savignyplatz. **Open** 9.30am-7pm Mon-Wed; 9.30am-8pm Thur-Fri; 9.30am-4pm Sat. **Credit** MC, V. **Map** p305 C4.
Rated by *Bookseller* as Europe's fourth best independent literary book shop, this excellent establishment, founded in 1930, includes a self-contained English-language section that, if not the largest selection in town, is one of the most interesting. Staff are sweet, helpful, know their stock and will track down anything that's not on their shelves.

St. Georges

Wörtherstrasse 27, Prenzlauer Berg (8179 8333/ www.saintgeorgesbookshop.com). Tram 1. **Open** *Winter* 1-7pm Mon-Fri; 11am-5pm Sat. *Summer* noon-8pm Mon-Fri; 11am-5pm Sat. **No credit cards. Map** p303 G2.
Stocks a decent and reasonably priced selection of second-hand English-language books, with a focus on biographies and contemporary lit. Reading areas are equipped with comfortable leather couches.

Children's clothes & toys

Wooden toys are a German speciality and, though pricey, are often worth the money. Puppets from the Dresdener puppet factory and tiny wooden figures from the Erzgebirge region are particularly distinctive. Stuffed toys are another traditional offering: Steiff (which claims to have invented the teddy bear) and its competitor Sigikid both offer beautifully made and collectable cuddly animals. For children's books *see p159* **Storytime Books** and *above* **Le Matou**.

Emma & Co

Niebuhrstrasse 1, Charlottenburg (882 7373). S3, S5, S7, S9, S75 Savignyplatz. **Open** 11am-7pm Mon-Wed; 11am-7.30pm Thur, Fri; 11am-4pm Sat. **Credit** MC, V. **Map** p304/p305 B/C4.
Melanie Wöltje's charming shop within Bramigk & Breer (*see p162*) offers well-made but not exorbitant children's wear, bedding, toys and gift items such as name books and terry-cloth teddies.

Heidi's Spielzeugladen

Kantstrasse 61, Charlottenburg (323 7556). U7 Wilmersdorfer Strasse. **Open** 9.30am-6.30pm Mon-Fri; 9.30am-4pm Sat. **Credit** MC, V. **Map** p304 B4.
Wooden toys, including cookery utensils and child-sized kitchens, are the attraction here. Heidi's is also known for stocking a good selection of books, puppets and wall-hangings.

H&M Kids

Kurfürstendamm 237, Charlottenburg (884 8760/ www.hm.com). U9, U15 Kurfürstendamm. **Open** 10am-8pm Mon-Sat. **Credit** AmEx, DC, MC, V. **Map** p305 C4.
The place for cute, cheap clothes for kids up to 14. This branch has the largest children's department.

Michas Bahnhof

Nürnberger Strasse 24A, Schöneberg (218 6611/ www.michas-bahnhof.de). U1 Augsburger Strasse. **Open** 10am-6.30pm Mon-Fri; 10am-4pm Sat. **Credit** AmEx, DC, MC, V. **Map** p305 D4.
Small shop packed with model trains both old and new, and everything that goes with them.

Nix Design

Heckmann Höfe, Oranienburger Strasse 32, Mitte (281 8044/www.nix.de). S1, S2, S25, S26 Oranienburger Strasse. **Open** 11am-8pm Mon-Fri; noon-6pm Sat. **Credit** AmEx, MC, V. **Map** p316/p302 F3.
Apart from her women's collection, avant-garde designer Barbara Gebhardt also does a wonderful children's line.

Peekaboo Kindermoden

Prenzlauer Allee 213, Prenzlauer Berg (4849 6092/www.peekaboo-kindermoden.de). Tram 1. **Open** 10am-6.30pm Mon-Fri; 10am-2pm Sat. **Credit** AmEx, MC, V. **Map** p303 G2.
Simply beautiful clothing for boys and girls up to age five. Wonderful selection of trendy designer handbags for little girls.

Tam Tam

Lietzenburger Strasse 92, Charlottenburg (882 1454). U15 Uhlandstrasse. **Open** 10am-6.30pm Mon-Fri; 10am-4pm Sat. **Credit** MC, V. **Map** p305 C4/5.
A bright, charming shop filled with stuffed animals and wooden toys, including building blocks, trains, trucks, dolls' houses, plus child-sized wooden stoves.

Dussmann Das KulturKaufhaus.

v. Kloeden

Wielandstrasse 24, Charlottenburg (8871 2512/ www.vonkloeden.de). U15 Uhlandstrasse. **Open** 9am-7pm Mon-Fri; 10am-4pm Sat. **Credit** AmEx, DC, MC, V. **Map** p305 C4.
Oldest and friendliest toy store in town, run by a brother-and-sister team who make it their policy to help you find the perfect present. The wide selection includes children's books in English, toys and reading material from the Montessori and Steiner schools, building blocks by German aviator Otto Lilienthal, handmade Käthe Kruse dolls, Erzgebirge wooden figures, and all kinds of modern-day fare.

Cosmetics

Belladonna

Bergmannstrasse 101, Kreuzberg (694 3731/ www.bella-donna.de). U7 Gneisenaustrasse. **Open** 10am-7pm Mon-Fri; 10am-4pm Sat. **Credit** AmEx, MC, V. **Map** p306 F5.
Natural and flower-essence products from Logona, Lavera, Dr Hauschka and Weleda, plus the entire range of Primavera essential oils and lamps to burn them in. The shop also stocks brushes, make-up and baby clothes.

MAC

Rosenthaler Strasse 36, Mitte (2404 8730/ www.maccosmetics.com) U8 Rosenthalerplatz. **Open** 11am-8pm Mon-Sat **Credit** DC, MC, V. **Map** p316/p302 F3.
This mirror-lined boutique is a cosmetic wonderland. This stuff is worn by every star who graces a red carpet these days, but the shop doesn't feel too exclusive: personal attention is excellent and you are encouraged to try on products. Splurge on some serious make-up drama, but save money and buy your sponges at Woolworth's.

Department stores

There is little to distinguish the four main chains, Hertie, Karstadt, Kaufhof and Wertheim. All offer everything you might need in decent quality and at similar prices.

Dussmann Das KulturKaufhaus

Friedrichstrasse 90, Mitte (20250/www.kulturkaufhaus.de). U6, S1, S2, S3, S5, S7, S9, S25, S26, S75 Friedrichstrasse. **Open** 10am-10pm Mon-Sat. **Credit** AmEx, MC, V. **Map** p316/p302 F3.
Intended as a 'cultural department store', this spacious four-floor retailer mixes books with CDs, videos with magazines, and has internet terminals, an interactive video-viewing room and DVD shop.

Galeries Lafayette

Französische Strasse 23, Mitte (209 480/ www.galerieslafayette.com). U2, U6 Stadtmitte. **Open** 10am-8pm Mon-Sat. **Credit** AmEx, DC, MC, V. **Map** p316/p302 F3.
The Jean Nouvel glass block that houses Galeries Lafayette offers a refreshing shopping experience. All merchandise is French, and though the selection of accessories, cosmetics and clothing is good (highlight is the Agnès B shop-in-shop on the first floor), the best feature is the food floor in the basement, where you'll feel transported to Paris among fresh cheeses, chocolates, wines, breads and condiments.

KaDeWe

Tauentzienstrasse 21-4, Schöneberg (21210/ www.kadewe.com). U1, U2, U15 Wittenbergplatz. **Open** 9.30am-8pm Mon-Fri; 10am-2pm Sat. **Credit** AmEx, DC, MC, V. **Map** p305 D4.
This is the largest department store in continental Europe and a top tourist attraction. But though it carries name brands in all departments, the presentation is bad and much of the merchandise merely average. KaDeWe is most famous for its lavish food hall, which takes up the entire sixth floor. The delicatessen is known for its specialities, the gourmet bars offer everything from oysters to smoked sausage, and special orders for more outré items can be made by phone (21211700). Some orders may take a few days but same-day delivery is possible until 4pm in Berlin and Potsdam.

Kaufhof

Alexanderplatz 9, Mitte (2474 3265/www.galleriakaufhof.de). U2, U5, U8, S3, S5, S7, S9, S75 Alexanderplatz. **Open** 9am-8pm Mon-Sat. **Credit** AmEx, DC, MC, V. **Map** p316/p303 G3.

The Kaufhof group bought the old GDR Centrum stores and dominates the eastern market. The façade of its Alexanderplatz branch looks so 1970s it's almost hip. This Kaufhof is structured on the shop-in-shop principle and expat London girls come here to stock up on Oasis. There's also an internet café and kids' cinema.

Naturkaufhaus

Schlossstrasse 101, Steglitz (797 3716). U9 Schlossstrasse. **Open** 10am-8pm Mon-Fri; 10am-6pm Sat. **Credit** AmEx, MC, V.

Berlin's first department store for organic goods is spread out over two floors of the Galleria mall in Steglitz. The selection ranges from the usual healthy foodstuffs you also find in smaller *Bioläden* to eco-friendly clothes, shoes and cosmetics as well as a selection of wines.

Quartier 206

Friedrichstrasse 71, Mitte (2094 6800). U2, U6 Stadtmitte. **Open** 10am-8pm Mon-Fri; 10am-6pm Sat. **Credit** AmEx, DC, MC, V. **Map** p316/p302 F3.

Reminiscent of New York's Takashimaya and designed by that city's Calvin Tsao, this upmarket department store offers not only the most lusted-after designer labels, but those labels' most definitive items. Cult cosmetics and centuries-old perfumes are sold on the ground floor along with a fantastic flower department, while the upstairs is devoted to women's and men's fashion, lingerie, jewellery, and shoes – including a Manolo Blahnik department – plus a home living section stocked with sinfully expensive design trends.

Design & household goods

For a while it seemed Berlin was so busy rebuilding someone forgot people needed to furnish all this new space. **stilwerk** (*see p164* **Design for living rooms**) came to the rescue, a project that has attracted other retailers to transform this stretch of **Kantstrasse** in Charlottenburg into an oasis for home improvers. The scene in Mitte is big on retro, and the **Alte** and **Neue Schönhauser Strassen** are good places to hunt for neo-cool eastern and western designs from the 1950s to 1970s. The 'ethno' look arrived late in Berlin and is still big here.

Bramigk & Breer

Niebuhrstrasse 1, Charlottenburg (882 7373). S3, S5, S7, S9, S75 Savignyplatz. **Open** 11am-6.30pm Mon-Wed; 11am-7.30pm Thur, Fri; 11am-4pm Sat. **Credit** MC, V. **Map** p304/p305 B/C4.

Strikes a balance between Mediterranean and Brandenburg country style with stripped-down furniture, warm lighting and irresistible ornaments. Highlights include a fine selection of natural linens, hand-blown coloured drinking glasses and realistic silk flowers. Also houses charming children's clothes and gift shop Emma & Co (*see p160*).

Coldampf's

Uhlandstrasse 54-5, Charlottenburg (883 9191/ www.coldampfs.de). U1 Hohenzollernplatz. **Open** 10am-8pm Mon-Fri; 10am-4pm Sat. **Credit** MC, V. **Map** p305 C5.

Stue. *See p163.*

Eat, Drink, Shop

An impressive stock of some 7,000 products to equip any kitchen, from high-tech cooking utensils to sturdy cocktail glasses. Also plates and glasses for hire. **Other locations**: Woertherstr 39, Prenzlauerberg, (4373 5225).

DIM

Oranienstrasse 26, Kreuzberg (902 986 612/ www.blindenanstalt.de). U1, U8, U15 Kottbusser Tor. **Open** 9am-5pm Mon-Wed; 10am-5.30pm Thur; 9am-3pm Fri. **No credit cards. Map** p307 G4/5.
A Design Institute initiative for the blind. Witty, high-style brushes, baskets and other wicker items, all high-quality and hand-made on the premises.

Dopo Domani

Kantstrasse 148, Charlottenburg (882 2242/ www.dopo-domani.com). S3, S5, S7, S9, S75 Savignyplatz. **Open** 10.30am-7pm Mon-Fri; 10am-6pm Sat. **Credit** AmEx, MC, V. **Map** p305 C4.
A temple for design aficionados installed over three levels of an old town house. Combining an interior design practice with a well-stocked shop, the focus is on Italian outfitters and the presentation creates an environment you'll dream of calling your own.

Furniture

Sredzkistrasse 22, Prenzlauer Berg (4434 2157). U2 Eberswalder Strasse. **Open** 2-7pm Mon; 12.30-8pm Wed, Fri; 12.30-6pm Sat. **No credit cards. Map** p303 G2.
Shagedelic Baby! Retro furniture, TVs, radios, clocks, lamps and wallpaper from the 1960s and 1970s. If you're into plastic stuff in burnt orange and brown, this is the place for you.

Formgeber Berlin

Goltzstrasse 13B, Schöneberg (2362 4920). U7 Eisenacher Strasse. **Open** 10am-8pm Mon-Fri; 10am-4pm Sat. **Credit** MC, V. **Map** p305 D5.
Pragmatic furniture and accessories for streamlined, style-conscious living with a touch of 1970s irony. Appealing ceramics in sleek and inventive shapes.

Leinenkontor

Tucholskystrasse 22, Mitte (2839 0277/www. leinenkontor.de). S1, S2, S25, S26 Oranienburger Strasse. **Open** 10am-6pm Tue-Sat. **Credit** MC, V. **Map** p316/p302 F3.
Textile designer Eva Endruweit's shop has linens for table and bed from her own no-frills collection, and from the exquisite Austrian company Leitner and Sweden's royal purveyor Ekelund. Also shirts, nightdresses and christening gowns.

Ruby

Oranienburger Strasse 32, Mitte (2838 6030). S1, S2, S25, S26 Oranienburger Strasse. **Open** 11am-8pm Mon-Fri; 11am-6pm Sat. **Credit** AmEx, MC, V. **Map** p316/p302 F3.
Flying the minimalist banner, this small shop in the beautifully restored courtyard offers Spencer Fung's architectural furniture, Bowls & Linares lamps, Henry Dean glass as well as rugs, fabrics, candles and an alluring selection of ceramics in earth tones.

Schlafwandel

Kantstrasse 21, Charlottenburg (312 6523). S3, S5, S7, S9, S75 Savignyplatz. **Open** 10am-6.30pm Mon-Fri; 10am-6pm Sat. **No credit cards. Map** p305 C4.
Top brands in towelling and linen for bath and bed, plus a huge selection of robes and pyjamas.

Strauss Innovation

Greifswalder Strasse 81-84, Prenzlauer Berg (420 102 301/www.strauss1902.de). S8, S41, S42 Greifswalder Strasse. **Open** 10am-8pm Mon-Fri; 10am-4pm Sat. **No credit cards. Map** p303 G/H2.
Among an odd assortment of merchandise there are cheap, good quality goose-down and feather pillows, plus imported Italian wine and preserved foods. **Other locations**: Friedrichstrasse 149, Mitte (2061 3230); Wilmersdorferstr 126-127, Charlottenburg (3110 2490).

Stue

Alte Schönhauser Strasse 48, Mitte (2472 7650). U8 Weinmeisterstrasse. **Open** 2-7pm Tue-Fri; 1-5pm Sat. **Credit** AmEx, MC, V. **Map** p316/p303 G3.
The name means 'living room' in Danish, and owner Heike-Marie Rädeker stocks furniture, art and interior design from Denmark, including stunningly restored Danish Modern pieces and contemporary designs at reasonable prices. Also working antique Bang & Olufsen equipment. Will ship items anywhere in the world.

Glass & ceramics

Bürgel-Haus

Friedrichstrasse 154, Mitte (204 4519). U6 Französische Strasse. **Open** 10am-8pm Mon-Sat. **Credit** AmEx, MC, V. **Map** p316/p302 F3.
This distinctive blue-and-cream pottery from the state of Thüringen makes an inexpensive present for lovers of cosy kitchenware.

Keramikladen am Prenzlauer Berg

Rykestrasse 49, Prenzlauer Berg (441 9109). U2 Senefelderplatz. **Open** 1-6.30pm Mon-Fri; 11am-4pm Sat. **No credit cards. Map** p303 G2.
Bright, inexpensive, humorous household ceramics from this collective of four potters. Upstairs there's a café and shop. In the basement workshop you can buy an unfired ceramic piece, paint it, glaze it, and pick up the finished item 24 hours later.

KPM

Wegelystrasse 1, Tiergarten (3900 9215/www.kpm-berlin.de). S3, S5, S7, S9, S75 Tiergarten. **Open** 10am-7pm Mon-Fri; 9.30am-4pm Sat. **Credit** AmEx, DC, MC, V. **Map** p305 D4.
Frederick the Great liked porcelain so much that he bought the company: Königliche Porzellan Manufaktur. Eat from a king's plate, inexpensively too if you pick up some seconds at this factory shop. The full-priced version is at the Kempinski branch. **Other locations**: Kempinski Hotel Kurfürstendamm 27, Charlottenburg (886 7210); Unter den Linden 35, Mitte (206 4150).

Design for living rooms

Home of the Bauhaus and buildings by such greats as Gropius and Mies van der Rohe, Berlin is no stranger to good design. And as the city settles into its new shape, design is once more coming into its own. **stilwerk** on Kantstrasse is the centrepiece of an increasingly style-conscious city. A theme centre for high-end products, opened in 1999, it's a 20,000 square-metre (215,000 square-foot) designer mall for more than 50 retailers offering a huge range of the finest in modern furnishings, state-of-the-art kitchens, high-tech lighting, as well as luxurious bath fittings, hi-fis, fabrics, floor coverings – even grand pianos. From Alessi to Zanotta, you'll find the major players in the world of interiors, with showrooms rented out by the likes of B&B Italia, Rolf Benz, Bulthaup and Cassina.

For the city's architects and designers, stilwerk is a reference point, a place to see the items that made the headlines and show clients what they mean when they talk about a 15,000 kitchen. For consumers it's a one-stop shop and for those who can't pay the prices, a glitzy place to goggle at a stylised world. But it's not all glossy. Antiques also have a place here, and beautiful European wooden furniture from Grüne Erde and Flötotto balance the modern with the classic.

The best way to approach stilwerk is to take one of the lifts at the back to the top. There's a fantastic view from the fifth floor, which can be rented out for exhibitions and events. In summer the roof garden is popular for parties, some of them open to the (trend-making) public. From the upper floors start your descent via the staircase.

Be sure to check out the Design & Crafts Platform on the fourth floor. It showcases local talents who have shops elsewhere in town – vitrines present such handcrafted goods as jewellery, pottery and unique design accessories, all of which can be purchased, and there are presentations of things you'll have to order, like innovative wall finishes or wrought iron fences. Get a quick fix on the other end of this floor at the espresso bar, which also sells dazzling coffee machinery.

Design-related exhibitions are regularly featured in the atrium on the ground floor, as well as evening events such as award ceremonies for design competitions. There are also periodic piano concerts sponsored by Bechstein Piano. And the Soultrane jazz club at street level features visitors such as Herbie Hancock or Ute Lemper.

And if you haven't already seen enough design, just step outside into Kantstrasse. stilwerk's influence has drawn a variety of other interior and design-related businesses to the area, transforming this corner of the west end into a haven of good taste and home improvement.

stilwerk

Kantstrasse 17, Charlottenburg (315 150). S3, S5, S7, S9, S75 Savignyplatz. **Open** 10am-8pm Mon-Fri; 10am-4pm Sat. *Viewing only* 2-6pm Sun. **Credit** varies. **Map** p304 C4.

Fashion

The best area for stylish, affordable clothing is to be found in and around the **Hackesche Höfe**, the **Heckmann Höfe** and the surrounding streets in Mitte, where younger designers often have their ateliers as well as their retail outlets. Several innovative local labels have also set up shop on the **Kastanienallee** in Prenzlauer Berg.

More hefty designers have moved into the retail developments on **Friedrichstrasse**, where new shopfronts are filling with high-profile international labels. And there is still the Ku'damm and its affluent offshoots, home to all the brand-name clothing giants. Around **Fasanenstrasse** you'll find the likes of Gucci, Chanel, Tiffany and Bvlgari – and lots of Russians shopping with wads of cash.

Accessories

Blush

Rosa-Luxemburg-Strasse 22, Mitte (2809 3580/ www.blush-berlin.com). U2 Rosa-Luxemburg-Platz. **Open** noon-7pm Mon-Wed; noon-8pm Thur, Fri; noon-6pm Sat. **Credit** MC, V. **Map** p316/p303 G3.

Beautiful lingerie in lace and silk. Imports from France and Italy as well as German brands.

Les Dessous

Fasanenstrasse 42, Wilmersdorf (883 3632/www. les-dessous.de). U1, U9 Spichernstrasse. **Open** 11am-7pm Mon-Fri; 10am-3pm Sat. **Credit** AmEx, DC, MC, V. **Map** p305 C4/C5.

A beautiful shop featuring luxurious lingerie, silk dressing gowns and striking swimwear by Capucine, Eres, Dior, La Perla and Andres Sarda. **Other locations**: Schlüterstrasse 36, Charlottenburg (881 3660).

Fiona Bennett

Grosse Hamburger Strasse 25, Mitte (2809 6330/ www.fionabennett.com). S3, S5, S7, S9, S75 Hackescher Markt. **Open** noon-6pm Tue-Fri; noon-6pm Sat. **Credit** AmEx, DC, MC, V. **Map** p316/p302 F3.

Fiona Bennett's hats are works of art. Redefining traditional shapes, her imagination leaves trends by the wayside to create horned headdresses, feathered fedoras, hats reminiscent of insects or sea urchins, and delicate hairpieces made of a single feather shaped into a curl or shimmering sequins spilling into a filigree fountain. For all their theatrics, the hats always display their maker's sense for beauty.

Fishbelly

Sophienstrasse 7A, Mitte (2804 5180/ www.fishbelly.de). U8 Weinmeisterstrasse. **Open** 12.30-7pm Mon-Fri; noon-6pm Sat. **Credit** AmEx, DC, MC, V. **Map** p316/p302 F3.

Often compared to London's Agent Provocateur, this tiny Hackesche Höfe shop is licensed to thrill with its selection of extravagant under- and bathing garments by designers such as Dolce & Gabbana Intimo, Christian Dior and Capucine Puerari. Also be sure to check out Fishbelly's own-brand line of imaginative lingerie.

Knopf Paul

Zossener Strasse 10, Kreuzberg (692 1212). U7 Gneisenaustrasse. **Open** 9am-6pm Tue, Fri; 2-6pm Wed, Thur. **No credit cards**. **Map** p306 F5.

A Kreuzberg institution that stocks buttons in every imaginable shape, colour, material and style. The selection numbers in the tens of thousands. Whatever you're seeking in the button department, Paul Knopf ('button') will help you find it. In fact, his wonderfully patient and amiable service is particularly remarkable considering that most transactions are for tiny sums.

Mane Lange Korsetts

Hagenauer Strasse 13, Prenzlauer Berg, (4432 8482/www.manelange.de) U2 Eberswalder Strasse. **Open** 2-7pm Wed-Fri; noon-6pm Sat; or by appointment. **No credit cards**. **Map** p303 G1/2.

Lovely original corsets in lush materials, hand-made on the premises by local designer Mane Lange. Bustiers come off the rack, otherwise custom orders require a fitting and are completed in 24 hours.

Roeckl

Kurfürstendamm 216, Charlottenburg (881 5379/ www.roeckl.de). U1, U15 Uhlandstrasse. **Open** 10am-7pm Mon-Fri; 10am-4pm Sat. **Credit** AmEx, DC, MC, V. **Map** p305 C4.

Gloves in all colours and materials, plus scarves, pashminas and shawls by international designers.

Tagebau

Rosenthaler Strasse 19, Mitte (2839 0890). U8 Weinmeisterstrasse or S3, S5, S7, S9, S75 Hackescher Markt. **Open** 11am-8pm Mon-Fri; 11am-6pm Sat. **Credit** MC. **Map** p316/p302 F3.

The six young designers who share this airy, spacious store-cum-workshop specialise in jewellery, fashion, millinery and furniture. Their work also shares a sculptural quality that, in this generous space and with subtle spotlighting, gives the whole establishment the feel of a gallery. Note: when this guide went to press, Tagebau was planning to move to a new location.

Costume & formal-wear hire

Graichen

Klosterstrasse 32, Spandau (331 3587/ www.kostumehause-graichen.de). U7 Rathaus Spandau. **Open** 10am-6pm Mon-Fri; 10am-1pm Sat; or by appointment. **Credit** MC.

Tuxedos for men, short and long evening wear for women. Bridal gowns too.

Theaterkunst

Eisenzahnstrasse 43-4, Wilmersdorf (864 7270/ www.theaterkunst.de). U1, U7 Fehrbelliner Platz. **Open** 8am-4.30pm Mon-Thur; 8am-3.30pm Fri. **No credit cards**. **Map** p304 B5.

Three warehouses crammed with period costumes for any historical fantasy. The choice is immense so allow time to browse and be fitted and go back later to collect. Founded in 1908, the impressive collection was destroyed during the last war and re-established in 1951. Staff know their stuff and give good advice, and there's a free alterations service.

Designer: international

Antonie Setzer

Bleibtreustrasse 19, Charlottenburg (883 1350/ www.antoniesetzer.de). S3, S5, S7, S9, S75 Savignyplatz. **Open** 10am-7pm Mon-Fri; 10am-8pm Thur-Fri; 10am-4pm Sat. **Credit** AmEx, DC, MC, V. **Map** p305 C4.

Fashion for women with an intelligent selection of styles from Capucine, D&G, Miu Miu, Strenesse and the unusual designs of Italian label Gembalies.

Harvey's

Kurfürstendamm 156, Charlottenburg (883 3803/ www.harveys-berlin.de). U15 Uhlandstrasse. **Open** 10.30am-8pm Mon-Fri; 10am-6pm Sat. **Credit** AmEx, DC, MC, V. **Map** p305 C4.

Frieder Böhnisch has held the fort of cutting-edge men's labels for 20 years. Now he stocks clothes and shoes by the Japanese (Yohji Yamamoto, Comme des Garçons) and the Belgians (Bikkembergs, Martin Margiela). His enthusiasm may persuade you to splurge, but there are no hard feelings if you don't.

Mientus Studio 2002

Wilmersdorfer Strasse 73, Charlottenburg (323 9077). U7 Wilmersdorfstrasse. **Open** 10am-7pm Mon-Fri; 10am-6pm Sat. **Credit** AmEx, DC, MC, V. **Map** p304 B4.

Clean cuts for sharp men from a range of collections including Dsquared, Neil Barrett, Helmut Lang, Miu Miu, Andrew Mackenzie and German rave labels.

Other locations: Schlüterstrasse 26, Charlottenburg (323 9077); Kurfürstendamm 52, Charlottenburg (323 9077).

Patrick Hellman

Fasanenstrasse 29, Charlottenburg (8848 7712/ www.patrickhellmann.com). U15 Uhlandstrasse. **Open** 10am-7pm Mon-Fri; 10am-8pm Thur; 10am-4pm Sat. **Credit** AmEx, DC, MC, V. **Map** p305 C5.

Prolific Berlin retailer with five stores to his name, specialising in international chic for men and women. A bespoke tailoring service offers men the choice of the Hellman design range in a variety of luxurious fabrics, including some by Italian textile maestro Ermenegildo Zegna.

T&G

Rosenthaler Strasse 34-5, Mitte (2809 2790). U8 Weinmeisterstrasse or S3, S5, S7, S9, S75 Hackescher Markt. **Open** 10am-8pm Mon-Fri; 10am-4pm Sat. **Credit** MC, V. **Map** p316/p302 F3.

Kai Angladegies is not the first to fuse fashion and fine art, but 'Tools & Gallery' is a bold, stylish and enjoyably pretentious attempt. The interior is camply rococo, with candelabras and muslin-draped cubicles, and the clothing selection is equally impressive. Menswear is especially strong and often nothing short of outrageous. Names for men and women include Givenchy, Alexander McQueen and Vivienne Westwood. The gallery is accessed via a beautiful 1860 wrought-iron staircase and features exhibitions of fine art, design and haute couture.

Designer: local

Chiton

Goltzstrasse 12, Schöneberg (216 6013/ www.chiton.de). U7 Eisenacher Strasse. **Open** noon-6.30pm Mon-Fri; 11am-6.30pm Sat. **Credit** AmEx, MC, V. **Map** p305 D5.

Fiona Bennett. *See p165.*

Husband-and-wife team Robert and Friederike Jorzig make beautiful bridal and evening gowns. Created using high-quality fabrics, their striking cuts – from the very simple to designs recalling early Hollywood sophistication – attract customers from Britain and America. They also put out summer and winter collections in their signature reductionist style. You should allow two or three weeks for gowns and men's suits; dresses, on the other hand, can be done in three days.

Claudia Skoda Level

Linienstrasse 156, Mitte (280 7211). U6 Oranienburger Tor. **Open** 11am-7pm Mon-Fri. **Credit** AmEx, DC, MC, V. **Map** p316/p302 F3.
Berlin's most established womenswear designer has extended her creative energies to include men. These days, she showcases designs for both sexes in this Mitte loft space. Using high-tech yarns and innovative knitting techniques, the collections bear her signature combination of stretch fabrics and graceful drape effects.

Hut Up

Oranienburger Strasse 32, Mitte (2838 6105/ www.hutup.de). S1, S2, S25, S26 Oranienburger Strasse. **Open** 11am-6pm Mon-Sat. **Credit** AmEx, DC, MC, V. **Map** p316/p302 F3.
Christine Birkle's imaginative felt designs come in bold colours. Her wares are handcrafted in one piece shaped from raw wool using traditional methods. The clothes combine felt with silk or gauze, and there's a witty range of accessories for the body or home including hats, slippers, vases, hot-water bottles, mobile phone cases, wine coolers and egg cosies shaped like dunce hats.

Lisa D

Hackesche Höfe, Rosenthaler Strasse 40-41, Mitte (282 9061). U8 Weinmeisterstrasse or S3, S5, S7, S9, S75 Hackescher Markt. **Open** noon-6.30pm Mon-Sat. **Credit** AmEx, DC, MC, V. **Map** p316/p302 F3.
Long, flowing womenswear in subdued shades from this avant-garde designer. Austrian-born Lisa D is well known on the Berlin fashion scene and was one of the first to move into the Hackesche Höfe.

Little Red Riding Hood

Friedrichstrasse 148, Mitte (2005 8755/www. littleredridinghood.de). U6, S1, S2, S3, S5, S7, S9, S25, S26, S75 Friedrichstrasse. **Open** 11am-8pm Mon-Sat. **Credit** AmEx, MC, V. **Map** p316/p302 F3.
The Unisex Line offers a sportily elegant range of variable trouser styles and sophisticated, designed skirts. Colours range from black, white and grey to violet. Strong details combined with body-fitting fabrics such as cotton/lycra mix, soft leather and canvas create an androgynous feel.

Molotow

Gneisenaustrasse 112, Kreuzberg (693 0818/ www.molotowberlin.de). U7 Mehringdamm. **Open** 2-8pm Mon-Fri; noon-4pm Sat. **Credit** AmEx, DC, MC, V. **Map** p306 F5.
Showcasing local talent, Molotow sells a selection of fashion and millinery from Berlin designers for men and women. The clothes are fresh and eye-catching, ranging from futuristic creations to classical sharp tailoring. Custom tailoring available.

RespectMen

Neue Schönhauser Strasse 14, Mitte (283 5010). U8 Weinmeisterstrasse. **Open** noon-8pm Mon-Fri; 12am-6pm Sat. **Credit** AmEx, MC, V. **Map** p316/p303 G3.

Seen on the rail, Dirk Seidel and Karin Warburg's menswear seems to be traditionally tailored, yet when worn it shows off a body-conscious, contemporary cut. Suits, trousers, jackets and coats can be made to order from the many fabrics on offer. Also stocks Bikkenbergs and Paul Smith.

Yoshiharu Ito

Auguststrasse 19, Mitte (4404 4490/www.itofashion.com). S1,S2, S25, S26 Oranienburger Strasse. **Open** noon-8pm Mon-Sat. **Credit** AmEx, DC, MC, V. **Map** p316/p302 F3.

Tokyo-born Ito's showroom offers his purist collections for men and women in the tradition of Asian designers like Yamamoto but with strong European influences. His styles are practical, with great attention to detail like perfectly worked pockets and seams in unusual places. With a nod to the avant-garde, Ito mixes a futuristic style with classic wool or lacquered cotton for fun and wearable clothes.

Dry-cleaning & alterations

Good laundry and dry-cleaning services are in short supply. Many designers offer alterations or a made-to-measure service included in the price, or for a small charge. To get a zip fixed or rip mended, alterations shops usually provide a next-day service. Consult the *Gelbe Seiten* (*Yellow Pages*) under *Änderungsschneidereien*.

Eva Boeelke

Torstrasse 56, Mitte (281 2372). U2 Rosa-Luxemburg-Platz. **Open** 9am-1pm, 2pm-6pm Mon-Fri. **No credit cards**. **Map** p303 G2/3.

When the top designer shops on Neue Schoenhauser Strasse need alterations and repairs, Frau Boeelke's small shop is where they send thework.

Jet-Clean

Memhardstrasse 1, Mitte (242 3974). U2, U5, U8, S3, S5, S7, S9, S75 Alexanderplatz. **Open** 8am-7pm Mon-Fri. **No credit cards**. **Map** p316/303 G3.

No-nonsense dry cleaner used by the Mitte boutique crowd and touted by *GQ*. They offer a one-day service in this large, bright establishment, but can do a rush service even quicker for no extra charge. Specialists in leather, suede and fine fabrics as well as household linens and shirts. No service at weekends, though.

Kim Jang Woon

Pestalozzistrasse 69, Charlottenburg (327 5151). U7 Wilmersdorfer Strasse. **Open** 9am-2pm Mon-Fri; 9am-1pm Sat. **No credit cards**. **Map** p304 B4.

Quick turnaround for all manner of alterations.

Kleenothek

Schönhauser Allee 186, Prenzlauer Berg (449 5833/www.kleentheck24.de). U2 Rosa-Luxemburg-Platz. **Open** 7.30am-8pm Mon-Fri; 9am-2pm Sat. **Credit** AmEx, MC, V. **Map** p303 G2.

Reliable dry-cleaners that will also take in laundry for service (machine) washing.

Michael Klemm

Wörtherstrasse 31, Prenzlauer Berg (442 4549). U2 Senefelderplatz. **Open** 10am-noon, 1-6pm Mon-Fri. **No credit cards**. **Map** p303 G2.

Friendly tailor for all types of alterations. Will also run up garments on request.

Fetish

Black Style

Seelower Strasse 5, Prenzlauer Berg (4468 8595/www.blackstyle.de). U2, S4, S8 Schönhauser Allee. **Open** 1-6.30pm Mon-Wed; 1-8pm Thur; 11am-4pm Fri; 10am-2pm Sat. **Credit** AmEx, DC, MC, V. **Map** p303 G1.

From black fashion to butt plugs – if it can be made out of rubber or latex, chances are they've got it here. High quality, reasonable prices and big variety. Mail order service available.

Leathers

Schliemannstrasse 38, Prenzlauer Berg (442 7786/www.leathers-berlin.de). U2 Eberswalder Strasse. **Open** noon-7.30pm Tue-Fri; noon-4pm Sat. **Credit** AmEx, MC, V. **Map** p303 G2.

This workshop produces leather and SM articles of the highest quality, as well as top-notch furniture. There's no smut here – just well-presented products and helpful staff.

Schwarze Mode

Uhlandstrasse 71, Wilmersdorf (784 5922/www.schwarzemode.de). U7 Kleistpark. **Open** 10am-8pm Mon-Fri; 10am-6pm Sat. **Credit** AmEx, DC, MC, V. **Map** p305 C5.

Leatherette, rubber and vinyl are among the delicacies stocked here for *Gummi* (rubber) enthusiasts. As well as the fetish fashions, erotic and SM literature, comics, videos, CDs and magazines are on offer next door in Schwarze Medien.

Mid-range

Luzifer

Alte Schönhauser Strasse 33, Mitte (2804 2335/hanf@luzifer.com). U8 Weinmeisterstrasse. **Open** 10am-8pm Mon-Fri; 10am-6pm Sat. **Credit** AmEx, MC, V. **Map** p316/p303 G3.

Large selection of natural hemp and linen clothing for men and women, mostly unstructured and in simple shapes.

Other locations: Adalbertstrasse 89, Kreuzberg (615 2239).

To Die For

Neue Schönhauser Strasse 10, Mitte (2838 6834). U8 Weinmeisterstrasse. **Open** noon-8pm Mon-Fri; 11am-6pm Sat. **Credit** AmEx, DC, MC, V. **Map** p316/p303 G3.

Ready-to-wear collections from the likes of D&G to slip into instant party mode.

Other locations: Alte Schönhauser Strasse 41, Mitte (2463 9643).

Fishbelly. *See p165.*

Lisa D. See p167.

Second-hand clothes & shoes

Berlin has a huge market in cheaper clothing, with several flea markets, junk shops and second-hand stores. The best hunting ground is around Mehringdamm in Kreuzberg.

Calypso – High Heels For Ever

Rosenthaler Strasse 23 Mitte (2854 5415/www.calypso-shoes.com). U8 Weinmeisterstrasse. **Open** noon-8pm Mon-Fri; noon-4pm Sat. **No credit cards**. **Map** p316/p303 G3.

Hundreds of stilettos, wedges and platforms in vivid shades and exotic shapes from the 1930s to 1980s, almost all in fine condition. Also a selection of stilettoed, thigh-high fetish boots, some in men's sizes. **Other locations**: Oderberger Strasse 61, Prenzlauer Berg (281 6165).

Colours

1st courtyard, Bergmannstrasse 102, Kreuzberg (694 3348). U7 Gneisenaustrasse. **Open** 11am-7pm Mon-Fri; 11am-6pm Sat. **Credit** MC, V. **Map** p306 F5.

Rows of jeans, leather jackets and dresses, including party stunners and fetching Bavarian dirndls, plus the odd gem from the 1950s or 1960s.

Garage

Ahornstrasse 2, Schöneberg (211 2760/www.kleidermarkt.de). U1, U2, U4, U15 Nollendorfplatz. **Open** 11am-7pm Mon-Wed; 11am-8pm Thur, Fri; 11am-6pm Sat. **Credit** MC, V. **Map** p305 D4.

Cheap second-hand shop, clothing priced per kilo. Well organised, given the barracks-like nature of the place. Good for cheap, last-minute party outfits.

Made in Berlin

Potsdamer Strasse 105, Tiergarten (262 2431/www.kleidermarkt.de). U1, U15 Kurfürstenstrasse. **Open** 10.30am-7pm Mon-Fri; 11am-6pm Sat. **Credit** DC, MC, V. **Map** p306 E4/5.

Sister store of Garage (*see above*), where the 'better stuff' supposedly goes. It's still pretty cheap though.

Sgt Peppers

Kastanienallee 91-2, Prenzlauer Berg (448 1121/www.fdt-pepper-berlin.de). U2 Eberswalder Strasse. **Open** 11am-8pm Mon-Sat. **Credit** MC, V. **Map** p303 G2.

Vivid and colourful gear from the 1960s to 1980s, arranged by size. Great t-shirts and airline bags.

Sterling Gold

Oranienburger Strasse 32, Mitte (2809 6500/www.sterlinggold.de). S1, S2, S25, S26 Oranienburger Strasse. **Open** noon-8pm Mon-Fri; noon-6pm Sat. **Credit** AmEx, MC, V. **Map** p316/p302 F3.

Michael Boenke couldn't believe his luck when he was offered a warehouse full of 'prom' dresses during a trip to America. He shipped themto Berlin and has done so well with them he's opened this second shop in the Heckmann Höfe. These fab ball- and cocktail gowns, in every conceivable shade and fabric from the '50s to the '80s, are in terrific condition.

Shoes & leather goods

Bleibgrün

Bleibtreustrasse 29-30, Charlottenburg (882 1689/www.bleibgruen.de). S3, S5, S7, S9, S75 Savignyplatz. **Open** 11.30am-6.30pm Mon-Fri; 11am-4pm Sat. **Credit** AmEx, DC, MC, V. **Map** p305 C4.

Berlin's best designer shoe shop, with a nifty selection from the likes of Lagerfeld, Maud Frizon and Jan Jansen. Bleibgrün has opened a swanky boutique next door at No.30 that has an equally discriminating choice of cutting-edge womenswear.

Bree

Kurfürstendamm 44, Charlottenburg (883 7462). U15 Uhlandstrasse. **Open** 10am-7pm Mon-Fri; 10am-6pm Sat. **Credit** AmEx, MC, V. **Map** p305 C4.

German leather goods company whose practical and durable handbags, briefcases, rucksacks and suitcases are sported by many a German professional.

Budapester Schuhe

Kurfürstendamm 43, Charlottenburg (8862 4206). U15 Uhlandstrasse. **Open** 10am-7pm Mon-Fri; 10am-6pm Sat. **Credit** AmEx, DC, MC, V. **Map** p305 C4.
Impressive selection of designer footwear for men and women at this chain. This is the largest of four Berlin branches, offering the latest by the like of Prada, Dolce & Gabbana, Sergio Rossi, JP Tod's and Miu Miu. Across the street at Kurfürstendamm 199, you'll find a conservative range for men, including handmade classics from Austrian Ludwig Reiter. At the Bleibtreustrasse branch, prices are slashed by up to 50% for last year's models, remainders and hard-to-sell sizes.
Other locations: Bleibtreustrasse 24, Charlottenburg (881 7001); Friedrichstrasse 81, Mitte (2038 8110); Kurfürstendamm 199, Charlottenburg (8811 1707).

Oxford & Co

Akazienstrasse 18, Schöneberg (7871 7310). U7 Eisenacher Strasse. **Open** 10am-8pm Mon-Fri; 10am-5pm Sat. **Credit** AmEx, MC, V. **Map** p305 D5.
Good quality men's and women's shoes from sporty trainers to boots, pumps and wingtips. The Kastanienallee branch also features children's shoes.

Penthesileia

Tucholskystrasse 31, Mitte (282 1152/ www.penthesileia.de). U6 Oranienburger Tor. **Open** 10am-7pm Mon-Fri; 10am-4pm Sat. **Credit** MC, V. **Map** p302/316 F3.
Showroom, shop and workspace for Sylvia Müller and Anke Runge, who design and make a highly imaginative range of handbags and rucksacks. Shapes are novel and organic – sunflowers, cones, shells, hearts, for example. Products are crafted from calfskin and nubuck.

Trainer – Sole Box

Alte Schönhauser Strasse 50, Mitte (9789 4610/ www.solebox.de). U8 Weinmeisterstrasse. **Open** 1-7.30pm Mon-Thur; 1-8 pm Fri; 1-6pm Sat. **Credit** MC, V. **Map** p316/p303 G3.
For those rare and collectible limited-edition Pumas, Nikes or Adidas, no longer available in New York, London or elsewhere. Japanese tour groups have been known to buy out the entire store in an hour. Sales staff are very helpful and well informed.
Other locations: Oderberger Strasse 13, Prenzlauer Berg (9120 6690).

Shoemakers

See also p179 **Repairs**.

Breitenbach

Bergmannstrasse 30, Kreuzberg (692 3570/ www.schuhzauber.de). U7 Gneisenaustrasse. **Open** 9am-6.30pm Mon-Fri; 10am-2pm Sat. **Credit** AmEx, MC, V. **Map** p306 F5.
This respected men's shoe- and bootmaker also provides a first-class repair service for men's and women's footwear.

Masschumhmacherei

Sophienstrasse 28-29, Mitte (4004 2861/www. massschuhmacherei.de). S3, S5, S7, S9, S75 Hackescher Markt. **Open** 12-7pm Tues-Fri; 11am-4pm Sat. **No credit cards**. **Map** p316/p302 F3.
Hand-made shoes in understated, classic designs. They also do repairs.

Sports gear

Karstadt Sport

Joachimstaler Strasse 5-6, Charlottenburg (8802 4153). U2, U9, S5, S7, S9 S75 Zoologischer Garten. **Open** 10am-8pm, Mon-Sat. **Credit** AmEx, DC, MC, V. **Map** p305 D4.
Three-level megastore with a wide selection of gear by both name brands and cheaper alternatives. Also US sportswear, German football paraphernalia and children's clothes. Includes skating area, ski simulator, internet terminals and sports restaurant.
Other locations: Schlosstrasse 7-10, Steglitz (0900 1604).

Montk

Kastanienallee 83, Prenzlauer Berg (448 2590/ www.mont-k.de). U2 Eberswalder Strasse. **Open** 10am-8pm Mon-Fri; 10am-4pm Sat. **Credit** AmEx, MC, V. **Map** p303 G2.
If you are a serious camper, skier, canoeist or climber, Montk can outfit you with serious equipment, outerwear and footgear.

Niketown Berlin

Tauentzienstrasse 7B-7C, Schöneberg (250 70). U1, U2, U15 Wittenbergplatz. **Open** 10am-8pm Mon-Sat. **Credit** AmEx, DC, MC, V. **Map** p305 D4.
Monster retail outlet for the monster US company in state-of-the art glass and neon design. Training gear – jerseys, sweatpants, trainers, even sunglasses and watches – all embossed with the Nike trademark.

360°

Pariser Strasse 23-4, Wilmersdorf (883 8596/ www.360berlin.de). U7 Adenauerplatz. **Open** 11am-7.30pm Mon-Fri; 10am-4pm Sat. **Credit** AmEx, DC, MC, V. **Map** p305 C5.
Designer sportswear and accessories from Stüssy, Quicksilver, Sky & High and Vans, plus in-line skates, snowboards and windsurfing gear.

Street/clubwear

Eisdieler

Kastanienallee 12, Prenzlauer Berg (285 7351/ www.eisdieler.de). U2 Eberswalder Strasse. **Open** noon-8pm Mon-Fri; noon-7pm Sat. **Credit** AmEx, MC, V. **Map** p302 F3.
Five young designers pooled resources to transform this former ice shop and each manages a label under the Eisdieler banner – clubwear, second-hand gear,

Shopping by area

Mitte

Antiques Emma Emmelie *p157.* **Books** Berlin Story *p159;* Le Matou *p160;* ProQM *p159.* **Children's clothes & toys** Nix Design *p160.* **Computer repairs** JE *p159.* **Cosmetics** MAC *p161.* **Department stores** Dussman Das KulturKaufhaus *p161*; Galeries Lafayette *p161*; Kaufhof *p161*; Naturkaufhaus *p162*; Quartier 206 *p162.* **Design & household goods** Bürgel-Haus *p163*; KPM *p163*; Leinenkontor *p163*; Ruby *p163*; Stue *p163.* **Dry cleaning & alterations** Eva Boeelke *p168*; Jet-Clean *p168.* **Fashion** Blush *p164*; Calypso – High Heels For Ever *p170*; Claudia Skoda Level *p167;* Fiona Bennett *p165*; Fishbelly *p165*; Flex *p172*; Hut Up *p167*; Lisa D *p167*; Little Red Riding Hood *p167*; Luzifer *p168*; Sterling Gold *p170*; Tagebau *p166*; To Die For *p168.* T&G *p166*; Yoshiharu Ito *p167.* **Food** Mitte Meer *p174.* **Hair salons** Hanley's Hair Company *p174.* **Jewellery** Glanzstücke *p175.* **Markets** Berliner Antik & Flohmarkt *p176*; Kunst und Nostalgie *p176.* **Music: CDs & records** DNS *p177*; Neurotitan *p178*; Saturn *p178.* **Opticians** Brille 54 *p178*; Brilliant *p178*; Fielmann *p178*; ic! *p178.* **Photography** PPS *p178.* **Shoes & leather goods** Budapester Schuhe *p171;* Masschuhmacherei *p170*; Penthesileia *p171*; Trainer – Sole Box *p171.* **Souvenirs** Johanna Petzoldt *p180.* **Stationery & art supplies** J Müller *p180*; OK *p180*; RSVP *p180.* **Wine & spirits** Whisky & Cigars *p175.*

Prenzlauer Berg & Friedrichshain

Books St. Georges *p160.* **Children's clothes & toys** Peekaboo Kindermoden *p160.* **Design & household goods** Coldampf's *p162*; Furniture *p163*; Keramikladen am P'Berg *p163*; Strauss Innovation *p163.* **Dry-cleaning & alterations** Kleenothek *p168*; Michael Klemm *p167.* **Fashion** Black Style *p167*; Eisdieler *p171;* Leathers *p168;* Mane Lange Korsetts *p165;* Montk *p171;* Sgt Peppers *p170.* **Jewellery** Scuderi *p175.* **Markets** Kollwitzplatz *p176.* **Music: CDs & records** DaCapo *p176*; D-Fens *p176.* **Souvenirs** Fanshop *p180*; Mondos Arts *p180.* **Stationery** Künstler Magazin *p180.*

Kreuzberg

Antiques Radio Art *p158.* **Books** Another Country *p159*; Bücherbogen *p159*; Fair Exchange *p159*; Hammett *p159;* Modern Graphics *p159.* **Cosmetics** Belladonna *p161.* **Design & household goods** DIM *p162.* **Fashion** Colours *p170*; Knopf Paul *p165;* Molotow *p167.* **Flowers** Fleurop *p172.* **Food** Broken English *p173.* **Jewellery** Fritz *p175.* **Music: CDs & records** Space Hall

casual wear and street style. Till Fuhrmann's jewellery, crafted fromsilver and wood, is particularly distinctive. Look out for his spiky ironwork, which adorns the façade.

Flex

Neue Schönhauser Strasse 2, Mitte (283 4836/ 4844). U8 Weinmeisterstrasse. **Open** noon-6pm Sat. **Credit** AmEx, DC, MC, V. **Map** p316/p303 G3.

Clubwear store and dance record shop in one – this is one of the buzziest stores on the street, especially in the evening when Mitte's young, bad and beautiful pick out an outfit from German labels including Sabotage and Thatchers.

Planet

Schlüterstrasse 35, Charlottenburg (885 2717). U15 Uhlandstrasse. **Open** 10.30am-7.30pm Mon-Fri; 11am-6pm Sat. **Credit** AmEx, DC, MC, V. **Map** p305 C4.

Owners Wera Wonder and Mik Moon have been kitting out Berlin's club scene in hip gear since 1985. Their DJ friends pump out deafening music to put you in club mode, and the rails and shelves are brimming with sparkling spandex shirts, fluffy vests and dance durable footwear.

Flowers

Blumen 31

Bleibtreustrasse 31, Charlottenburg (8847 4604). U15 Uhlandstrasse. **Open** 9am-8pm Mon-Fri; 9am-6pm Sat. **Credit** AmEx, DC, MC, V. **Map** p305 C4.

This first-rate florist specialises in roses from Ecuador, which are creatively combined into bouquets with little more than an array of greens. Delivery service.

Fleurop

Lindenstrasse 3-4, Kreuzberg (713 710). **Open** 8am-6.30pm Mon-Fri; 8am-2pm Sat. *U6, U1, U15 Hallesches Tor.* **Credit** AmEx, DC, MC, V. **Map** p306 F4.

Call to have flowers delivered anywhere in the western world. Within Germany, flowers can arrive in an hour via any one of 7,000 shops nationwide.

p178. **Shoemakers** Breitenbach *p171*. **Stationery & arts supplies** Grüne Papeterie *p180*; Propolis *p180*.

Schöneberg & Tiergarten

Antiques Deco Arts *p157*; Fingers *p158*. **Beauty salons** Hautfit Bio Kosmetik *p158*. **Books** Storytime Books *p158*. **Children's toys** Michas Bahnhof *p160*. **Computer repairs** Petra Koch *p179*. **Department stores** KaDeWe *p161*. **Design & household goods** Formgeber Berlin *p163*; KPM *p163*. **Fashion** Chiton *p166*; Garage *p170*; Made in Berlin *p170*; Niketown *p171*. **Food** Vinh-Loi *p174*. **Hair salons** Jonnycut *p175*. **Luggage repairs** Witt *p179*. **Markets** Farmers' Market *p175*; Strasse des 17.Juni *p176*; Winterfeldt Markt *p176*. **Music: CDs & records** Mr Dead & Mrs Free *p177*; WOM *p178*. **Shoes** Oxford & Co *p171*. **Shoe repairs** Picobello *p179*. **Stationery & art supplies** Ferdinand Braune *p179;* Otto Ebeling *p180*. **Wine & spirits** Getränke Hoffmann *p174*; Vendemmia *p174*.

Charlottenburg & Wilmersdorf

Antiques Lehmanns Colonialwaren *p158*; Wolfgang Haas *p158*. **Beauty salons** Vivera *p158*; Marie France *p158*. **Books** Antiquariat Senzel *p159*; Books in Berlin *p159*; Bücherbogen *p159*; Düwal *p159*; Hugendubel *p159*; Kohlhaas & Company *p159;* Marga Schoeller Bücherstube *p160*. **Children's clothes & toys** Emma & Co *p159*; Heidi's Spielzeugladen *p160*; H&M Kids *p160*; Tam Tam *p160*; v. Kloeden *p161*. **Design & household goods** Bramigk & Breer *p162*; Coldampf's *p162*; Dopo Domani *p163*; KPM *p163*; Schlafwandel *p162*; stilwerk *p164*: **Dry-cleaning & alterations** Kim Jang Woon *p168*. **Fashion** Antonie Setzer *p166*; Les Dessous *p164*; Harvey's *p165*; Karstadt Sport *p171*; Mientus Studio 2002 *p166*; Patrick Hellman *p166*; Planet *p172*; Roeckl *p165*; Schwarze Mode *p168*; Theaterkunst *p166;* 360° *p171*. **Flowers** Blumen 31 *p172*. **Food** Königsberger Marzipan *p174*; Leysieffer *p174*; Lindenberg *p174*; Weichardt-Brot *p174*. **Hair salons** Udo Walz *p175*. **Jewellery** Fritz *p175*; Rio *p175*. **Luggage repairs** Kofferhaus Gabriel *p179*. **Markets** Zille-Hof *p176*. **Music: CDs & records** Gelbe Musik *p177*; Hans Riedl Musikalienhandel *p177*; MakroMarkt *p178*. **Opticians** Brilliant *p178*. **Photography** Fix Foto *p178*; Wüstefeld *p179*. **Shoes & leather goods** Bleibgrün *p170*; Bree *p170*; Budapester Schuhe *p171*. **Souvenirs** Berliner Zinnfiguren Kabinett *p180*. **Wine & spirits** Klemke Wein & Spirituosenhandel *p174;* Vineyard *p175*.

Food

Supermarket shopping in Berlin is not very interesting. Stores are often small and cramped, and even the larger chains generally have bland selections, long check-out queues, and don't take all credit cards. The alternative are specialist shops, from ethnic to gourmet, which range from expensive Italian delis to cheap Asian mini-markets. The organic food market is booming and the variety of produce sold in *Bioläden* is huge and subject to strict controls. Several department stores have impressive food halls. Those particularly worth a visit include **Galeries Lafayette** (*see p161*) and **KaDeWe** (*see p161*).

Broken English

Körtestrasse 10, Kreuzberg (691 1227/ www.brokenenglish.de). U7 Südstern. **Open** 11am-6.30pm Mon-Fri; 10am-6pm Sat. **Credit** MC, V. **Map** p307 G5.

Cosy shop choc-a-bloc with everything UK expats need to keep the homesick blues at bay. There's a massive selection of teas, biscuits, crisps and sweets; ingredients such as self-raising flour and clotted cream; a selection of cheeses and deep-frozen pies; and essentials such as Heinz baked beans, salad cream and Marmite. The gift section includes children's tapes, cookbooks, mugs and malts.

Other locations: British Shop, Sophienstrasse 10, Mitte (2859 9307).

ExPat Shopping

Kieler Strasse 1-2, Steglitz (5165 5800/www. expatshopping.com). U9 Schlossstrasse. **Open** 10am-8pm Mon-Fri; 10am-6pm Sat. **Credit** MC.

Groceries from the US and UK, some of which seem pricey until compared with similar stuff sold at KaDeWe. Americans can stock up on old favourites like Ocean Spray Cranberry Sauce and Jell-O. Brits will find Lemsip, Heinz baby foods and haggis. But it's the gift packages (€20-25) which commend this place. The Essential Box comes laden with Marmite, marmalade, tea, baked beans and other staples. The

ExPat Shopping – stocking up on Marmite, crisps and Campbell's soup. *See p173.*

Kids' Box is stuffed with British sweets and crisps for homesick youngsters. The shop also imports items from Australia.

Königsberger Marzipan

Pestalozzistrasse 54A, Charlottenburg (323 8254). S3, S5, S7, S9, S75 Charlottenburg. **Open** 11am-6pm Mon, Wed; 2-6pm Tue, Thur, Fri; 11am-2pm Sat. **No credit cards. Map** p304 B4.

Irmgard Wald and her late husband moved from Kaliningrad to Berlin after the war and began again in the confectionery trade. With her smiling American-born granddaughter, Frau Wald still produces fresh, soft, melt-in-your-mouth marzipan. Small boxes of assorted sweets make great gifts.

Leysieffer

Kurfürstendamm 218, Charlottenburg (885 7480/ www.leysieffer.de). U15 Uhlandstrasse. **Open** 10am-8pm Mon-Fri; 11am-7pm Sat; 11am-6pm Sun. **Credit** AmEx, DC, MC, V. **Map** p305 C4.

Beautifully packaged confitures, teas and handmade chocolates from German fine food company make perfect gifts. Café upstairs and bakery attached.

Lindenberg

Morsestrasse 2, Charlottenburg (3908 1523). U9 Turmstrasse. **Open** 8am-8pm Tue-Fri; 8am-2pm Sat. **No credit cards. Map** p301 D3.

Wholesaler where the city's pro and amateur chefs stock up on live lobster, fresh seafood, New Zealand lamb, local ducks, out-of-season fruit and veg, assorted French cheeses, and wines and spirits. Anyone can walk in but most things are sold only in industrial quantities. Advance orders taken.

Mitte Meer

Invalidenstrasse 50-51, Mitte (398 0163/www.mitte-meer.de). S5, S7, S9, S75 Hauptbahnhof-Lehrter Bahnhof. **Open** 9am-8pm Mon-Fri; 9am-4pm Sat. **No credit cards. Map** p302 E3/F2.

Wholesaler and retailer offering Spanish and Italian imports in industrial quantities. There's a huge Spanish wine selection, two large refrigerated rooms filled with sausages and cheeses and yet another stocked with fresh Mediterranean seafood. Also a vast frozen selection. One-stop tapas shopping.

Vinh-Loi

Ansbacher Strasse 16, Schöneberg (235 0900). U1, U2, U15 Wittenbergplatz. **Open** 9am-7pm Mon-Fri; 9am-5pm Sat. **No credit cards. Map** p305 D5.

Asian groceries including Thai fruit, veg and herbs fresh from the airport on Mondays and Thursdays. Plus woks, rice steamers and Chinese crockery.

Weichardt-Brot

Mehlitzstrasse 7, Wilmersdorf (873 8099/ www.weichardt.de). U7, U9 Berliner Strasse. **Open** 8am-6.30pm Tue-Fri; 8am-1pm Sat. **No credit cards. Map** p305 C5.

The very best bakery in town, Weichardt-Brot grew out of a Berlin collective from the 1960s. Stone-ground organic flour and natural leavens make this a mecca for bread lovers.

General markets

See p176.

Wine & spirits

Getränke Hoffmann

Kleiststrasse 23-6, Schöneberg (2147 3096). U1, U2, U15 Wittenbergplatz. **Open** 9am-8pm Mon-Fri; 8am-6pm Sat. **No credit cards. Map** p305 D4.

Branches all over town offer a wide range of everyday booze at everyday prices. Call 2147 3096 to make orders for delivery anywhere in Berlin.

Other locations: Schönfliesser Strasse 19, Prenzlauer Berg (444 0682).

Klemke Wein & Spirituosenhandel

Mommsenstrasse 9, Charlottenburg (8855 1260). S3, S5, S7, S9, S75 Savignyplatz. **Open** 9am-7pm Mon-Fri; 8am-2.30pm Sat. **No credit cards. Map** p305 C4.

Respected specialists in French and Italian wines from the tiniest vineyard to the grandest chateau. Also digestifs and whiskies. Free delivery in Berlin.

Vendemmia

Akazienstrasse 20, Schöneberg (784 2728/ www.vendemmia.de). U7 Eisenacher Strasse. **Open** 10am-7pm Mon-Fri; 10am-3pm Sat. **No credit cards. Map** p305 D5.

Bulk importers of first-class Italian wines that are decanted into bottles with photocopied labels. Not the most impressive bottle to take to a party, but it's good stuff and very cheap. Several other good wine and spirits shops on this street, plus an Italian deli with a good wine selection.

Vineyard

Salzufer 13-14, Charlottenberg (390 4900/ www.vineyard.de). S5, S7, S9, S75 Tiergarten. **Open** noon-6pm Mon-Wed; noon-8pm Thur, Fri; 11am-2pm Sat. **Credit** AmEx, MC, V. **Map** p301 C3.

Specialists in Australian, South African and American wines, but also carrying a large selection of wines from elsewhere around the world. Phone orders with a one-hour delivery service in Berlin.

Whisky & Cigars

Sophienstrasse 23, Mitte (282 0376/www.whisky-cigars.de). S3, S5, S7, S9, S75 Hackescher Markt. **Open** noon-7pm Mon-Fri; 11am-4pm Sat. **Credit** MC, V. **Map** p316/p302 F3.

Two friends sharing a love of single malts are behind this shop, which stocks 450 whiskies, and cigars from Cuba, Jamaica and Honduras. They hold regular whisky-tasting and cigar-smoking evenings and will deliver or even ship orders.

Hair salons

Berlin hair stylists' technical skills tend to outmatch their judgement or taste. In fact, the state of the average Berlin barnet might convince you never to trust your crowning glory to the locals. That said, the city does boast a few stylists and colourists that can do a pretty fair job, not to mention some international salons that can cut it with the best of them.

Beige

Auguststrasse 83, Mitte (2759 4051/www.salon-beige.de). U6 Oranienburger Tor. **Open** noon-9pm Tue-Fri; 3-9pm Sat. **No credit cards. Map** p316/p302 F3.

Exclusive salon on the garden level of a private apartment building. The waiting-room features a light installation and doubles as a gallery space. The two client rooms are decorated in 1960s and baroque styles respectively. Hair designer Oliver Weidner, who boasts international clients from Japan, the US and Europe, specialises in modern colours and cuts. Reasonably priced but by appointment only.

Hanley's Hair Company

Hackesche Höfe, Rosenthaler Strasse 40-41, Mitte (281 3179). U8 Weinmeisterstrasse or S3, S5, S7, S9, S75 Hackescher Markt. **Open** 9am-8pm Mon-Fri; 10am-8pm Sat. **No credit cards. Map** p316/p302 F3.

Friendly, trendy salon run by Thomas Schweizer and Deborah Hanley – who does amazing colour jobs. Full range of styling and treatments, offering wash, cut and head massage.

Jonnycut

Yorckstrasse 43, Schöneberg (217 0941). U7, S1, S2, S25 Yorckstrasse. **Open** noon-6pm Mon; 11am-8pm Tue-Fri; 11am-5pm Sat. **Credit** MC, V. **Map** p306 E5.

Jonny Pazzo is a versatile stylist who shuttles between shoots for glossy magazines and record covers to appointments in his small salon. Decked out with pictures of angels, Buddhas, reggae musicians and children, it's frequented by many an established and rising scene star.

Udo Walz

Kempinski-Plaza, Uhlandstrasse 181-3, Charlottenburg (882 7457/www.udo-walz.de). U15 Uhlandstrasse. **Open** 9am-7pm Tue-Fri; 9am-3pm Sat. **Credit** AmEx, MC, V. **Map** p305 C4.

Udo Walz is the darling of the Berlin hair brigade, and likes to have his picture taken with the likes of Claudia Schiffer. His stylists are well trained, imaginative and friendly.

Other locations: Hohenzollerndamm 92, Wilmersdorf (826 6108).

Jewellery

Fritz

Dresdener Strasse 20, Kreuzberg (615 1700). U1, U8, U15 Kottbusser Tor. **Open** 11am-6pm Tue-Fri; 11am-2pm Sat. **Credit** V. **Map** p307 G4.

Bold designs by this Berliner are sold alongside interesting hand-crafted work in a range of materials by smiths based elsewhere in Germany and Europe. The selection of rings attracts many brides and grooms-to-be, with prices ranging from hundreds to thousands of euros.

Glanzstücke

Sophienstrasse 7, Mitte (208 2676). S3, S5, S7, S9, S75 Hackescher Markt. **Open** noon-7pm Mon-Fri; noon-6pm Sat. **Credit** AmEx, MC, V. **Map** p316/p302 F3.

Original 20th-century costume jewellery with a strong emphasis on art nouveau and art deco. Owner Kirstin Pax hunts down glittering treasures in rhinestone and glass, and does good trade with American dealers, who find prices for items in her Bakelite collection a steal.

Rio

Bleibtreustrasse 52, Charlottenburg (313 3152). S3, S5, S7, S9, S75 Savignyplatz. **Open** 11am-6.30pm Mon-Wed; 11am-7pm Thur; 11am-6.30pm Fri; 10am-4pm Sat. **Credit** V. **Map** p305 C4.

Eye-catching costume jewellery, with a stunning array of earrings from the likes of Vivienne Westwood, Armani and Herv van der Straeten. Plus Rio's own range of luminescent frosted-glass necklaces, bracelets and earrings designed by shop owner Barbara Kranz.

Scuderi

Wörther Strasse 32, Prenzlauer Berg (4737 4240). U2 Senefelderplatz. **Open** 11am-7pm Mon-Fri; 11am-3pm Sat. **Credit** MC, V. **Map** p303 G2.

The four women who share this space work magic with gold and silver, pearls, stones and hand-rolled glass, creating lightweight ornaments that make a strong statement.

Markets

Flea markets

Berliner Antik & Flohmarkt

Bahnhof Friedrichstrasse, S-Bahnbogen 190-203, Mitte (208 2645/www.antikmarkt-berlin.de). U6, S1, S2, S3, S5, S7, S9, S25, S26, S75 Friedrichstrasse. **Open** 11am-6pm Mon, Wed-Sun. **Map** p316/p302 F3.

More than 60 dealers have taken up residence in the renovated arches under the S-Bahn tracks, selling furniture, jewellery, paintings and vintage clothing, some of it from the 1920s and 1930s.

Kunst und Nostalgie Markt

Museumsinsel, by Zeughaus, Mitte (03341 309 411). U6, S1, S2, S3, S5, S7, S9, S25, S26, S75, Friedrichstrasse. **Open** 11am-5pm Sat, Sun. **Map** p316/p302 F3.

One of the few places you can still find true GDR relics, with anything from old signs advertising coal briquets to framed pictures of Honecker.

Strasse des 17.Juni

Strasse des 17.Juni, Tiergarten (2655 0096). U2 Ernst-Reuter-Platz or S3, S5, S7, S9, S75 Tiergarten. **Open** 10am-5pm Sat, Sun. **Map** p305 C4.

Early 20th-century objects of a high quality with prices to match, alongside a jumble of vintage and alternative clothing, second-hand records, CDs and books. Arts and crafts further along the street. Best flea market in town, albeit an insanely cramped one.

Zille-Hof

Fasanenstrasse 14, Charlottenburg (313 4333). U15 Uhlandstrasse. **Open** 8am-5.30pm Mon-Fri; 8am-1pm Sat. **Map** p305 C4.

Almost next door to the Kempinski Hotel (*see p61*), a neat and tidy junk market where you can track down everything from an antique hatpin to a chest of drawers. The better bric-a-brac is indoors, while the real bargains lurk in the courtyard outside.

General markets

Berlin's many *Wochenmärkte* usually sell cheaper, fresher produce than regular stores.

Farmers' Market

Wittenbergplatz, Schöneberg. U1, U2, U15 Wittenbergplatz. **Open** 8am-2pm Tue-Fri; 10am-7.30pm Thur. **Map** p305 D4.

Predominantly organic produce, including 'bio' cheese, bread, fresh pasta and meat stands, plus fruit and vegetables from farms in the region. Also inedible items such as wooden brushes and sheepskins.

Kollwitzplatz

Kollwitzplatz, Prenzlauer Berg. U2 Senefelderplatz. **Open** noon-7pm Thur, Sat. **Map** p303 G2.

Open-air food markets are still rare in the east. This one is a small and unassuming organic market, more lively in summer, though nothing could be more *gemütlich* in winter than the scene around the stand serving mugs of steaming punch and fresh whole-grain cinnamon waffles.

Türkischer Markt

Maybachufer, Neukölln. U1, U8, U15 Kottbusser Tor. **Open** noon-6.30pm Tue, Fri. **Map** p307 G5.

A noisy, crowded market just across the canal from Kreuzberg, meeting the needs of the local Turkish community. Fresh vegetables, great spices.

Winterfeldt Markt

Winterfeldtplatz, Schöneberg. U1, U2, U4, U15 Nollendorfplatz. **Open** 8am-2pm Wed, Sat. **Map** p305 D5.

Saturday's multicultural experience. Everybody shows up to buy their vegetables, cheese, whole-grain breads, Wurst, meats, flowers, clothes, pet supplies and toys; or simply to meet over a coffee, beer or falafel at one of the many cafés off the square.

Music: CDs & records

See also p172 **Flex** and *p161* **Dussmann Das KulturKaufhaus**. Go to www.platten.net for a complete guide to every record shop in Berlin.

DaCapo Records

Kastanienallee 96, Prenzlauer Berg (448 1771/www.dacapo-vinyl.de). U2 Eberswalder Strasse. **Open** 11am-7pm Mon-Fri; 11am-4pm Sat. **Credit** MC, V. **Map** p303 G2.

Pricey but wide selection of used vinyl, releases on GDR label Amiga plus rare 1950s 10-inch records and jazz singles.

D-Fens

Greifswalder Strasse 224, Prenzlauer Berg (4434 2250/www.d-fens-berlin.de). Tram 2, 3, 4. **Open** noon-7pm Mon-Fri; noon-3pm Sat. **No credit cards**. **Map** p303 G3.

Small DJ shop in a revamped garage, specialising in house, trance, electro, techno and disco. Home base of Berlin labels Formaldahyde and BCC. Owner

Lenin's on sale again

The plot of the movie *Goodbye Lenin!* made much of the difficulty of finding old GDR products. That story was set not long after Reunification, when the economy of East German had been rolled over and its citizens were snapping up fancy new western goods. Now the wheel has come full circle. Communist brands are a mark of eastern identity, retro GDR styling is cool, and a jar of Spreewald pickles is probably easier to come by than it was ten years ago.

In fact, you can find said pickles at **Ostkost** (Lychener Strasse 54, Prenzlauer Berg, 4465 3623, www.ostkost.de), next to Bautzener mustard, Werder ketchup, Othello chocolate biscuits and other communist-era comestibles. Or if it's old GDR cosmetics, sweets or wine that you're after, **M. Koos Ostprodukte** (in Alexanderplatz U-Bahn station, 242 5791) will sell you not only those, but also a GDR trade fair bag to carry them home. Even ordinary super-markets often have display cases of eastern jam or honey labelled 'Ost-Power!'.

In one form or another, the old East is on sale all over the place. **Da Capo** (*see p176*) on Kastanienallee has a huge selection of old vinyl from the GDR state-owned record label, Amiga. But you don't need to pay collector's prices to hear some Ostrock. **Saturn** (*see p178*) at Alexanderplatz has a special bin next to the cashier for CD reissues of GDR bands such as the Puhdys or Silly. And if you want something to read while you're listening, **Antiquariat Revers** (Gabelsbergerstrasse 5, Friedrichshain, 422 7133) has shelves full of used books from East German publishers.

Street vendors at **Checkpoint Charlie** can supply hats, badges, binoculars and other paraphernalia from the days of the Volksarmee. Most of it's authentic, if grossly overpriced, but steer clear of the 'Wall' chunks. For the more discerning collector, **Intershop 2000** (Ehrenberg-strasse 3-7, Friedrichshain, 3180 0364, www.ddr-alltagskultur.de), housed in an old GDR *Raumerweiterungshalle* – a sort of telescoping container building – has items such as miniature editions of Marx, orange plastic chicken-shaped egg cups and Mitropa coffee pots. The display is assembled by a society devoted to preserving artefacts from East German daily life.

Of course nothing is sacred, and the iconography of the communist era has become fair game for all. The young designers at **Eastberlin** (Kastanienallee 13, Prenzlauer Berg, 4404 6090, www.eastberlin.net) happily desecrate the symbolism of Germanies east and west on new clothes and jewellery. **Berlin Story** (*see p159*) is full of East-inspired souvenirs, from card games to 'GDR kits'. The high-street fashion chain **Coliseum II** (am Treptower Park 14, Treptow, 5321 1295) offers replica GDR Olympic jerseys and tracksuits. And both **Mondos Arts** (Schreinerstrasse 6, Friedrichshain, 4201 0778, www.mondosarts.de) and **Ampelmännchen Galerie** (Hof 5, Rosenthaler Strasse 40-41, 4404 8809, www.ampelmann.de) sell a huge variety of stuff emblazoned with the old East's most enduring symbol: the jaunty red and green traffic-light men.

Ralph Ballschuh, a DJ himself, is happy to turn up the volume on any track you wish. Tricky to find so follow the signs for the Knaack Klub.

DNS

Alte Schönhauser Strasse 39-40, Mitte (247 9835). U8 Weinmeisterstrasse. **Open** 11am-6pm Mon-Fri; 11am-4pm Sat. **Credit** AmEx, DC, MC, V. **Map** p316/p303 G3.

Old vinyl, including some rare finds, as well as the latest pressings in the world of techno.

Gelbe Musik

Schaperstrasse 11, Wilmersdorf (211 3962). U1 Augsburger Strasse. **Open** 1-6pm Tue-Fri; 11am-2pm Sat. **Credit** MC, V. **Map** p305 C5.

One of Europe's most important avant-garde outlets has racks stacked with minimalist, electronic, world, industrial and extreme noise. Rare vinyl and import CDs, music press and sound objects make for absorbing browsing.

Hans Riedl Musikalienhandel

Uhlandstrasse 38, Wilmersdorf (882 7395). U15 Uhlandstrasse. **Open** 8am-6.30pm Mon-Fri; 9am-2pm Sat. **Credit** MC, V. **Map** p306 F4.

Probably the best address for classical music in Berlin, this huge, slightly old-fashioned shop stocks a wide selection of CDs and sheet music, as well as string and brass instruments.

Mr Dead & Mrs Free

Bülowstrasse 5, Schöneberg (215 1449/www.deadandfree.com). U1, U2, U4, U15 Nollendorfplatz. **Open** 11am-7pm Fri; 11am-4pm Sat. **Credit** V. **Map** p306 D/E5.

Berlin's leading address for independent and underground rock, with bucketloads of British, US and Australian imports, a huge vinyl section, and staff who know and love their music.

Neurotitan

Rosenthaler Strasse 39, Mitte (3087 2573/ www.neurotitan.de). S3, S5, S7, S9, S75 Hackescher Markt. **Open** 2pm-10pm Mon, Wed-Fri; 2-8pm Sat. **No credit cards Map** p316/p302 F3.
At the end of an alley on the second floor, one of Berlin's most interesting art book and record stores. Featuring hand-made and small press art books, original artwork, and small label CDs and vinyl.

Space Hall

Zossenerstrasse 33, Kreuzberg (694 7664/www. space-hall.de). U7 Gneisenaustrasse. **Open** 11am-7pm Mon-Wed; 11am-8pm Thur, Fri; 10.30am-5pm Sat. **Credit** AmEx, MC, V. **Map** p306 F5.
A spacious shop offering a broad range of new and second-hand CDs at competitive prices and with a huge techno/house vinyl room at the back. There are a couple more good record shops on Zossenerstrasse and still more round the corner on Bergmannstrasse.

Wagadu

Pannierstrasse 6, Neukölln (6273 2467/www. wagadu.de). U7, U8 Hermannplatz. **Open** 11am-7.30pm Mon-Fri; 10am-4pm Sat. **Credit** MC, V. **Map** p307 H5.
Large selection of African and Afro-Caribbean CDs.

Chain stores

MakroMarkt

Kurfürstendamm 206, Charlottenburg (886 886/ www.makromarkt.de). U15 Uhlandstrasse. **Open** 10am-8pm Mon-Fri; 10am-6pm Sat. **Credit** AmEx, V. **Map** p305 C4.
This branch of the chain has a good selection of club sounds. Also mainstream English-language videos.
Other locations: across the city.

Saturn

Alexanderplatz 8, Mitte (247 516). U2, U5, U8, S3, S5, S7, S9, S75 Alexanderplatz. **Open** 9am-8pm Mon-Sat; 9am-4pm Sat. **Credit** AmEx, DC, MC, V. **Map** p316/p303 G3.
This chain is one of the cheapest in town, with stacks of new releases and a good range of back catalogue. CDs only.
Other locations: Potsdamer Platz, Alte Potsdamer Strasse 7 (3025 9240).

WOM

Augsburger Strasse 36-42, Schöneberg (885 7240). U1 Augsburger Strasse. **Open** 10am-8pm Mon-Fri; 9am-4pm Sat. **Credit** AmEx, MC, V. **Map** p305 D4.
The World of Music chain offers a no-nonsense, no-frills approach to music retailing, and its wide selection of CDs includes a good array of jazz recordings.
Other locations: Hertie Wilmersdorfer Strasse 118, Charlottenburg (315 9170).

Opticians

Brille 54

Friedrichstrasse 71, Mitte (2094 6060/www. brille54.de). U6 Französische Strasse. **Open** 10am-8pm Mon-Fri; 10am-6pm Sat. **Credit** AmEx, DC, MC, V. **Map** p316/p306 F4.
A small but functionally sleek space in Quartier 206 designed by hot young Berlin architects Plajer & Franz. In stock are Armani, Gucci, Oliver Peoples, Lunor, Paul Smith, Prada and Miu Miu.
Other locations: Rosenthaler Strasse 36, Mitte (2804 0818).

Brilliant

Schlüterstrasse 53, Charlottenburg (324 1991/ www.brilliant-augenoptik.de). S3, S5, S7, S9, S75 Savignyplatz. **Open** 11am-7pm Mon-Wed; 11am-8pm Thur, Fri; 10am-4pm Sat. **Credit** AmEx, MC, V. **Map** p305 C4.
Sip tea or espresso in this chic spot while trying out frames by Vivienne Westwood, Helmut Lang, Romeo Gigli or German institution Zeiss. The Mitte branch carries a range of buffalo-horn rims.
Other locations: Reinhardtstrasse 9, Mitte (2790 8991).

Fielmann

Passage, Alexanderplatz, Mitte (242 4507). U2, U5, U8, S3, S5, S7, S9, S75 Alexanderplatz. **Open** 9am-8pm Mon-Fri; 9am-6pm Sat. **Credit** AmEx, DC, MC, V. **Map** p316/p303 G3.
Germany's biggest chain of opticians offers a large selection of frames at competitive prices.
Other locations: across the city.

ic!

Max-Beer-Strasse 17, Mitte (417 1770/www.ic-berlin.de). U8 Weinmeisterstrasse. **Open** 1-7pm Mon -Fri. **Credit** AmEx, DC, MC. **Map** p316/p303 G3.
Berlin's hippest eyewear store for adults and children with both prescription glasses and sunglasses.

Photography

Everyday developing, usually a 2-3 day service, can be done at branches of **Rossmann and Schlecker** all over town. Branches of **Saturn** (*see above*) provide several processing services.

Fix Foto

Kurfürstendamm 213, Charlottenburg (882 7267). U15 Uhlandstrasse. **Open** 9am-10pm Mon-Sat; 11am-7pm Sun. **Credit** AmEx, MC, V. **Map** p305 C4.
Half-hour developing from black and white or colour film or slides, enlargements, CD-Rom and other fast services at unusually generous opening hours.
Other locations: across the city.

PPS

Alexanderplatz 2, Mitte (726 109 209). U2, U5, U8, S3, S5, S7, S9, S75 Alexanderplatz. **Open** 8am-9pm Mon-Fri; noon-5pm Sat, Sun. **Credit** AmEx, DC, MC, V. **Map** p316/p303 G3.

Endangered traffic-light men seek refuge in mugs and bottles at **Mondos Arts**. *See p180.*

Professional colour lab offering two-hour developing, digital service, scanning, black-and-white hand-developed enlargements, large format print and other services. Also sells cameras, rents out sophisticated equipment and sends off repairs.

Wüstefeld

Grolmanstrasse 36, Charlottenburg (883 7593). U15 Uhlandstrasse or S3, S5, S7, S9, S75 Savignyplatz. **Open** 10am-7pm Mon-Fri; 10am-4pm Sat. **Credit** MC, V. **Map** p305 C4.
In exchange for a glance at your ID and a credit card deposit, you can rent Nikon, Canon, Hasselblad and Leica cameras and photo equipment here. Also professional processing service.

Repairs

There are surprisingly few 24-hour emergency repair services dealing with plumbing, electricity, heating, locks, cars and carpentry.

Computer repairs

Petra Koch

Katzlerstrasse 4, Schöneberg (2403 5999/www.homepage.mac.com/macpe). U7 Yorkstrasse. **Open** by appointment. **No credit cards**.
Mac repair shop. Koch speaks English, and will even come to your home.

JE

Poststrasse 12, Mitte (2472 1741/www.je-computer.de). U2 Klosterstrasse. **Open** 10am-8pm Mon-Sat. **No credit cards**. **Map** p316/p303 G3.
PCs repaired, software sold and classes given.

Lock-opening & repairs

For a local locksmith, look in the *Gelbe Seiten* (*Yellow Pages*) under Schlösser. **Schlossdienst** (834 2292) offers 24-hour emergency assistance.

Luggage repairs

Kofferhaus Gabriel

Meinekestrasse 25, Wilmersdorf (882 2262). U9, U15 Kurfürstendamm. **Open** 10.30am-6pm Mon-Fri; 10am-4pm Sat. **Credit** AmEx, DC, MC, V. **Map** p305 C4.
Specialists in Samsonite, Delsey, Airline, Traveller, Rimova and Picard. The staff will be pleased to repair your suitcases within three working days and deliver new ones within the Berlin city limits.

Witt

Hauptstrasse 9, Schöneberg (781 4937). U7 Kleistpark. **Open** 9am-6pm Mon-Fri; 9am-2pm Sat. **Credit** AmEx, DC, MC, V. **Map** p306 E5.
Probably Berlin's most extensive assortment of suitcase spare parts, including patches. Luggage repairs can be completed in a day, and if damage has happened during a flight and you have written airline confirmation, the repairs will be billed to the airline. Evening delivery possible.

Shoe repairs

See also p171 **Breitenbach**.

Picobello

KaDeWe, Tauentzienstrasse 21, Schöneberg (2121 2349). U1, U2, U15 Wittenbergplatz. **Open** 9.30am-8pm Mon-Fri; 9.30am-8pm Sat. **Credit** AmEx, DC, MC, V. **Map** p305 D4.
Staff will heel and sole shoes while you wait, and also engrave and cut keys. There are branches scattered all over Berlin, many of which can be found in department stores.

Water, gas & heating

In an emergency, try **Meisterbetrieb** (703 5050), **Ex-Rohr** (6719 8909) or **Kempinger** (851 5111).

Souvenirs

You'll find stands selling Communist relics such as Party cards, Russian hats or Soviet binoculars plus bits of graffitied plaster, said to be from the Wall, at Checkpoint Charlie. The **Haus am Checkpoint Charlie** (*see p177*) sells items such as key rings, lighters and mouse pads on a 'You Are Leaving The American Sector' theme. The **Kunst und Nostalgie Markt** and **Strasse des 17.Juni** flea markets (for both, *see p176*) have stalls devoted to artefacts from the old East. **Berlin Story** (*see p159*) has a big selection of toy Trabbies, historical maps, mounted wall chunks and other souvenirs. *See also p177* **Lenin's on sale again**.

Berliner Zinnfiguren Kabinett

Knesebeckstrasse 88, Charlottenburg (313 0802/ www.zinnfigur.com). S3, S5, S7, S9, S75 Savignyplatz. **Open** 10am-6pm Mon-Fri; 10am-3pm Sat. **Credit** AmEx, MC, V. **Map** p305 C4.

Armies of tin soldiers line up alongside farm animals and historical characters, all handworked in tin and painted in incredible detail. You could take home an entire battalion of Prussian Grenadiers. Also a fascinating collection of books on Prussian military history.

Fanshop

Wittstockerstrasse 24, Moabit (294 7691/294 7691). U9 Birkenstrasse. **Open** 11am-3pm Mon, Fri; 11am-6pm Tue, Thur; 10am-12.30pm Sat. **No credit cards**.

Should either of Berlin's major soccer clubs have captured your heart, this is the place to stock up on Hertha or Union caps, shawls and T-shirts.

Johanna Petzoldt

Sophienstrasse 9, Mitte (282 6754/www. originalerzegebirgskuenst.de). U8 Weinmeisterstrasse or S3, S5, S7, S9, S75 Hackescher Markt. **Open** 11am-7pm Mon-Fri; 10am-6pm Sat. **Credit** AmEx, DC, MC, V. **Map** p316/p302 F3.

Tiny, charming shop filled with traditional handmade wooden figurines, musical boxes and candle-mobiles from the Erzgebirge region. Some of the quirky figures depict rural German life; others are themed around Christmas or the military. Appropriate or appealing souvenirs.

Mondos Arts

Schreinerstrasse 6, Friedrichshain (4201 0778/ www.mondosarts.de). U5 Samariter Strasse. **Open** 10am-7pm Mon-Fri; 11am-4pm Sat. **Credit** AmEx, MC, V. **Map** p88.

The best of what's left of the east. All types of GDR memorabilia, including flags, posters, clocks, border signs, CDs of Ost-Rock, videos and various products embossed with the endangered *Ampelmännchen* – the characterful stop-and-go men on a dwindling number of traffic lights in eastern Berlin.

Stationery & art supplies

Ferdinand Braune

Grunewaldstrasse 87, Schöneberg (7870 3773/ www.braune-kunstlerbedarf.de). U7 Kleistpark. **Open** 10am-6.30pm Mon-Fri; 10am-2pm Sat. **Credit** MC, V. **Map** p305/p306 D/E5.

Berlin's painters flock here for Herr Braune's hand-blended oil paints, acrylics, sketchbooks and the finest canvas stretches. Delivery service available.

Grüne Papeterie

Oranienstrasse 196, Kreuzberg (618 5355). **Open** 10am-7.30pm Mon-Fri; 10am-4pm Sat. **No credit cards**. **Map** p307 G4.

Eco-friendly stationery, wrapping paper, wooden fountain pens as well as small gifts and toys.

J Müller

Neue Schönhauser Strasse 16, Mitte (283 2532/ www.truckerei-mueller-berlin.de). U8 Weinmeisterstrasse. **Open** 8am-6pm Mon-Fri. **No credit cards**. **Map** p316/p303 G3.

Family-run business selling fine stationery and rubber stamps. Also prints signs and business cards.

Künstler Magazin

Kastanienallee 33, Prenzlauer Berg (448 4447/ www.kuenstlermagazin.de). U2 Eberswalder Strasse. **Open** 9am-8pm Mon-Fri; 10am-6pm Sat. **No credit cards. Map** p303 G2.

Full selection of art supplies including canvas, paint, brushes, paper and easels at reasonable prices.

OK

Alte Schönhauser Strasse 36/37, Mitte (2463 8746/ www.okVersand.com). U8 Weinmeisterstrasse. **Open** noon-8pm Mon-Fri; noon-5pm Sat. **Credit** MC, V. **Map** p316/p303 G3.

Kitsch inexpensive stationery, office items, bags, toys and household items from Japan and Mexico.

Otto Ebeling

Fuggerstrasse 43-45, Schöneberg (211 4627). U1, U2, U15 Wittenbergplatz. **Open** 8.30am-7pm Mon-Fri; 10am-4pm Sat. **Credit** AmEx, MC, V. **Map** p305 D5.

Complete offering of art supplies, paper and portfolios. Carries Schmincke Artist Colours in oil and watercolours. Ships German brands internationally.

Propolis

Oranienstrasse 19A, Kreuzberg (615 2464). U1, U8, U15 Kottbusser Tor. **Open** 10am-6pm Mon-Fri. **No credit cards**. **Map** p307 G4.

Carries over 300 pigments, plus recipes and ingredients for wall finishes. Also available are paints, resins, gold and silver leaf, brushes and canvases.

RSVP

Mulackstrasse 14, Mitte (2809 4644/www.rsvp-berlin.de). U8 Weinmeister Strasse. **Open** noon-7pm Tue-Fri. **Credit** MC, V. **Map** p316/p303 G3.

Stationery for the aesthete: unusual paper for every occasion, plus rubber stamps and Japanese knives.

Arts & Entertainment

Features

Festivals & Events

Berlin's calendar is crammed – carnivals, conferences and culture on demand.

Berlin is alive 24/7, all year round. Spring is ushered in by the traditional May Day Riots, when local anarchists take to the streets for their annual battle with police. In summer, the city hosts parades celebrating everything from hemp and gay life to multiculturalism, sex and techno music. In winter, cultural venues like the Philharmonie and the opera houses are packed for seasonal performances. Christmas markets and ice-skating rinks spring up around the city, giving Berlin a traditional, old-fashioned flair.

Spring

Zeitfenster – Biennale für alte Musik

Konzerthaus, Gendarmenmarkt 2, Mitte (203 090/www.konzerthaus.de). U2, U6 Stadtmitte. **Tickets** varies. **Credit** AmEx, MC, V. **Map** p316/p306 F4. **Date** 1wk in Apr, every 2yrs (2006, 2008).

The Biennial Festival of Early Music at the impressive Konzerthaus (*p237*) in the Gendarmenmarkt focuses on 16th- and 17th-century baroque sounds.

May Day Riots

Around Kottbusser Tor, Kreuzberg. U1, U8, U15 Kottbusser Tor. **Map** p307 G5. **Date** 1 May.

An annual event since 1987, when *Autonomen* engaged in violent clashes with police. Its traditions go back to the early 20th century, however, when Communists and anarchists did the same. The riots are worth checking out only from a distance – police sometimes use batons and water cannons, and some anarchists lob Molotov cocktails and loot shops.

Deutschland Pokal-Endspiele

Olympiastadion, Olympischer Platz 3, Charlottenburg (300 633). U2 Olympia-Stadion or S5 Olympiastadion. Information & tickets: Deutscher Fussball-Bund (tickets@dfb.de/fax 069 678 8266). **Tickets** varies. **No credit cards**. **Date** early May.

The domestic football cup final has been taking place at the Olympiastadion every year since 1985. It regularly attracts some 65,000 football fans.

International Aerospace Exhibition

Flughafen Schönefeld (3038 2014/www.ila-berlin.de/ 6091 1620). S9, S45 Flughafen Schönefeld. **Tickets** varies. **No credit cards**. **Date** 1wk in May, every 2yrs (2006, 2008).

This increasingly popular biennial event, held at Schönefeld airport, features some 1,000 exhibitors from 40 countries, with aircraft of all kinds on display, as well as a serious focus on space.

Eurocard Ladies German Open

LTTC Rot-Weiss, Gottfried-von-Cramm-Weg 47-55, Grunewald (ticket hotline 308 785 685/www.german-open.org). S7 Grunewald. **Tickets** varies. **Credit** AmEx, DC, MC, V. **Date** 1st or 2nd wk in May.

The world's fifth largest international women's tennis championship is also a week-long get-together for Germany's rich and famous. After match point, the focus switches to a gala ball and other glitzy social affairs. Tickets are hard to come by.

Theatertreffen Berlin

Various venues. Organisers: Berliner Festspiele, Schaperstrasse 24, Charlottenburg (2548 9100/ www.berlinerfestspiele.de). **Tickets** varies. **Credit** AmEx, MC, V. **Date** 3wks in May.

The 'Berlin Theatre Meeting' presents the best in German-language productions. A jury chooses ten of the most innovative and controversial new productions from companies in Germany, Austria and Switzerland. The winners come to Berlin to perform their pieces during the festival.

Karneval der Kulturen

Kreuzberg (6097 7022/www.karneval-berlin.de). **Tickets** free. **Date** 4 days in May/June.

Inspired by the Notting Hill Carnival and intended as a celebration of Berlin's ethnic and cultural diversity, the long weekend (always Pentecost) includes a street festival, parties and a 'multi-kulti' parade involving dozens of floats, hundreds of musicians and thousands of spectators. The route changes every year, so check details. *See p184* **Don't stop the Karneval**.

Museumsinselfestival

Museumsinsel, Mitte (www.museumsinselfestival.info). S3, S5, S7, S9, S75 Hackescher Markt. **Map** p316 F4. **Date** May-Sept.

An open-air season of rock and classical concerts, readings, plays and film screenings, with events staged both on Museuminsel itself and at the Kulturforum complex near Potsdamer Platz.

Summer

In Transit

Haus der Kulturen der Welt, John-Foster-Dulles-Allee 10, Tiergarten (3978 7175/www.hkw.de). Bus 100. **Tickets** varies. **Credit** DC, MC, V. **Map** p316 F4. **Date** 3wks in early summer (2004, 2006).

Dance and performance artists from around the world collaborate with Berlin groups at this event. Artists can be viewed as they work or in the resulting evening performances.

Berlin International Film Festival: a bit of glitz in the dead of winter. *See p186.*

Schwul-Lesbisches Strassenfest

Nollendorfplatz, Schöneberg (216 8008/www.csd-berlin.de). U1, U2, U4, U15 Nollendorfplatz.
Tickets free. **Map** p305 D5. **Date** 2 days in June.
The traditional summer Gay and Lesbian Street Fair takes over Schöneberg every year, filling several blocks in west Berlin's gay quarter. Participating bars, clubs, food stands and musical acts make this a dizzying non-stop event. The fair also serves as kick-off for the following week's Christopher Street Day Parade (*see below*).

Berlin Philharmonie at the Waldbühne

Waldbühne, Glockenturmstrasse, Charlottenburg (809 9090). S5 Pichelsburg, then shuttle bus.
Tickets €18-€46. **Credit** AmEx, MC, V.
Date 1 day in June.
The Philharmonie ends its season with an open-air concert at the atmospheric 'forest theatre'. The event marks the beginning of summer for more than 20,000 Berliners, who light up the venue with candles once darkness falls.

Fête de la Musique

Various venues (449 2594/www.fetedelamusique.de).
Tickets free. **Date** 21 June.
A regular summer solstice happening since 1995, this music extravaganza takes place all over town and features hundreds of bands and DJs. The music selection is a mixed bag, with DJs playing everything from heavy metal to *Schlager*.

Christopher Street Day Parade

Route varies (2362 8632/www.csd-berlin.de).
Date Sat in late June.
Originally organised to commemorate the 1969 riots at the Stonewall Bar on Christopher Street in New York, which marked the beginning of gay liberation, the parade has become one of the summer's most flamboyant street parties. It attracts both gays and straights and is an exciting event for visitors to the city. The parade usually takes place on the Saturday nearest to 22 June.

Classic Open Air

Gendarmenmarkt, Mitte (Media On-Line 315 7540/ www.classicopenair.de). U6 Französische Strasse, U2, U6 Stadmitte or U2 Hausvogteiplatz. **Tickets** €30-€80. **Credit** AmEx, MC. **Map** p316/p306 F4.
Date 4-7 days in early July.
Big names usually open this concert series held in one of Berlin's most beautiful squares. Many local orchestras take part, as well as soloists from around Europe. Tickets can be booked online.

Love Parade

Tiergarten (Planetcom 284 620/www.loveparade.net). **Tickets** *Parade* free. *Evening parties* varies.
Map p316/p302 E4. **Date** 2nd Sat in July.
Still attracting over half a million visitors, techno's annual carneval includes dozens of floats sponsored by clubs. It has become increasingly controversial in recent years, however, with many locals opposing the Parade's route through the Tiergarten.

Fuck Parade

069 9435 9090/www.fuckparade.de. **Tickets** free.
Date 1st or 2nd Sat in July.
Launched in 1997 as a sort of anti-Love Parade, the Fuck Parade is meant to represent the edgier, non-commercial side of electronic music. It attracts a few thousand ravers and floats from techno, drum 'n' bass and gabba clubs. The route varies, usually meandering through eastern backstreets.

Heimatklänge

Various venues (318 6140/www.musikadelmondo.de). **Tickets** €6. **Credit** varies. **Date** 1wk in Aug.
Berlin's biggest world music festival, featuring acts from around the globe. Expect anything from Balkan brass bands to Brazilian jazz.

Tanz im August

Various venues. Organisers: HAU, Hallesches Ufer 32, Kreuzberg (2590 0427/www.hebbel-am-ufer.de).
Tickets varies. **Credit** varies. **Date** 3wks in Aug.
Germany's leading dance festival is an annual showcase for dance trends from around the world.

Don't stop the Karneval

Sound systems blasting out rhythms from all over the world, straws slurping Caipirinhas, young and old bumping and grinding – welcome to **Karneval der Kulturen**, Berlin's answer to Mardi Gras, Rio or the Notting Hill Carnival. Every year, for four days over Pentecost weekend, Kreuzberg becomes the hub of street parties, live music and a multicultural fairground, culminating in a parade on Pentecost Sunday which in 2003 attracted a crowd of 700,000 – more than that year's Love Parade.

Plans for a carnival-like spectacle in Berlin had been bandied about for ages, but most merely tried to copy other carnivals without adding a Berlin-specific vibe. Considering Berlin's non-German population of 440,000, the largest in Germany, the Neukölln-based multicultural initiative Werkstatt der Kulturen decided to use that potential to stage a 'multi-kulti' carnival that truly reflected the creativity and diversity of the city. The first carnival in 1998 attracted 500,000 visitors

Deutsch-Französisches Volksfest

Zentraler Festplatz am Kurt-Schumacher-Damm, Kurt-Schumacher-Damm 207-45, Reinickendorf (639 030/www.berlinervolksfeste.de/seiten/dfv.htm). U6 Kurt-Schumacher-Platz. **Tickets** €1.50. **No credit cards**. **Date** 4wks in June/July.

A survivor from the days when the northern part of West Berlin was the French Sector, the month-long German-French Festival offers a range of rides, French music and cuisine. On 14 July 14 Bastille Day, there is a fireworks display.

Deutsch-Amerikanisches Volksfest

Truman Plaza, Hüttenweg/Clayallee, Zehlendorf (0172 390 0930/www.deutsch-amerikanisches-volksfest.de). U1 Oskar-Helene-Heim. **Tickets** €1.50; children free. **No credit cards**. **Date** 4wks in July/Aug.

Originally established by the US forces stationed in West Berlin, the German-American Festival continues to delight Berliners – both adults and children – with a tacky mix of carnival rides, cowboys doing lasso tricks, candy floss, hamburgers, hot dogs and plenty of Yankee beer.

Internationales Berliner Bierfestival

Karl-Marx-Allee, from Strausberger Platz to Frankfurter Tor, Friedrichshain (508 6822/ www.bierfestival-berlin.de). U5 Frankfurter Tor. **Map** p303 G3/H3. **Date** 1 weekend in Aug.

The annual Berlin International Beer Festival showcases hundreds of beers from more than 60 different countries. Stalls are set up along the Stalinist-style Karl-Marx-Allee.

Young Euro Classic

Konzerthaus, Am Gendarmenmarkt 2, Mitte (203 092 101/www.young-euro-classic.de). **Tickets** varies. **No credit cards**. **Map** p306 F4. **Date** 2wks in Aug.

This annual summer music programme brings together youth orchestras from around Europe for a series of recommended concerts.

Lange Nacht der Museen

2839 7444/www.lange-nacht-der-museen.de. **Tickets** €12; €8 concessions. **Date** 1 evening in late Aug.

and involved 3,500 people in the organisational and creative side. In the next years the parade alone would attract that many people and more. Berlin now boasted its own four days of 'peace and music'. Even the competition for Best Float was friendly, and the sneaky Berlin weather usually played along.

The idea to use the carnival as vehicle of integration seems to be working. Not only are Berliners exposed to different cultures in a fun way, the preparation groups give migrants 'the rare opportunity to actively contribute to something, regardless of their social status,' as the Werkstatt sees it, diminishing a sense of alienation and promoting communication between groups.

As the Karneval grew it spawned a cottage industry (including four CDs from participating musicians) and cries of commercialisation can be heard, bemoaning everything from the increasingly banal floats to hikes in Caipirinha prices. Of course, this may be unavoidable for an event of this scope. But for the time being the Karneval is still the better Love Parade – more diversity, a crowd big enough to feel part of a common celebration, but not so large as to feel smothered, and an underlying message more in tune with the times.

Twice a year 80 museums stay open into the early hours. In addition to their collections, the 'Long Night of the Museums' offers concerts, readings and stage acts. Museum-hoppers can shuttle between venues by bus, tram or boat. *See also p186.*

Berliner Comic Festival

Various venues. Organisers: Neue Gesellschaft für Literatur, Spreeufer 5 (283 3983/2887 9890/www.berliner-comicfestival.de). **Date** 5 days in late August.

These five days of exhibitions, cartoon screenings, lectures, drawing contests and a comic publisher fair attract both the geeks and those who have read about Art Spiegelman in the arts pages. Manga is heavily represented. No festival will be held in 2004.

Kreuzberger Festliche Tage

Viktoria Park, Katzbachstrasse, Kreuzberg (4340 7905/www.kreuzberg-festliche-tage.de). U6, U7, S2, S25 Yorkstrasse. **Tickets** free. **Map** p306 F6. **Date** 2wks in late Aug/early Sept.

This annual late summer festival in Kreuzberg's Viktoria Park offers music, games, beer and food.

Autumn

Hanfparade

Hallesches Tor to Rotes Rathaus (2472 0233/ www.hanfparade.de). **Tickets** free. **Date** usually 1 Sept; (2004) 14 Aug.

Celebrating the utility of the fibrous weed, organisers of the Hemp Parade seek total legalisation of the use and possession of cannabis. The route sometimes changes; check local press for details.

Berliner Festwochen

Various venues. Organisers: Berliner Festspiele, Schaperstrasse 24, Charlottenburg (2548 9218/ www.berlinerfestspiele.de). **Tickets** varies. **Credit** varies. **Date** Sept-Jan.

Summer fades into winter with a few months of events, concerts and performances. Classical music, theatre and dance are accompanied by exhibitions and readings based on a specific region or theme.

Popkomm

Messe Berlin, Messedamm 22, Charlottenburg (3038 2269/www.popkomm.de). U2 Kaiserdamm, S75 Messe Süd, S41, S42 Messe Nord. **Map** p304 A4. **Date** 3 days in Sept.

Europe's largest domestic music industry trade fair arrives in Berlin from Cologne, bringing three days of business schmoozing and lots of music. As well as a trade-only conference, Berlin's clubs and live venues will host a myriad of showcases and events.

Art Forum Berlin

Messegelände am Funkturm, Messedamm 22 Charlottenburg (3038 2076/www.art-forum-berlin.de). U2 Kaiserdamm, S75 Messe Süd, S41, S42 Messe Nord. **Map** p304 A4. **Date** 5 days in late Sept/early Oct.

Since 1996, the Art Forum Berlin has sought to bring together gallery-owners and artists during this five-day trade fair of contemporary art. The event attracts many of Europe's leading galleries plus thousands of lay enthusiasts.

Berlin Marathon

Organisers: Berlin-Marathon, Glockenturmstrasse 23, 14055 (302 8810/3012 8820www.berlin-marathon.com). **Admission** €50-€90. **Credit** call for details. **Date** last Sun in Sept.

The city's biggest sporting event takes 30,000 participants from around the world, including wheelchair racers and in-line skaters, past most of the city's landmarks on its 42-km (26-mile) trek through seven boroughs.

JazzFest Berlin

Various venues. Organisers: Berliner Festspiele, Schaperstrasse 24, Charlottenburg (2548 9100/ www.berlinerfestspiele.de). **Tickets** varies. **Credit** varies. **Date** 4 days late Oct/early Nov.

A wide spectrum of jazz from an array of internationally renowned artists, and a fixture since 1964. The concurrent Fringe Jazz Festival (organised by JazzRadio) showcases less established acts.

Winter

Berliner Märchentage

Various venues (282 9140/www.berlin-maerchentage.de). **Tickets** varies. **Credit** varies. **Date** 11 days in mid Nov.

The Berlin Fairytale Festival celebrates tales from around the world with storytelling, music and a carnival atmosphere: some 400 events at 150 locations. Past festivals have been themed around the Arabian Nights and the world of Russian fairytales.

Tanznacht Berlin

Various venues. Organisers: HAU, Hallesches Ufer 32, Kreuzberg (2590 0427/www.hebbel-am-ufer.de). U1, U6, U15 Hallesches Tor. **Tickets** varies. **Credit** varies. **Date** one night in mid Dec (2005, 2007).

Biennial event aiming to showcase the quality and diversity of contemporary dance in Berlin, presenting up to 20 different acts in one long night.

Christmas Markets

Kaiser-Wilhelm-Gedächtniskirche, Breitscheidplatz, Charlottenburg. U2, U9, S3, S5, S7, S9 Zoologischer Garten. **Open** 11am-8pm Mon-Thur, Sun; 11am-9pm Fri, Sat. **Map** p305 D4.

Traditional markets spring up all over Berlin during the Christmas season, offering traditional toys, mulled wine, gingerbread and other goodies or gifts. This is one of the biggest and most central.

Berliner Silvesterlauf

Grunewald (302 5370/www.berlin-marathon.com/events/silvester/anmeldung). S5, S75 Eichkamp. **Tickets** free. **Date** 31 Dec.

A local tradition for almost 30 years, the New Year's Eve Run, also known as the 'pancake run', starts in Grunewald at the intersection of Waldschulallee and Harbigstrasse at the foot of Teufelsberg.

Silvester

Date 31 Dec.

With Berliners' enthusiasm for tossing firecrackers and launching rockets from windows, New Year's Eve is always vivid and noisy. Thousands celebrate at the Brandenburger Tor. Thousands more trek up to the Teufelsberg at the northern tip of Grunewald or Viktoria Park in Kreuzberg to watch fireworks.

Internationale Grüne Woche

Messegelände am Funkturm, Messedamm 22, Charlottenburg (3038 2267/www.messe-berlin.de). U2 Kaiserdamm, S75 Messe Süd, S41, S42 Messe Nord. **Open** 10am-6pm daily. **Tickets** varies. **No credit cards**. **Map** p304 A4. **Date** 10 days in Jan.

A ten-day orgy of food and drink from the far corners of Germany and the world.

UltraSchall

Various venues. Organisers: DeutschlandRadio Berlin, Hans-Rosenthal-Platz, Schöneberg (850 30/www.dradio.de/dlr). **Tickets** varies. **Credit** varies. **Date** 10 days in mid Jan.

New music presented in high-profile venues by some of the world's leading specialist ensembles. Concerts are often broadcast live by DeutschlandRadio and Rundfunk Berlin Brandenburg.

Tanztage

Sophiensaele, Sophienstrasse 18, Mitte (283 5266/www.sophiensaele.de). U8 Weinmeisterstrasse or S3, S5, S7, S9, S75 Hackescher Markt. **Tickets** varies. **No credit cards**. **Map** p316/p302 F3. **Date** 2 wks in mid Jan.

New talent featured in a fortnight of dance events.

Lange Nacht der Museen

2839 7444/www.lange-nacht-der-museen.de. **Date** 1 evening in Feb. **Admission** (€12; €8 concessions).

Late-night museum opening. *See p184.*

Transmediale

Haus der Kulturen der Welt, John-Foster-Dulles-Allee 10, Tiergarten (3978 7175/www.hkw.de). Bus 100, 248. **Open** *Buro* 10am-6pm Mon; 10am-8pm Tue-Sun. **Tickets** varies. **Credit** AmEx, MC, V. **Map** p302 E3. **Date** 5 days in early Feb.

One of the world's largest international media art festivals, presenting exhibitions from artists working with video, television, computer animation, internet and other visual media and digital technologies. The offshoot Club Transmediale, which takes place at Maria am Ufer (*see p220*), offers performances, discussions and media art about electronic music.

Berlin International Film Festival

Potsdamer Platz, Tiergarten & other venues (259 2000/www.berlinale.de). U2, S1, S2, S25, S26 Potsdamer Platz. **Tickets** €7-€16; €140. **Credit** call for details. **Date** 1-2wks in mid Feb.

Now over 50 years old, this is one of the world's major cinema festivals, featuring over 300 movies from around the world. It is held at the Potsdamer Platz cinemas and attended by international stars, providing this normally glamour-proof city with a bit of glitz in the dead of winter. *See p192.*

MärzMusik – Festival für aktuelle Musik

Various venues. Organisers: Berliner Festspiele, Schaperstrasse 24, Tiergarten (2548 9100/www.berlinfestspiele.de). **Tickets** varies. **Credit** varies. **Date** 1-2wks in Mar.

A holdover from the more culture-conscious days of the old East Germany, this annual festival highlights trends in contemporary music. The event invites international avant-garde composers and musicians to present new works.

International Tourism Fair

Messegelände am Funkturm, Messedamm 22 Charlottenburg (3038-2275/www.itb-berlin.de). U2 Kaiserdamm or S75 Messe Süd or S41, S42 Messe Nord. **Open** 10am-6pm daily. **Tickets** varies. **No credit cards**. **Date** 5 days in mid-March.

The world is your oyster at this trade fair where tourism boards, travel agents and hotels present themselves to satisfy Berliner wanderlust.

Children

All corners of town are cool for kids.

Children are well-integrated into daily Berlin life, and there are plenty of areas created especially for them. So seek out the playgrounds in most parks and the children's sections in many museums and your kids will enjoy the city as much as you do. Most locals respond well to children, and you will find it pretty easy to get around. Using public transport with children (or with a buggy) is not a problem, as main U- and S-Bahn stations have lifts. Buses allow for easy entry with a buggy through the rear doors.

The best way to make sense of Berlin with children is to take a geographical approach to the city. Each of Berlin's districts is distinct, and offers a range of different attractions.

Mitte

There's no shortage of things to see and do in Mitte. Most museums are around here, many on **Museumsinsel** (*see p76*), which, with its weekend flea market, is a lovely, lively spot to pass a few hours. Nearby **Monbijou Park** on Oranienburger Strasse has greenery, playgrounds and, in summer, a great wading pool for kids, the Kinderbad Monbijou. A pleasant way to orient yourself in Berlin is by a boat tour, many of which operate from in front of the **Pergamonmuseum** on Museumsinsel. From here you can set out west towards Charlottenburg and the Havel river, the **Wannsee** (*see p116*) and **Potsdam** (*see p256*) or head east to the **Müggelsee** in Köpenick (*see p118*) and the **Spreewald** forest (*see p262*). Another way to get the lie of the land is to take in the panorama from the top of Berlin's highest landmark, the **Fernsehturm** (TV Tower; *see p86*) on Alexanderplatz. Down below, kids cool off and wade about in the **Neptunebrunnen** (*see p84*) in summer.

Of Mitte's many museums, children will enjoy the dinosaur skeletons at the **Museum für Naturkunde** (Museum of Natural History; *see p82*), the interactive exhibits and robots at the **Museum für Kommunikation** (*see p82*), and the ancient architecture on a grand scale at the **Pergamonmuseum** (*see p78*). The **Museum Kindheit und Jugend** (Museum of Childhood and Youth; *see p86*) has old toys, and childhood and classroom artefacts from the last century. For entertainment, the **Hackesches Hof Theater** at Rosenthaler Strasse 40-41 (283 2587) puts on an enjoyable Sunday brunch show, with clowns and puppets, from 10am onwards. **Milch und Honig** ('milk and honey', 6162 5761) presents Jewish life in Berlin and offers cultural events for parents and children (6162 5761/www.milch-und-honig.com/kinderseite.htm).

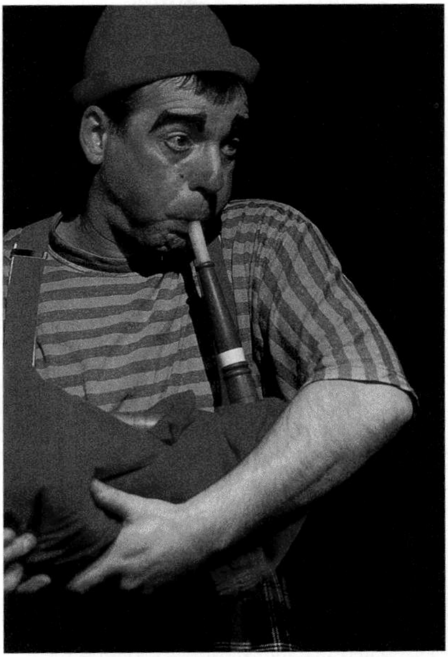

Hackesches Hof Theatre: clowns at brunch.

At Mitte's south-western corner, the gleaming **Potsdamer Platz** complex contains three multiplex cinemas which screen children's and family films (though dubbed into German) each afternoon. Many of the movies at the **Kinderfilmfest**, an offshoot of the annual grown-up FilmFest (*see p192*), are screened around here. Every February there are about 25 new children's films from around the world, and a prize for the best one is awarded by a jury of kids aged between 11 and 14.

Many restaurants in Mitte have children's menus, but the area around Hackesche Höfe and Rosenthaler Strasse offers the richest pickings.

The great indoors

Put 'em down. Let 'em loose. And watch 'em go! That's the latest trend among parents in Berlin who have discovered a safe way to promote juvenile exhaustion. Right across town, huge, empty industrial spaces have been converted to indoor playgrounds. For a small entry fee, kids can jump, run, scream, ride, climb, and raise hell till they drop. On a typical Saturday afternoon at Jolos Kinderwelt in Kreuzberg, for example, you'll find hundreds of kids scrambling to the top of an inflatable mountain, or tumbling out of the gaping jaws of Jolo the giant crocodile. Some of them will be riding a dorky locomotive in the back, or tooling around in auto-scooters up front. There are net-enclosed trampolines, sliding boards, and table football and air hockey tables. Rubber balls of every size litter the 1,500-square-metre (16, 145-square-feet) complex (formerly an annex of the Schultheiss brewery). Supervisors keep the rowdies in check, so parents can chill in the roped-off dining area next to the snack bar, which features reasonably priced drinks, chips and Wiener Würstchen.

Jacks Fun World

Miraustrasse 38, Tegel (419 00 242/ www.jacks-fun-world.de). S25 Eichborndamm. **Open** 10am-8.30pm Sat, Sun. **Admission** €9 Mon-Fri; €12 Sat, Sun.

Jolos Kinderwelt

Am Tempelhofer Berg 7d, 10965 Kreuzberg (612 02796/www.jolo-berlin.de). U6 Platz der Luftbrücke. **Open** 2pm-7pm Mon-Fri 11am-7pm Sat, Sun. **Admission** *Children* €6. *Adult* €3.50. *2nd adult* free. **Map** p306 F5.

Pups

Kochstrasse 73, Mitte (2594 2910/ www.pups.de). U6 Kochstrasse. **Open** 10am-8pm daily. **Admission** €3/hr (higher during school holidays). **Map** p306 F4.

Try the **Hackescher Hof** at Rosenthaler Strasse 40 (283 5293), the American **Catherine's** (2025 1555) at Friedrichstrasse 90, **Der Kartoffelkeller** (282 8548) with regional German food at Albrechtstrasse 14B.

Mitte's newest attraction is **AquaDom & Sealife** on Spandauer Strasse 3 (*see p85*). There are 13 aquariums, including the mightyAquaDom itself, a huge salt-water tank that's home to 2,500 varieties of fish. You can take a ride in a lift up through the middle of it. There's also a 'petting aquarium' where kids can touch the fish, plus plenty of hands-on gadgetry.

Prenzlauer Berg & Friedrichshain

More children are currently being born in Prenzlauer Berg than in any other part of Germany, but there are few parks or specific attractions for kids. There are, however, plenty of cafés, restaurants, squares and playgrounds, particularly in the area around Kollwitzplatz.

Among the restaurants that offer special children's menus are the **Italian Istoria** (Kollwitzstrasse 64, 4405 0208), **Zander** (No.50, 4405 7678), **Prater** (Kastanienallee 7; *see p149*) with German food; and the **Indian Maharadsha** 2 (Schönhauser Allee 142, 448 5172).

Die Schaubude (Greifswalder Strasse 81-4, 423 4314) is a high-quality puppet theatre, used by a variety of local and visiting troupes. **Volkspark Friedrichshain** has half-pipes and skater routes, and the Märchenbrunnen ('fairy tale fountain') features figures from stories by the Brothers Grimm.

Kreuzberg

This colourful borough has lots of small shops, plenty of good, cheap restaurants, and a vibrant, child-friendly atmosphere.The **Haus am Checkpoint Charlie** (*see p95*) has plenty to interest older children, including the old cars and balloons that people used to circumvent the Wall. Older kids will also enjoy the **Grusel Kabinett** (*see p95*), a spooky chamber of horrors in an old World War II bunker. The **Deutsches Technikmuseum Berlin** (*see p95*) in Trebbiner Strasse 9 offers old locomotives and cars to explore, computers and gadgets to play with, and a new 'Maritime Wing' with boats. **New City Bowling** on Hasenheide (*see p248*) has 12 lanes for children and is open from 10am daily.

Leafy **Viktoriapark** has a hill to climb, with good views from the top. In summer, a waterfall cascades down to street level; in winter the hill is great for tobogganing. The park also has an excellent playground, a tiny zoo, and hosts the occasional circus or funfair. Nearby are plenty of eating options, such as **Osteria No.1** (*see p133*) at Kreuzbergstrasse 71, the **Lon Men** at Grossbeerenstrasse 57a (*see p135*).

At the other end of the borough, the highlight of **Görlitzer Park** is the Kinderbauernhof, a petting zoo (611 7424).

Schöneberg

Schöneberg is a huge, disparate district, but the area around Winterfeldplatz is a pleasant focal point, with an outdoor market each Wednesday and Saturday, and lots of cafés and restaurants (there's good, cheap fast food on Golzstrasse). There are plenty of parks and playgrounds in the district, but there aren't many specific attractions. It's worth the trek to the **Planetarium am Insulaner** (Munsterdamm 90, 790 0930), about 20 minutes by S-Bahn (S2, S25, S26 Priesterweg) from the centre of town. Two to four times a week the planetarium offers programmes for children.

The huge **Volkspark Wilmersdorf**, stretching from the district of Dahlem via Wilmersdorf into Schöneberg, offers myriad slides, playground paraphernalia and a ski lift ride. At the park's eastern end is one of Berlin's best indoor swimming pools (Hauptstrasse).

There are good, child-friendly restaurants all over Schöneberg. Try the tartes flambées at **Storch** (Wartburgstrasse 54, *see p135*), the hearty pasta dishes at **Petite Europe** (Langenscheidtstrasse 1, *see p136*) or the burgers and bagels at **Tim's Canadian Deli** (Maasenstrasse 11, *see p155*).

South of Schöneberg, in Friedenau, the children's book shop **Storytime Books** (*see p159*) is worth a visit.

Tiergarten

The major draw in Tiergarten is the park itself. Paddle and rowing boats can be hired near the **Café am Neuen See** (*see p156*). Meanwhile, along Strasse des 17.Juni, the main road through the park, there is an interesting flea market, which takes place on Saturdays and Sundays (*see p176*).

In the park's south-western corner is Berlin's beautifully landscaped Zoo and, good for rainy days, its sizeable **Aquarium** (for both, *see p103*). The excellent **Gemäldegalerie** in Matthäikirchplatz (*see p102*) runs Sunday afternoon tours for children, and the **Haus der Kulturen der Welt** (*see p99*), on the north side of the park, has programmes for kids.

Gadgets to get them going at the **Deutsches Technikmuseum Berlin**. *See p188.*

Charlottenburg

The area around Zooligischer Garten and the Ku'damm can seem busy and unappealing. But away from the main thoroughfares the atmosphere is pleasant, with good restaurants, shops and outdoor markets. The Saturday market at Karl-August-Platz, for example, is a gathering point for families, with a playground, cafés, and top-notch ice cream at **Micha's Eisdiele** (Pestalozzistrasse 85).

Fifteen minutes' walk west of here is the small but pretty **Lietzenseepark**, with a lake, three playgrounds, two cafés (open April-October) and two sports areas.

Of more interest to children than the **Schloss Charlottenburg** (*see p107*) is the **Ägyptisches Museum** (*see p107*) over the road – a great place for mummy-mad kids. There are special tours for children above the age of eight (places are limited, call 266 2951 in advance). There are child-friendly restaurants all over Charlottenburg, particularly in the east part. At **Charlottchen** (Droysenstrasse 1, 324 4717) parents eat in the dining room (the food is nothing special) while their kids let their hair down in a rumpus room. There are theatre performances on Sundays (11.30am, 3.30pm).

The relaxed Italian attitude to kids is evident at **La Cantina** (Bleibtreustrasse 33, 883 2156) or **Toto** (corner of Bleibtreustrasse and Pestalozzistrasse, 312 5449).

Other districts

The UFA Fabrik cultural centre in the southern district of **Tempelhof** (Viktoriastrasse 10-18, 755 030, www.ufafabrik.de) has a farm for kids, a circus and a variety of courses and workshops. It's right by U-Bahn Ullsteinstrasse (U6) and has several restaurants and cafés.

South-west of the city, the vast **Grunewald woods** (*see p115*) are great for long walks, and the Kronprinzessinnenweg in its centre is an ideal track for rollerblading and cycling. There are various lakes where bathing is possible, and **Strandbad Wannsee** (*see p116*) is Europe's largest inland beach; there's a playground, cafés and pedalos for hire.

It's possible to visit **Pfaueninsel** (Peacock Island; *see p116*) with its nature reserve and an eccentric castle built by Friedrich Wilhelm II, or you can take a boat tour southwards through various small lakes and canals to Potsdam. The nearby **Filmpark Babelsberg** (*see p258*) offers behind-the-scenes action and stunts.

To the east of the Grunewald, **Domäne Dahlem** (*see p113*) is a 17th-century-style working farm, featuring demonstrations by blacksmiths, carpenters, bakers and potters. At weekends children can ride ponies, tractors and hay-wagons. Going further back in time, **Museumsdorf Düppel** (*see p117*) is a reconstructed 14th-century village around archaeological excavations near the Düppel forest. Kids can witness craftspeople at work, medieval technology, old farming techniques and ride ox-carts (Apr-Oct).

In the district of Gatow to the west of the Havel is the small **British-German Yacht Club** (Kladower Damm 217A, 365 4010), which has a good team of sailing teachers (4pm Tue, 11am Sat, closed Nov-Mar) and a British pub, where parents drink and snack at the waterside, while the youngsters mess about on the water. In the centre of Gatow, children clamber in and out of the military aircraft on view at the **Luftwaffenmuseum** (*see p112*).

You can avoid summer crowds on the Havel and Wannsee by visiting the **Tegeler See** to the north-west of the centre. North-east of Tegel, in the quaint village of Alt Lübars, is **Jugendfarm Lübars**, (S1 to Wittenau, then bus 221, 415 7027, closed Oct-Mar, Mon, Sat) where children can see farm animals, watch craftspeople at work and eat at the restaurant. Adjacent is a playground and a hill of World War II rubble to climb.

It's worth the half-hour trip on the S3 to **FEZ in der Wuhlheide** (An der Wuhlheide 250, 5307 1257), deep in the woods south-east of the centre. This Communist-era children's park has a narrow-gauge railway, swimming and wading pools, forts, trampolines and picnic areas. The **Mellowpark** in nearby Köpenick (Friedrichshagener Strasse 10-12) offers supervised play for older children. Activities, daily from 2pm in summer, include skating, boarding, basketball and breakdancing on the banks of the Spree.

Also to the east is the **Tierpark Berlin-Friedrichsfelde** (*see p118*), a lovely, huge park and zoo, featuring grassland animals, like giraffes and deer, playgrounds, a petting zoo and snack stands. Still further east, the **Müggelsee** (*see p118*) is another beautiful sailing and swimming area. A boat tour from Mitte to the Müggelsee and back occupies a full day, but is worth it in good weather.

Babysitters

There's a good online search engine (in German) for babysitters at www.berlinonline.de/service/familie/babysitter/.html/b/b_suchen.htm.

Aufgepasst

851 3723. **Rates** €10/hr. **No credit cards**.

Biene Maja

344 3973/www.babysitteragentur.de. **Rates** €9.50-€13/hr. **No credit cards**.

Film

With its prestigious film festival, historic cinemas, new multiplexes and cool video shops, Berlin is ready for its close-up.

Recent years have seen a worldwide proliferation of multiplex culture, and Berlin is no exception. Not so long ago a place where repertory cinema flourished in various neighbourhoods, the Berlin of today boasts a massive array of multi-screen malls all showing basically the same thing – the latest Hollywood fare, a sprinkling of British and occasional French crossover 'hits', with mainstream German product just about holding down its own, albeit modest, niche.

The result of all this is that English-language programming, once the speciality of the small and daring, has become more and more the domain of the large, and largely conservative, multiplex chains. Even the **Berlin International Film Festival** (*see p186 and p192*) – both one of the world's most important international film festivals, and one of Berlin's major cultural events – has forsaken historic landmark venues for two multiplexes in the mighty shopping mall that is Potsdamer Platz.

While last year saw the closing of a couple of mainstay English-language cinemas, the eight-screen Cinestar in the Sony Center at Potsdamer Platz is now exclusively English-language, which means the English screen count has actually risen.

Those whose tastes run to the mainstream will feel right at home in the modern multiplex of Cinestar or its competing neighbour, Cinemaxx Potsdamer Platz (two to three of its 19 screens in English). Though the historically less conservative all-English houses such as a Odeon or Babylon have been veering towards the middle of the road, their old-style homey atmosphere is still a welcome change of pace.

But rabid cineastes should be advised that all is not totally lost. Berlin is a city with not one but two Cinematheques: the Arsenal and the Filmkunsthaus Babylon, respectively representing the former West and East. Also, this year sees the long awaited reopening of the Zeughaus Kino, the cinema of the **Deutsches Historisches Museum** (*see p76*), which despite its name, has historically offered many English-language classic film series. The bad news is that the dependable Eiszeit, Central and Xenon kinos are being cut loose by their owners, but the good news is that they are being taken over by their respective principal programmers. With luck they'll continue the film-freak tradition that originally made them famous.

One typical Berlin phenomenon that remains very much alive is the city's fascination with silent films, often presented with live musical accompaniment, ranging from simple piano to full symphony orchestra with the occasional hard-core band for variety. Recurring favourites include German historical hits such as *Metropolis*, *Berlin: Sinfonie einer Grosstadt* (Symphony of a City) and *The Cabinet of Dr. Caligari*, though almost anything could show up. The most likely venues are currently Filmkunsthaus Babylon (with a recently installed organ), Arsenal or any of the outdoor cinemas (*see below*), and the Filmfest inevitably has at least one major special event of this kind.

Another popular tradition is the outdoor cinema, the *Frieluftkino*, though with Berlin's unpredictable weather, the screen count varies from year to year. Unfortunately, almost everything, apart from silent films, is shown synchronised into German, but things in English do pop up occasionally at the Freiluftkino Kreuzberg (*see p195*) and on a clement night it can be really fun.

FESTIVALS

A more reliable way to while away the summer evenings is the **Fantasy Film Festival** (www.fantasyfilmfest.com) which shows both classics and the latest in fantasy, horror and sci-fi from America, Hong Kong, Japan and Europe. Films are often premières, with occasional previews, programmed retrospectives and assorted rarities. Aside from the occasional German film, all shows have been in English or with English subtitles. Venues seem to change periodically but recent years have found it at the Cinemaxx (*see p195*). Dates are flexible but seem to hover around mid August.

The most recent addition to the Berlin summer calendar is the **B-Film Digital Vision Festival** (www.bfilm.de). Begun as part of a conference on new media, the film programme has taken on a life of its own, featuring panels and seminars on digital film-making as well as showing wild and strange productions ranging from off-Hollywood to Swedish gang films to Malaysian road movies

Berlin International Film Festival

As the Love Parade slowly loses steam, the Internationale Filmfestspiele Berlin (*see also p186*) is re-emerging as the city's biggest annual event. Born out of the Cold War, it developed from a propaganda event supported by the Allies into a genuine meeting place – or maybe collision point – for East and West during the post-War, Cold War and post-Cold War periods. Whether it was the French boycott in 1959 over the showing of *Paths Of Glory*, Stanley Kubrick's controversial indictment of war, the jury revolt of 1970 over the pro-Vietnamese film, *OK*, or the East Bloc walkout in 1979 over the depiction of Vietnamese people in *The Deer Hunter*, the drama of the festival was not confined to the screens. The years immediately following the fall of the Berlin Wall were particularly exciting: the mood and energy of the festival reflected the joy and chaos of the city's changing landscape. Recent years have seen it move more towards the glamour and celebrity of its two major rivals, Cannes and Venice. It also coincides with the announcement of the Oscar nominations, which always cause a flurry of excitement for nominated festival guests.

The last few years have seen the festival settle comfortably into a new home in Potsdamer Platz (*pictured*). Some miss watching the films in the historical landmark cinemas scattered around the former West Berlin, but staging it in one central location is more convenient and heightens the festival atmosphere. In addition, the presence of the recently completed Film Museum in the nearby Sony Center (*see p196*) has increased the profile of the Retrospective section (*see below*) and added opportunities for special exhibitions. The festival's new director, Dieter Kosslick, has also brought a more open and energetic atmosphere to the proceedings, adding various symposia and an outreach programme for developing filmmakers (*see below* **Talent Campus**). And for those who still yearn for the old landmark theatres, the Delphi, a former pre-war dance palace, The International, formerly one of East Berlin's premiere theaters, and the splendid 1950s-designed Zoo Palast, are still used as venues for repeat performances.

What remains the same, however, is the chance to see what is arguably the widest and most eclectic mix of any film festival anywhere. And unlike its two sister festivals, Berlin is at least as much about the audiences as it is about the industry. Every February, it seems like the entire city turns out to see literally hundreds of films, presented in eight sections – the most important of which are listed below.

THE INTERNATIONAL COMPETITION

If the most visible part in terms of glamour and publicity, this is also by nature the most conservative in selection. Concentrating on major, big-budget productions from all over the world, with a heavy (and often heavily criticised) accent on America, these films usually make it to general release. Films compete for the Gold and Silver Bears and there is often a furore accompanying the announcement of the winners. Since the evening galas are the most expensive and most likely to sell out, go for the afternoon shows or the repeats in the neighbourhood cinemas. All shows in the Berlinale Palast come with simultaneous translation over headphones. Repeats are at Royal Palast and Kino International.

THE INTERNATIONAL FORUM OF YOUNG CINEMA

Born out of the revolt that dissolved the Competition in the 1970 festival, the Forum provides challenging and eclectic fare that you wouldn't see elsewhere: devotees claim this is the real Berlin festival. Anything can happen here, from the latest American indie film, to African cinema, to midnight shows of Hong Kong action films. The likes of George Clooney can look pretty small waving from the stage of the Berlinale Palast but at the Forum, dialogues between audience and filmmaker are *de rigueur*. Shows at CinemaxX, Arsenal, as well as repeat shows at the Delphi, have instant translation.

PANORAMA

Originally intended to showcase films that fell outside the strict guidelines of the Competition, the Panorama gives the Forum a run for its money in terms of innovative programming. But Panorama films are less serious than the Forum, with a spotlight on world independent movies, gay and lesbian and political films. Panorama films show in

CinemaxX and Zoo Palast with repeats at CinemaxX, CineStar and International. No translation, but most films show with English subtitles.

PERSPEKTIVE DEUTSCHES KINO AND NEW GERMAN CINEMA

The recently created 'Perspektive' reflects the festival's increased focus on New German cinema, with a range of interesting and provocative fare. If German cinema has a bad rep, this festival subverts the stereotypes. All films shown with English subtitles.

RETROSPECTIVE

Perhaps the festival's surest bet for sheer movie-going pleasure. While the Retrospective often concentrates on the established mainstream, it's an opportunity to see classics on the big screen. Themes have ranged from great directors such as Erich von Stroheim, William Wyler or Fritz Lang, to subjects like Cinemascope, The Cold War, Hollywood Mavericks and even Nazi entertainment films. There is also an hommage section, which celebrates the work of stars such as Kirk Douglas, Catherine Deneuve or Shirley McLaine. It's often accompanied by an exhibition and seminars at the nearby Film Museum (see below). Films show in the CinemaXX and Zeughaus Kino. English and subtitles.

TALENT CAMPUS

Not a film series *per se*, this newly created event offers a chance for young filmmakers from all over the world to come together, show their work and collaborate with global peers. Guest speakers and participants have included Anthony Minghella (*The English Patient, Cold Mountain*) Spike Lee and Wim Wenders and even John Cale, who did a lecture/demo on film scoring. Information and applications can be found on the Berlinale website.

TICKETS

Tickets can be bought up to three days in advance (four days for Competition repeats) at the main ticket office in the **Arkaden am Potsdamer Platz** (Alte Potsdamer Strasse, Tiergarten, 259 2000), the **Europa Center** (2nd floor, Breitscheidplatz 5, Charlottenburg, 348 0088) or at **Kino International** (Karl-Marx-Allee 33, corner of Schillingstrasse, Mitte, 242 5826). A limited number of tickets are also available for online booking. On the day of performance they must be bought at the theatre box office and last-minute tickets are often available. Queues for advance tickets can be absurdly long so it pays to come early and buy as much as you can at once. Films in the Competition and Panorama are described in a catalogue which you can pick up for a nominal price at the Arkaden am Potsdamer Platz. The Forum has its own programme booklet, available free at every Forum theatre. There is also a free daily Festival Journal available at all theatres with news, articles and screening information. Films are usually shown three times.

Ticket prices usually range from €7-€16 (hint: Berlinale Palast is cheaper during the day; all films showing on the last day play at reduced prices. A limited number of full festival passes (*Dauerkarte*) are available at the Arkaden am Potsdamer Platz or by mail (see website, below, for details). The last reported price was €140 (bring two passport photos). It's supposed to be good for all sections and showings but check the website for details to avoid disappointment. Information for each year goes up in January at www.berlinale.de. Ticket sales begin two or three days prior to opening.

High End 54 im Kunsthaus Tacheles, *p195.*

or Slovenian rock video retrospectives. All non-German films are in English or with English subtitles. This takes place in September at the Central and other venues.

Another new addition to the festival circuit is **Britspotting**, or British Independent Film Festival (www.britspotting.de), an annual compilation of the freshest low-budget contributions to celluloid coming out of the UK. Organised by the British Council, it shows up each May at the Central, Hackesche Höfe and other venues around town.

Berlin's status as a queer-friendly city is reflected in two film festivals, both in autumn, that spotlight gay and lesbian films. The more elaborate of the two is **Versaubert: The International Queer Film Festival** (www.queer-view.com/verzaubert), run by the same bunch who do the Fantasy Film Fest. Presented in November at the Hackesche Höfe, it offers a high-profile survey of gay cinema from around the world.

The Lesben Film Festival (www.lesbenfilmfestival.de) manifests itself every October with a wide international selection of films. Having found a home at the Arsenal, it flies in the face of the new mall culture of Potsdamer Platz. Many events are for women only, though some things might be screened again later at Arsenal or Xenon.

INFORMATION

The best way to find out what's going on is to check the listings in *tip* and *Zitty*, as well as *(030)* which is available free in most bars. You can also look at the English-language monthly, *Ex-Berliner*, but beware of dodgy listings information. Check for the notation **OV** or **OF** (original version or *Originalfassung*), **OmU** (original with subtitles) or **OmE** (original with English subtitles). But watch out, OmU could just as easily be a French or Chinese movie with German titles. The cinemas listed here are those most likely to be showing films in English but keep your eyes open for other venues.

Cinemas

Arsenal

Potsdamer Strasse 2, Potsdamer Platz (2695 5100/ www.fdk-berlin.de). U2, S1, S2, S25, S26 Potsdamer Platz. **Tickets** €6; €4 concessions. **No credit cards. Map** p316/306 E4.

This is the Berlin Cinematheque in everything but name. Its brazenly eclectic programming ranges from classic Hollywood to contemporary Middle Eastern cinema, from Russian art films to Italian horror movies, from Third World documentaries to silent films with live accompaniment. It shows many English-language films and sometimes foreign films with English subtitles. Occasionally filmmakers show up to present their work. The Arsenal's two state-of-the-art screening rooms in the Sony Center places it in the belly of the great Hollywood Beast, which is probably right where we need it. Like its bigger neighbours, the Arsenal is a major venue for the Berlin International Film Festival.

Babylon Kreuzberg (A&B)

Dresdener Strasse 126, Kreuzberg, 10999 (6160 9693). U1, U15, U8 Kottbusser Tor/bus 247. **Tickets** €4.50-€7. **No credit cards. Map** p307 G4.

This twin-screen theatre runs a varied programme featuring off-Hollywood, indie crossover and UK films. Formerly a neighbourhood Turkish cinema, its programme is now almost all English-language and this place offers a homey respite from the multiplex experience. Not to be confused with Filmkunsthaus Babylon (*see p195*).

Central

Rosenthaler Strasse 39, Mitte (2859 9973/www.eyz-kino.de). U8 Weinmeisterstrasse or S3, S5, S7, S9, S75 Hackescher Markt. **Tickets** €4-€6. **No credit cards. Map** p316/p302 F3.

On the edge of busy Hackesche Höfe, this duplex only occasionally offers its regular programming in English, except for special midnight shows (ranging from Pam Grier retros to Pamela Anderson sex tapes and a whole lot in between) and movies shown as part of the Berlin Beta Film Festival, Britspotting and other special events. It's a good bet that new management will keep up the programming policy.

CinemaxX Potsdamer Platz

Potsdamer Strasse 5, Potsdamer Platz, Tiergarten (2592 2111/www.cinemaxx.de). U2 or S1, S2, S25, S26 Potsdamer Platz. **Tickets** €3-€10. **No credit cards. Map** p316/p306 E4.

The biggest multiplex in town with 19 screens, two or three of which usually show something in English. The programming is strictly Hollywood mainstream in bland mall surroundings. A main venue for the Berlin International Film Festival.

CineStar Sony Center

Potsdamer Strasse 4, Tiergarten (2606 6400/ www.cinestar.de). U2, S1, S2, S25, S26, Potsdamer Platz. **Tickets** €4-€7.70; €4.50 concessions. **No credit cards. Map** p316/p306 E4.

Programming is much the same as its Potsdamer Platz neighbour, CinemaxX (*see above*), but, at the time of going to press, every screen was showing films in their original languages, mostly English. This eight-screen multiplex has been showing Hollywood films almost exclusively in their original English for the last two years. Despite a few random sparks of creativity, it is basically mainstream fare. Counteract their high prices by buying the 5-Star ticket – five entries for €27. Also a main venue for the Berlin International Film Festival.

Eiszeit

Zeughofstrasse 20, Kreuzberg (611 6016/2431 3030/www.eyz-kino.de). U1, U15 Görlitzer Bahnhof. **Tickets** €5-€6; €3 concessions. **No credit cards. Map** p307 H4.

In recent years, this has been the most energetic cinema in town, established by total film nuts compelled to inflict their unique tastes upon the world. No longer a down-at-heel cinema, its renovation, which saw the addition of plush seats and Dolby Surround, also brought in a more conservative selection of films to pay the bill. Still, this also means that you can sit in comfort to watch Eiszeit's own special blend of German underground, Hong Kong films, Japanimation, slash movies, gangsta films, US indies and assorted weirdness. Let's hope new management keeps it all going. Eiszeit is also a venue for the Britspotting festival and hosts occasional special events.

Filmkunsthaus Babylon

Rosa-Luxemburg-Strasse 30, Mitte (242 5076/ www.fkh-babylon.de). U2, U5, U8, S3, S5, S7, S75 Alexanderplatz or U2 Rosa-Luxemburg-Platz. **Tickets** €5.50-€6.50; €5.50 concessions. **No credit cards. Map** p316/p303 G3.

Not to be confused with Babylon Kreuzberg, this was once a premier East German theatre, housed in a landmark building by Hans Poelzig, who also designed the classic German silent film, *The Golem*. After years of renovation, the cinema is finally back to its full Weimar glory and it's worth a visit just for that. Heavy on retrospectives and thematic programming, it can show some interesting old East bloc films as well as occasional Hollywood films in English and foreign films with English subtitles. Its cosy auxiliary kino around the corner shows a lot of the English-language programming and you can count on a few surprises there.

Freiluftkino Kreuzberg

Mariannenplatz 2, courtyard of Haus Bethanien, Kreuzberg (www.eyz-kino.de). U1, U8 Kottbusser Tor or S3, S5, S9, S75 Ostbahnhof. **Tickets** €5.50. **No credit cards. Map** p307 G4.

This big-screen Dolby Stereo outdoor summer cinema, open June through August, offers a mix of past cinema hits, cult films and independent movies. There are occasional live events, including DJs before and after the films, a wide selection of food and drink, plus a playground featuring basketball and other games. Some shows are in English. Bring a pillow. And maybe an umbrella.

FSK

Segitzdamm 2, Kreuzberg (614 2464/www.fsk-kino.de). U1, U8 Kottbusser Tor or U8 Moritzplatz. **Tickets** €4.50-€6. **No credit cards. Map** p307 G4.

Named for the state film rating board, this two-screen cinema is deep in the heart of Turkish Kreuzberg, convenient for a range of bars and cafés. They usually get the German versions, but they occasionally have American or British indie films and documentaries, and some Taiwan or Hong Kong films with English subtitles.

Hackesche Höfe

Rosenthaler Strasse 40/41, Mitte (tickets from 2.30pm 283 4603/www.hackesche-hoefe.org). U8 Weinmeisterstrasse or S3, S5, S9, S75 Hackescher Markt. **Tickets** €4-€7. **No credit cards. Map** p316/p302 F3.

Being a four-flight walk-up hasn't stopped this from being one of the area's most well attended cinemas. Claiming to have the longest bar in Berlin probably helps. It shows mostly foreign films, with feature-length documentaries and occasional indie features in English. Venue for Verzaubert: International Queer Film Festival and other special events.

High End 54 im Kunsthaus Tacheles

Oranienburger Strasse 54-6, Mitte (283 1498/ Tacheles office 282 6185/www.highend54.de). U6 Oranienburger Tor or S1, S2, S25, S26 Oranienburger Strasse. **Tickets** €4.50-€6. **No credit cards. Map** p316/p302 F3.

Part of the multi-purpose Tacheles' many venues, with film programming that offers an undefinable mishmash of independent and off-Hollywood films as well as some interesting foreign movies. The two-screen cinema was once the screening room for the GDR State Film Archive. Films in original English seem to show as often as not, and foreign films sometimes have English subtitles.

Moviemento

Kottbusser Damm 22, Kreuzberg (692 4785/ www.moviemento.de). U7, U8 Hermannplatz, U8 Schönleinestrasse. **Tickets** €4.50-€6; €5.50 concessions. **No credit cards. Map** p307 G5.

Marlene on the wall

Founded in 1963, the Deutsche Kinemathek (German Cinematheque) has amassed a major collection of films, memorabilia, documentation and apparatus chronicling the history of German Cinema – including its transposition to Hollywood via Third Reich exiles. For years it was a sort of museum-without-portfolio, but with the move to Potsdamer Platz in 2000 the collection is now accessible by the public.

With a large exhibition space on two floors of the Filmhaus in the Sony Center, it is not only comprehensive but visually striking, with its posters, photos and maquettes. Particularly noteworthy is the two-storey-high video wall of disasters from Fritz Lang's adventure films and an exhibition space for films from the Third Reich that resembles a morgue. On a lighter note, highlights include a collection of clay animation figures from Ray Harryhausen films, such as the *Seven Voyages of Sinbad* and *Jason and the Argonauts.*

The main attraction, though, is the Marlene Dietrich collection, which displays personal effects, home movies, designer clothes and some revealing (and occasionally bitchy) correspondence. With regular exhibitions, often with accompanying films at the Arsenal cinema downstairs, plus the yearly retrospective programming at the Berlin Film Festival, there's always a lot to see. The vertigo-inducing entrance hall alone is worth the admission.

Filmmuseum Berlin

Potsdamer Strasse, Tiergarten (300 9030/ www.filmmuseum-berlin.de). U2, S1, S2, S25, S26 Potsdamer Platz. **Open** 10am-6pm Tue, Wed, Fri-Sun; 10am-8pm Thur. **Admission** €6; concessions €4. **No credit cards. Map** p306, p316 E4

This laid-back and youthful cinema, situated on the edge of Kreuzberg, shows a few films in English in three small screening rooms (232 seats altogether).

Odeon

Hauptstrasse 116, Schöneberg (7870 4019/ www.york.de/odeon.php3). U4, S45, S46 Innsbrucker Platz, S1, S4 Schöneberg. **Tickets** €4-€7.50, €5 concessions. **No credit cards. Map** p305 D6.

Berlin's favourite English-language cinema, deep in the heart of Schöneberg. It's a big old-fashioned single screen cinema, popular with the locals. Shows a reasonably intelligent, though increasingly mainstream, selection of Hollywood and UK fare.

Xenon

Kolonnenstrasse 5/6, Schöneberg (782 8850/ www.xenon-kino.de). U7 Kleistpark. **Tickets** €4-€6; €2.50 concessions. **No credit cards. Map** p306 E6.

A cosy cinema mostly dedicated to gay and lesbian programming. Mostly from the US and UK, the films are largely in English.

Zeughaus Kino

Unter den Linden 2, Mitte (203 0421/tickets 2030 4670). U8 Weinmeister Strasse, S3, S5, S7, S9, S75 Hackescher Markt. **Tickets** €5. **No credit cards. Map** p316/p302 F3.

Probably the last place one would look for English-language films is in the Deutsches Historisches Museum (*see p76*), but the Zeughaus Kino often hosts travelling retrospective shows and also programmes a variety of interesting series. They make a concerted effort to get the original versions and occasionally foreign films have English subtitles.

Video rental

If home video can be blamed for the decline of repertory cinema, Berlin has several video rental outlets that almost make up for the loss. (Note that all outlets require ID and proof of residency to open an account.)

The **Amerika-Gedenk-bibliothek** (Blücherplatz, Kreuzberg, 9022 6105/ www.zlb.de; closed Sun) has a good range of classics, silents, musicals, sci-fi, westerns and war films (movies are free). **The British Council Library** (Hackescher Markt 1, Mitte, 3110 9910/www.britcoun.de /e/berlin; closed Sun) has a large collection of British classic and contemporary films and TV shows. **Film Galerie 451** (Torstrasse 231, Mitte, 2345 7911/www.filmgalerie451.de) has a decent selection of English-language fare, including foreign films and TV series.

Incredibly Strange Video (Eisenacher Strasse 1, Schöneberg, 215 1770/www. incredibly.de, closed Sun) covers sci-fi, horror, crime, comedy, foreign films and TV shows. **Negativeland** (Dunkerstrasse 9, Prenzlauer Berg (447 7447/www.negativeland; closed Sun) has a meaty selection of Japanimation, biker films, lesbian vampire, documentaries and *Star Trek*. The amazing **Videodrom** (Mittenwalder Strasse 11, Kreuzberg, 695 740 611; closed Sun) offers 15,000 titles, encompassing mainstream, Japanimation, splatter, Hong Kong, women-in-prison films and cult TV shows.

Galleries

The established scene keeps on moving, the alternative begins to settle down.

Despite and/or because of its current economic difficulties, Berlin continues to act as a magnet for resident artists and their gallerists. And though the home market may be sluggish, Berlin artists enjoy an increasing international presence – represented at such major venues as Art/Basel and Art/Basel Miami Beach, for example, and New York's revived Armory Show. Then there's the growing success of two major home-grown events: the **Berlin Art Forum**, an art fair which takes place every autumn at the Messegelände (www.art-forum-berlin.de; *see p185*); and the **Biennale**, now taking place every two years, though at no fixed date (www.berlinbiennale.de). From February to September 2004, the **Neue Nationalgalerie** (*see p102*) hosted 200 masterworks from the Permanent Collection of New York's Museum of Modern Art. And we estimate that approaching a thousand other exhibitions and events will take place by the end of this year. Berlin can justifiably claim to be an established international art capital.

After the past decade's often chaotic recharting of art in Berlin, the map is more or less complete. Charlottenburg remains the classic showplace for some of (former West) Berlin's oldest established dealers, specialising in classic-contemporary pre-1990s art. More of the city's galleries cluster in and around Mitte's historic Scheunenviertel, spilling over into the Mitte Nord area above Torstrasse. But the main drag, Auguststrasse, is buckling under bus-loads of non-buying tourists and yuppie bar-hoppers. In the last few years, some of the more successful galleries have left the fraying edges of the tourist park for more rarefied, though still accessible, parts of Mitte. In a turn-of-the-century enclave on Zimmerstrasse, near Checkpoint Charlie, we find such luminaries as Arndt & Partner, Barbara Weiss, Volker Diehl, Max Hetzler, Klosterfelde and Nordenhake. Elsewhere, the likes of Büro Friedrich, Carlier/Gebauer, Chouakri Brahms and the second Max Hetzler gallery cluster under the arches of Jannowitzbrücke station, while Müllerdechiara, Johann König and Christian Nagel share the ground floor of a large art-deco building across from the Volksbühne on Rosa-Luxemburg-Platz. The Viertel is still an important stop, though. A Galerienrundgang, or walkabout, takes place three times a year for galleries around Auguststrasse, and an informal collective called KunstMitteNord now sponsors an Open Weekend (check local listings for the exact dates of these events).

Contemporary Fine Arts: solid. *See p200.*

Though the promise of a more-than-localised culture-boom in Friedrichshain still hasn't panned out – at least in part because of its isolated location – there are rumblings of a renaissance around Schlesisches Tor. And the alternative scene, though no less alternative, has finally found a few fixed addresses (see *p198* **Addressing the alternative**). Gentrifying trends will continue, of course: who knows what our next edition will report?

LISTINGS AND INFORMATION

Artery is the most complete art guide for Berlin and environs. It is published every two months and is sold at several galleries and book stores. *Berliner Galerien* serves all of Berlin but is more selective, and *Index* lists only those in Mitte. Both of these are free and available in most

Addressing the alternative

Berlin has always been known for having a lively alternative art scene. Up until recently, though, it could be hard to know just how and where to find it. In the early post-Wall period, the city was filled with unused and often unusable spaces. 'Openings' would pop up in fly-by-night 'galleries' occupying former border defences or abandoned factories. It was a wild scene, but limited to certain grapevines and often overlooked by the mainstream. The results were correspondingly private and somewhat localised.

Sweeping gentrification long ago wiped out the cheap and temporary spaces that made all that possible. And the internet has also altered the nature of 'alternative'. Information can be spread without depending on word of mouth. Artists communicate internationally, work travels more easily, and the whole framework to which it's possible to be alternative is now broader based.

In this new context, temporary spaces are more likely to be virtual than physical, while non-commercial and artist-run efforts have acquired more permanent addresses. These come in an assortment of shapes and sizes.

Close to the traditional model, **WBD** is an artist-run commercial gallery. It was founded in September 2000 by Martin Städeli, Michael Dethleffsen and Thomas Ravens with the simple aim of remaining independent of constraining institutions. They hold six shows a year, featuring not only their own work but also that of young artists such as Thaddäus Huppi, Joachim Grommek and Rudi Molacek.

Less traditionally, Ina Bierstadt, Bettina Carl and Alena Meier established **Capri** in 2001 as a purely non-commercial showcase both for themselves and for other independent artists such as Geka Heinke, Tina Habor or WBD's Thomas Ravens. In what was formerly a florist's (some of the fixtures are still intact), they present more project-oriented showings every two weeks, and pre-arrange on a three-month basis, allowing for well-organised press work and web updates.

And when **Rocket Shop** lost its premises to gentrification, co-founder Laura Schleussner began independently curating ambitious international projects in a variety of spaces. These included a five-day event of art, music and performance at Büro Friedrich (*see p199*). Rocket Shop has now landed at **Zentralbüro** (*pictured*), an impressive independent project centre for art, architecture and 'media development'. Their extraordinary space, in the former university book shop near Alexanderplatz, recently hosted a group effort including French art group Le Linéaire and Berlin's Subspace. Itself an independent project room begun by Jane Morren and Heiko Blankenstein, **Subspace** in turn invited young American artists to participate in their own first group showings in 2003.

galleries and museums. *U_Spot*, a newer bi-monthly in both German and English, lists many of the alternative spaces (again, concentrating mainly upon Mitte). And *tip* and *Zitty*, the two Berlin listings fortnightlies, cover most current showings throughout the city. Almost every gallery has a website, many in English. For those with serviceable German, www.art-in-berlin.de provides up-to-date information on current events and the inner workings of the market.

Mitte

Arndt & Partner

Zimmerstrasse 90-91 (280 8123/www.arndt-partner.de). U6 Kochstrasse. **Open** 11am-6pm Tue-Sat. **Credit cards** V, MC. **Map** p306 F4.

At this high-powered, high-quality establishment, gallerist Matthias Arndt shows excellent examples from the more accessible side of experimental work. Artists represented here include Sophie Calle, Thomas Hirschhorn, Mathilde ter Heijne, Keith Tyson and Massimo Vitali.

Galerie Barbara Thumm

Dircksenstrasse 41 (2839 0347/www.bthumm.de). U2, U5, U8 or S3, S5, S7, S9, S75 Alexanderplatz. **Open** 11am-6pm Tue-Fri; 1-6pm Sat. **Credit** MC, V. **Map** p303/316 G3.

A respected gallerist both here and abroad, Barbara Thumm delivers a solid program of established names like (e.) Twin Gabriel, Sabine Hornig, and Alex Katz, and newer artists Martin Dammann, Christian Hoischen and Ralf Ziervogel.

Galerie Barbara Weiss

Zimmerstrasse 88-89 (262 4284/www.galerie barbaraweiss.de). U6 Kochstrasse or U2 Stadtmitte. **Open** 11am-6pm Tue-Sat. **No credit cards**. **Map** p306 F4.

This beautiful gallery's rather spare, modest atmosphere is reflected in its style of exhibition. Gallerist Barbara Weiss specialises in serious, no-frills pre-

This kind of connection and cooperation among younger artists, often involving participation from other cities and scenes, is the hallmark of Berlin's new alternative – ambitious, adventurous and no longer merely local.

Capri
Brunnenstrasse 149, Mitte (6956 5383/ 4467 6649/www.capri-berlin.de). U8 Bernauer Strasse. **Open** 4-7pm Thur-Sat; & by appointment. **No credit cards. Map** p302 F1.

Subspace
Richard-Sorge-Strasse 30, Friedrichshain (4208 9774/subspaceberlin@yahoo.com). U5 Frankfurter Tor. **Open** 2-8pm Thur, Sat. **No credit cards. Map** p303 H3.

Rocket Shop
www.rocketshop.net

WBD
Brunnenstrasse 9, Mitte (2180 4657/ www.webede.com). U8 Rosenthaler Platz. **Open** 4-7pm Thur-Sat. **No credit cards. Map** p302 F2.

Zentralbüro
Spandauer Strasse 2, Mitte (0179 667 7950/www.zentralbuero-berlin.org). S3, S5, S7, S9, S75 Hackescher Markt. **Open** 4-8pm Tue-Sat. **No credit cards. Map** p316/p303 G3.

sentations of such international conceptually oriented artists as Frederike Feldmann, Boris Mikhailov and Jean-Fréderic Schnyder.

Galerie Berinson
Auguststrasse 22 (2838 7990/www.berinson.de). S1, S2, S25 Oranienburger Strasse. **Open** 2-7pm Tue-Sat. **No credit cards. Map** p302 F3.

A tiny, classic gem on the main drag, Hendrik Berinson's gallery is best known for exhibits of fine vintage photography by such 20th-century masters as Weegee and Peter Hujar. Other photographers in his collection include Lee Miller, Moholy-Nagy and even Stanley Kubrick.

Büro Friedrich
Holzmarktstrasse 15-18, S-Bahn Arches 53/54 (2016 5115/www.buerofriedrich.org). U8 or S3, S5, S7, S9, S75 Jannowitzbrücke. **Open** noon-6pm Tue-Sat. **No credit cards. Map** p303 G3.

Waling Boers began this non-profit venue to house internationally collaborative 'projects' with an interesting cultural-studies bent such as Higher Truth 2 (A Project on Fashion), work by Kurdish videographer Fikret Atay, and the 5-day Launch Option festival co-produced by Rocket Shop (*see p198* **Addressing the alternative**).

Carlier/Gebauer
Holzmarktstrasse 15-18, S-Bahn Arches 51/52 (280 8110/www.carliergebauer.com). U8 Jannowitzbrücke or S3, S5, S7, S9, S75. **Open** 11am-6pm Tue-Sat. **No credit cards. Map** p303 G3.

Ulrich Gebauer (who once worked with Barbara Thumm) and co-director Marie Blanche Carlier present a truly varied programme of larger-scale installations and work in various media by international and politically minded contemporary artists such as Luc Tuymans, Janaina Tschäpe and South African photographer Santu Mofokeng.

Chouakri Brahms Berlin
Holzmarktstrasse 15-18, S-Bahn Arches 47 (2839 1153/www.chouakri-brahms-berlin.com). U8 or S3, S5, S7, S9, S75 Jannowitzbrücke. **Open** 11am-6pm Tue-Sat. **No credit cards. Map** p303 G3.

In sleek, sparse surroundings, Mehdi Chouakri features both emerging artists and established international names such as Sylvie Fleurie, John M. Armleder and Mathieu Mercier.

C/O Berlin

Linienstrasse 144 (2809 1925/www.co-berlin.com). U6 Oranienburger Tor or S1, S2, S25 Oranienburger Strasse. **Open** 11am-7pm daily. **Admission** €5. **No credit cards. Map** p302 F3.

Co-founded by photographer Stephan Erfurt, this magnificent building contains studios, a rooftop lounge and a first-class space for exhibits by internationally known photographers such as Margaret Bourke-White, Alfred Eisenstaedt, André Rival and James Nachtway.

Contemporary Fine Arts

Sophienstrasse 21 (288 7870/www.cfa-berlin.com). U8 Weinmeisterstrasse or S3, S5, S7, S9, S75 Hackescher Markt. **Open** 10am-1pm, 2-6pm Mon-Fri; 11am-5pm Sat. **No credit cards. Map** p316/p302 F3.

Well-established off a quiet courtyard in the Sophie-Gips-Höfen, Brunno Brunnet and Nicole Hackert exhibit contemporary works by such solid representative artists as Cecily Brown, Daniel Richter, Raymond Pettibon, Juergen Teller and Gavin Turk.

Galerie Crone, Andreas Osarek

Kochstrasse 60 (2589 9370/www.cronegalerie.de). U6 Kochstrasse. **Open** 11am-6pm Tue-Sat. **No credit cards. Map** p306 F4.

Near Checkpoint Charlie, Andreas Osarek continues the tradition begun in Hamburg by his late partner, Ascan Crone. A wide spectrum of contemporary work from Rosemarie Trockel and Gilbert & George to Marc Brandenburg and Bjarne Melgaard.

Galerie Eigen + Art

Auguststrasse 26 (280 6605/www.eigen-art.com). S1, S2, S25 Oranienburger Strasse. **Open** 11am-6pm Tue-Sat. **No credit cards. Map** p302 F3.

From his Leipzig living room in the early 1980s (his gallery down there is still going strong today), to the Advisory Board of Art Forum, the ever-active Gerd Harry 'Judy' Lybke presents such luminaries as Tim Eitel, Carsten Nicolai and Neo Rauch.

Galerie Giti Nourbakhsch

Rosenthaler Strasse 72 (4404 6781/www.nourbakhsch.de). U8 Rosenthaler Platz. **Open** 11am-6pm Wed-Sat. **No credit cards. Map** p316/p302 F3.

This former hair salon remains as refreshing and brash as a quasi-established gallery can get, with a continuous, often difficult mix of known and emerging artists such as Piotr Janas, Zoe Leonard, Ryan McGinley, Vincent Tavenne and Hayley Tompkins.

Galerie Jette Rudolph

Joachimstrasse 3-4 (6130 3887/www.jette-rudolph.de). U8 Weinmeisterstrasse or Rosenthaler Platz. **Open** 1-7pm Tue-Fri; 11-4pm Sat. **No credit cards. Map** p316/p302 F3.

Young art historian Jette Rudolph's great eye actively pursues the work of emerging contemporary talent from Europe and America, such as Philip Argent (UK), Marcy Freedman (USA) and Alex Tennigkeit (D), while occasionally staging motorbike races and music fests along the way.

Johann König

Weydingerstrasse 10 (3088 2688/www.johannkoenig.de). U2 Rosa-Luxemburg-Platz. **Open** 11am-7pm Tue-Sat. **No credit cards Map** p303 G3.

A newer but active presence on the domestic and international scene, Johann König often presents sparse, politically oriented and conceptualised works by artists such as Tue Greenfort, Jeppe Hein and David Zink.

Klosterfelde

Zimmerstrasse 90/91 (283 5305/ww.klosterfelde.de). U6 Kochstrasse. **Open** 11am-6pm Tue-Sat. **No credit cards. Map** p306 F4.

Among the more varied of gallery menus, with occasional showings by invited guests, and seeming little method to the madness. Martin Klosterfelde focuses principally upon younger artists in as interesting and wide a range as Vibeke Tandberg, Steve Pippin and Nader Ahrinan.

Kuckei + Kuckei

Linienstrasse 158 (courtyard) (883 4354 www.kuckei-kuckei.de). U6 Oranienburger Tor or S1, S2, S25 Oranienburger Strasse. **Open** 11am-6pm Tue-Fri; 11-5pm Sat. **No credit cards. Map** p302 F3.

Ben and Hannes Kuckei continue to present young, more concept-related artists such as Anne Berning, Ingmar Alge, Hlynur Hallsson and Oliver van den Berg. The sensibility is uniformly interesting, clean and sparse.

Kunst-Werke

Augustrasse 69 (243 4590/www.kw-berlin.de). U6 Oranienburger Tor or S1, S2, S25 Oranienburger Strasse. **Open** noon-6pm Tue-Sun. **No credit cards. Map** p302 F3.

In a baroque former margarine factory (with a courtyard designed by Dan Graham; check out the winding slide), this co-host of the Biennale is the major non-profit showcase for culturally themed exhibits of contemporary artists, such as Terry Richardson's *Too Much* and the controversial RAF exhibit which, after much argument, should finally happen at the end of 2004. This is a good starting point for a gallery walk in Mitte.

Galerie Marcus Richter

Schröderstrasse 13 (2804 7283/www.galeriemarkusrichter.de). S1, S2, S25 Nordbahnhof. **Open** noon-7pm Tue-Sat. **Credit** AmEx, V. **Map** p302 F3.

In this sleek and perfect space in Mitte Nord, Marcus Richter concentrates on dramatic exhibits of contemporary minimal and conceptual work by artists like Colin Ardley, Beat Zoderer and David Tremlett.

Schipper & Krome: heady projects and cutting-edge greats. *See p202.*

Galerie Max Hetzler (1)

Zimmerstrasse 90-91 (229 2437/www.maxhetzler.com). U6 Kochstrasse. **Open** 11am-6pm Tue-Sat. **No credit cards. Map** p306 F4.

With two differently dramatic and versatile spaces, this wonderful gallery (in business long before its Berlin days began in 1994) represents an amazing roster of talent, including Darren Almond, Cady Noland, Christopher Wool and Albert Oehlen. A recent exhibit, Goat, celebrated publication of the Jeff Koons-designed book tribute to Mohammed Ali.

Other locations: Holzmarktstrasse 15-18, Arches 48 (2404 5630).

Maschenmode: Galerie Guido W Baudach

Torstrasse 230 (2804 7727/www.maschenmode-berlin.de). U6 Oranienburger Tor. **Open** noon-6pm Tue-Sat. **No credit cards. Map** p302 F3.

Behind its original shop facade, Maschenmode is now at the forefront of young Berlin galleries featuring new, emerging and wonderfully colourful local talent such as Tine Furler, Joep van Liefland and rising star Thomas Zipp.

Müllerdechiara

Weydingerstrasse 10 (3903 2040/www.mullerdechiara.com). U2 Rosa-Luxemburg-Platz. **Open** noon-7pm Tue-Sat. **No credit cards. Map** p303 G3.

New York gallerist Laurie De Chiara and Berlin art historian Sönke Magnus have chosen to debut young international conceptual artists in Berlin. Art featured includes exciting and difficult work by Christoph Draeger, Warren Neidlich, Jeffrey Reed and Mark Dean Veca.

Murata & Friends

Rosenthaler Strasse 39 (2809 9071/www.murataandfriends.de). U8 Weinmeisterstrasse or S3, S5, S7, S9, S75 Hackescher Markt. **Open** 1-7pm Wed-Fri; noon-6pm Sat. **No credit cards. Map** p316/p302 F3.

In this tiny, romantically warm atelier, tucked in above a courtyard by the Hackescher Höfe, Manabi Murata primarily features the work of young emerging contemporary Japanese artists (one of the rooms serves as visiting guest quarters) such as Tatsuya Higuchi, Yoshiaki Kaihtasu, and Tsuneo Shinano. The place has a distinctly uncommercial feel.

Neuer Berliner Kunstverein

Chauseestrasse 128-129 (280 7020/www.nbk.org). U6 Oranienburger Tor. **Open** noon-6pm Tue-Fri; 2-6pm Sat-Sun. **No credit cards. Map** p302 F2.

This non-profit organisation was founded in 1969 through a citizens' initiative, with the purpose of bringing contemporary art to a wider public. In addition to lectures, a video archive and art-lending library, it features exhibitions by young talent, with an emphasis on photography and video.

Neugerriemschneider

Linienstrasse 155 (courtyard) (2887 7277). U6 Oranienburger Tor or S1, S2, S25 Oranienburger Strasse. **Open** 11am-6pm Tue-Sat. **No credit cards. Map** p302 F3.

At the back of a courtyard, Tim Neuger and Burkhard Riemschneider have made a bright, friendly viewing-space in which to show the latest and hippest art from America and Europe, plus a host of works by local talent. Names include Franz Ackermann, Keith Edmier, Sharon Lockhart, Jorge Pardo and Elizabeth Peyton.

Prüss & Ochs

Sophienstrasse 18 (2839 1387/www.pruess-ochs-gallery.de). U8 Weinmeisterstrasse or S3, S5, S7, S9, S75 Hackescher Markt. **Open** noon-6pm Tue-Fri; 11-6pm Sat. **No credit cards. Map** p302 F3.

Begun in 1997 as part of their European cultural exchange with China, Prüss and Ochs mostly feature important young Chinese artists such as Fang Lijun, Yin Xiuzhen and Xu Bing, with occasional showings from other South-east Asian countries.

Schipper & Krome

Linienstrasse 85 (2839 0139/www.schipper-krome.com). U8 Rosenthaler Platz. **Open** 11am-6pm Tue-Sat. **No credit cards. Map** p302 F3.

Since their beginnings in the early 1990s, Esther Schipper and Michael Krome have always had a penchant for heady projects and cutting-edge greats, and their tradition continues with Angela Bulloch, Nathan Carter, Carsten Höller and Atelier van Lieshout, to name a few.

Galerie Volker Diehl

Zimmerstrasse 88-91 (2248 7922/www.dv-art.com). U6 Kochstrasse. **Open** 11am-6pm Tue-Sat. **No credit cards. Map** p306 F4.

One of the original organisers of the Berlin Art Forum, Volker Diehl has long been an established and prominent member of the international art world, concentrating his efforts upon younger contemporary artists including Angela Dwyer, Marcel Dzama and Jaume Plensa.

Galerie Weisser Elefant

Auguststrasse 21 (2888 4454). S1, S2, S25 Oranienburger Strasse. **Open** 2-7pm Tue-Fri; 1-5pm Sat. **No credit cards. Map** p302 F3.

Ralf Bartolomaüs has exhibited often difficult and challenging work by younger artists since before Reunification. Here, situated in and supported by the Kulturamt Mitte, he continues with recent work by Kai Feldschur, Pia Linz and a series of new artists from Korea. Unlike some of the other sharks in the business, Bartolomaüs isn't in it for the money: he has a great eye and loves art.

Galerie Wieland

Ackerstrasse 5 (2838 5751/www.galerie-wieland.de). U8 Rosenthaler Platz. **Open** 2-7pm Wed-Fri; noon-5pm Sat. **No credit cards. Map** p302 F2.

With often surprisingly satisfying results, Angelika Wieland's small and unassuming gallery remains true to her creed of presenting work by mid-career artists whose use of sophisticated form challenges the boundaries between high and low art, such as Eva Castringius, Maverick and David Rothman.

Wohnmaschine

Tucholskystrasse 35 (3087 2015/www.wohnmaschine.de). S1, S2, S25 Oranienburger Strasse. **Open** 11am-6pm Tue-Sat. **No credit cards. Map** p302 F3.

Friedrich Loock first began the gallery in his nearby apartment in 1988, giving it the German name for Le Corbusier's *machine à habiter*: living with art and in art. Now he offers interesting, sometimes minimal propositions, often through the work of young Japanese artists such as Yoshihiro Suda and Takehito Koganezawa, as well as Robert Lippok and Holly Zausner.

Zwinger Galerie

Gipsstrasse 3 (859 8907). U8 Weinmeisterstrasse or Rosenthaler Platz. **Open** 2-7pm Tue-Fri; 11am-5pm Sat. **No credit cards. Map** p302 F3.

In this tiny and intimate courtyard gallery, Werner Müller, a long-established member of the art community, turns enthusiasm and a reputable eye towards younger talents such as Ueli Etter, Tobias Hauser, Theresa Lükenwerk and Susi Pop.

Prenzlauer Berg

Akira Ikeda Gallery Berlin

Pfefferberg, Schönhauser Allée 176 (4432 8510/www.akiraikedagallery.com). U2 Senefelderplatz. **Open** 11am-6pm Tue-Sat. **No credit cards. Map** p303 G2.

Hidden at the back of a dilapidated 19th-century brewery, this magnificent third branch of the Japan/NY gallery, specialising in work post-1945, has room enough for the mammoth di Suveros, older and new, and works by the Starn Twins, Imi Knoebel and Noriyuki Haraguchi.

Galerie Vostell Berlin im Pfefferberg

Pfefferberg, Schönhauser Allée 176 (885 2280/www.vostell.de). U2 Senefelderplatz. **Open** noon-6pm Tue-Sat. **No credit cards. Map** p303 G2.

In a new location directly across from Akira Ikeda, Rafael Vostell continues to champion such 1960s luminaries as Yoko Ono, Naim June Paik and his father, Fluxus pioneer Wolf Vostell. Plus emerging international artists such as Qin Yufen and Constantino Ciervo.

Kreuzberg

Künstlerhaus Bethanien

Mariannenplatz 2 (616 9030/www.bethanien.de). U1, U8, U15 Kottbusser Tor or U1, U15 Görlitzer Bahnhof. **Open** 2-7pm Tue-Sun. **Map** p307 G4.

Housed in a former 19th-century hospital complex, this Berlin institution began as an art-squat in the '70s, and has since developed a major studio-residency program for foreign artists in Berlin. Though funding cuts loom larger than ever, its three main galleries are always occupied.

Laura Mars Group

Sorauerstrasse 3 (6107 4630/www.lauramars.de). U1, U15 Schlesiches Tor. **Open** noon-7pm Tue-Fri. **No credit cards. Map** p307 H5.

In this wonderful surprise of a small space on a quiet residential street near the slowly up-and-coming Schlesische Strasse, Gundula Schmitz and Oliver Koerner bring the likes of Kerstin Drechsel, Marc Brandenburg and Louvre Boutique to a once art-neglected corner of Kreuzberg.

NGBK

Oranienstrasse 25 (615 3031/www.ngbk.de). U1, U8 Kottbusser Tor. **Open** noon-6:30pm daily. **No credit cards. Map** p307 G4.

Begun in the smokey haze of the late 1960s, the NGBK is still confrontational and energetic, continuing their group-based projects with a social

Camera Work.
See p204.

conscience – legal/illegal, as a recent example, featured work by Dennis Oppenheim and Abbie Hoffman. The entrance is through the bookstore.

Tiergarten

Daadgalerie

Kurfürstenstrasse 58 (2613640/www.berliner-kuenstlerprogramm.de). U1, U2, U4 Nollendorfplatz. **Open** 12:30-7pm daily. **No credit cards.** **Map** p305 D4.

Above the Café Einstein, the gallery of the 40-year-old Berlin Artists-in-Residence Program continues to invite important and aspiring artists to Berlin. Stan Douglas, Rachel Whiteread and Damien Hirst have all passed through here.

Galerie Eva Poll

Lützowplatz 7 (261 7091/www.poll-berlin.de). U1, U2, U4 Nollendorfplatz. **Open** 10am-1pm Mon; 11am-6:30pm Tue-Fri; 11am-3pm Sat. **No credit cards.** **Map** p305 D4.

Opened in 1968 with her collection of critical realists from the 1960s, Eva Poll's beautiful gallery (her private apartment is still in the back) includes, among others, Sabina Grzimek, Kubiak & Rauch, Peter Sorge and Genny Wiegmann. Her Stiftung Eva Poll, at Gipsstrasse 3 in Mitte, also exhibits photography.

Haus am Lützowplatz

Lützowplatz 9 (261 3805/www.hausamluetzowplatz-berlin.de). U1, U2, U4 Nollendorfplatz. **Open** 11am-6pm Tue-Sun. **No credit cards.** **Map** p305 D4.

Though exhibits were held in this building as early as 1949, the non-profit society which has occupied it since the early '60s (Elvira Bach is on the board) maintains a pledge to present both unknown Berlin artists and guests such as Dorothy Iannone, Mario Mertz and Emmett Williams.

Charlottenburg

Galerie Anselm Dreher

Pfalzburger Strasse 80 (883 5249/796 5572/www.galerie-anselm-dreher.com). U1 Hohenzollernplatz, U1, U9 Spichernstrasse or U15 Uhlandstrasse. **Open** 2-6:30pm Tue-Fri; 11am-2pm Sat. **No credit cards.** **Map** p305 C5.

Since opening his gallery on the Wilmersdorf border in 1967, Anselm Dreher continues the lonely task of championing hard-core minimalist and concrete works by newcomers and old masters such as Dennis Oppenheim, Joseph Kosuth and Carl Andre, and he does it wonderfully.

Camera Work

Kantstrasse 149 (3150 4783/www.camerawork.de). S3, S5, S7, S9, S75 Savignyplatz. **Open** 10am-6pm Tue-Fri; 11am-4pm Sat. **No credit cards.** **Map** p305 C4.

Named for the magazine started by Alfred Stieglitz, this magnificent courtyard space offers prime viewing of some of the most important photographic work of the century, including comprehensive exhibitions of Irving Penn, Leni Riefenstahl, Peter Beard and Helmut Newton.

Galerie Georg Nothelfer

Uhlandstrasse 184 (881 4405). U15 Uhlandstrasse. **Open** 11am-6:30pm Tue-Fri; 10am-2pm Sat. **Credit** V. **Map** p305 C4.

Longtime doyen Nothelfer quietly and importantly pursues his love of Informel and Tachist work, best exemplified by artists such as Walter Stöhner, Henri Michaux, and Jan Voss.

Other locations: *Corneliusstrasse 3, Tiergarten (575 9806).*

Galerie Haas & Fuchs

Niebuhrstrasse 5 (8892 9190/www.haasundfuchs.de). U15 Uhlandstrasse or S3, S5, S7, S9, S75 Savignyplatz. **Open** 10am-6pm Tue-Fri; 11am-2pm Sat. **No credit cards.** **Map** p305 C4.

Next door to his original Galerie Michael Haas, which now specialises in classic contemporary art post-1945, Michael Haas and his partner Michael Fuchs here feature such varied artists as Howard Hodgkin, Richard Jordan and Frank Thiel.

Raab Galerie Berlin

Kantdreieck, Fasanenstrasse 81 (261 9217/www.raab-galerie.de). U2, U9 or S3, S5, S7, S9, S75 Zoologischer Garten. **Open** 10am-7pm Mon-Fri; 10am-4pm Sat. **No credit cards.** **Map** p305 C4.

Since her monumental first show of Jungen Wilden in 1978, Ingrid Raab has been a grand champion of work by young artists such as Paul Vergier, Ben Henriques and Christian Sauer, and stalwarts like Lüpertz, Castelli and the wonderful Odd Nerdrum. Her enthusiasm is contagious.

Galerie Springer & Winckler

Fasanenstrasse 13 (315 7220/www.artnet.com). U2, U9, S3, S5, S7, S9, S75 Zoologischer Garten or U9, U15 Kurfürstendamm. **Open** 10am-1pm, 2-6pm Tue-Fri; 11am-3pm Sat. **No credit cards.** **Map** p305 C4.

Originally the gallery of Rudolph Springer (one of the grand old men of Berlin's art world, who'd been in the business since 1948), this space is now run by his son Robert and partner Gerald Winkler. These days, the pair concentrate mainly on lush German post-war artists such as Georg Baselitz, Markus Lüpertz, Sigmar Polke and Gerhard Richter.

Galerie Thomas Schulte

Mommsenstrasse 56 (324 0044/www.galeriethomasschulte.de). U7 Adenauerplatz or Wilmersdorfer Strasse or S3, S5, S7, S9, S75 Charlottenburg. **Open** 11am-6pm Mon-Fri; 11am-3pm Sat. **No credit cards. Map** p304 B4.

New Yorker Thomas Schulte and Swiss-born Eric Franck opened their doors in 1991, hoping to breathe some life into the local market. This is now one of Berlin's finer, more upmarket galleries, featuring work by the likes of Richard Artschwager, Rebecca Horn, Robert Mapplethorpe Gordon Matta-Clark and Tony Oursler.

Gay & Lesbian

Even the mayor says, 'I'm gay, and that's OK.'

SchwuZ. *See p212.*

Berlin has a long tradition of open-mindedness. As early as the 18th century it had the reputation of being extremely tolerant towards people of other faiths and sexual orientation, being the capital of a Kingdom whose king himself, Frederick the Great, was rumoured to love 'in the Greek fashion'.

In 1897 the first institution in the world with an emancipatory homosexual agenda was founded in Berlin – the Wissenschaftlich-Humanitäres Komitee (Scientific-Humanitarian Committee). Its main aims were legal reform, scientific research into the 'Third Gender' and the publication of emancipatory literature.

In the 1920s Berlin became the first city in the world to have what we might recognise as a large gay and lesbian community, frequented by such diverse people as Marlene Dietrich, Ernst Röhm and Christopher Isherwood. After 1933, Hitler put a stop to all that. Gays were persecuted and forced to wear the Pink Triangle in concentration camps. They are commemorated on a plaque outside Nollendorfplatz station.

In the late 1960s Berlin resumed its role as one of the world's homosexual meccas. The gay and lesbian scenes today are big and bold, mostly concentrated in Schöneberg, Kreuzberg, Mitte and Prenzlauer Berg. Summer is the most exciting time of year, when all contingents come together and enjoy themselves. **The Schwullesbisches Strassenfest** (*see p183*) on Motzstrasse in mid-June is followed by **Christopher Street Day Parade** (*see p183*), a flamboyant annual event where up to 500,000 gays and lesbians unite to commemorate the Stonewall riots.

The scene includes much more than just the venues listed here, especially in terms of cultural events such as plays, drag performances or the Gay Teddy award for the best gay film at the **Berlin International Film Festival** (*see p186*). Queer films can be seen Mondays at Kino International (Karl-Marx-Allee 33, Mitte; 242 5826). The Wong Show at SchwuZ invites the audience to fight, literally, over the quality of the trashy acts performing on stage. Gay art and history is documented at the **Schwules Museum** (*see p96*) which also has an archive. If you want to, you can live an entirely queer life in Berlin, what with the numerous gay and lesbian

Party info and free publications can be picked up at **Café Melitta Sundström**. *See p207.*

businesses cropping up around the city (*see p208* **The community of enterprise**). And of course there is gay sex, any time of the day or night, any day of the week. The Berlin scene offers sex parties for every taste and perversion, from pub darkrooms to dance clubs.

In June 2001, before being nominated by his party to be the new mayor of Berlin, Klaus Wowereit took the wind out of the tabloids' sails by telling them: 'I am gay, and that's OK!' ('Ich bin schwul, und das ist auch gut so!') His epigram became the catchphrase of the year. Lo and behold, a century after the first cautious attempts at viewing gay sexuality in an open-minded way, Berlin is governed by an openly gay man. And the tabloids even like his partner.

INFO AND PUBLICATIONS

For gay and lesbian helplines, information and counselling services, *see p275.*

Sergej (www.sergej.de) and *Siegessäule* (www.siegessaeule.de) are monthly listings freebies that can be found at most venues. Apart from a what's-on calendar, both list all gay and lesbian venues and pinpoint them on a city map. *Sergej* also lists clubs, parties and fetish venues separately.

A free *Berlin Fun Map* (www.gaymap.info-english) pinpointing places of interest can be picked up at many venues, as can the free *Siegessäule Kompass* (www.siegessaeule-kompass.de), a classified directory of everything gay or lesbian.

Mixed

In West Berlin gays and lesbians trod separate paths for decades, but in the East things were different. Homosexuals of both genders shared bars and clubs, making common cause under the Communists, a tradition that hasn't disappeared despite the emergence of male-only cruise bars in Prenzlauer Berg.

That said, the western half of the city has changed. The late 1990s saw an increase in the number of mixed gay and lesbian venues, and lesbians made their voices felt in formerly gay-only organisations and political institutions. One-nighters now usually target both gays and lesbians. Below we list a selection of mixed cafés, bars and clubs.

Bars & cafés

Prenzlauer Berg

Café Amsterdam

Gleimstrasse 24 (448 0792/www.pension-amsterdam.de). U2, S4, S8, S10 Schönhauser Allee. **Open** 3pm-4am Mon-Sat; 9am-4am Sun. **Credit** AmEx, MC, V. **Map** p303 G1.
Nice café in daytime. At night a good bar to get wrecked in, with loud house and techno music. Snacks and salads. Mostly youngish crowd. Central location. Popular.

Schall & Rauch
Gleimstrasse 23 (443 3970/4433 9722/www.schall-und-rauch-berlin.de). U2, S4, S8, S10 Schönhauser Allee. **Open** 9am-3am daily. **No credit cards. Map** p303 G1.
Relaxed and friendly atmosphere, good selection of food, central location – an ideal place to spend the afternoon or kick off an evening in Prenzlauer Berg.

Friedrichshain

HT
Kopernikusstrasse 23 (2900 4965/www.hat-berlin.de). U5 Frankfurter Tor. **Open** 5pm-2am daily. **No credit cards. Map** p88.
Comfortable but quiet café and bar in a popular nightlife district. Good service, friendly staff.

Kreuzberg

Barbie Bar
Mehringdamm 77 (6956 8610/www.barbiebar.de). U6, U7 Mehringdamm. **Open** *Summer* 2pm-4am daily. *Winter* 4pm-4am daily. **No credit cards. Map** p306 F5.
Tacky and camp, with lots of dolls and pictures of drag queens adorning the walls, the Barbie Bar is also a stylish place, with comfortable easy chairs and quiet music, which makes it good for chatting. Small terrace in summer.

Café Melitta Sundström
Mehringdamm 61 (692 4414). U6, U7 Mehringdamm. **Open** 10am-late daily. **No credit cards. Map** p306 F5.
Daytimes, this place serves as a café where students discuss relationships and why they have a problem getting up in the morning. In the evenings, it's full of gays too lazy to go to Schöneberg and lesbians who wouldn't go to Schöneberg anyway. At weekends, it's the entrance to SchwuZ (*see below*) and the place is hectic and fun. Best in summer, when the big terrace is open late, luring all of queer Kreuzberg.

Möbel Olfe
End of Dresner Strasse/Kotbusser Tor (6165 9612/www.moebel-olfe.de). U1, U15, U8 Kottbusser Tor. **Open** 6pm-late Tue-Sun. **No credit cards. Map** p307 G4.
Not an ideal situation for a gay bar, wedged among Turkish snack bars and empty shops in a down-at-heel 1960s development at Kottbusser Tor, and open to hostile gazes through large glass windows on both sides. But this place has been packed since the day it opened. Unpretentious, crowded and fun.

Roses
Oranienstrasse 187 (615 6570). U1, U15, U8 Kottbusser Tor. **Open** 10pm-5am daily. **No credit cards. Map** p307 G4.
Whatever state you're in (the more of a state, the better) you'll fit in just fine at this boisterous den of glitter. It draws customers from right across the sexual spectrum, who mix and mingle and indulge in excessive drinking amid the plush, kitsch decor. No place for uptights, always full, very Kreuzbergish.

Schöneberg

Neues Ufer
Hauptstrasse 157 (7895 7900). U7 Kleistpark. **Open** 11am-2am Mon-Sun. **No credit cards. Map** p306 E5.
Established in the early 1970s, this is the city's oldest gay café, now run by new management. The former name Anderes Ufer (The Other Side) was changed to Neues Ufer (The New Side), symbolising a new beginning. Relaxed daytime scene.

Clubs & one-nighters

Mitte

Blu
Neue Schönhauser Strasse 20 (443 1980/www.blu-club.de/club/index.php). U8 Weinmeisterstrasse. **Open** 11pm-late Fri-Sun; 9pm-late Wed; 8pm-1am Sun. **Admission** €5. **No credit cards. Map** p316/p303 G3.
Newest addition to the club scene in Mitte pulls a see-and-be-seen crowd of youngish guys and girls, and claims to have the longest bar in Europe. Friday parties are hosted by various drag queens; third Saturday of the month is GaymeBoy (*see p211*); first Saturday of the month is S.L.U.T Club (pervy party); second and fourth Saturday is Diamonds and Pearls (party for lesbians, men in female company only); Sundays is the Real T-Dance (mixed party).

Friedrichshain

Die Busche
Mühlenstrasse 11-12 (296 0800/www.diebusche.de). U1, U15, S3, S5, S6, S7, S9 Warschauer Strasse. **Open** 10pm-5am Wed, Sun; 10pm-6am Fri, Sat. **Admission** €3.50-€5. **No credit cards. Map** p307 H4.
An East German relic: loud, tacky, mixed and packed, this is one of east Berlin's oldest discos, full of stylish lesbians, gay teens and their girlfriends. A must for kitsch addicts and Abba fans; a no-go area for guys who like a masculine atmosphere.

Kreuzberg

SO36
Oranienstrasse 190 (6140 1306/www.so36.de). U1, U12, U15, U8 Kottbusser Tor. **Open** 10pm-late, Mon, Wed; 7pm-late every 2nd Tue; 10pm-late 1st Fri/mth, last Sat/mth; 6pm-late Sun. **Admission** *Parties* €3-€8. *Concerts* €8-€20. **No credit cards. Map** p307 G4.
A key venue for both gays and lesbians. Monday (Electric Ballroom) is not completely gay, but the

The community of enterprise

Browse through the **Siegessäule-Kompass** (www.siegessaeule-kompass.de), the 150-page classified directory of everything gay or lesbian in Berlin, and you'll see that, if you wish, you can live an exclusively gay or lesbian life here. You can work at a gay company, work out at a gay gym. You can use a gay internet provider, buy clothes at a gay shop, eat in a gay restaurant, and pay for it all with a gay credit card. And when it's time to go, a gay undertaker can supply you with pink coffin or leather urn.

And as unemployment worsens, more and more gays and lesbians are trying their luck as entrepreneurs, often with businesses catering specifically to a gay clientele. But they don't do it purely for business reasons. They do it to be part of the scene.

Once such business is **030-Workstation** (www.030-workstation.de), a gay and lesbian employment agency set up by Rainer Calmer in mid-2002 after 18 years of being an employee himself. Originally Calmer's thinking was that gays and lesbians constituted 20 per cent of Berlin's workforce and had never been targeted. But he also found something he wasn't expecting. Because 030-Workstation was part of the scene, clients felt able to be frank and open about their employment problems. This extension of his business beyond the merely economic makes Calmer proud. He perceives it as a contribution towards the solidarity, freedom and independence of gays and lesbians.

Personal freedom and independence were also reasons why Jenny Danger (*pictured*) set up her antique accessories shop, **Antik-Zubehör** (Mittenwalder Strasse 50, Kreuzberg, 6950 4057, www.antiq-zubehoer.de). Danger doesn't have a target group but she does have an agenda. She wants and expects customers to see that she and her partner, who also works in the shop, are lesbians. And she hopes that this realisation will help fuel wider acceptance.

The most successful new enterprise is **gayromeo.com** (www.gayromeo.com), a gay cruising website. With over 100,000 users and hundreds more registering every day, it has become Germany's largest such website since its October 2002 launch. About 30 per cent of its users are non-German and this number is also rising fast.

Group identity is an important part of it, as many gayromeo staff are volunteers. Payments are also voluntary and there is no advertising – something that site-owners Jens Schmidt and Manuel Abraham insist they will not change. Apart from making a satisfactory living from donations, they also feel a responsibility to those who rely on their website to make gay contacts – gays in rural areas, say, or gays in non-democratic countries. Schmidt says his biggest satisfaction would be if two Iranians came together through his website, had good sex – and the mullahs could do nothing about it.

It's noticeable that younger gay or lesbian enterprises in Berlin all have one thing in common: the tone is less formal than elsewhere. It's 'Du' rather than 'Sie'. Why? Because apart from the act of purchase, there's also a spirit of community, which in turn has the economic benefit of ensuring customer loyalty. The result of all this is 'community enterprises', and they're thriving like never before.

hard techno sounds draw a largely male following. Last Saturday in the month is Gay Oriental Night (Gayhane), with belly-dancing, transvestites and Turkish hits. Monthly m.appeal parties (first Friday of the month) bring together every imaginable manifestation of womanhood (plus gay friends) to dance to house and disco. Sunday is Café Fatal, where gays and lesbians get into ballroom dancing. Every second Tuesday, Bingo Bar attracts a colourful mixture of guys and girls, who cross out numbers to the sounds of trash-queen announcers.

Gay

You don't need to look for the gay scene in Berlin. It'll find you in about ten minutes. Some areas, however, are gayer than others, especially Schöneberg's Motzstrasse and Fuggerstrasse, and the area around Schönhauser Allee station in Prenzlauer Berg. Bars, clubs, shops and saunas are so many and various it's impossible to take them all in on one visit.

The age of consent is 16 – same as for everyone else. Gays making contact in public is rarely of interest to passers-by, but bigots do exist and so does anti-gay violence. In the west it tends to be by gangs of Turkish teenagers, in the east by right-wing skinhead Germans. But violence is rare and compared to other cities, Berlin is an easy-going place.

The scene is always shifting, so the places listed here may have changed or new ones might have sprung up by the time you read this. *Siegessäule* and *Sergej* are the best sources of current information.

Where to stay

Most hotels know gays are important to the tourist industry and are courteous and helpful. Here are some catering specifically for gay men.

Art Hotel-Connection Berlin

Fuggerstrasse 33, Schöneberg, 10777 (210 218 800/fax 210 218 830/www.arthotel-connection.de. U1, U2, U12, U15 Wittenbergplatz. **Rates** €60-85 single; €85-€110 double; €130. **Credit** AmEx, MC, V. **Map** p305 D5.

Comfortable and spacious rooms (most en suite), sumptuous breakfast included, prime location right in the middle of Schöneberg's gay area. The SM room is fitted with a sling, stocks and a cage.

Eastside

Schönhauser Allee 41, Prenzlauer Berg, 10435 (4373 5484/fax 4373 5485/www.eastside-gayllery.de). U2 Eberswalder Strasse. **Rates** €34-€39 single; €64-€74 double. **Credit** AmEx, MC, V. **Map** p303 G1.

Quiet guesthouse in the centre of Prenzlauer Berg, convenient for the gay scene. All rooms have TV/VCR and private bath.

Enjoy Bed & Breakfast

c/o Mann-O-Meter, Bülowstrasse 106, Schöneberg, 10783 (2362 3610/fax 2362 3619/www.ebab.de). U1, U2, U4 Nollendorfplatz. **No credit cards. Map** p305 D5.

This excellent accommodation service caters to both gays and lesbians, and can fix you up with a room in the private apartment of fellow queers for as little as €20 a night. You can view and book rooms on their website.

LGHEI - Lesbian & Gay Hospitality Exchange International

c/o J. Wiley, Schönleinstrasse 20, Kreuzberg, 10967 (691 9537/fax 691 9537/www.lghei.org). U8 Schönleinstrasse.

This organisation is comprised of a worldwide network of lesbians and gay men who offer each other the gift of short-term hospitality during their travels on the basis of reciprocity. No sex.

RoB Play & Stay Apartments

c/o RoB, Fuggerstrasse 19, Schöneberg (2196 7400/ www.rob.nl). U1, U2, U15 Wittenbergplatz. **Open** noon-8pm Mon-Sat. **Rates** (min 3-night stay) €120-€145 single; €145 double. **Credit** AmEx, MC, V. **Map** p305 D5.

Two apartments to rent including kitchen, bathroom, TV, VCR, internet access, own mobile telephone number – and a playroom.

Schall und Rauch

Gleimstrasse 23, Prenzlauer Berg, 10437 (443 3970/ fax 4433 9722/www.schall-und-rauch-berlin.de). U2, S4, S8, S10 Schönhauser Allee. **Rates** €40 single; €75 double. **No credit cards. Map** p303 G1.

Clean, modern rooms next door to the café of the same name (above). All rooms are en suite, complete with TV and telephone; rate includes breakfast and decreases the longer you stay.

Tom's House

Eisenacher Strasse 10, Schöneberg, 10777 (218 5544/www.toms-house-alster-berlin.de). U1, U2, U4, U15 Nollendorfplatz. **Rates** €35-€65 single; €85 double. **Credit** AmEx, DC, MC, V. **Map** p305 D5.

An eccentric and unpredictable establishment deep in the heart of gay Schöneberg, with seven double rooms, a single one and first-rate buffet brunches, served from 10am to 1pm.

Bars, cafés & restaurants

Prenzlauer Berg

Flax

Chodowieckistrasse 41 (4404 6988/www.flax-berlin.de). U2, S4, S8, S10 Schönhauser Allee. **Open** 5pm-3am Mon-Fri; 3pm-2am Sat; 10am-2am Sun. **No credit cards. Map** p303 H2.

It may be on the edge of the Prenzlauer Berg gay scene, but the Flax has developed into one of the most popular café/bars in the east, mainly pulling a young, mixed crowd.

Greifbar

Wichertstrasse 10 (444 0828/www.greifbar.net). U2 S4, S8, S10 Schönhauser Allee. **Open** 10pm-late daily. **No credit cards**. **Map** p303 G1.
Cruisy bar with a younger Prenzlauer Berg crowd looking for adventure and pleasure, either by picking someone up or by roaming about in the large darkrooms. There's also a good atmosphere if you just want to spend the night drinking.

Guppi

Gleimstrasse 31 (4373 9611/www.guppi-berlin.de). U2, S4, S8, S10 Schönhauser Allee. **Open** 2pm-2am daily. **No credit cards**. **Map** p303 G1.
Stylish two-storey bar with high ceilings and easy chairs. Low music and warm colours make it a relaxing place for coffee and cake in daytime or drinks at night. Occasional house parties, mixed crowd.

Pick Ab!

Greifenhagener Strasse 16 (445 8523/www.pickab.com). U2, S4, S8, S10 Schönhauser Allee. **Open** 10pm-6am daily. **No credit cards**. **Map** p303 G1.
Late-night cruise bar decorated in camp taste. Like most bars of this kind, it fills up best during winter, when cruising heated backrooms is more comfortable than roaming freezing parks.

Stiller Don

Erich-Weinert-Strasse 67 (283 4392/www.stillerdon.de). U2, S4, S8, S10 Schönhauser Allee. **Open** 8pm-late daily. **No credit cards**. **Map** p303 G1.
Formerly home to the local avant-garde, now attracting a mixed crowd from all over Berlin. The set-up is like a cosy café, but it gets high-spirited at weekends and on Mondays.

Kreuzberg

Bargelb

Mehringdamm 62 (7889 9299). U6, U7 Mehringdamm. **Open** 8pm-late daily. **No credit cards**. **Map** p306 F5.
This plush and somewhat tacky bar is a good place for those who feel like prolonging their long night into morning, or for taking a first drink on an evening out. Free and easy atmosphere. Across the street from SchwuZ.

Triebwerk

Urbanstrasse 64 (6950 5203/www.triebwerk-t-online.de). U7, U8 Hermannplatz. **Open** 10pm-late Mon, Thur-Sat; 9pm-late Tue; 4pm-late Sun. **Credit** AmEx, MC, V. **Map** p307 H5.
Small comfortable bar with a huge video screen and a darkroom maze in the basement. Mainly Kreuzberg gays of every denomination. Mondays two for one drinks; Naked & Underwear Parties on Tuesdays, Fridays and Sundays.

Schöneberg

Berio

Maassenstrasse 7 (216 1946/www.berio.de). U1, U2, U4, U15 Nollendorfplatz. **Open** 8am-1am daily. **No credit cards**. **Map** p305 D5.
One of the best daytime cafés in Berlin, full of good-looking, trendy young men (including the waiters), with a good people-watching terrace in summer.

Hafen

Motzstrasse 19 (2114 1180/www.hafen-berlin.de). U1, U2, U4, U15 Nollendorfplatz. **Open** 8pm-late daily. **No credit cards**. **Map** p305 D5.
A red, plush and vaguely psychedelic bar in the centre of Schöneberg's gay triangle. Popular with the fashion- and body-conscious, especially at weekends, when it provides a safe haven from nearby heavy cruising dens. Usually very crowded.

Mutschmanns

Martin-Luther-Strasse 19 (2191 9640/www.mutschmanns.de). U1, U2, U4, U15 Nollendorfplatz. **Open** 10pm-late Tue, Thur; 11pm-late Fri, Sat; 9pm-2am Sun. **Admission** varies. **No credit cards**. **Map** p305 D5/6.
Newish addition to the hardcore Motzstrasse scene. Communicative bar with large darkroom in the basement. Suitable for cruising or just hanging out, but with a dress code of leather, rubber or uniform. Naked parties on Thursdays and Sundays, Rubber Night the first Saturday of the month.

Prinzknecht

Fuggerstrasse 33 (2362 7444/www.prinzknecht.de). U1, U2, U15 Wittenbergplatz. **Open** 3pm-3am daily. **No credit cards**. **Map** p305 D5.
With a large but underused darkroom out back, this huge, open bar draws in gays from the neighbourhood as well as leather and more hardcore men. The place is somewhat provincial in feel, but nice for a chat and a beer.

Tom's Bar

Motzstrasse 19 (213 4570/www.tomsbar.de). U1, U2, U4, U15 Nollendorfplatz. **Open** 10pm-6am Mon-Thur, Sun; 10pm-late Fri-Sat. **No credit cards**. **Map** p305 D5.
Once described by *Der Spiegel* as the climax, or crash-landing of the night. The front bar is fairly chatty, but the closer you get to the steps down to the darkroom, the more intense things become. Men only, but men of all ages and styles. Very popular, especially Monday, when you can get two drinks for the price of one.

Clubs & one-nighters

With only a few real discos (Die Busche, SchwuZ, Connection, Blu; *see below*), one-nighters are all the rage. Some come and go; others run and run. Check *Siegessäule*, *Sergej* or look out for flyers in bars, cafés and shops.

Come dancing at **SO36**'s Café Fatal. *See p207.*

Mitte

GaymeBoy

c/o Blu, Neue Schönhauser Strasse 20 (443 1980/www.gaymeboy.com). U8 Weinmeisterstrasse. **Open** 9pm-late 3rd Sat/mth. **Admission** €5-€7. **No credit cards. Map** p316/p303 G3.

GaymeBoy only lets you in if you're under 26 (or look it) so shy boys are not overwhelmed by dispassionate and cool nightlife, and the not-so-shy are not put off by wrinkling skin, sagging bottoms and leering stares. Old men over 26 admitted after 1am.

GMF

c/o Nachtbar Moskau, Karl-Marx-Allee 34, 10178. (2809 5396/www.gmf-berlin.de). U5 Schillingstrasse. **Open** 11pm-late Sun. **Admission** €8. **No credit cards. Map** p303 G3/H3.

The ultimate Sunday Tea-Dance with an unbeatable DJ line-up including Divinity and Westbam. Located in the Café Moskau in all of its 1950s glory, the dancefloor is intense and the cocktail lounge sociable and buzzing. Stylish and youngish crowd with lots of energy. Very popular, always packed.

Klub International

c/o Kino International, Karl-Marx-Allee 33 (2475 6011/www.kino-international.com). U5 Schillingstrasse. **Open** 11pm-late 1st Sat/mth. **Admission** €8. **No credit cards. Map** p303 G3.

Taking place in a 1950s GDR cinema, this club is worth a look for the interior alone. It's one of the biggest parties in town, regularly attracting up to 1,500 youngish guests in their tightest t-shirts. There are two dancefloors and DJs play a mix of house and mainstream music.

Nite Club

c/o Sage Club, Köpenicker Strasse 76 (278 9830/ www.sage-club.de). U8 Heinrich-Heine-Strasse. **Open** 12pm-late Sun, Mon. **No credit cards. Map** p307 G4/H4.

There are those for whom a whole weekend of partying is not enough. They cannot sleep, they have nothing to do, they do not have to get up on Monday. And so they go to Sage, for wicked techno and house in an interestingly styled club. Fullest around 5am, when GMF tips out.

Studio 69

c/o Kino International, Karl-Marx-Allee 33 (2475 6011/www.dissentertainment.de). U5 Schillingstrasse. **Open** 11pm-late, one Sat/mth. **Admission** €6-€7.50. **No credit cards. Map** p303 G3/H3.

Offers a wicked mix of music from the 1960s, 1970s, and 1980s. The club mostly attracts a shrieking youngish crowd, who really get into the old tunes. All kinds of activities and action included.

Prenzlauer Berg

Irrenhouse

GeburtstagsKlub, Am Friedrichshain 33 (4202 1406 /www.ninaqueer.com). Tram 2,3,4 Am Friedrichshain. **Open** 11pm-late 3rd Sat mth. **No credit cards. Map** p303 H2.

Popular one-nighter true to its name: 'Madhouse'. A bizarre mixture of party kids, trashy drag queens and flotsam of the night, partying to house and chart music under even more bizarre porn installations. Popular and shrill. Don't hesitate to misbehave – hostess Nina Queer does it all the time.

Kreuzberg

MS Edelweiss

Köpenicker Strasse 22-25 (at Schilling brigde) (www.edelweissberlin.de). N44, N65, 140, 265 Koepenicker Strasse/Manteuffelstrasse. **Open** 11pm-late Sat. **No credit cards. Map** p307 G4/H4.
Newish addition to the techno and house scene, on a boat moored on the Spree. Be prepared for loud music and lots of smiling, raving skinheads and other hardcore gays, ravers and party kids. Although new, it's already very popular.

SchwuZ

Mehringdamm 61 (693 7025/www.schwuz.de). U6, U7 Mehringdamm. **Open** 11pm-late Fri, Sat. **Admission** €4-€8. **No credit cards. Map** p306 F5.
Saturday is the main disco night at the Schwulen Zentrum ('Gay Centre'), Berlin's longest-running dance institution. The club attracts a mixed crowd, covering all ages and styles. There are two, sometimes three dancefloors (one of them featuring house music) and much mingling between the three bars and Café Melitta Sundström (*p207*) at the front. Friday hosts an assortment of one-nighters: first Friday of the month is Popstarrz, with independent and pop music; second Friday of the month there's Subterra, a very popular lesbian party; third Friday of the month, Subworxx offers indie and rock music and on every fourth Friday of the month the vibe is R&B, hip hop, soul and funk at Bootilicious. Special events here include trashy drag shows staged in the small theatre.

Schöneberg

Connection

Fuggerstrasse 33 (218 1432/www.connection-berlin.com/connection.php4). U1, U2, U15 Wittenbergplatz. **Open** 11pm-late Fri, Sat. **Admission** €7 (includes drink ticket). **Map** p305 D5.
Especially popular on men-only Saturdays, when DJs play a mixture of esoteric and Top 40 sounds; the dancefloor is usually packed. If you're bored with dancing, you can always cruise the vast dungeons of Connection Garage (below). In fact, this is where most guests spend their time.

Leather, sex & fetish venues

The hardcore and fetish scene in Berlin is huge. These days, leather gays are outnumbered by a younger hardcore crowd and skinhead-type gays, who prefer donning rubber and uniforms. Places to obtain your preferred garb are plentiful, as are opportunities to show it off, including the eternally crowded Leather Meeting over the Easter holidays, the annual Gay Skinhead Meeting or various fetish parties and events. Most of the parties are men-only affairs and have a strict dress code.

Prenzlauer Berg

Darkroom

Rodenbergstrasse 23 (444 9321/www.darkroom-berlin.de). U2, S4, S8, S10 Schönhauser Allee. **Open** 10pm-late daily. **Map** p303 G1.
Yes, there is a darkroom in this small bar. Actually there's more darkroom than bar. And with the help of camouflage netting and urinals (in the actual darkroom) the place pulls in a slightly 'harder' clientele, though on less busy nights things sometimes feel a bit desperate. The Naked Sex Party on Friday and Saturday's Golden Shower Party are particularly popular. After disposing of your clothes in a dustbin liner, feel free to roam about like the piece of trash you truly are.

Midnight Sun

Paul-Robeson-Strasse 50 (4471 6395/www.themidnightsun.de/www.bssunday.de/www.afterworksexparty.de). U2, S4, S8, S10 Schönhauser Allee. **Open** 10pm-6am Mon, Wed, Thu; 7pm-6am Tue; 10pm-noon Fri-Sat; 4pm-6am Sun. **Admission** €6. **No credit cards. Map** p303 G1.
Cruising fetish bar, popular with skinheads and hardcore types. Sex parties are on Tuesdays and Sundays, when it opens its second darkroom in the basement. Tuesdays it's the After Work Sex Party, while the 'Bastard Sunday' themes vary: Coffee & Cream (first of the month); fist afternoon (second Sun); Gang Bang (third); rubber, skins and bikers (fourth). Dress code: naked, erotic, fetish.

Stahlrohr

Greifenhagener Strasse 54 (4473 2747/www.stahlrohr.com). U2, S4, S8, S10 Schönhauser Allee. **Open** 10pm-6am daily. **Admission** €5. **No credit cards. Map** p303 G1.
Small hardcore pub in the front and a huge darkroom in the back. Sex parties for every taste, including Fist, Gangbang and Youngster parties. Check the gay press or website for details.

Kreuzberg

Bodies in Emotion

c/o AHA, Mehringdamm 61 (692 3600/www.aha-berlin.de). U6, U7 Mehringdamm. **Open** 9pm-5am every 2nd Fri. **Admission** €6. **No credit cards. Map** p306 F5.
Every second Friday, this sex party is popular with guys under 30 (or who look it – no hairy chests here). What you wear is your business, but most put on sexy shorts, which they then take off in the sex area, where mattresses and slings invite you to have fun – if you can find an empty one.

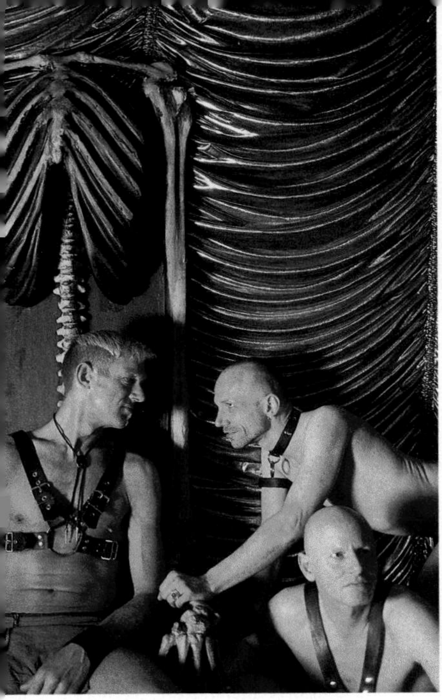

Diverse sex parties at **Club Culture Houze**.

Club Culture Houze

Görlitzer Strasse 71 (6170 9669/www.club-culture-houze.de). U1, U15 Görlitzer Bahnhof. **Open** 7pm-late Mon, Thu; 8pm-late Wed, Fri; 10pm-late Sat. **Admission** €7.60. **Map** p307 H5.
Diverse sex parties (some of them mixed), ranging from 'naked' to 'SM and Fetish'. Exclusive gay nights on Monday (Naked Sex), Thursday (After Work), Friday (Fist & Fuck Factory) and Saturday (Gay Sex Party). Mostly body-conscious night owls visit these kitsch rooms. Mattresses encourage people to lie down, but they do it everywhere.

Quälgeist

Körtestrasse 15-17 (2nd backyard) (788 5799/ www.quaelgeist-berlin.de). U7 Südstern.
Open varies. **Admission** €8-15. **No credit cards**. **Map** p306 D5.
First institution established solely to organise SM parties, which include SM for beginners, bondage, slave-market and fist nights. Pick up their flyers at any leather bar or Mann-O-Meter (*see p276*). Usually a dress code.

Schöneberg

Ajpnia

Eisenacher Strasse 23 (2191 8881/www.ajpnia.de). U1, U2, U4, U15 Nollendorfplatz. **Open** 7pm-2am Wed; 9pm-7am Fri, Sat. **Admission** €5-€6. **No credit cards**. **Map** p306 D5.
Two-storey sex club frequented by men of all ages. Every first and third Saturday is Posithiv Verkehr, a party by and for HIV-positives; every second and fourth Saturday is Nachtverkehr ('Night Traffic') and Wednesday is Feierabendverkehr ('After Work Traffic'). Note: *Verkehr* also means 'intercourse'.

Kit Kat Club

Bessemerstrasse 2 (no phone/www.kitkatclub.de). U6 Alt-Tempelhof or S2, S4 Papestrasse. **Open** 9pm-late, Thur; 11pm-late Fri, Sat; 8pm-late Sun. **No credit cards**.
Essentially a mixed/straight sex and techno club with a gay night on the first Monday of the month. Saturday parties are also frequented by gays but the most popular evening is Sunday's 'Peepshow', open 8am-7pm. Most parties have a dress code; the least you have to do is take off your shirt. Laid-back and high-spirited, but out of the way: take a taxi.

New Action

Kleiststrasse 35 (211 8256/www.new-action-berlin.de). U1, U2, U4, U15 Nollendorfplatz.
Open Mon-Sat 8pm-late; Sun 1pm-late.
No credit cards. **Map** p305 D5.
Atmospheric, custom-designed hardcore bar with small darkroom. In early morning it can become quite a gathering of eccentrics who either don't want to go to bed yet or else just got up. Leather, rubber, uniform, jeans, but also the odd woollen pullover creates a casual atmosphere. Don't be sober.

Scheune

Motzstrasse 25 (213 8580/www.scheune-berlin.de). U1, U2, U4, U12 Nollendorfplatz. **Open** 9pm-7am Fri-Sun. **Admission** varies. **No credit cards**. **Map** p306 D5.
Small and popular leather hardcore bar. Action in the cellar is late and heavy. 'Naked Sex Party' Sunday afternoon (entrance 4-6.30pm) and rubber nights every second Friday. Very popular.

Other districts

Böse Buben

Lichtenrader Strasse 32 (2nd backyard), Neukölln (6270 5610/www.boesebubenberlin.de). U8 Leinestrasse. **Open** 4pm-4am Wed; 9pm-4am Fri-Sat. **Admission** €5. **No credit cards**. **Map** p307 G6.
Fetish sex party club with imaginatively furnished and decorated rooms. Tiled piss room, sling room, bondage cross and cheap drinks make this quite a grotto of hedonism. Wednesday is the After Work Sex Party; weekends have different parties like hard SM, fist, bondage or spanking.

Saunas

Saunas are popular and you may have to queue, especially on cheaper days. In-house bills are run up on your locker or cabin number and settled on leaving. No open cabins, only personal ones.

Sex counselling, conflict mediation and a variety of dildos at **Sexclusivitäten**. *See p216*.

Apollo City Sauna

Kurfürstenstrasse 101, Schöneberg (213 2424). U1, U2, U15 Wittenbergplatz. **Open** 1pm-7am daily. **Admission** €14.50/day; *locker* €13/mth; *cabin* €19.50 . **No credit cards**. **Map** p306 D5.

A sprawling labyrinth of sin – with 130 lockers and 60 cabins. Dry and steam saunas, porn video den, TV lounge, weights room, sunbeds and a well-stocked bar. If you don't end up in one of the cabins, there's plenty of action in the dark, cruisy steam bath downstairs.

Steam Sauna

Kurfürstenstrasse 113, Tiergarten (218 4060/ www.steam-sauna.de). U1, U2, U15 Wittenbergplatz. **Open** 11am-7am Mon-Thur; 24 hrs Fri-Sun. **Admission** €12.50-€15; €6 for cabin. **No credit cards**. **Map** p305 D4.

Classic sauna with 180 lockers and 38 cabins. Sex is plentiful, sometimes hardcore. Clientele of all ages plus sauna and steam rooms, whirlpool, bar and TV room showing porn. Saturday is slightly cheaper and gets packed; clubbers drift along early on Sunday mornings and stay for the day.

Treibhaus Sauna

Schönhauser Allee 132, Prenzlauer Berg (448 4503/ 449 3494/www.treibhaussauna.de). U2 Eberswalder Strasse. **Open** 1pm-7am Mon-Thur; 24 hrs noon Fri-late Sun. **Admission** €9.50; €17 (10hrs incl. drink ticket); cabin €5. **No credit cards**. **Map** p303 G2.

Tucked in the first courtyard (buzz for entry), this has become a big favourite, especially with students and youngsters. Facilities include dry sauna, steam room, whirlpool, cycle jet, solarium, a shop stocked with toys and lubricants and cabins equipped with TV and VCR on a first-come, first-served basis. During the week, there's a variety of medicinal and therapeutic massage treatments on offer.

Cruising

Cruising is a popular and legal pursuit in Berlin. Most action takes place in the parks. Don't panic or jump into a bush when encountering the police – they are actually there to protect you from gay bashers and they never hassle cruisers. One way or another, it's actually very safe to go roaming about at night in Berlin. Summer seems to bring out all of Berlin's finery and there is no taboo attached to nudity in parks.

Grunewald

S7 Grunewald.

Go to the woods behind the car park at Pappelplatz. Walk about 500m (1,640ft) along Eichkampstrasse until it passes under the Autobahn, then turn to the right into the woods. From there it's about another 50m (164ft) to the car park. This is a popular day-time spot but it's also well frequented at night, when bikers and harder guys mingle among the trees.

Tiergarten
S3, S5, S7, S9 Tiergarten. **Map** p305 D4.
The Löwenbrücke (where the Grosser Weg crosses the Neuer See) is the cruising focal point – but the whole corner south-west of the Siegessäule becomes a bit of a gay theme park in summer, when daytime finds hundreds of gays sunning themselves on the 'Tuntenwiese' ('faggots meadow').

Volkspark Friedrichshain
U2, U5, U8 or S3, S5, S7, S9 Alexanderplatz/bus 100, 157, 257. **Map** p303 H3.
After sundown, the area around and behind the Märchenbrunnen fills with horny lads. Busy at night. Some activity by day, but it involves searching the nearby slopes for it.

Shops

Books & art

Bruno's
Nollendorfplatz/Bülow Strasse 106, Schöneberg (2147 3293/www.brunos.de). U1, U2, U4, U15 Nollendorfplatz. **Open** 10am-10pm Mon-Sat; 1pm-9pm Sun. **Credit** AmEx, MC, V. **Map** p305 D4.
Large and rather plush shop with an extensive selection of reading and viewing material, plus cards, calendars, videos and other paraphernalia.

Prinz Eisenherz Buchladen
Lietzenburger Strasse 9a, Schöneberg (313 9936/fax 313 1795/www.prinz-eisenherz.com). U1, U2, U15 Wittenbergplatz. **Open** 10am-8pm Mon-Fri; 10am-6pm Sat. **Credit** MC, V. **Map** p305 D4.
One of the finest gay book shops in Europe, including, among its large English-language stock, many titles unavailable in Britain. There's a good art and photography section, plus magazines, postcards and news of book readings and other events.

Toys & fetish outfits

Black Style
Seelower Strasse 5, Prenzlauer Berg (4468 8595/www.blackstyle.de). U2 Schönhauser Allee, S4, S8, S10. **Open** 1-6.30pm Mon-Wed; 1-8pm Thu, Fri; 11am-4pm Sat. **Credit** AmEx, DC, MC, V. **Map** p303 G1.
From black fashion of all kinds to butt plugs – if it's made out of rubber or latex they've got it. High quality, reasonable prices and big variety. Mail order.

Connection Garage
Fuggerstrasse 33, Schöneberg (218 1432/www.connection-berlin.com/www.gayonline sexshop.de). U1, U2, U15 Wittenbergplatz. **Open** 10am-1am Mon-Sat; 2pm-1am Sun. **Credit** MC, V. **Map** p305 D5.
Huge selection of rubber and leather novelties, clothing, SM accessories, magazines. The cruising area comes alive at weekends when it amalgamates with Connection Disco (*see p212*).

The Jaxx
Motzstrasse 19, Schöneberg (213 8103). U1, U2, U4, U15 Nollendorfplatz. **Open** noon-3am Mon-Sat; 1pm-3am Sun. **Admission** €8; €6 Tue. **Credit** MC, V. **Map** p305 D5.
A good selection of toys and videos is available here, plus video cabins and a cruising area. Very popular with younger guys.

Leathers
Schliemannstrasse 38, Prenzlauer Berg (442 7786/www.leathers.de). U2 Eberswalder Strasse. **Open** noon-7.30pm Mon-Fri; noon-4pm Sat. **Credit** AmEx, MC, V. **Map** p303 G2.
A workshop which produces leather and SM articles of the highest quality. No smut here – just a range of well-presented products and helpful staff.

Mr B
Nollendorfstrasse 23, Schöneberg (2199 7704/www.misterb.com). U1, U2, U4, U15 Nollendorfplatz. **Open** noon-8pm Mon-Fri; 11am-6pm Sat. **Credit** AmEx, DC, MC, V. **Map** p305 D5.
Everything for the hardcore crowd can be found here. The place is known particularly for its leather and rubber outfits, metal accessories and toys, SM articles, lubricants and clothing. Mr B also hosts the occasional art exhibition.

Lesbian

Few cities can compete with Berlin's network of lesbian institutions, but there are few lesbian-only bars. For mixed bars and club nights, check *Siegessäule* or *L-mag* (www.L-mag.de), a quarterly free lesbian mag. Many young lesbians favour mixed venues such as **SchwuZ** (*see p212*), **SO36** or **Die Busche** (*see p207*).

Cafés & bars

Mitte

Café Seidenfaden
Dircksenstrasse 47 (283 2783/www.FrauSucht Zukunft.de). S3, S5, S7, S9 Hackescher Markt. **Open** 12am-6pm Mon, Tue, Thu, Fri; 12am-9pm Wed; 11am-8pm Sun. **No credit cards. Map** p303 G3.
Run by women from a therapy group of former addicts. There are readings and exhibitions but absolutely no drugs or alcohol. Packed at lunchtime, quiet at night.

Friedrichshain

Frieda Frauenzentrum
Proskauer Strasse 7 (422 4276/www.frieda-frauenzentrum.de). U5 Samariterstrasse. **Open** 9am-10pm Tue, Thur; 1pm-midnight Fri; 11am-2pm Sun. **No credit cards. Map** p88.

Lesbenabend ('Lesbian Night') on Fridays, and Lesbenfrühstück ('Breakfast for Lesbians') 10.30am-2pm Saturdays. Mother and senior groups too.

Kreuzberg

Schoko Café

Mariannenstrasse 6 (615 1561/www.schokofabrik.de). U1, U8 Kottbusser Tor. **Open** 5pm-late Mon-Sat. **No credit cards. Map** p307 G5.

Part of the Schoko-Fabrik women's centre, mostly frequented by lesbians. Snacks, occasional parties.

Schöneberg

Begine

Potsdamer Strasse 139 (215 1414/www.begine.de). U2 Bülowstrasse. **Open** 5pm-1am Mon-Sat. **No credit cards. Map** p306 E5.

Women-only café frequented by lesbians. Part of the 'Meeting point and Culture for Women' centre.

Charlottenburg

Neue Bar

Knesebeckstrasse 16 (3150 3062/www.neuebar.de). S3, S5, S7, S9 Savignyplatz. **Open** 6pm-late Tue-Sun. **Map** p305 C4.

Small pub for women and lesbians. Talkative atmosphere. Wednesday 'Vinyl-Lounge' from 7pm-late.

Clubs & one-nighters

Mitte

Metrobabes

c/o Sage Club/Kantina Berlin Barcelona, Köpenicker Strasse 76 (0171 897 1812/www.www.mbabes.de). U8 Heinrich-Heine-Strasse. **Open** 11pm-late 4th Sat/mth. **Admission** €6, €7. **No credit cards. Map** p307 G/H4.

House party for lesbians and their gay friends. Known for its exuberant atmosphere.

Prenzlauer Berg

Frauenparty im EWA e.V. Frauenzentrum

Prenzlauer Allee 6 (442 8023/www-ewa-frauenzentrum.de). U2 Rosa-Luxemburg-Platz. **Open** 10pm-3am Sat. **No credit cards. Map** p303 G3.

Dance party for women every Saturday. Check the press for other events at this venue.

Kreuzberg

m.appeal

c/o SO36, Oranienstrasse 190 (6140 1306/www.so36.de). U1, U8 Kottbusser Tor. **Open** 10pm-late. **Map** p307 G4. **No credit cards.**

Every first Friday of the month, youngish progressive lesbians party in a slightly trashy atmosphere. Drag welcome; gays are only admitted in lesbian company. Go-go dancers. Wild.

Salsa Theka

c/o Schoko Café, Mariannenstrasse 6 (615 1561). U1, U8 Kottbusser Tor. **Open** from 9pm 2nd Fri/mth. **Admission** €3.50. **No credit cards. Map** p307 G5.

Women's Latin dance party.

subterra

c/o SchwuZ, Mehringdamm 61 (693 7025/www.megadyke.de/www.schwuz.de). U6, U7 Mehringdamm. **Open** 10pm-late every 2nd Fri. **Admission** €6-€8. **No credit cards. Map** p306 F5.

Mixed party with distinctly more lesbians than gays, downstairs in SchwuZ, organised by Megadyke Productions. Two dancefloors and a massage corner in the candlelight lounge, where a professional masseuse will knead anyone's flesh. Often full to capacity.

Tiergarten

Die 2

Rathenower Strasse 19, Tiergarten (3983 8969). U9 Turmstrasse, bus 227, N27. **Open** 7pm-late Wed, Thu; 10pm-late Fri, Sat. **Map** p301 D2/3.

Easy-going atmosphere for more sophisticated and mature lesbians. Wednesday 'After-Work-Party', Thursday 'Cultural Thursday' – readings, exhibitions, Friday and Saturday disco.

Shops & services

Lustwandel

Raumerstrasse 20, Prenzlauer Berg (4404 0860/www.lustwandel.de). U2 Eberswalder Strasse. **Open** noon-8pm Mon-Fri; 10am-16pm Sat. **Credit** MC, V. **Map** p303 G1/2.

Women's book store with erotic literature for every taste, plus fiction, art and illustrated books.

Playstixx

Waldemarstrasse 24, Kreuzberg (6165 9500/www.playstixx.de). U1, U8 Kottbusser Tor. **Open** 2-6pm Wed, Thu; 2-5pm Fri; 11am-3pm 2nd & 4th Sat mth. **No credit cards. Map** p307 G4.

The dildos on offer at this workshop, run by sculptress Stefanie Dörr, come in the form of bananas, whales, fists or dolphins rather than phalluses. Most are made of non-allergenic, highly durable silicon.

Sexclusivitäten

c/o Laura Merrit, Fürbringerstrasse 2, Kreuzberg (693 6666/www.sexclusivitaeten.de). U7 Gneisenaustrasse. **No credit cards. Map** p306 F5.

Laura Merrit calls herself a feminist linguist and sexpert, offering sex counselling, conflict mediation and a big selection of sex toys. Shop for a variety of dildos, vibrators and other items. By appointment only.

Music: Rock, World & Jazz

Going overground! The mainstream has arrived in Berlin, but will this prove blessing or curse for a city of independent scenes?

Rock Boys at **Kirche von unten.** *See p219.*

Berlin has always been a place to catch seminal shows by live acts great and small. Simple Minds even name-checked a legendary Charlottenburg venue with their 1981 instrumental 'Kant-Kino'. But though East Berlin was the hub of the GDR record business, the recording industry before 1989 largely shunned the western half of the city.

All that has changed. Both Sony Music Germany and Universal Germany are established here. V2 Records is also in Berlin, and MTV Germany has arrived from Munich. With the Popkomm trade fair (*see p219* **Pop komms to Berlin**) wrested away from Cologne, Berlin is now arguably Germany's music biz capital.

A whopping 60 per cent of German music-related revenue is generated in Berlin by about 570 companies, including those major labels and around 150 indies, among them such internationally known imprints as Kitty-yo, Monika Enterprises, Bungalow, Basic Channel, Low Spirit, !K7, City Slang, Klangkrieg and Chicks On Speed Records (C.O.S.). US electroclash feminists Le Tigre chose C.O.S. as their home and Finnish lounge eccentric Jimi Tenor is now on Kitty-yo, demonstrating Berlin labels' attractiveness for non-German talent.

Conversely, the venerable mini-major Mute (now an EMI subsidiary) opened an office in Kreuzberg, paying tribute to Berlin connections which have long bolstered its revenue and reputation: Einstürzende Neubauten, the Birthday Party/Nick Cave and various offshoots, Depeche Mode's recordings at Hansa Studios, and newer releases by Westbam, Pole and Mediengruppe Telekommander.

The arrival of the mainstreams has aroused mixed feelings in the independent scene. On the one hand, it has renewed old anxieties about the fruits of smaller labels' years of loving support being snatched away by the majors' cash at the expense of the artists' innovation and integrity. On the other, indie label owners such as Monika Enterprises' Gudrun Gut are optimistic, hoping for trickle-down effects and a mutually beneficial 'co-opetition' (as a city official termed it) between majors and indies.

Wir Sind Helden: anthemically yearning.

As for a Berlin 'brand', the only unifying characteristic is the sheer diversity. A huge number of interesting acts record and perform in Berlin. Electronica remains a focus: Kyborg, Rechenzentrum, Guido Möbius and Monolake are names to check out. Reggae-inspired vibes are represented by SEEED's precise groove attack at one end of the spectrum and Rhythm & Sound's abstract dub at the other. Perhaps as a counterweight to that male-dominated idiom, the C.O.S. label has paved the way for a number of post-post feminist voices: queercore electroclash by Rhythm King and Her Friends, keyboardist-singer-songwriter Barbara Morgenstern's technical brilliance transcending gender discussions, hardrockin' Cobra Killer who wouldn't seem out of place in *Faster Pussycat, Kill, Kill!*.

But the two big recent success stories were of a retro nature. The first was Sven Regener's novel *Herr Lehmann* (published in English as *Berlin Blues*). This laconic portrait of late 1980s Kreuzberg, penned by the frontman of veteran band Element of Crime, soon became a major motion picture and soundtrack album – fittingly on Mute and featuring Element of Crime, Nick Cave, and the late Fad Gadget (whose 1984 'Collapsing New People' had satirised the West Berlin scene). The interest *Herr Lehmann* sparked in pre-1989 West Berlin was a companion phenomenon to the Ostalgia earlier inspired by *Goodbye, Lenin!*

The other surprise success came from a four-piece band discovered in a Prenzlauer Berg goth and alt.rock club. Wir sind Helden, taking their name from David Bowie's Berlin-era signature tune 'Heroes', caught the ear thanks to catchy, anthemic, new wave-like tunes. But it was lyrics by fetching singer, guitarist and cultural studies grad Judith Holofernes, playfully addressing the yearning for meaning and value amid a consumer culture gone rampant, that have won them a broad audience.

It remains to be seen whether the commercial spotlight now shining on Berlin will scorch more delicate seedlings or allow a whole new underground to thrive in its shadows. A hopeful harbinger is the city's continued lure for creative spirits from all over the world and the potential for cultural and stylistic boundary-transcending this entails.

As the distinction between live music and DJ sets has become blurred, most clubs offer some live events several times a week. The selection that follows includes venues devoted mainly to live performances or with an especially noteworthy booking policy.

Check *Zitty* and *tip* for gig listings. Radio Eins (95.8FM) and Radio Fritz (102.6FM) also inform about upcoming events. Another good source of information is the bilingual site www.dorfdisco.de, which covers local and international acts as well as offering a trial of legal, artist-friendly filesharing service Potato.

Rock venues

The primarily sports venues **Max-Schmeling-Halle** and **Velodrom** (*for both, see p244*) also host occasional music events.

Arena Treptow

Eichenstrasse 4, Treptow (533 7333/www.arena-berlin.de). S4, S6, S8, S9 Treptower Park/bus 265, N65. **Open** *Tickets* 10am-6pm Mon-Fri. *Concert* varies. **No credit cards. Map** p88.

This former bus garage now hosts big concerts by the likes of Pink as well as events such as the German adaptation of *The Vagina Monologues*. Techno and house parties are held sporadically at Glashaus next door.

Bastard @ Prater

Kastanienallee 7-9, Prenzlauer Berg (4404 9669/www.praterteam.de). U2 Eberswalder Strasse/bus N52. **Open** *Office* 1-4pm Tue-Fri. *Concerts* varies. **Admission** varies. **No credit cards. Map** p303 G2.

Concert and club space with living-room charm – if one's living room was four metres high and covered with pictures torn from fashion and news magazines. Local and international alternative and electronica acts perform here several times a week in addition to club nights.

ColumbiaFritz
Columbiadamm 9-11, Tempelhof (6981 280/ www.columbiafritz.de). U6 Platz der Luftbrücke. **Open** *Concerts* varies. *Disco* 11pm-6am Sat. **Admission** *Concerts* €10-€13. *Disco* €5.50. **No credit cards. Map** p306 F6.
Former US Forces cinema showcases lower profile rock and alt.rock acts, but has lost the cream of booking to comparable venues like Magnet (*see p227*) or Maria am Ufer (*see p220*). Youth radio station Fritz hosts the Emergenza series of local talent concerts.

Columbiahalle
Columbiadamm 13-21, Tempelhof (698 0980). U6 Platz der Luftbrücke. **Open** *Concerts* varies. *Box office* 10am-6pm Mon-Fri. **Admission** €5-€40. **No credit cards. Map** p306 F6.
Belle & Sebastian, Limp Bizkit and AIR have all played this roomy venue next door to ColumbiaFritz.

Huxley's Neue Welt
Hasenheide 107-118 Neukölln (6290 4088). U7, U8 Hermannplatz/late bus N4, N6, N19, N40, N44. **Open** varies **Admission** varies. **No credit cards. Map** p307 G5/6.
Legendary 1980s West Berlin venue, once a roller rink. Ryan Adams and Sugababes have played here.

Kirche von unten
Kremmener Strasse 9-11, Mitte (449 1172/448 93 41/www.kvu-berlin.de). U8 Bernauer Strasse, U2 Eberswalder Strasse, Tram 20. **Open** 9pm-late. **Admission** call for details. **No credit cards. Map** p302/p303 F/G2.

Pop komms to Berlin

Starting in 2004, **Popkomm** – the largest domestic music industry trade fair in Europe – is relocating from Cologne to Berlin. This move was heavily lobbied by newly Berlin-based majors such as Sony and Universal – and specifically by Universal's former head, Tim Renner, a postpunk wunderkind who nurtured acts such as Element Of Crime and Rammstein and envisioned a globally competitive German rock scene with Berlin as its epicentre. And when the city-owned Messe Berlin corporation, which also manages trade fairs such as Internationale Grüne Woche (*see p186*) or the International Tourism Fair (*see p186*), got involved, the trade fair complex at the Funkturm (*see p110*) soon became Popkomm's new home.

Popkomm was first held in 1989 as a small indie market in Düsseldorf. Back then the German music industry was still meekly tail-ending its US and UK counterparts. Popkomm then spent 1990-2003 as a long mid-August weekend in Cologne. Its ascension to an industry mega-event comparable to Austin's South by Southwest or Midem in Cannes dovetailed with Germany's post-1989 development into a major music market and exporter of internationally successful trends.

It also went hand in hand with the 1993 emergence of German-language music video channel VIVA, masterminded by Popkomm founder Dieter Gorny. VIVA has been involved in various incarnations of the company running the fair, and that channel's Komet music prize is awarded during Popkomm.

Staged in conjunction with live showcases and a club festival, Popkomm became an annual fixture for industry professionals. This was all made possible by lavish subsidies from the government of Nord-Rhein-Westfalen, which supported Popkomm as part of its plan to make Cologne into the media capital of Germany. For a while, as Popkomm saw off its early trade fair rival, Berlin Independence Days (1988-1993), that plan seemed to be working.

But Popkomm peaked in 2000 with almost 1,000 exhibitors. The following years saw a steady decrease in exhibitor and visitor figures. The New Economy nosedive and perceived threat of filesharing had wounded both the industry in general and Popkomm in particular.

With relocation to Berlin, the ailing Popkomm, now staged in late September, hopes to regain momentum by refocusing on indies, strengthening partnerships with healthier music markets such as France, casting an eye on emerging markets in Eastern Europe and 'by integrating related areas such as fashion, games, film and telecommunications into new business models,' as Popkomm project manager Claudia Bittner explains.

The Berlin indie labels that Popkomm hopes to court have mixed feelings. Amid fears of being co-opted by a stronger major presence, the fair is also seen as an 'opportunity to get indie issues on the agenda,' as major to indie renegade Jörg Heidemann offers.

Whether Popkomm can both reinvent itself and help turn around a moribund industry remains to be seen. But as in Cologne, there will be a myriad of music showcases and a club festival. And that alone might worth the price of admission.

A continuation of the 1980s East Berlin movement whereby punks, environmentalists and other dissidents gathered under the umbrella of the Protestant church. The current secular incarnation offers politically charged live punk and doubles as meeting place for what's left of the squat scene.

Knaack Club

Greifswalder Strasse 224, Prenzlauer Berg (442 7061/www.knaack-berlin.de). Tram 2, 3, 4/bus N54. **Open** *Bar* 6pm-late daily. *Disco* 9pm-late Wed, Fri, Sat. **Admission** *Concerts* €6-€15. *Disco* €2.50 Wed, before 11pm Fri, Sat; €5 after 11pm Fri, Sat. **No credit cards. Map** p303 H2.

Booking policy covers the full spectrum of alternative rock. Both dancefloors and performance spaces lurk within this multi-level complex. A concert ticket gets you into club events, but not vice versa.

Maria am Ufer

An der Schillingbrücke, Friedrichshain (2123 8190/www.clubmaria.de). S3, S5, S7, S9, S75 Ostbahnhof/bus N44. **Open** 8pm-late **Admission** €8-€15. **No credit cards. Map** p307 H4.

Relocated from Ostbahnhof, Maria is the premier venue for live and DJ sets of electronica, alternative and post rock. Other attractions are the stylish post-industrial design and labyrinth of lounges.

Neues Tempodrom

Möckernstrasse 10, Kreuzberg (6953 3885/www.tempodrom.de). S, S2, S25, S26 Anhalter Bahnhof/bus N29. **Open** *Events* varies. *Box office* noon-6.30pm Mon-Fri; 11am-2pm Sat. **No credit cards. Map** p306 F4.

The original Tempodrom, two circus tents first at Potsdamer Platz, then across the street from the Reichstag, hosted some seminal events, including the 1981 Geniale Dilettanten festival that put Einstürzende Neubauten on the map, and the Heimatklänge world music concerts. In 1998 construction of the Federal Chancellery forced the Tempodrom to move to this new location at the former Anhalter Bahnhof. Now a permanent structure with vaguely tent-like appearance, it houses a 3,400-capacity venue, a smaller arena for 500, and the Liquidrom (*see p253*) a sauna complex including a domed saline pool with soothing music. Booking is a grab bag of everything from Vanessa Mae to Kraftwerk to Neubauten. At press time, the money-losing venue was in the throes of a financing scandal reaching the upper echelons of city government.

Parkbühne Wuhlheide

An der Wuhlheide 8, Köpenick. S3 Wuhlheide.

Radiohead and REM have graced this open-air stage, more intimate than the Waldbühne.

Podewil

Klosterstrasse 68-70, Mitte (247 496/tickets 2474 9777/www.podewil.de). U2 Klosterstrasse/bus N52. **Open** varies. **Admission** €5-€18; €3-€15 concessions. **Open** *Box office* 9am-8pm Mon-Fri. *Concerts* varies. **Credit** MC, V. **Map** p316/p303 G3.

The former HQ of the GDR youth organisation, FDJ has become Berlin's premier venue for avant-rock and experimental music. Also hosts performance art, video installations and the Total Music Meeting.

Volksbühne

Rosa-Luxemburg-Platz, Mitte (4401 7400/www.roter-salon.de). U2 Rosa-Luxemburg-Platz. **Open** *Box office* noon-6pm Fri. **Admission** €5-€8. **No credit cards. Map** p316/p303 G3.

A popular and controversial theatre, the Volksbühne also lends its stage to acts such as Laibach or Suicide. The smaller Roter Salon, with its own side entrance, stucco moulding and chandeliers, hosts club nights and marginal concerts; *tangeros* and swing kids shake a leg at the Grüner Salon on the other side of the building.

Wabe

Danziger Strasse 101, Prenzlauer Berg (4240 2525/www.wabe-berlin.de). S4, S8, S85 Greifswalder Strasse/bus N54. **Open** varies. **Admission** varies. **No credit cards. Map** p303 H3.

A GDR-era cultural centre in Ernst-Thälmann-Park, this octagonal space is a good place to trace the legacy of 'Ostrock'. Both mainstream and underground acts from the old East play here, such as Engerling and Iron Hennig, as well as ska-punk outfit Blascore or Frank Schoebel, the GDR's answer to Elvis.

Waldbühne

Waldbühne, Glockenturmstrasse, Charlottenburg (office 810 750/tics 01805 332 433). S5, S75 Pichelsberg. **Open** *Box office* 10am-6pm Mon-Fri. **Admission** €30-€70. **No credit cards.**

In summer this 22,000-seat amphitheatre in the woods near Olympiastadion hosts the likes of Neil Young, Sting and Depeche Mode.

World, folk & Latino

The term 'world music' has become somewhat obsolete – jazz, rock and avant-garde have all absorbed non-European elements, while indigenous music has been 'watered down' for Western ears. Also, many newer 'world' acts eschew tradition and purism, cutting and mixing influences and styles. Berlin's worldbeat scene reflects this trend: Di Grine Kuzine's Italian-Balkan-Klezmer fusion, Genetic Drugs' digital travelogues of the Indian subcontinent, 17 Hippies playing just as many styles.

Berlin also offers a broad selection of traditional music, with Klezmer, Irish pub folk and anything vaguely 'Latino' the most popular. Music from the Balkans and the former Soviet Union has also found a following. African music enjoys an ongoing if lower key presence, with Kwaito, house-influenced dance music from South Africa, gaining a toehold.

For info tune to Radio MultiKulti on 106.8FM, or scan music listings in *tip* and *Zitty*.

Frank Mead blows **Soultrane**. *See p222.*

Hackesches Hof Theater

Rosenthaler Strasse 40-1, Mitte (283 2587/www.hackescher-hoftheater.de). S3, S5, S7, S9, S75 Hackescher Markt or U8 Weinmeisterstrasse. **Open** *Box office* 11am-3pm Mon-Fri. **Admission** *Theatre* €14; €9 concessions. *Concerts* €12; €9 concessions. **No credit cards**. **Map** p316/p302 F3.

Intimate seated space offers regular concerts of Klezmer, Yiddish and East European folk music.

Haus der Kulturen der Welt

John-Foster-Dulles Allee 10, Tiergarten (office 397 870/tickets 3978 7175/www.hkw.de). S3, S5, S7, S9 Bellevue/bus 100. **Open** *Box office* 10am-9pm Tue-Sun. **Credit** DC, MC, V. **Map** p302 E3.

Berlin's largest world music venue. The Café Global, overlooking the Spree, often hosts live bands.

Havanna Club

Hauptstrasse 30, Schöneberg (784 8565/www.havanna-berlin.de). U7 Eisenacher Strasse. **Open** 9pm-late Wed; 10pm-late Fri, Sat. **Admission** €2.50 Wed; €6.50 Fri; €7 Sat. **No credit cards**. **Map** p305 D6.

Three dancefloors with salsa, merengue and R&B. Popular with South American and Cubans.

Kulturbrauerei

Schönhauser Allee 36 (entrance also from Knaackstrasse 97) Prenzlauer Berg (4431 5151/www.kulturbrauerei-berlin.de). U2 Eberswalder Strasse/bus N52. **Open** 10.30am-5.30pm. **Admission** varies. **No credit cards. Map** p303 G2.

This concert space, formerly a brewery, hosts a variety of music from East of the Elbe, such as Budapest dance-pop sensation Anima Sound System and St. Petersburg rude boys Spitfire.

Tam Tam

Wiener Strasse 34, Kreuzberg (6162 1714/www.tamtam-afrodisco.de). U1, 15 Görlitzer Bahnhof/ bus N29. **Open** 10pm-late Wed, Fri, Sat. **Admission** €5. **No credit cards**. **Map** p307 H5.

African-run club offering a variety of classic and contemporary African, Afro-Caribbean and African-American music, including N'Dombolo, Soukouss, Merengue, Yankadi, Zouk, Soul, Reggae and Soca.

Werkstatt der Kulturen

Wissmannstrasse 31-42, Neukölln (622 2024/609 7700/www.werkstatt-der-kulturen.de). U7, U8 Hermannplatz. **Open** varies. **Admission** varies. **No credit cards**. **Map** p307 G6.

Small, community centre-style venue for more traditional, grass roots music from around the world as well as ethno-jazz performances and club nights.

Jazz

Berlin's jazz scene is large and encompasses everything from pub jam sessions to major international festivals. The city also boasts Germany's only 24-hour jazz radio station, JazzRadio, which favours polite, melodic sounds. The scene in general leans towards the more traditional. A dedicated following sustains 30 or so venues, and initiatives such as the Berlin Jazz & Blues Awards and the Jazz Radio-sponsored Fringe Jazz Festival hope to bring the city's diverse scene to wider attention.

Events such as the Total Music Meeting showcase more entropic forms, and the city's avant-jazz and improv scenes are renowned. There is also fertile cross-pollination between jazz and club music, as demonstrated on groovy releases by Jazzanova and Maxwell Implosion.

Check Jazz Radio 101.9 (bilingual website www.jazzradio.net) or www.jazzdimensions.de for gig listings and background info.

Atalante

Richardstrasse 112, Neukölln (681 8497/www.esskultur-berlin.de). U7 Karl-Marx-Strasse. **Open** varies. **Admission** €3-€5. **No credit cards. Map** p307 H6.

Jazz, art and fine food are the refined pleasures at this bistro-like club in unrefined Neukölln. As well as free Thursday jam sessions and Friday jazz or blues concerts, also hosts readings and exhibitions.

A-Trane

Bleibtreustrasse 1, Charlottenburg (313 2550/www.a-trane.de). S3, S5, S7, S9, S75 Savignyplatz. **Open** 9pm-2am Sun-Thur; 9pm-late Fri, Sat. *Concerts* from 10pm daily. **Admission** €5-€15. **Credit** (starting Sept 2004). **Credit** AmEx, DC, MC, V. **Map** p305 C4.

Swanky attempt at a New York-style jazz bar where events are occasionally interesting enough to be audible over the yuppie trimmings.

Badenscher Hof

Badensche Strasse 29, Wilmersdorf (861 0080/www.badenscher-hof.de). U7, U9 Berliner Strasse. **Open** 4pm-late Mon-Sat. **Admission** €10-€12. **No credit cards. Map** p305 D6.

Small, friendly club offers semi-avant jazz with a mostly African-American cast. Summer garden.

B-Flat

Rosenthaler Strasse 13, Mitte (283 3123/www.b-flat-berlin.de). U8 Rosenthaler Platz/bus N8, N52. **Open** from 9pm daily. **Admission** €4-€10. **No credit cards. Map** p302 F3.

Cavernous bar fills up for mostly local, mostly hoity-toity, lily-white mainstream jazz acts and DJ sets.

Junction Bar

Gneisenaustrasse 18, Kreuzberg (694 6602/www.junction-bar.de). U7 Gneisenaustrasse. **Open** *Café* 11-2am daily. *Club* 8pm-5am daily. *Concerts* 9pm Thur-Sun; 10pm Fri, Sat. **Admission** €3-€6. **No credit cards. Map** p306 F5.

Jazz in all varieties – swing, Latin, contemporary, jazz poetry. Occasionally some blues and rock too. After-show DJs spin soul, funk and R&B.

Kunstfabrik Schlot

Chausseestrasse 18 (entrance Schlegelstrasse 26), Mitte (448 2160/www.kunstfabrik-schlot.de). U6 Zinnowitzer Strasse. **Open** 8pm-late daily. **Admission** *Concerts* €5-€10. *Cabaret* €7-€8. **No credit cards. Map** p302 E2.

The Prenzlauer Berg jazz club now in a refunctioned Mitte industrial complex. Intriguing Polish and Czech jazz, cabaret and improv theatre.

Quasimodo

Kantstrasse 12A, Charlottenburg (312 8086/www.quasimodo.de). U2, U9, S3, S5, S7, S9 Zoologischer Garten. **Open** *Office* 11am-6pm Mon-Fri. *Concerts* from 9pm daily. **Admission** €8-€25. **No credit cards. Map** p305 C4.

Small, cramped and a stopping-off point for many US bands touring Europe. The booking policy now also includes 1970s rock, blues, roots and R&B.

Soultrane

Kantstrasse 17, Charlottenburg (315 1860/www.soultrane.de). S3, S5, S7, S9, S75 Savignyplatz/bus N49. **Open** 10am-2am Tue-Thur; 10am-late Fri-Sun. **Admission** €12-€18 Sat, Sun. **Credit** AmEx. **Map** p305 C4.

High-end dining and exclusive sets by Herbie Hancock, Ute Lemper and Til Brönner as well as by local fixtures like Tony Hurdle and Gary Wiggins. In the former restaurant (interiors by Terence Conran) of the stilwerk (*see p164*) design mall.

Tränenpalast

Reichstagsufer 17, Mitte (office 206 1000/tickets 2061 0011/www.traenenpalast.de). U6, S1, S2, S3, S5, S7, S9 Friedrichstrasse. **Open** *Box office* from 6pm daily. *Concerts* phone for details. **Admission** €8-€30. **Credit** phone for details. **Map** p316/p302 F3.

This former checkpoint is now a cosy venue not only for jazz notables such as Pharaoh Sanders, but also cabaret, laid-back rock acts and comedians.

Yorckschlösschen

Yorckstrasse 15, Kreuzberg (215 8070/www.yorckschloesschen.de). U6, U7 Mehringdamm. **Open** 9am-3am Mon-Thur, Sun; 9am-4am, Fri, Sat. **Admission** varies. **Credit** AmEx, DC, MC, V. **Map** p306 E5/F5.

Century-old Berliner *Eckkneipe* mutated into a jazz hangout in the early 1970s and is still going strong. Largely trad jazz with a smidgeon of R&B and funk on Wednesday, Friday and Saturday nights as well as Sunday afternoon concerts. Noteworthy for the garden, good *Weizenbier* and CD shop.

Nightlife

City of night, but not of sleep.

Sternradio. *See p226.*

Newcomers to Berlin may find themselves either mystified or daunted by the variety, intensity, stamina and tolerance that characterises nightlife in this shadowy city. But soon, the visitor happily joins native Berliners on the enticing and bountiful club, bar and cabaret trails.

Clubs

Hanging out with beer bottle or cocktail glass in hand and/or swaying to the beat on the dancefloor have always been among the city's favourite pastimes. Until the end of the 1980s, the walled city attracted radicals with its military service-exemption and subsidised dissidence. Geopolitical circumstances also made it hard to get out of town at weekends, so drinking and nightclubbing became the central get-away-from-it-all form of leisure.

After the Wall fell many scenes moved east, converting abandoned warehouses, industrial buildings and youth clubs into techno and house dancefloors that opened for days at a time. As the Love Parade grew and the underground scene spilled out on to the streets and into the mainstream, at times it seemed like the whole city was a club that wouldn't close. Liberal licensing laws still do not specify any closing hours, and evenings out follow the classic continental time-frame, with restaurants serving until 11pm or midnight and clubs peaking between 2am and 4am.

Much of the variety of Berlin after dark is due to the fact that it's still a city of independent bar and club owners. While stalwarts of the post-Wall squat scene and 1990s club culture zenith such as IM Eimer, Ostgut, WMF and Maria have since closed or relocated, things seem to have settled for the time being. Given Germany's economic downturn, it's heartening that new places still open and stay open. And while stylish newcomers like 12/34 or Watergate are a far cry from the dank cellars and techno bunkers of yore, the city still remains impervious to the charms of elitist, upscale nightclubs.

While a comprehensive survey of Berlin clubland would require a whole book, musically

► *For more late-night drinking options, see chapter* **Cafes, Bars & Pubs**.

KingKongKlub. *See p225.*

oriented stylistic indicators can give rough impressions of particular Berlin scenes. Techno, house, trance, drum 'n' bass, hip hop, electroclash, Balkan Beats and Russian Disco, African, R&B/soul, blaxploitation funk, biker, neo-rockabilly, headbanger, Goth, neo-grunge, industrial, neo-wave, post punk, lounge-core and Latin scenes all make their presence felt in regular and one-off venues around Berlin.

And everything comes and goes. The listings here are as current as we can make them, but anything could have happened in a year's time. Particularly for clubs, we recommend you cross-check against local listings. Happily, Berlin has a highly developed information infrastructure. Pamphlets and party flyers can be found on bar tops and in postcard and newspaper racks in cafés across the city. The clubradio website (www.klubradio.de) features streams from Tresor and WMF, and many bars and clubs have websites. The Club Commission, an umbrella lobby organisation, also has an informative site at www.clubcommission.de

The distinction between bars and nightclubs is often blurred, with many bars offering DJs and dancefloors and nightly changes of theme and atmosphere, and some putting on bands. And recurring parties without home venues may be thrown in several places over the course of a season (*see p231* **A moveable Fest**).

We've organised our listings by area partly because the different areas have different characters of nightlife, but also because any system of categorisation squelches particularities of scene and venue.

Mitte is still the epicentre of the city's clubscape, although the centre of gravity is gradually shifting north from the Hackescher Markt/Oranienburger Strasse area towards Rosenthaler Platz and into the district's northwestern and southeastern fringes. Sub-centres are emerging in various Friedrichshain, Prenzlauer Berg and even Kreuzberg neighbourhoods.

Mitte

For an overview of the café, pub and bar scene in Mitte, *see p142*.

Bergwerk

Bergstrasse 68 (280 8876/www.bergwerk.de). U8 Rosenthaler Platz/bus N8. **Open** 5pm-late daily. **Admission** free; €2-€4 for special events. **No credit cards. Map** p302 F2.

Dependable basement club for young-ish, no-nonsense crowd eager to avoid posey places and pricey beer. Lock, pop and slam to alternative, crossover and hip hop.

Club der polnischen Versager

Torstrasse 66 (2809 3779/www.polnischeversager.de). U2 Rosa-Luxemburg-Platz/bus N2. **Open** 7pm-1am daily. **Admission** €2. **No credit cards. Map** p303 G2/3.

The 'club of Polish losers' is a living-room-sized space offering a rich programme of exhibitions, readings, film screenings and, on Thursdays, music and DJs from Poland and Berlin's Polish expat community. A fun way to get acquainted with the new EU neighbours. Membership can be purchased at the bar along with vodka and Baltika beer.

Cookie's

Charlottenstrasse 44 (no phone/www.cookies-berlin.de). U6, S1, S2, S3, S5, S7, S9, S25, S26, S75 Friedrichstrasse/bus N5, N84. **Open** varies. **Admission** varies. **No credit cards. Map** p316/p302 F3.

This big ballroom-like venue is usually packed with a fashion-conscious crowd writhing to techno or minimal house, or chattering at the bar. The slickly designed, unisex, flimsily walled toilets resemble an art installation; not recommended, then, for the introverted or faint-hearted. Perennially hip, including the monthly classical night, Yellow Lounge (*see p234* **Roll over Beethoven**).

Hotelbar

Zionskirchstrasse 5 (4432 8577/www.hotelbar-berlin.de). U8 Bernauer Strasse/bus N2, N8. **Open** 10pm-late Mon-Sat. **Admission** free. **No credit cards. Map** p303 G2.

Stylish retro 1970s dancefloor below the Roberta (*see p145*) and Urban Comfort Food snack bar (*see p123*) with DJs spinning a range of grooves from R&B and disco to house with some big beat and even punk thrown in. Also regular film screenings.

Kaffee Burger

Torstrasse 60 (2804 6495/www.kaffeeburger.de). U2 Rosa-Luxemburg-Platz/bus N2. **Open** 5pm-late Mon-Thur; 9pm-late Fri, Sat. **Admission** €3-€5. **No credit cards. Map** p303 G2.

Former haunt of the pre-1989 Prenzlauer Berg underground literary scene, reopened in 1999. Poet Bert Papenfuss is a co-owner, so the written and spoken word still figure strongly, with regular readings of poetry, prose and subversive non-fiction. Russian expat cult author Vladimir Kaminer DJs Russian Disco nights (www.russendisko.de) twice monthly. But that's only part of the eclectic and enjoyable programme, which includes regular film screenings, live music from local and east European acts and *Schallplattenunterhalter* ('record entertainers': East German term for DJ) spinning anything from soul to 'thrillbient', crime jazz to East Berlin punk.

KingKongKlub

Brunnenstrasse 173 (2859 8538/www.king-kong-klub.de). U8 Rosenthaler Platz/bus N8, N84. **Open** 9pm-late Mon-Sat. **Admission** varies. **No credit cards. Map** p302 F1/2.

Quirky and comfy club offering DJ sets and live sets in both new and retro flavours. Genres include anything from French neo-chanson electropop and post-punk to Polish alternative and Roma beats. Highly affordable beer and pleasant bar staff. Also readings focusing on music journalism.

Kinzo Club

Karl-Liebknecht-Strasse 11 (9700 4820/ www.kinzo-berlin.de). U2, U5, U8, S3, S5, S7, S9, S75 Alexanderplatz. **Open** 11pm-late Wed, Sat. **Admission** €4-€6. **No credit cards. Map** p316/p303 G3.

Minimalist, cutting-edge club on the cusp of nightlife and media arts boasting top DJs such as Chica and the Folder, Erobique, Le Hammond Inferno or Eric D. of Whirlpool Productions. Also VJ sets, film screenings and sound art.

Mudd Club

Grosse Hamburger Strasse 17 (4403 6299/www.muddclub.de). S3, S5, S7, S9, S75 Hackescher Markt/bus N2, N5, N8, N84. **Open** 9.30pm-late Wed, Thur-Sat. **Admission** €4. **No credit cards. Map** p316/p302 F3.

Launched and run by Steve Maas, impresario of the original early 1980s NYC Mudd Club, at the time the hub of new wave postmodern clubbing. In Berlin, Maas has set up shop in the dank and cavernous basement of a courtyard complex off Oranienburger Strasse. The Mudd Club focuses on Russian and other eastern European music, with bi-monthly Balkan Beat nights (www.balkanbeats.de) and other live and DJ events.

Oxymoron

Hof 1, Hackesche Höfe, Rosenthaler Strasse 40-1 (2839 1886/www.oxymoron-berlin.de). U8 Weinmeisterstrasse or S3, S5, S7, S9, S75 Hackescher Markt/bus N2, N5, N8, N84. **Open** *Club* 8pm-1am Wed; 11pm-late Sat. *Restaurant/café* 11am-late daily. **Admission** *Club* €5-€10. **Credit** AmEx, V. **Map** p316/p302 F3.

A salon-à-club with elegantly recessed booths in the heart of the Hackescher Markt leisure mall, Oxymoron is a book begging to be judged by its expensive cover charges. In the restaurant/café, tourists and ad execs vie with couples from Charlottenburg for the attention of demi-mondettes modelling waitress aprons. The club (in the rear) is small but efficient, catering to guests who would be

The best Clubs

For a good all-round Saturday night
The **WMF** at Café Moskau has got it all: great DJs, classic location, long tradition and a crowd that's both fun and fashionable. *See p227.*

For well-heeled lounging
Minimal house with cocktails and waterfront views at **12/34**. *See p228.*

For drum 'n' bass
Prenzlauer Berg's **Icon** remains Berlin's breakbeat central. *See p227.*

For good old-fashioned techno
Veteran trance and techno workhorses such as Dr Motte and Paul van Dyk continue to rock the high street at **Casino**. *See p228.*

For Russian disco and a literary vibe
Cult author Wladimir Kaminer twice monthly as DJ is only one of **Kaffee Burger**'s eclectic attractions. *See p225.*

For shagging in public
The infamous **KitKatClub** is no place to be shy. *See p229.*

For not being fashionable
DJs play anything that someone'll dance to and no one cares what you wear at **Sophienclub**. *See p226.*

For a punk queer drag kind of sensibility
Black Girls Coalition has its own angle on fun. *See p228.*

WMF. *See p227.*

very hip in Munich. DJs play anything from house to acid jazz to package-tour dance.

Polar.TV

Heidestrasse 73 (246 259 320/www.no-ufos.de). S3, S5, S7, S9, S75 Hauptbahnhof-Lehrter Bahnhof/ bus N41. **Open** 11pm-late Sat. **Admission** €10. **No credit cards. Map** p302 E2.

Techno and house parties (courtesy of the No Ufos crew, *see p231* **A moveable Fest**) in a former commercial building on the fringe of what could be called Mitte. The generous space accommodates crowds happily grooving to local and international DJs and the occasional live act. In summer, there's also Polar.park, an outdoor chillout area complete with 'Wimbledon' lawn.

Sage-Club

Köpenicker Strasse 76 (278 9830/www.sage-club.de). U8 Heinrich-Heine-Strasse/bus N8. **Open** 10pm-late Thur; 11pm-late Fri-Sun. **Admission** €6-€11. **No credit cards. Map** p307 G4.

Large, labyrinthine complex of half a dozen dancefloors and bars under the Heinrich-Heine-Strasse U-Bahn station, catering to a fashion-conscious, twentysomething crowd into anything from techno (Saturdays) to rock (Thursdays) or R&B ('Funky Fridays'). In a separate, street-level part of the same complex, the Cantina Berlin Barcelona also hosts an assortment of club nights.

Salon Tbilisi

Torstrasse 164/Linienstrasse 98 (2790 7101/ www.salon-tbilisi.de). U8 Rosenthaler Platz/bus N2, N8. **Open** 6pm-late daily. **Admission** €3-€5. **No credit cards. Map** p303 F2.

Courtyard club, accessible from parallel streets. Just opened at press time but a promising-looking enterprise from Whirlpool Productions' Eric D. Clark, aiming for a stylish house-music kind of crowd.

Sophienclub

Sophienstrasse 6 (282 4552/www.sophienclub.de). U8 Weinmeisterstrasse or S3, S5, S7, S9, S75 Hackescher Markt/bus N8. **Open** 10pm-late Tue, Thur, Fri-Sun. **Admission** €3-€5 Tue, Thur; €5 Fri; €6 Sat. **No credit cards. Map** p316/p302 F3.

One of a handful of youth-oriented clubs in East Berlin before reunification, the club always ignored musical trends and still does. There's hip hop and R&B downstairs, and anything from new wave to chart hits upstairs. Good for people looking to party but not terribly concerned about being fashionable.

Sternradio

Alexanderplatz 5 (2472 4982/www.sternradio-berlin.de). S3, S5, S7, S9, S75, U2, U5, U8 Alexanderplatz/bus N5, N8. **Open** 11pm-late Fri, Sat. **Admission** €8 Fri; €10 Sat. **No credit cards. Map** p316/p303 G3.

Named after an old East German radio brand and located in a typical late 1960s edifice, Sternradio has become a popular old-school house and techno venue, thanks in part to residencies by Woody, Clé (latterly of Märtini Brös fame) and Tamito.

Tresor/Globus

Leipziger Strasse 126A (6953 7714/www.tresor-berlin.de). U2, S1, S2, S25, S26, Potsdamer Platz/bus N2, N84. **Open** 11pm-late Wed-Sat. **Admission** €3-€10. **No credit cards. Map** p306 E4.

Pioneering no-man's-land club, partly in the subterranean safe-deposit box room of the otherwise vanished pre-war Wertheim department store, partly in the old Globus bank building at ground level. This was the place in techno's good old days, and the legend just about lingers. Still good for catching Juan Atkins, Blake Baxter, Jeff Mills and other Detroit greats when they're in town. The summer Trancegarden out back, with tables and fairy lights among the shrubbery, is the club's finest feature, complementing two internal dancefloors and a bar. Rumours of Tresor's imminent demise always turn out to have been somewhat exaggerated.

WMF

Karl-Marx-Allee 34 (2887 88910/www.wmfclub.de). U5 Schillingstrasse/bus N5. **Open** 11pm-late Thur-Sat. **Admission** €8-€10. **No credit cards. Map** p316/p302 F3.

In its sixth incarnation – now at the former Café Moskau, East Berlin's showcase Russian restaurant – WMF remains among the city's best techno/house venues, attracting a stream of top local and international acts and DJs. Most events take place in the spacious basement bar still retaining much original GDR design, but on special occasions all floors of this landmark building are opened.

Prenzlauer Berg

For an overview of the café, pub and bar scene in Prenzlauer Berg, *see p147.*

Ausland

Lychener Strasse 60 (447 7008/www.ausland-berlin.de). U2 Eberswalder Strasse/bus N2. **Open** varies. **Admission** €3-€5. **No credit cards. Map** p303 G1.

In keeping with a trend for clubs to offer added intellectual value, this subterranean location calls itself a 'space for interdisciplinary art, music and theory'. Don't let that scare you away from some interesting electronica club nights and experimental concerts. For those who can't make it to the club, Ausland also has a show on Berlin's only free radio, reboot.fm (104.1/www.reboot.fm/stream), which can be heard on Wednesdays from 7pm to 9pm.

Icon

Cantianstrasse 15 (4849 2878 /www.iconberlin.de). U2 Eberswalder Strasse or U2, S4, S8 Schönhauser Allee/bus N2, N55. **Open** 11pm-late Tue; 11.30pm-late Fri, Sat. **Admission** €3-€6; special events €10. **No credit cards. Map** p303 G1.

A tricky-to-locate entrance in the courtyard just north of the junction with Milastrasse leads to an interesting space cascading down several levels into a long stone cellar. It's a well-ventilated little labyrinth, with an intense dancefloor space, imaginative lighting, good sound and a separate bar. Sometimes breakbeat, sometimes drum 'n' bass. Best when the core crowd of young locals is augmented by a wider audience for some special event.

Knaack

Greifswalder Strasse 224 (442 7060/www.knaack-berlin.de). S4, S8, S10 Greifswalder Strasse/tram N54. **Open** *Bar* 6pm-late daily. *Club* 8pm-late Wed; 9pm-late Fri, Sat. **Admission** *Club* €2.50 Wed; €2.50-€5 Fri, Sat. *Concerts* €6-€18. **No credit cards. Map** p303 H2.

Veteran multi-level club attracting a young audience with a changing programme of hard, aggressive music in the basement, and generic party music upstairs. The concert hall books a steady stream of interesting international acts (*see p219*).

Magnet Club

Greifswalder Strasse 212-13 Prenzlauer Berg (4285 1335/www.magnet-club.de). S4, S8, S10 Greifswalder Strasse/tram N54. **Open** 11pm-late Fri, Sat; 8pm-late Sun. **Admission** €5-€8. **No credit cards. Map** p303 H2.

Live music in the back, lounge and dancefloor space up front with Swinging London-style lighting and decor. During the week, Magnet showcases an array of local talent; weekends are usually devoted to funk, R&B, disco and indie club nights, such as Karrera Klub (*see p231* **A moveable Fest**).

nbi

Schönhauser Allee 157 (www.neueberlinerinitiative.de). U2 Senefelderplatz/bus N2. **Open** 8pm-late daily. **Admission** free Mon-Wed; free-€3 Thur-Sun. **No credit cards. Map** p303 G1/2.

In the building on the right side of the courtyard, the Neuer Berliner Initiative promotes cutting-edge electronica from local and international acts, including those on their own label (Kyborg, Frank Bretschneider). There's free entry to rehearsals and workshops. Freizeitheim, a separate club in the front of the same building, serves up trashier electronics for your dancing and lounging pleasure.

Soda-Club

Knaackstrasse 97 (4405 8707/www.soda-berlin.de). U2 Eberswalder Strasse or U2, S4, S8 Schönhauser Allee/bus N2. **Open** varies-6am Thur-Sun. **Admission** *Club* €3-€10. **Credit** V (restaurant only). **Map** p303 G2.

In the Kulturbrauerei entertainment complex, the bar is a serviceable meeting point but the upstairs club-by-numbers with its unimaginative 'black music' policy is highly avoidable, save for the Thursday salsa nights (with instruction) which attract a devoted following and are usually a good place to meet people.

Taucher Club

Saarbrücker Strasse 36a (5664 2639/www.taucher-berlin.de). U2, U5, U8, S3, S5, S7, S9, S75 Alexanderplatz/Bus N5, N8. **Open** 11pm-late Thur-Sat. **Admission** free-€8. **No credit cards. Map** p303 G2.

In a former bakery which once housed Cookies and Casino, this large club specialises in French House by the likes of Cassius, Alex Gopher and Etienne de Crecy. Rooftop lounge in summer.

Friedrichshain

Nightlife in Friedrichshain is concentrated in **Oberbaum City** (the area around Warschauer Strasse station) for bigger venues catering to a younger, dancefloor kind of crowd. Hipper neighbourhoods are centred around **Simon-Dach-Strasse** (more upscale), further east near **Samariterstrasse U-Bahn** (rougher, ex-squat vibe) and **Karl-Marx-Allee** (east retro chic).

For an overview of the café, pub and bar scene in Friedrichshain, *see p150*.

Astro Bar

Simon-Dach-Strasse 40 (no phone). U5 Frankfurter Tor/bus N5, N29. **Open** 6pm-late daily. **Admission** free. **No credit cards. Map** p88.

Charming dusk-till-dawn venue with control panels in the back room that could have come from a *Thunderbirds* set, and DJs playing anything from Slim Galliard to Atari Teenage Riot.

Black Girls Coalition

Samariterstrasse 32 (6953 4300/www.blackgirls coalition.de). U5 Samariterstrasse/bus N5. **Open** 9-4am Mon & last Thur of month. **Admission** €2-€3. **No credit cards. Map** p88.

Owned by a black drag queen, BGC (as this small club is familiarly known) is a unique synthesis of punk and queer sensibilities. Cheap drinks, drag performances, live music.

Butter Club

Scharnweberstrasse 54 (www.butterclub.de). U5 Samariterstrasse/bus N5. **Open** Wed-Sun 10pm-late. **Admission** varies. **No credit cards. Map** p88.

Formerly the anglophone indie hangout DeziBel, now hosting both live and DJ events varying from punk, alternative, electrofolk and emo to good old-fashioned hard rock. Frequented by a grungy, beer-drinking crowd.

Casino

Mühlenstrasse26-30 (2900 9799/www.casino-bln.de). S3, S5, S7, S9, S75 Ostbahnhof/bus N29, N44. **Open** 11pm-late Fri, Sat. **Admission** €3-€10. **No credit cards. Map** p307 H4.

This spacious techno club and live venue, divided into main floor and lounge, is the last holdover in a disused industrial complex which also once housed the Ostgut. Names such as Dr Motte, Clé and resident Paul van Dyk continue to pack 'em in.

GeburtstagsKlub

Am Friedrichshain 33 (4202 1406/www. geburtstagsklub.de). Tram 2, 3, 4/bus N54. **Open** 11pm-late Mon, Fri, Sat. **Admission** €5-€8. **No credit cards. Map** p303 H2.

House, breakbeats, electro, funk and disco are writ large in this subterranean club, which is decorated with light and slide projections. Reggae, ragga and dancehall feature on Monday nights. Also monthly drag performances.

K17

Pettenkoferstrasse 17 (4208 9300/www.k17.de). U5, S8, S9, S41, S42 Frankfurter Allee/bus N5. **Open** 10pm-late Tue-Wed, Fri. **Admission** free-€4. **No credit cards. Map** p88.

Goth, EBM, industrial and metal are undead and well in this three-floor club. The mid-week Jailbreak concert series features live earaches inflicted by hardcore, nu-metal and crossover bands.

Matrix

Warschauer Platz 18 (2949 1047/www.matrix-berlin.de). U1, U12, S3, S5, S6, S7, S9, S75 Warschauer Strasse/bus N29. **Open** 9pm-5am Tue, Thur; 10pm-5am Wed; 10pm-6am Fri, Sat. **Admission** €3-€6. **Credit** AmEx, MC, V. **Map** p307 H4.

Four dancefloors, six bars and numerous chillout zones under the U-Bahn arches attract a young, very mixed (gay and straight) crowd. The music policy has been mainstreamed somewhat from the hard techno and later nu-metal days of yore, with classic 1970s and 1980s disco, R&B, house and chart fare now dominating the decks.

Pavillion im Volkspark Friedrichshain

Friedenstrasse corner Platz der Vereinten Nationen (0172 750 4724/www.pavillion-berlin.de). Tram 5, 15/bus N94. **Open** 9pm-late Tue; 10pm-late Fri, Sat. **Admission** €5-€6. **No credit cards. Map** p303 H3.

Shake your blaxploitation booty to a mix of funk, disco, dancehall and house in this parkside pavilion. Summer beer garden and barbecue.

12/34

Stralauer Allee 1 (52007 2301/www.fritzfischer.de). U1, U12, S3, S5, S6, S7, S9, S75 Warschauer Strasse/bus N29. **Open** 11pm-late Fri, Sat. **Admission** €5-€8. **No credit cards. Map** p316/p303 G3.

Above the Fritz Fischer restaurant (*see p130*) in the new Universal Music headquarters by the Spree, with minimalist red design and house music attracting a young, well-heeled crowd. Local DJs on Fridays. Good views over the river from the terrace.

Kreuzberg

For an overview of the café, pub and bar scene in Kreuzberg, *see p152*.

Konrad Tönz

Falckensteinstrasse 30 (612 3252/www.konrad toenz.de). U1, U15 Schlesisches Tor/bus N29, N65. **Open** 8.15pm-2am Tue-Thur; 8.15-late Fri-Sun. **Admission** free. **No credit cards. Map** p307 H5.

Named after the Swiss correspondent of popular true crime show *Aktenzeichen XY ungelöst*, this lounge with small dancefloor also embraces a retro, shaken-not-stirred aesthetic with patterned wallpaper and suave jazzy and twangy grooves from mono record players. DJs from 9pm at weekends.

Polar.TV. *See p226.*

Mandingo

Mehringdamm 107 (6950 6800). U6, U7 Mehringdamm/bus N4, N19. **Open** 10pm-6am Fri, Sat. **Admission** €5. **No credit cards**. **Map** p306 F5.

A friendly and unpretentious meeting place for Berlin's African community and other lovers of zouk, highlife, rai, reggae, ragga, funk, R&B and hip hop – a full spectrum of African, Afro-Caribbean and African-American musical styles.

Privat Club

Pücklerstrasse 34 (611 3302/www.privatclub-berlin.de). U1, U15 Görlitzer Bahnhof/bus N29, N44. **Open** 11pm-late Fri, Sat. **Admission** €5. **No credit cards**. **Map** p307 H4.

This long, low space in the basement of the Markthalle (*see p84*) hosts a variety of events, from occasional live acts to retro parties and dance music of all stripes. Worth a look, though it's hard to predict just what you'll find.

SO36

Oranienstrasse 190 (6140 1306/www.so36.de). U1, U8, U15 Kottbusser Tor/bus N8, N29. **Open** 9pm-late daily. **Admission** €3-€8; concerts €8-€20. **No credit cards**. **Map** p307 G4.

Predominantly a gay and lesbian venue, though Monday house and techno nights attract a mixed cross-section (though mostly male) less defined by sexuality than the desire to dance. Recently refurbished. See also *p207*.

Watergate

Falckensteinstrasse 49 (6128 0395/www.water-gate.de). U1, U15 Schlesisches Tor/bus N29, N65. **Open** 11pm-late Tue, Thur-Sat. **Admission** €6-€10. **No credit cards**. **Map** p88.

The unassuming entrance belies a spacious glass-fronted club that offers a view of the Spree for those sipping cocktails or dancing to breakbeats, hip hop or deep house. Lounge in the basement.

Schöneberg

For an overview of the café, pub and bar scene in Schöneberg, *see p154*.

KitKatClub

Bessemerstrasse 4, Schöneberg (no phone/www.kitkatclub.de). Bus 204, N6, N46. **Open** 9pm-late Thur; 11pm-late Fri, Sat; 8pm-late Sun. **Admission** varies. **No credit cards**.

You thought the days of true Berlin decadence were a thing of the past? Think again. Although Berlin's best-known sex club is not in the least bit seedy, this is still no place for the narrow-minded, with half the crowd in fetish gear, the other half in no gear at all, and every kind of sexual activity taking place in full view. In its way KitKat is the most relaxing club night in Berlin. No one has anything to prove and everyone knows why they're there, and will almost certainly get it. But if you're not dressed up (or down) enough, you probably won't get in: there's a rigorous door policy.

90°

Dennewitzstrasse 37 (2300 5954/www.90grad.com). U1, U15 Kurfürstenstrasse/bus N5, N19. **Open** 7pm-2am Wed; 11pm-late Fri, Sat. **Admission** varies Wed; €10 Fri, Sat. **Credit** AmEx, V. **Map** p306 E5.

Not to be confused with the overheated, oversexed joint of yore. Populated mainly by minor visiting celebs and wannabes. Dress code and door policy.

Tiergarten

Adagio

Marlene-Dietrich-Platz 1 (2592 9550/www.adagio.de). U2, S1, S2, S25, S26 Potsdamer Platz/bus N2, N5, N19. **Open** 7pm-2am Wed-Thur, Sun; 10pm-4am Fri; 10pm-5am Sat (occasionally closed for private events). **Admission** €5-€10. **Credit** AmEx, V. **Map** p306 E4.

Spin-off of a chichi Zurich disco, its 'medieval' decor and Renaissance frescos are jarringly at odds with the Renzo Piano-designed Musicaltheater whose basement it occupies. Pricey drinks, abundant members-only areas and a music policy of disco, polite house and oldies cater to fortysomething tourists and locals willing to shell out for a semblance of exclusivity. Dress code (no jeans or sports shoes).

Dorian Gray

Marlene-Dietrich-Platz 4 (office: 2529 2172/club: 2593 0660/www.doriangrayberlin.de). U2, S1, S2, S25, S26 Potsdamer Platz/bus N2, N5, N19. **Open** 10pm-late Thur-Sat. **Admission** €8-€10. **Credit** MC, V. **Map** p306 E4.

The space vacated by the unpopular Blu was recently taken over by the crew of Frankfurt's legendary nightspot of the same name. Softer sounds (funk, electro pop, house) than the earlier incarnation's techno policy, but just as exclusive – dress code, Davidoff lounge on the top floor and even over-21 admission for some events. Gay night on Thursday.

Trompete

Lützowplatz 9 (2300 4794/www.trompete-berlin.de). U1, U2, U4, Nollendorfplatz/bus N5, N19. **Open** 6pm-late Thur; 10pm-late Fri, Sat. **Admission** free; dance events €5-€6. **Credit** AmEx, DC, MC, V. **Map** p305 D4.

Actor Ben Becker is the not-so-silent partner in this heavily publicised nightlife joint venture. Has found its niche thanks to the popular After Work Lounge on Thursdays, from 6pm with DJs from RadioEins spinning sounds to forget the day's stress by.

Charlottenburg

For an overview of the café, pub and bar scene in Charlottenburg, *see p156*.

Abraxas

Kantstrasse 134 (312 9493). U7 Wilmersdorfer Strasse or S3, S5, S7, S9, S75 Savignyplatz/bus N49. **Open** 10pm-late Tue-Sat. **Admission** free Tue-Thur; €5 Fri, Sat. **Credit** V. **Map** p304 B4.

A dusky, relaxed disco where you don't have to dress up to get in and where academics, social workers, bank clerks and midwives populate the floor. Flirtation rules. Dance to funk, soul, Latino and jazz.

Big Eden

Kurfürstendamm 202 (882 6120/www.big-eden.de). U15 Uhlandstrasse/bus N10, N19, N21, N29. **Open** 10pm-late Wed, Thur; 11pm-late Fri, Sat. **Admission** €10. **Credit** MC, V. **Map** p305 C4.

One-time watering hole of the old West Berlin 'jet-set', formerly owned by Viagra-charged geriatric playboy Rolf Eden, now offers club nights programmed by Kitty-yo, Ministry of Sound and Alexander Hacke of Einstürzende Neubauten.

Other districts

Insel

Alt-Treptow 6, Treptow (5360 8020/www.insel-berlin.com). S6, S8, S10 Plänterwald/bus N65. **Open** 7pm-1am Wed; 10pm-late Fri, Sat. **Admission** free Wed; €5-€10 Fri, Sat. **No credit cards**.

Out of the way, but brilliant – like a miniature castle on a tiny Spree island, with several levels and a top-floor balcony. Once a Communist youth club, now a live venue/colourful club – with lots of neon and ultra-violet, crusties and hippies, techno and hip hop, punk and metal. Great in summer.

MS Hoppetosse

Eichenstrasse 4, Treptow (533 7169/www.arena-berlin.de/location/hoppe/intro.html). S8, S9, S41, S42 Treptower Park/bus N65. **Open** 10pm-late Fri-Sun. **Admission** varies. **Credit** MC, V. **Map** p88.

This docked boat on the Spree near Arena Treptow (*see p218*) is a restaurant by day and a disco by night. Electro, reggae and chart pop. On Friday night music journalists man the turntables.

Cabaret

Several venues have invested big money into recreating the look of old Berlin cabaret, but it's mostly wishful thinking. Places like Wintergarten and Friedrichstadtpalast are perfect examples. Here expect the type of show known as *Varieté*, with clowns, magicians, acrobats and expensive table service.

Modern Cabaret is a little less pretentious and cheaper. At venues like Bar Jeder Vernunft and BKA, you can see anything from gender-bending stand-up comedy to lascivious chansons. Watch out for *die O-Tonpiraten* (clever drag cabaret/theatre) or the anglophone entertainer Gayle Tufts ('denglish' stand-up comedy with pop). Modern Cabaret crosses over into the area of Improv-theater, stand-up comedy and a variety of music.

But this is not what the Germans call *Kabarett*, which has a strong following in Berlin. *Kabarett* is political satire sprinkled with original songs and sketches, and happens at venues such as Kartoon, Kneifzange, or Distel (watch out for press listings). But if you don't speak perfect German and have a good understanding of local politics such shows will be above your head. Finally there is *Travestie*, basically drag revue. Berlin offers some of the best you can get.

A moveable *Fest*

Some nightspots have such a strong identity that clubgoers hang out there regardless of any particular night's musical offerings. Others are vessels for a variety of travelling DJ crews or party concepts which are themselves the main attraction, making the rounds of suitable venues either by accident or design. Everyone wins in this floating crap game: partymakers have regular venues without the overheads of owning a club; venues have audiences and brand identity without worrying about booking policy; partygoers have fun. Here are some noteworthy party nomads and special events.

Dangerous Drums

www.dangerous-drums.de

Since 1999, Dangerous Drummers Ed 2000 and DJ Vela have been pounding out 'Modern Urban Funk' – essentially breakbeat, garage and neurofunk – with local DJs and international guests. The DD imprint issues mostly vinyl releases by Ed 2000 and kindred acts like Elektronauten or Circuit Breaker. Maria am Ufer (*see p220*) is a regular venue.

Karrera Klub

www.karrera-klub.de

Since 1996 DJs Tim, Spencer and Christian have been spinning an Anglophile selection of Britpop, indie, electroclash and bigbeat in Frankfurt and Berlin. Catch them at the Roter Salon in the Volksbühne (*see p220*), Bastard (*see p218*), Magnet (*see p227*), Mudd Club (*see p225*), Sophienclub (*see p226*), Kaffee Burger (*see p225*), Privat Club (*see p229*) or Maria am Ufer (*see p220*).

Ma Baker, Daddy Cool

www.mabaker.de, www.daddy-cool-party.de

Every 1st and 3rd Saturday of the month get out your leisure suits and platform shoes and head to Ma Baker at the BKA Luftschloss (Schlossplatz, Mitte) to shake those booties to 1970s dancefloor (Abba, Bee Gees and of course Boney M). A nightlife institution since 1992, Daddy Cool on the 2nd Saturday at the same venue has a broader spectrum: expect to hear the Stones, glam rock, Duran Duran and Neue Deutsche Welle added to the mix.

No Ufos

www.no-ufos.de

Since 1997 resident DJs like Clé, Phonique and Woody, often with top-flight international guests such as Laurent Garnier or Andrew Weatherall, have been heating up the crowds with techno and house. In 2002 a home base of sorts was established at Polar.TV (*see p226*) where No Ufos parties take flight every Saturday. No Ufos also land regularly at Sternradio (*see p226*).

Die schöne Party

www.schoeneparty.de

Danceability of a high order at this immensely popular bi-weekly party (every 2nd and 4th Saturday each month) sponsored since 2000 by RadioEins (which provides the DJs) and *tip* magazine. House, dance, rock and pop bring the dancefloor of the Kalkscheune (Johannisstrasse 2, Mitte) to boiling point while the Basement, Blue and Red Lounges offer more specialised sounds from rotating guest DJs. Prides itself on having first broken Manu Chao and Berlin electropop sensations 2Raumwohnung. Advance ticket purchase recommended.

The Sonic Pop Allnighter

Dance to 'Independent, Punk, New Wave and 60s Sound' at Kaffee Burger (*see p225*), 8mm Bar (*see p147*) and other smallish clubs around town.

Varieté & revues

Chamäleon Varieté

Hackesche Höfe, Rosenthaler Strasse 40-41, Mitte (282 7118/www.chamaeleonberlin.de). S3, S5, S7, S9, S75 Hackescher Markt. **Open** *Box office* noon-9pm Mon-Sat; 4-7pm Sun. *Showtimes* 8.30pm Mon, Wed-Sat; 7pm Sun; extra shows midnight Fri, Sat. **Tickets** €23 Mon, Wed, Thur, Sun; €28 Fri, Sat; €17 concessions. **No credit cards. Map** p302 F3.

Beautiful old theatre with classy table seating. As Hackesche Höfe becomes increasingly commercialised and touristy, there's a risk this club may become a sort of Wintergarten-Ost. Until then it still attracts a very diverse audience.

Friedrichstadtpalast

Friedrichstrasse 107, Mitte (2326 2326). U6, S1, S2, S3, S5, S7, S9, S25, S26, S75 Friedrichstrasse. **Open** 6pm-1am daily. *Box office* 10am-6pm Mon, Sun; 10am-7pm Tue-Sat. *Showtimes* 8pm Tue-Fri; 4pm, 8pm Sat; 4pm Sun. **Tickets** €15-€51 Tue-Thur, Sat, Sun matinee; €19-€59 Fri, Sat. **Credit** AmEx. **Map** p316/p302 F3.

Big, Las Vegas-style musical revues with Vegas-style prices to match. Mostly packed with coachloads of German tourists.

Kleine Nachtrevue

Kurfürstenstrasse 116, Schöneberg (218 8950/ www.Kleine-Nachtrevue.de). U1, U2, U12, U15 Wittenbergplatz. **Open** 7pm-3am Tue-Sat. *Showtimes* 10.45pm; (sometimes) 8.30pm Fri, Sat. **Admission** €15-€25. **Credit** AmEx, DC, MC, V. **Map** p305 D4.

As close as you can get to real nostalgic German cabaret – saucy, risqué and spiced with Berliner *Schnauze*. Nightly shows consist of short song or dance numbers sprinkled with tasteful nudity. Special weekend shows at 9pm vary from erotic opera or a four-course meal to songs from the male reincarnation of Marlene Dietrich.

Pomp, Duck and Circumstance

Spiegelpalast Salon Zazou, Gleisdreieck/ Möckernstrasse 26, Kreuzberg (2694 9200/www. pompduck.de). U1, U7, U15 Möckernbrücke. **Open** *Box office* 9am-8pm Mon-Fri; 12-8pm Sat, Sun. *Showtimes* 8pm Mon-Sat; 7pm Sun. **Tickets** €110 Wed-Thur, Sun; €120 Fri, Sat. **Credit** MC. **Map** p306 F4.

A *Varieté* extravaganza in an old-fashioned tent, where the show comes with a four-course meal – yes, usually including duck. Performers work the audience constantly and are first rate; the food is less reliable. Very expensive, but always packed.

La Vie en Rose

Flughafen Tempelhof, Tempelhof (6951 3000/www. lavieenrose-berlin.de). U6 Platz der Luftbrücke. **Open** *Box office* 11am-9pm daily. *Showtimes* 8pm Tue-Sun. **Admission** €25-€39 show only; €55 show & dine. **Credit** AmEx, DC, MC, V.

Revue theatre and restaurant/piano bar, to the left of Tempelhof Airport's main entrance. Dancing girls, soft porn, pricey drinks and maximum cheese.

Wintergarten Varieté

Potsdamer Strasse 96, Tiergarten (250 0880/hotline 2500 8888). U1, U12 Kurfürstenstrasse. **Open** *Box office* 10am-4pm Mon-Sat. *Showtimes* 8pm Mon; 4pm, 8pm Wed; 8pm Thur, Fri; 5pm, 8pm Sat; 3pm, 6pm Sun. **Tickets** €15-€55 show only; €66-€76 show & dine. **Credit** AmEx, MC, V. **Map** p306 E4.

A classy place. Shows are slick and professional, though sometimes of mixed quality. Excellent acrobats and magicians, but some awful comedy acts.

Modern

Bar Jeder Vernunft

Spiegelzelt, Schaperstrasse 24, Wilmersdorf (883 1582/www.bar-jeder-vernunft.de). U1, U9 Spichernstrasse. **Open** *Box office* noon-7pm daily; 3-6pm Sat, Sun. *Showtime* 8.30pm Mon-Thur; 8pm Fri, Sun. **Tickets** €15-€30. **Credit** AmEx, MC, V. **Map** p305 C5.

In this snazzy circus tent of many mirrors, you can see some of Berlin's most celebrated entertainers, and some polished English entertainers too. The Friday and Saturday late-night shows are generally free but can vary from a lovely surprise to a lame excuse. Watch out for the drink prices.

BKA Theater

Mehringdamm 34, Kreuzberg (202 2007/www.bka-luftschluss.de). U6, U7 Mehringdamm. **Open** 11am-8:30pm Mon-Fri; 2pm-8:30pm Sat. *Show* 8pm daily. **Tickets** €9-€24. **Credit** AmEx, MC, V. **Map** p306 F5.

Fresh and sassy *Hoftheater* (meaning it's located in the backyard) hosts varied acts such as the Nina Hagen Talk Show and drag comedian Ades Zabel.

Chez Nous

Marburger Strasse 14, Charlottenburg (213 1810). U2, U9, U12, S3, S5, S7, S9, S75 Zoologischer Garten. **Open** *Box office* 10am-1pm, 1.30-6.30pm Mon-Sat. *Showtimes* 8.30pm, 11pm daily. **Admission** €35. **Credit** AmEx, MC. **Map** p305 D4.

Revue with classic drag queen numbers.

Scheinbar

Monumentenstrasse 9, Schöneberg (784 5539/ www.scheinbar.de). U7 Kleistpark. **Open** *Box office* 7.30pm-after the show daily. *Showtimes* 8.30pm. **Admission** €11 Mon; €8 concessions; €6 Tue concessions; €6.50 Wed, Thur; €8 Fri, Sat. **No credit cards**. **Map** p306 E4.

Experimental, fun-loving cabaret in a hip, intimate club exploding with fresh talent.

Theater im Keller

Weserstrasse 211, Neukölln (623 1452). U7, U8 Hermannplatz. **Open** *Shows* Fri, Sat 8pm; Sun 7pm. **Admission** €23.40. **Credit** AmEx, MC, V. **Map** p307 H5/6.

Intimate, quaint little club where regular drag revue is somehow done with a more whimsical touch.

Cafe Theater Schalotte

Behaimstrasse 22, Charlottenburg (341 1485/ www.schalotte.de). U7 Richard-Wagner-Platz. **Open** *Box office* varies. *Showtimes* 4-8pm variable days. **Tickets** €10-€15. **No credit cards**. **Map** p300 B3.

Not very comfy, but fun shows. The O-Tonpiraten, a clever kind of drag theatre troupe, plays here often.

Tipi-Das Zelt

Grossquerallee btwn Kanzleramt & Haus d. Kulturen d. Welt, Tiergarten (0180 327 9358/www.tipi-das-zeit.de). Bus 100, 248 to Platz der Republik. **Open** *Box office* noon-7pm Mon-Sat; 3-6pm Sun. *Showtimes* 8.30pm Tue-Sat; 7.30pm Sun. **Tickets** €18.50-€42. **Credit** AmEx, V. **Map** p302 E3.

Circus tent in the Tiergarten with cool international performers, such as Italian Ennio and his amazing paper costumes, and England's Tiger Lilies.

Tränenpalast

Reichstagufer 17, Mitte (2061 0011/www. tranenpalast.de). U6, S1, S25, S5, S2 Friedrichstrasse. **Open** 6pm-9pm Mon-Sat; 4.30-9.30pm Sun. *Showtime* varies. **Tickets** varies. **No credit cards**. **Map** p316/p302 E3/F3.

In the days of division this was the entrance to the Friedrichstrasse checkpoint, scene of many a sad farewell. Shows vary from tango or salsa to political Kabarett and musical comedy.

Performing Arts

Though funding crises rumble on, Berlin remains on the front line of classical music, dance and theatre.

Lobby Hero at **Friends of Italian Opera**. *See p241.*

Music: Classical & Opera

There's no city in the world that can compete with Berlin in terms of the sheer number of orchestras (six, plus various private ones), opera houses (three, not counting several independent houses and companies) and venues (two major concert halls, plus a myriad of smaller venues). And it's not only quantity. The Berlin Philharmonic is arguably the world's finest symphony orchestra, and there are top-notch performances of one kind or another in Berlin pretty much every night of the year.

The profusion of companies and venues, however, is not only a legacy of the city's long artistic heritage, but also of its Cold War division. Berlin quite literally has enough classical music for any two normal cities. But how long can it continue to afford it? Belt-tightening has already begun. In March 2004, the Berlin Symphoniker closed after being refused further public funding by culture senator Thomas Flierl, reducing the city's major orchestra count from seven to six.

Meanwhile, rationalisation of Berlin's opera houses was initiated by Federal Minister of Culture Christina Weiss. The three houses are now incorporated into one foundation, and there are hopes that this will result in clearer artistic identities and more coordinated programming. Right now, not one of them is open in the summer when Berlin fills with tourists. Nor did any of them get it together to commemorate Hector Berlioz's 200th anniversary. But at the time of writing, they still hadn't found a Generalintendant for the new body, and Georg Vierthaler, managing director of the Staatsoper, faced the daunting task of also running the foundation. Meanwhile, unless both efficiency and ticket prices soar to match cuts in subsidy, one of the three houses is likely to close.

The **Deutsche Oper** was shaken by the sudden death of long-time intendant Götz Friedrich in December 2000. Friedrich's successor, Udo Zimmermann, had little success in modernising the profile of the house. Faced with both political opposition and audience resistance when he tried to appoint Fabio Luisi as new musical director, Zimmermann was forced to resign after little more than a year. At press time, Kiel intendant Kirsten Harms seemed the likely candidate for the post.

Meanwhile, the **Staatsoper Unter den Linden** has appointed the neurologist Peter Mussbach as intendant, succeeding the brief and uninspired reign of Georg Quander. While comfortably situated in Mitte and enjoying its proximity to German politics, the house itself is in desperate need of some renovation. The underground passage connecting the main house and administrative offices is regularly flooded; several performances even had to be stopped midway due to security hazards. Quite who will pay to sort all this out and where productions will be staged during the necessary closure remains unclear. Its orchestra, the **Berliner Staatskapelle**, founded in 1570 by royal decree and today directed by Daniel Barenboim, is regarded as Berlin's finest opera orchestra.

With Barenboim at the Staatsoper and Christian Thielemann still at the Deutsche Oper, Berlin has Germany's two best Wagner directors and is the only city in the world with two complete Ring cycles. (With Kyrill Petrenko taking over at the Komische Oper, even Berlin's third opera company now has a head conductor

Roll over Beethoven

You might think that, with all its concert halls, opera houses and performing ensembles, Berlin already offered enough opportunities to hear classical music. But the **Yellow Lounge** events (www.yellowlounge.de) at Cookie's (*see p224*) – usually first Monday of the month – are something different.

The concept is a classical club night: DJs spinning anything from Gesualdo to Górecki, abstract projections and visual effects by VJs from Pfadfinderei (motto: 'First-class digital shit') who jam along with the music, and with some kind of live performance providing the evening's centrepiece. Artists appearing so far have included Yundi Li, the Emerson String Quartet, Anna Gourari, Andreas Scholl, Micha Maisky, Musica Antiqua Köln and the Deutsches Kammerorchester. There have also been guest DJs, such as Rupert Huber from Vienna, Richard Dorfmeister's partner in Tosca, who challenged the audience with a set of Berg, Webern and Varèse.

Though it's not unknown for people to start waltzing when the DJ drops some Johann Strauss, dancing inevitably takes a back seat on these nights. Large areas of the floor are instead filled with big beds, where guests can recline and listen. Usually there's too much background conversation for anything pianissimo to work, and DJs have to mix from one piece to another, rarely letting anything play right through. The result can be a strange mish-mash of periods and styles, or a sort of symphonic wall of sound.

'You hear everything from Monteverdi to Ligeti,' explains David Canisius, the Yellow Lounge organiser and DJ who also plays violin with the Deutsches Kammerorchester. 'I string the pieces together without a break. For instance, I might take the secondary theme from Schubert's *Death and the Maiden* and lead into the second movement of a Górecki piece. That's a completely different epoch and they really don't have anything to do with each other. But at the very moment when the music works, I've reached someone.'

Yellow Lounge is ultimately an initiative of Universal Music, which owns Deutsches Grammophon and is looking for new ways to market its catalogue. The club nights have already resulted in two Yellow Lounge classical mix CDs, with Yellow Lounge tours to support their release. But if the events allow club-goers to encounter classical music in a relaxed, unpretentious context, they've also provided musicians with a performing experience considerably more immediate than that to be had within the conventions of a traditional classical performance space.

Canisius again: 'When we performed with the Deutsches Kammerorchester, I was completely wired: the place was totally packed. There were beer cans everywhere and we had to clear the way to our music stands. All at once the tremendous noise level sank and you could have heard a pin drop. Everyone could see the puddles forming on our fingerboards. We were practically rubbing shoulders with the audience – and not distanced from them like in a concert hall. An unbelievably magical exchange.'

Yellow Lounge is proving so successful that there have been queues around the block as Cookie's packs to capacity. If you're heading along, arrive early.

who made his name doing Wagner.) While Barenboim has just resigned his second post with the Chicago Symphony Orchestra to concentrate on Berlin, Thielemann is rarely seen at the Deutsche Oper, and is likely to be seen even less once he succeeds James Levine at the Munich Philharmonic.

For more avant-garde operatic fare, don't neglect the **Neuköllner Oper**, which puts on witty and imaginative productions from companies such as the **Neue Opernbühne**, **Zeitgenössische Oper** and **Berliner Kammeroper**. Highly promising is the newly founded company **Novoflot** (www.novoflot.de), gathered around energetic director Sven Holm and usually performing at the Sophiensaele. Expect innovative music and theatre of surprising quality despite low budgets.

ORCHESTRAL MANOEUVRES

Meanwhile, despite the closure of the Berliner Symphoniker, Berlin's orchestral scene is as vibrant as ever. The **Deutsches Symphonie Orchester** (www.dso-berlin.de) still boasts fairly substantial subsidies, which Kent Nagano negotiated before signing his contract, and remains the best place in town to hear avant-garde compositions. But the orchestra's artistic future remains uncertain: Nagano has accepted the chief post at the Bayrische Staatsoper from 2006 and will simultaneously be chief in Montreal. How he will manage to conduct four concerts a year with the DSO and also take care of Los Angeles Opera is a question only he can answer.

Groundbreaking 20th-century composers, from Hindemith to Prokofiev and Schönberg to Penderecki, have conducted their own work with the **Rundfunk-Sinfonieorchester Berlin** (www.rsb-online.de). The orchestra, founded in 1923 to provide programming for the new medium of radio, looks set to continue with its tradition of drawing attention to contemporary works under the competent hand of musical director Marek Janowski, who debuts in the 2002-03 season.

Fans of the old masters are still well served by the **Berliner Sinfonie-Orchester** (www.berliner-sinfonie-orchester.de), which plays at the splendid Konzerthaus, under ambitious conductor Eliahu Inbal. The feisty group – founded after the building of the Wall as the East's answer to the Philharmonic – has a loyal following of its own, but one that prefers more familiar works.

Berlin's chamber orchestras also offer a steady stream of first-rate concerts. One of the finest groups is **Ensemble Oriol** (www.ensemble-oriol.de) with a strong emphasis on contemporary music. The **Kammerorchester Berlin** (www.koberlin.de) remains popular but predictable, with works usually ranging from Vivaldi to Mozart and back again. The **Deutsches Kammerorchester Berlin** (www-dko-berlin.de) under manager Stefan Fragner has acquired an excellent reputation for working with rising star conductors and soloists, and providing innovative though still audience-friendly programmes. It's also the only orchestra to have played at the **Yellow Lounge** classical nights at Cookie's. *See p234* **Roll over Beethoven**.

And finally, there's the mighty **Berliner Philharmoniker** (www.berliner-philharmoniker.de) which goes from strength to strength under Sir Simon Rattle. He arrived at the Phil a bit like David Beckham at Real Madrid – effortlessly matching all the huge expectations. He also gathered the ensemble behind him by refusing to sign his contract until extra private funding was secured for musicians' salaries.

Rattle had promised to bring adventure to the programme and attract younger audiences. From his very first concert, he introduced an emphasis on contemporary composers such as Thomas Adès, Heiner Goebbels and Marc Anthony Turnage. He's also worked with jazz musicians and improvisers. But at the same time Rattle has put the ensemble through more traditional paces via an emphasis on Haydn and an early performance of Schubert's *Eighth*. He's also launched a new education programme with events such as a ballet performance of Stravinsky's *Sacre du Printemps* at the Arena Treptow (*see p218*) involving students from local schools. Right now, everyone loves him to bits.

FESTIVALS

Music festivals pepper Berlin's calendar. **MärzMusik – Festival für aktuelle Musik** (*see p186*) takes place annually over one to two weeks in March at various venues, and showcases trends in contemporary music. The **Ultraschall** (*see p186*) festival of new music, organised by DeutschlandRadio and Rundfunk Berlin-Brandenburg every January, presents many of the world's leading specialist ensembles. The biennial **Zeitfenster – Biennale für alte Musik** (*see p182*) at the Konzerthaus focuses on 17th-century baroque music for one week in April (2006). Major-name orchestras and soloists often open the **Classic Open Air** concert series *(see p183)* on Gendarmenmarkt over several days in early July. There is less focus on food, drink and socialising at **Young Euro Classic** (*see p184*), which assembles youth orchestras from across Europe over a couple of weeks in August. From

September to November the **Berliner Festwochen** (*see p185*) includes several classical performances at various venues.

TICKETS

Getting seats at the **Philharmonie** (*see p237*) is notoriously difficult, especially to see big-name stars or when the Berlin Phil itself is in residence; tickets for concerts by visiting performers are often easier to come by. If you can plan at least eight weeks ahead, you can order tickets by post or online with a credit card, but not by phone. Likewise, if you are coming to town for the annual **Berliner Festwochen** (*see p185*), which brings some of the world's best performers to town, it's best to book well in advance (www.berliner-philharmoniker.de).

Otherwise it's worth scanning the listings in daily papers or *tip* and *Zitty*, and phoning venues to see what's available. If all else fails, try positioning yourself outside the venue with a sign reading '*Suche eine Karte*' ('seeking a ticket'), or chatting up arriving concert-goers ('*Haben Sie vielleicht eine Karte übrig?*' means 'Got a spare ticket?'). You may also see people with extras for sale ('*Karte(n) zu verkaufen*'), but beware of ticket sharks.

Some of the former East Berlin venues – especially the Konzerthaus and the Komische Oper – remain more affordable than their western counterparts, but the days of socialist subsidies and dirt-cheap tickets are long gone. Standing-room at the top of the Konzerthaus actually gives a decent view, but before buying cheap seats for the Staatsoper ask how much of the stage you can see.

At the Komische Oper, all unsold tickets for that evening's performance are available from the box office half-price after 11am. Most venues offer student discounts; students can save even more by queuing 30 minutes before performance time at the Staatsoper, when leftover balcony seats are sold for €10.

If you're under 27 and plan to attend several events, it's worth investing in the **Classic Card**, which costs €25 for the season and gives you the right to the best available tickets on the night of a performance for between €5 and €10. So far it works at the Berlin Phil, the Deutsche Oper and the Konzerthaus, but other venues may also join the scheme. You can buy the card at the box offices of any of the three houses, or order online at www.staatsoper-berlin.org.

TICKET AGENCIES

Tickets are sold at concert hall box offices or through ticket agencies, called *Theaterkassen*. At box offices, seats are generally sold up to one hour before the performance. You can also make reservations by phone, except for concerts of the Berlin Phil. *Theaterkassen* provide the easiest means of buying a ticket, but be prepared to pay for the convenience as commissions can run as high as 17 per cent. Below are details of some centrally located agencies. For the 50 or so others around the city, look in the *Gelbe Seiten* (*Yellow Pages*) under *Theaterkassen*. Note that many places may not accept credit cards.

Hekticket

Hardenbergstrasse 29D, Charlottenburg (230 9930/ www.hekticket.de). U2, U9, U12, S3, S5, S7, S9, S75 Zoologischer Garten. **Open** 10am-8pm Mon-Sat; 2pm-6pm Sun. **Credit** AmEx, DC, MC, V. **Map** p305 C4.
Hekticket offers discounts of up to 50% on theatre and concert tickets, so it should be your first choice if using a ticket agency. For a small commission, its staff will sell you tickets for the same evening's performance. Tickets for Sunday matinées are available on Saturday. You can check ticket availability online, though not everything is listed. This branch is in a kiosk just south of the S-Bahn bridge. The one below, near Zoo station, is open 10am-8pm Mon-Sat and 2-6pm Sun.
Other locations: Hardenbergstrasse 29D, Charlottenburg (2309 9233).

Kant-Kasse

Krumme Strasse 55, Charlottenburg (313 4554/booking 834 4073/www.telecard.de). U7 Wilmersdorfer Strasse. **Open** 10am-6.30pm Mon-Fri; 10am-2pm Sat. **No credit cards**. **Map** p304 B4.

Major venues

Deutsche Oper

Richard Wagner Strasse 10, Charlottenburg (343 8401/freephone 0800 248 9842/www.deutsche-oper.berlin.de). U2 Deutsche Oper. **Open** *Box office* 11am-30 mins before performance Mon-Fri; 10am-2pm Sat. **Tickets** €12-€114. **Credit** AmEx, DC, V. **Map** 304 B4.
With roots dating back to 1912, the Deutsche Oper built its present 1,900-seat hall in 1961, just in time to carry the operatic torch for West Berlin during the Wall years. It has lost out in profile to the more elegant and central Staatsoper since reunification, but retains a reputation for blockbuster productions of the classics. Unsold tickets are available at a discount half an hour before performances.

Komische Oper

Behrenstrasse 55-7, Mitte (202 600/tickets 4799 7400/www.komische-oper-berlin.de). U6, S1, S2, S25, S26 Unter den Linden or Französische Strasse. **Open** *Box office* 11am-7pm Mon-Sat; 1pm-2hrs before performance Sun. **Tickets** €11-€62. **Credit** AmEx, MC, V. **Map** p316/p302 F3.
Despite its name, the Komische Oper puts on a broader range than just comic works, and, after its founding in 1947, made its name by breaking with

Staatsoper Unter den Linden: grand façade but in need of renovation. *See p238.*

the old operatic tradition of 'costumed concerts' – singers standing around on stage – and putting an emphasis on 'opera as theatre', with real acting skill demanded of its young ensemble. Outgoing artistic director Harry Kupfer strove for intelligent opera that speaks to the public – one reason why the Komische sings most of its productions in German. Telephone bookings can be made 9am-8pm Mon-Sat and 2-8pm Sun. Discounts available for tickets sold immediately before performances.

Konzerthaus

Gendarmenmarkt 2, Mitte (2030 92101/ www.konzerthaus.de). U6 Französische Strasse. **Open** *Box office* 11am-7pm Mon-Sat; noon-4pm Sun. **Tickets** €7-€99; some half-price concessions. **Credit** AmEx, MC, V. **Map** p316/p306 F4.

Formerly the Schauspielhaus am Gendarmenmarkt, this 1821 architectural gem by Schinkel was all but destroyed in the war. Lovingly restored, it was reopened in 1984 with three main spaces for concerts: the Grosser Konzertsaal for orchestras, and the Kleiner Saal for chamber music, and the recently opened Werner-Otto-Saal, named after the businessman who financed the construction. Organ recitals in the large concert hall are a treat, played on the massive Jehmlich organ at the back of the stage. The Berliner Sinfonie-Orchester is based here, presenting a healthy mixture of the classic, the new and the rediscovered. There are also occasional informal concerts in the cosy little Musik Club in the depths of the building. The Deutsches Sinfonie-Orchester also plays here, and is particularly noteworthy for its performances of contemporary music.

Philharmonie

Herbert-von-Karajan Strasse 1, Tiergarten (2548 8999/www.berlin-philharmonic.com). U2, S1, S2, S25, S26 Potsdamer Platz. **Open** *Box office* 9am-6pm daily. **Tickets** €7-€109. **Credit** AmEx, MC, V. **Map** p306 E4.

Berlin's most famous concert hall, home to the world-renowned Berlin Philharmonic Orchestra, is also its most architecturally daring; a marvellous, puckish piece of organic modernism. The hall, with its golden vaulting roof, was designed by Hans Scharoun and opened in 1963. The sad news is that this wonderful building is now dwarfed by newer structures at Potsdamer Platz. Its reputation for superb acoustics is accurate, but it does depend on where you sit in the hall. Behind the orchestra the acoustics leave plenty to be desired, but in front (where it is much more expensive) the sound is heavenly. The structure also incorporates a smaller hall, the Kammermusiksaal, about which the same acoustical notes apply. The unique Berliner Philharmoniker was founded in 1882 by 54 musicians keen to break away from the penurious Benjamin Bilse, in whose orchestra they played. Over the last 120 years it has been led by some of the world's greatest conductors, as well as by composers such as Peter Tchaikovsky, Edvard Grieg, Richard Strauss and Gustav Mahler. Its greatest fame came under the baton of Herbert von Karajan, who led the orchestra between 1955 and 1989, and was succeeded by Claudio Abbado. Since 2002, it has been under the leadership of the popular Sir Simon Rattle. The Berlin Phil gives about 100 performances in Berlin during its August to June sea-

St Matthäus Kirche am Kulturforum: monks, organs and exquisite acoustics. *See p239.*

son, and puts on another 20 to 30 concerts around the world. Some tickets are available at a discount immediately before performances.

Staatsoper Unter den Linden

Unter den Linden 5-7, Mitte (203 540/tickets 2035 4555/www.staatsoper-berlin.de). U2 Hausvogteiplatz. **Open** *Box office* 10am-8pm Mon-Sat; 2pm-8pm Sun. **Tickets** €5-€120. **Credit** AmEx, MC, V. **Map** p316/p305 F3.

The Staatsoper was founded as Prussia's Royal Court Opera for Frederick the Great in 1742, and designed along the lines of a Greek temple. Although the present building dates from 1955, the façade faithfully copies that of Knobelsdorff's original, twice destroyed in World War II. The elegant interior gives an immediate sense of the house's past glory, with huge chandeliers and elaborate wall paintings. Chamber music is performed in the small, ornate Apollo Saal, housed within the main building and now also open for occasional club nights and electronica performances. Half an hour before the performance, unsold tickets are available for €10.

Other venues

Many churches offer organ recitals. It's also worth enquiring if concerts are going to be staged in any of the area's castles or museums, especially in the summer months. Telephones are often erratically staffed, so check *tip* or *Zitty* for information.

Akademie der Künste

Hanseatenweg 10 (390 760/www.adk.de). U9 Hansaplatz or S3, S5, S7, S9 Bellevue. **Open** 11am-6pm Mon, Tue, Fri-Sun; 10am-8pm Thur. **Tickets** €5-€8. **No credit cards. Map** p301 D3.

Founded by Prince Friedrich III in 1696, this is one of the oldest cultural institutions in Berlin. By 1938, however, the Nazis had forced virtually all of its prominent members into exile. It was re-established in West Berlin in 1954, in this fine new building from architect Werner Duttmann, to serve as 'a community of exceptional artists' from around the world. Apart from performances of 20th-century compositions, its programme offers a variety of other events, from jazz and poetry readings to film screenings and art exhibitions. Despite portions of the now reunified Akademie moving into a new building at its prewar address on Pariser Platz, most performances and exhibitions remain here at Hanseatenweg.

Other locations: Pariser Platz 4, Mitte.

Ballhaus Naunynstrasse

Naunynstrasse 27, Kreuzberg (9029 86644/ www.kulturamt.de). U1, U8 Kottbusser Tor. **Open** *Box office* 1hr before performance Mon-Fri. **Tickets** €6-€12. **No credit cards. Map** p307 G4.

Don't expect to hear anything ordinary at this Kreuzberg cultural centre. A varied assortment of western and oriental music is on the menu, with drinks and snacks in the café out front. The long, rectangular hall, which seats 150, plays host to the excellent Berlin Chamber Opera, among others.

Berliner Dom

Lustgarten 1, Mitte (2026 9136/www.berliner-dom.de). S3, S5, S7, S9, S75 Hackescher Markt. **Open** *Box office* 10am-6pm Mon-Fri. **Tickets** €7-€30. **No credit cards. Map** p316/p302 F3.

Berlin's restored cathedral now hosts some recommendable concerts, usually of the organ or choral variety. *See also p78.*

Meistersaal

Köthener Strasse 38, Kreuzberg (5200 0060/www.meistersaal.de). U2, S1, S2, S25, S26 Potsdamer Platz. **Open** *Box office* 10am-5pm Mon-Fri. **Tickets** varies. **Credit** MC, V. **Map** p306 E4.

What was once the Hansa recording studio now hosts solo instrumentalists and chamber groups that can't afford to book the Kammermusiksaal of the Philharmonie. But don't let that fool you. Music-making of the highest rank occurs here in this warm and welcoming little salon, which is notable for its superb acoustics. Back when this was a studio, David Bowie and Iggy Pop recorded here during the 1970s (*see p92* **Home for 'Heroes'**).

Musikhochschule Hanns Eisler

Charlottenstrasse 55, Gendarmenmarkt, Mitte (9029 6841). U2, U6 Stadtmitte. **Tickets** varies (usually free). **No credit cards. Map** p316/p306 F4.

Opposite the Konzerthaus, this musical academy was founded in 1950 and named after the composer of the East German national anthem. It offers students the chance to study under some of the stars of Berlin's major orchestras and operas. Rehearsals and master classes are often open to the public for free, and student performances, some of them top-notch, are held in the Konzerthaus. Other events are held in the annexe at Wilhelmstrasse 53, Mitte.

Neuköllner Oper

Karl-Marx-Strasse 131-3, Neuköln (6889 0777/www.neuköllneroper.de). U7 Karl-Marx-Strasse. **Open** *Box office* 3-7pm Tue-Fri. **Tickets** €9-€21. **Credit** MC, V. **Map** p307 H6.

No grand opera here, but a constantly changing programme of chamber operas and music-theatre works much-loved by the Neuköllners who come to see lighter, bubblier (and much less expensive) works than those offered by Berlin's big three opera houses. This is an informal alternative to the champagne-and-chandeliers atmosphere of the Deutsche, Komische or Staatsoper. Current artistic director Peter Lund is one of Berlin's most promising young theatre directors. Pity about the acoustics.

Palast der Republik

Schlossplatz, Mitte (2887 9818/www.zwischen palastnutzung.de). S3, S5, S7, S9, S75 Hackescher Markt. **Tickets** varies. **Credit** varies. **Map** p316/p302 F3.

Controversy still shrouds the future of the colossal GDR Palace of the Republic. Parliament decided to demolish it and reconstruct the Stadtschloss which formerly stood here, but progress has foundered due to lack of funding. Meanwhile the site has attracted organisers and producers who are keen to stage performances in the gutted and finally asbestos-free interior. An interim solution has been found to enable events to be staged here.

Staatsbibliothek – Otto-Braun Saal

Potsdamer Strasse 33, Tiergarten (2660/www.staatsbibliothek-berlin.de). U2, S1, S2 Potsdamer Platz. **Open** *Box office* Times vary, call for details. **Tickets** varies. **No credit cards. Map** p306 E4.

This smaller ensembles provide the lion's share of the music in this chamber of the state library.

St Matthäus Kirche am Kulturforum

Matthaeikirchplatz, Tiergarten (2262 1202/www.stiftung-stmatthaeus.de). U2, S1, S2, S25, S26 Potsdamer Platz. **Open** *Box office* noon-6pm Tue-Sun. **Tickets** varies. **No credit cards. Map** p306 E4.

Concerts here might be anything from a free organ recital to a chorus of Russian Orthodox monks. Exquisite acoustics.

Universität der Künste

Hardenbergstrasse 33, corner of Fasanenstrasse, Tiergarten (3185 2374). U2, U9, S3, S5, S7, S9, S75 Zoologischer Garten. **Open** *Box office* 3-6.30pm Tue-Fri; 11am-2pm Sat. **Tickets** varies. **No credit cards. Map** p305 C4.

This place may be grotesquely ugly, but it is nonetheless a functional hall, hosting both student soloists and orchestras, as well as performances by lesser-known professional groups.

Theatre

There have lately been some big changes in Berlin theatre, the biggest of which has been organisational: the amalgamation in November 2003 of the Hebbel Theater, Theater am Halleschen Ufer and Theater am Ufer into one unit with a coordinated programme for experimental theatre and dance. The new body is called the **HAU** (*see p240*) and the intendant is Matthias Lilienthal, formerly at the Volksbühne, a man whose goal is to 'keep things at a chaotic level for three years'. The theatre world is waiting to see what happens next, but the hope is that this will provide more support for new directors and playwrights.

In the meantime, watch out for independent companies such as She She Pop, Nico and the Navigators, Riminiprotokoll and Lubricat, which are all creating original works including elements of dance, video and docu-drama.

Berlin's **Theatertreffen** (*see p182*) in May remains the major festival for German-language work. Between November 2004 and January 2005 comes the first edition of a new festival, **Spielzeiteuropa** (www.berlinerfestspiele.de), intended to highlight work from elsewhere in

Europe. The Netherlands is the focus in 2004-05; the following year it will be the Balkans.

For ticket agencies *see p236*.

Civic theatres

Berliner Ensemble

Bertolt-Brecht-Platz 1, Mitte (2840 8155/www.berliner-ensemble.de). U6,S1, S2, S3, S5, S7, S9, S25, S75 Friedrich Strasse. **Open** *Box office* 8am-6pm Mon-Fri; 11am 6pm Sat, Sun. **Tickets** €5-€30; €5 concessions. **Credit** AmEx, DC, MC, V. **Map** p316/p302 F3.

Constructed in 1891, and still with an elaborate period interior, this place is best known for its association with Brecht – first during the Weimar period (this was where the *Threepenny Opera* was first staged in 1928) and later under the Communists when Brecht ran the place from 1948 until his death in 1956. Under current intendant Claus Peymann, expect a repertoire where modern productions of Brecht rub shoulders with pieces by living German and Austrian writers.

Deutsches Theater/Kammerspiele des Deutschen Theaters

Schumannstrasse 13A, Mitte (Box office 2844 1225/information 2844 1221/www.deutschestheater.de). U6, S1, S2, S3, S5, S7, S9, S25, S26, S75 Friedrichstrasse. **Open** *Box office* 11am-6.30pm Mon-Sat; 3-6.30pm Sun. **Tickets** €4-€42. **Credit** AmEx, MC, V. **Map** p316/p302 E/F3.

After years suffering from mildew of the classics, the former East German state theatre has been spruced up with a programme of new interpretations of the classics mixed with high-class contemporary and international dramas, courtesy of new intendant Bernd Wilms and the crowd of young directors he brought with him.

Maxim Gorki Theatre & Studiobühne

Am Festungsgraben 2, Mitte (box office 2022 1115/information 2022 1129/www.gorki.de). U6, S1, S2, S3, S5, S7, S9, S25, S26, S75 Friedrichstrasse. **Open** *Box office* noon-6.30pm Mon-Sat; 4-6.30pm Sun. **Tickets** €13-€30. **Credit** MC, V. **Map** p316/p302 F3.

The primary house for progressive Russian and east European drama, known for its naturalistic, down-to-earth style. Actress and director Katharina Thalbach is a major attraction here.

Schaubühne am Lehniner Platz

Kurfürstendamm 153, Charlottenburg (890 023/www.schaubühne.de). U7 Adenauerplatz or S3, S5, S7, S9, S75 Charlottenburg. **Open** *Box office* 11am-6.30pm Mon-Sat; 3-6.30pm Sun. **Tickets** €10-€30; €8 concessions. **Credit** AmEx, MC, V. **Map** p305 F5.

One of the places to be for the theatrical in-crowd, offering modern drama from young authors played by great stage actors. The programme is almost exclusively contemporary drama and dance, including some English-language works (plays by Sarah Kane, Nicky Silver, Mark Ravenhill and Caryl Churchill have all featured).

Berliner Ensemble: elaborate 1891 interior.

HAU 1-2-3

Main office, HAU 2, Hallesches Ufer 32, Kreuzberg. (Box office 2590 0427/www.hebbel-am-ufer.de). U7 Möckernbrücke or U1, U6 Hallesches Tor. **Open** *Box office* noon-7pm daily. **Tickets** €10-€15; €6 concessions. **Credit** AmEx, MC, V. **Map** p306 F5.

With the amalgamation of the former Hebbel Theater (HAU1), Theater am Hallesches Ufer (HAU2) and Theater am Ufer (HAU3) under intendant Matthias Lilienthal, it is now possible to develop, rehearse and present internationally renowned guest ensembles, innovative theatre projects and dance productions – all at the same time. The added perk for performers and artists is that while working on concurrent projects they will be able to view and discuss each others' work. This is what creates the whirlwind of excitement around HAU. The international dance festival, Tanz im August (*see p183*) continues its success here, further dance and theatre festivals are in the planning stages, and there are thematic weekends throughout the year including discussion, debates and docu-dramas on a wide range of social issues.

Other locations: Hau 1, Stresemannstrasse 29, Kreuzberg; Hau 3 Tempelhofer Ufer 10, Kreuzberg.

Arts & Entertainment

Prater

Prater Kastanienallee 79, Prenzlauer Berg (247 6772/www.volksbühne-berin.de). U2 Eberswalder Strasse. **Open** *Box office* noon-6pm daily. **Tickets** €10-€21; €6 concessions. **Credit** MC, V (no credit cards over phone). **Map** p303 G2.

Artistic director Rene Pollesch is developing a reputation as a non-conformist both here and overseas. Under his leadership, Prater has stepped out from the shadow of the Volksbühne (see below), which still manages it, and into its own limelight.

Renaissance

Hardenbergstrasse 6, Charlottenburg (312 4202/ www.renaissance-theatre.de). U2 Ernst-Reuter-Platz. **Open** *Box office* 10:30am-7pm Mon-Sat; 3-6pm Sun. **Tickets** €11-€32. **Credit** AmEx, MC, V. **Map** p305 C4.

If you want famous actors and a classy location, then this is the place to come. Some of Germany's best-known performers appear in shows such as the hit play *Art* (*Kunst*), running from summer 2004. And the building is one of only two remaining examples of work by Oskar Kaufmann, a premier Berlin theatre architect of the early 20th century. The art deco style is also a great backdrop to the Chansons evenings that are served up with a full dinner in the upstairs salon.

Volksbühne

Rosa-Luxemburg-Platz, Mitte (247 6772/ www.volksbühne-berlin.de). U2 Rosa-Luxemburg-Platz. **Open** *Box office* noon-6pm daily. **Tickets** €10-€21; €6 concessions. **Credit** MC, V (no credit cards over phone). **Map** p303 G2.

This landmark theatre on Rosa-Luxemburg-Platz was hovering on the brink of closure when Frank Castorf became intendant, but it's bounced back: Castorf's provocative interpretations have regenerated the popularity of the 'Peoples' Stage'. To create contact with wider audiences, a summer project has been launched with Prater, the Rollende Road Schau. This mobile event steps outside of genre limitations and features audience participation as it visits Berliners in their suburbs.

Fringe & English-language theatre

Berlin once boasted 100 fringe companies; only about two dozen exist today. Fringe theatre, known to Germans as Off-Theater, has been growing in profile over the past several years, but remains dangerously reliant on shrinking public funds. The spaces occupied are often rough and ready, but performances can be revelatory. Quality does vary considerably, but prices will always be lowish and the audience unstuffy.

English-language theatre is of a high standard in Berlin. Several local groups feature excellent mother-tongue actors, and top-notch touring companies (particularly Irish and British) often perform here, generally at the Friends of Italian Opera (see below).

Unless otherwise indicated, box offices open one hour before a performance and sell tickets for that performance only. Tickets are around €8-€15 and an international student ID card should get you a discount at most of the local and fringe theatres on the night.

Brotfabrik

Caligariplatz (Reservations 471 4001/2/ www.brotfabrik-berlin.de). S8, S41, S42 PrenzlauerAllee. **Open** *Box office* 1hr before performance. **Tickets** €10; €8 concessions. **Credit** MC, V. **Map** p303 G1.

A former bread factory which was used as a youth centre during the GDR period. In its current incarnation, Brotfabrik houses a cinema and café with an amiable summer courtyard and a smaller, experimental theatre. Productions here are performed in a variety of languages.

Friends of Italian Opera

Fidicinstrasse 40, Kreuzberg (box office 691 1211/information 693 5692/www.thefriends.de). U6 Platz der Luftbrücke. **Open** *Box office* from 7pm daily. **Tickets** €7-€14; €8 concessions. **No credit cards**. **Map** p306 F5.

Two German Anglophiles run this gem of a fringe venue snuggled away in a Kreuzberg courtyard, and you won't find a more exciting English-language theatre on the continent. The programme varies from touring companies from all over the western world to some suprisingly high-quality work from resident expats. Also regular readings of brand new work, poetry and performance evenings.

Sophiensaele

Sophienstrasse 18, Mitte (information 2789 0030/tickets 283 5266/www.sophiensaele.com). U8 Weinmeisterstrasse or S3, S5, S7, S9, S75 Hackescher Markt. **Open** 1hr before show daily. **Tickets** €13; €8 concessions. **No credit cards**. **Map** p316/p302 F3.

Expect a contemporary programme of dance, theatre, music and opera, with up-and-coming groups from around the world. If avant-garde is ever crowd-pleasing, then this is the place. Venue for assorted festivals, including Theatertreffen (*see p182*), Tanz im August (*see p183*) and Ultraschall (*see p186*).

Theater unterm Dach

Danziger Strasse 101, Im Kulturhaus im Ernst-Thlmann-Park, Prenzlauer Berg (4240 1080). S4, S8 Greifswalder Strasse. **Open** phone bookings only. **Tickets** €8; €5 concessions. **No credit cards**. **Map** p303 G2.

In the large attic of a converted factory, this is the place to see new German fringe theatre groups. The artistic director searches for the country's most promising young directors or companies and gives them a chance in the capital. Productions are always full of energy and can be quite inspiring.

Just another provocative interpretation at the **Volksbühne**. *See p241.*

Theaterdiscounter

Monbijoustrasse 1, Ecke Oranienburger Strasse, Mitte (4404 8561/tickets@theaterdiscounter.de). S1, S2, S25, S26 Oranienburger Strasse. **Open** *Box office* from 7pm daily. *Show times* 8pm. **Tickets** €10 max. **No credit cards. Map** p316/p302 F3.

Opened in 2003 in an old telegraph office, this is where an intense group of ten actors and various directors perform original pieces. It's anti-illusion theatre with interactive possibilities – very fresh and happening. Shows are for audiences of up to 50.

Vagantenbühne

Kantstrasse 12a, Charlottenburg (3124 529/ www.vaganten.de). U2, U9, S3, S5, S7, S75 Zoologischer Garten. **Open** *Box office* 10am-4pm Mon; 10am-8pm Tue, Fri; 2-8pm Sat. **Tickets** €9-€17. **No credit cards. Map** p305 C4.

A comfortable 99-seater featuring international plays, some classics, performed in German. Works hard to promote itself to younger theatregoers.

Dance

During the last 15 years, Berlin has asserted itself as one of the world's leading centres for contemporary dance. There is hardly an international festival these days that doesn't feature a production from the German capital, and the city continues to attract adventurous international choreographers from all over the world, inspired by the processes taking place in a city seeking to redefine itself on all levels.

On a purely physical level, Berlin offers myriad possibilities to stage productions in incongruous settings: in structures waiting to be torn down or revamped, such as Palast der Republik, the Jahndorf storehouse (Constanza Macras), abandoned underground stations (Anna Huber), anonymous apartments (Two Fish) or leftover World War II shelters (Ausland). And then there is the cross-fertilisation phenomenon. Choreographers frequently team up with leading lights in the new media, fine arts or music scenes.

The influx of dancers in the independent scene has upped the competitive edge. That, in turn, has created more professional training opportunities. There is now a handful of schools, such as Dock 11 in Prenzlauer Berg (see below) or Tanzfabrik in Kreuzberg, though the city still lacks a state-funded institution.

Nevertheless, standards have improved tremendously. Half the productions showcased at the biennial **Tanzplattform**, which rotates around German cities, come from Berlin.

For information on current performances, check *tip* or *Zitty* or the free *Tanzkalender*, which can be picked up around town.

For ticket agencies *see p236*.

Major venues & festivals

While the focus at the **Sophiensaele** (*see p241*) is now more on theatre, dance still features in its own two-week **Tanztage** festival (*see p186*) in January. It presents new local talent, often giving dancers from the ballet corps of the opera houses their first crack at choreography of their own.

As well as holding classes, **Dock 11** (Kastanienallee, Prenzlauer Berg; 448 1222/ www.dock11-berlin.de) continues to host an adventurous programme of modern dance and dance-theatre.

Tanzwerkstatt is based at the **Podewil** cultural centre (*see p220*). It scouts out fresh, promising talent at international festivals and books young choreographers for Berlin events and Podewil's own stage. Workshops often run parallel to performances. Look out for productions by choreographers in Podewil's artist-in-residence programme.

Newly established is the **HAU** (*see p240*) theatre agglomeration in Kreuzberg. Composed of three venues, it offers an entirely new context for dance and theatre productions and will also now be in charge of Berlin's major dance event, the annual **Tanz im August** festival (*see p183*), as well as organising **Tanznacht Berlin** (*see p186*), a new biennial all-night event. Next edition is in December 2005.

In Transit (*see p182*) is another new festival to watch out for. Launched in 2002 by the **Haus der Kulturen der Welt** (*see p99*), it commissions a different, non-European curator every two years to travel the world and book dance and performance artists to work with Berlin groups during a three-week period in early summer. The results of their collaboration will be on show both while they are working and as evening productions.

Contemporary companies & choreographers

Jo Fabian/Department

Image wiz Fabian began his career as an actor and director in East Germany. Since founding what he calls his 'theatre of moving architecture', he has sought to break down boundaries between drama, dance, music performance and installation. Fabian's prize-winning productions are packed with visionary power and make good use of video and shadow-play. In recent years, he has been developing an encoded language of movement based on the rules of writing, which he calls the 'Alphasystem', whereby dancers 'write' with their movements.

Thomas Lehmen

Born in the Ruhr and trained as a choreographer in Amsterdam, Lehmen bridges performance and choreographic art. Since summer 2003 he has been working on a performance called *Stationen*, in which he invites people 'of all types of professions' to join in and talk about their work. His *Schreibstück* is a written score for a dance piece handed out to different choreographers for interpretation. In 2004 he is presenting a new work that has been developed with choreographers in Tallinn, Zagreb and Sofia.

Felix Ruckert

Based at Dock 11, Ruckert (formerly a dancer with Pina Bausch) and his company explore all aspects of audience participation – including nudity, touch, and the infliction of pain. Ruckert's company tours extensively, but he has also worked for Strasbourg's National Ballet Company with great success.

Constanza Macras

Born in Buenos Aires, Macras came to Berlin via New York and Amsterdam. With her company Dorky Park she developed serial projects such as *MIR – A love story*, *PORNOsotros* and *Back to the Present*, a hit in 2003. The production has now been invited to the Avignon summer festival in France.

Sasha Waltz

Germany's leading proponent of postmodern dance-theatre, Sasha Waltz has been co-director of the prestigious and previously drama-only Schaubühne am Lehniner Platz (*see p240*) since 1999. Her first production there, *Körper*, was a huge success. Waltz's site-specific projects have taken audiences on to the roof of the Schaubühne and inside the shell of Libeskind's Jüdisches Museum before it opened.

Ballet

A city struggling to finance three different opera houses can't also afford three ballet companies. Therefore, the **Komische Oper** (*see p236*) is closing down its Tanztheater department at the end of the 2003-04 season.

The Staatsoper Unter den Linden (*see p238*) has boasted 'dancer of the century' Vladimir Malakhov as ballet director since 2002, and his roots in the Russian academic tradition have guaranteed the Staatsoper's profile as home of the all-time classics. But the 64-member Staatsoper ballet will soon merge with the 30-strong corps at the Deutsche Oper (*see p236*), meaning no more competition between the two companies, and just one streamlined troupe to perform in all three opera houses.

Sport & Fitness

Offering every activity from athletics to yoga, Berlin is one big playground.

Laps of luxury at **Club Olympus Spa & Fitness**. *See p250.*

For the serious player, there are countless organisations and clubs. For the more anarchic, there are the parks. In the summer, if you take a walk through one of Berlin's green spaces, you're bound to come across some motley crew playing football or chucking a frisbee around. If you spot a game going on with an uneven number of players, you'll probably be welcomed if you want to join in. Spectator sports, meanwhile, are reasonably priced and you can often just show up and pay at the turnstiles; only the really big events sell out in advance.

Major stadiums & arenas

Max-Schmeling-Halle

Am Falkplatz, Prenzlauer Berg (443 045/ www.velomax.de). U2 Eberswalder Strasse or U2, S4, S8 Schönhauser Allee. **Map** p303 G1.

Named after the German boxer who knocked out the seemingly invincible Joe Louis in 1936 (Louis settled the score two years later), this state-of-the-art indoor arena is better known now as the home of Berlin's basketball hotshots ALBA (*see p245*). The 11,000-capacity hall also hosts a variety of international sporting events, rock concerts and conferences.

Olympiastadion

Olympischer Platz 3, Charlottenburg (300 633). U2 Olympia-Stadion or S5, S75 Olympiastadion.

Designed by March as the centrepiece for the 1936 Olympics, the Olympiastadion is one of the best surviving examples of Nazi monumentalism. After years of neglect, and although a protected building, the 76,000-seater is being given a new roof, slated for completion by December 2004. This huge bowl hosts Berlin's top football club, Hertha BSC (*see p245*), the Deutschland Pokalendspiele (the German football cup final; *see p182*), American football's Berlin Thunder (*see p245*) and the ISTAF annual athletics meeting (*see p245*) as well as rock concerts and other events. It's also the venue for the 2006 World Cup Final.

Velodrom

Paul-Heyse-Strasse 26, Prenzlauer Berg (administration 443 045/tickets 4430 4430/ www.velomax.de). S4, S8 Landsberger Allee. **Map** p303 H2.

Opened in 1997, this multifunctional sports and entertainment venue was designed by renowned architect Dominique Perrault for the annual six-day cycling race, and boasts a cycling track handmade from Siberian spruce. It also accommodates equestrian and super-cross events, as well as pop concerts, trade fairs and conferences.

Spectator sports

American Football

Berlin Thunder

Friesenhof 1, Hanns-Braun Strasse, Charlottenburg. U2/S5 Olympiastadion (3006 4444/www.berlin-thunder.de). **Tickets** €8-€31.50. **Credit** (advance booking only) AmEx, V. **Map** p303 G1.

The NFL Europe has grown in stature and popularity since it started in the early 1990s. Initially viewed as a last-chance saloon for players who couldn't make it in the NFL, it has earned a reputation as something of a finishing school, especially for quarterbacks. Berlin Thunder won two successive World Bowls in 2001 and 2002, and now play at the prestigious Olympiastadion (*see p244*). Attendance rose by an impressive 23% in 2003, even though Thunder came last in the league.

Athletics

ISTAF Athletics Meeting

2433 1990/www.istaf.de. **Tickets** €7.50-€45; €6.50-€40.50 concessions.

First held in 1937, this international one-day meet, held at the Olympiastadion (*see p244*), is the last of four events in the International Association of Athletics Federations' Golden League. The $1 million prize money is shared between athletes who win their disciplines at all four Golden League meetings. With that kind of wealth and prestige at stake, the crowd is often treated to new world records. The 2004 event is on 12 September.

Basketball

ALBA

308 785 685/www.albaticket.de. **Tickets** €6.50-€27. **Credit** AmEx, MC, V.

Berlin's representatives in the top division of German basketball take their name from their sponsors, waste disposal and recycling firm, ALBA. And they've cleaned up domestically in recent years, winning seven league titles in a row and the cup three times in the same period. ALBA has not so far made a similar mark on the Euro League, but can count on a loyal following to fill the Max-Schmeling-Halle (*see p244*) and fund the team.

Football

German football got a major boost in 2002 when the national team surprised everybody by going all the way to the World Cup final. Germany is host nation in 2006 and the final will be played at Berlin's Olympiastadion (*see p244*). By then, football here could probably also use a boost. After returning to the top division in 1997, Berlin's biggest club, Hertha BSC, appeared to have established itself with regular top-six finishes and forays into Europe. Then everything started coming apart (*see below*). The only other team making news is the eastern club FC Union.

Hertha BSC

0180 518 9200/www.herthabsc.de. **Tickets** €9-€43. **No credit cards** (except online bookings).

At the beginning of the 2003-04 season, Hertha's players bragged that they would be contenders for the league title. Instead, they crashed straight out of the UEFA Cup, fell at the third hurdle in the German Cup and were soon stuck at the bottom of the table. At press time they were on their second coach of the season and relegation loomed. Hertha play at the Olympiastadion (*see p244*).

1. FC Union

Stadion An der Alten Försterei 263, Köpenick (6566 8861/www.fc-union-berlin.de). S3 Köpenick. **Tickets** €7.50-€22. **No credit cards**.

Having struggled under both Communism and capitalism, 'Iron Union' finally seem to have their finances sorted. The club's fan base, drawn from the industrial working class, is arguably the city's best and, true to tradition, the side is largely made up of players from the former East bloc. Union made it to the German Cup Final in 2001 and were rewarded with a UEFA Cup slot, but have yet to net their most prized goal: joining Hertha in the big time. Far from it: at the time of going to press, Union looked in danger of being relegated to the Third Division.

Horse racing

Galopprennbahn-Hoppegarten

Goetheallee 1, Dahlwitz-Hoppegarten (0334 238 9323/tickets 033 389 323/www.galopprennbahn-hoppegarten.de). S5 Hoppegarten. **Tickets** €5-€20. **Credit** AmEx, MC, V.

Thoroughbred races are held between April and October. The Oleander restaurant is a meeting place for horse owners, trainers and race enthusiasts. The betting is run along the lines of the British tote system. All money bet on horses in a race goes into a 'pot' which is shared out between all those who have placed winning bets. The main difference to gambling with an independent bookmaker is that you don't know what a winning wager will pay.

Pferdesportpark

Treskowallee 129, Karlshorst (5001 7121/www.psp-sportpark.de). S3 Karlshorst.
Tickets €2 daytime; free evenings.

This and its partner track Mariendorf (*see p246*) host trotting events, aka harness racing. This entails riders pelting about in modern-day chariots, a kind of *Ben Hur* in tweeds. Meetings are held all year round on Wednesdays at about 6pm.

Trabrennbahn Mariendorf

Mariendorfer Damm 222/298, Mariendorf (740 1212/www.berlintrab.de). U6 Alt-Mariendorf, then bus X76, 176, 179. **Tickets** €2.50. **No credit cards.**

Race meetings take place on Sundays at 1.30pm and Tuesdays at 6pm as well as other selected occasions. Derby Week in August has become a major international event.

Ice hockey

Since German ice hockey clubs set up a private national league in 1994, the sport has become big business. For now, the Eisbären ('polar bears'), the old eastern club, have seen off their western rivals, the Capitals. The Caps have nosedived from the top flight and, at the time this guide went to press, had just filed for bankruptcy protection.

EHC Eisbären Berlin

Wellblechpalast, Steffenstrasse, Hohenschönhausen (971 8400/tickets 9718 4040/www.eisbaeren.de). S8, S10 Landsberger Allee, then tram 5, 15. **Tickets** €15-€30. **No credit cards.**

Berlin's leading club, the Eisbären are also shaping up to be a major force on the national scene, appearing regularly in the play-offs of the Deutsche Eishockey-Liga. Some might miss their boisterous derbies against the Capitals, but the club's been

The gymnastics revolution

Turngemeinde in Berlin 1848 ('Gymnastics Community in Berlin 1848') is the city's oldest surviving sports club, and perhaps its most diverse. As its rather archaic name suggests, it was founded in 1848. The list of sports it caters for is almost as long as its history, ranging from aikido to volleyball, and its continual adoption of modern sporting trends goes hand in hand with its pioneering role in German sports.

Fittingly, the club is based beside the Hasenheide park, where **Friedrich Ludwig Jahn**, 'the father of German gymnastics' established the country's first physical education facility in 1811. To this day, the club's coat of arms features the 'four Fs' Jahn used for his own crest. They stood for 'Frisch, Frei, Frölisch und Fromm' (fresh, free, cheerful and pious).

But Jahn wasn't just a fitness fanatic. He was motivated by a patriotic desire to prepare his countrymen for a war of liberation that would rid the land of French occupying forces and unite the nation. The aim of physical education was to develop sturdy citizen-soldiers with a love of their homeland and the strength to throw off the oppressor. And Jahn led a volunteer corps that fought with distinction as part of the Prussian force at Waterloo in 1815.

Once Napoleon had been defeated, Jahn and the Turnvereine – the patriotic gymnastic societies he had inspired – continued in a political vein, fighting for greater personal and political freedoms. This, however, was too much for German monarchs, who banned the clubs and jailed Jahn in 1819. He was released five years later, but only on condition that he stay away from university cities and desist from teaching. He was pardoned by Kaiser Friedrich Wilhelm IV in 1840 and finally decorated with the Iron Cross for his services decades earlier. His political opinions, especially his belief in uniting the various German-speaking mini-states, played an important role in the liberal movement that led to the failed uprisings of 1848 – the year Turngemeinde in Berlin was founded.

Jahn died in 1852 but remains a controversial figure. The Nazis idolised him, claiming him as a kind of prophet, a man 'a hundred years ahead of his time'. Jahn certainly extolled racial purity: Poles, French and Jews were persona non grata in his organisation. It's another of the many ironies of German history that the GDR also tried to establish an ideological link, and there's a park named after him in Prenzlauer Berg.

In the Hasenheide, there's an odd-looking monument to the man (or at least to his efforts), based on some of the devices he used to train his followers. To this day, the park is a favourite haunt of joggers and footballers, volleyball teams and frisbee wizards. And the nearby Turngemeinde in Berlin 1848 continues to provide facilities for dozens of other sports. Although Jahn was living proof that sport and politics can never be truly separated, it's safe to say that his most lasting legacy is a healthy one.

Turngemeinde in Berlin 1848

Columbiadamm 111, Neukölln (6110 1020/ www.tib1848ev.de). U7 Südstern or U8 Boddinstrasse. **Open** 9am-11pm daily. **Rates** *Badminton* €7.50-€13/hr. *Tennis* €17-€24/hr. *Sauna* €6/day. **No credit cards.** **Map** p307 G6.

EHC Eisbären Berlin – shaping up as a national force. *See p246.*

doing much better since the city has only had to support one top-flight outfit. The stadium name means 'corrugated iron palace'.

Motor sports

Eurospeedway Lausitz

Lausitzallee 1, Klettwitz (035754 31110/tickets 01805 880288/www.eurospeedway.de). Train RB14 Senftenberg, then shuttle bus (racing days only). **Tickets** €7.50-€257.70. **Credit** AmEx, DC, MC, V.

Located 130km (81 miles) south-east of Berlin, the largest racing facility on the Continent opened in 2000 to roaring crowds. Less than two years later, it was bankrupt. But with local government covering losses until 2008, the course is still open for business. Prestige events include the German Touring Car Masters (DTM), the Porsche GTP weekend and the International German Motorbike Championship (IDM). Budding race drivers can test their nerves and ability in their own cars (and at their own risk) on selected days. Eurospeedway can be reached via the A13 motorway or by train to Senftenberg.

Tennis

The Eurocard Ladies' German Open, held each May as a warm-up tournament for the French Open, is the world's fifth largest international women's tennis championship, and usually attracts most of the big names. *See p182.*

LTTC Rot-Weiss

Gottfried-von-Cramm-Weg 47-55, Grunewald (Tickets 8957 5520/www.rot-weiss-berlin.de). S3, S7 Grunewald. **Open** 8am-5pm Mon-Thur; 8am-noon Fri. **Tickets** €15-€65; €7.50-€10 concessions. **No credit cards**.

Venue for the German Open, played on clay courts. LTTC stands for Lawn Tennis Tournament Club.

Water polo

Wasserfreunde Spandau 04 have practically owned the German league title for the last 25 years, so don't expect much excitement at a Bundesliga match. They face stiffer competition in the Euroleague; it's worth catching a game if you want to do something different. Grab a seat in the stands with a thousand others or book a table at the poolside and take in a three-course meal and pre-match show, both themed on the opponents' home country. There's free beer for everyone for an hour after the match. Games are at the Sport- und Lehrschwimmhalle in Schöneberg in winter and the Olympiastadion (*see p244*) in summer. For more details visit www.spandau04.net.

Sport- und Lehrschwimmhalle

Sachsendamm 11, Schöneberg (3510 2272). S1, S41, S42, S45, S46, S47 Schöneberg. **Tickets** €5-€15; €50 for dinner & drinks package. **No credit cards**. **Map** p305 D6.

Active sports/fitness

Berlin is a dream for the DIY athlete. This chapter only covers a fraction of what's on offer; if you don't find what you're looking for, contact one of the organisations listed. *Verbände* are the umbrella 'associations' that co-ordinate sports.

Landessportbund Berlin (LSB)

Jesse-Owens-Allee 2, Charlottenburg (300 020/ www.lsb-berlin.org). U2 Olympia-Stadion or S5 Olympiastadion. **Open** 9am-3pm Mon-Thur; 9am-2pm Fri.

The Berlin Regional Sports Association's central office provides general information and co-ordinates other offices in charge of specific sports. The Landesauschuss Frauensport, Regional Committee for Women's Sport, is at the same address.

Athletics

Berlin Marathon

Glockenturm 23, Charlottenburg (3012 8810/ www.berlin-marathon.com). **Entrance fee.** €50-€90. **Date** last Sun in Sept.

More than 30,000 people take part in the world's third-largest marathon. And because Berlin is flat and the weather moderate in September, the race is conducive to record-breaking performances. The 2003 finish, when Kenya's Paul Tergat not only slashed 45 seconds off the previous best to come home in two hours, four minutes and 55 seconds, but also crossed the line just one second ahead of compatriot Sammy Korir, was thrilling. The less ambitious can try the Berlin Half-Marathon in early April or 'City Night' in August, a 10km (6-mile) trot up and down the Ku'damm. There's also the New Year Fun Run every 1 January, when Berliners work off their hangovers. It starts at the Soviet War Memorial near the Brandenburg Gate.

Badminton

Most tennis facilities (*see p254*) also have badminton courts.

Sportoase & Lady Line & Himaxx

Stromstrasse 11-17, Moabit (390 6620/ www.sportoase.de). U9 Turmstrasse. **Open** 8am-11pm Mon; 8am-10pm Fri; 9am-10pm Sat, Sun. **Rates** vary. **No credit cards. Map** p301 D2/3.

This impressive complex, housed in a former brewery, has 15 badminton and eight squash courts, a mixed fitness room, a women-only fitness centre called Lady Line, and Himaxx, a high-altitude training centre, where oxygen levels are dosed to reproduce the thin air of the mountains. There's a pleasant pub/restaurant too.

Beach volleyball

The Volleyball-Verband Berlin (3199 9933/ www.vvb-online.de) is the sport's umbrella organisation. Their website lists all permanent beach volleyball facilities in Berlin.

City Beach

Michelangelostrasse/Hanns-Eisler-Strasse, Prenzlauer Berg (0177 247 6907/www.city-beach-berlin.de). S8, S41, S42 Greifswalder Strasse. **Open** 10am-11pm daily. **Rates** €20-€22/hr. **Map** p303 H1.

Central indoor facility with three courts.

City Beach am Friedrichshain

Kniprodestrasse/Danziger Strasse, Prenzlauer Berg (0177 247 6907/www.city-beach-berlin.de). Tram 20 Kniprodestrasse/Danziger Strasse. **Open** call for details. **Rates** €10/hr. **Map** p303 H2.

Outdoor nine-court facility that's theoretically open all year, though little used in bad weather. 'Beach bar' in summer. Call in advance to book a court.

Indoor Beachsport Center

Königshorster Strasse 11/13, Wittenau (4140 8888/www.beachberlin.de). U8, S1 Wittenau. **Open** 10am-midnight daily. **Rates** €15/hr 10am-2pm; €20/hr 2pm-5pm; €30/hr 5pm-midnight.

This place isn't central, and it's a ten- to 15-minute walk from the U-Bahn, but it's very well equipped nonetheless, with six playing areas for beach volleyball, soccer and handball. It also has saunas, two cocktail bars and serves food.

Bowling

There are more than 50 bowling alleys in Berlin, all listed at www.bowlingzone.de.

Bowling Center am Alex

Rathausstrasse 5, Mitte (242 6657). U2, U5, U8, S3, S5, S7, S9 Alexanderplatz. **Open** 11am-midnight Mon-Thur; 11am-2am Fri, Sat; 10am-midnight Sun. **Rates** €12.60-€19.20/hr. **No credit cards. Map** p316/p303 G3.

This GDR relic now boasts all mod cons: 18 lanes with scorers, pool tables, darts, pinball machines and a restaurant. Look for the big neon sign and head down the steps.

New City Bowling Hasenheide

Hasenheide 107-9, Kreuzberg (622 2038/www.bowling-hasenheide.de). U7, U8 Hermannplatz. **Open** 10am-midnight daily. **Rates** €1.80-€3.30/person/game. **No credit cards. Map** p307 G5.

Top international competitions are hosted at this recently renovated 28-lane facility. There are also 12 lanes for children and a bar/restaurant.

Canoeing & kayaking

Der Bootsladen

Brandensteinweg 8, Spandau (362 5685/www.der-bootsladen.de). Bus 149. **Open** *Mar-Oct* noon-7pm Tue-Fri; 9am-7pm Sat, Sun. *Nov-Feb* 1-4pm Fri; 10am-4pm Sat. **Rates** *Kayak* €5.50/hr. *Canadian double* €6.50/hr. **Credit** V.

Berlin's urban waterway network is unique in central Europe. This is a good place for canoe and kayak tours of the western river and canal system. If you want a boat for more than three hours, you'll save money by booking for a whole day.

Kanu Connection

Köpenicker Strasse 9, Kreuzberg (612 2686/ www.kanu-connection.de). U1, U15 Schlesisches Tor. **Open** 10am-7pm Mon-Fri; 9am-1pm Sat. **Rates** €20-€27/person/day; €45-€60/wknd; €90-€110/wk. **No credit cards. Map** p307 H4.

Kreuzberg itself is a nice area to paddle through, or you could head east to the forests. This outfit can provide you with maps and guides.

Bowling Center am Alex. *See p248.*

Climbing

There are two options for climbing in Berlin: go to one of the two big commercial halls or join a club. The latter is worthwhile for beginners because clubs offer good value introductory courses, and for experienced climbers because it allows access to some fantastic outdoor venues. The website www.klettern-in-berlin.de lists official and unofficial climbing venues in Berlin, along with a colour-coded legality guide.

Alpinclub Berlin

Spielhagenstrasse 4, Charlottenburg (3450 8804/www.alpinclub-berlin.de). U2 Bismarkstrasse. **Open** 4-6pm Mon-Fri. **Map** p300 B3.

Club can provide information and both beginners' and advanced climbing courses; also organises mountaineering expeditions.

Deutscher Alpenverein (DAV)

Markgrafenstrasse 11, Kreuzberg (251 0943/www.alpenverein-berlin.de). U6 Kochstrasse. **Open** 2-7pm Mon, Wed; 9am-1pm Fri. **Admission** *Membership* €67; (18-26) €37; (17) €31. **No credit cards. Map** p306 F4.

This club offers information and a series of courses. Membership also accords a couple of special privileges: it allows you to climb both the north face of the World War II flak tower in Humboldthain, which was converted into a climbing facility in 1998, and the Kirchbachspitze, a tower built to resemble a cliff face on Kirchbachstrasse in Schöneberg.

Magic Mountain

Böttgerstrasse 20-26, Wedding (8871 5790 www.magicmountain.de). U8, S1 Gesundbrunnen. **Open** noon-midnight Mon-Wed, Fri; 10am-midnight Thur; 11am-10pm Sat, Sun. **Admission** €12-€20. **Credit** MC, V.

Pleasantly designed indoor climbing hall, featuring a range of walls up to 50ft (15m) high. It's also got a 'donut boulder' for experts, and there's a café/restaurant, plus a wellness area equipped with saunas.

T-Hall

Thiemannstrasse 1, Neukölln (6808 9864/www.t-hall.de). U7 Karl-Marx-Strasse or S4 Sonnenallee. **Open** *June-Sept* 10am-11pm Tue; 1-11pm Wed-Fri. *Oct-May* 2pm-midnight Mon, Wed-Fri; 11am-midnight Tue, Sat, Sun). **Rates** €10-€12/day; €6-€9.50 concessions. **No credit cards**.

Spacious indoor climbing facility that reproduces the challenges posed by natural mountains and cliffs. You can take a course, or if you know your stuff, sign the necessary declaration and the 36ft (11m) high ceiling's the limit.

TeamVenture SportsBerlin

Hauptstrasse 2, Rummelsburg (5515 1359/www.teamventure.de). S3, S41, S42, S5, S7, S75, S8, S9 Ostkreuz. **Open** *Mar-Oct* 5-10pm Mon-Fri; 11am-10pm Sat, Sun. *Nov-Feb* by appointment. **No credit cards**.

Offers a high ropes course with more than 20 elements, canoeing and kayaking, beach volleyball, soccer and a small beer garden. Don't be fooled by the website photos. The setting is more urban wasteland than riverside idyll.

Cricket

Cricket has been played in Berlin since the mid-19th century, and though history has bowled it repeated googlies, it's managed to hang in there. The sport is run by the Berlin Cricket Komitee (6950 9065/www.berlin-cricket.de). Six teams currently play competitively; in summer there are games every Saturday and Sunday.

If you want to play, the Berlin Cricket Club (6950 9065/www.berlincc.de), nicknamed 'the Refugees', is a multinational, English-speaking team of expats and locals who are always on the lookout for new members. If you want to watch, the games start at 11am in one of the most beautiful grounds in mainland Europe (Körner Platz, Hanns-Braun-Strasse, Charlottenburg, U2 Olympia-Stadion). At press time, they were intending to open a café/pub during the 2004 season.

Cycling

Cycling is an ideal way to get around Berlin, as the city is flat and well supplied with cycle lanes. In fact, it can be a particularly scenic way to see the city, as bike lanes run through parks and alongside canals. Sport cycling is also popular, and Berlin has produced several internationally renowned riders. The city's level hinterland is also ideal for touring. For bike rental, *see p273*.

Allgemeiner DeutsFahrrad-Club

Brunnenstrasse 28, Mitte (448 4724/www.adfc-berlin.de). U8 Bernauer Strasse. **Open** noon-8pm Mon-Fri; 10am-4pm Sat. **Map** p316/p302.

Has an information and meeting point for cyclists and a do-it-yourself repair station. Contact them for a copy of their Berlin cycle path map or details of routes in and around Berlin.

Berliner Radsport-Verband

Paul-Heyse-Strasse 29, Prenzlauer Berg (4210 5145/www.bdr-radsport.de/ber). S4 Landsberger Allee. **Open** 9am-1pm Tue, Fri; 2-5pm Thur. **Map** p303 H2.

Info on clubs, races and events. The Tour de Berlin, a five-stage, 600km/375-mile race, is held annually at the end of May.

Disabled

There are dozens of clubs and organisations for disabled athletes in Berlin. Phone Behinderten-Sportverband Berlin (3009 9675) for details or visit the national website at www.behindertensport.de and click 'Vereine' to find the nearest one.

Fitness centres

There are hundreds of health and fitness clubs in Berlin – everything from sweaty body-building basements to luxurious spa-like penthouses. Courses offered match those in any big city; there are branches of all the chains, such as Kieser, Swiss Training or Gold's.

Aspria

Karlsruher Strasse 20, Wilmersdorf (890 688 810/www.aspria.de). S45, S46 Halensee. **Open** 6am-11pm Mon-Fri; 9am-10pm Sat, Sun. **Rates** from €70/month (no day pass). **Credit** AmEx, DC, MC, V. **Map** p304 B5.

Five-floor complex with a health and beauty centre, 25m pool, saunas, steam room, ice room, restaurants, bars, sun terrace with solariums and a view of central Berlin. The club offers massages, beauty treatments, fitness courses and customised workouts.

Axxel City Fitness

Bülowstrasse 57, Schöneberg (2175 3000/www.axxel24.de). U2 Bülowstrasse, U7, S1, S2 Yorckstrasse. **Open** 24hrs daily. **Rates** €30-70/mth (2yr contract €33). **No credit cards**. **Map** p304 B5.

For insomniac fitness freaks.

Club Olympus Spa & Fitness

Marlene-Dietrich-Platz 2, Tiergarten (2553 1890/www.berlin.grand.hyatt.com). U2, S1, S2, S25 Potsdamer Platz. **Open** 6.30am-10.30pm Mon-Fri; 7.30am-9pm Sat, Sun. **Rates** €60/day. **Credit** AmEx, DC, MC, V. **Map** p306 E4.

Luxurious, expensive fitness centre on the roof of the Grand Hyatt hotel (*see p58*).

Jason's City Fitness

Wilmersdorfer Strasse 82/83, Charlottenburg (324 1025/www.jasons.cityfitness.de.vu). U7 Adenauerplatz. **Open** 10am-11pm Mon, Wed, Fri; 7am-11pm Tue, Thur; 10am-10pm Sat, Sun. **Rates** vary. **No credit cards. Map** p304.

This place was planning major renovations for the summer of 2004, so ring before you go there. Men only; gays welcome, but it's not exclusively gay.

Jopp Frauen Fitness

Tauentzienstrasse 13A, Charlottenburg (210 111/www.jopp.de). U9, U15 Kurfürstendamm or U1, U15, U2 Wittenbergplatz. **Open** 7am-11pm Mon-Fri, 10am-8pm Sat, Sun. **Rates** €66/mth (3/mth contract). **Map** p305 D4.

This women-only chain has branches across Berlin. **Other locations**: Friedrichstrasse 50, Mitte (2045 8585); Karl-Liebknecht-Strasse 13, Mitte (2434 9355).

Gay & lesbian sports

Berlin's openly homosexual mayor, Klaus Wowereit, has given his backing to a bid to host the Gay Games in 2010. Berlin is the first German city to bid for the event. The Gay Games in Sydney in 2002 attracted more than 11,000 athletes from more than 70 nations. See www.vorspiel.de for details of local sports.

Golf

Golfpark Schloss Wilkendorf

Am Weiher 1, OT Wilkendorf, Gielsdorf (03341 330 960/www.golfpark-schloss-wilkendorf.com). S5 Strausberg Nord, then walk/taxi. **Open** *Nov-Feb* 9am-5pm daily. *Mar-Oct* 8am-7pm. **Rates** *Westside Platz* (18 holes) €28-€54 Mon-Fri; €45 Sat, Sun. *Sandy-Lyle-Platz* (18 holes; members only) €25-€55 Mon-Fri; €50 Sat, Sun. *Public course* (6 holes) €10-€15. **Credit** MC, V.

The only 18-hole course in the area open to non-members: at weekends only, with a Platzreife –'German Golf Certificate' – obtainable with any golf membership or by taking a test. Call for details.

Öffentliche Golf-Übungsanlage Berlin-Adlershof

Rudower Chaussee 4, Adlershof (7076 1188/www.go-for-golf.de). S4, S6, S8, S9 Adlershof. **Open** 10am-dusk daily. **Rates** €7.50/day Mon-Sat; €5 concessions; €5-€10 Sun; €3.75-€7.50 concessions. Golf club rental €0.50. **No credit cards.**

'Public golf for all', four par-three holes, driving range and indoor practice facility.

Öffentliches Golf-Zentrum Berlin-Mitte

Chausseestrasse 94, Mitte. Office: Habersaathstrasse 34, Mitte (2804 7070/www.golfzentrum-berlin.de). U6 Zinnowitzer Strasse. **Open** 7am-dusk daily. **Rates** free. Golf club rental €1. **Credit** AmEx, V. **Map** p302 E2.

A 100,000 sq m (350,000 sq ft) facility with 64-tee driving range and a partially roofed putting green. Free entry, free lessons for kids, weather permitting, usually on Thursdays, call first. Also a BMX course.

Ice skating

The Christmas market at Alexanderplatz has a small outdoor rink, and you can try your hand at curling in the Sony Center at Potsdamer Platz from late November to early January.

Eisstadion Berlin Wilmersdorf

Fritz-Wildung-Strasse 9, Wilmersdorf (824 1012/www.horst-dohm-eisstadion.de). S4 Hohenzollerndamm. **Open** *Oct-mid Mar* 9am-6.30pm, 7.30-10pm Mon, Wed, Fri; 9am-5.30pm, 7.30-10pm Tue, Thur; 9am-10pm Sat; 10am-6pm Sun. **Rates** €3/2hrs; €1.50 concessions. **No credit cards. Map** p304 B6.

With an outer ring for speed skating and an inner field for figure skaters. Skate rental, too.

Erika-Hess-Eisstadion-Mitte

Erika-Hess-Stadion, Müllerstrasse 185, Wedding (200 945 550). U6 Wedding. **Open** *Oct-Mar* 9am-noon, 3-5.30pm Mon, Sun; 9am-noon, 3-5.30pm, 7.30-9.30pm Tue-Sat. **Admission** €3.30; €1.50 concessions. **No credit cards. Map** p302 E1.

Eisstadion Berlin Wilmersdorf.

Life's a beach

You're more likely to think of the Copacabana in Rio de Janeiro when you hear the words **beach volleyball**, but every year, the sport's top pros make the trip across the pond to landlocked Berlin, one of four cities that host a grand slam tournament. The German Open, with a $600,000 purse, is the most lucrative on the European circuit. In 2004 it takes place 20-27 June.

Some 3,000 tonnes of fine sand, twice-washed and laboratory-tested, are trucked from a nearby quarry and dumped on the Schlossplatz (Unter den Linden) to create a total of eight courts, including a centre court with room for 6,000 spectators. The result is world-class sport played in a holiday atmosphere by sunkissed athletes in skimpy swimwear – right in the middle of downtown Berlin.

Of course, rain can put a damper on the occasion. But if the sun shines, it's a real party, entry is free and the standard of play is world class. You should arrive early, especially if it's sunny and the competition is in its final phase.

Beach volleyball, also known simply as 'beach', has come a long way since it was first played in Santa Monica during the Great Depression, when families took a ball and net to the beach and tried to forget about their troubles. The first official tournament wasn't held until the 1940s: the prize was a crate of Pepsi-Cola. Sponsored tournaments were held in the US in the 1970s and the first world championships were held in Rio de Janeiro in 1987. By the 1990s, it was being played all over the world and it became a full medal Olympic sport in 1996.

Santa Monica may be the birthplace of the sport and the Copacabana its spiritual home, but Berlin is now firmly on the international beach volleyball map. Jean-Pierre Seppey, head of volleyball's international governing body, FIVB, said he believed Berlin would become the beach volleyball capital of the world in the coming years. He may just have been trying to flatter his guests, but the World Championships are coming to Berlin in 2005 (20-26 June) with $1 million in prize money up for grabs.

Cheapest public rink in town. Admission gets you up to three hours of skating. The venue also holds important skating competitions.

Karting

Formula one stars such as Michael and Ralf Schumacher and Heinz-Harald Frentzen cut their teeth on the kart track. It's an expensive way to spend an afternoon, though.

Kart-World & Freizeit Park

Am Juliusturm 15-19, Spandau (3549 3100/3549 3113/www.kart-world-berlin.de). U7 Zitadelle or Haselhorst/bus 133. **Open** 3pm-midnight Mon-Thur; noon-midnight Fri; 10am-midnight Sat, Sun. **Rates** €9.20/8 mins; €7.70 concessions. *10 admissions* €70; €52 concessions. **No credit cards**.
Good indoor track including a bridge and tunnel. Bar and bistro with video projection for watching races live. On Formula One race days, if you guess the result you can ride a cart all day for free.

Rok Kart

Grossbeerenstrasse 148-58, Mariendorf (7479 2827/www.rok-kart.de). S2 Marienfelde, then bus 127. **Open** 3-10pm Mon-Thur; 3pm-midnight Fri; 11am-midnight Sat; 11am-10pm Sun. **Rates** €11/10 mins; €7.50 concessions. *5 admissions* €40; €30 concessions. *For 10 karts* €480/hr. **Credit** MC, V.
First-rate indoor track well-suited to beginners.

Sailing & motor boating

Berlin is amazing for water rats. It boasts 50 lakes and a 200-kilometre (125-mile) network of navigable rivers, estuaries and canals. The city is bordered on the west by the Havel river and to the south by the Dahme, while the Spree forms an east-west axis through the centre. If you're planning a longer stay, you might join one of the clubs or associations listed at www.wassersport-in-berlin.de. But there are also opportunities for the short-term visitor.

You need a licence for boating and sailing. If you have one from your native country, bring it. Boat rental places may then issue you a charter pass for sailboats or motor boats.

The Berlin-Brandenburg Water Sports Association (Wassertourismus Förderverband; www.wtb-brb.de) publishes a waterway and tourism map with speed limits and landings. The Berliner Segler-Verband (3083 9908/ www.berliner-segler-verband.de) has info on sailing in and around Berlin.

The Wassersportzentrum Berlin (www.wassersportzentrum.de) runs two sailing/diving/motor boat centres with marinas at the Müggelsee in south-east Berlin. For contacts on the Wannsee, to the west, try www.yachthafen-marina-wannsee.de.

Yachtcharter Berlin
Müggelseedamm 70, Köpenick (6409 4310/ www.yachtcharter-berlin.de). Tram 61. **Rates** call for details. **Open** *Apr-Oct* 9am-6pm daily. *Nov-Mar* 10am-noon Mon; 4-6pm Thur. **No credit cards**.
Motor boat charter company.

Sauna & Turkish baths

Many of Berlin's public baths have cheapish saunas and massage services. *See below.*

Hamam Turkish Bath
Schoko-Fabrik, Naunynstrasse 72, Kreuzberg (615 1464/615 2999/www.schokofabrik.de). U1, U8, U15 Kottbusser Tor. **Open** *Sept-Apr* 3-11pm Mon; noon-10pm Tue-Sun. *May-June* call for hours. **Rates** €12/3 hrs. **No credit cards. Map** p307 G4.
Under the glass cupola of the main hall, women sit in alcoves, soaking in warm water. A friendly and laid-back place, attracting a mixed clientele. Enjoy Turkish tea and a reviving massage afterwards. Children are not permitted on Tuesday and Fridays but Thursday is kids' day. It's women only but boys up to age of six are allowed in.

Liquidrom
Möckernstrasse 10, Kreuzberg (7473 7171/ www.liquidrom.com) U7 Möckernbrücke, S1, S2, S25 Anhalter Bahnhof. **Open** 10am-10pm Sun-Thurs; 10am-midnight, Fri, Sat. **Rates** €15/2 hrs; €25 day pass). **No credit cards. Map** p306 F4.
The new facility under the roof of the recently built Neues Tempodrom (*see p220*) cultural and entertainment arena features pools, saunas, steam and thermal baths, an open-air Japanese Onsen pool, massages and a terrace and bar. The highlight is 'liquid sound', a domed pool with music and light effects. Stretch out, put your head back (salt water keeps you afloat) and savour the watery ambience.

Sultan Hamam
Bülowstrasse 57, Schöneberg (2175 3375/ www.sultan-hamam.de). U2 Bülowstrasse. **Open** noon-11pm daily. **Rates** €14/3hrs; €11 peel; €16 massage. **No credit cards. Map** p306 E4.
Traditional massages and peelings, as well as more modern cosmetic treatments. Monday is men's day, Sunday is families' day; during the rest of the week it's women only.

Thermen am Europa-Center
Europa-Center, Nürnberger Strasse 7, Charlottenburg (257 5760/www.thermen-berlin.de). U1, U2, U15 Wittenbergplatz. **Open** 10am-midnight Mon-Sat; 10am-9pm Sun. **Rates** €17.90/day; €9.20 1st hr; €4.10 2nd hr. *10 admissions* €154. **No credit cards. Map** p305 D4.
Big, central, mixed facility offering Finnish saunas, steam baths, hot and cool pools, and a garden (open until October). There is a pool where you can swim outside on the roof, even in the depths of winter. Thermen also boasts a café, pool-side loungers, table tennis, billiards and massage.

Skateboarding, in-line skating & BMX

Berlin is a skater-friendly city, with small facilities dotted across town and several bigger complexes, all listed by district at www.skatespots.de.

The city's skaters occasionally disrupt street traffic by holding demonstrations for equal rights. Routes vary; check www.berlinparade.de for dates and starting points.

Erlebniswerkstatt des Projektes Erlebnisräume
Sterndamm 82, Treptow (631 0911/ www.erlebnisraume.de). S4, S6, S8, S9, S10 Schöneweide. **Open** call for appointment. **Admission** free.
Berlin's only trial track with jump ramps, and a good place to connect with what's going on. Projekt Erlebnisräume builds and maintains skateboarding, skating and climbing facilities around town and organises competitions and events.

Liberty Park
Senftenberger Strasse/corner Kastanienallee, Hellersdorf. U5 Hellersdorf.
The largest BMX and skater complex in Berlin, with half-pipe and mini-ramps.

Squash

Most tennis facilities also have squash courts.

TSB City Sport
Brandenburgische Strasse 53, Wilmersdorf (873 9097/www.city-sports-berlin.com). U7 Konstanzer Strasse. **Open** 7am-midnight Mon-Fri; 8am-midnight Sat, Sun. **Rates** *Tennis* €17-€32. *Squash* €10-€18. *Badminton* €9-€15.60. *Sauna* €2.50-€7.50. **Credit** V. **Map** p305 C5.
Offers four tennis courts, nine squash courts and 12 badminton courts, plus a sauna, solarium, restaurant and beer garden. Coaching is available for all three sports, along with aerobics and classical dance.

Swimming (indoor)

Every district has an indoor pool. Check the phone book under Stadtbad or visit www.berlinerbaederbetriebe.de for the nearest.

Schwimm- und Sprunghalle im Europapark
Paul-Heyse-Strasse 26, Prenzlauer Berg (4218 6120). S4, S8, S10 Landsberger Allee. **Open** 6.30-10pm Mon-Thur; 9-10pm Fri; 12-7pm Sat; 10am-6pm Sun. **Admission** €3; €2.50 concessions. **No credit cards. Map** p303 H2.
This immense facility is one of the largest swimming pools in Europe. It often hosts international swimming competitions, and is right next door to the Velodrom (*see p244*).

Stadtbad Mitte

Gartenstrasse 5, Mitte (3088 0910). S1, S2 Nordbahnhof/tram 8, 50. **Open** 6.30am-10pm Mon; 10am-4pm Tue; 6.30am-10pm Wed; 6.30-8am Thur; 6.30-10pm Fri; 2-9pm Sat, Sun. **Admission** €3; €2.50 concessions. **No credit cards. Map** p302 F2/p316.
Built in 1928, this place has a 50m (164ft) pool.

Stadtbad Neukölln

Ganghoferstrasse 3, Neukölln (6824 9812). U7 Rathaus Neukölln. **Open** 2-5pm Mon; 6:45am-6:30pm Tue, Wed; 6:45am-10pm Thur, Fri; 8am-4pm Sat. **Admission** €4; €2.50 concessions. **Map** p307 H6.
Described as 'Europe's most beautiful baths' when opened in 1914, they survived the 20th century unscathed. Built in Greco-Roman style, the complex features two splendid pools flanked by Ionic columns, with original tiling, wood panelling and stained-glass windows.

Stadtbad Schöneberg

Hauptstrasse 39, Schöneberg (780 9930/ www.berlinerbaederbetriebe.de). U7 Eisenacher Strasse. **Open** 7am-10pm Mon-Fri; 9am-10pm Sat, Sun. **Admission** €5; €4 concessions. **Map** p305 D6.
Great mixture of old and new. Kids can play in the wave pool while you recharge batteries in the sauna. Busy at peak times, such as Saturday afternoon.

Swimming (open-air)

Before setting out to a pool, phone first to make sure it's open (or the Berlin service hotline on 0180 310 2020) as the city's financial woes affect pool opening times. Details of all outdoor public pools at www.berlinerbaederbetriebe.de.

There is also plenty of lake swimming in Berlin. Schlachtensee and Krumme Lanke in the west are clean, set in attractive woodland and easily accessible by public transport.

Freibad Müggelsee

Fürstenwalder Damm 838, Rahnsdorf (648 7777). 3 Rahnsdorf. **Open** *Summer* call for times. **Admission** €4; €2 concessions. **No credit cards.**
North shore bathing beach, complete with nudist camp, on the bank of east Berlin's biggest lake.

Sommerbad Kreuzberg

Prinzenstrasse 113-119, Kreuzberg (616 1080). U1 Prinzenstrasse. **Admission** €4; €2 concessions. **No credit cards. Map** p306 F5.
Known as Prinzenbad, a popular outdoor complex for swimming and sunbathing. It has a 50m (164ft) pool and one for non-swimmers. Disabled access, nudist area and refreshments.

Strandbad Wannsee

Wannseebadweg, Nikolassee (803 5612/www. berlinerbaederbetriebe.de). S1, S7 Nikolassee. **Admission** €4; €2.50 concessions. **No credit cards.**
Europe's largest inland beach, with sand, sunbeds, water slides, pedalos, snack stalls and beer garden.

Tennis

An expensive habit in Berlin. The cheapest time to hire a court is in the mornings and even then it can cost €15-€30 an hour for an indoor court. Many badminton and squash establishments also have tennis courts. The Tennis-Verband Berlin-Brandenburg (8972 8730/www.tvbb.de) has information about local leagues and clubs.

Tennis Center Weissensee

Roelckestrasse 106, Weissensee (927 4594/ www.twww.tcwsports.com). S4, S8, S10 Greifswalder Strasse. **Open** 7am-midnight Mon-Fri; 8am-midnight Sat, Sun. **Rates** call for details. **No credit cards. Map** p303 H1.
Seven clay-style tennis courts, 16 badminton courts and four fun ball courts for the kids, all indoors. Prices include use of the sauna (10am-10pm).

TSF

Richard-Tauber-Damm 36, Marienfelde (742 1091/ www.tsf-sport.de). U6 Alt-Mariendorf. **Open** 7am-12.30pm daily. **Rates** *Winter* €16-€24. *Summer* €12-€19. **No credit cards.**
Offers nine quality indoor tennis courts, six squash courts, gymnastics, massage, sauna and restaurant facilities. No membership fee.
Other locations: Galenstrasse 33-45, Spandau (333 4083).

Windsurfing, waterskiing, wakeboarding & surfing

360°

Pariser Strasse 23/24, Charlottenburg (883 8596/ www.360berlin.com). U1, U9 Spichernstrasse. **Open** 11am-7.30pm Mon-Fri; 10am-4pm Sat. **Credit** AmEx, MC, V. **Map** p305 C5.
Fashion, hardware, kite courses, snowboards, skating, in-line, surfing, wakeboarding and windsurfing.

Wakeboard & Wasserski Grossbeeren

Bahnhofstrasse 49, Grossbeeren (033701 90873/ www.wassersport-grosbeeren.de). S25, S26 Lichterfelde Süd, then RB32. **Open** *Swimming area* Apr-Sept; call for times. **Rates** €12.50/hr; €10 concessions. €29/day; €23 concessions. *Board rental* €5/2hrs; €16-€21/day. *Wetsuit rental* €6/2hrs; €12/day. **No credit cards.**
One of Europe's most modern waterskiing facilities.

Wet & Wild Wasserski-Seilbahn Berlin-Velten

Am Bernsteinsee, Am Autobahndreieck Oranienburg, Ausfart Velten (0330 945 1563/www. wakeboard-berlin.de). **Open** Apr-Oct; call for times. **Rates** (Mon-Fri) €18/2hrs; €27/day; €12-€19 concessions. (Sat, Sun) €20/2 hrs; €14 concessions. €29/day; €23 concessions. **No credit cards.**
Waterskiing without a boat. Imagine a ski lift in the water and you get the picture.

Trips Out of Town

Features

Maps

Trips Out of Town

Potsdam palaces, Saxon cities, Baltic islands and watery wilderness.

The Russia house: Potsdam's **Alexandrowka** district. *See p259.*

Berlin is a city in the middle of nowhere. For miles around, fields, lakes and dense woods are scarcely interrupted by a scattering of small towns and villages. In fact, water and greenery crowd into the city from all sides, providing a wealth of opportunities for walking, cycling and swimming (*see p111* **Other Districts** for a nature escape within the city limits).

By far the most popular day trip from the city is to **Potsdam**, which is to Berlin what Versailles is to Paris. There's easily enough here to fill a couple of days. Neighbouring **Babelsberg** has the old UFA film studios, Germany's answer to Hollywood. Another worthwhile, though more sombre, trip is just north of the city to the former concentration camp **Sachsenhausen** (*see p262*).

If you fancy travelling a little further in search of nature, the **Spreewald**, a forest scattered with small streams, is good for a stroll or boat ride, and can be reached in about an hour by train. If only the seaside will do, then head up north to the Baltic coast and the island of **Rügen**, but plan on staying at least overnight.

Two other excellent trips are south to historic cities of former East Germany. In terms of its compact picturesque centre, **Leipzig** is probably the most rewarding, though **Dresden**'s history, flamboyant baroque architecture and art collections are impressive. Both are around two hours from Berlin by train.

Around Berlin

Potsdam & Babelsberg

Potsdam is capital of the state of Brandenburg and, just outside the city limits to the south-west, Berlin's most beautiful neighbour. Known for its 18th-century baroque architecture, it's a magnet for tourists. The summer weekend crowds can be overwhelming; visit outside of peak times, if you can.

For centuries, Potsdam was the summer residence of the Hohenzollerns, who were attracted by the area's gently rolling landscape, rivers and lakes. Despite the damage wrought during World War II and by East Germany's socialist planners, much remains of the legacy of these Prussian kings. The best-known landmark is **Sanssouci** (*see p259*) the huge landscaped park created by Frederick the Great, one of three royal parks flanking the town.

At the moment, Potsdam is undergoing a fascinating process of redefinition. The town has changed considerably since reunification. In East German times Potsdam's associations with the monarchy were regarded with suspicion; the lack of political will and economic means led to much of the town's historic fabric falling into disrepair or being destroyed. But in 1990 Potsdam was assigned UNESCO world heritage status; some 80 per cent of the town's historic buildings have been subsequently restored.

The end of East Germany also marked the end of Potsdam's historic role as a garrison town. Until the Soviet withdrawal, some 10,000 troops were stationed here. With their departure, vast barracks and tracts of land to the north of the town were abandoned. The area is currently being redeveloped for civilian use, including the BUGA or Volkspark, with its nature museum, the **Biosphäre** (*see p261*).

THE OLD TOWN

One of the most dominant – if not the prettiest – buildings of historical interest in the old town is the 19th-century **Nikolaikirche**. It is hard to miss the huge dome, inspired by St Paul's in London. Rather more graceful is the mid-18th century **Altes Rathaus**, diagonally opposite, whose tower was used a prison until 1875. Nowadays, the former town hall is used for exhibitions and lectures. Both the Nikolaikirche and the Altes Rathaus were badly damaged in the war and rebuilt in the 1960s. They are all that remains of the original Alter Markt, once one of Potsdam's most beautiful squares.

The Stadtschloss, in the centre of town, was substantially damaged during the war and the East German authorities demolished the rest of it in 1960. There are plans to rebuild it, but funding problems mean this is unlikely to happen soon. Private sponsors have already funded the reconstruction of the Fortunaportal, one decorative former entrance to the palace, in the Alter Markt. To get an impression of this square before 1945, take a look at the model in the foyer of the Altes Rathaus.

The area behind the gargantuan Hotel Mercure was once part of the palace gardens. Later, Friedrich Wilhelm I, the Soldier King, turned it into a parade ground. Now it has become a park. If you walk up Breite Strasse, you can see all that is left of the old Stadtschloss. The low red building that now houses the **Filmmuseum** (*see p261*) is the former *Marstall*, or royal stables. Dating from 1685 and originally an orangery, it is one of the oldest buildings in the town.

The nearby Neuer Markt survived the war intact. At number 1 is the house where Friedrich Wilhelm II was born. The Kutschstall, originally a royal stables, now houses the new **Haus der Brandenburgisch-Preussischen Geschichte** (*see p261*) with its exhibition charting 800 years of Brandenburg history.

BAROQUE AROUND THE BLOCK

Potsdam's impressive baroque quarter is bounded by Schopenhauerstrasse, Hegelallee, Hebbelstrasse and Charlottenstrasse. Some of the best houses can be found in Gutenbergstrasse and Brandenburger Strasse, Potsdam's pedestrianised shopping drag. Note the pitched roofs with space to accommodate troops – the Soldier King built the quarter in the 1730s. Around the corner is Lindenstrasse 54, once the house of a Prussian officer, later a Stasi detention centre (you can now tour the cells).

Three baroque town gates – the Nauener Tor, Jäger Tor and the Brandenburger Tor – stand on the northern and western edges of the quarter. The latter predates its Berlin namesake by 18 years. On the quarter's eastern edge, two churches bear witness to Potsdam's cosmopolitan past. The Great Elector's 1685 Edict of Potsdam promised refuge to Protestants suffering from religious persecution in their homelands, sparking waves of immigration. The Französische Kirche was built for the town's Huguenot community while St Peter and Paul's in Bassinplatz was built for Catholic immigrants who came to this Protestant area in response to the Prussian kings' drive to attract skilled workers and soldiers.

Hollywood Babelsberg

Regimes may come and go, but movies have been made at **Babelsberg** for almost a century. A Berlin cameraman built the first studio here in 1911 and started production with his company Bioscop the following year. To this day, movies, including a number of major international co-productions such as Roman Polanski's *The Pianist*, are still being made at studios now owned by Vivendi Universal. Medienstadt Babelsberg is also the headquarters for a number of film institutions, such as the Filmboard Berlin-Brandenburg.

Babelsberg really took off in 1917 after the German General Staff decided the war effort was suffering from inferior propaganda. The Universum Film AG (Ufa), a partly state-owned production company, was set up as a result. By the 1920s the studio had become the largest in the world outside Hollywood. Masterpieces such as the Expressionist *Cabinet of Dr Caligari*, Fritz Lang's *Metropolis*, and Josef von Sternberg's *The Blue Angel* starring Marlene Dietrich were produced here. The studio's success rubbed off on the town, as film stars began settling in the 19th-century villas close to Lake Griebnitzsee.

After the Nazis took power, the studio's Jewish employees were sacked and many of Ufa's big names left for the USA. Propaganda minister Joseph Goebbels assumed control over film production. During the Nazi period, the studios mainly churned out thrillers, family drama and light entertainment. But there were also those with a more overt Nazi message, such as Leni Riefenstahl's *Triumph of the Will* and Veit Harlan's *Jud Süss*.

Film production resumed quickly after the end of the war. Until the founding of East Germany in 1949, the Soviets were chiefly interested in using film as a tool for de-Nazification. The first film from this period and one of its most striking is Wolfgang Staudte's *Die Mörder sind unter uns* set in immediate post-war Germany. Only in the early 1950s did film policy become more aesthetically and politically proscriptive. Throughout DEFA's history the contemporary political climate determined the degree of censorship. More than 700 feature films were produced here in the Communist era, including 150 for children, as well as more than 600 TV movies. At the Filmmuseum Potsdam (*see p261*) you can gain an interesting insight into the various phases of film-making at DEFA.

After reunification, the studios were privatised. Now there are state-of-the-art facilities for all phases of TV and film production. Sections of the studios are open to the public in tacky theme-park form. Admission includes tours of production facilities, various shows and stunt displays.

Filmpark Babelsberg

August-Bebel-Strasse 26-53, entrance on Grossbeerenstrasse (0331 721 2717/ www.filmpark.de). Train to Medienstadt Babelsberg/S1 Babelsberg. **Open** *Apr-Oct* 10am-6pm daily. **Admission** €17; €15.50 concessions. **No credit cards**.

Holländisches Viertel, Potsdam.

The **Holländisches Viertel**, or Dutch quarter, is the most attractive part of Friedrich Wilhelm I's new town extension. As part of a failed strategy to attract skilled Dutch immigrants to the town, the king had Dutch builders construct 134 gable-fronted houses. But in this era, Brandenburg was backward and sparsely populated, as a result of war and epidemics, while Holland was one of Europe's most progressive nations. In the **Jan Bouman Haus** (*see p261*) in Mittelstrasse 8 you can see an original interior. Today this quarter is filled with upmarket boutiques and restaurants.

THE RUSSIAN INFLUENCE

Another Potsdam curiosity is the Russian Colony of **Alexandrowka**, 15 minutes' walk north of the town centre. The settlement consists of 13 wooden clad, two-storey dwellings with steeply pitched roofs laid out in the form of a St Andrew's Cross. There is even a Russian orthodox church with onion dome on the rise behind the houses. Regular services are still held in the Alexander-Newski-Kapelle. Alexandrowka was built in 1826 by Friedrich Wilhelm III to commemorate the death of Tsar Alexander I, a friend from the Wars of Liberation against Napoleon. The settlement became home to surviving members of a troupe of Russian musicians given into Prussian service by the Tsar in 1812. Two of the houses are still inhabited by the descendants of these men. At the Teehaus Russische Kolonie (Alexandrowka 1, 0331 200 6478, closed Mon, main course €15), Russian specialities are served by waitresses in folkloric costume.

The area around and to the north of Alexandrowka became the focus of a different Russian presence during the Cold War. The late Wilhelmine villas served as offices to the Soviet administration or as officers' homes. Soviet forces took over buildings used by the Prussian army in the 19th century and later by the Nazis. One such is the castle-like Garde-Ulanen-Kaserne in Jäger Allee, close to the junction with Reiterweg. The recently restored Belvedere, at the top of the hill to the north of Alexandrowka, is the town's highest observation point. It fell into disuse after the Wall went up in 1961, when people were banned from enjoying views over West Berlin.

POTSDAM'S ROYAL PARKS

Back towards the town centre is Potsdam's biggest tourist magnet, **Park Sanssouci**. It's beautiful, but be warned: its main avenues can become overrun and it is not always easy to get into the palaces (guided tours are compulsory and numbers limited). The park is a legacy of King Frederick the Great, who was attracted to the area by its fine views. He initially had terraced gardens built here before adding a palace. Sanssouci means 'without worries' and reveals the king's desire for a sanctuary where he could pursue his philosophical, musical and literary interests. Voltaire was among his guests. His nearby Bildergalerie was the first purpose-built museum in Germany.

After victory in the Seven Year War, Frederick the Great built the huge **Neues Palais** on the park's western edge. Friedrich II's sumptuous suite, as well as the Grottensaal

No worries! **Sanssouci** was Frederick the Great's sanctuary. *See p259.*

(Grotto Room), Marmorsaal (Marble Room) and Schlosstheater (Palace Theatre), are worth a visit. Other attractions in the park include the **Orangery**; the **Spielfestung**, or toy fortress, built for Wilhelm II's sons, complete with a toy cannon which can be fired; the **Chinesisches Teehaus** (Chinese Teahouse) with its collection of Chinese and Meissen porcelain and the **Drachenhaus** (Dragonhouse), a pagoda-style café. In the park's south-west corner lies **Schloss Charlottenhof**, with its blue-glazed entrance and Kupferstichzimmer (copper-plate engraving room), built in the 1830s on the orders of crown prince Friedrich Wilhelm IV. Outside Sanssouci in the Breite Strasse is the **Dampfmaschinenhaus** that pumped water for Sanssouci's fountains, but was built to look like a mosque.

North-east of the town centre is yet another large park complex, the **Neuer Garten**, designed on the orders of Frederick the Great's nephew and successor to the throne, Friedrich Wilhelm II. In the neo-classical **Marmorpalais** the king died a premature death allegedly as a result of his dissolute lifestyle. At the park's most northern corner is **Schloss Cecilienhof**, the last royal palace to be built in Potsdam. This incongruous, mock-Tudor mansion was built for the Kaiser's son and his wife. Spared wartime damage, in summer 1945 it hosted the Potsdam Conference, where Stalin, Truman and Churchill met to discuss Germany's future. Inside you can see the round table where the delegates negotiated the settlement.

During the conference, the Allied leaders lived across the Havel in one of Babelsberg's secluded 19th-century villa districts. Stalin stayed in Karl-Marx-Strasse 27, Churchill in the Villa Urbig at Virchowstrasse 23, one of Mies van der Rohe's early buildings, and Truman in the Truman-Villa in Karl-Marx-Strasse 2. All buildings can be viewed from the outside only.

Potsdam's third and most recent royal park, **Park Babelsberg**, also makes for a good walk. In East German times this fell into neglect because it lay so close to the border. Schloss Babelsberg, a neo-Gothic extravaganza inspired by Windsor Castle, nestles among its wooded slopes. Another architectural curiosity is the **Flatowturm**, an observation point in mock medieval style close to the Glienicker See.

Also on the east side of the Havel close to Potsdam's main station is the Telegraphenberg – once the site of a telegraph station. In 1921 it became the site of Erich Mendelsohn's Expressionist **Einsteinturm**, commissioned to house an observatory that could confirm the General Theory of Relativity. A wonderfully whimsical building, it was one of the first products of the inter-war avant-garde.

On the nearby Brauhausberg, there is one last reminder of Potsdam's complex, multi-layered past. The square tower rising up from the trees is the present seat of Brandenburg's state parliament. In East German days, the building was known as the Kremlin because it served as local Communist party headquarters. Originally, it was the 'Kriegsschule' – the war school – where young men trained to be officers in the German imperial army.

Altes Rathaus

Am Alten Markt. (0331 289 6336/ www.altesrathauspotsdam.de). **Open** 10am-6pm Tue-Sun. **Admission** €3; €2 concessions. **No credit cards.**

Biosphäre

Georg-Hermann-Allee 99 (0331 550 740/ www.biosphaere.net). **Open** 9am-6pm (last entry 4.30pm) Mon-Fri; 10am-7pm (last entry 5.30pm) Sat, Sun. **Admission** €9.50; €8 concessions; €6.50 under-14s. **No credit cards.**

Filmmuseum Potsdam

Marstall (0331 271810). **Open** 10am-6pm daily. **Admission** €3; €2 concessions. **No credit cards.**

The museum's permanent exhibition opened in April 2004. Exploring 90 years of film-making at the Babelsberg studios, it focuses on the history of DEFA, East Germany's sole film-making company.

Gedenkstätte Lindenstrasse

Lindenstrasse 54 (0331 289 6136). **Open** 9am-5pm Tue, Thur, Sat. **Admission** €1.50. **No credit cards.**

East German secret police interrogated people in this labyrinthine complex of cells.

Haus der Brandenburgisch-Preussischen Geschichte

Kutschstall, Am Neuen Markt (0331 200 56355). **Open** 10am-6pm Tue, Thur-Sun; 10am-8pm Wed. **Admission** €4; €3 concessions. **No credit cards.**

Jan Bouman Haus

Mittelstrasse 8 (0331 280 3773). **Open** 1-6pm Mon, Fri; 11am-6pm Sat, Sun. **Admission** €2; €1 concessions. **No credit cards.**

Marmorpalais

Im Neuen Garten (0331 969 4246/www.spsg.de). **Open** *Apr-Oct* 10am-5pm Tue-Sun. *Nov-Mar* 10am-12.30pm, 1-4pm Sat, Sun. **Admission** €3; €2 concessions. **No credit cards.**

Nikolaikirche

Am Alten Markt (0331 291 682/www. nikolaipotsdam.de). **Open** 2pm-5pm Mon; 10am-5pm Tue-Sun. **Admission** free.

Sanssouci

Potsdam (0331 969 4202/www.spsg.de). **Open** *Palace & exhibition buildings* Apr-Oct 9am-5pm Tue-Sun; Nov-Mar 9am-4pm daily. *Park* 9am-dusk daily. **Admission** *Palace & exhibition buildings* €8; €5 concessions. *Park* free. **Credit** MC, V.

Each of the palaces and buildings has its own closing days each month and some are only open mid May to mid October. Phone for full details.

Schloss Cecilienhof

Im Neuen Garten (0331 969 4244/www.spsg.de). **Open** *Apr-Oct* 9am-5pm Tue-Sun. *Nov-Mar* 9am-4pm Tue-Sun. **Admission** €5; €4 concessions. **No credit cards.**

Where to eat & drink

B-West (Zeppelinstrasse 146, 0331 951 0798, closed Sun, main course €6-€10) attracts a lively, young crowd and serves simple German cuisine. The cosy **Café Heider** (Friedrich-Ebert-Strasse 29, 0331 270 5596, main course €3-€15) offers excellent coffee and cake, plus a wide range of main dishes. **Kinocafé Melodie** (Friedrich-Ebert-Strasse 12, 0331 620 0699, admission €3) serves no food, but is a popular watering hole. **Matschkes Galerie Café** (Alleestrasse 10, 0331 280 5111, main course €4-€8) serves good simple German and Russian cooking at a reasonable price and has some outdoor courtyard seating. In an old Dutch house, the **M18** (Mittelstrasse 18, 0331 2701 818) pub has a great selection of whisky and beer and a garden. **Villa Kellermann** (Mangerstrasse 34-36, 0331 291 572, closed Mon Oct-Mar, main course €14) serves first-rate Italian food in a 19th century villa, with terrace views over Heiligensee and the Neue Garten.

Theatre & nightlife

Lindenpark (Stahnsdorfer Strasse 76-78, 01805 170517/www.lindenpark.de) in Babelsberg has regular club nights and gigs. **Theater im Schiff** (Lange Brücke, 0331 280 0100), anchored close to the Hans-Otto-Theater, is a ship offering theatre, cinema, cabaret and discos. **Waschhaus** (Schiffbauergasse, 0331 271 560, www. waschhaus.de), a large club just outside Potsdam centre, offers DJs and live gigs.

Getting there

By train

Both Potsdam and Babelsberg can be reached via the S1 S-Bahn line (it takes just under an hour from Mitte; be sure to buy a ticket that covers the 'C' zone). For Babelsberg, there's a direct regional train from Zooligischer Garten to Medienstadt Babelsberg that takes just 15mins (leaving around ten minutes past the hour, every hour), and a number of regional trains to Potsdam Hauptbahnhof from Zooligischer Garten that leave every 20 mins and take 20-30 mins.

Tourist information

Potsdam Tourismus Service

Friedrich-Ebertstrasse 5 (0331 275 580/ www.potsdam.de). **Open** 10am-6pm Mon-Fri; 10am-2pm Sat, Sun.

Sachsenhausen

Many Nazi concentration camps have been preserved and opened to the public as memorials and museums. Sachsenhausen is the one nearest to Berlin.

Immediately upon coming to power, Hitler set about rounding up and interning his opponents. From 1933 to 1935 an old brewery on this site was used to hold them. The present camp received its first prisoners in July 1936. It was designated with cynical euphemism as a *Schutzhaftlager* ('Protective Custody Camp'). The first *Schutzhaftlagern* were political opponents of the government: Communists, social democrats, trade unionists. Soon, the variety of prisoners widened to include anyone guilty of 'anti-social' behaviour, gays and Jews.

About 6,000 Jews were forcibly brought here after Kristallnacht alone. It was here that some of the first experiments in organised mass murder were made: thousands of POWs from the Eastern Front were killed at 'Station Z'.

The SS evacuated the camp in 1945 and began marching 33,000 inmates to the Baltic, where they were to be packed into boats and sunk in the sea. Some 6,000 died during the march before the survivors were rescued by the Allies. Another 3,000 prisoners were found in the camp's hospital when it was captured on 22 April 1945.

But the horror did not end here. After the German capitulation, the Russian secret police, the MVD, reopened Sachsenhausen as 'Camp 7' for the detention of war criminals; in fact, it was filled with anyone suspected of opposition. Following the fall of the GDR, mass graves were discovered, containing the remains of an estimated 10,000 prisoners.

On 23 April 1961, the partially restored camp was opened to the public as a national monument and memorial. The inscription over the entrance, *Arbeit Macht Frei* ('Work Sets You Free'), could be found over the gates of all concentration camps.

The parade ground, where morning roll-call was taken, and from where inmates were required to witness executions on the gallows, stands before the two remaining barrack blocks. One is now a museum and the other a memorial hall and cinema, where a film about the history of the camp is shown. Next door stands the prison block.

There are another couple of small exhibitions in buildings in the centre of the camp (no English labelling), but perhaps the grimmest site here is the subsiding remains of Station Z, the surprisingly small extermination block. A map traces the path the condemned would follow, depending upon whether they were to be shot (the bullets were retrieved and reused) or gassed. All ended up in the neighbouring ovens.

All this can be disturbing, but so it should be: there are still people who pretend that none of it happened – some of them burned buildings here in 1992. Note: it's a good idea to hire an audio guide (available in English) at the gate.

KZ Sachsenhausen

Strasse der Nationen 22, Oranienburg (03301 8037 1517/www.gedenkstaette-sachsenhausen.de). **Open** *Apr-Sept* 8.30am-6pm Tue-Sun. *Oct-Mar* 8.30am-4.30pm Tue-Sun. **Admission** free.

Getting there

By train

Oranienburg is at the end of the S1 S-Bahn line (40mins from Mitte). From the station follow signs to 'Gedenkstätte Sachsenhausen'; a 20-min walk.

Further Afield

Spreewald

This filigree network of tiny rivers, streams and canals, dividing patches of deciduous forest and farmland, is one of the loveliest excursions from Berlin. German author Theodor Fontane described the Spreewald as how Venice would have looked 1,500 years ago. It gets crowded in season, particularly at weekends, giving the lie to its claim to be one of the most perfect wilderness areas in Europe. Still, out of season, you can have the area to yourself.

Located about 100 kilometres (60 miles) south-east of Berlin, the Spree bisects the area into the Unterspreewald and Oberspreewald. For the former, Schepzig or Lübben are the best starting points; for the latter go 15 kilometres (nine miles) further on the train to Lübbenau.

The character of both sections is very similar. The Oberspreewald is perhaps better, for its 500 square kilometres (190 square miles) of territory contain more than 300 natural and artificial channels, called *Fliesse*. You can travel around these on hand-propelled punts – rent your own or join a larger group – and also take out kayaks. Motorised boats are forbidden. Here and there in the forest are restaurants and small hotels. The tourist information centre in Lübbenau provide maps and walk routes.

The local population belongs to the Sorbisch minority, a Slav people related to Czechs and Slovaks. Their own language is found in street names, newspapers and so on. This adds an air of exoticism, unlike the folk festivals laid on for tourists in the high season.

Dresden's **Aldstadt** is getting a makeover for its 800th birthday. *See p265.*

Where to eat & drink

There are plenty of eating and drinking options in Lübben and Lübbenau, and little to choose between most of them. Follow your nose.

Getting there

By train

There are direct trains every hour to Lübben and Lübbenau. The fastest is 52mins from Ostbahnhof and 1hr 16mins from Zoo to Lübben. Lübbenau is a further 17mins.

Tourist information

Tourist websites (www.spreewald-info.com or www.spreewald-online.de) are good sources of information about the area and allow you to book hotel rooms online.

Haus für Mensch & Natur

Schulstrasse 9, Lübbenau (03542 89210/892130). **Open** *Apr-Oct* 10am-5pm daily. **Admission** free.

In an old schoolhouse, the 'House for Mankind & Nature' is the visitor centre for the Spreewald Biosphere Reservation. It has an exhibition about the environmental importance of the Spreewald.

Spreewald Information

Ehm-Welk-Strasse 15, Lübbenau (035 423 668/ www.spreewald-online.de). **Open** *Apr-Oct* 9am-6pm Mon-Fri; 9am-1pm Sat, Sun. *Nov-Mar* 9am-4pm Mon-Fri.

Rügen

The Baltic coast was the favoured holiday destination of the GDR citizen; post-reunification it is still the most accessible stretch of seaside for Berliners. The coast forms the northern boundary of the modern state of Mecklenburg-Vorpommern. Bismarck famously said of the area: 'When the end of the world comes, I shall go to Mecklenburg, because there everything happens a hundred years later.'

The large island of **Rügen** is gradually resuming its rivalry with Sylt in the North Sea – both islands claim to be the principal north German resort. The island is undoubtedly beautiful, with its white chalk cliffs, beechwoods and beaches. Most people stay in the resorts on the east coast, such as Binz (the largest and best known), Sellin and Göhren. In July and August Rügen can get crowded (don't go without pre-booked accommodation), and the island's handful of restaurants and lack of late-night bars mean visitors are early to bed and early to rise. Go out of season and enjoy the solitude.

Where to stay & eat

Most accommodation on Rügen is in private houses. Your best bet is to contact the local tourist office (*see below*), which will help you find a room. Camping is very popular on Rügen. Binz offers the best selection of places to eat.

Dresden's **Neue Synagoge**. *See p265.*

Getting there

By train

Most trains to Rügen terminate at Stralsund; it takes around 3hrs 30mins to reach Stralsund, then 30mins or so more to Rügen. There's one direct train a day from Ostbahnhof/Zoo to Bergen on Rügen, taking about 3hrs 30mins.

Tourist information

Tourismus Zentrale Rügen

Markt 4, Bergen, Rügen (0383 880770).
Open 8am-6pm Mon-Fri.
Heinrich-Heine-Strasse 7, Binz (03839 3148148).
Open 9am-4pm Mon-Fri; 11am-4pm, Sat, Sun.
Postrasse 9, Göhren (03830866709).
Open *Summer* 9am-noon, 1-6pm Mon-Fri; 9am-noon Sat. *Winter* 9am-noon, 1-4pm Mon, Wed, Thur; 9am-noon, 1-6pm Tue; 9am-noon, 1-3pm Fri.
Wilhelmstrasse 40, Sellin (03830 387006).
Open 9am-4pm Mon-Fri.
The Bergen head office provides information, but cannot book rooms; try the other offices for bookings. Visit www.ruegen.net for general information.

Dresden

Destroyed twice and rebuilt one and a half times, the capital of Saxony – 100 kilometres (60 miles) south of Berlin – boasts one of Germany's best art museums and many historic buildings.

Modern Dresden is built on the ruins of its past. A fire consumed Altendresden on the bank of the Elbe in 1685, and the city was rebuilt. On the night of 13 February 1945, the biggest of Sir Arthur 'Bomber' Harris's raids caused huge fire storms killing up to 100,000 people. After the war, Dresden was twinned with Coventry, and Benjamin Britten's *War Requiem* was given its first performance in the Hofkirche by musicians from both towns. Under the GDR reconstruction was erratic, but a maze of cranes and scaffolding sprang up in the 1990s – Dresden is making up for lost time.

An unappealing resemblance to Coventry is apparent walking from the station to the centre along hideous Prager Strasse. But press on through the tower blocks and 1960s shopping arcades (stopping at the tourist office for a map) and the older city starts to assert itself.

Dresden's major attractions are the buildings from the reign of Augustus the Strong (1670-1733). The Hofkirche and the Zwinger complex are fine examples of the city's baroque legacy.

Dresden's main draw for art lovers is the **Gemäldegalerie Alte Meister** in the Zwinger. There's more art at the **Albertinum**, which contains the Grünes Gewölbe, a collection of Augustus's jewels and trinkets.

Building was continued by Augustus's successor, Augustus III, who then lost to Prussia in the Seven Years War (1756-63). Frederick the Great destroyed much of the city during the war, though not the lovely riverside promenade of the Brühlsche Terrasse in the old part of town. A victorious Napoleon ordered the demolition of the city's defences in 1809.

By the Zwinger is the **Semperoper** opera house, named after its architect Gottfried Semper (1838-41), which was fully restored to its earlier elegance in 1985.

The industrialisation of Dresden heralded a new phase of construction that produced the Rathaus (Town Hall, 1905-10) at Dr-Külz-Ring, the Hauptbahnhof (1892-5) at the end of Prager Strasse, the Yenidze cigarette factory (1912) in Könneritzstrasse, designed to look like a mosque, and the grandiose Landtagsgebäude (completed to plans by Paul Wallot, designer of Berlin's Reichstag, in 1907) at Heinrich-Zille-Strasse 11. The finest example of inter-war architecture is Wilhelm Kreis' Deutsches Hygienemuseum (1929) at Lingner Platz 1, built to house the German Institute of Hygiene.

The **Neue Synagoge** was dedicated in Dresden (Rathenauplatz) in November 2001, 63 years after its predecessor (built by Semper in 1838-40) was destroyed in the Nazi pogroms.

The ongoing reconstruction of the Frauenkirche at Neumarkt, the Schloss, and the **Altstadt** (Old Town), should see the city in its best light for its 800th anniversary in 2006.

The Striezelmarkt (named after the savoury pretzel you will see everyone eating) is held on Altstädtermarkt every December. The Christmas market is one of the most colourful events of the year. Dresden is also home to the best *Stollen*, a German variety of yuletide cake.

In the GDR days, this part of the country, behind the Saxon hills, could not receive Western television or radio broadcasts and was called 'Tal der Ahnungslosen' ('Valley of the Clueless'). As a result, a vibrant alternative scene developed in the Neustadt, particularly in the bars and cafés on and around Alaunstrasse.

The Neustadt – on the north bank of the Elbe – literally means 'new town', although it is over 300 years old. Having escaped major damage during the war, the Neustadt has much of its original architecture intact.

When Augustus the Strong commissioned the rebuilding of Dresden in 1685, he pictured a new Venice. The Neustadt doesn't quite measure up, but the 18th-century town houses in Hauptstrasse and Königstrasse are charming.

To avoid the tourist spillover from the Altstadt, head north and east of Albertplatz. Recently, a wealth of boutiques, cafés and bars has sprung up here in the cobblestone streets.

Albertinum

Brühlsche Terrasse (0351 491 4622). **Open** 10am-6pm Mon-Wed, Fri-Sun. **Admission** €6; €3 concessions. **No credit cards.**

Houses two major collections of paintings and treasures – the Gemäldegalerie Neue Meister and the Grünes Gewölbe (Green Vault) – as well as coin and sculpture collections.

Gemäldegalerie Alte Meister

Zwinger, Theaterplatz (0351 491 4622/ www.staatl-kunstsammlungen-dresden.de). **Open** 10am-6pm Tue-Sun. **Admission** €6; €3.50 concessions. **No credit cards.**

A superb collection of Old Masters, particularly Italian Renaissance and Flemish. There is also porcelain from nearby Meissen, and collections of armour, weapons, clocks and scientific equipment

Semperoper

Tickets: Aldstädter Wache, Theaterplatz (0351 49110). **Open** *Box office* 10am-6pm Mon-Fri; 10am-1pm Sat. **Tickets** €4.50-€56.50 concessions. **No credit cards.**

Where to stay

The trendy **Arthotel Dresden** (Ostra-Allee 33, 0351 49220/www.artotels.de, rates €77-€130) is decorated with 600 works by local painter AR Penck. **Bastei/Königstein/ Lilienstein** (Pragerstrasse 0351 4856 6661/ 0351 4856 6662/0351 4856 6663/www.ibis-hotel.de, rates €53-€96) are three functional tower-block hotels on Pragerstrasse between the rail station and Altstadt. The **Hotel Bayerischer Hof Dresden** (Antonstrasse 33-35, 0351 829370, www.bayerischer-hof-dresden.de, rates €80-€160) has comfy rooms and a personal feel; the **Bülow-Residenz** (Rähnitzgasse 19, 0351 80030/www.buelow-residenz.de, rates €120-€225) offers elegant, old-world luxury. In the Neustadt, the **Hostel Mondpalast** (Katharinenstrasse 11-13, 0351 804 6061, rates €13.50-€34) is a decent budget option. **Hotel Smetana** (Schlüterstrasse 25, 0351 256 080/www.hotel-smetana.de, rates €65-€109) is a pleasant three-star, east of the centre.

Where to eat & drink

Caroussel, Caroussel (Bülow-Residenz, Rähnitzgasse 19, 0351 80030, closed Sun, Mon, main course €30-€40), a contemporary German restaurant, offers fine cooking and has a leafy courtyard in summer. **Der Drachen** (Bautzener Strasse 72, 0351 804 1188, closed Mon in winter, main course €15-€22) is a decent modern German eaterie beside the Elbe. **Piccola Capri** (Alaunstrasse 93, 801 4774, closed Sun, main course €6.50-€15.50) is one of the Neustadt's best Italians.

Nightlife

The Neustadt is best for nightlife. Clubs such as **Déjà-Vu** (Rothenburgerstrasse 37, 0351 802 3040) and **Flower Power** (Eschenstrasse 11, 0351 804 9814) have different DJs every night.

Getting there

By train

Direct trains run every 2hrs from Berlin, and take 2hrs from Ostbahnhof and 2hrs 15mins from Zoo.

Tourist information

Dresden Tourist Information

Ostra Allee 11 (0351 491 920/www.dresden-tourist.de). **Open** 9.30am-6pm Mon-Fri; 9.30am-4pm Sat. *Schinkelwache, Theaterplatz (0351 491 920/ www.dresden-tourist.de).* **Open** 10am-6pm Mon-Fri; 9.30am-4pm Sat.

Leipzig

One of Germany's most important trade centres and former second city of the GDR, Leipzig is Bach's city, a centre of education and culture and the place where East Germany's mass movement for political change began. The city, once one of Germany's industrial strongholds, has also been famed for its fairs for centuries; in fact, these days, trade fairs (*Messen*) are its bread and butter. Its pedestrianised, recently restored old centre is another attraction: with its Renaissance and baroque churches, narrow lanes, old street markets and the ancient university, it's hard to believe that it was bombed to bits during World War II. The area is also crammed with enough sights, bars and restaurants to fill a visit of a day or two.

In Saxony, around 130 kilometres (80 miles) south-west of Berlin, Leipzig traces its origins back to a settlement founded by the Sorbs, a Slavic people who venerated the lime tree, some time between the seventh to ninth centuries. The Sorbs called it Lipzk ('place of limes').

Most visitors arrive at **Leipzig Hauptbahnhof**, the huge, renovated central train station (the largest in Europe; it contains a three-level shopping mall). The station stands on the north-east edge of the compact city centre, and is surrounded by a ring road that follows the course of the old city walls. Much of the ring road is lined with parks; most of the city's attractions can be found within its limits.

The first place to head is the **Leipzig Tourist Service** office, diagonally left across tram-strewn Willy-Brand-Platz from the front of the train station. Pick up a guide to the city in English (which includes a map) and head for

Markt, the old market square, to get your bearings. The eastern side of the square is occupied by the lovely Renaissance **Altes Rathaus** (Old Town Hall), built in 1556-7. It now houses the **Stadtgeschichtliches Museum** (Town Museum). On the square's south side are the huge bay windows of the Könighaus, once a haunt of Saxony's rulers when visiting the city (the notoriously rowdy Peter the Great of Russia also once stayed here).

The church off the south-west corner of Markt is the **Thomaskirche**, where Johan Sebastian Bach spent 27 years as *Kappellmeister*, choirmaster of the famous St Thomas's Boys Choir; the great man is buried in the chancel and his statue stands outside the church. Here too is the prefab Thomasshop, which details on its side a Bach-themed stroll around the city. Opposite the church in the Bosehaus is the **Bach-Museum**.

South from the Thomaskirche towards the south-west corner of the ring road is the Neues Rathaus (New Town Hall), whose origins are 16th century, though the current buildings are only about 100 years old.

Back at the Altes Rathaus, immediately behind the building, is the delightful little chocolate box of the Alte Börse (Old Stock Exchange), built in 1687, and fronted by a statue of Goethe, who studied at Leipzig University. Follow his gaze towards the entrance to Mädler Passage, Leipzig's finest shopping arcade, within which is **Auerbachs Keller**, one of the oldest and most famous restaurants in Germany. It was in Auerbachs, where he often used to drink, that Goethe set a scene in *Faust*, which saw Faust and Mephistopheles boozing with students before riding off on a barrel.

The **Altes Rathaus** in Leipzig.

North of the Alte Börse is Sachsenplatz, site of the city's main outdoor market, and new home of the **Museum der Bildenden Künste** (Museum of Arts Picture Gallery).

Just south-east of here is the **Nikolaikirche**, Leipzig's proud symbol of its new freedom. This medieval church, with its baroque interior, is the place where regular free-speech meetings started in 1982. These evolved into the 'Swords to Ploughshares' peace movement, which led to the first anti-GDR demonstration on 4 September 1989 in the Nikolaikirchhof.

West of here, on the edge of the ring road, is the **Museum in der 'Runde Ecke'** (Museum in the 'Round Corner', nickname of the building that once housed the local Stasi headquarters and now has an exhibition detailing its nefarious methods). North of here, outside the ring road, is **Leipzig Zoo**.

In the south-east corner of the ring road rises the drab tower block of Leipzig University. Rebuilt in 1970 to resemble an opened book on its side, this modern monstrosity is ironically one of Europe's oldest centres of learning. Alumni, besides Goethe, include Nietzche, Schumann and Wagner. The university runs the **Ägyptisches Museum**; nearby is the **Grassi Museum für Kunsthandwerk**.

The university tower stands at the south-eastern corner of Augustplatz, a project of GDR Communist Party leader Walter Ulbricht, himself a Leipziger. Next door to it are the brown glass-fronted buildings of the **Gewandhaus**, home of the Leipziger Gewandhaus Orchester, one of the world's finest orchestras. On the square's northern side stands the **Opernhaus Leipzig** (opened in 1960), which also has an excellent reputation.

Ägyptisches Museum

Burgstrasse 21 (0341 973 7010/www.uni-leipzig.de/~egypt). **Open** 1-5pm Tue-Sat; 10am-1pm Sun. **Admission** €2; €1 concessions. **Credit** AmEx, MC, V.

Bach-Museum

Thomaskirchhof 16 (0341 913 7202/www.bach-leipzig.de). **Open** 10am-5pm daily. **Admission** €3; €2 concessions. *With tour* €6; €4 concessions. **No credit cards.**

Documents, instruments and furniture from Bach's time illustrate the work and influence of the great man.

Gewandhaus

Augustusplatz 8 (0341 12700/127 080/280 www.gewandhaus.de). **Open** *Box office* 10am-6pm Mon-Fri; 10am-2pm Sat. **Tickets** vary. **Credit** AmEx, DC, MC.

Grassi Museum für Kunsthandwerk

Neumarkt 20 (0341 213 3719/ www.grassimuseum.de). **Open** 10am-6pm Tue, Thur-Sun; 10am-8pm Wed. **Admission** €4; €2 concessions. **No credit cards.**

Founded in 1874 and now in a temporary home, this was a major centre for applied art in the 1920s.

Leipzig Zoo

Pfaffendorfer Strasse 29 (0341 593 3500/ www.zooleipzig.de). **Open** *May-Sept* 9am-7pm daily. *Apr, Oct* 9am-6pm Mon-Fri; 9am-5pm Sat, Sun. *Nov-Mar* 9am-5pm daily. **Admission** €10; €4.50-€6.50 concessions. **No credit cards.**

All the usual family favourites are here: lions, tigers, orang-utans, polar bears and hippos.

Museum der Bildenden Künste

Katarienen Strasse 10 (216 9914/www.leipzig.de/ museum-d-bil-kuenste.htm). **Open** 10am-6pm Tue, Thur-Sun; 1-9.30pm Wed. **Admission** €2.50; €1 concessions; free 2nd Sun of mth. *Temporary exhibitions* €4; €2 concessions. **No credit cards.**

Due to re-open at the above address in December 2004. The gallery's 2,200-strong collection stretches from 15th- and 16th-century Dutch, Flemish and German paintings to expressionism and GDR art. Artists include Dürer, Rembrandt and Rubens.

Museum in der 'Runde Ecke'

Dittrichring 24 (0341 961 2443/www.runde-ecke-leipzig.de). **Open** 10am-6pm daily. *Tour* 3pm daily. **Admission** free. *Tour* €3; €2 concessions. **No credit cards.**

An interesting (despite the lack of English labelling) look at the Stasi's frightening yet ridiculous methods – collecting scents of suspected people in jars, say – and a hilarious section on Stasi disguises.

Nikolaikirche

Nikolaikirchhof 3 (0341 960 5270/ www.nikolaikirche-leipzig.de). **Open** 10am-noon Mon, Tue, Thur, Fri; 4-6pm Wed. **Admission** free.

Opernhaus Leipzig

Augustusplatz 12 (0341 12610/www.leipzig-online.de/oper). **Open** *Box office* 10am-8pm Mon-Fri; 10am-4pm Sat; 1hr before performances Sun. **Tickets** varies. **No credit cards.**

Call for information about tours of the building.

Stadtgeschichtliches Museum

Altes Rathaus, Markt 1 (1 341 965 1316). **Open** 2-8pm Tue; 10am-6pm Tue-Sun. **Admission** €2.50; €2 concessions. **No credit cards.**

Thomaskirche

Thomaskirchhof 18 (0341 960 2855/ www.thomaskirche.org). **Open** 9am-6pm daily. **Admission** free.

Where to stay

North of the rail station are the luxury chains (Kempinski, Marriott, etc). The **Accento Hotel Leipzig** (Taucher Strasse 260, 01341 92620, www.accento-hotel.de, rates €92-€153) has stylish rooms and polite staff. **Adagio Minotel Leipzig** (Seeburgstrasse 96, 0341 216 699/www.hotel-adagio.de, rates €67-€102) offers individually furnished rooms and a central location. **Hotel Mercure Leipzig** (Augustusplatz 5-6, 0341 21460/www.hotel-mercure-leipzig.de, rates €66-€112) isn't very characterful, but it's centrally located. For art nouveau luxury, try the **Seaside Park Hotel** (Richard-Wagner-Strasse 7, 0341 98520, www.parkhotelleipzig.de, rates €110-€160). The Leipzig Tourist Service (*see below*) can help with budget options.

Where to eat

Apels Garten (Kolonnadenstrasse 2, 0341 960 7777, main course €8-€12) is a pretty restaurant with imaginative German cooking. **Auerbachs Keller** (Mädlerpassage, Grimmaische Strasse 2-4, 0341 216 100, set menus €11-24), set in a 1525 beer hall, has a gourmet menu and a cheaper version: both serve classic Saxon cuisine (schnitzel, dumplings, pork and sauerkraut). **Barthels Hof** (Hainstrasse 1, 0341 141 310, main course €9.50-€17) offers hearty Saxon cooking in a cosy panelled *Gasthaus*. **El Matador** (Friedrich-Ebert-Strasse 108, 0341 980 0876, closed Sun, main course €8-€15) serves decent Spanish food.

Nightlife

With its major university, Leipzig is a party town: wander the streets around Markt for late-night quaffing. For dancing, try **Distillery** (Kurt-Eisner-Strasse 4, 0341 3559 7400, admission €3) or **Tanzpalast** (Bose-strasse 1, 0341 960 0596, admission €5), a huge club (live music Wed, Fri). **Live Music** (Moritz-bastei, 0341 702 590) features live jazz and blues.

Tourist information

Leipzig Tourist Service

Richard-Wagner-Strasse 1 (0341 710 4260/4265/ www.leipzig.de). **Open** 9am-7pm Mon-Fri; 9am-4pm Sat; 10am-2pm Sun.

Getting there

By train

Direct trains from Berlin every 2hrs; the fastest takes 1hr 34mins from Ostbahnhof, 1hr 51mins from Zoo.

Directory

Features

Directory

Getting Around

Arriving & leaving

By air

Until the new **Berlin-Brandenburg International Airport** is built (2007 at the earliest), Berlin is served by three airports: **Tegel**, **Schönefeld** and **Tempelhof**. Information in English on all of these airports (including live departures and arrivals) can be found at www.berlin-airport.de. Note: most of Berlin's hotels are in Mitte, the revived centre of the united city, or in the area served by Bahnhof Zoo (Zoo Station), pivotal point of the west end.

Tegel Airport

Airport Information (0180 5000 186/www.berlin-airport.de). **Open** 4am-midnight daily. **Map** p300 B1.

Most flights to and from Berlin use compact Tegel Airport, which is a mere 8km (5 miles) north-west of Mitte. The airport contains tourist information, exchange facilities, shops, restaurants, bars and car rental desks. A cab can drop you right by the check-in desk and departure gate.

Buses 109 and **X9** (the express version) run via Luisenplatz and the Kurfürstendamm to Zoologischer Garten (known as Zoo Station, Bahnof Zoo or just Zoo) in western Berlin. Tickets cost €2 (and can also be used on U-Bahn and S-Bahn services). Buses run every five to 15 minutes, and take 30-40 minutes to reach Zoo. From Zoo you can connect by bus, U-Bahn or S-Bahn to anywhere in the city (same tickets are valid). There are rail and tourist information offices at Zoo (*see p271*).

The direct link to Mitte is the JetExpressBus TXL. This runs from Tegel to Alexanderplatz with useful stops at Beusselstrasse S-Bahn (connects with the Ringbahn), Turmstrasse U-Bahn (U9), Unter den Linden S-Bahn (S1, S2, S25) and Französische Strasse U-Bahn (U6). It costs €2, runs every 15 or 20 minutes between 6am-11pm, and takes 30-40 minutes. You can take bus 109 to Jacob-Kaiser-Platz U-Bahn (U7), or bus 128 to Kurt-Schumacher-Platz U-Bahn (U6), and proceed on the underground from there. One ticket can be used for the combined journey (€2).

A taxi to anywhere central will cost around €20-€25, and takes 20-30 minutes, depending on traffic and precise destination.

Schönefeld Airport

Airport Information (0180 5000 186/www.berlin-airport.de). **Open** 24hrs daily.

The former airport of East Berlin is 18km (11 miles) south-east of the city centre. It's small, and serves mainly eastern Europe, the Middle and Far East – but budget airlines from the UK also use it. The usual foreign exchange, shops, snack bars and car hire facilities can be found here.

Train is the best means of reaching the city centre. **S-Bahn Flughafen Schönefeld** is a five-minute walk from the terminal (a free S-Bahn shuttle bus runs every ten minutes between 6am-10pm from outside the terminal; at other times, bus 171 also runs to the station). From here, the **Airport Express** train runs to Mitte (25 minutes to Alexanderplatz) and Zoo (35 minutes) every half hour from 5am-11.30pm at 27 minutes (route RE4) and 54 minutes (route RE5) past the hour. Be warned that the final destination of the trains varies, so check the timetable for your stop. You also take S-Bahn line S9, which runs into the centre every 20 minutes (40 minutes to Alexanderplatz, 50 minutes to Zoo). The S45 line from Schönefeld connects with the Ringbahn, also running every 20 minutes. **Bus 171** from the airport takes you to Rudow U-Bahn (U7), from where you can connect with the underground.

Tickets from the airport to the city cost €2, and can be used on any combination of bus, U-Bahn, S-Bahn and tram. There are ticket machines at the airport and at the station.

A **taxi** to Zoo or Mitte is pricey: €30-€35, and takes 45-60 minutes.

Tempelhof Airport

Airport Information (0180 5000 186/www.berlin-airport.de). Flight Information (6951 2288). **Open** 5am-11pm daily. **Map** p306 F6.

Berlin's third airport, Tempelhof is a mere 4km (2.5 miles) south of Mitte, but few airlines use it. The airport has basic shops, snack bars, currency exchange and car hire desks.

Connections to the rest of Berlin are easy. **Platz der Luftbrücke** U-Bahn station (U6 – direct to Mitte in around ten minutes) is a short walk from the terminal building, as are bus connections. **Bus 109** goes from the airport to the Europa-Center, near Bahnhof Zoo, in the west end (journey time: 20 minutes).

All tickets from Tempelhof to the centre cost €2, and can be used on any combination of bus, U-Bahn and S-Bahn services.

A **taxi** to Mitte or Zoo will cost €12-€18, and will take about 15 minutes and 20 minutes, respectively.

Airlines

From outside Germany dial the international access code (usually 00), then 49 for Germany, then the number (omitting any initial zero). All operators speak English.

Air Berlin 0180 573 7800/ www.airberlin.com
Air France 0180 583 0830/ www.airfrance.de
Alitalia 0180 507 4747/ www.alitalia.de
British Airways 0180 526 6522/ www.britishairways.com
DBA 0180 535 9322/ www.flydba.com
EasyJet 0180 365 4321/ www.easyjet.com
German Wings 0180 595 5855/ www. germanwings.com
Iberia 0180 500 6735/www.iberia.de
KLM 0180 521 4201/www.klm.de
Lufthansa 0180 380 3803/ www.lufthansa.de
RyanAir 0190 170 100/ www.ryanair.com

By rail

Bahnhof Zoo

Deutsche Bahn Information, Bahnhof Zoo, Hardenbergplatz, Charlottenburg (11 861/ www.bahn.de). **Open** 5.30am-11pm daily. **Map** p304 C4.

Bahnhof Zoo is the point of arrival from most destinations to the west. Most trains also carry on to **Ostbahnhof**. Bahnhof Zoo has excellent bus, U-Bahn and S-Bahn links with the rest of the city, as well as left luggage facilities, lockers, currency exchange, an information counter (which can book hotels) and the helpful **EurAide** office (*see p285*), which offers advice in English and also sells rail tickets. This is also close to the main tourist office (*see p285*), and there are plenty of shops and restaurants with extended opening hours. If you call the information number, you can request someone who speaks English.

Bahnhof Lichtenberg, out in the wilds of east Berlin on U-Bahn line U5, and S-Bahn lines S5, S7 and S75, is the main station for destinations to the south and east, including Vienna, Warsaw, Prague, Budapest, Dresden and Leipzig. It's a small place, with limited lockers and an information desk.

These stations will be superseded when the major rail terminus at **Lehrter Stadtbahnhof** (north of Tiergarten) is completed in 2006.

By bus

Zentraler Omnibus Bahnhof (ZOB)

Masurenallee 4-6, Charlottenburg (Information 301 0380/ www.zobreisebuero.de). **Open** 6am-7.30pm Mon-Fri; 6am-3pm Sat, Sun. **Map** p304 A4.

Buses arrive in western Berlin at the Central Bus Station, opposite the Funkturm and the ICC (International Congress Centrum). From here, U-Bahn line U2 runs into the centre. There's also a left luggage office. East Berlin has no bus station.

Getting around

Berlin is served by a comprehensive and interlinked network of buses, trains, trams and ferries. It's efficient and punctual, though not particularly cheap.

With the completion of the Ringbahn in 2002, the former East and West Berlin transport systems were finally sewn back together, though it can still sometimes be complicated travelling between eastern and western destinations. Even within one half of the city, journeys can involve several changes of route or mode of transport. But services are usually regular and frequent, timetables can be trusted, and one ticket can be used for two hours on all legs of the journey and all forms of transport.

The Berlin transport authority, the **BVG**, operates **bus**, **U-Bahn** (underground) and tram networks, and a few ferry services on the outlying lakes. The **S-Bahn** (overground railway) is run by its own authority, but services are completely integrated within the same three-zone tariff system (see below **Fares & tickets**).

Information

There are **BVG information centres** at **Turmstrasse** U-Bahn (U9; open 6.30am-8.30pm Mon-Fri, 9am-3.30pm Sat) and at Zoo Pavillon, Hardenburger Strasse, outside **Bahnhof Zoo** (open 6am-10pm daily). In addition, the BVG website (**www.bvg.de**) has a wealth of information (in English) on city transport. The S-Bahn has its own website at www.s-bahn-berlin.de.

The **Liniennetz**, a map of U-Bahn, S-Bahn, bus and tram routes for Berlin and Potsdam, is available free from info centres and ticket offices. It includes a city centre map. A map of the U- and S-Bahn can also be picked up free at ticket offices or from the grey-uniformed *Zugabfertiger* – passenger assistance personnel – who appear in the larger U-Bahn and S-Bahn stations.

Fares & tickets

The bus, tram, U-Bahn, S-Bahn and ferry services operate on an integrated **three-zone system**. Zone A covers central Berlin, zone B extends out to the edge of the suburbs and zone C stretches into Brandenburg. See the public transport map at the back of this guide for specific details of precisely what area is covered by each zone.

The basic single ticket is the €2 *Normaltarif* (zones A and B). Unless going to Potsdam, few visitors are likely to travel beyond zone B, making this in effect a flat-fare system.

Apart from the *Zeitkarten* (longer-term tickets, *see p272*), tickets for Berlin's public transport system can be bought from the yellow or orange machines at U- or S-Bahn stations, and by some bus stops. These take coins and sometimes notes, give change and have a limited explanation of the ticket system in English. Once you've purchased your ticket, validate it in the small red or yellow box next to the machine, which stamps it with the time and date. (Tickets bought on trams or buses are usually already validated.) If an inspector catches you without a valid ticket, you will be fined €40 on the spot. Ticket inspections are frequent, particularly at weekends and at the beginning of the month.

Single ticket (Normaltarif)

Single tickets cost €2 (€1.40 for children between the ages of six and 14) for travel within zones A and B, €2.25 (€1.55) for zones B and C, and €2.60 (€1.90) for all three zones. A ticket allows use of the BVG network for two hours, with as many changes between bus, tram, U-Bahn and S-Bahn as necessary travelling in one direction.

Short-distance ticket (Kurzstreckentarif)

The *Kurzstreckentarif* (ask for a *Kurzstrecke*) costs €1.20 (€1 concessions) and is valid for three U- or S-Bahn stops, or six stops on the tram or bus. No transfers allowed.

Day ticket (Tageskarte)

A *Tageskarte* for zones A and B costs €5.60 (€4.20 concessions), or €6 (€4.50) for all three zones. A day ticket lasts until 3am the day after validating.

Longer-term tickets (Zeitkarten)

If you're in Berlin for a week, it makes sense to buy a *Sieben-Tage-Karte* ('seven-day ticket') at €24.30 for zones A and B, or €30 for all three zones (no concessions).

A stay of a month or more makes it worth buying a *Monatskarte* ('month ticket'), which costs €64 for zones A and B, or €79.50 for all three zones.

U-Bahn

The first stretch of Berlin's U-Bahn was opened in 1902 and the network now consists of nine lines and 170 stations. (Many of the most interesting old stations – such as Wittenbergplatz – were renovated for the U-Bahn's 100th birthday in 2002.) The first trains run shortly after 4am; the last between midnight and 1am, except on Fridays and Saturdays when trains run all night on lines U2, U5, U6, U7, U8, U9 and U15. The direction of travel is indicated by the name of the last stop on the line.

S-Bahn

Especially useful in eastern Berlin, the S-Bahn covers long distances faster than the U-Bahn and is a more efficient means of getting to outlying areas. The recent completion of the Ringbahn, which circles central Berlin in around an hour, was the final piece of the S-Bahn system to be renovated, though there are still temporary disruptions here and there.

Buses

Berlin has a dense network of 161 bus routes, of which 54 run in the early hours. The day lines run from 4.30am to about 1am the next morning. Enter at the front of the bus and exit in the middle. The driver sells only individual tickets, but all tickets from machines on the U- or S-Bahn are valid. Most bus stops have clear timetables and route maps.

Trams

There are 27 tram lines (five of which run all night), mainly in the east, though some have now been extended a few kilometres into the western half of the city, mostly in Wedding. **Hackescher Markt** is the site of the main tram terminus. Tickets are available from machines on the trams, at the termini and in U-Bahn stations.

Other rail services

Berlin is also served by the **Regionalbahn** ('regional railway'), which in former times connected East Berlin with Potsdam via the suburbs and small towns that had been left outside the Wall. It still circumnavigates the entire city. The Regionalbahn is run by Deutsche Bahn and ticket prices vary according to the journey.

For timetable and ticket information in English, go to Deutsche Bahn's website at www.bahn.de and click on 'international guests'.

Travelling at night

Berlin has a comprehensive **Nachtliniennetz** ('night-line network') that covers all parts of town via 59 bus and tram routes running every 30 minutes between 12.30am and 4.30am. Before and after these times the regular timetable for bus and tram routes applies.

Night-line network maps and timetables are available from BVG information kiosks at stations, and large maps of the night services are usually found next to the normal BVG map on station platforms. Ticket prices are the same as during the day. Buses and trams that run at night are distinguished by an 'N' in front of the number.

On lines N11, N35 and N41, the bus will actually take you right to your front door if it's close to the official route. The BVG also operates a **Taxi-Ruf-System** ('taxi calling service') on the U-Bahn for female passengers and people with disabilities from 8pm every evening until the network closes. Just ask the uniformed BVG employee in the platform booth to phone, giving your destination and method of payment.

Truncated versions of U-Bahn lines U2, U5, U6, U7, U8, U9 and U15 run all night on Fridays and Saturdays, with trains every 15 minutes. The S-Bahn also runs on weekend nights, with lines S1, S2, S3, S5, S7, S8, S9, S25, S41, S42, S46, S47, S75 in service.

Boat trips

Getting about by water is more of a leisure activity than a practical means of getting around the city, but the BVG network does include a handful of boat services on Berlin's lakes. There are also several private companies offering tours of Berlin's waterways:

Reederei Heinz Riedel

Planufer 78, Kreuzberg (691 3782). U8 Schönleinstrasse. **Open** *March-Sept* 6am-9pm Mon-Fri, 8am-6pm Sat, 10am-3pm Sun. *Oct* 8am-5pm Mon-Fri; 8am-6pm Sat; 10am-3pm Sun. *Nov-Feb* 8am-4pm Mon-Fri. **Map** p306 F5.

This company operates excursions that start in the city and pass through industrial suburbs into rural Berlin. A tour through the city's network of rivers and canals costs €5-€15.

Stern und Kreisschiffahrt

Puschkinallee 16-17, Treptow (536 3600/www.sternundkreis.de). S6, S8, S9, S10 Treptower Park. **Open** 9am-4pm Mon-Thur, 9am-2pm Fri.

Offers around 25 different cruises along the Spree and around lakes in the Berlin area. Departure points and times vary. A 3hr 30min tour costs €15.50.

Taxis

Berlin taxis are pricey, efficient and numerous, yet sometimes hard to find.

The starting fee is €2.50 and thereafter the fare is €1.53 per kilometre (about €3.06 per mile). The rate remains the same at night. For short journeys ask for a Kurzstrecke – up to two kilometres for €3, but only available when you've hailed a cab and not from taxi ranks. Taxi stands are numerous, especially in central areas near stations and at major intersections.

You can phone for a cab 24 hours daily on 261 026. Cabs ordered by phone are charged at the same rates. Most taxi firms can transport people with disabilities, but require advance notice. Cabs accept all credit cards except Diners Club, subject to a €0.50 charge.

The majority of cabs are Mercedes. If you want an estate car (station wagon), ask for a 'combi'. As well as normal taxis, **Funk Taxi Berlin** operates vans capable of transporting up to seven people and has two vehicles for people with disabilities. Call 813 2613.

Driving

Despite congestion, driving in Berlin, with its wide, straight roads, presents few problems. Visitors from the UK and US should bear in mind that, in the absence of signals, drivers must yield to traffic from the right, except at crossings that are marked by a diamond-shaped yellow sign. And in the east, trams always have right of way. An *Einbahnstrasse* is a one-way street.

Breakdown services

The following garage offers 24-hour assistance at a rate of about €60 an hour. But it won't take credit cards.

ADAC

Bundesallee 29-30, Wilmersdorf (0180 222 2222)

Filling stations

Both of the places below are open 24 hours a day.

Aral

Holzmarktstrasse 12, Mitte (2472 0748). **Credit** AmEx, MC, V. **Map** p307 G4.

BP-Oil

Kurfürstendamm 128, Wilmersdorf (8909 6972). **Credit** AmEx, MC, V. **Map** p304 B5.

Parking

Parking is free in Berlin side streets, but spaces are hard to find. On busier streets you may have to buy a ticket (€1 per hour) from a nearby machine. Without a ticket, or if you park illegally (pedestrian crossing, loading zone, bus lane), you risk getting your car clamped or towed away.

There are long-term car parks at Schönefeld and Tegel airports (*see p270*). Otherwise there are numerous *Parkgaragen* and *Parkhäuser* (multi-storey and underground car parks) around the city, open 24 hours, that charge around €2 an hour.

Schönefeld Airport Car Park

0180 500 0186. **Rates** *Per day* €12-€15. *Per week* €60-€70. **Credit** V.

Tegel Airport Car Park

0180 500 0186. **Rates** *Per day* €13-€20. *Per week* €80-€150. **No credit cards.**

Tempelhof Airport

0180 5000 186. **Rates** *Per day* €12. *Per week* €70. **No credit cards.**

Vehicle hire

Car hire in Germany is not expensive and all major companies are represented in Berlin. There are car hire desks at all three of the city's airports, including the major international names. Look under *Autovermietung* in the *Gelbe Seiten* (*Yellow Pages*).

Cycling

The western half of Berlin is wonderful for cycling – flat, with lots of cycle paths, parks to scoot through and canals to cruise beside. East Berlin has fewer cycle paths and more cobblestones and tram lines.

On the U-Bahn, there is a limit of two cycles at the end of carriages that have a bicycle sign on them. Bikes may not be taken on the U-Bahn during rush hour (6-9am and 2-5pm). More may be taken on to S-Bahn carriages, and at any time of day. In each case an extra ticket (€2.60) must be bought for each bike. The **ADFC Fahrradstadtplan**, available in bike shops (€6.50), is a good guide to cycle routes. The companies below will rent bikes. Or look under *Fahrradverleih* in the *Yellow Pages*.

Fahrradstation

Bahnhof Friedrichstrasse, Mitte (2045 4500/www.fahrradstation.de). S1, S2, S3, S5, S7, S9, S25, S26, S75, U6 Friedrichstrasse. **Open** 8am-8pm Mon-Fri, 10am-4pm Sat, Sun. **Rates** *Per day* from €10. **No credit cards. Map** p302 F3. **Other locations:** Bergmannstrasse 9, Kreuzberg (215 1566); Hackesche Höfe, Mitte (2838 4848).

Pedalpower

Grossbeerenstrasse 53, Kreuzberg (5515 3270/www.pedalpower.de). U1, U7 Möckernbrücke. **Open** 10am-6.30pm Mon-Fri, 11am-2pm Sat. **Rates** *Per day* from €10. **No credit cards. Map** p306 F5. **Other locations:** Pfarrstrasse 115, Lichtenberg (5515 3270).

Walking

Berlin is a good walking city, but it's spread out. Getting around, say, Mitte is most pleasant on foot, but if you then want to check out Charlottenburg, you'll next need to take a bus or train.

Resources A-Z

Addresses

The house/building number always follows the street name (eg Friedrichstrasse 21), and numbers sometimes run up one side of the street and back down the other side. *Strasse* (street) is often abbreviated to *Str* and not usually written separately but appended to the street name, as in the example above. Exceptions are when the street name is the adjectival form of a place name (eg Potsdamer Strasse) or the full name of an individual (eg Heinrich-Heine-Strasse).

Within buildings: EG means *Erdgeschoss*, the ground floor; 1. *OG* (*Obergeschoss*) is the first floor; *VH* means *Vorderhaus*, or the front part of the building; *HH* means *Hinterhaus*, the part of the building off the *Hinterhof*, the 'back courtyard'; *SF* is *Seitenflügel*, stairs that go off to the side from the *Hinterhof*. In big, industrial complexes, stairwells are often numbered or lettered. *Treppenhaus B*, or sometimes just *Haus B*, would indicate a particular staircase off the courtyard.

Age restrictions

The legal age for drinking is 16; for smoking it is 16; for driving it is 18; and the age of consent for both heterosexual and homosexual sex is 16.

Business

Conferences

Messe Berlin

Messedamm 22, Charlottenburg (303 80/www.messe-berlin.de). U2 Theodor-Heuss-Platz. **Open** 10am-6pm Mon-Fri; 10am-2pm Sat. **Map** p304 A4.
The city's official trade fair and conference organisation can advise on setting up small seminars and congresses, or big trade fairs.

Couriers

A package up to 5kg delivered within Germany costs about €7; to the UK about €17; and to North America about €30. The post office runs a cheaper express service (*see p282*).

DHL

Kaiserin-Augusta-Allee 16-24, Tiergarten (0180 5345 2255/ www.dhl.de). U9 Turmstrasse. **Open** 7am-8pm Mon-Fri; 7am-6pm Sat; 7am-noon Sun. **No credit cards. Map** p301 C3.
Delivers to 180 countries worldwide.

Regus Business Centre

Kurfürstendamm 21, Charlottenburg (887 060/fax 887 061 200/www.regus.de). S3, S5, S7, S9, S75, U2, U9 Zoologischer Garten. **Open** 8.30am-6pm Mon-Fri. **Map** p305 C4.
Offices for rent, secretarial services and conference facilities.
Other locations: Lindencorso, Unter den Linden, Mitte (2092 4000).

UPS

Lengeder Strasse 17-19, Reinickendorf (00800 882 6630/www.ups.com). S25 Alt Reinickendorf. **Open** 8am-7pm Mon-Fri. **Credit** AmEx, MC, V.
Office hire & secretarial services.

Relocation services

The following offers assistance in looking for homes and schools, and will help deal with residence and work permits.

Hardenberg Concept

Burgunder Strasse 5, Zehlendorf (8040 2646). S1, S7 Nikolassee. **Open** 10am-4pm Mon-Fri.

Translators & interpreters

See also *Übersetzungen* in the *Gelbe Seiten* (*Yellow Pages*).

K Hilau Übersetzungsdienst

Innsbrucker Strasse 58, Schöneberg (781 7584). U4, U7 Bayerischer Platz. **Open** 1-6pm Mon-Fri. **Map** p305 D6.

Intertext Fremdsprachendienst e.G

Greifswalder Strasse 5, Prenzlauer Berg (4210 1755). Tram 2,3,4 Friedrichschain. Open 8am-6pm Mon-Fri. **Map** p303 G2.

Useful organisations

American Chamber of Commerce

Charlottenstrasse 42, Mitte (261 5586) U2, U6 Stadtmitte. **Open** 9am-5pm Mon-Fri. **Map** p305 D4.

American Embassy Commercial Dept

Neustädtische Kirchstrasse 4-5, Mitte (8305 2730). U6, S1, S2, S3, S5, S7, S9, S25, S26, S75 Friedrichstrasse. **Open** 8.30am-5.30pm Mon-Fri. **Map** p302 E3.

Berlin Chamber of Commerce

Fasanenstrasse 85, Charlottenburg (315 100). **Open** 9am-3pm Mon-Fri. **Map** p305 C4.

British Embassy Commercial Dept

Wilhelmstrasse 70, Mitte (204 570/fax 245 7577). S1, S2, S25, S26 Unter den Linden. **Open** 9-11am, noon-4pm Mon-Fri. **Map** p316 E3.
Basic advice for British businesses.

Partner für Berlin

Charlottenstrasse 65, Mitte (2024 0100). U2, U6 Stadtmitte. **Open** 9am-5.30pm Mon-Fri. **Map** p316/p302 F3.
City marketing agency.

Customs

EU nationals over 17 years of age can import limitless goods for personal use, if bought tax paid. For non-EU citizens and for duty-free goods, the following limits apply:

- 200 cigarettes or 50 cigars or 250 grams of tobacco
- 1 litre of spirits (over 22 per cent alcohol), or 2 litres of fortified wine (under 22 per cent alcohol), or 2 litres of non-sparkling and sparkling wine
- 50 grams of perfume
- 500 grams of coffee

• Other goods to the value of €175 for non-commercial use
• The import of meat, meat products, fruit, plants, flowers and protected animals is restricted or forbidden.

Disabled

Only some U- and S-Bahn stations have wheelchair facilities; the map of the transport network (*see p271*; look for the wheelchair symbol) indicates which ones do. The BVG is improving things slowly, adding facilities here and there, but it's still a long way from being a wheelchair-friendly system. You may prefer to use the **Telebus** (*see below*), a bus service for people with disabilities.

Berlin Tourismus Marketing (*see p285*) can give details about which of the city's hotels have disabled access, but if you require more specific information, try the **Beschäftigungswerk des BBV** or the **Touristik Union International**.

Beschäftigungswerk des BBV

Bizetstrasse 51-5, Weissensee (927 0360). S4, S8, S10 Greifswalder Strasse. **Open** 8am-4pm Mon-Fri.
The Berlin Centre for the Disabled provides legal and social advice, together with a transport service and travel information.

Telebus-Zentrale

Ollenhauerstrasse 98a, Reinickendorf (410 200). U6 Kurt-Schumacher-Platz. **Open** *Office* 7am-5pm Mon-Fri.
The Telebus is available to tourists if they contact this organisation in advance. A pass has to be issued for each user, though, so be sure to give plenty of notice.

Touristik Union International (TUI)

Unter den Linden 17, Mitte (200 583 100/www.tui.com). S1, S2, S25, S26 Unter den Linden. **Open** (by appointment) 9am-6pm Mon-Fri. **Map** p304 B5.
This service provides information on accommodation and travel in Germany for the disabled.

Drugs

Berlin is relatively liberal in its attitude towards drugs. In recent years, possession of hash or grass has been effectively decriminalised. Anyone caught with an amount under ten grams is liable to have the stuff confiscated, but can expect no further retribution. Joint smoking is tolerated in some of Berlin's younger bars and cafés. It's usually easy to tell whether you're in one. Anyone caught with small amounts of hard drugs will net a fine, but is unlikely to be incarcerated.

For **Drogen Notdienst** (Emergency Drug Service), *see p277*.

Electricity

Electricity in Germany runs on 220v. To use British appliances (240v), change the plug or use an adaptor. (These are available at most UK electric shops). US appliances (110v) require a converter.

Embassies & consulates

Australian Embassy

Wallstrasse 76-79, Mitte (880 0880). U2 Märkisches Museum. **Open** 8.30am-1pm, 2-5pm Mon-Thur; 8.30am-4.15pm Fri. **Map** p305 C4.

British Embassy

Wilhelmstrasse 70, Mitte (204 570). S1, S2, S25, S26 Unter den Linden. **Open** 9-11am, noon-4pm Mon-Fri. **Map** p316 E3.

Irish Consulate

Friedrichstrasse 200, Mitte (220 720). U2, U6 Stadtmitte. **Open** 9.30am-12.30pm, 2.30-4.45pm daily. **Map** p305 C4.

US Consulate

Clayallee 170, Zehlendorf (832 9233/visa enquiries 0190 850 055). U1 Oscar-Helene-Heim. **Open** *Consular enquiries* 8.30am-noon Mon-Fri. *Visa enquiries* 8.30-11.30am Mon-Fri.

US Embassy

Neustädtische Kirchstrasse 4, Mitte (830 50). S1, S2, S25, S26 Unter den Linden. **Open** 24hrs daily. **Map** p302 F3.

Emergencies

In the event of an emergency, call the numbers below. See also *p277* **Helplines**.

Police 110.
Ambulance/Fire Brigade 112.

Gay & lesbian

Help & information

Lesbenberatung e.V.

Kulmer Strasse 20A, Schöneberg (215 2000/www.lesbenberatung-berlin.de). U7, S1, S2, Yorckstrasse. **Open** 4-7pm Mon, Tue, Thur; 10am-1pm Wed; 2-5pm Fri. **Map** p306 E5.

Travel advice

For up-to-date information on travelling to a specific country – including the latest news on safety and security, health issues, local laws and customs – contact your home country government's department of foreign affairs. Most of them have websites that are packed with useful advice for would-be travellers.

Australia
www.dfat.gov.au/travel
Canada
www.voyage.gc.ca
New Zealand
www.mft.govt.nz/travel
Republic of Ireland
www.irlgov.ie/iveagh
UK
www.fco.gov.uk/travel
USA
www.state.gov/travel

Directory

The Lesbian Advice Centre offers counselling in all areas of lesbian life as well as self-help groups, courses, cultural events and an info-café.

Mann-O-Meter

Bülowstrasse 106, Schöneberg (216 3336/ www.mann-o-meter.de). U1, U2, U4 Nollendorfplatz. **Open** 5-7pm daily. **Map** p305 D5.

Drop-in centre and helpline. Advice about AIDS prevention, jobs, flats, gay contacts, plus cheap stocks of safer sex materials. English spoken.

Schwulenberatung

Mommsenstrasse 45, Charlottenburg (office 2336 9070/counselling 19446/www.schwulenberatungberlin.de). U7 Adenauerplatz. **Open** 9am-8pm Mon-Thur; 9am-6pm Fri. **Map** p305 C4.

The Gay Advice Centre provides info and counselling about HIV and AIDS, crisis intervention and advice on all aspects of gay life.

Health

EU countries have reciprocal medical treatment arrangements with Germany. All EU citizens will need the E111 form. UK citizens can obtain this by filling in the application form in leaflet SA30, available in all DSS offices or over any post office counter. You should get your E111 at least two weeks before you leave. It does not cover all medical costs (for example dental treatment), so private insurance is not a bad idea.

Citizens from non-EU countries should take out private medical insurance. German medical treatment is expensive: the minimum charge is roughly €35-€40.

The British Embassy (*see p275*) publishes a list of English-speaking doctors and dentists, as well as lawyers and interpreters. Should you fall ill in Berlin, take a completed E111 form to the **AOK** (*see below*). Staff will exchange it for a *Krankenschein* (medical certificate). Show this to your doctor or to the hospital in an emergency.

If you require non-emergency hospital treatment, the doctor will issue you with a *Notwendigkeitsbescheinigung* ('Certificate of Necessity'), which you must take to the **AOK**. Staff there will give you a *Kostenübernahmeschein* ('Cost Transferral Certificate'), which entitles you to hospital treatment in a public ward.

All hospitals have a 24-hour emergency ward. Otherwise, patients are admitted to hospital via a physician. Hospitals are listed in the *Gelbe Seiten* (*Yellow Pages*) under *Krankenhäuser/ Kliniken*.

AOK Auslandsschalter

Karl-Marx-Allee 3, Mitte (253 10/www.aokberlin.de). U2, U5, U8, S3, S5, S7, S9, S75 Alexanderplatz. **Open** 8am-2pm Mon, Wed; 8am-6pm Tue, Thur; 8am-noon Fri. **Map** p316/p303 G3.

Accident & emergency

The following are the most central hospitals. All have 24-hour emergency wards.

Charité

Schumann Strasse 20-21, Mitte (450 50/www.charite.de). U6, S1, S2, S3, S5, S7, S9, S25, S26, S75 Friedrichstrasse/bus 147. **Map** p302 F3.

Klinikum Am Urban

Dieffenbachstrasse 1, Kreuzberg (6970). U7 Südstern/bus 241, 248. **Map** p307 G5.

Krankenhaus Moabit

Turmstrasse 21, Tiergarten (3976 4000/www.krankenhaus-moabit.de). U9 Turmstrasse. **Map** p301 D3.

St Hedwig Krankenhaus

Grosse Hamburger Strasse 5, Mitte (23110). S3, S5, S7, S9, S75 Hackescher Markt or S1, S2, S25, S26 Oranienburger Strasse. **Map** p302 F3.

Complementary medicine

There is a long tradition of alternative medicine (*Heilpraxis*) in Germany, and your medical insurance will usually cover treatment costs. For a full list of practitioners, look up *Heilpraktiker* in the *Gelbe Seiten* (*Yellow Pages*). There you'll find a complete list of chiropractors, osteopaths, acupuncturists, homoeopaths and healers of various kinds. Homoeopathic medicines are harder to get hold of and much more expensive than in the UK, and it's generally harder to find an osteopath or chiropractor.

Contraception, abortion & childbirth

Family-planning clinics are thin on the ground in Germany, and generally you have to go to a gynaecologist (*Frauenarzt*).

The abortion law was amended in 1995 to take into account the differing systems that existed in east and west. East Germany had abortion on demand; in the West, abortion was only allowed in extenuating circumstances, such as when the health of the foetus or mother was at risk. In a complicated compromise, abortion is still technically illegal, but is not punishable. Women wishing to terminate a pregnancy can do so only after receiving certification from a counsellor. Counselling is offered by state, lay and church bodies.

Feministisches Frauengesundheitzentrum (FFGZ)

Bamberger Strasse 51, Schöneberg (213 9597). U4, U7 Bayerischer Platz. **Open** 10am-1pm Tue; 10am-1pm, 5-7pm Thur. **Map** p305 D5.

Courses and lectures are offered on natural contraception, pregnancy, cancer, abortion, AIDS, migraines and sexuality. Self-help and preventative medicine are stressed. Information on gynaecologists, health institutions and organisations can also be obtained.

Pro Familia

Kalkreuthstrasse 4, Schöneberg (2147 6414). U1, U2, U15 Wittenbergplatz. **Open** 3-6pm Mon, Tue, Thur; 9am-noon Wed, Sat. **Map** p305 D5.

Free advice about sex, contraception and abortion is offered here. Call for an appointment.

Dentists

Dr Andreas Bothe

Kurfürstendamm 210, Charlottenburg (882 6767). U15 Uhlandstrasse. **Open** 8am-2pm Mon, Fri; 2-8pm Tue, Thur. **Map** p305 C4.

Mr Pankaj Mehta

Schlangenbader Strasse 25, Wilmersdorf (823 3010). U1 Rüdesheimer Platz. **Open** 9am-noon, 2-6pm Mon, Tue, Thur; 8am-noon Wed; 8am-1pm Fri. **Map** p304 B6.

Doctors

If you don't know of any doctors, or are too ill to leave your bed, phone the Emergency Doctor's Service (*Ärztlicher Bereitschaftdienst* 310 031). This service specialises in dispatching doctors for house calls. Charges vary according to treatment.

In Germany, you choose your doctor according to his or her speciality. You don't need a referral from a GP. The British Embassy (*see p275*) can provide a list of English-speaking doctors, but many doctors can speak some English. All will be expensive, so either have your E111 at hand, or your private insurance document.

The following doctors all speak good English.

Herr Dr U Beck

Bundesratufer 2, Tiergarten (391 2808). U9 Turmstrasse. **Open** 9.30am-noon, 4-6pm Mon, Thur; 9.30am-noon Tue; 9am-noon Fri. **Map** p305 D5.

Frau Dr I Dorow

Rüsternallee 14-16, Charlottenburg (302 4690). U2 Neu-Westend. **Open** 9-11.30am, 4-6pm Mon, Tue, Thur; 9-11.30am Fri. **Map** p300 A3.

Dr Christine Rommelspacher

Bornholmer Strasse 12, Prenzlauer Berg (392 2075). S1, S2, S8, S25 Bornholmer Strasse. **Open** 9am-noon Mon; 3-6pm Tue; 9am-noon, 3-6pm Fri. **Map** p302 F1.

Gynaecologist

Dr Lutz Opitz

Tegeler Weg 4, Charlottenburg (344 4001). U7 Mierendorffplatz. **Open** 8am-2pm Mon; 3-7pm Tue, Thur; 8am-noon Wed, Fri. **Map** p300 B3.

Pharmacies

Prescription and non-prescription drugs (including aspirin) are sold only at pharmacies (*Apotheken*). You can recognise these by a red 'A' outside the front door.
A list of pharmacies open on Sundays and in the evening should be displayed at every pharmacy. Phone **Emergency Pharmaceutical Services** on 19292 for information.

STDs, HIV & AIDS

For most STDs, see a doctor.

Berliner Aids-Hilfe (BAH)

Büro 15, Meinekestrasse 12, Wilmersdorf (885 6400/Advice line 19411). U9, U15 Kurfürstendamm. **Open** noon-6pm Mon-Thur; noon-3pm Fri. *Advice line* 10am-midnight daily. **Map** p305 C4.
Information is given on all aspects of HIV and AIDS. Free consultations, condoms and lubricant are also provided.

Helplines

Berliner Krisendienst

Mitte, Friedrichshain, Kreuzberg, Tiergarten & Wedding (390 6310). Charlottenburg & Wilmersdorf (390 6320). Prenzlauer Berg, Weissensee & Pankow (390 6340). Schöneberg, Tempelhof, Steglitz (390 6360).
For most problems, this is the best place to call. The service offers help and/or counselling on a range of subjects, and if they can't provide exactly what you're looking for, they'll put you in touch with someone who can. The phone lines, organised by district, are staffed 24 hours daily. Counsellors will also come and visit you in your house if necessary.

Drogen Notdienst

Ansbacher Strasse 11, Schöneberg (192 37). U1, U2, U15 Wittenbergplatz. **Open** *Advice* 8.30am-10pm Mon-Fri; 2-9.30pm Sat, Sun. **Map** p305 D4.
At the 'drug emergency service', no appointment is necessary if you're coming for advice.

Frauenkrisentelefon

Mon-Fri 615 4243; Sat, Sun 615 7596. **Open** 10am-noon Mon, Thur; 9am-9pm Tue, Wed, Fri; 5-7pm Sat, Sun.
Offers advice and information for women on anything and everything.

ID

By law you are required to carry some form of ID, which, for UK and US citizens, means a passport. If police catch you without one, they may accompany you to wherever you've left it.

Internet

For internet access, try one of the cybercafés listed below. For long stays, **Snafu** is reputed to be a good internet service provider. Call on 0180 252 42 or check its website at www.snafu.de. For Berlin-related websites, *see p289*.

British Council

Hackescher Markt 1, Mitte (311 0990/www.britcoun.de/e/berlin). S3, S5, S7, S9, S75 Hackescher Markt. **Open** 9am-7pm Mon-Fri; 9am-5.45pm Sat. **Map** p316/p302 F3.
Half an hour of internet access is free at one of the terminals to the left of the reception desk.

easyInternetCafé

Kurfürstendamm 224, Charlottenburg (www.easyinternetcafe.com). U2, U9, S3, S5, S7, S9, S75 Zoologischer Garten or U9, U15 Kurfürstendamm. **Open** 6.30am-2am. **No credit cards. Map** p305 C4.
Hundreds of computers, two floors, no staff, mechanised system to buy time online, and a Dunkin' Donuts. **Other locations**: Karl-Marx-Strasse 78, Neukölln; Schlossstrasse 102, Steglitz.

Internet Café Alpha

Dunckerstrasse 72, Prenzlauer Berg (447 9067/www.alpha-icafe.de). U2 Eberswalder Strasse. **Open** noon-midnight daily. **No credit cards. Map** p303 G1.
Using one of the 12 computers costs €2.50 per hour. Wine, beer and a range of snacks can fuel your surfing. Also available: CD burners, scanners and games.

Left luggage

Airports

There is a left luggage office at **Tegel** (*see p270*; 0180 5000 186; open 5am-10.30pm daily) and lockers at **Schönefeld** (*see p270*; in the Multi Parking Garage P4) and at **Tempelhof** (*see p270*; in Parking Area P1).

Rail & bus stations

There are lockers and left luggage facilities at Bahnhof Zoo (*see p270*), and 24-hour lockers at Friedrichstrasse and Alexanderplatz stations. Zentraler Omnibus Bahnhof (ZOB; *see p271*) also has facilities.

Legal help

If you get into legal difficulties, contact the British Embassy (*see p275*): it can provide you with a list of English-speaking lawyers in Berlin.

Libraries

Berlin has hundreds of *Bibliotheken/Büchereien* (public libraries). To borrow books, you will be required to bring two things: an *Anmeldungsformular* ('Certificate of Registration'; *see p285*) and a passport.

Amerika-Gedenkbibliothek

Blücherplatz 1, Kreuzberg (9022 6105/www.zlb.de). U1, U6 Hallesches Tor. **Open** 3-7pm Mon; 11am-7pm Tue, Thur-Sat. **Membership** *Per year* €10; students €5. **Map** p306 F5.
This library only contains a small collection of English and American literature, but it has an excellent collection of videos.

British Council

Hackescher Markt 1, Mitte (3110 9910/www.britcoun.de/e/berlin). S3, S5, S7, S9, S75 Hackescher Markt. **Open** 1-7.30pm Mon, Tue, Thur, Fri; 1-4pm Sat. **Membership** *Per year* €45; students, teachers & journalists €35. **Map** p302 F3.
The Information Centre at the British Council holds 2,500 English-language videos, plus a range of DVDs and CD-ROMs.

Staatsbibliothek

Potsdamer Strasse 33, Tiergarten (2660/www.sbb.spk-berlin.de). S1, S2, S25, S26, U2 Potsdamer Platz. **Open** 9am-9pm Mon-Fri; 9am-7pm Sat. **Map** p306 E4.
Books in English on every subject are available at this branch of the State Library, which you may recognise from Wim Wenders' *Wings of Desire*.

Staatsbibliothek

Unter den Linden 8, Mitte (2660/www.sbb.spk-berlin.de). U6, S1, S2, S3, S5, S7, S9, S25, S26, S75 Friedrichstrasse. **Open** 9am-9pm Mon-Fri; 9am-5pm Sat. **Map** p316/p302 F3.
A smaller range of English books than the branch above, but it's still worth a visit, not least for its café.

Lost/stolen property

If your belongings are stolen, you should go immediately to the police station nearest to where the incident occurred (listed in the *Gelbe Seiten/ Yellow Pages* under Polizei) and report the theft. There you will be required to fill in report forms for insurance purposes. If you can't speak German, don't worry: the police will call in one of their interpreters, a service that is provided free of charge.

For information about what to do concerning lost or stolen credit cards, *see p281*.

BVG Fundbüro

Potsdamer Strasse 180-182, Schöneberg (194 49). U7 Kleistpark. **Open** *Office* 9am-6pm Mon-Thur; 9am-2pm Fri. *Call centre* 24 hrs daily. **Map** p306 E5.
You should contact this office if you have any queries about property lost on Berlin's public transport system. If you are robbed on one of their vehicles, you can ask about the surveillance video.

Zentrales Fundbüro

Platz der Luftbrücke 6, Tempelhof (756 00). U6 Platz der Luftbrücke. **Open** 7.30am-2pm Mon; 8.30am-4pm Tue; noon-6.30pm Wed; 1-7pm Thur; 7.30am-noon Fri. **Map** p306 F6.
This is the central police lost property office.

Weather report

	Average max. temperature	Average min. temperature	Average daily hrs of sunshine	Average rainfall
January	2°C/36°F	-3°C/27°F	2	43mm/0.17in
February	3°C/37°F	-2°C/28°F	3	38mm/0.15in
March	8°C/46°F	0°C/32°F	5	38mm/0.15in
April	13°C/55°F	4°C/39°F	6	43mm/0.17in
May	18°C/64°F	8°C/46°F	8	56mm/0.22in
June	22°C/72°F	11°C/52°F	8	71mm/0.28in
July	23°C/73°F	13°C/55°F	8	53mm/0.21in
August	23°C/73°F	12°C/54°F	7	66mm/0.26in
September	18°C/64°F	9°C/48°F	6	46mm/0.18in
October	13°C/55°F	6°C/43°F	4	36mm/0.14in
November	7°C/45°F	2°C/36°F	2	51mm/0.20in
December	3°C/37°F	-1°C/30°F	1	56mm/0.22in

Media

Foreign press

International publications are available at main stations, the **Europa-Center** (*see p104*) and various **Internationale Presse** newsagents. Book retailers **Dussmann** (*see p161*) and **Hugendubel** (*see p160*) also carry international titles. The monthly *Ex-Berliner* magazine offers listings as well as articles on cultural and political topics in English.

National newspapers

BILD

Flagship tabloid of the Axel Springer group. Though its credibility varies from story to story, *BILD* leverages the journalistic resources of the Springer empire and its four-million circulation to land regular scoops, so even the German intelligentsia pays attention to its daily riot of polemic.

Financial Times Deutschland

Since hitting newsstands in 2000, the *FTD* has overcome lukewarm circulation predictions, as well as shaky and hesitant reporting. Its circulation is steadily increasing, and though it's not likely to dethrone *Handelsblatt*, FTD's success proves there's room for different approaches within the business trade market.

Frankfurter Allgemeine Zeitung

Germany's *de facto* newspaper of record. Stolid, exhaustive coverage of daily events, plus lots of analysis, particularly on the business pages. Designers are itching to give it a facelift, but the FAZ is too busy being serious. Weekly English language supplement.

Handelsblatt

The closest thing Germany can offer to the *Wall Street Journal,* the *Handelsblatt* co-operates with that paper's European offshoot. Competition from the *Financial Times Deutschland* has shaken *Handelsblatt* out of its complacency and energised its reporting.

Sueddeutsche Zeitung

Based in Munich, the *Sueddeutsche* blends first-rate journalism with enlightened commentary and, not unusual in the German press, uninspired visuals.

die tageszeitung

Set up in Berlin's rebellious Kreuzberg district in the 1970s, the '*taz*' was an attempt to balance the provincial world view offered by West German newspapers and give coverage to alternative political and social issues. Today, with many of its charter readers now making mainstream policies in the Bundestag, the *taz* is floundering. Still, the Berlin edition keeps watch on crooks in local government.

Die Welt

Springer's *Die Welt* moved its main editorial office to Berlin well in advance of the government's arrival, appointed a new editor-in-chief and went through a redesign. Once a lacklustre mouthpiece of conservative, provincial thinking, *Die Welt* has widened its political horizons. But at a circulation of around 17,000 for its Berlin edition, it's a non-starter in the capital. Recently pooled its personnel resources with the Springer-owned local daily *Berliner Morgenpost* (*see below*) to cut costs.

Local newspapers

Berliner Morgenpost

Fat, fresh and self-conscious, this broadsheet is the favourite of the petty bourgeois. Good local coverage, and gradually gaining readers in the east through the introduction of neighbourhood editions, but no depth on the national and international pages and not helped by the fusion of the paper's staff with that of *Die Welt*. Comprehensive employment opportunities section on Saturday.

Berliner Zeitung

A black hole of investment since Gruner + Jahr bought it from Robert Maxwell in the early 1990s, this east Berlin newspaper sopped up the best journalistic talent and was redesigned in a bid to become the voice of Berlin. Gains through huge marketing in western strongholds only partly offset losses from its haemorrhaging core readership in the east. Running out of gimmicks just as the competition was preparing its own, the paper now lacks the spit and vigour of a few years ago, but remains a lively, though unauthoritative, read.

BZ

The daily riot of polemic and pictures hasn't let up since it was demonised by the left in the 1970s – but its circulation has. Although still Berlin's largest seller with 270,000 copies daily, BZ sales are down by over 70,000 copies since 1991.

Der Tagesspiegel

Solid but predictable, this is the staple of Wilmersdorf solicitors and Dahlem academics. Once thought vulnerable to the *Berliner Zeitung's* advance, its circulation has emerged as Berlin's most stable, and a new, younger editor-in-chief has managed to bring a fresher viewpoint. Losing money hand over fist, *Der Tagesspiegel* is a matter of prestige for owner Holtzbrinck.

Weekly newspapers

Jungle World

Defiantly left, graphically switched-on and commercially undaunted, the editors of this Berlin-based weekly can be relied on to mock anything approaching the comfortable views of the mainstream press. Born of an ideological dispute with the publishers of *Junge Welt*, a former East Berlin youth title, *Jungle World* lacks sales but packs a punch.

Die Zeit

Every major post-war intellectual debate in Germany has been carried out in the pages of *Die Zeit*, the newspaper that proved to a suspicious world that a liberal tradition was alive and well in a country best known for excesses of intolerance. Unforunately, the wandering style of its elite authors makes for a difficult read.

Freitag

'The East-West weekly paper' is a post-1989 relaunch of a GDR intellectual weekly. Worth a look for its political and cultural articles.

Magazines

Focus

Once, its spare, to-the-point articles, four-colour graphics and service features were a welcome innovation. But the gloss has faded, and *Focus* has established itself as a non-thinking man's *Der Spiegel*, whose answer to the upstart was simply to print more colour pages and become warm and fuzzy by adding bylines.

Der Spiegel

Few journalistic institutions in Germany possess the resources and clout to pursue a major story like *Der Spiegel*, one of the best and most aggressive news weeklies in Europe. After years of firing barbs at the ruling Christian Democrats, *Der Spiegel* was caught off guard when the Social Democrats were elected in 1999, but remains a must-read for anyone interested in Germany's power structure.

Stern

The heyday of news pictorials may have long gone, but Stern still manages to shift around a million copies a week of big colour spreads detailing the horrors of war, the beauties of nature and the curves of the female body. Nevertheless, its reputation has never really recovered from the Hitler diaries fiasco in the early 1980s.

Scheinschlag

This free monthly was established in 1991 to chronicle and critique the post-1989 developments in Berlin's inner city districts. It remains a must-read for anyone interested in local politics, urbanisation and contemporary culture, with the bonus of skewed cartoons.

Listings magazines

Berlin is awash with listings freebies, notably *[030]* (music, nightlife, film), *Partysan* (a pocket-sized club guide), *Siegessaeule* and *Sergej* (both gay). These can be picked up in bars and restaurants. Two newsstand fortnightlies, *Zitty* and *tip*, come out on alternate weeks and, at least for cinema information, it pays to get the current title.

tip

A glossier version of *Zitty* in every respect, tip gets better marks for its overall presentation and readability, largely due to higher quality paper, full-colour throughout and a space-saving TV insert. This makes it more appealing to display advertisers – a double-edged sword depending on why you buy a listings magazine in the first place.

Zitty

Having lost some counter-cultural edge since its foundation in 1977, *Zitty* remains a vital force on the Berlin media scene, providing a fortnightly blend of close-to-the-bone civic journalism, alternative cultural coverage and comprehensive listings interspersed with wry, often arcane German comics. The Harte Welle ('hardcore') department of its Lonely Hearts classifieds is legendary.

Television

At its best, German TV produces solid investigative programmes and clever drama series. At its worst, there are cheesy 'erotic' shows, vapid folk-music programmes featuring rhythmically clapping studio audiences and German adaptations of reality TV and casting shows like *Big Brother* and *Star Search*. Late-night TV, in particular, is chock-a-block with imported action series and European soft porn, interspersed with nipple-pinching and finger-sucking adverts for telephone sex numbers.

A basic channel shakedown looks like this: two national public networks, **ARD** and **ZDF**, a handful of no-holds-barred commercial channels, and a load of special-interest channels.

ARD's daily *Tagesschau* at 8pm is the most authoritative news broadcast nationally. **N-tv** is Germany's all-news cable channel, owned partly by CNN, but lacking the satellite broadcaster's ability to cover a breaking story. **TVBerlin** is the city's experiment with local commercial television and, though more ambitious under new management, it's still catching up with ARD's local affiliate **RBB** (a merger of Berlin and Brandenburg stations SFB and ORB), which covers local news with more insight.

RTL, **Pro 7** and **SAT.1** are privately owned services offering a predictable mix of Hollywood re-runs and imported series, plus their own sensational magazine programmes and sometimes surprisingly good TV movies.

Special interest channels run from **Kinderkanal** for kids to **Eurosport**, **MTV Europe** and its German-language competitors **Viva** and more offbeat **Onyx**, to **Arte**, an enlightened French-German cultural channel with high-quality films and documentaries.

Channels broadcasting regularly in English include **CNN**, **NBC**, **MTV Europe** and **BBC World**. British or American films on ARD or ZDF are sometimes broadcast with a simultaneous soundtrack in English for stereo-equipped TV sets.

Radio

Some 33 stations compete for audiences in Berlin, so even tiny shifts in market share have huge consequences for broadcasters. The race for ratings in the greater metropolitan area is thwarted by a clear split between the urban audience in both east and west and a rural one in the hinterland. The main four stations in the region have their audiences based in either Berlin (**Berliner Rundfunk**, 91.4; **r.s.2**, 94.3) or **Brandenburg** (BB Radio, 107.5; Antenne Brandenburg, 99.7). No single station can pull in everyone.

Commercial stations **104,6 RTL** (104.6), **Energy 103,4** (103.4) and **Hundert,6** (100.6) offer standard chart pop spiced with news. **RadioEins** (95.8) and **Fritz** (102.6) are a bit more adventurous but still far from cutting-edge. **RockStar FM**'s (87.9) rock format and **Voice of America** news broadcasts look back to the days when the frequency was occupied by the US Armed Forces Network in Berlin. Jazz is round the clock on **Jazz Radio** (101.9). Information-based stations such as **Info Radio** (93.1) are increasing in popularity. The **BBC World Service** (90.2) is available 24 hours a day. **Radio Multikulti** (96.3) broadcasts in 18 languages besides German and serves up global sounds. The **reboot.fm** collective transmits from vacant frequencies and is trying to establish a WFMU or Resonance FM style free radio in Berlin.

Money

On 1 January 2002, the Mark ceased to be legal tender and Germany adopted the euro (€). One euro is made up of 100 cents. There are seven new banknotes, and eight coins. The notes are of differing colours and sizes (€5 is the smallest, €500 the largest) and each of their designs represent a different period of European architecture. They are: €5 (grey), €10 (red), €20 (blue), €50 (orange), €100 (green), €200 (yellow-brown), €500 (purple).

The eight denominations of coins vary in colour, size and thickness. They share one common side; the other features a country-specific design (all can be used in any participating state). They are: €2, €1, 50 cents, 20 cents, 10 cents, 5 cents, 2 cents, 1 cent.

For more information on the euro, see www.euro.ecb.int. At the time of going to press, the exchange rate was £1 = €0.70 and US$1 = €1.29.

ATMs

ATMs are found throughout the centre of Berlin, and are the most convenient way of obtaining cash. Most major credit cards are accepted, as well as debit cards that are part of the Cirrus, Plus, Star or Maestro systems. You will normally be charged a fee for withdrawing cash, but the exchange rate is usually good.

Banks & bureaux de change

Foreign currency and travellers' cheques can be exchanged in most banks.

Wechselstuben (bureaux de change) are open outside normal banking hours and give better rates than banks, where changing money often involves long queues.

Reisebank AG

Zoo Station, Hardenbergplatz, Charlottenburg (881 7117). S3, S5, S7, S9, S75, U2, U9 Zoologischer Garten. **Open** 7.30am-10pm daily. **Map** p305 C4.

The Wechselstuben of the Reisebank offer good exchange rates. Branches at Alexanderplatz, Ostbahnhof and Bahnhof Lichtenberg.

Credit cards

Many Berliners prefer to use cash for most transactions, although larger hotels, shops and restaurants often accept major credit cards (American Express, Diners Club, MasterCard, Visa) and many will take Eurocheques with guarantee cards, and travellers' cheques with ID. In general, German banking and retail systems are less enthusiastic about credit than their UK or US equivalents, though this is changing.

If you want to take out cash on your credit card, some banks will give an advance against Visa and MasterCard cards. But you may not be able to withdraw less than the equivalent of US$100. A better option is using an ATM machine.

American Express

Bayreuther Strasse 37, Schöneberg (214 9830). U1, U2, U15 Wittenbergplatz. **Open** 9am-7pm Mon-Fri; 10am-1pm Sat. **Map** p305 D5.

Holders of an American Express card can use the company's facilities here, including the cash advance service.

Lost/stolen cards

If you've lost a credit card, or had one stolen, phone one of the 24-hour emergency numbers listed below.

American Express 0180 523 2377.
Diners Club 0697 254 0440.
MasterCard/Visa 0697 933 1910.

Tax

Non-EU citizens can claim back German value-added tax (*Mehrwertsteuer* or MwSt) on goods purchased in the country (it's only worth the hassle on sizeable purchases). Ask to be issued with a Tax-Free Shopping Cheque for the amount of the refund and present this, with the receipt, at the airport's refund office (before checking in bags).

Opening hours

Most banks are open 9am to noon Monday to Friday, and 1pm to 3pm or 2pm to 6pm on varied weekdays.

Shops can stay open until 8.30pm on weekdays, and 4pm on Saturdays, though many close earlier. Most big stores open their doors at 8.30am, newsagents a little earlier, and smaller or independent shops open around 10am or later.

An increasing number of all-purpose neighbourhood shops open around 5pm and close around midnight. Many Turkish shops are open on Saturday afternoons and on Sundays from 1pm to 5pm. Many bakers open to sell cakes on Sundays from 2pm to 4pm. Most 24-hour fuel stations also sell basic groceries.

The opening times of bars vary , but many are open during the day, and most stay open until at least 1am, if not through until morning.

Most post offices are open 8am to 6pm Monday to Friday and 8am to 1pm on Saturdays.

Police stations

You are unlikely to come in contact with the *Polizei*, unless you commit a crime or are the victim of one. There are very few pedestrian patrols or traffic checks (and local radio news often announces where to look out for them).

The central police HQ is at Platz der Luftbrücke 6, Tempelhof (466 40), and there are local stations at: Jägerstrasse 48, Mitte (466 462 242); Joachimsthaler Strasse 15-17, Charlottenburg (466 452

842); Friesenstrasse 16, Kreuzberg (466 433 242); Hauptstrasse 44, Schönberg (466 457 042); Eberswalder Strasse 6-9 (466 446 642).

Postal services

Most post offices (simply *Post* in German) are open from 8am to 6pm Monday to Friday, and 8am to 1pm Saturday.

For non-local mail, use the *Andere Richtungen* ('other destinations') slot in post-boxes. Letters of up to 20 grams (7oz) to anywhere in Germany and the EU need €0.55 in postage. Postcards require €0.45. For anywhere outside the EU, a 20-gram airmail letter costs €1.55, a postcard €1.

Postamt Friedrichstrasse

Georgenstrasse 12, Mitte. U6, S1, S2, S3, S5, S7, S9, S25, S26, S75 Friedrichstrasse. **Open** 8am-10pm daily. **Map** p302/p316 F3.

Berlin has no main post office. This branch, actually inside Friedrichstrasse station, has the longest opening hours.

Poste restante

Poste restante facilities are available at the main post offices of each district. Address them to the recipient '*Postlagernd,*' followed by the address of the post office, or collect them from the counter marked *Postlagernde Sendungen*. Take your passport.

Public holidays

On public holidays (*Feiertagen*) it can be difficult to get things done in Berlin. However, most cafés, bars and restaurants stay open – except on the evening of 24 December, when almost everything closes.

Public holidays are: **New Year's Day** (1 Jan); **Good Friday** (Mar/Apr); **Easter Monday** (Mar/Apr); **May/Labour Day** (1 May); **Ascension Day** (May/June; ten days before Whitsun/Pentacost, the 7th Sun after Easter); **Whit/Pentacost Monday** (May/June); **Day of German Unity** (3 Oct); **Day of Prayer and National Repentance** (3rd Wed in Nov); **Christmas Eve** (24 Dec); **Christmas Day** (25 Dec); **Boxing Day** (26 Dec).

Religion

For lists of places of worship for the major religions, the website **www.berlinfo.com** is useful (click on the link for 'community').

Safety & security

Though crime is increasing, Berlin remains a safe city by western standards. Even for a woman, it's pretty safe to walk around alone at night in most central areas of the city. However, avoid the eastern suburbs if you look gay or non-German. Pickpockets are not unknown around major tourist areas. Use some common sense and you're unlikely to get into any trouble.

Smoking

Many Berliners smoke, and, though the habit is in decline, there is less stigma attached than in the UK or US. Smoking is banned on public transport, in theatres and many public institutions, but is tolerated almost everywhere else.

Study

There are more than 140,000 students in Berlin, spread between four universities and 16 subject-specific colleges (*Fachhochschulen*). Studies last at least four years but most students take longer.

Since reunification the lot of students has worsened. Rents have risen, libraries and lecture halls are congested, while the city government demands ever harsher spending cuts, entailing closing faculties, introducing tuition fees and restricting admissions.

Language classes

Goethe-Institut

Neue Schönhauser Strasse 20, Mitte (25 90 63/www.goethe.de/ins/de/ort/gst/ber/ins/deindex.htm). U8 Weinmeisterstrasse or S3, S5, S7, S9, S75 Hackescher Markt. **Map** p306 F4.

The Goethe-Institut is well organised, solid and reliable. Facilities include a cultural extension programme (theatre, film and museum visits), accommodation for students, and a media centre with computers. A four-week intensive course costs €1405 with accommodation; eight-week courses cost €2645. Exams can be taken at the end of each level.

Tandem

Lychenerstrasse 7, Prenzlauer Berg (441 3003/www.tandem-berlin.de). U2 Eberswalder Strasse. **Map** p303 G1.

For €15 Tandem will put you in touch with two German speakers who want to learn English, and are prepared to teach you German. Language classes available.

Universities

Freie Universitaet Berlin

Central administration, Kaiserswertherstrasse 16-18, Dahlem (8381/www.FU-Berlin.de). U1 Dahlem-Dorf.

What is today Germany's biggest university was founded by a group of students in 1948 after the Humboldt was taken over by the East German authorities. It began with a few books, a Dahlem villa provided by the US military government and a constitution that gave students a vote on all decision-making bodies. It was intended to be free of government interference. But today the huge anonymous university is far from being a community of professors, tutors and students. The AStA (*Allgemeiner Studentenausschuss*, 'General Student Committee'), elected by the student parliament, now has no decision-making powers. The financial situation is also getting worse: more students, fewer books, professors, tutors and services.

Watching the wildlife

Every city has its wildlife, and Berlin is home to all the usual suspects, though with more rats and fewer pigeons than in many places. Berlin's symbol is the bear, but outside of the two zoos (*see p103 and p118*), the only place you'll encounter one is in the bearpit in Köllnischer Park near the Märkisches Museum (*see p85*) – home to Schnute, Maxi and Tilo, the official Berlin bears.

During the Cold War, Berlin was noted for its rabbits, which hopped around happily in no-man's land and other barren spaces. But Reunification seems to have killed the bunnies off. That and the increase in foxes, often spotted scavenging around the city.

But the biggest increase has been in Berlin's wild boar population. The papers have been full of Wildschwein stories: a 54-year-old man in Dahlem finds a boar under his dining table, which bites him when he tries to shoo it away; Hertha BSC training sessions disrupted by wild boar, who were tearing up one of the training pitches. A pair of wild boar were even seen in Alexanderplatz, nosing around for food.

These are not shy, retiring creatures. These are undomesticated pigs, typically weighing between 90 to 136 kilograms (200-300 pounds), with five-inch tusks and a nasty temper – particularly females with children. If you encounter one, best treat it with respect.

Still, many people like them, and leave out food. The abundant supply of eats in the city is one reason for the increase in numbers, along with warmer winters. Experts estimate the population to be around 8,000, bossing the forests, rooting around parks, and settling on overgrown railway embankments.

Wild boar have been here longer than Berlin. Racoons are a more recent arrival. A bunch of them escaped when a stray Allied bomb hit a racoon farm near Berlin during World War II. Half a century later, these furry aliens have spread across Germany and soon will be all over Europe.

Racoons have started leaving their natural habitat near streams or lakes and moving into the city, where food and shelter – someone's attic or cellar, say – are easy to find. Racoons shin up drainpipes, jump on to roofs from trees, or wander in via the cat flap. They can even turn knobs and open latches.

Once racoons have made themselves at home in your garage or gable, it's difficult to get them out again. Studies show that the more of them people trap and kill, the more they simply breed. Urban racoon experts instead recommend preventative measures: trimming tree branches, covering drainpipes. But whatever measures do or don't prove effective, suburban Berliners are on the front line of this furry invasion.

Humboldt-Universitaet zu Berlin (HUB)

Unter den Linden 6, Mitte (20930/www.hu-berlin.de). U6, S1, S2, S3, S5, S7, S9, S25, S26, S75 Friedrichstrasse. **Map** p316/p303 F3.

Berlin's first university was founded by the humanist Wilhelm von Humboldt in 1810. Hegel taught here in the 1820s, making Berlin the centre of German philosophy. His pupils included Karl Marx. Other departments have boasted Nobel Prize-winning chemists van t'Hoff and Otto Hahn; physicists Max Planck, Albert Einstein and Werner Heisenberg; and physicians Rudolf Virchow and Robert Koch. During the Nazi period, books were burned, students and professors expelled and murdered. When the Soviets reopened the university in 1946, there were hopes of a fresh start but these were stifled. After the 1989 revolution, students fought, with partial success, against plans to close some faculties. In 2003 Chancellor Schröder publicly pondered establishing world-class elite universities in Germany, with the HU as a possible candidate.

Technische Universitaet Berlin (TU)

Strasse des 17. Juni 135, Tiergarten (3140/www.TU-Berlin.de). U2 Ernst-Reuter-Platz. **Map** p305 C4.

The Technical University, or TU, started life as a mining, building and gardening academy in the 18th century. With its focus on engineering, machinery and business, the university was given priority by the Nazi government. It was reopened in 1946 with an expanded remit including the social sciences, philosophy, psychology, business studies, computers and analytical chemistry. With roughly 30,000 students, the TU is one of Germany's ten largest universities. It also has the highest number of foreign students (19%). There are special supplementary classes and a Language and Cultural Exchange Programme for foreigners (Sprach- und Kulturboerse, SKB; see below), where you can take intensive language courses, join conversational groups and attend seminars on international issues and apply for language exchange partnerships. The SKB services are open to students at any Berlin university.

Sprach- und Kulturbörse an der TU Berlin

Ernst-Reuter-Platz 7, Charlottenburg (3142 2730/www.skb.tub-fk1.de). U2 Ernst-Reuter-Platz. **Open** 3.30-5.30pm Tue, Thur. **Map** p304 C4.

Universität der Künste Berlin (UdK)

Hardenbergstrasse 33, Charlottenburg (318 50/www.udk-berlin.de). U2, U9, S3, S5, S7, S9, S75 Zoologischer Garten. **Map** p305 C4.

Directory

Founded in 1975 with the merger of the traditional Fine and Applied Arts, Drama, Music and Printing Colleges, the UdK offers a rare combination of artistic and academic disciplines and attracts renowned teachers such as Vivienne Westwood. With newer faculties such as Theory and Practice of Communication, the Electronic Business School or Experimental Film and Media, the UdK keeps in tune with changing demands of aesthetic discourse and the job market.

Useful organisations

Studentenwerk Berlin

Hardenbergstrasse 34, Charlottenburg (311 20/ www.studentenwerk-berlin.de). U2, U9, S3, S5, S7, S9, S75 Zoologischer Garten. **Open** 9am-3pm Mon-Thur; 9am-1pm Fri. **Map** p305 C4.

The central organisation for student affairs runs hostels, restaurants and job agencies.

Telephones

All phone numbers in this guide are local Berlin numbers (other than those in the chapter **Trips Out of Town**) but note that numbers beginning with 0180 have higher tarifs. To call from outside the city, *see below*.

Dialling & codes

To phone Berlin from abroad, dial the international access code (00 from the UK, 011 from the US, 0011 from Australia), then 49 (for Germany) and 30 (for Berlin), followed by the local number.

To phone abroad from Germany dial 00, then the appropriate country-code:
Australia 61;
Canada 1;
Ireland 353;
New Zealand 64;
United Kingdom 44;
United States 1.
And then the local area code (minus the initial zero) and the local number.

To call Berlin from elsewhere in Germany, dial 030 and then the local number.

Making a call

Calls within Berlin from 9am-6pm cost €0.10 per minute. Numbers prefixed 0180 are charged at €0.12 per minute.

A call from Berlin to the UK and Ireland costs €0.60 per minute, to the US and Canada €0.90 per minute and to Australia €2.60 per minute.

Both local and international calls can be a lot cheaper if you simply dial a prefix before the international code. There are various numbers and they change from time to time. Look in local newspapers or visit www.tariftip.de.

Public phones

At post offices you'll find both coin- and card-operated phones, but most pavement phone boxes are card-only.

You can sometimes find a coin-operated phone in a bar or café. Phonecards can be bought at post offices and in newsagents for various sums from €5 to €50. There are also phonecard machines in Alexanderplatz and Zoo stations.

To make international calls, look for phone boxes marked 'international' and with a ringing-bell symbol – you can be called back on them.

Operator services

For online directory enquiries (available in English), go to **www.teleauskunft.de**.

Alarm calls/Weckruf 0180 114 1033 (automated, in German).
International directory enquiries 11834.
Operator assistance/German directory enquiries 11833 (11837 English-speaking only).
Phone repairs/Störungsannahme 080 0330 2000.
Telegram (Telegrammaufnahme) 01805 121 210.
Time (Zeitansage) 01191 (automated, in German).
Weather (Wettervorhersage) 0190 116 400 (automated, in German).

Mobile phones

German mobile phones networks operate at 900MHz (in common with those in the UK and Australia), so all UK and Australian mobiles should work in Berlin (if roaming is activated). US and Canadian cell phones users (whose phones operate at 1900MHz) should check whether their phones can switch to 900MHz.

Time

Germany is on Central European Time – one hour ahead of Greenwich Mean Time. Daylight-saving time comes into operation on the last Sunday in March (clocks go forward one hour), and on the last Sunday in October (clocks go back one hour).

When daylight-saving is not in effect, London is one hour behind Berlin, New York is six hours behind, San Francisco is nine hours behind, and Sydney is nine hours ahead.

Germany uses a 24-hour system. 8am is '8 Uhr' (usually written 8h), noon is '12 Uhr Mittags' or just '12 Uhr', 5pm is '17 Uhr' and midnight is '12 Uhr Mitternachts' or just 'Mitternacht'.

8.15 is '8 Uhr 15' or 'Viertel nach 8'; 8.30 is '8 Uhr 30' or 'halb 9'; and 8.45 is '8 Uhr 45' or 'Viertel vor 9'.

Tipping

The standard tip in restaurants is around ten per cent, but tipping is not obligatory. Check for the words *Bedienung Inclusiv* (service included) on your bill. In a taxi round up the bill to the nearest euro.

Toilets

Berlin public toilets can be pretty scummy but the authorities have been trying to clean them up. Single-occupancy, coin-operated 'City Toilets' are becoming the norm. The toilets in main stations are looked after by an attendant and are pretty clean. Restaurants and cafés have to let you use their toilets by law and legally they can't refuse you a glass of water.

Tourist information

Berlin Tourismus Marketing (BTM)

Europa-Center, Budapester Strasse, Charlottenburg (250 025/www.btm.de). S3, S5, S7, S9, S75, U2, U9 Zoologischer Garten. **Open** 10am-6pm daily. **Map** p305 D4.

Berlin's official (though private) tourist organisation. The branch below is open 9.30am-9pm daily.

Other location: Brandenburg Gate.

EurAide

Main hall, Bahnhof Zoologischer Garten, Charlottenburg (www.euraide.de). U2, U9, S3, S5, S7, S9, S75 Zoologischer Garten. **Open** *June-Oct* 8.30am-12.30pm, 1.30-4.30pm Mon-Fri. *Nov-May* 9am-12.30pm, 1.30-4.30pm Mon-Fri. **Map** p305 C4.

Behind the Reisezentrum in Bahnhof Zoo, this excellent office offers advice and info in English for travellers. Staff can advise on sights, hostels, tours and local transport, and can sell you rail tickets.

Visas & immigration

A passport valid for at least three months beyond the length of stay is all that is required for UK, EU, US, Canadian and Australian citizens for a stay in Germany of up to three months. Citizens of EU countries with valid national ID cards need only show their ID cards.

Citizens of other countries should check with their local German embassy or consulate whether a visa is required.

As with any trip, you should confirm visa requirements with your country's embassy well before you plan to travel.

Residence permits

For stays of longer than three months, you'll need a residence permit. EU citizens, and those of Andorra, Australia, Canada, Cyprus, Israel, Japan, Malta, New Zealand and the US can obtain this from the **Landeseinwohneramt Berlin**. It is free and can be obtained on the day of application. Appointments are not required, but expect to wait. Bring your passport, two photos and proof of an address in Germany (your *Anmeldungsbestätigung* – a form confirming you have registered at the *Anmeldungsamt*, or registration office). If you have a work contract, bring it – you may be granted a longer stay.

If unsure about your status, contact the German Embassy in your country of origin, or your own embassy or consulate in Berlin. *See p275* **Embassies & consulates**.

Landeseinwohneramt Berlin

Charlottenstrasse 90, Mitte, 10958 (902 690). U6 Kochstrasse. **Open** 8am-3pm Mon, Wed; 11am-6pm Tue, Thur; 8am-1pm Fri. **Map** p302/p316 F2/3.

When to go

Berlin has a continental climate, hot in summer and cold in winter. In January and February Berlin often ices over. Spring begins in late March/April. For more info, *see p278* **Weather report**.

Women

See also *p277* **Helplines** and *p276* **Health**.

Women's centres

EWA Frauenzentrum

Prenzlauer Allee 6, Prenzlauer Berg (442 5542/www.ewa-frauenzentrum.de). U2 Senefelderplatz. **Open** 10am-6pm Mon-Fri; (disco) 10pm-3am Sat. *Café & gallery* 6-11pm Mon-Thur. **Map** p303 G2.

Offers legal advice and counselling, courses, readings and discussion groups. The media workshop has PCs, a darkroom, an editing suite, archive and library.

Working in Berlin

Berlin offers a decent range of working opportunities, but the job market is beginning to shrink.

The small ads in the magazines *Zitty*, *tip* (*see p280*) and *Zweite Hand* are good places to look for work. Teaching English is popular: there is always a demand for native English speakers.

If you're studying in Berlin, try the **Studenten Vermittlung Arbeitsamt** ('Student Job Service'). You'll need your passport, student card and a *Lohnsteuerkarte* ('tax card'), available from your local *Finanzamt* ('tax office' – listed in the *Yellow Pages*). Tax is reclaimable. Students looking for summer work can contact the **Zentralstelle für Arbeitsvermittlung**.

The German equivalent of the Job Centre is the *Arbeitsamt* ('Employment Service'). There are very few private agencies. To find the address of your nearest office in Germany, look in the *Gelbe Seiten* under *Arbeitsämter*.

EU nationals have the right to live and work in Germany without a work permit.

Studenten Vermittlung Arbeitsamt

Hardenbergstrasse 35, Charlottenburg (315 9340). U2 Ernst-Reuter-Platz. **Open** 8am-5pm Mon-Fri. **Map** p305 C4.

Zentralstelle für Arbeitsvermittlung (ZAV)

Kurfürstendamm 206, Charlottenburg (885 9060). U15 Uhlandstrasse. **Open** 8.15am-4pm Mon-Wed; 8.30am-6pm Thur; 8.15am-2pm Fri. **Map** p305 C4.

Vocabulary

Pronunciation

z – pronounced ts
w – like English v
v – like English f
s – like English z, but softer
r – like a throaty French r
a – as in f**a**ther
e – as in d**a**y
i – as in s**ee**k
o – as in n**o**te
u – as in l**oo**t
ch – as in Scottish lo**ch**
ä – combination of a and e, sometimes like **ai** in p**ai**d and sometimes like **e** in s**e**t
ö – combination of o and e, as in French **eu**
ü – combination of u and e, like tr**ue**
ai – like p**ie**
au – like h**ou**se
ie – like fr**ee**
ei – like f**i**ne
eu – like c**oi**l

Useful phrases

hello/good day – *guten Tag*
goodbye – *aufwiedersehen,*
goodbye (informal) – *tschüss*
good morning – *guten Morgen*
good evening – *guten Abend*
good night – *gute Nacht*
yes – *ja;* (emphatic) *jawohl*
no – *nein, nee*
maybe – *vielleicht*
please – *bitte*
thank you – *danke*
thank you very much – *danke schön*
excuse me – *entschuldigen Sie mir bitte*
sorry! – *Verzeihung!*
I'm sorry, I don't speak German – *Entschuldigung, ich spreche kein Deutsch*
do you speak English? – *sprechen Sie Englisch?*
can you speak more slowly, please? – *können Sie bitte langsamer sprechen?*
my name is… – *ich heisse…*
do you have a light? – *haben Sie Feuer?*
open/closed – *geöffnet/geschlossen*
with/without – *mit/ohne*
cheap/expensive – *billig/teuer*
big/small – *gross/klein*
entrance/exit – *Eingang/Ausgang*
push/pull – *drücken/ziehen*
I would like... – *ich möchte...*
how much is... ? – *wieviel kostet... ?*
could I have a receipt? – *darf ich bitte eine Quittung haben?*
how do I get to... ? – *wie komme ich nach... ?*
how far is it to... ? – *wie weit ist es nach... ?*
where is... ? – *wo ist... ?*
airport – *der Flughafen*
railway station – *der Bahnhof*
bus station – *der Busbahnhof*
metro – *die U-Bahn*
petrol – *das Benzin*
lead-free – *bleifrei*
can you call me a cab? – *können Sie bitte mir ein Taxi rufen?*
left – *links*
right – *rechts*
straight ahead – *gerade aus*
far – *weit*
near – *nah*
street – *die Strasse*
square – *der Platz*
help! – *Hilfe!*
I feel ill – *ich bin krank*
doctor – *der Arzt*
pharmacy – *die Apotheke*
hospital – *das Krankenhaus*

Numbers

0 *null*; 1 *eins*; 2 *zwei*; 3 *drei*; 4 *vier*; 5 *fünf*; 6 *sechs*; 7 *sieben*; 8 *acht*; 9 *neun*; 10 *zehn*; 11 *elf*; 12 *zwölf*; 13 *dreizehn*; 14 *vierzehn*; 15 *fünfzehn*; 16 *sechszehn*; 17 *siebzehn*; 18 *achtzehn*; 19 *neunzehn*; 20 *zwanzig*; 21 *einundzwanzig*; 22 *zweiundzwanzig*; 30 *dreissig*; 40 *vierzig*; 50 *fünfzig*; 60 *sechszig*; 70 *siebzig*; 80 *achtzig*; 90 *neunzig*; 100 *hundert*; 101 *hunderteins*; 110 *hundertzehn*; 200 *zweihundert*; 201 *zweihunderteins*; 1,000 *tausend;* 2,000 *zweitausend.*

Beautiful party evening!

Everyday Deutsch is rich in bizarre idioms. Here we present some crucial colloquialisms.

Arsch

Arsch ('arse') is German's most common amplifier. Weather can be *arschkalt* (very cold), goods are often *arschteuer* (extremely expensive) and someone who talks crap is an *Arschgeige* ('arse violin'). When everything's going wrong you say there's an *Arschprogramm* going on. Be warned: *Arschloch* ('arsehole') is a more serious insult than it is in English. Don't use it unless you want to end up *am Arsch* (fucked up).

Feierabend

Literally 'party evening', but when a bar keeper announces this at 4am, don't take it as an invitation to dance on the tables. It's actually a more poetic version of the British 'knocking-off time'. Bond with your local shopkeeper by wishing him a *schön Feierabend* ('beautiful party evening') and then nip out for a *Feierabendsbier* yourself.

Geil

The German equivalent of the English 'wicked' or American 'awesome' literally means 'horny'. Berliners deliver the dipthong with gusto: 'Guy-ull!'

Scheissladen

A handy term. Literally 'shit shop', but *Laden* also means restaurant, bar or any place where one parts with money and expects value in return. When the waiter forgets your order, the barman brings the wrong drink, or you queue for 20 minutes only to find some obvious item is out of stock and then get barked at by the shopkeeper, communicate your disdain for their useless establishment by muttering *Scheissladen*!

Further Reference

Books

We've chosen these books for quality and interest as much as for availability. Most are currently in print, but some will only be found in libraries or second-hand. Date given is that of the first publication in English.

Fiction

Deighton, Len *Berlin Game, Mexico Set, London Match* (London 1983, 1984, 1985)
Epic espionage trilogy with labyrinthine plot set against an accurate picture of 1980s Berlin. The next six books in the series aren't bad either.
Döblin, Alfred *Berlin-Alexanderplatz* (London 1975)
Devastating expressionist portrait of the inter-war underworld in the working class quarters of Alexanderplatz.
Eckhart, Gabriele *Hitchhiking* (Lincoln, Nebraska 1992)
Short stories viewing East Berlin through the eyes of street cleaners and a female construction worker.
Grass, Gunther *Local Anaesthetic* (New York 1970)
The Berlin angst of a schoolboy who threatens to burn a dog outside a Ku'damm café to protest against the Vietnam War is firmly satirised, albeit in Grass's irritating schoolmasterly way.
Harris, Robert *Fatherland* (London 1992)
Alternative history and detective novel set in a 1964 Berlin as the Nazis might have built it.
Isherwood, Christopher *Mr Norris Changes Trains*, *Goodbye To Berlin* (London 1935, 1939)
Isherwood's two Berlin novels, the basis of the movie *Cabaret*, offer finely drawn characters and a sharp picture of the city as it tipped over into Nazism.
Johnson, Uwe *Two Views* (New York 1966)
Love story across the East-West divide, strong on the mood of Berlin in the late 1950s and early 1960s.
Kaminer, Wladimir *Russian Disco* (London 2002)
Best-selling collection of short tales from cult Kaffe Burger DJ.
Kerr, Philip *Berlin Noir* (London 1994)
The Bernie Gunther trilogy, about a private detective in Nazi Berlin, now in one volume.
Markstein, George *Ultimate Issue* (London 1981)
Stark thriller of political expediency leading to uncomfortable conclusion about why the Wall went up.
McEwan, Ian *The Innocent* (London 1990)
Tale of naive young Englishman recruited into Cold War machinations with tragi-comic results.
Müller, Heiner *The Battle* (New York 1989)
Collection of plays and pieces strong on the grimness of Stalinism and false temptations from the West.
Nabokov, Vladimir *The Gift* (New York 1963)
Written and set in 1920s Berlin, where impoverished Russian émigré dreams of writing a book very like this one.
Regener, Sven *Berlin Blues* (London 2003)
Irresponsibility and childhood's end in the bars of late 1980s Kreuzberg – a western version of the ostalgic mindset.
Schneider, Peter *The Wall Jumper* (London 1984)
Somewhere between novel, prose poem and artful reportage, a meditation on the madhouse absurdities of the Wall.

Children

Kästner, Erich *Emil And The Detectives* (London 1931)
Classic set mostly around Bahnhof Zoo and Nollendorfplatz.

Biography & memoir

Baumann, Bommi *How It All Began* (Vancouver 1977)
Frank and funny account of the Berlin origins of West German terrorism, by a former member of the June 2nd Movement.
Bielenberg, Christabel *The Past Is Myself* (London 1968)
Fascinating autobiography of an English woman who married a German lawyer and lived through the war in Berlin.
Friedrich, Ruth Andreas *The Berlin Underground* 1938-45 (New York 1947)
A few courageous souls formed anti-Nazi resistance groups in Berlin. The journalist-author's diaries capture the day-to-day fear.
Rimmer, Dave *Once Upon A Time In The East* (London 1992)
The collapse of communism seen stoned and from ground level – strange tales of games between East and West Berlin and travels through assorted East European revolutions.
Schirer, William L *Berlin Diaries* (New York 1941)
Foreign correspondent in Berlin 1931-1941 bears appalled witness to Europe's plunge into Armageddon.

History

Friedrich, Otto *Before The Deluge* (New York, 1972)
Vivid portrait of 1920s Berlin, based on interviews with those who survived what followed.
Garton Ash, Timothy *We The People* (London 1990)
Instant history of the 1989 revolutions.
Gelb, Norman *The Berlin Wall* (New York 1986)
Gripping narrative history of how the Wall went up.
Jelavich, Peter *Berlin Cabaret* (Harvard 1993)
Definitive history of Berlin cabaret from 1901to Nazi times.
Levenson, Thomas *Einstein in Berlin* (New York 2003)
Absorbing mainstream account of the historical deal between physicist and the city.
McElvoy, Anne *The Saddled Cow* (London 1992)
Lively history of East Germany by a former Berlin Times correspondent.
Read, Anthony and Fisher, David *Berlin – The Biography Of A City* (London 1994)
Readable, lightweight history.
Richie, Alexandra *Faust's Metropolis* (London 1998)
Best one-volume history of Berlin, but too heavy for holiday reading and with a too conservative agenda.
Schirer, William L *The Rise And Fall Of The Third Reich* (New York 1960)
Still the most readable history of Nazi Germany.
Tusa, Ann & John *The Berlin Blockade* (London 1988)
Absorbing account of the 11 months when the Allied sector was fed from the air and Berlin, Germany and Europe proceeded to fall into two.

Architecture

Ladd, Brian *The Ghosts Of Berlin: Confronting German History In The Urban Landscape* (Chicago, 1997)
Erudite and insightful look into the relationship between architecture, urbanism and Berlin's violent political history.
Berlin: Open City (Berlin 2001)
Excellent guide to both new building and extant architectural curiosities, built around walks detailed in fine fold-out maps.

Miscellaneous

Bertsch, Georg C & Hedler, Ernst *SED* (Cologne 1990)
Schöne Einheits Design: over 200 illustrations of crazy East German consumer product designs.

Friedrich, Thomas *Berlin – A Photographic Portrait Of The Weimar Years 1918-1933* (London 1991)
Superb photographs of lost Berlin, its personalities and daily life; foreword by Stephen Spender.

Film

Cabaret (Bob Fosse, 1972)
Liza Minelli as Sally Bowles, the very definition of the Berlin myth, and the last great Hollywood musical.

Christiane F. (Uli Edel, 1981)
To hell and back in the housing estates and heroin scene of late 1970s West Berlin, with Bowie soundtrack.

A Foreign Affair (Billy Wilder, 1948)
Marlene Dietrich sings 'Black Market' among the romantically rendered ruins of post-war Berlin.

Funeral In Berlin (Guy Hamilton, 1966)
Adaptation of Len Deighton's novel: Michael Caine in entertaining, puzzling Cold War yarn.

Good bye, Lenin! (Wolfgang Becker, 2003)
Ostalgia, the movie – a comic eulogy for the GDR, in which socialism gets a different kind of send-off.

It's Not The Homosexual Who Is Perverse But The Situation In Which He Lives (Rosa von Praunheim, 1973)
The best of the flamboyant von Praunheim's many films, a laundry list of the follies of Berlin's gay population.

M (Fritz Lang, 1931)
Paedophilia and vigilantism as Peter Lorre's child murderer stalks an expressionistic Weimar Berlin.

Olympia (Leni Riefenstahl, 1937)
In filming the 1936 Olympics, the Nazis' favourite director invented all the conventions of modern sportscasting.

One, Two, Three (Billy Wilder, 1961)
James Cagney is brilliant as the Pepsi exec whose daughter falls for East Berlin Communist Horst Buchholz. Hilarious torture scene involving 'Itsy Bitsy Teeny Weeny Yellow Polka Dot Bikini'.

The Legend Of Paul And Paula (Heiner Carow, 1974)
Cult GDR love story that delivered a stinging slap to the unromantic regime. No longer banned, it still plays regularly with English subtitles. Soundtrack by the also legendary Pudhys.

The Spy Who Came In From The Cold (Martin Ritt, 1965)
Intense atmosphere, brilliant Richard Burton performance, and an ending that shatteringly brings home the obscenity of the Wall.

Westler (Wieland Speck, 1985)
Low-budget gay romance between West and East Berliners and all you need know about the Wall in one checkpoint strip-search scene.

Wings of Desire (Wim Wenders, 1987)
Bruno Ganz in love, Peter Falk in a bunker, Nick Cave in concert, and an angel on the Siegessäule – Wenders has never surpassed his (double) vision of the divided city.

Music

AG Geige *Raabe?* (Zensor)
One of the first post-1989 discs to emerge from the East Berlin underground came from a bizarre electronica outfit rooted in The Residents and Die Tödliche Doris.

Ash Ra Tempel *Join Inn* (Temple/Spalax)
The 1972 hippy freakout incarnation of guitarist Manuel Göttsching, before he was reborn as techno's most baffling muse.

Meret Becker *Noctambule* (Ego)
Actress/chanteuse Becker restages Weimar alongside Berliner Krankheit classics like Neubauten's Schwarz.

The Birthday Party *Mutiny/The Bad Seed* EP (4AD)
Nick Cave and cohorts escaped drab London for the fevered creativity of early 1980s Berlin to record their two most intense EPs, here compressed into one volatile CD.

David Bowie *Heroes* (EMI)
In which Bowie romanticises the Wall and captures the atmosphere of (misspelt) Neuköln.

David Bowie *Low* (EMI)
Begun in France, completed at Hansa Studios, the album that heralded Bowie's new career in a new town.

Brecht/Weill *Die Dreigroschenoper Berlin 1930* (Teldec)
Historic shellac transcriptions from 1930 featuring a young and shrill Lotte Lenya, who also contributes a brace of *Mahagony* songs.

Caspar Brötzmann/FM Einheit *Merry Christmas* (Blast First/Rough Trade Deutschland)
Guitarist son Caspar is no less noisy than père Brötzmann, especially on this frenzy of feedback and distortion kicked up with ex-Neubauten man-mountain FM Einheit on, er, stones.

Peter Brötzmann *No Nothing* (FMP)
Uncharacteristically introspective recording from the sax colossus of German improvisation for Berlin's vital Free Music Production label, which he co-founded 30 years ago.

Ernst Busch *Der Rote Orpheus/Der Barrikaden Tauber* (BARBArossa)
Two-CD survey of the revolutionary tenor's 1930s recordings covers Brecht, Eisler and Weill.

Nick Cave *From Her To Eternity* (Mute)
Cave in best Berlinerisch debauched and desperate mode, with a title track later featured in *Wings of Desire*.

Comedian Harmonists *Ihre grossen Erfolge* (Laserlight)
Sublime six-part harmonies from the Weimar sensations whose career was cut short during the Third Reich.

Crime & The City Solution *Paradise Discotheque* (Mute)
Underrated Berlin-Australian group's finest disc (1990) is an oblique commentary on the heady 'neo-black market burnt-out ruins' amorality of the immediate post-1989 era.

DAF *Kebabträume* (Mute)
Exhilarating German punk satire of Berlin's Cold War neuroses, culminating in the coda 'We are the Turks of tomorrow'.

Marlene Dietrich *On Screen, Stage And Radio* (Legend)
From 'I Am The Sexy Lola' through 'Ruins Of Berlin', the sultry Schöneberg songstress embodies the mood of decadent Berlin.

Einstürzende Neubauten *Berlin Babylon Soundtrack* (Zomba)
More Neubauten 'Strategies Against Architecture' accompanying a highly watchable documentary about the head-spinning changes in Berlin's urban landscape and the movers and shakers behind them.

Alec Empire *The Geist Of…* (Geist)
Wonderful triple CD compilation of ATR mainman Empire's less combative electronica explorations for Frankfurt brainiac label Force Inc/Mille Plateaux.

Manuel Göttsching *E2-E4* (Racket)
Great lost waveform guitar album by ex-Ash Ra Tempel leader.

Gudrun Gut & Various *The Ocean Club* (Alternation)
Ex-Malaria! member Gudrun Gut's Ocean Club is a congenial cyberport for ambient song collaborations between singers, artists and programmers as disparate as Blixa Bargeld, Anita Lane, Thomas Fehlmann and Johnny Klimek.

Die Haut Head On (What's So Funny About)
Avantish Berlin equivalent of The Ventures lay down Morricone-meets-Loony-Tunes backdrops for guest singers like Alan Vega, Lydia Lunch, Kim Gordon and Jeffrey Lee Pierce.

Liaisons Dangereuses *Liaisons Dangereuses* (Roadrunner)
Formed by ex-DAF member Chrislo Haas, their solitary 1982 album of chipped beats and industrial atmospheres was a key influence on Detroit's techno pioneers.

Malaria! *Compiled* (Moabit Musik)
What with their tell-tale song titles – 'Passion', 'Jealousy', 'Power' and 'Death' – and suffocating swirls of synths and heavy-stepping beats, Malaria! was girl-pop, Berlin-style.
Maurizio *M* (M)
Essential CD compilation of Basic Channel mainman Moritz Von Oswald's vinyl releases, which lights up Chicago house with streaming beats diverted from the Berlin-Detroit techno grid.
Monolake *Momentum* (Imbalance)
Robert Hencke's post-techno pulses in some vast acoustic space, like last night's riffs still echoing around a distant corner of the club.
Barbara Morgenstern *Vermona ET-61* (Monika)
Morgenstern's everywoman voice, simple lyrics and clever accompaniment on a GDR home organ grow after repeated listenings, but the achingly beautiful instrumentals are the true highlights.
Pole *CD1* (Kiff SM)
Ex-Basic Channel engineer Stefan Betke is now at the cutting edge of the digidub school of blunted beats and vinyl glitches.
Iggy Pop *The Idiot* (Virgin America)
With Bowie in the producer's chair, Iggy begins to absorb the influence of early German electronica and the city of bright, white clubbing.
Iggy Pop *Lust For Life* (Virgin America)
Way back in West Berlin, Iggy the passenger cruises through the divided city's ripped-back sides and finds himself full of lust for life.
Lou Reed *Berlin* (RCA)
Although he'd never even been to the city, Lou somehow still got it right in this melancholy Meisterwerk.
Rhythm & Sound w/ the artists (Indigo)
Techno meets reggae at the mixing desk of Mark Ernestus and Moritz von Oswald. Eight singles (and vocalists) compiled on this and companion b-side CD, the versions.
Spacebow Big Waves (Noteworks)
Extraordinary reverberating metallic sound sculptures hewn from Berlin-based American expatriate artist Robert Rutman's steel cellos.
Stereo Total *My Melody* (Bungalow)
Demented chansons with cheesy lounge backing – Mitte's kitsch aesthetic plus a Francophone spin.
Tangerine Dream *Zeit* (Jive Electro)
Where cosmic consciousness and electronic minimalism first met by the Wall.
Terranova *Hitchhiking Non-Stop With No Particular Destination* (K7)
Heavy and intelligent trip hop from the WMF axis. Guest appearances by Ari Upp, Cath Coffey and Mike Ladd.
Ton Steine *Scherben Keine Macht Für Niemand* (David Volksmund)
Ernst Busch reincarnated as the early 1970s rock commune which provided Kreuzberg's anarchists with their most enduring anthems.
U2 *Achtung Baby!* (Island)
It took Zoo station and post-Wall Berlin to inspire the U2 album for people who don't like U2.
Paul van Dyk *Seven Ways* (MFS)
Eisenhüttenstadt's prime export is trance's one-trick pony, but here shows it off at its best.
Various *alaska.de Soundtrack* (Kitty-yo)
CD One is a serviceable sampler of recent Kitty-yo hits by Peaches, Gonzales, Surrogat et al. CD Two harbours meyermoserdöring's moody score, evoking Berlin ennui with fewer clichés than the film's visuals.
Various *Das Beste Aus Der DDR Parts I-III* (Amiga)
Three-part DDR rock retrospective, divided into rock, pop and 'Kult', including Ostalgia stalwarts like Puhdys, Silly and Karat plus Sandow's alt anthem 'Born in the GDR' and an early Nina Hagen ditty.
Various *Berlin 1992* (Tresor)
On the first of several Tresor compilations, Berlin techno is captured in its early, apocalyptic phase. Includes Love Parade anthem 'Der Klang der Familie' by 3Phase (at that time, Dr Motte & Sven Röhrig).
Various *Digital Hardcore Recordings… Riot Zone* (DHR)
Atari Teenage Riot's 1997 riotbeat label compilation also showcases the anarcho-comicbook radicalism of acolytes Shizuo, Christoph De Babalon and EC8OR.
Various *Freischwimmer* (Kitty-Yo)
Sampler covering five years of work on Mitte's premier post-rock indie label. Acts include Laub, Tarwater, Raz O'Hara, Gonzalez.
Various *Hotel-Stadt-Berlin* (Hausmusik/Kompakt/Indigo)
Label showcase bodes well for the future, with local electronica musicians exploring paths off the beaten track of techno and trance.
Various *Pop 2000* (Grönland/Spiegel Edition)
Eight-CD companion to TV chronicle of postwar German culture in East and West. 'Ostrock' is a bit under-represented, but otherwise an engaging compilation of the obvious and the obscure.
Various *Tranceformed From Beyond* (MFS)
Compilation that defined Berlin trance. Selection includes Cosmic Baby, Microglobe and Effective Force and others.
Westbam *A Practising Maniac At Work* (Low Spirit)
Effectively summarises the best of Berlin's best-known DJ, veering from stomping techno to twisted disco.
Wir Sind Helden *Die Reklamation* (Reklamation Records)
Simple but addictive tunes, lyrics asking modern consumer culture to 'give me my life back', touched a nerve with leftish alterna-teens and charmed older intelligentsia into believing that music still matters.

Websites

Time Out
www.timeout.com/berlin
Contains general information and history, plus shop, restaurant, café, bar and hotel reviews, all written by residents.
berlinfo.com
www.berlinfo.com
Up-to-date information about many aspects of life in Berlin, designed for residents and visitors alike. It contains film and theatre listings, as well as handy lists of professionals – doctors, lawyers, tax accountants – who speak English.
Berlin Info
www.berlin-info.de/index_e.html
Fairly comprehensive source of information and links, but the English translation is often painful (and sometimes missing). Operated by the official tourist board BTM (*see p285*) and oriented to upmarket tourism.
berlin.de
www.berlin.de
Berlin's official site – run by the tourist board (BTM) – is inevitably not its most objective but is nonethelessless well-written.
HotelGuide
berlin.hotelguide.net
A commercial site that sends you to the most expensive hotels, but then they're the ones which have online reservation services.
SMPK
www.smb.spk-berlin.de
Smart bilingual site with information on more than 20 Berlin museums run by SMPK.
stadtplandienst
www.stadtplandienst.de
An interactive map that can pinpoint any address in the city; zoomable so you can figure out how to get there.
Stadtmuseum Berlin
www.stadtmuseum.de
Comprehensive information on Berlin's museums and useful links. In German only.
BVG
www.bvg.de/e_index.html
Online timetable and public transport information for Berlin/Brandenburg.
Zitty
www.zitty.de
The online sister of Berlin's main listings publication. This rather crowded site contains listing information and has search functions. In German only.

Index

Note: Page numbers in **bold** indicate key information on a topic; *italics* indicate photographs.

t

u

v

w

Accommodation

Cafés, bars & pubs

Restaurants

Advertisers' Index

Please refer to the relevant sections for addresses/telephone numbers

Place of interest and/or entertainment	(shaded box)
Railway station	(shaded box)
Park	(shaded box)
Hospital/university	(shaded box)
Pedestrian Area	(shaded box)
Church	✚
S-Bahn Station	S
U-Bahn Station	U
S-Bahn line	S1
U-Bahn line	U1
District boundary	(line)
Course of Wall	(line)
Area	MITTE

Maps

Berlin & Around

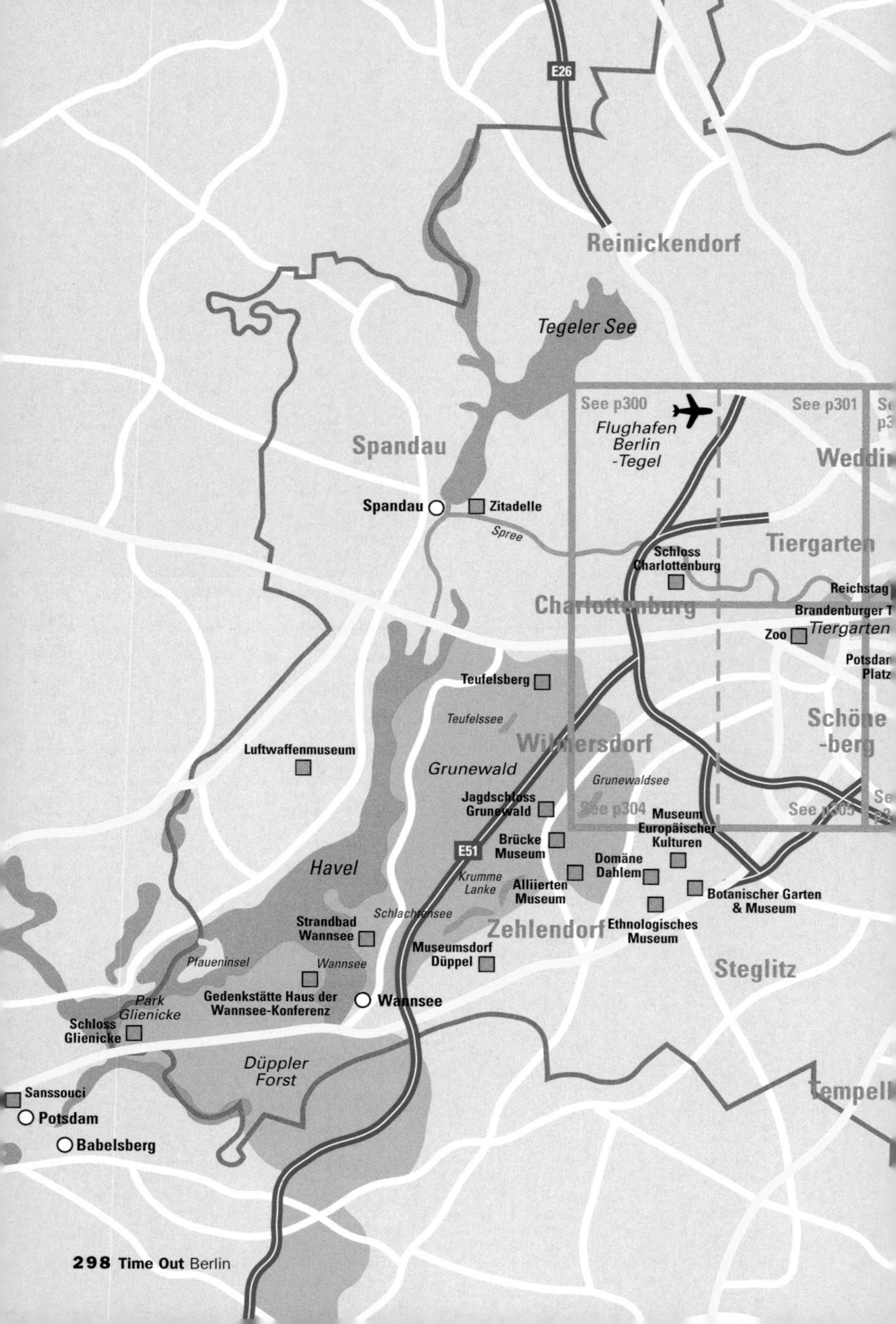

E26
Reinickendorf
Tegeler See
See p300
Flughafen Berlin -Tegel
See p301
Weddi
Spandau
Spandau
Zitadelle
Spree
Tiergarten
Schloss Charlottenburg
Reichstag
Charlottenburg
Brandenburger T
Zoo
Tiergarten
Potsdar Platz
Teufelsberg
Teufelssee
Schöne -berg
Wilmersdorf
Luftwaffenmuseum
Grunewald
Grunewaldsee
Jagdschloss Grunewald
See p304
Museum Europäischer Kulturen
See p305
Brücke Museum
E51
Domäne Dahlem
Havel
Krumme Lanke
Alliierten Museum
Botanischer Garten & Museum
Strandbad Wannsee
Schlachtensee
Zehlendorf
Ethnologisches Museum
Museumsdorf Düppel
Pfaueninsel
Wannsee
Steglitz
Park Glienicke
Gedenkstätte Haus der Wannsee-Konferenz
Wannsee
Schloss Glienicke
Düppler Forst
Sanssouci
Potsdam
Babelsberg
Tempel

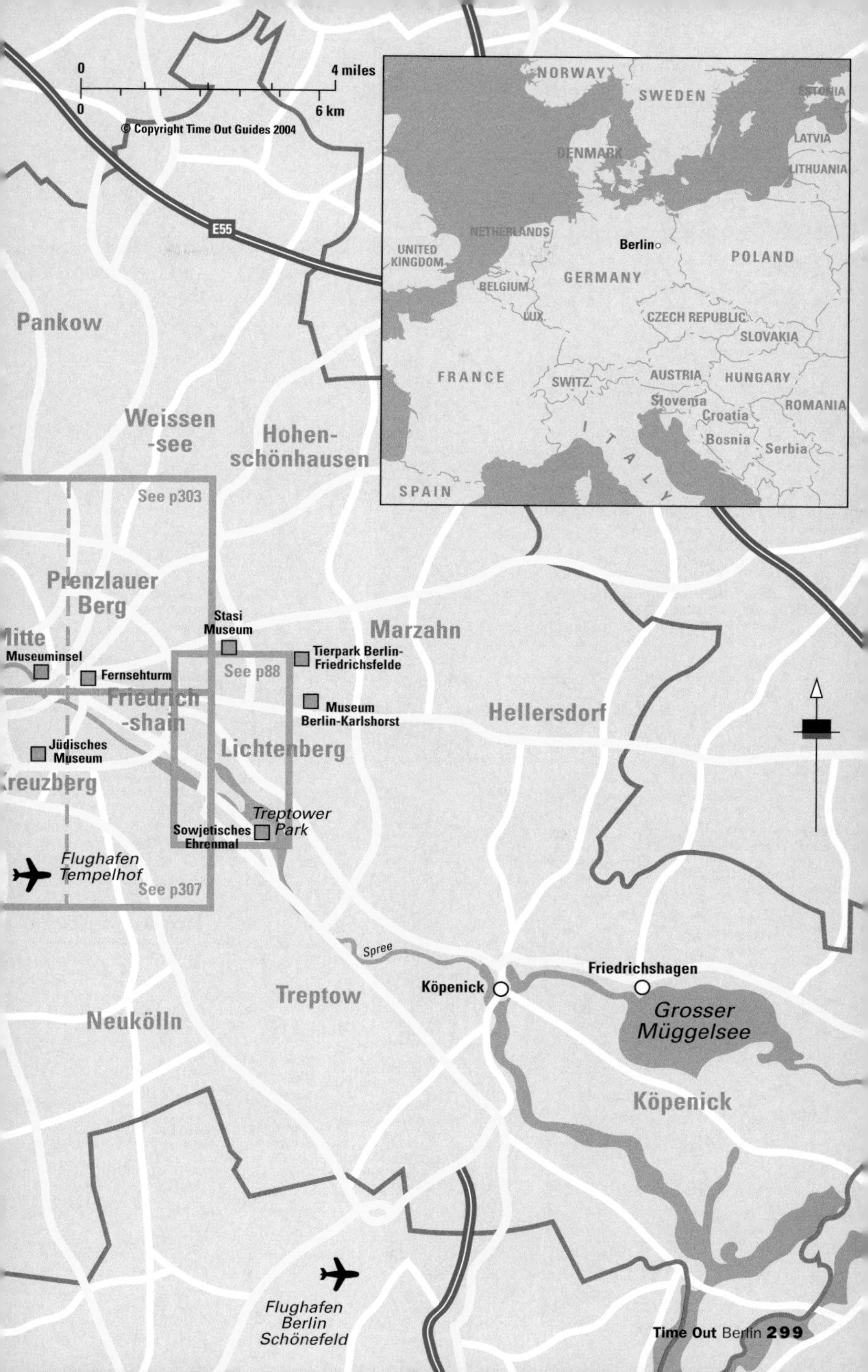
0
4 miles
0
6 km
© Copyright Time Out Guides 2004
E55
NORWAY
SWEDEN
ESTONIA
LATVIA
LITHUANIA
DENMARK
NETHERLANDS
UNITED KINGDOM
Berlin
POLAND
GERMANY
BELGIUM
LUX.
CZECH REPUBLIC
SLOVAKIA
FRANCE
SWITZ.
AUSTRIA
HUNGARY
Slovenia
Croatia
ROMANIA
ITALY
Bosnia
Serbia
SPAIN
Pankow
Weissen -see
Hohen-schönhausen
See p303
Prenzlauer Berg
Mitte
Museuminsel
Fernsehturm
Stasi Museum
See p88
Tierpark Berlin-Friedrichsfelde
Marzahn
Friedrich -shain
Museum Berlin-Karlshorst
Hellersdorf
Jüdisches Museum
Lichtenberg
Kreuzberg
Treptower Park
Sowjetisches Ehrenmal
Flughafen Tempelhof
See p307
Spree
Friedrichshagen
Köpenick
Treptow
Grosser Müggelsee
Neukölln
Köpenick
Flughafen Berlin Schönefeld

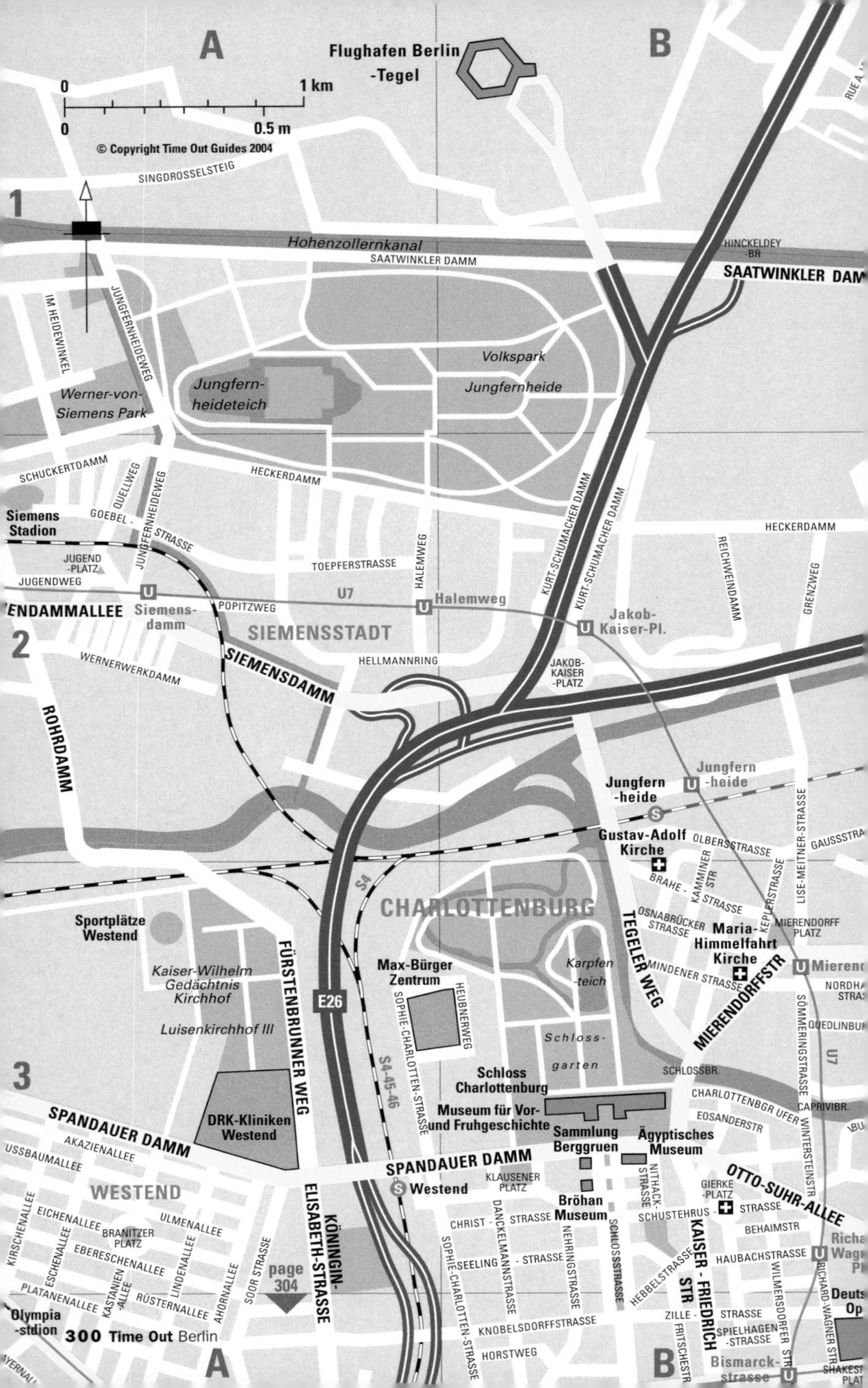
A
B
Flughafen Berlin
-Tegel
0
1 km
0
0.5 m
© Copyright Time Out Guides 2004
SINGDROSSELSTEIG
1
Hohenzollernkanal
SAATWINKLER DAMM
HINCKELDEY
-BR
SAATWINKLER DAM
IM HEIDEWINKEL
JUNGFERNHEIDEWEG
Werner-von-
Siemens Park
Jungfern-
heideteich
Volkspark
Jungfernheide
SCHUCKERTDAMM
QUELLWEG
HECKERDAMM
Siemens
Stadion
GOEBEL - STRASSE
JUNGFERNHEIDEWEG
JUGEND
-PLATZ
JUGENDWEG
TOEPFERSTRASSE
HALEMWEG
KURT-SCHUMACHER DAMM
KURT-SCHUMACHER DAMM
HECKERDAMM
REICHWEINDAMM
GRENZWEG
U7
ENDAMMALLEE
Siemens-
damm
POPITZWEG
Halemweg
Jakob-
Kaiser-Pl.
2
SIEMENSSTADT
WERNERWERKDAMM
SIEMENSDAMM
HELLMANNRING
JAKOB-
KAISER
-PLATZ
ROHRDAMM
Jungfern
-heide
Jungfern
-heide
Gustav-Adolf
Kirche
OLBERSSTRASSE
GAUSSSTRA
S4
CHARLOTTENBURG
BRAHE - STRASSE
KAMMINER
STR
KEPLERSTRASSE
LISE-MEITNER-STRASSE
OSNABRÜCKER
STRASSE
Maria-
Himmelfahrt
Kirche
MIERENDORFF
PLATZ
Sportplätze
Westend
TEGELER WEG
MINDENER STRASSE
Mierend
Kaiser-Wilhelm
Gedächtnis
Kirchhof
FÜRSTENBRUNNER WEG
Max-Bürger
Zentrum
Karpfen
-teich
MIERENDORFFSTR
NORDHA
STRA
E26
SOPHIE-CHARLOTTEN-STRASSE
HEUBNERWEG
SÖMMERINGSTRASSE
Luisenkirchhof III
QUEDLINBU
S4-45-46
Schloss-
garten
U7
3
Schloss
Charlottenburg
SCHLOSSBR.
CHARLOTTENBGR UFER
CAPRIVIBR.
Museum für Vor-
und Fruhgeschichte
EOSANDERSTR
WINTERSTEINSTR
SPANDAUER DAMM
DRK-Kliniken
Westend
Sammlung
Berggruen
Ägyptisches
Museum
AKAZIENALLEE
USSBAUMALLEE
SPANDAUER DAMM
OTTO-SUHR-ALLEE
KLAUSENER
PLATZ
NITHACK-
STRASSE
GIERKE
-PLATZ
WESTEND
Westend
Bröhan
Museum
KIRSCHENALLEE
EICHENALLEE
ULMENALLEE
BRANITZER
PLATZ
CHRIST - STRASSE
DANCKELMANNSTRASSE
SCHUSTEHRUS - STRASSE
BEHAIMSTR
Richa
Wagn
ESCHENALLEE
EBERESCHENALLEE
LINDENALLEE
SOOR STRASSE
page
304
KÖNINGIN-
ELISABETH-STRASSE
SOPHIE-CHARLOTTEN-STRASSE
SEELING - STRASSE
NEHRINGSTRASSE
SCHLOSSSTRASSE
HEBBELSTRASSE
KAISER - FRIEDRICH
STR
HAUBACHSTRASSE
WILMERSDORFER STR
RICHARD-WAGNER STR
PLATANENALLEE
KASTANIEN
-ALLEE
RÜSTERNALLEE
AHORNALLEE
Deuts
Op
Olympia
-stdion
ZILLE - STRASSE
SPIELHAGEN
-STRASSE
KNOBELSDORFFSTRASSE
HORSTWEG
FRITSCHESTR
Bismarck-
strasse
SHAKESP
PLAT

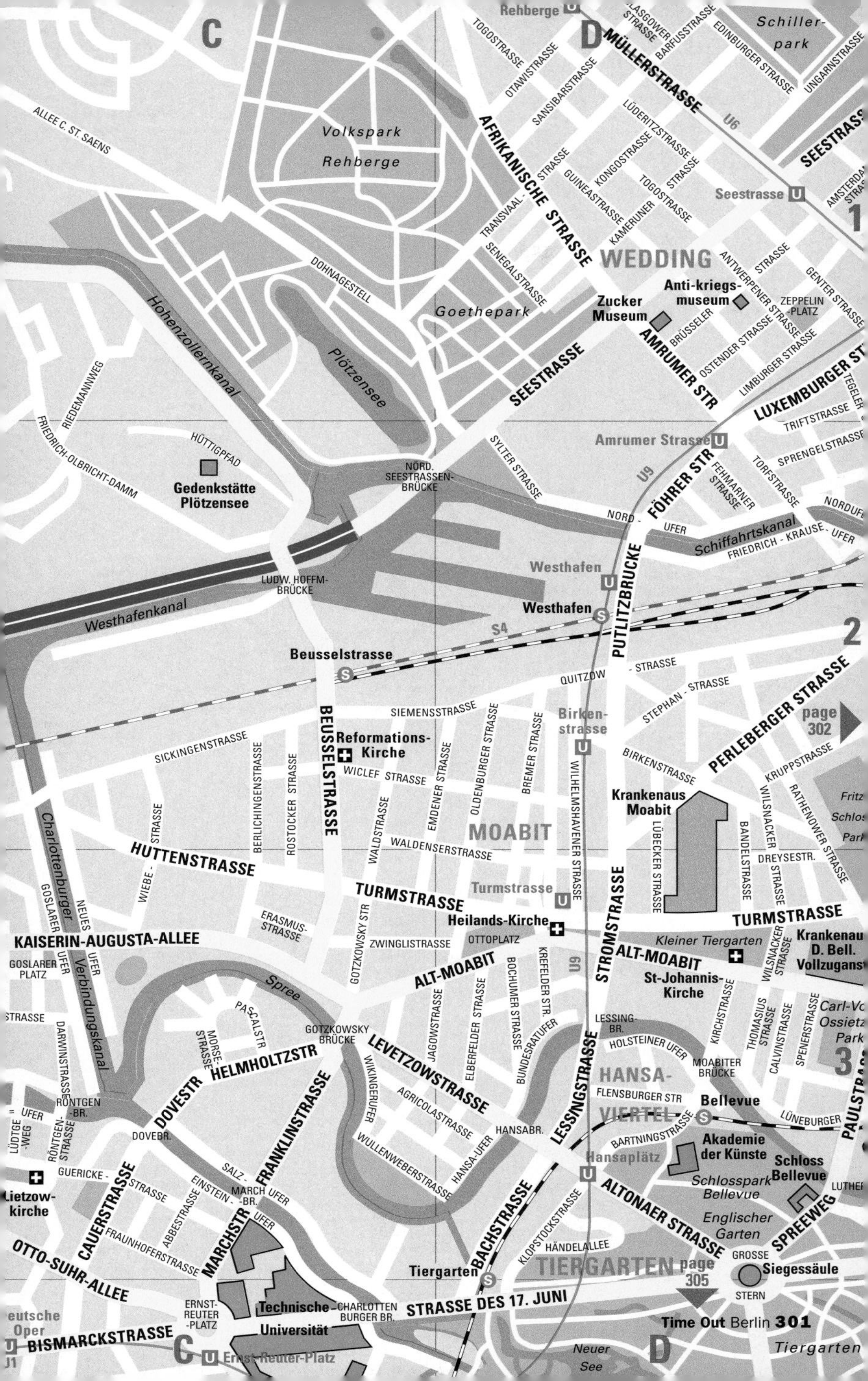
C
D
1
2
3
Rehberge
Volkspark
Rehberge
Schiller-
park
WEDDING
Seestrasse
Anti-kriegs-
museum
Zucker
Museum
Goethepark
Plötzensee
Hohenzollernkanal
Gedenkstätte
Plötzensee
Amrumer Strasse
Westhafen
Westhafenkanal
Schiffahrtskanal
Beusselstrasse
Reformations-
Kirche
Birken-
strasse
Krankenaus
Moabit
MOABIT
Turmstrasse
Heilands-Kirche
Kleiner Tiergarten
St-Johannis-
Kirche
Krankenau
D. Bell.
Vollzugans
Carl-Vo
Ossietz
Park
Fritz
Schlos
Park
Spree
HANSA-
VIERTEL
Bellevue
Akademie
der Künste
Schloss
Bellevue
Schlosspark
Bellevue
Englischer
Garten
Hansaplätz
Tiergarten
TIERGARTEN
Siegessäule
Technische
Universität
Ernst-Reuter-Platz
Lietzow-
kirche
eutsche
Oper
Neuer
See
Tiergarten
page
302
page
305
MÜLLERSTRASSE
SEESTRASSE
AFRIKANISCHE STRASSE
AMRUMER STR
LUXEMBURGER STR
FÖHRER STR
PUTLITZBRÜCKE
PERLEBERGER STRASSE
BEUSSELSTRASSE
HUTTENSTRASSE
TURMSTRASSE
KAISERIN-AUGUSTA-ALLEE
ALT-MOABIT
STROMSTRASSE
LESSINGSTRASSE
LEVETZOWSTRASSE
HELMHOLTZSTR
DOVESTR
FRANKLINSTRASSE
CAUERSTRASSE
MARCHSTR
OTTO-SUHR-ALLEE
BISMARCKSTRASSE
STRASSE DES 17. JUNI
BACHSTRASSE
ALTONAER STRASSE
SPREEWEG
PAULSTRASSE
U6
U9
S4

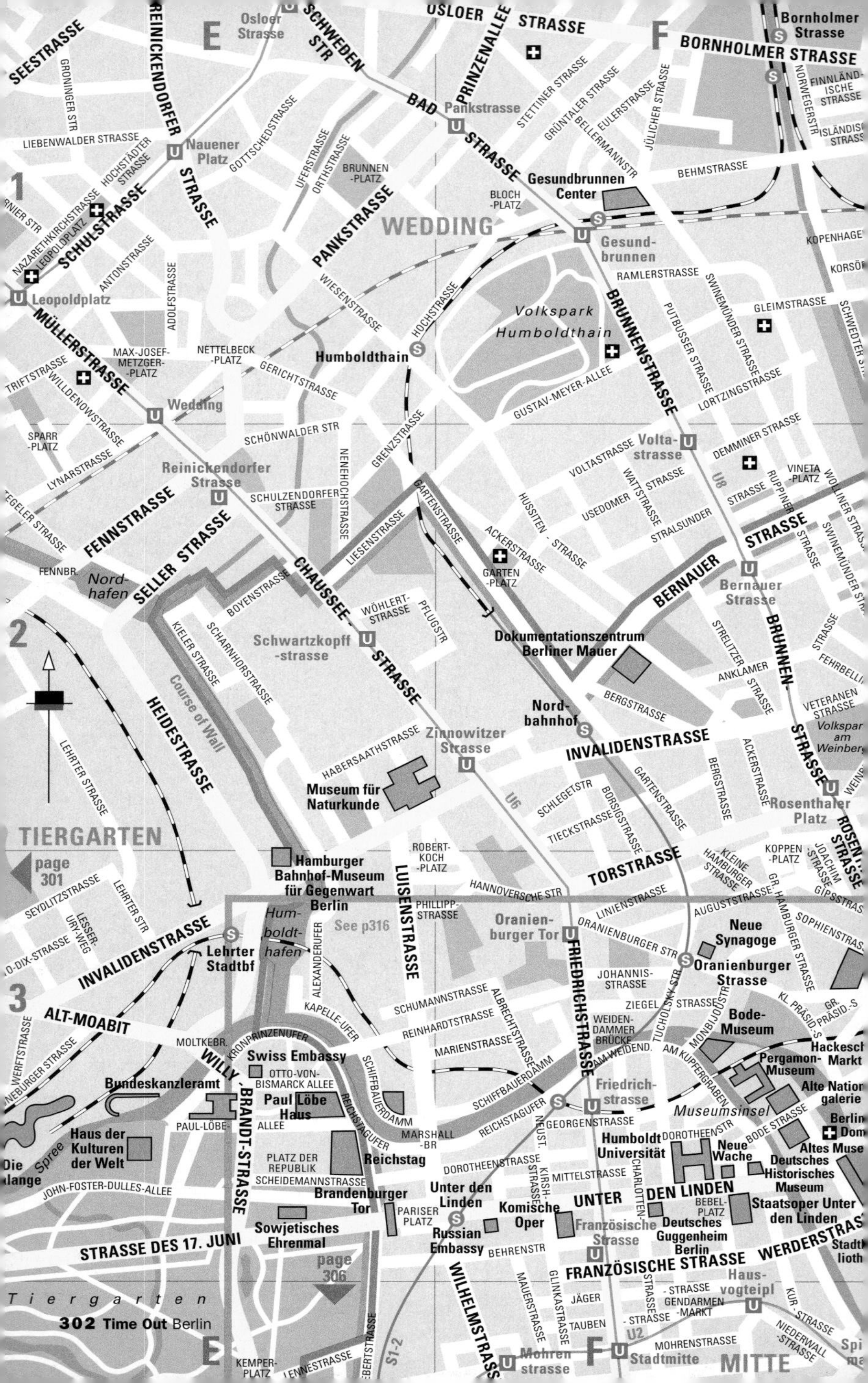
E
F
1
2
3
SEESTRASSE
REINICKENDORFER STRASSE
Osloer Strasse
SCHWEDEN STR
USLOER STRASSE
PRINZENALLEE
Bornholmer Strasse
BORNHOLMER STRASSE
FINNLÄNDISCHE STRASSE
NORWEGERSTR
ISLÄNDISCHE STRASSE
GRONINGER STR
LIEBENWALDER STRASSE
HOCHSTÄDTER STRASSE
Nauener Platz
GOTTSCHEDSTRASSE
BAD STRASSE
Pankstrasse
STETTINER STRASSE
GRÜNTALER STRASSE
BELLERMANNSTR
EULERSTRASSE
JÜLICHER STRASSE
BEHMSTRASSE
UFERSTRASSE
ORTHSTRASSE
BRUNNEN-PLATZ
PANKSTRASSE
BLOCH-PLATZ
Gesundbrunnen Center
NAZARETHKIRCHSTRASSE
LEOPOLDPLATZ
SCHULSTRASSE
ANTONSTRASSE
ADOLFSTRASSE
Leopoldplatz
WEDDING
Gesundbrunnen
KOPENHAGENER
KORSÖR
RAMLERSTRASSE
SCHWEDTER STR
MÜLLERSTRASSE
WIESENSTRASSE
HOCHSTRASSE
Volkspark Humboldthain
BRUNNENSTRASSE
PUTBUSSER STRASSE
SWINEMÜNDER STRASSE
GLEIMSTRASSE
MAX-JOSEF-METZGER-PLATZ
NETTELBECK-PLATZ
Humboldthain
GERICHTSTRASSE
TRIFTSTRASSE
WILDENOWSTRASSE
GUSTAV-MEYER-ALLEE
LORTZINGSTRASSE
Wedding
SPARR-PLATZ
SCHÖNWALDER STR
GRENZSTRASSE
Voltastrasse
DEMMINER STRASSE
LYNARSTRASSE
Reinickendorfer Strasse
NENEHOCHSTRASSE
VOLTASTRASSE
WATTSTRASSE
HUSSITENSTRASSE
USEDOMER STRASSE
U8
RUPPINER STRASSE
VINETA-PLATZ
WOLLINER STRASSE
SCHULZENDORFER STRASSE
GARTENSTRASSE
STRALSUNDER
TEGELER STRASSE
FENNSTRASSE
SELLER STRASSE
LIESENSTRASSE
ACKERSTRASSE
GARTEN-PLATZ
BERNAUER STRASSE
SWINEMÜNDER STRASSE
FENNBR.
Nordhafen
BOYENSTRASSE
CHAUSSEESTRASSE
WÖHLERTSTRASSE
PFLUGSTR
Bernauer Strasse
BRUNNENSTRASSE
Schwartzkopffstrasse
Dokumentationszentrum Berliner Mauer
KIELER STRASSE
SCHARNHORSTSTRASSE
Course of Wall
STRELITZER STRASSE
ANKLAMER
FEHRBELLINER
HEIDESTRASSE
BERGSTRASSE
VETERANENSTRASSE
Nordbahnhof
Volkspark am Weinberg
LEHRTER STRASSE
HABERSAATHSTRASSE
Zinnowitzer Strasse
INVALIDENSTRASSE
Museum für Naturkunde
U6
SCHLEGELSTR
BORSIGSTRASSE
GARTENSTRASSE
BERGSTRASSE
ACKERSTRASSE
WEINBERG
TIERGARTEN
TIECKSTRASSE
Rosenthaler Platz
ROSENTHALER STRASSE
page 301
ROBERT-KOCH-PLATZ
Hamburger Bahnhof-Museum für Gegenwart Berlin
LUISENSTRASSE
TORSTRASSE
KLEINE HAMBURGER STRASSE
KOPPEN-PLATZ
JOACHIMSTRASSE
SEYDLITZSTRASSE
LEHRTER STR
LESSER-URY-WEG
HANNOVERSCHE STR
PHILLIPPSTRASSE
LINIENSTRASSE
AUGUSTSTRASSE
GR. HAMBURGER STRASSE
GIPSSTRASSE
Humboldthafen
See p316
Oranienburger Tor
ORANIENBURGER STR
SOPHIENSTRASSE
OTTO-DIX-STRASSE
INVALIDENSTRASSE
Lehrter Stadtbf
ALEXANDERUFER
FRIEDRICHSTRASSE
Neue Synagoge
Oranienburger Strasse
JOHANNISSTRASSE
TUCHOLSKYSTR
ALT-MOABIT
SCHUMANNSTRASSE
ALBRECHTSTRASSE
ZIEGELSTRASSE
MONBIJOUSTR
KL. PRÄSIDENTENSTR
GR. PRÄSIDENTENSTR
KAPELLE-UFER
REINHARDTSTRASSE
Bode-Museum
WERFTSTRASSE
MOLTKEBR.
KRONPRINZENUFER
MARIENSTRASSE
WEIDENDAMMER BRÜCKE
AM WEIDEND.
AM KUPFERGRABEN
Hackescher Markt
Swiss Embassy
WILLY-BRANDT-STRASSE
OTTO-VON-BISMARCK ALLEE
SCHIFFBAUERDAMM
Pergamon-Museum
Alte Nationalgalerie
Bundeskanzleramt
Paul Löbe Haus
Friedrichstrasse
Museumsinsel
REICHSTAGUFER
GEORGENSTRASSE
PAUL-LÖBE-ALLEE
MARSHALL-BR
BODE STRASSE
Berliner Dom
Haus der Kulturen der Welt
Humboldt Universität
DOROTHEENSTR
Neue Wache
Altes Museum
Spree
Reichstag
PLATZ DER REPUBLIK
DOROTHEENSTRASSE
NEUST. KIRCHSTRASSE
MITTELSTRASSE
CHARLOTTENSTRASSE
Deutsches Historisches Museum
JOHN-FOSTER-DULLES-ALLEE
SCHEIDEMANNSTRASSE
Brandenburger Tor
Unter den Linden
Komische Oper
UNTER DEN LINDEN
BEBEL-PLATZ
Staatsoper Unter den Linden
PARISER PLATZ
Russian Embassy
Französische Strasse
Deutsches Guggenheim Berlin
Sowjetisches Ehrenmal
STRASSE DES 17. JUNI
BEHRENSTR
FRANZÖSISCHE STRASSE
WERDERSTRASSE
page 306
WILHELMSTRASSE
MAUERSTRASSE
GLINKASTRASSE
JÄGERSTRASSE
GENDARMENMARKT
Hausvogteiplatz
KURSTRASSE
Tiergarten
TAUBENSTRASSE
NIEDERWALLSTRASSE
S1-2
U2
MOHRENSTRASSE
KEMPER-PLATZ
LENNÉSTRASSE
EBERTSTRASSE
Mohrenstrasse
Stadtmitte
MITTE

G
H
1
2
3
IBSENSTRASSE
STAVANGER-STRASSE
ESCHENGRABEN
THULESTRASSE
NEUMANNSTRASSE
TALSTRASSE
PRENZLAUER PROM.
JACOBSOHNSTRASSE
PISTORIUSSTRASSE
BORNHOLMER STRASSE
SCHONENSCHE STRASSE
CHARLOTTENBURGER STRASSE
MIRBACH PLATZ
ZARNIKAUER STR
PAUL-ROBESON-STRASSE
WISBYER STRASSE
GUSTAV-ADOLF-STRASSE
GOETHESTRASSE
LANGHANSSTRASSE
MAX-STEIN
ARNIM -PLATZ
SEELOWER STRASSE
U2
KUGLERSTRASSE
ERICH-WEINERT STRASSE
RODENBERG-STRASSE
STREUSTRASSE
LEHDERSTRASSE
ROELCKESTRASSE
BEHAIMSTRASSE
DÄNENSTRASSE
SCHÖNHAUSER ALLEE
Schönhauser Allee
GUDVANGER STRASSE
KRÜGER STRASSE
HUMANN -PLATZ
STAHLHEIMER
WICHERTSTRASSE
PRENZLAUER ALLEE
SÜLTSTRASSE
OSTSEESTRASSE
SONNENBURGER STRASSE
GREIFENHAGENER STRASSE
Gethsemane -Kirche
S4-8-10
GUBITZSTRASSE
ERICH-WEINERT-STRASSE
HOSEMANN STRASSE
BERLINER ALLEE
GÜRTEL
GAUDYSTRASSE
CANTIANSTRASSE
MILA-STR
Max-Schmeling-Halle
STARGARDER STRASSE
Prenzlauer Allee
GREIFSWALDER STR
MICHELANGELOSTR
HANNS-EISLER-STRASSE
Friedrich-Ludwig Jahn Sportpark
PAPPELALLEE
LYCHENER STRASSE
HELMHOLTZ -PLATZ
GRELLSTRASSE
Stadium
TOPSSTRASSE
RAUMER-STR
DUNCKERSTRASSE
SENEFELDERSTRASSE
STUBBENKAMMERSTR
Zeiss-Grossplanetarium
EBERSWALDER STR
Eberswalder Strasse
FRÖBEL-STR
DIESTERWEGSTRASSE
ELLA-KAY-STRASSE
Greifswalder Strasse
Kulturbrauerei
HAGENAUER STRASSE
KNAACKSTR
DANZIGER STR
Ernst-Thälmann-Park
EINSTEINSTRASSE
STORKOWER STRASSE
ODERBERGER STRASSE
SREDZKISTRASSE
HUSEMANN STRASSE
PRENZLAUER BERG
Volkspark Anton-Saefkow
ANTON-SAEFKOW-STRASSE
KASTANIENALLEE
CHODOWIECKISTRASSE
JABLONSKISTRASSE
CHRISTBURGER STRASSE
WÖRTHER STRASSE
RYKESTR
KOLLWITZ -PLATZ
B.-LICHTENBERG-STR
KURISCHE STRASSE
BÖTZOWSTR
R.-SCHWARZ-STRASSE
KNIPRODESTRASSE
Jüdische Friedhof
Synagoge Rykestrasse
MARIENBURGER STRASSE
Wasserturm
DIETRICH-BONHOEFFER-STR
ARNSWALDER PLATZ
HANS-OTTO-STRASSE
CHORINER STRASSE
SCHWEDTER STRASSE
KOLLWITZSTRASSE
BELFORTER STR
IMMANUELKIRCHSTRASSE
Immanuel-Kirche
WINSSTRASSE
PASTEURSTRASSE
HUFELANDSTRASSE
L.-HERMANN-STRASSE
BÖTZOW-STRASSE
THORNER STRASSE
FÜRSTENBERGSTR
Senefelderplatz
TEUTOBURGER -PLATZ
METZER STRASSE
HEINR.ROLLER-STRASSE
KÄTHE-NIEDERKIRCHNER-STR
PAUL-HEYSE-STRASSE
DANZIGER STRASSE
CHRISTINENSTRASSE
SAARBRÜCKER STRASSE
GREIFSWALDER STRASSE
Friedhof
STRASSBURGER STRASSE
AM FRIEDRICHSHAIN
TORSTRASSE
Rosa-Luxemburg-Platz
ROSA-LUXEMBURG-PLATZ
Volksbühne
Volkspark Friedrichshain
BARNIMSTRASSE
WEINSTRASSE
BÜSCHINGSTRASSE
FRIEDENSTRASSE
LANDSBERGER ALLEE
WEYDINGER STRASSE
HIRTENSTRASSE
ALTE SCHÖNHAUSER STRASSE
MAX-BEER-STR
ALMSTADT-STR
WADZECKSTR
KEIBELSTRASSE
OTTO-BRAUN-STRASSE
MOLLSTRASSE
0
1 km
0
0.5 m
© Copyright Time Out Guides 2004
R.-LUXEMBURG-STR
MEMHARD-STR
U8
KARL-LIEBKNECHT-STRASSE
ROCHSTRASSE
Hackesche Höfe
ALEXANDER PLATZ
Alexanderplatz
BEROLINASTRASSE
Schillingstrasse
RICHARD SORGE-STR
PUFENDORFSTRASSE
See p88
Fernsehturm
GRUNERSTR
KARL-MARX-ALLEE
WEYDEMEYERSTRASSE
Marien-Kirche
RATHAUSSTRASSE
MITTE
JACOBYSTRASSE
PALISADENSTRASSE
FRIEDRICHSHAIN
AUERSTRASSE
SPANDAUER STRASSE
Berliner Rathaus
ALEXANDERSTRASSE
DIRCKSENSTRASSE
LITTENSTRASSE
MAGAZINSTRASSE
SCHILLINGSTRASSE
U5
BLUMENSTRASSE
Strausberger Pl
WELDENWEG
Klosterstrasse
Weberwiese
Nikolai-Viertel
Hanf Museum
Nikolaikirche
STRALAUER STR
LICHTENBERGER STRASSE
SINGERSTRASSE
H.-JADAMOWITZ-STRASSE
MÜHLENDAMM
ROLANDUFER
Spree
Jannowitzbr
HOLZMARKT
page 307
ANDREASSTRASSE
STRASSE DER PARISER KOMMUNE
MARCHLEWSKISTR
FREDERSDORFER STR
GUBENER STRASSE
Fischerinsel
FISCHERINSEL
Märkisches Museum
Märkisches Museum
JANNOWITZBR.
BRÜCKENSTR
RUNGESTR
G
H

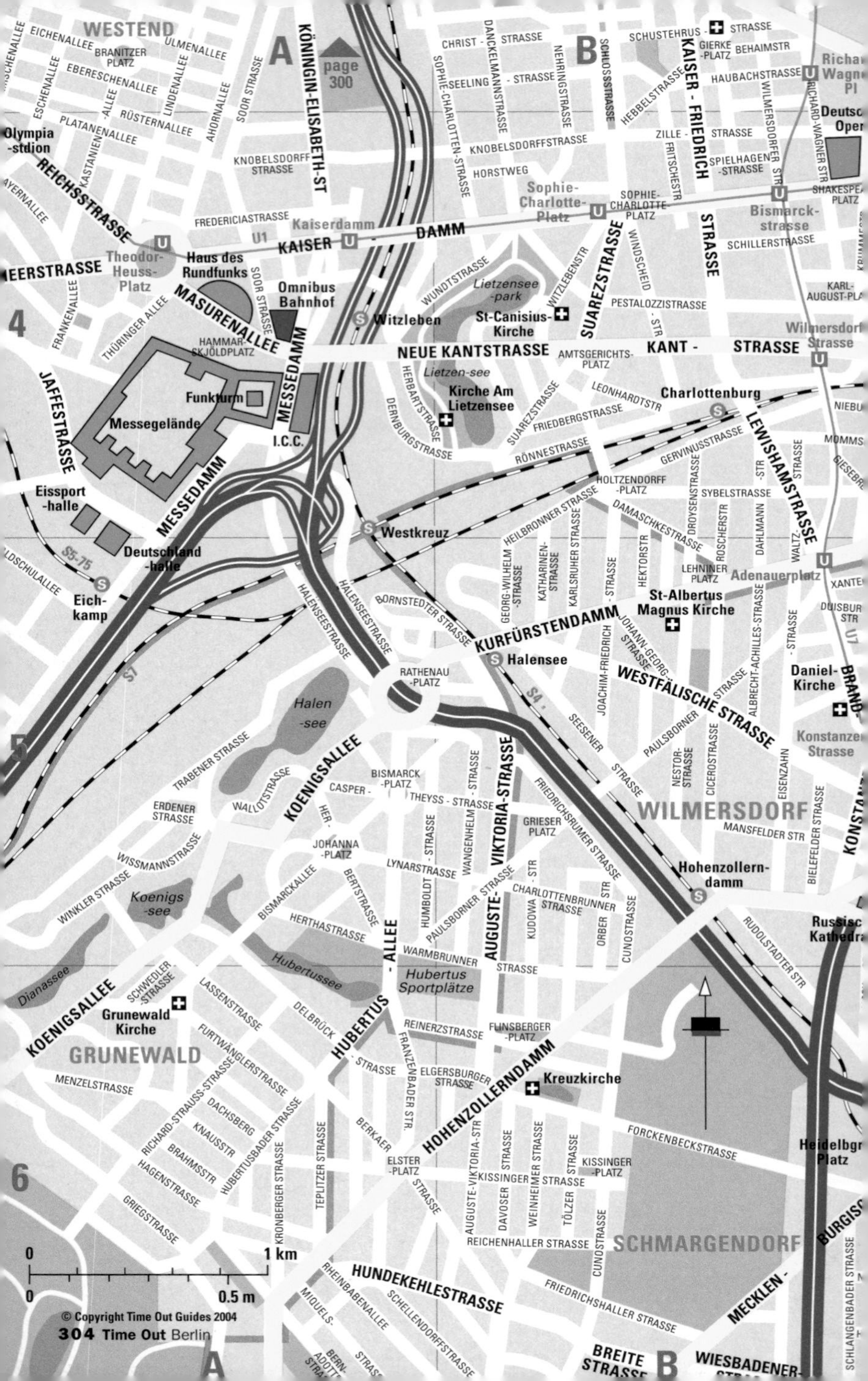
WESTEND
A
B
page 300
4
5
6
EICHENALLEE
BRANITZER PLATZ
ULMENALLEE
EBERESCHENALLEE
ESCHENALLEE
LINDENALLEE
RÜSTERNALLEE
PLATANENALLEE
AHORNALLEE
SOOR STRASSE
Olympia -stdion
KASTANIENALLEE
REICHSSTRASSE
KNOBELSDORFF STRASSE
KÖNINGIN-ELISABETH-ST
FREDERICIASTRASSE
Kaiserdamm
U1
KAISER DAMM
Theodor-Heuss-Platz
Haus des Rundfunks
HEERSTRASSE
Omnibus Bahnhof
MASURENALLEE
FRANKENALLEE
THÜRINGER ALLEE
HAMMARSKJÖLDPLATZ
JAFFESTRASSE
Funkturm
Messegelände
MESSEDAMM
I.C.C.
Eissport -halle
Deutschland -halle
S5-75
Eichkamp
S7
CHRIST - STRASSE
DANCKELMANNSTRASSE
SOPHIE-CHARLOTTEN-STRASSE
SEELING - STRASSE
NEHRINGSTRASSE
SCHLOSSSTRASSE
KNOBELSDORFFSTRASSE
HORSTWEG
Sophie-Charlotte-Platz
SOPHIE-CHARLOTTE-PLATZ
SCHUSTEHRUS - STRASSE
GIERKE -PLATZ
BEHAIMSTR
HEBBELSTRASSE
KAISER - FRIEDRICH STRASSE
HAUBACHSTRASSE
ZILLE - STRASSE
FRITSCHESTR
SPIELHAGEN -STRASSE
WILMERSDORFER STR
RICHARD-WAGNER STR
Richard-Wagner Pl
Deutsche Oper
SHAKESPEARE PLATZ
Bismarck-strasse
SCHILLERSTRASSE
KARL-AUGUST-PLATZ
WUNDTSTRASSE
Lietzensee -park
WITZLEBENSTR
SUAREZSTRASSE
WINDSCHEID STR
PESTALOZZISTRASSE
Witzleben
St-Canisius-Kirche
NEUE KANTSTRASSE
AMTSGERICHTS-PLATZ
KANT - STRASSE
Wilmersdorfer Strasse
Lietzen-see
HERBARTSTRASSE
Kirche Am Lietzensee
DERNBURGSTRASSE
LEONHARDTSTR
FRIEDBERGSTRASSE
SUAREZSTRASSE
Charlottenburg
LEWISHAMSTRASSE
RÖNNESTRASSE
GERVINUSSTRASSE
HOLTZENDORFF -PLATZ
SYBELSTRASSE
DROYSENSTRASSE
DAHLMANN -STR
WALTZ-STRASSE
NIEBUHR
MOMMSEN
GIESEBRECHT
HEILBRONNER STRASSE
DAMASCHKESTRASSE
Westkreuz
GEORG-WILHELM -STRASSE
KATHARINEN-STRASSE
KARLSRUHER STRASSE
HEKTORSTR
ROSCHERSTR
LEHNINER PLATZ
Adenauerplatz
XANTENER
DUISBURGER STR
U7
HALENSEESTRASSE
BORNSTEDTER STRASSE
KURFÜRSTENDAMM
St-Albertus Magnus Kirche
Halensee
JOHANN-GEORG-STRASSE
JOACHIM-FRIEDRICH-STRASSE
WESTFÄLISCHE STRASSE
ALBRECHT-ACHILLES-STRASSE
Daniel-Kirche
BRANDENBURGISCHE
RATHENAU -PLATZ
S4
SEESENER STRASSE
PAULSBORNER STRASSE
Konstanzer Strasse
Halen -see
TRABENER STRASSE
KOENIGSALLEE
BISMARCK -PLATZ
CASPER - THEYSS - STRASSE
WANGENHELM - STRASSE
VIKTORIA-STRASSE
FRIEDRICHSRUHER STRASSE
NESTOR-STRASSE
CICEROSTRASSE
EISENZAHN
WILMERSDORF
KONSTANZER
ERDENER STRASSE
WALLOTSTRASSE
HER-
JOHANNA -PLATZ
HUMBOLDT - STRASSE
GRIESER PLATZ
MANSFELDER STR
BIELEFELDER STRASSE
WISSMANNSTRASSE
LYNARSTRASSE
BERTSTRASSE
PAULSBORNER STRASSE
AUGUSTE-
KUDOWA - STR
ORBER STR
CHARLOTTENBRUNNER STRASSE
CUNOSTRASSE
Hohenzollern-damm
WINKLER STRASSE
Koenigs -see
BISMARCKALLEE
HERTHASTRASSE
HUBERTUS - ALLEE
WARMBRUNNER STRASSE
RUDOLSTADTER STR
Russische Kathedrale
Dianassee
Hubertussee
Hubertus Sportplätze
KOENIGSALLEE
SCHWEDLER-STRASSE
LASSENSTRASSE
DELBRÜCK STRASSE
REINERZSTRASSE
FLINSBERGER -PLATZ
Grunewald Kirche
FURTWÄNGLERSTRASSE
FRANZENSBADER STR.
HOHENZOLLERNDAMM
GRUNEWALD
ELGERSBURGER STRASSE
Kreuzkirche
MENZELSTRASSE
RICHARD-STRAUSS-STRASSE
DACHSBERG
HUBERTUSBADER STRASSE
BERKAER STRASSE
FORCKENBECKSTRASSE
Heidelberger Platz
KNAUSSTR
BRAHMSSTR
HAGENSTRASSE
KRONBERGER STRASSE
TEPLITZER STRASSE
ELSTER -PLATZ
AUGUSTE-VIKTORIA-STR
DAVOSER STRASSE
WEINHEIMER STRASSE
KISSINGER STRASSE
TÖLZER STRASSE
KISSINGER -PLATZ
GRIEGSTRASSE
CUNOSTRASSE
REICHENHALLER STRASSE
SCHMARGENDORF
BURGGRAFEN
0
1 km
0
0.5 m
RHEINBABENALLEE
HUNDEKEHLESTRASSE
SCHELLENDORFFSTRASSE
FRIEDRICHSHALLER STRASSE
MECKLEN-
SCHLANGENBADER STRASSE
MIQUELS-
BERN-ADOTTE-STR
BREITE STRASSE
WIESBADENER-

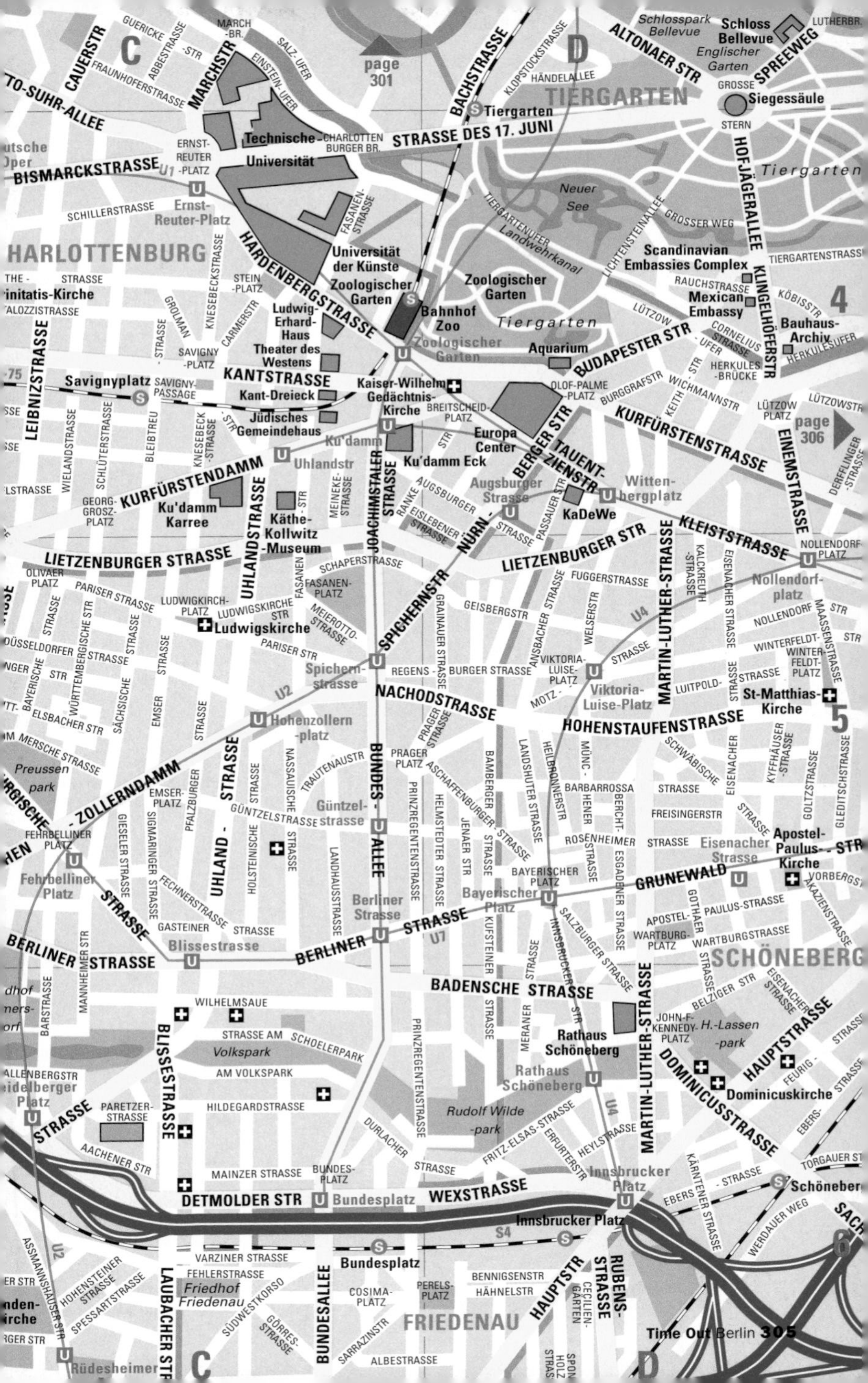
C
D
page 301
page 306
4
5
6
Schlosspark Bellevue
Schloss Bellevue
Englischer Garten
LUTHERBR.
ALTONAER STR
SPREEWEG
TIERGARTEN
GROSSE STERN
Siegessäule
HÄNDELALLEE
KLOPSTOCKSTRASSE
BACHSTRASSE
Tiergarten
STRASSE DES 17. JUNI
CHARLOTTEN BURGER BR.
MARCH -BR.
GUERICKE
ABBESTRASSE
SALZ-UFER
EINSTEIN-UFER
CAUERSTR
FRAUNHOFERSTRASSE
MARCHSTR
OTTO-SUHR-ALLEE
ERNST-REUTER-PLATZ
Technische Universität
BISMARCKSTRASSE
U1
Ernst-Reuter-Platz
SCHILLERSTRASSE
FASANENSTRASSE
HARDENBERGSTRASSE
CHARLOTTENBURG
Universität der Künste
Zoologischer Garten
Bahnhof Zoo
Zoologischer Garten
Neuer See
TIERGARTENUFER
Landwehrkanal
LICHTENSTEINALLEE
GROSSER WEG
HOFJÄGERALLEE
Tiergarten
TIERGARTENSTRASSE
Scandinavian Embassies Complex
RAUCHSTRASSE
Mexican Embassy
KÖBISSTR
KLINGELHÖFERSTR
Bauhaus-Archiv
HERKULESUFER
LÜTZOW
CORNELIUSSTRASSE
-UFER
HERKULES-BRÜCKE
Aquarium
BUDAPESTER STR
OLOF-PALME-PLATZ
BURGGRAFSTR
WICHMANNSTR
LÜTZOWPLATZ
LÜTZOWSTR
KURFÜRSTENSTRASSE
EINEMSTRASSE
DERFFLINGERSTRASSE
KEITHSTR
TAUENTZIENSTR
NÜRNBERGER STR
Europa Center
Kaiser-Wilhelm Gedächtnis-Kirche
BREITSCHEID-PLATZ
Ku'damm
Ku'damm Eck
Uhlandstr
KURFÜRSTENDAMM
Ku'damm Karree
Käthe-Kollwitz-Museum
STEIN-PLATZ
KNESEBECKSTRASSE
CARMERSTR
GROLMANSTRASSE
SAVIGNY-PLATZ
Ludwig-Erhard-Haus
Theater des Westens
KANTSTRASSE
Kant-Dreieck
Jüdisches Gemeindehaus
Savignyplatz
SAVIGNY-PASSAGE
LEIBNIZSTRASSE
WIELANDSTRASSE
SCHLÜTERSTRASSE
BLEIBTREU
KNESEBECKSTRASSE
GEORG-GROSZ-PLATZ
UHLANDSTRASSE
MEINEKESTRASSE
JOACHIMSTALER STRASSE
RANKE
AUGSBURGER
EISLEBENER STRASSE
Augsburger Strasse
Witten-bergplatz
KaDeWe
PASSAUER STR
KLEISTSTRASSE
NOLLENDORF-PLATZ
LIETZENBURGER STRASSE
LIETZENBURGER STR
OLIVAER PLATZ
SCHAPERSTRASSE
FASANEN-PLATZ
PARISER STRASSE
LUDWIGKIRCH-PLATZ
LUDWIGSKIRCHSTR
Ludwigskirche
MEIEROTTOSTRASSE
SPICHERNSTR
GRAINAUER STRASSE
GEISBERGSTR
FUGGERSTRASSE
ANSBACHER STRASSE
WELSERSTR
MARTIN-LUTHER-STRASSE
KALCKREUTH-STRASSE
EISENACHER STRASSE
Nollendorf-platz
NOLLENDORF STR
MAASSENSTRASSE
U4
DÜSSELDORFER STRASSE
PARISER STR
Spichern-strasse
REGENSBURGER STRASSE
VIKTORIA-LUISE-PLATZ
Viktoria-Luise-Platz
LUITPOLD-STRASSE
WINTERFELDT-STRASSE
WINTERFELDT-PLATZ
St-Matthias-Kirche
NACHODSTRASSE
MOTZ-
HOHENSTAUFENSTRASSE
U2
Hohenzollern-platz
BAYERISCHE STR
WÜRTTEMBERGISCHE STR
SÄCHSISCHE
EMSER
ELSBACHER STR
Preussen park
HOHENZOLLERNDAMM
EMSER-PLATZ
PFALZBURGER
UHLANDSTRASSE
NASSAUISCHE STRASSE
TRAUTENAUSTR
BUNDESALLEE
PRAGER PLATZ
PRAGER STRASSE
ASCHAFFENBURGER STRASSE
BAMBERGER STRASSE
LANDSHUTER STRASSE
HEILBRONNERSTR
MÜNCHENER STRASSE
BARBAROSSA STRASSE
SCHWÄBISCHE STRASSE
KYFFHÄUSERSTRASSE
GOLTZSTRASSE
GLEDITSCHSTRASSE
Güntzel-strasse
GÜNTZELSTRASSE
HOLSTEINISCHE STRASSE
LANDHAUSSTRASSE
PRINZREGENTENSTRASSE
HELMSTEDTER STRASSE
JENAER STR
FREISINGERSTR
ROSENHEIMER STRASSE
BERCHTESGADENER STRASSE
Eisenacher Strasse
Apostel-Paulus-Kirche
VORBERGSTR
AKAZIENSTRASSE
FEHRBELLINER PLATZ
Fehrbelliner Platz
GIESELER STRASSE
SIGMARINGER STRASSE
FECHNERSTRASSE
BAYERISCHER PLATZ
Bayerischer Platz
GRUNEWALD STRASSE
Berliner Strasse
BERLINER STRASSE
U7
KUFSTEINER STRASSE
SALZBURGER STRASSE
INNSBRUCKER STR
APOSTEL-PAULUS-STRASSE
WARTBURG-PLATZ
WARTBURGSTRASSE
GOTHAER STRASSE
SCHÖNEBERG
GASTEINER STRASSE
Blissestrasse
BERLINER STRASSE
MANNHEIMER STR
BARSTRASSE
BADENSCHE STRASSE
MERANER STRASSE
EISENACHER STRASSE
BELZIGER STR
JOHN-F-KENNEDY-PLATZ
H.-Lassen-park
HAUPTSTRASSE
WILHELMSAUE
STRASSE AM SCHOELERPARK
Volkspark
AM VOLKSPARK
Rathaus Schöneberg
Rathaus Schöneberg
DOMINICUSSTRASSE
Dominicuskirche
FEURIGSTRASSE
EBERSSTRASSE
BLISSESTRASSE
HILDEGARDSTRASSE
PARETZER-STRASSE
Rudolf Wilde -park
DURLACHER STRASSE
FRITZ-ELSAS-STRASSE
ERFURTERSTR
HEYLSTRASSE
MARTIN-LUTHER-STRASSE
KÄRNTENER STRASSE
TORGAUER ST
AACHENER STR
MAINZER STRASSE
BUNDES-PLATZ
Innsbrucker Platz
Schöneberg
EBERS-STRASSE
WERDAUER WEG
DETMOLDER STR
Bundesplatz
WEXSTRASSE
Innsbrucker Platz
S4
VARZINER STRASSE
FEHLERSTRASSE
Friedhof Friedenau
Bundesplatz
BENNIGSENSTR
HÄHNELSTR
HAUPTSTR
RUBENSSTRASSE
CECILIENGARTEN
ASSMANNSHAUSER STR
HOHENSTEINER STRASSE
SPESSARTSTRASSE
LAUBACHER STR
SÜDWESTKORSO
GÖRRESSTRASSE
BUNDESALLEE
COSIMA-PLATZ
PERELS-PLATZ
SARRAZINSTR
FRIEDENAU
ALBESTRASSE
Rüdesheimer

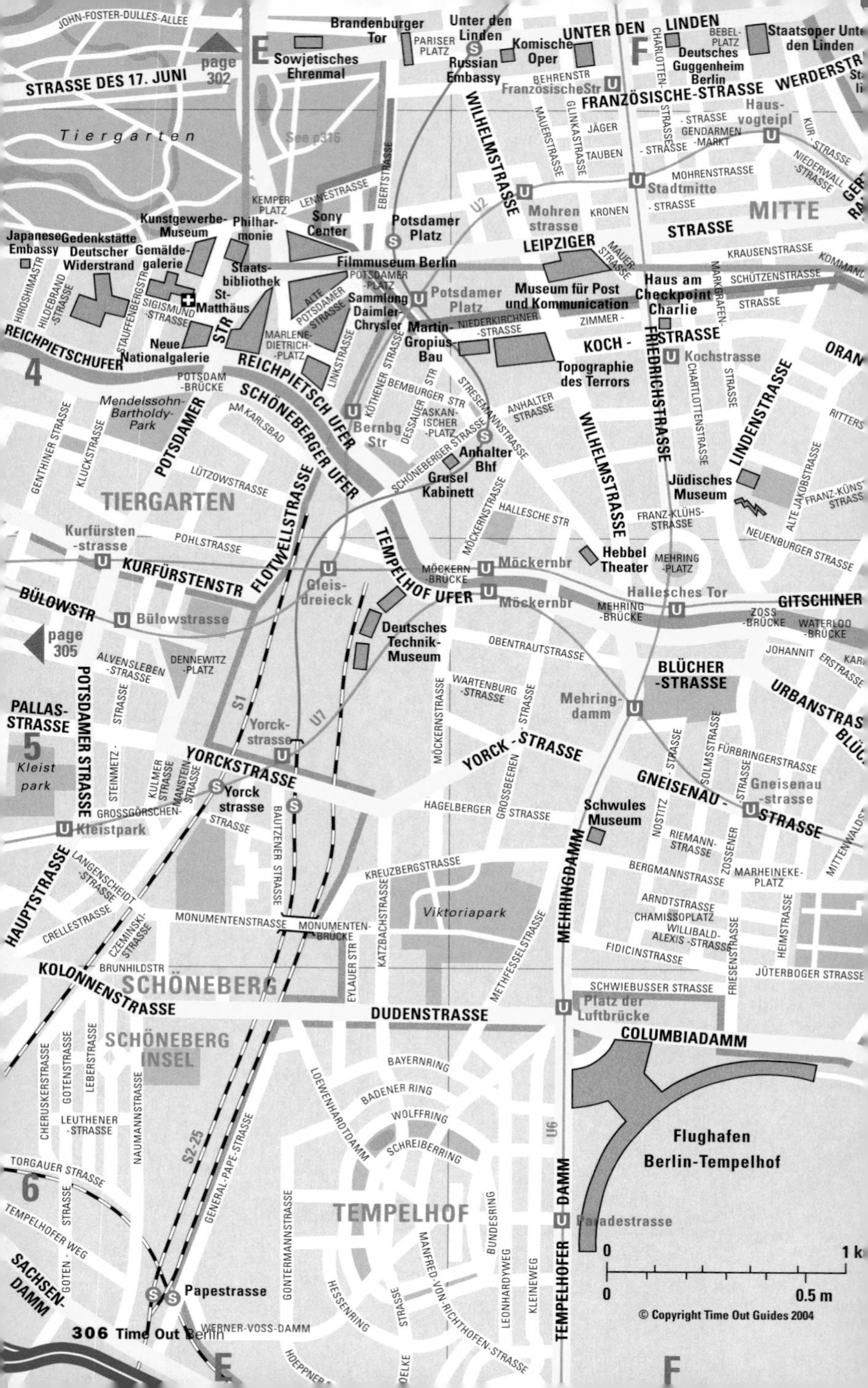

JOHN-FOSTER-DULLES-ALLEE
page 302
E
F
STRASSE DES 17. JUNI
Tiergarten
Brandenburger Tor
Sowjetisches Ehrenmal
PARISER PLATZ
Unter den Linden
Russian Embassy
Komische Oper
UNTER DEN LINDEN
BEBEL-PLATZ
Staatsoper Unter den Linden
Deutsches Guggenheim Berlin
CHARLOTTEN-STRASSE
BEHRENSTR
Französische Str
FRANZÖSISCHE-STRASSE
WERDERSTR
Hausvogteiplatz
GENDARMEN-MARKT
JÄGER-STRASSE
TAUBEN-STRASSE
MAUERSTRASSE
GLINKASTRASSE
WILHELMSTRASSE
KUR-STRASSE
NIEDERWALL-STRASSE
MOHRENSTRASSE
Stadtmitte
Mohrenstrasse
KRONEN-STRASSE
MITTE
See p316
EBERTSTRASSE
KEMPER-PLATZ
LENNESTRASSE
U2
Kunstgewerbe-Museum
Philharmonie
Sony Center
Potsdamer Platz
LEIPZIGER STRASSE
MAUER-STRASSE
KRAUSENSTRASSE
KOMMANDANTENSTRASSE
Japanese Embassy
Gedenkstätte Deutscher Widerstand
Gemäldegalerie
Staatsbibliothek
Filmmuseum Berlin
POTSDAMER PLATZ
Museum für Post und Kommunication
Haus am Checkpoint Charlie
SCHÜTZENSTRASSE
MARKGRAFEN-STRASSE
HIROSHIMASTR
HILDEBRANDSTRASSE
STAUFFENBERGSTR
SIGISMUNDSTRASSE
St-Matthäus
ALTE POTSDAMER STRASSE
Sammlung Daimler-Chrysler
Potsdamer Platz
NIEDERKIRCHNERSTRASSE
ZIMMERSTRASSE
KOCH-STRASSE
FRIEDRICHSTRASSE
REICHPIETSCHUFER
Neue Nationalgalerie
STR
MARLENE-DIETRICH-PLATZ
LINKSTRASSE
Martin-Gropius-Bau
Topographie des Terrors
Kochstrasse
ORANIENSTRASSE
4
POTSDAM BRÜCKE
REICHPIETSCH UFER
KÖTHENER STRASSE
BEMBURGER STR
STRESEMANNSTRASSE
CHARLOTTENSTRASSE
LINDENSTRASSE
RITTERSTRASSE
Mendelssohn-Bartholdy-Park
POTSDAMER
AM KARLSBAD
SCHÖNEBERGER UFER
Bernbg Str
DESSAUER STR
ASKANISCHER PLATZ
ANHALTER STRASSE
Anhalter Bhf
GENTHINER STRASSE
KLUCKSTRASSE
LÜTZOWSTRASSE
FLOTWELLSTRASSE
SCHÖNEBERGER STRASSE
Grusel Kabinett
Jüdisches Museum
ALTE JAKOBSTRASSE
FRANZ-KÜNSTLER-STRASSE
TIERGARTEN
MÖCKERNSTRASSE
HALLESCHE STR
FRANZ-KLÜHS-STRASSE
Kurfürstenstrasse
POHLSTRASSE
TEMPELHOF UFER
NEUENBURGER STRASSE
KURFÜRSTENSTR
Gleisdreieck
MÖCKERN-BRÜCKE
Möckernbr
Hebbel Theater
MEHRING-PLATZ
BÜLOWSTR
Bülowstrasse
Hallesches Tor
GITSCHINER
MEHRING-BRÜCKE
ZOSS-BRÜCKE
WATERLOO-BRÜCKE
page 305
Deutsches Technik-Museum
OBENTRAUTSTRASSE
JOHANNITERSTRASSE
ALVENSLEBEN-STRASSE
DENNEWITZ-PLATZ
BLÜCHER-STRASSE
URBANSTRASSE
POTSDAMER STRASSE
WARTENBURG-STRASSE
Mehringdamm
PALLAS-STRASSE
S1
Yorckstrasse
U7
5
Kleist park
STEINMETZ-STRASSE
KULMER STRASSE
MANSTEIN-STRASSE
YORCKSTRASSE
YORCK-STRASSE
GROSSBEEREN STRASSE
FÜRBRINGERSTRASSE
SOLMSSTRASSE
GNEISENAU-STRASSE
Gneisenaustrasse
Yorck strasse
GROSSGÖRSCHEN-STRASSE
HAGELBERGER STRASSE
Schwules Museum
NOSTITZ STRASSE
Kleistpark
BAUTZENER STRASSE
RIEMANN-STRASSE
ZOSSENER STRASSE
MITTENWALDER
HAUPTSTRASSE
LANGENSCHEIDT-STRASSE
KREUZBERGSTRASSE
MEHRINGDAMM
BERGMANNSTRASSE
MARHEINEKE-PLATZ
CRELLESTRASSE
CZEMINSKI-STRASSE
MONUMENTENSTRASSE
MONUMENTEN-BRÜCKE
KATZBACHSTRASSE
Viktoriapark
ARNDTSTRASSE
CHAMISSOPLATZ
WILLIBALD-ALEXIS-STRASSE
METHFESSELSTRASSE
FIDICINSTRASSE
HEIMSTRASSE
FRIESENSTRASSE
BRUNHILDSTR
KOLONNENSTRASSE
SCHÖNEBERG
EYLAUER STR
JÜTERBOGER STRASSE
SCHWIEBUSSER STRASSE
DUDENSTRASSE
Platz der Luftbrücke
COLUMBIADAMM
SCHÖNEBERG INSEL
CHERUSKERSTRASSE
GOTENSTRASSE
LEBERSTRASSE
BAYERNRING
BADENER RING
WOLFFRING
SCHREIBERRING
LOEWENHARDTDAMM
LEUTHENER-STRASSE
NAUMANNSTRASSE
S2-25
GENERAL-PAPE-STRASSE
U6
Flughafen Berlin-Tempelhof
TORGAUER STRASSE
6
TEMPELHOFER WEG
TEMPELHOF
GONTERMANNSTRASSE
BUNDESRING
TEMPELHOFER DAMM
Paradestrasse
0
1 km
0.5 m
SACHSENDAMM
GOTENSTRASSE
Papestrasse
HESSENRING
MANFRED-VON-RICHTHOFEN-STRASSE
LEONHARDYWEG
KLEINEWEG
WERNER-VOSS-DAMM
HOEPPNERSTRASSE
© Copyright Time Out Guides 2004

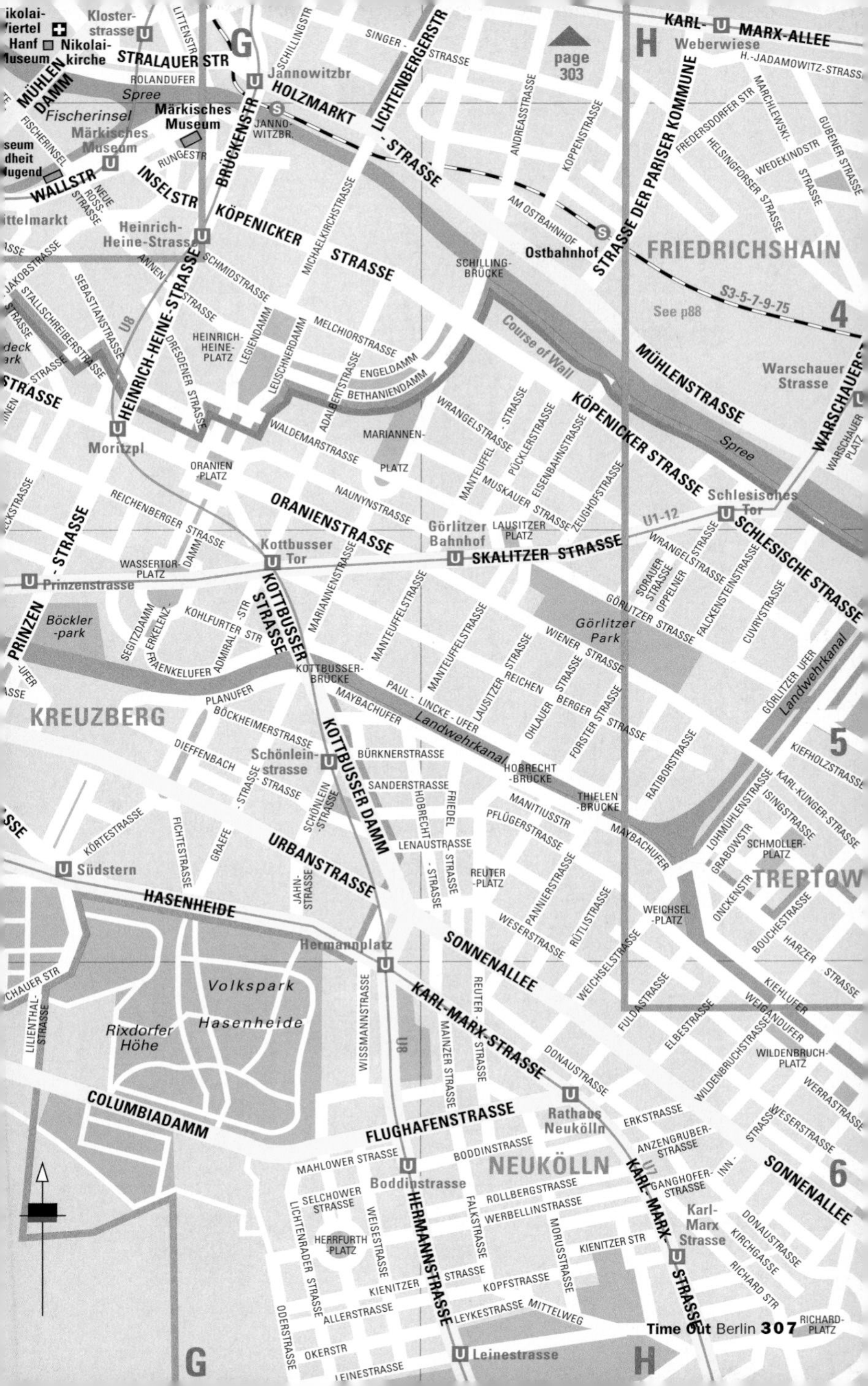

G
H
4
5
6
page 303
See p88
FRIEDRICHSHAIN
KREUZBERG
NEUKÖLLN
TREPTOW
Nikolai-Viertel
Hanf
Nikolai-Museum
Nikolaikirche
Klosterstrasse
Mühlendamm
Stralauer Str
Rolandufer
Spree
Fischerinsel
Märkisches Museum
Wallstr
Neue Ross-Strasse
Rungestr
Inselstr
Brückenstr
Jannowitzbr
Holzmarkt-Strasse
Lichtenbergerstr
Schillingstr
Littenstr
Singer-Strasse
Karl-Marx-Allee
Weberwiese
H.-Jadamowitz-Strasse
Andreasstrasse
Koppenstrasse
Strasse der Pariser Kommune
Fredersdorfer Str
Marchlewskistr
Wedekindstr
Helsingforser Strasse
Gubener Strasse
Am Ostbahnhof
Ostbahnhof
S3-5-7-9-75
Heinrich-Heine-Strasse
Köpenicker Strasse
Michaelkirchstrasse
Schillingbrücke
Course of Wall
Mühlenstrasse
Warschauer Strasse
Schmidstrasse
Annenstrasse
Jakobstrasse
Sebastianstrasse
Stallschreiberstrasse
Heinrich-Heine-Platz
Legiendamm
Leuschnerdamm
Dresdener Strasse
Melchiorstrasse
Engeldamm
Bethaniendamm
Adalbertstrasse
Waldemarstrasse
Mariannenplatz
Wrangelstrasse
Manteuffelstrasse
Pücklerstrasse
Eisenbahnstrasse
Muskauer Strasse
Zeughofstrasse
Moritzpl
U8
Oranienplatz
Reichenberger Strasse
Naunynstrasse
Oranienstrasse
Görlitzer Bahnhof
Lausitzer Platz
Schlesisches Tor
U1-12
Schlesische Strasse
Kottbusser Tor
Skalitzer Strasse
Wassertorplatz
Prinzenstrasse
Prinzen-Strasse
Böckler-park
Segitzdamm
Erkelenzdamm
Kohlfurter Str
Admiralstr
Fraenkelufer
Kottbusser Strasse
Mariannenstrasse
Manteuffelstrasse
Görlitzer Park
Görlitzer Strasse
Wiener Strasse
Sorauer Strasse
Oppelner Strasse
Falckensteinstrasse
Cuvrystrasse
Görlitzer Ufer
Landwehrkanal
Kottbusser-brücke
Planufer
Maybachufer
Paul-Lincke-Ufer
Lausitzer Strasse
Reichenberger Strasse
Ohlauer Strasse
Forster Strasse
Böckheimerstrasse
Dieffenbachstrasse
Schönleinstrasse
Kottbusser Damm
Bürknerstrasse
Sanderstrasse
Hobrechtbrücke
Thielenbrücke
Ratiborstrasse
Kiefholzstrasse
Karl-Kunger-Strasse
Lohmühlenstrasse
Isingstrasse
Grabowstr
Schmoller-Platz
Manitiusstr
Pflügerstrasse
Hobrechtstrasse
Friedelstrasse
Lenaustrasse
Reuterplatz
Pannierstrasse
Rütlistrasse
Weichselplatz
Onckenstr
Bouchestrasse
Harzer Strasse
Körtestrasse
Fichtestrasse
Graefestrasse
Urbanstrasse
Jahnstrasse
Südstern
Hasenheide
Hermannplatz
Sonnenallee
Weserstrasse
Weichselstrasse
Fuldastrasse
Elbestrasse
Kiehlufer
Weigandufer
Wildenbruchstrasse
Wildenbruchplatz
Werrastrasse
Volkspark Hasenheide
Rixdorfer Höhe
Wissmannstrasse
Karl-Marx-Strasse
Reuterstrasse
Mainzer Strasse
Donaustrasse
Rathaus Neukölln
Erkstrasse
Anzengruberstrasse
Columbiadamm
Flughafenstrasse
Boddinstrasse
Mahlower Strasse
Boddinstrasse
Selchower Strasse
Lichtenrader Strasse
Herrfurthplatz
Weisestrasse
Hermannstrasse
Falkstrasse
Rollbergstrasse
Werbellinstrasse
Morusstrasse
Kienitzer Str
Kienitzer Strasse
Kopfstrasse
Allerstrasse
Leykestrasse
Mittelweg
Oderstrasse
Okerstr
Leinestrasse
Leinestrasse
Ganghofer-Strasse
Innstrasse
Karl-Marx-Strasse
Karl-Marx-Strasse
U7
Donaustrasse
Kirchgasse
Richard Str
Richardplatz
Weserstrasse
Sonnenallee
Lilienthalstrasse
Kreuzberg

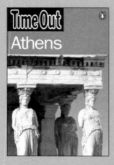

Street Index

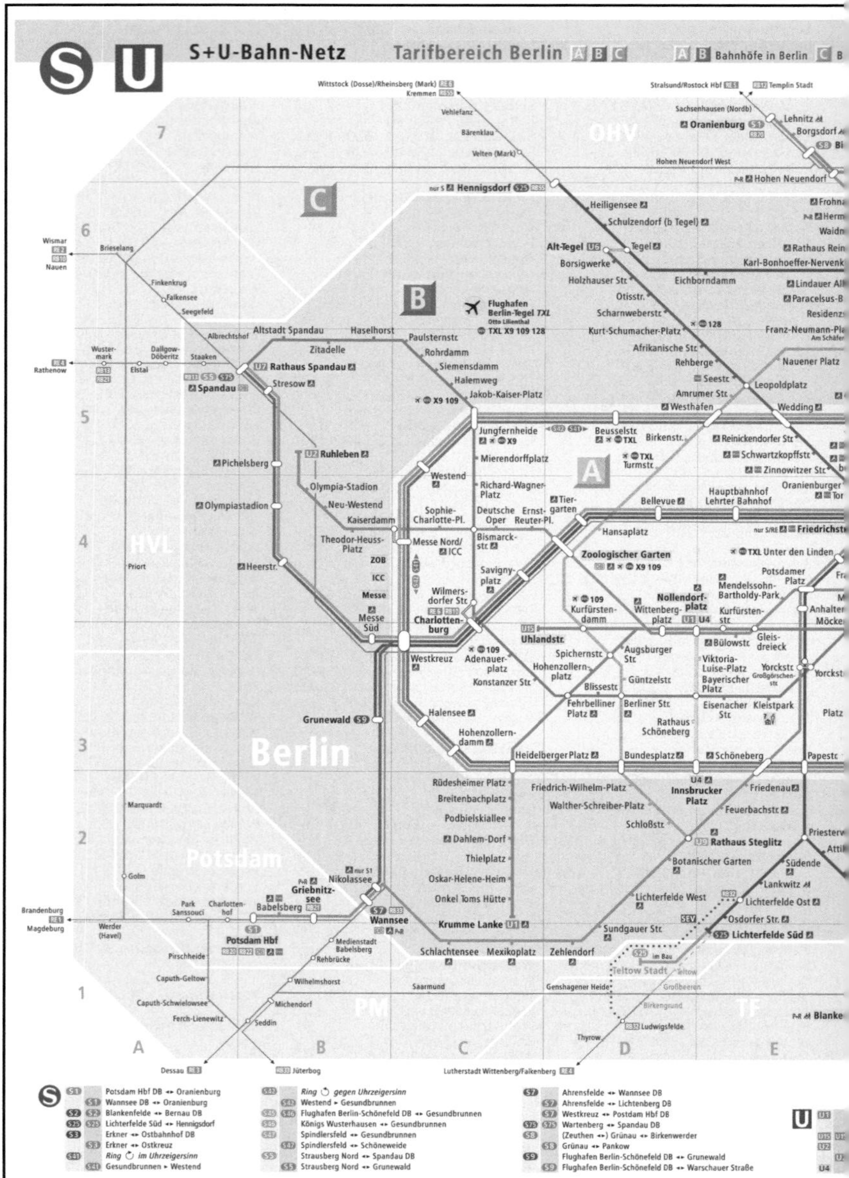
S U
S+U-Bahn-Netz
Tarifbereich Berlin A B C
A B Bahnhöfe in Berlin
Wittstock (Dosse)/Rheinsberg (Mark) RE6
Kremmen RB55
Stralsund/Rostock Hbf RE5
RB12 Templin Stadt
Sachsenhausen (Nordb)
Oranienburg S1
Lehnitz
Borgsdorf
Hohen Neuendorf West
Hohen Neuendorf
Vehlefanz
Bärenklau
Velten (Mark)
OHV
C
B
A
Hennigsdorf S25
Heiligensee
Schulzendorf (b Tegel)
Alt-Tegel U6
Tegel
Borsigwerke
Holzhauser Str.
Otisstr.
Scharnweberstr.
Kurt-Schumacher-Platz
Afrikanische Str.
Rehberge
Seestr.
Amrumer Str.
Westhafen
Eichborndamm
Karl-Bonhoeffer-Nervenk
Rathaus Rein
Lindauer All
Paracelsus-B
Franz-Neumann-Pla
Nauener Platz
Leopoldplatz
Wedding
Wismar
Nauen
Brieselang
Finkenkrug
Falkensee
Seegefeld
Albrechtshof
Wustermark
Dallgow-Döberitz
Staaken
Elstal
Rathenow
Flughafen Berlin-Tegel TXL
Otto Lilienthal
TXL X9 109 128
Altstadt Spandau
Haselhorst
Paulsternstr.
Zitadelle
Rohrdamm
Siemensdamm
Halemweg
Jakob-Kaiser-Platz
Rathaus Spandau
Spandau
Stresow
Ruhleben
Pichelsberg
Olympia-Stadion
Neu-Westend
Olympiastadion
Kaiserdamm
Theodor-Heuss-Platz
Heerstr.
ZOB
ICC
Messe
Messe Süd
Westend
Sophie-Charlotte-Pl.
Messe Nord/ICC
Jungfernheide
Beusselstr.
Birkenstr.
Mierendorffplatz
Richard-Wagner-Platz
Deutsche Oper
Ernst-Reuter-Pl.
Tiergarten
Bellevue
Hauptbahnhof Lehrter Bahnhof
Oranienburger Tor
Reinickendorfer Str.
Schwartzkopffstr.
Zinnowitzer Str.
Turmstr.
Hansaplatz
Friedrichstr.
Unter den Linden
Bismarckstr.
Zoologischer Garten
Savignyplatz
Wilmersdorfer Str.
Charlottenburg
Kurfürstendamm
Wittenbergplatz
Nollendorfplatz
Mendelssohn-Bartholdy-Park
Potsdamer Platz
Anhalter
Kurfürstenstr.
Gleisdreieck
Bülowstr.
Uhlandstr.
Augsburger Str.
Spichernstr.
Hohenzollernplatz
Westkreuz
Adenauerplatz
Konstanzer Str.
Güntzelstr.
Viktoria-Luise-Platz
Bayerischer Platz
Yorckstr.
Großgörschenstr.
Blissestr.
Fehrbelliner Platz
Berliner Str.
Eisenacher Str.
Kleistpark
Rathaus Schöneberg
Halensee
Hohenzollerndamm
Heidelberger Platz
Bundesplatz
Schöneberg
Papestr.
Grunewald S9
Berlin
HVL
Priort
Rüdesheimer Platz
Breitenbachplatz
Podbielskiallee
Dahlem-Dorf
Thielplatz
Oskar-Helene-Heim
Onkel Toms Hütte
Krumme Lanke U1
Friedrich-Wilhelm-Platz
Walther-Schreiber-Platz
Schloßstr.
Innsbrucker Platz
Friedenau
Feuerbachstr.
Rathaus Steglitz
Botanischer Garten
Südende
Priesterw
Lankwitz
Lichterfelde West
Lichterfelde Ost
Osdorfer Str.
Lichterfelde Süd
Sundgauer Str.
Marquardt
Potsdam
Golm
Nikolassee
Griebnitzsee
Babelsberg
Wannsee
Brandenburg
Magdeburg
Werder (Havel)
Park Sanssouci
Charlottenhof
Potsdam Hbf
Medienstadt Babelsberg
Rehbrücke
Schlachtensee
Mexikoplatz
Zehlendorf
Pirschheide
Caputh-Geltow
Wilhelmshorst
Caputh-Schwielowsee
Michendorf
Ferch-Lienewitz
Seddin
Saarmund
Genshagener Heide
Teltow Stadt
Großbeeren
Birkengrund
Ludwigsfelde
Thyrow
PM
TF
Dessau RE3
RE3 Jüterbog
Lutherstadt Wittenberg/Falkenberg RE4
A B C D E
1 2 3 4 5 6 7
S1 Potsdam Hbf DB ↔ Oranienburg
S1 Wannsee DB ↔ Oranienburg
S2 Blankenfelde ↔ Bernau DB
S25 Lichterfelde Süd ↔ Hennigsdorf
S3 Erkner ↔ Ostbahnhof DB
S3 Erkner ↔ Ostkreuz
S41 Ring im Uhrzeigersinn
S41 Gesundbrunnen ▸ Westend
S42 Ring gegen Uhrzeigersinn
S42 Westend ▸ Gesundbrunnen
S45 Flughafen Berlin-Schönefeld DB ↔ Gesundbrunnen
S46 Königs Wusterhausen ↔ Gesundbrunnen
S47 Spindlersfeld ↔ Gesundbrunnen
S47 Spindlersfeld ↔ Schöneweide
S5 Strausberg Nord ↔ Spandau DB
S5 Strausberg Nord ↔ Grunewald
S7 Ahrensfelde ↔ Wannsee DB
S7 Ahrensfelde ↔ Lichtenberg DB
S7 Westkreuz ↔ Postdam Hbf DB
S75 Wartenberg ↔ Spandau DB
S8 (Zeuthen ↔) Grünau ↔ Birkenwerder
S8 Grünau ↔ Pankow
S9 Flughafen Berlin-Schönefeld DB ↔ Grunewald
S9 Flughafen Berlin-Schönefeld DB ↔ Warschauer Straße

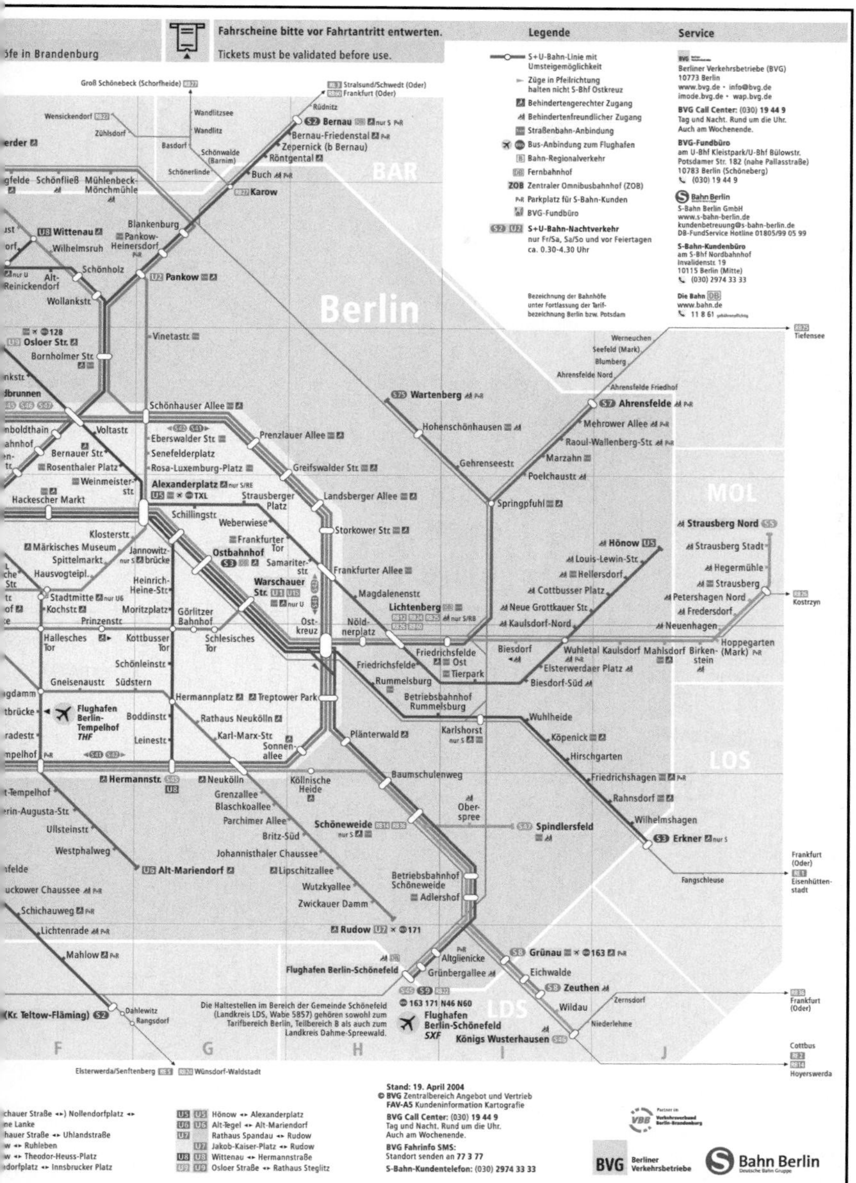
öfe in Brandenburg
Fahrscheine bitte vor Fahrtantritt entwerten.
Tickets must be validated before use.
Legende
S+U-Bahn-Linie mit Umsteigemöglichkeit
Züge in Pfeilrichtung halten nicht S-Bhf Ostkreuz
Behindertengerechter Zugang
Behindertenfreundlicher Zugang
Straßenbahn-Anbindung
Bus-Anbindung zum Flughafen
Bahn-Regionalverkehr
Fernbahnhof
ZOB Zentraler Omnibusbahnhof (ZOB)
Parkplatz für S-Bahn-Kunden
BVG-Fundbüro
S+U-Bahn-Nachtverkehr
nur Fr/Sa, Sa/So und vor Feiertagen ca. 0.30-4.30 Uhr
Bezeichnung der Bahnhöfe unter Fortlassung der Tarifbezeichnung Berlin bzw. Potsdam
Service
Berliner Verkehrsbetriebe (BVG)
10773 Berlin
www.bvg.de · info@bvg.de
imode.bvg.de · wap.bvg.de
BVG Call Center: (030) 19 44 9
Tag und Nacht. Rund um die Uhr. Auch am Wochenende.
BVG-Fundbüro
am U-Bhf Kleistpark/U-Bhf Bülowstr.
Potsdamer Str. 182 (nahe Pallasstraße)
10783 Berlin (Schöneberg)
(030) 19 44 9
S-Bahn Berlin GmbH
www.s-bahn-berlin.de
kundenbetreuung@s-bahn-berlin.de
DB-FundService Hotline 01805/99 05 99
S-Bahn-Kundenbüro
am S-Bhf Nordbahnhof
Invalidenstr. 19
10115 Berlin (Mitte)
(030) 2974 33 33
Die Bahn DB
www.bahn.de
11 8 61
BAR
Berlin
MOL
LOS
LDS
Groß Schönebeck (Schorfheide)
Stralsund/Schwedt (Oder)
Frankfurt (Oder)
Rüdnitz
Wensickendorf
Zühlsdorf
Wandlitzsee
Wandlitz
Basdorf
Schönwalde (Barnim)
Schönerlinde
S2 Bernau
Bernau-Friedenstal
Zepernick (b Bernau)
Röntgental
Buch
Karow
Blankenburg
Pankow-Heinersdorf
Wittenau
Wilhelmsruh
Schönholz
Pankow
Wollankstr.
Alt-Reinickendorf
Osloer Str.
Bornholmer Str.
Vinetastr.
Schönhauser Allee
Voltastr.
Bernauer Str.
Rosenthaler Platz
Weinmeisterstr.
Hackescher Markt
Eberswalder Str.
Senefelderplatz
Rosa-Luxemburg-Platz
Alexanderplatz
Prenzlauer Allee
Greifswalder Str.
Landsberger Allee
Storkower Str.
Frankfurter Allee
Strausberger Platz
Schillingstr.
Weberwiese
Frankfurter Tor
Klosterstr.
Märkisches Museum
Spittelmarkt
Jannowitzbrücke
Hausvogteipl.
Ostbahnhof
Samariterstr.
Warschauer Str.
Heinrich-Heine-Str.
Stadtmitte
Kochstr.
Moritzplatz
Görlitzer Bahnhof
Prinzenstr.
Hallesches Tor
Kottbusser Tor
Schlesisches Tor
Schönleinstr.
Gneisenaustr.
Südstern
Hermannplatz
Treptower Park
Ostkreuz
Nöldnerplatz
Magdalenenstr.
Lichtenberg
Friedrichsfelde
Friedrichsfelde Ost
Tierpark
Rummelsburg
Betriebsbahnhof Rummelsburg
Flughafen Berlin-Tempelhof THF
Boddinstr.
Leinestr.
Rathaus Neukölln
Karl-Marx-Str.
Sonnenallee
Hermannstr.
Neukölln
Köllnische Heide
Grenzallee
Blaschkoallee
Parchimer Allee
Britz-Süd
Johannisthaler Chaussee
Lipschitzallee
Wutzkyallee
Zwickauer Damm
Rudow
Alt-Mariendorf
Westphalweg
Ullsteinstr.
Schichauweg
Lichtenrade
Mahlow
Dahlewitz
Rangsdorf
Plänterwald
Baumschulenweg
Schöneweide
Oberspree
Spindlersfeld
Betriebsbahnhof Schöneweide
Adlershof
Karlshorst
Wuhlheide
Köpenick
Hirschgarten
Friedrichshagen
Rahnsdorf
Wilhelmshagen
Erkner
Fangschleuse
Altglienicke
Grünbergallee
Flughafen Berlin-Schönefeld
Grünau
Eichwalde
Zeuthen
Wildau
Königs Wusterhausen
Zernsdorf
Niederlehme
Flughafen Berlin-Schönefeld SXF
Wartenberg
Hohenschönhausen
Gehrenseestr.
Springpfuhl
Werneuchen
Seefeld (Mark)
Blumberg
Ahrensfelde Nord
Ahrensfelde Friedhof
Ahrensfelde
Mehrower Allee
Raoul-Wallenberg-Str.
Marzahn
Poelchaustr.
Hönow
Louis-Lewin-Str.
Hellersdorf
Cottbusser Platz
Neue Grottkauer Str.
Kaulsdorf-Nord
Strausberg Nord
Strausberg Stadt
Hegermühle
Strausberg
Petershagen Nord
Fredersdorf
Neuenhagen
Hoppegarten (Mark)
Biesdorf
Wuhletal
Kaulsdorf
Mahlsdorf
Birkenstein
Elsterwerdaer Platz
Biesdorf-Süd
Tiefensee
Kostrzyn
Frankfurt (Oder)
Eisenhüttenstadt
Cottbus
Hoyerswerda
Elsterwerda/Senftenberg
Wünsdorf-Waldstadt
(Kr. Teltow-Fläming)
Die Haltestellen im Bereich der Gemeinde Schönefeld (Landkreis LDS, Wabe 5857) gehören sowohl zum Tarifbereich Berlin, Teilbereich B als auch zum Landkreis Dahme-Spreewald.
F
G
H
I
J
Stand: 19. April 2004
© BVG Zentralbereich Angebot und Vertrieb
FAV-A5 Kundeninformation Kartografie
BVG Call Center: (030) 19 44 9
Tag und Nacht. Rund um die Uhr.
Auch am Wochenende.
BVG Fahrinfo SMS:
Standort senden an 77 3 77
S-Bahn-Kundentelefon: (030) 2974 33 33
chauer Straße ↔ Nollendorfplatz ↔
ne Lanke
hauer Straße ↔ Uhlandstraße
w ↔ Ruhleben
w ↔ Theodor-Heuss-Platz
dorfplatz ↔ Innsbrucker Platz
U5 Hönow ↔ Alexanderplatz
U6 Alt-Tegel ↔ Alt-Mariendorf
U7 Rathaus Spandau ↔ Rudow
U7 Jakob-Kaiser-Platz ↔ Rudow
U8 Wittenau ↔ Hermannstraße
U9 Osloer Straße ↔ Rathaus Steglitz
Partner im Verkehrsverbund Berlin-Brandenburg
BVG Berliner Verkehrsbetriebe
S Bahn Berlin
Deutsche Bahn Gruppe

Mitte

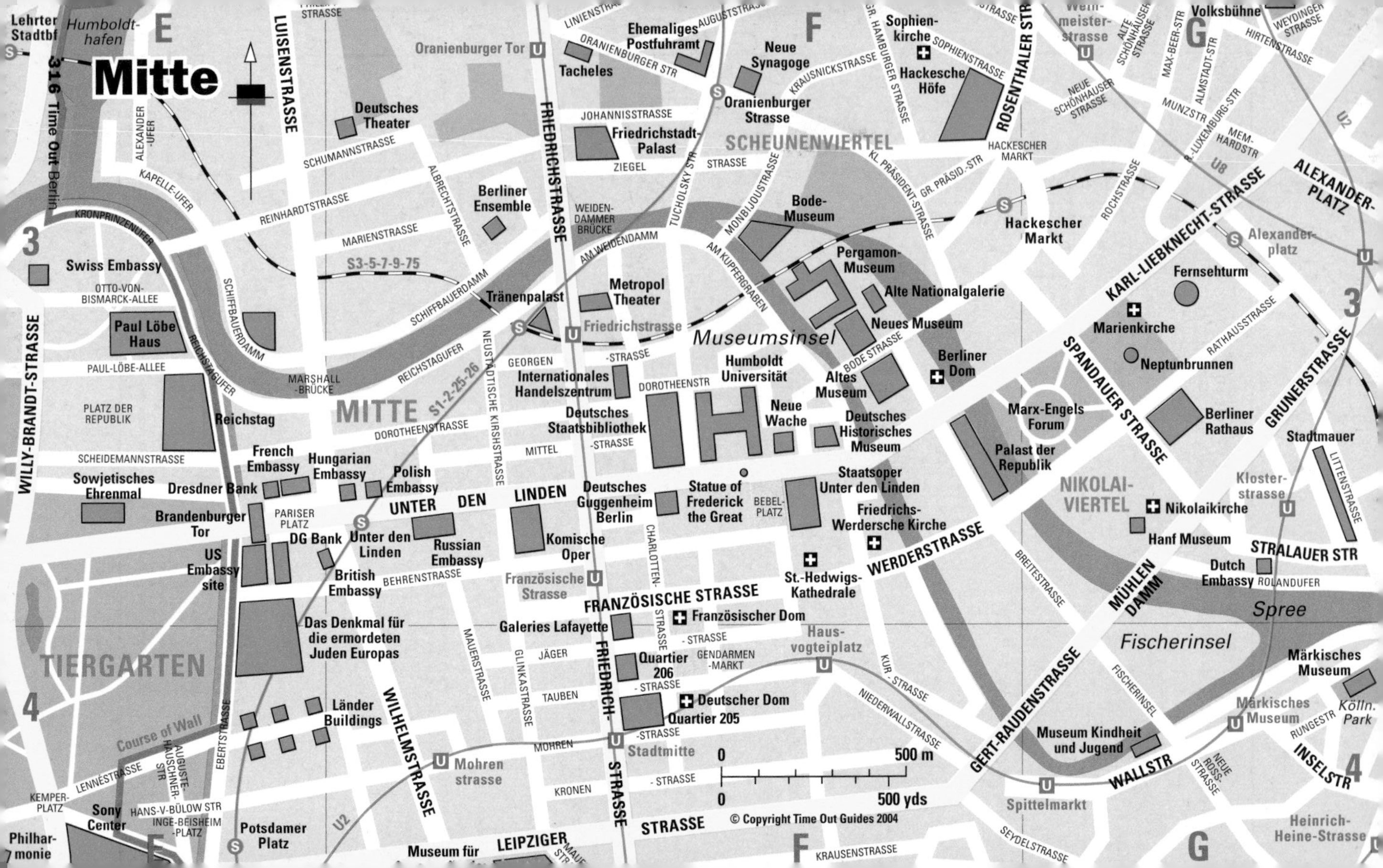
Lehrter Stadtbf
Humboldt-hafen
Oranienburger Tor
Deutsches Theater
Berliner Ensemble
Swiss Embassy
Paul Löbe Haus
Reichstag
Tränenpalast
Metropol Theater
Friedrichstrasse
Tacheles
Ehemaliges Postfuhramt
Neue Synagoge
Oranienburger Strasse
Friedrichstadt-Palast
SCHEUNENVIERTEL
Sophien-kirche
Hackesche Höfe
Hackescher Markt
Bode-Museum
Pergamon-Museum
Alte Nationalgalerie
Neues Museum
Museumsinsel
Altes Museum
Berliner Dom
Humboldt Universität
Neue Wache
Deutsches Historisches Museum
Internationales Handelszentrum
Deutsches Staatsbibliothek
MITTE
French Embassy
Hungarian Embassy
Polish Embassy
Sowjetisches Ehrenmal
Dresdner Bank
Brandenburger Tor
US Embassy site
DG Bank
Unter den Linden
Russian Embassy
British Embassy
UNTER DEN LINDEN
Komische Oper
Deutsches Guggenheim Berlin
Statue of Frederick the Great
Staatsoper Unter den Linden
Friedrichs-Werdersche Kirche
St.-Hedwigs-Kathedrale
Französische Strasse
Galeries Lafayette
Französischer Dom
Quartier 206
Deutscher Dom
Quartier 205
Hausvogteiplatz
Stadtmitte
Mohrenstrasse
Das Denkmal für die ermordeten Juden Europas
Länder Buildings
TIERGARTEN
Course of Wall
Sony Center
Potsdamer Platz
Philharmonie
Museum für
Volksbühne
Weinmeisterstrasse
Alexanderplatz
ALEXANDER-PLATZ
Fernsehturm
Marienkirche
Neptunbrunnen
Berliner Rathaus
Marx-Engels Forum
Palast der Republik
Stadtmauer
Klosterstrasse
NIKOLAI-VIERTEL
Nikolaikirche
Hanf Museum
Dutch Embassy
Spree
Fischerinsel
Märkisches Museum
Köllnischer Park
Museum Kindheit und Jugend
Spittelmarkt
Heinrich-Heine-Strasse
LUISENSTRASSE
FRIEDRICHSTRASSE
WILLY-BRANDT-STRASSE
WILHELMSTRASSE
LEIPZIGER STRASSE
ROSENTHALER STR
KARL-LIEBKNECHT-STRASSE
SPANDAUER STRASSE
GRUNERSTRASSE
WERDERSTRASSE
FRANZÖSISCHE STRASSE
GERT-RAUDENSTRASSE
MÜHLENDAMM
STRALAUER STR
WALLSTR
INSELSTR
S3-5-7-9-75
S1-2-25-26
U2
U8
0 500 m
0 500 yds
© Copyright Time Out Guides 2004